The Thomistic Response to the Nouvelle Théologie

The Thomistic Response to the Nouvelle Théologie

Concerning the Truth of Dogma and the Nature of Theology

Raymond-Léopold Bruckberger, OP
Réginald Garrigou-Lagrange, OP
Michel-Marie Labourdette, OP
and
Marie-Joseph Nicolas, OP

Edited and translated by Jon Kirwan
and Matthew K. Minerd

The Catholic University of America Press
Washington, D.C.

Introduction, bibliography, and English translations
(excluding those listed below)
Copyright © 2023
The Catholic University of America Press
All rights reserved

English translation of Réginald Garrigou-Lagrange, OP,
"Where is the New Theology Leading Us?"
Copyright © 2011 Josephinum Journal of Theology

English translation of Réginald Garrigou-Lagrange,
"Theology and the Life of Faith."
Copyright © 2019 Cluny Media

Cataloging-in-Publication Data is available from Library of Congress
ISBN: 978-0-8132-3663-6
eISBN: 978-0-8132-3664-3

"If at that age when great vocations and ardent fidelities emerge some ardent youths meditate on these pages and receive from them some taste and ambition for the task of theology, this exhausting labor in service to the divine truth, both will be well rewarded. For in an age of horrible famines—both material and spiritual—the words of the Gospel resound with an ominous tone: 'The harvest is plenty, but the laborers few.'"

—Raymond-Léopold Bruckberger, OP

"Jon Kirwan and Matthew Minerd have rendered the Catholic theological community a great service. The Dominican response to *La nouvelle théologie* has long been buried under the copious amounts of *ressourcement* discoveries and the subsequent rethinking of how to do Catholic theology that they generated. Today graduate theology students will find names like de Lubac and Daniélou familiar, whereas Labourdette and Marie-Joseph Nicolas would likely be known only to specialists. All four of these men were French Roman Catholic priests, two Jesuit and two Dominicans. After the Second Vatican Council, the Jesuits were honored with the cardinalate; the Dominicans were overlooked.

"The value of this book, however, rests not on the unearthing of a long-forgotten theological debate. In fact, the book provides a long and expert introduction to one of the most significant events in modern Catholic theology. For the first time, English readers have a translation of the objections that the Dominicans raised to the project that became known as 'The New Theology.' The most lasting monument to this twentieth-century novelty appears in the some 632 volumes published at Paris in the *Sources Chrétiennes* collection. Each volume presents a text by a patristic or medieval author that, as the title indicates, is considered one of the "sources" for doing Christian theology.

"Do you wonder why learned Dominicans would have taken exception to this project to supply fresh translations of the classical texts of the Christian tradition? If so, and one should, read what the Dominicans themselves wrote in their own defense. If you have noticed a certain destabilization of Catholic theology that seems to leave so many questions open to a variety of opinions, read this book. The Dominicans saw the crackup coming. If you are bothered by the fact that today much Catholic theology looks like an exercise in literary criticism instead of an exposition of eternal truth, this is the book for you. What is best, the long introduction and fine translations come from the pens of two devout Catholic laymen who, as far as I know, are not committed *a priori* to either Jesuit or Dominican ways of thinking. No. Kirwan and Minerd are concerned with the stabilization of Catholic truth."

Romanus Cessario, OP
Ave Maria University, FL

"The general shape of twentieth-century theology can be summarized as a movement away from first principles to sources and narratives. And herein lies the tremendous value of this book: it is an important source about first principles that challenges prevailing narratives about the history of Catholic thought. Even if one does not agree with everything found in this volume, no one can deny that these essays present nuanced analysis and coherent argumentation. The heated *nouvelle théologie* debates of yesteryear have ceased. The critical questions that Thomists asked about the *nouvelle théologie*, however, have not yet received adequate answer. Indeed, the analysis and argumentation found herein are ripe for reconsideration. English-speaking students of theology owe profound gratitude to Jon Kirwan and Matthew K. Minerd for the impressive erudition and remarkable industry that produced this book—a book that asks a fundamental, timeless and timely question: *what is sacred theology?*

Cajetan Cuddy, OP
Dominican House of Studies, Washington, DC

"What guarantees the unity and pluralism, the stability as well as the adaptability, of Catholic theology? What is the role of St Thomas Aquinas and his legacy for the theological enterprise today and in the future? Through this timely volume, Jon Kirwan and Matthew K. Minerd point us to the importance of past history in considering these contemporary questions. Not only do they uncover one root for today's challenges in the largely forgotten contours of a lively debate about theological method in France nearly a century ago, but they also make available in English translation some of its more neglected contributions from some prominent Dominican thinkers. While their thorough and useful introduction and chronology of the debate is sensitive to the different nuances of the friars of Toulouse and Rome, the editors helpfully discern some common approaches among the contributors and evaluate some of the reasons why dialogue was so unfortunately truncated to the detriment of Catholic theology. The publication of this volume can only serve to aid a renewed theological dialogue that can serve the Church's engagement with the modern world."

Simon Francis Gaine, OP
Pontifical University of St Thomas Aquinas, Rome

"Between the end of World War II and the opening of the Second Vatican Council, an exchange regarding theological method and the nature of doctrine was initiated by Dominican theologians in Europe with their Jesuit confreres. The actual nature of the Dominican concern—as the evidence demonstrates—was treated preponderantly by their interlocutors more as circumstantial polemical annoyance than as matter for sustained and serious conversation. In the time since, the exchange has come to be treated even more reductively, in an unhistorical and prooftext manner exhibiting many of the elements of a morality play. Much of the Dominican engagement—including importantly the response of Labourdette to Henri de Lubac—has been treated as mere 'flyover' country in the *soi dissant* 'historical' accounts that proceed remote from the texts. This volume provides the Dominican texts, and seeks to redress the postponement of a theological conversation already overdue when it began before the Second Vatican Council, a conversation arguably even more necessary today. The introductory essay alone is normative literature on this subject. The editors and translators, Kirwan and Minerd, are owed a debt of thanks for making these works at last available to the Anglophone world. May this 'dialogue delayed' be renewed with intensified charity and intelligence. This work is one of the most important theological publications of the past 50 years."

Steven Long
Ave Maria University, FL

"Gives voice to a theological concern that has been marginalized, especially in post-conciliar academic theological discourse. . . . As a great majority of these articles are only now appearing in English, a real historical-theological consideration of this debate can begin in the English-speaking world."

Andrew Meszaros
St. Patrick's College, Maynooth, Ireland

"This book makes available for the first time in English the most important texts that express Thomistic concerns about the Nouvelle Théologie. Its scholarly introduction exposes the way in which historians have uncritically accepted slanderous claims about the arguments, motives, and attitudes of twentieth century Thomistic theologians. It also shows how these theologians foresaw many problems that would arise in Catholic theology after Vatican II."

Thomas Osborne
University of St. Thomas, Houston, TX

"It's often the case in the history of Catholic theology that forgotten and unresolved disputes of the past become suddenly relevant and remembered again in the face of a new crisis. Kirwan and Minerd have heroically unearthed such a dispute. On one side were mid-20th century Jesuit fathers, Jean Daniélou and Henri Bouillard. On the other side were Réginald Garrigou-Lagrange and Michel Labourdette, representing two different Dominican provinces. The two sides were utterly divided on the very nature of truth, dogma, and the scientific character of theology itself. The result is an electrifying and dynamic set of dialogues within French Catholicism that's essential not only for our understanding of old debates over *nouvelle théologie*, but these disputes can also help us to renew and revive the very task and mission of theology in the Church today. Highly recommended."

C. C. Pecknold
The Catholic University of America

Contents

Translators' Introduction: A Dialogue Delayed 1

Part 1: The Toulouse Response: *Revue thomiste* and
Dialogue Théologique
   1. Theology: Faith Seeking Understanding 89
      Michel-Marie Labourdette, OP
   2. A Theological Dialogue 127
      Raymond-Léopold Bruckberger, OP
   3. Theology and Its Sources 133
      Michel-Marie Labourdette, OP
   4. Criticism in Theology: A Response 161
      Michel-Marie Labourdette, OP
   5. Theological Progress and Fidelity to St. Thomas 187
      Marie-Joseph Nicolas, OP
   6. The Analogy of Truth and the Unity of Theological Science . . 193
      Michel-Marie Labourdette, OP, and Marie-Joseph Nicolas, OP
   7. Closing Remarks Concerning Our Position 241
      Michel-Marie Labourdette, OP
   8. Discussion Surrounding Our 'Dialogue Théologique' 255
      Michel-Marie Labourdette, OP, and Marie-Joseph Nicolas, OP

Part 2: The Roman Response: Garrigou-Lagrange on Truth
and Dogma
   9. Theology and the Life of Faith 269
  10. Where is the New Theology Headed? 287
  11. Truth and the Immutability of Dogma 305
  12. Concerning Notions Consecrated by the Councils 319
  13. On the Need to Return to the Traditional Conception
      of Truth 331
  14. On the Immutability of Defined Truths, With Remarks
      on the Notion of the Supernatural 343
  15. Relativism and the Immutability of Dogma According to
      the [First] Vatican Council 357
  16. Correspondence 371
      Maurice Blondel and Réginald Garrigou-Lagrange, OP

Bibliography 375

Index 391

Translators' Introduction: A Dialogue Delayed

Jon Kirwan and Matthew K. Minerd

Erupting during the immediate aftermath of World War II, though with roots going back decades, the *nouvelle théologie* affair was a multi-year dispute that engaged a number of Catholic (and, at times, Protestant[1]) thinkers concerning a range of philosophical, theological, and political issues. To those interested in the controversy, it will come as a surprise that some of the most important texts in what is arguably the most important theological debate between the condemnation of modernism and the opening of the Second Vatican Council are all but forgotten,[2] despite its continued relevance concerning the questions of theological methodology posed today.[3] With the exception of a few sensational fragments that are frequently cited, though

---

[1] This aspect of the dialogue, not generally noted well enough, was addressed briefly in Marie-Michel Labourdette and Marie-Joseph Nicolas, "Autour du 'Dialogue théologique,'" *Revue thomiste* 47 (1947): 577–85. This essay is included in translation here as "Discussion Surrounding our 'Dialogue Théologique.'"

[2] See Étienne Fouilloux, "Dialogue théologique? (1946–1948)," in *Saint Thomas au XXe siecle: Actes du colloque Centenaire de la Revue Thomiste; Toulouse, 25–28 mars 1993*, ed. Serge-Thomas Bonino (Paris: Éditions Saint-Paul, 1994), 153.

[3] Writing over thirty years ago, and from a perspective differing from the present authors, Gerald McCool nonetheless made a perceptive observation which is as true today as it was under his pen at the time: "In contemporary Catholic theology, the relation between positive and speculative theology still remains a problem whose solution demands the use of a coherent system of epistemology and metaphysics. . . . For the contemporary debate over theological method is simply another phase in the dialectical movement of Catholic theology's response to the challenge of post-Enlightenment thought from the beginning of the nineteenth century through Vatican I, *Aeterni Patris*, the Modernist crisis, between-the-wars Thomism, *the New Theology controversy*, and Vatican II up to the present. *To understand where we are in Catholic scientific theology, we must understand where we have come from and how far we have traveled in the course of the last two centuries. The contemporary quest for an adequate method in Catholic theology has a history. The better that history is known, the clearer will be the theologian's understanding of his own discipline and his own scientific task*" (emphasis added). See Gerald A. McCool, *Nineteenth Century Scholasticism: The Search or a Unitary Method* (New York: Fordham University Press, 1989), 15–16. In a way that likely would have been unsuspected by McCool himself, we find ourselves in partial agreement, and in this volume, we also wish to play our own role in making clear all the details of the history of the "New Theology controversy."

often misunderstood, the articles involved in this exchange, scattered as they were throughout numerous French postwar journals, have been essentially lost to contemporary readers. This volume reassembles many of those writings from the most important exchange in the entire *ressourcement* controversy, in which the Toulouse and Roman Dominicans, on the one hand, and Fourvière Jesuits, on the other, debated the nature of truth, dogma, and theological methodology during the tumultuous post-war years. Nearly ten Dominican and Jesuit thinkers exchanged over twenty articles and other writings across five different journals over a period of almost four years. Sometimes the articles were written with grace and irenic magnanimity and other times with bitterness and acrimony. Some are theologically subtle and well-reasoned, while others stand as popular manifestos and calls to arms. Moreover, there is a great variance in theological quality. At times, it can be difficult to make sense of the entire affair, given that different responses to numerous charges and countercharges were bouncing back and forth quite rapidly across different publications. Adding to the complexity was a behind-the-scenes flurry of personal correspondence and political maneuvering.

While some aspects of the debate are timebound and outdated, constituting an interest only for historians, other aspects are still vitally important, with certain texts seeming as if they were written for our own time. Moreover, rereading these texts makes clear, in a pronounced way, what is already well known: one of the most important theological debates of modern times, one whose successful conclusion could have dramatically lowered the theological temperature of the pre-conciliar era, was largely in fact an unfortunate failure. What would have been an opportunity for both sides to come together, clarify their differences and agreements, strive to shore up weaknesses in their own theologies, and at some level work together, essentially burned itself out before any meaningful resolution could be reached.

Thus, by providing the missing pieces of the exchange, the translators / editors of this volume have two main aims in view. First, by presenting heretofore-unpublished texts, we hope to give voice to the position articulated by the Dominican parties, whose full position has been presented only in brief in English, and even then, in academic journals.[4] By bringing these thinkers to the table, we hope to provide a resource for a fuller understanding of the essential issues and nuanced positions taken by each side. Second, this volume intends to provide aid in assessing why in fact this exchange was cut short and failed to achieve resolution. The answer to the second question perhaps will call for some revision of received opinions concerning the

---

[4] See Philip J. Donnelly, "Current Theology: Theological Opinion on the Development of Dogma," *Theological Studies* 8, no. 1 (1947): 668–99; Aidan Nichols, "Thomism and the Nouvelle Théologie," *The Thomist* 64, no. 1 (2000): 1–19.

parties involved and, therefore, may in fact spark controversy today. Be that as it may, all of the opposing voices deserve to state their case, as pleasing or repellant as they may be, in their own words.

Given this possible controversy, it would be beneficial for us to state, up front, the historiographical assumptions that will direct this introduction, which on certain key points follow the lead of the historian Thomas Haskell, who argues that although historical neutrality is impossible, objectivity must be sought at all costs.[5] Objectivity here bears no resemblance to the antiquated notions that a history, facilitated by a "pure detachment" and able to discern an equally-pure history, essentially "is as it was." For Haskell, the historical skill of detachment is exercised not through "self-immolation" but, rather, through "self-control," where "the demand is for detachment and fairness, not disengagement from life." This "detachment" simply strives after a basic fairness that is characterized by the historian momentarily, at least, stepping outside of his viewpoint to seek the

> vital minimum of ascetic self-discipline that enables a person to do such things as abandon wishful thinking, assimilate bad news, discard pleasing interpretations that cannot pass elementary tests of evidence and logic, and, most important of all, suspend or bracket one's own perceptions long enough to enter sympathetically into the alien and possibly repugnant perspectives of rival thinkers. All of these mental acts—especially coming to grips with a rival's perspective—require detachment, an undeniably ascetic capacity to achieve some distance from one's own spontaneous perceptions and convictions, to imagine how the world appears in another's eyes, to experimentally adopt perspectives that do not come naturally.[6]

Sadly, this detachment is often absent from histories of twentieth- century Catholic thought, and it is difficult to think of an academically more-unpopular task than that of offering a kind of historical defense, or at least qualification, for the Dominican Thomists involved in the *nouvelle théologie* affair. They are regularly branded as anti-modern and anti-historical symbols of Roman authoritarianism and Scholastic excess. While in some cases this assessment may have been true, nonetheless, as the texts gathered in this volume will exhibit, this generally-received narrative[7] is at times sadly unfair to the Dominicans involved, who often were voices of peace and reasoned

---

[5] Thomas Haskell, "Objectivity Is Not Neutrality: Rhetoric vs. Practice in Peter Novick's *That Noble Dream*," *History and Theory* 29, no. 2 (May 1990): 129–57.

[6] Haskell, "Objectivity," 132.

[7] Reflected quite clearly in, for example, Jürgen Mettepenningen, *Nouvelle Théologie, New Theology: Inheritor of Modernism, Precursor of Vatican II* (London: T & T Clark, 2010).

dialogue, at times even seeking to find common ground and showing theological affinity for historical studies and the needs of modernity. However, this side of the debate is often insufficiently acknowledged.

Reproducing this exchange is important not only in order to have a complete historical record of a complex debate that is often grossly simplified but also to dispel misleading and highly charged characterizations that envision a "Thomist attack" against a reticent and irenic *ressourcement* simply wanting to survive in peace.[8] These characterizations do little beyond reigniting pre-conciliar acrimony. The reality is, as readers will soon see, that both sides were intensely engaged, with both sides "attacking" and both sides looking for dialogue at various points. From the time of their formation in the 1920s, the *nouveaux théologiens* had no small disdain for Scholasticism, above all in its post-Tridentine form, and from their ordinations around 1930 sought unequivocally, in the words of Yves Congar, to "liquidate" it primarily through the production of various historical studies.[9] Moreover, the debate was not over *history* or *dialogue*, which the Thomists agreed had a place in theological research, but rather, over the controlling use of a certain philosophy of history championed by the *nouveaux théologiens*, or, in some cases, their enthusiastic appropriation of aspects of existentialist thought.

As the table of contents attests, this volume contains only one side of the debate, the Thomist side, and this was not our original intention. At the start of this project, we sketched out a volume containing texts from both sides of the debate over truth, dogma, and theological methodology, presented in chronological order. However, this aim was altered by the very recent publication of the *ressourcement* reader by Patricia Kelly, a wide-ranging collection covering a number of different thinkers and debates from different time periods in the *nouvelle théologie* affair.[10] The volume in question provides merely a sampling of articles from various debates and focuses primarily on articles written by the proponents of the *nouvelle théologie*, in a way that is

---

[8] This sort of tone is echoed in the introductory essay in the recent volume by Patricia Kelly, *Ressourcement Theology: A Source Book* (London: T&T Clark, 2020). The consistently negative tone of the introduction to the volume, along with the particular slant of its text selection, is discussed by the two translators of this volume in book reviews to be published in *New Blackfriars* and the English edition of *Nova et Vetera*. Moreover, as is discussed in those two reviews, Kelly's translation at times suffers from certain infelicities regarding technical terminology and also, without warning, excises content from the articles being translated, particularly longer footnote texts.

[9] For an account of their formation in the 20s, see Jon Kirwan, *An Avant-garde Theological Generation* (Oxford: Oxford University Press, 2018), 96–134; for the quote from Congar, see Kirwan, *Avant-garde*, 162.

[10] Concerning problems with the translations in the volume, see note 8.

arguably somewhat decontextualized,[11] not following any lines of debate from beginning to end. Thus, in order to avoid undue overlap between these volumes,[12] we pivoted to cover the Thomist articles. Thus, in its current state, this volume presents a departure from our original approach, the aim of which from the beginning has been to reproduce the debate over dogma and theology from beginning to end. English translations of most of the missing *ressourcement* voices exist elsewhere and will be referenced here, so that readers can piece together and read both sides of the exchange.

A DIALOGUE WITH THE MODERN WORLD: THE BEGINNINGS OF THE DEBATE

The postwar eruption of the *nouvelle théologie* debate over the nature of speculative truth, dogma, and theological methodology was initiated by two works, both written by Fourvière Jesuits, Jean Daniélou's 1946 article "Les Orientations présentes de la pensée religieuse" and Henri Bouillard's 1944 book *Conversion et grâce chez S. Thomas d'Aquin*, the latter being published during the closing years of the war.[13] Two responses developed, which we here will refer to as the Toulouse response, led by Michel Labourdette, Marie-Joseph Nicholas, and Raymond-Léopold Bruckberger, all Dominican fathers of the Toulouse province, gathered around the *Revue thomiste*, and the Roman response, led by Garrigou-Lagrange and published primarily in the journal *Angelicum*. We have made this differentiation in order to organize and clarify the exchanges, as they both responded to the Fourvière Jesuits and were essentially embroiled in separate back-and-forth exchanges. Let us begin with a general overview of the texts by Daniélou and Bouillard.

In the heady days after the Second World War, what had been an intense and almost uninterrupted debate within the world of French Catholicism

---

[11] For example, the text is organized thematically in such a way that a response to Labourdette is presented *before* Labourdette's own article. Moreover, his own response is not presented. Rather, his text, along with a later text penned by him and Marie-Joseph Nicolas, is presented in a section partisanly entitled, "Attacks on 'The New Theology.'"

[12] However, we do have two points of overlap, namely Labourdette's "Theology and its Sources" and Garrigou-Lagrange's "Where is the 'New Theology' Headed?" This was needed for full context. Due to concerns addressed above related to Kelly's recent volume, we have included our own translation of Michel Labourdette and Marie-Joseph Nicolas, "L'analogie de la vérité et l'unité de la science théologique," *Revue thomiste* 47 (1947): 411–66.

[13] See Jean Daniélou, "Les Orientations présentes de la pensée religieuse," *Études* 249 (1946): 5–21, translated as "Present Orientations of Religious Thought," *Josephinum Journal of Theology* 18, no. 1 (2011): 51–62; Henri Bouillard, *Conversion et grâce chez S. Thomas d'Aquin* (Paris: Aubier, 1944), translated as "Conversion and Grace in Aquinas," in Kelly, *Ressourcement*, 33–40.

over the value of Neo-Thomism and modern thought boiled over and gained international attention. There had been three generations of critics against Neo-Thomism, and in 1946, the movement that in 1942 had received the appellation *nouvelle théologie* took center stage.[14] What had been central to the years of criticism was the demand for the abandonment of what was called the "static" Aristotelianism of Neo-Thomism and the embrace of a fruitful dialogue with certain currents of modern thought built on central categories of history, lived experience, engagement, and evolutionary science. The Jesuit Jean Daniélou, a central figure in this movement, published a series of writings throughout the mid-40s surveying the broad currents of intellectual thought *en vogue* in France at the time and stridently called for a dialogue with them.[15] In fact, Daniélou wrote a full-length book entitled *Dialogues*, in which he sought a fruitful exchange with Marxists, existentialists, protestants, and Jews, declaring that the "living forces of French thought are beginning to sketch out their outlines, and we want to seize the moment, conscious of how this enterprise is presumptuous, but also convinced of its importance."[16] He continued by stating that "this dialogue will fill the decades which we are entering" as "it is certain that the moment has come when it is necessary, using the considerable enrichments that science, phenomenological descriptions, and historical events have brought over the last fifty years, and which exist in fragments. We should work to build a new vision of the world, as was done by Proclus, Thomas Aquinas, or Hegel."[17] For Daniélou, the fruit of this dialogue would be nothing short of the renewal of the modern world: "All this fills us with immense hope, but also makes us aware of a great responsibility. If Christians understand this state of affairs aright, they will bring salvific answers to the questions being raised by the world."[18]

In the article "Present Orientations of Religious Thought," still regarded as the defining charter and manifesto of *ressourcement* and the *nouvelle théologie*, Daniélou lays out precisely the intellectual boundaries of this dialogue which must be the pillars of Catholic theology, history, subjectivity, and

---

14 For a history of the movement, see Kirwan, *Avant-garde*.

15 Jean Daniélou, "La Vie intellectuelle en France: Communisme, Existentialisme, Christianisme," *Études* (September 1945): 241–54; Jean Daniélou, "Christianisme et histoire," *Études* 254, no. 8 (1947): 166–84; Jean Daniélou, "Existentialisme et Théologie de l'Histoire," *Dieu Vivant* 15 (1950): 131–35; Jean Daniélou, "Existentialism and the Theology of History," *The Month* 1 (1949): 66–70.

16 Jean Daniélou, *Dialogues: avec les marxistes, les existentialistes, les protestants, les juifs, l'hindouisme* (Paris: Le Portulan, 1948), 9.

17 Daniélou, *Dialogues*, 26.

18 Daniélou, *Dialogues*, 28.

engagement. In his explication, Daniélou lists a who's who of French intellectual life, including secular champions of this methodology, such as Jean-Paul Sartre, Maurice Merleau-Ponty, and Simone de Beauvoir. Daniélou's enthusiasm for the promises of modern thought can barely be contained as he appeals to the "men of today" repeatedly to begin building a new world and new man.

Daniélou's call for an engagement with history had been taken up four years earlier by fellow Jesuit Henri Bouillard in a controversial work, *Conversion et grâce chez S. Thomas d'Aquin*, initially overlooked during the war years. As is indicated by its title, this text, the fruit of his studies directed in part by the conservative Jesuit theologian Charles Boyer, was dedicated to the doctrine of grace and the act of conversion in St. Thomas's thought. Published as the first volume in the new Jesuit-edited series, *Théologie*, this text would have resounding effects because of certain claims made in its closing section, where Bouillard voiced broad-brush comments concerning the nature of doctrinal and theological development.

In the now-infamous conclusion, Bouillard criticized Thomism as static and ahistorical, "a ready-made science of immutable notions, timeless problems, and definitive arguments."[19] However, a "historical study reveals, on the contrary, to what extent theology is time-bound and connected to the becoming of the human mind. It shows what is contingent in it: the relativity of notions, the evolution of problems, the temporary obscuring of certain important truths."[20] After a strong critique of the Aristotelian influence on Aquinas, and the theological turns which led him to his position,[21] which he stated was merely the adoption of the categories of the day, he declared that Christian truth never remains in a pure state: "It is always embedded in contingent concepts and schemata that determine its rational structure. It is not possible to isolate it from them. It can emancipate itself from one system of concepts only by passing into another."[22] However, a historically-conscious theology "causes us to see the permanence of divine truth and, at the same time, reveals to us what is contingent in the notions and systems in which

---

[19] Bouillard, *Conversion*, 211.

[20] Bouillard, *Conversion*, 211.

[21] Bouillard does generally affirm the doctrinal continuity of Aquinas with the Fathers without going into depth, and the reader can only assume that Bouillard primarily refers to Aristotelian accretions as the source of most points of rupture. See Bouillard, *Conversion*, 216: "Certainly, we do not intend to deny the doctrinal continuity that connects St. Thomas to the Fathers and the moderns to St. Thomas. If we do not insist on it, it is because it is fairly obvious and has often been emphasized. By contrast, in this historical study, it has been useful to bring out the dissimilarities, which are less noticeable."

[22] Bouillard, *Conversion*, 219.

we receive it."²³ For Bouillard, hindsight provides the historical theologian the vantage to see clearly the unifying threads that run through the tradition beneath transient concepts and categories. Thus, according to Bouillard, history does not lead to relativism, for it "allows one to grasp an absolute within theological development [*évolution*]. This is not an absolute in representation, but an absolute in affirmation." This notion of absolute affirmation but relative formulation will come to be central to the debate, as Bouillard's point remains vague and is not clearly spelled out in his brief concluding chapter.²⁴ Indeed, the seeds of controversy are plain as he explains further that history "manifests to the times the relativity of notions and schemata in which theology takes its shape as well as the permanent affirmation that dominates them. It reveals the temporal character of theology and at the same time provides the faith with the absolute affirmation, the divine Word, which is incarnated in it."²⁵ As will become clear throughout the debate, the two parties held two *completely* different theories of judgment. This profound (and arguably insuperable) philosophical difference likely precluded any fully peaceful rapprochement.

Bouillard continues that this epistemological dynamic (an absolute affirmation expressed in a time-bound, relative formulation) applies to dogma and the first principles of the mind, in which the absolute is contained *within* the formulation. To highlight this dynamic, Bouillard utilized the example of the notion of formal causality used in the definition of justification expressed dogmatically by the Council of Trent in its *Decree on Justification*. He asks whether the Council wanted to consecrate this use and confer on the

---

[23] Bouillard, *Conversion*, 220. In our translations, we have generally chosen to retain "notion" as the English translation for the same word in French. For Garrigou-Lagrange, there are several places where "notion" vs. "concept" might be tracking the later-scholastic distinction between the "objective concept" and the "formal concept."

[24] He goes on to say (Bouillard, *Conversion*, 220–21):

> Moreover, these affirmations themselves, in order to preserve their meaning in a new intellectual universe, determine the new notions, methods, and systems that correspond with this universe. If it were otherwise, old formulas, were they to remain, would lose their primary meaning. The mind that receives a formula strives, in fact, to understand it by connecting it to the ensemble of its conceptions. The mind interprets it according to what it knows. It reconstructs it according to personal schemata. Only in this way can the mind understand it. But do we not see that, in a single formula, or even several correlative formulas, if one of the concepts or notions is unconsciously modified, all the others must be modified correlatively so that these affirmations retain their meaning? By passing from one mind to another that is notably different, an affirmation passes from one system to another. This is what we have observed in the medieval theology concerning the preparation for grace.

[25] Bouillard, *Conversion*, 221.

concept of grace-form a definitive character? He responds: "By no means. It was certainly not the intention of the Council to canonize an Aristotelian notion, nor even a theological notion conceived under the influence of Aristotle."[26] Trent simply wanted to affirm that justification was an interior renewal, against Protestant notions of the imputation of the merits of Christ. This claim will be the source of great vexation for the Dominicans, above all for Garrigou-Lagrange, who will come to write a number of articles in response to it.

Thus, according to Bouillard, it is the task of historical theology to recognize "obsolete explanations, aged schemata, and dead notions,"[27] which are like old-fashioned garments or outdated tools that hamper the process of theological reflection, akin to the outmoded aspects of Aristotelian physics which must be abandoned by contemporary thought. Bouillard concedes that it is sometimes difficult to untangle these concepts "without error, from the absolute truth with which they overlap," but, nonetheless, in a line that will resound down to this day, igniting a furious debate, he states, "A theology that would not be contemporary would be a false theology."[28] Garrigou's interventions will almost completely be occupied with challenging Bouillard's conclusion (and with what he believed to be the Blondellian background to it) and will incite his famous assertion that the *nouvelle théologie* was leading Catholic thought back to the errors of modernism.

THE TOULOUSE RESPONSE

During the immediate postwar years, the controversy between the Thomists and *ressourcement* thinkers became prominent, and the unquestioned authority on the history of modern French Catholic thought, Étienne Fouilloux, writes that "this debate was not confined to specialized clerical circles but had a certain echo amongst the clergy at the time."[29] Moreover, in the postwar climate of Marxism and existentialism, Thomism seemed irrelevant and outdated. Capturing this sentiment, Charles Journet wrote to Jacques Maritain that in "this disintegration of the world, one seems a fool for trying to remain faithful to St. Thomas."[30] Throughout the 1930s, there were sustained and strident attacks against Thomism by the *ressourcement* thinkers, with critics accusing it of being an intellectual corruption, not only imperiling the very substance of the faith but likewise causing the very phenomenon of secularism

---

26 Bouillard, *Conversion*, 221–22.
27 Bouillard, *Conversion*, 224.
28 Bouillard, *Conversion*, 219.
29 Fouilloux, "Dialogue," 153.
30 Fouilloux, "Dialogue," 158.

itself.³¹ Indeed, we now know that certain *ressourcement* thinkers had no intention of broaching a kind of rapprochement, but even in 1936 hatched a plan to "liquidate" it through a campaign of historical studies. With this in mind, it is striking that there was such little theological push back from Thomists, and only in 1942³² did the Roman authorities step in to correct what were interpreted as being problematic notions of truth, theological science, and dogma put forth by Marie-Dominique Chenu and Louis Charlier, the former in his lecture, published in limited circulation as *Une école de théologie: Le Saulchoir*,³³ and the latter in *Essai sur le problème théologique*.³⁴

Although he names no interlocutors, the Thomist articulation of the nature of theology, concerned above all with maintaining its scientific character, can be found in Michel Labourdette's "Theology: Faith Seeking Understanding," published in the *Revue thomiste* in 1946.³⁵ Carefully treating notions of science, faith, and the structure of theology, Labourdette provides a crystal-clear expression of the notion of theology articulated within the *schola Thomae*. His defense of theology as a science is part of a long, ongoing debate that might be seen as the main current that unites all of the various exchanges of the *nouvelle théologie* affair throughout the 1930s and 1940s.³⁶

---

31 For example, one might consider de Lubac's 1942 inaugural lecture, as well as his famous claims against Thomas de Vio Cajetan in relation to the distinction between the natural and supernatural orders.

32 Richard Peddicord, relying on the 1985 work of Fouilloux, holds that "Garrigou made it clear that while he was in agreement with the decision [against Chenu], he had not instigated the investigation and had not been one of the prime movers behind the condemnation." See Peddicord, *The Sacred Monster of Thomism: An Introduction to the Life and Legacy of Reginald Garrigou-Lagrange* (South Bend, IN: St. Augustine's Press, 2005), 107. See Étienne Fouilloux, "Le Saulchoir en procès (1937–1942)," in Marie-Dominique Chenu, *Une école de théologie: Le Saulchoir* (Paris: Éditions du Cerf, 1985), 37–60. For a much more detailed and updated review of the entire Chenu affair, see Fouilloux, "L'affaire Chenu 1937–1943," *Revue des sciences philosophiques et théologiques* 98, no. 2 (April–June 2014): 261–352.

33 Marie-Dominique Chenu, *Une école de théologie: Le Saulchoir* (Kain: Le Saulchoir, 1937); republished by Éditions du Cerf in 1985.

34 Louis Charlier, *Essai sur le problème théologique* (Thuillies: Ramgal, 1938). For a general account of these two condemnations, see Mettepenningen, *Nouvelle Théologie*, 47–57 and 61–69; Mettepenningen, "L'Essai de Louis Charlier (1938): une contribution à la Nouvelle Théologie," *Revue théologique de Louvain* 32 (2008): 211–38.

35 Marie-Michel Labourdette, "Théologie, intelligence de la foi," *Revue thomiste* 46, no. 1 (1946): 5–44.

36 See Marie-Dominique Chenu, "Position de la théologie," *Revue des sciences philosophiques et théologiques* 24 (1935): 232–57, reprinted as *La foi dans l'intelligence* in Chenu's *La parole de Dieu*, vol. 1 (Paris: Éditions du Cerf, 1964), 115–38; Chenu, *Une école de théologie: le Saulchoir*; Louis Charlier, *Essai sur le problème théologique*, Bibliothèque Orientations: Section scientifique, 1 (Thuillies: Ramgal, 1938); Jean-François

Indeed, for his developed notion of science, Labourdette depends on Jacques Maritain's *Degrees of Knowledge*, which emerged, at least in part, in the context of the conversations which culminated in the debate over Christian philosophy in the 1930s (1930–1936).[37] Labourdette begins by giving a brief definition of science, its types, and the nature of observation, all influenced by Aristotle's *Posterior Analytics* and the Scholastic tradition. A lengthy treatment of the object of faith follows, and one should remember that this was an ongoing and highly charged topic that had been developing since the Modernist crisis, especially after the publication of Pierre Rousselot's *The Eyes of Faith*.[38] Labourdette argues that Revelation's mode of expression is in an "ensemble of statements, through which God makes Himself known to humanity."[39] Striking a laudable balance, he writes "What grandeur and poverty are involved in our formulas of faith!" On the one hand they are an "inferior kind of packaging given to the supernatural," however, they "lead our mind to this Sovereign Reality which exceeds them; this is what they *conform* it to; this Object is what our intellect is assimilated to through them."[40] Far

---

Bonnefoy, "La théologie comme science et l'explication de la foi selon saint Thomas d'Aquin," *Ephemerides theologicae Lovanienses* 14 (1937): 421–46, 600–31; Marie-Rosaire Gagnebet, "La nature de la théologie spéculative," *Revue thomiste* 44 (1938): 1–39, 213–55, 645–74.

[37] Jacques Maritain, *Degrees of Knowledge*, trans. Gerald Phelan et al. (South Bend: University of Notre Dame Press, 1995). For the Christian philosophy debate, see Gregory Sadler, *Reason Fulfilled by Revelation: The 1930s Christian Philosophy Debate in France* (Washington DC: The Catholic University of America Press, 2011); and Ralph McInerny, *Preambula Fidei: Thomism and the God of the Philosophers* (Washington DC: The Catholic University of America Press, 2006).

[38] For a complete survey of the debate written at the time, see Roger Aubert, *Le Problème de l'acte de foi: Données traditionnelles et résultats des controversies récentes*, 3rd ed. (Louvain: Universitas Catholica Lovaniensis, 1958). For Labourdette's treatment of the act of faith, one may consult, "La foi théologale et la connaissance mystique d'après saint Jean de la Croix," *Revue thomiste* 41 (1936): 593–629; 42 (1937): 16–57 and 191–229; "Le développement vital de la foi théologale," *Revue thomiste* 43 (1937): 101–15; "Foi et crédibilité (chronique)," *Revue thomiste* 52 (1952): 215–25; "La vie théologale selon saint Thomas, L'objet de la foi," *Revue thomiste* 58 (1958): 597–622; "La vie théologale selon Thomas d'Aquin, L'affection dans la foi," *Revue thomiste* 60 (1960): 364–80; *La foi*, "Grand cours" de théologie morale, vol. 8 (Paris: Parole et Silence, 2015). For Garrigou-Lagrange's most comprehensive treatment of the formal resolution of faith, see *On Divine Revelation*, vol. 1, trans. Matthew K. Minerd (Steubenville, OH: Emmaus Academic, 2021), 655–775.

[39] Labourdette, "Theology: Faith Seeking Understanding," 99 below.

[40] Labourdette, "Theology: Faith Seeking Understanding," 99 below. The status of these formulas had been intensely debated, and for an example of a radicalization of Rousselot, in which concepts are minimized, even denigrated, see Marie-Dominique Chenu, "The Eyes of Faith," in *Faith and Theology*, trans. Denis Hickey (New York: Macmillan, 1968), 8–14. For an exposition in line with Labourdette's own theological position, see Romanus

from being dead propositions, cut off from "life," in them we find the *means* for "elevating us to divine knowledge [and there] we find our spirit's true and profound nourishment."[41] He then spells out the ecclesiology that flows from this theology of faith, defending against the reductionist charge that Thomistic ecclesiology is merely doctrinaire and authoritarian. True, the Church defines these formulas, fixes their meaning, and explains them, and thus, they appeal to authority. Nevertheless, authority is not the "true and fundamental motive" for our supernatural adherence. What motivates faith's adherence is supernatural revelation, God Himself as revealing, and the Church's mediation safeguards an "authentic encounter" with God who reveals.[42]

While outlining the nature of theology, Labourdette develops a nuanced position within the Thomist school's own notion of theological science,[43] explaining that theology does not come forth, strictly speaking, from the exercise of the virtue of faith, since faith does not reason or analyze, but instead, is ordered to *assent to revealed truths*. However, neither is theology merely an application of reason to the data of faith. Instead, theology is "brought about through supernatural faith *placing in its service* all of our intellectual resources with the goal of bringing, as far as is possible, the intelligibility of the truths of faith to the perfect state of knowledge which we call science."[44]

In treating the structure of theology, Labourdette makes a critical move by defending the importance of history and its relationship with speculative theology, attempting to dispel the simplistic notion that Thomism is fundamentally ahistorical. He argues that historical reflection provides indispensable service "in determining what is revealed and in understanding it," while still maintaining that speculative theology is the crowning achievement of theological science.[45] This subordination of historical investigation to spec-

---

Cessario, *Christian Faith and the Theological Life* (Washington, DC: The Catholic University of America Press, 1996).

[41] Labourdette, "Theology: Faith Seeking Understanding," 101 below.

[42] In this, Labourdette is echoing with great fidelity, what can be found at length in the text of Garrigou-Lagrange cited in note 38. This teaching was consistently found in the various editions of Garrigou-Lagrange's text.

[43] A number of texts are cited regarding this topic in Matthew Minerd, "Wisdom be Attentive: The Noetic Structure of Sapiential Knowledge," *Nova et Vetera* (English edition) 18, no. 4 (2020): 1103–46; also see Reginald Garrigou-Lagrange, "Remarks Concerning the Metaphysical Character of St. Thomas's Moral Theology, in Particular as It Is Related to Prudence and Conscience," trans. Matthew K. Minerd, *Nova et Vetera* 17, no. 1 (2019): 261–66 ("Translator's Appendix 1: Concerning the Formal Object of Acquired Theology").

[44] Labourdette, "Theology: Faith Seeking Understanding," 105 below.

[45] Labourdette is echoing a sentiment that one can find in the posthumous remarks about Ambroise Gardeil written by Jacques Maritain in his introduction to Ambroise Gardeil, *La vraie vie chrétienne* (Paris: Desclée de Brouwer, 1935), viii: "He maintained

ulative thought will be a significant point of difference between the Thomist and *ressourcement* thinkers. However, Labourdette never posits the compartmentalized reduction of history that his interlocutors charge, as theology is never in a finished state here below, and there is a "continual back-and-forth" between speculative theology and historical theology, which remain closely intertwined. Nonetheless, he recognizes the limits of history and its provisional character, that it cannot shackle the speculative work of the theologian: "We do not need to completely traverse the entire field of positive theology in its multiple developments in order to then begin our reflection on the intelligibility of the revealed datum as well as on the possibility of developing it into a science."[46] Underscoring this unity, he writes that "at the same time, historical and critical reflection will develop themselves along with their own proper methodologies. If both remain theological, each will benefit from the other's progress."[47]

Without formally engaging in a debate, Labourdette draws this article to a close by succinctly articulating that what divides Thomism from the *ressourcement* thinkers is precisely the powers of the human intellect. Indeed it was the question of Aristotle that hung over the debate since the Modernist crisis when Édouard Le Roy accused Thomists of requiring a double conversion, first to Aristotle and then to Christianity.[48] The defining Scholastic response to this criticism emerged out of this debate in Garrigou-Lagrange's *Le sens commun*, which Gardeil adopted.[49] The response to this charge by Le Roy might be summarized in Gardeil's response: "Must the simple concepts of revelation embrace the modalities of Aristotelianism? Yes and no. No, if it is the systematic and personal mentality of the philosopher. Yes, if it is the human mentality itself, to the extent that it is present in the Aristotelian

---

speculative studies at the level that is rightfully due to them, not ceasing to show, at once, their primacy over so-called positive studies, as well as their harmony with them."

[46] Labourdette, "Theology: Faith Seeking Understanding," 107 below. The influence of Ambroise Gardeil is readily apparent, and this is a position that Garrigou-Lagrange would broadly align himself with. See Ambroise Gardeil, *Le Donné de Révélé* (Juvisy: Cerf, 1909; 2nd ed. 1932).

[47] Labourdette, "Theology: Faith Seeking Understanding," 107 below. For a summary of the discussions concerning positive theology at around this time, see Celestine Luke Salm, "The Problem of Positive Theology," S.T.D. Dissertation, The Catholic University of America, 1955.

[48] See Guy Mansini, *What is Dogma? The Meaning and Truth of Dogma in Edouard Le Roy and His Scholastic Opponents* (Rome: Gregorian University, 1985).

[49] See Reginald Garrigou-Lagrange, *Thomistic Common Sense: The Philosophy of Being and the Development of Doctrine*, trans. Matthew K. Minerd (Steubenville, OH: Emmaus Academic, 2021).

mentality by the data of common sense."⁵⁰ Near the conclusion of his own article, Labourdette reiterates this point emphatically:

> The outlooks that we find ourselves fighting against profoundly underrate the powers of the human intellect and cast suspicion on everything that is a "conceptual construction." These attitudes are connected with quite different currents of thought than those animating St. Thomas's own and, indeed, clash with what quite obviously was his constant practice as a theologian. Thus, the problem must be transferred to philosophy's terrain and, most especially, that of the critique of knowledge.... This difference of philosophical outlooks, which, without always being explicit, is profound, is not the only motive for the low esteem many have for the great theological syntheses and, along with them, for speculative theology itself. Many join to it a desire that testifies to their Christian sense and their zeal for God's House: does not speculative theology run the risk of incorporating a "philosophical system" into Christian doctrine? Will this not involve (and compromise) the faith in our speculations? ... In point of fact, what theology claims to offer to faith as *an instrument of scientific explanation* is not the doctrine of this or that author, Aristotle, Plato, Confucius, or Shankara, but rather, those notions which best assure us of attaining *definitive truths* and imperishable values, whose scope is not temporal or relative but, instead, supra-temporal.... What theology wishes to use (and, moreover, what the Church likewise uses in the more precise formulations of her dogmas) are not truth values that are relative to a given author or to a given time. Rather, she wishes to use absolute truth values, by which it reaches a particular, unchangeable aspect of reality. Here, the fact that such truth values do indeed exist is still a philosophical problem whose resolution depends on the notion that one forms for oneself concerning the intellect and its scope, as well as concerning the unity and permanence of human *nature*.⁵¹

Although "Theology: Faith Seeking Understanding" stands on its own, it will be explicitly presupposed in the later debate, which is chronicled in the sequence of articles following it in the present volume. The next four articles to be discussed constitute a whole and were published as a small book

---

50 Gardeil, *Le Donné*, 307. For an important discussion of this theme, noting how philosophical explication is and is not involved in this connecting of dogmas to common sense (superelevated by supernatural faith), see Garrigou-Lagrange, *Thomistic Common Sense*, 278–86. For recent discussion of this topic (with some critical words concerning Gardeil and Garrigou-Lagrange), see Guy Mansini, "The Historicity of Dogma and Common Sense: Ambroise Gardeil, Reginald Garrigou-Lagrange, Yves Congar, and the Modern Magisterium," *Nova et Vetera* (English edition) 18, no. 1 (2020): 111–38. Some systematic discussion of this issue will be undertaken below.

51 Labourdette, "Theology: Faith Seeking Understanding," 123 below.

on account of publication delays with the *Revue thomiste*. The Thomists saw Daniélou's aforementioned article in the popular Jesuit journal *Études* as an unprovoked attack, and Labourdette wrote that Daniélou had "deeply wounded several of us," and he wanted to "respond as quickly and as clearly as possible to what was understood at the time to be real act of anti-Thomist aggression."[52]

Gathering together the texts in a single volume, the Toulouse Dominicans wished to bring together their relevant pieces, together with an anonymous Jesuit *Response*, written by de Lubac,[53] and not included here on account of its publication elsewhere.[54] The small volume constitutes the definitive Toulouse response to the Jesuits of Fourvière.[55] The complete exchange looks like the following:

1. Raymond-Léopold Bruckberger, "A Theological Dialogue"
2. Michel Labourdette, "Theology and its Sources"
3. Anonymous Jesuits, "Response"
4. Michel Labourdette, "Criticism in Theology: A Response"
5. Marie-Joseph Nicolas, "Conclusion: Theological Progress and Fidelity to St. Thomas"

Labourdette's "Theology and Its Sources," directly questioned the animating spirit of recent work by Jesuit authors reflected in their parallel series *Théologie* and *Sources Chrétienne*, and Fouilloux states, "Theology and Its Sources" is anything but polemical: "the tone is meant to be modest, serene, and even explicitly benevolent."[56] Despite this, Labourdette's article resulted in a swift and sharp anonymous reply from the Jesuits published in their journal *Recherches de science religieuse*.[57] Due to the aforementioned postwar delays with the *Revue thomiste*, a volume apart was published as *Dialogue théologique*, containing both articles, a response from Labourdette ("Criticism in Theology: A Response"), along with a stentorian introduction by Raymond-Léopold Bruckberger,[58] and a conclusion by Marie-Joseph Nicolas,

---

52 Fouilloux, "Dialogue," 157.

53 See note 68.

54 Fouilloux, "Dialogue," 174; Anon., "Response to 'The Sources of Theology'[sic]," in Kelly, *Ressourcement Theology*, 73–82.

55 For the definitive history of this exchange, see Fouilloux, "Dialogue," 154–59.

56 Marie-Michel Labourdette, "La Théologie et ses sources," *Revue thomiste* 11 (1946): 353–71; Fouilloux, "Dialogue," 155.

57 Henri de Lubac et al. (anonymously written), "Théologie et ses sources: Reponse," *Recherches de science religieuse* 33 (1946): 385–401.

58 Bruckberger, a now-forgotten figure, was a larger-than life Dominican from this era. The primary chaplain to the French resistance during World War II, he would come to have

"Conclusion: Theological Progress and Fidelity to St. Thomas." The fascicule was published as *Dialogue théologique*.[59]

In his introduction, Bruckberger appeals for a "theological dialogue" in what is certainly a provocative attempt to insert Thomistic thought into a dialogue to which it was not invited, Daniélou's appeal for dialogue with the modern world. Indeed, this appeal explicitly excluded a repudiated Scholastic thought from the conversation. Thus, "A Theological Dialogue," is very much a manifesto for a return to Thomism and can in every sense be seen as a kind of counter-manifesto to Daniélou's "Present Orientations." A side-by-side comparison offers the clearest picture of the underlying mentality of the differing sides. Both men were writing barely a year after the weapons of the Second World War had been silenced, and the stark differences of their cultural, intellectual, and religious analyses are striking. Daniélou's exuberant, almost triumphal piece cries out to the "men of today" that "now is the time" to build a new theology, new man, new Christianity, and new civilization on the rubrics of the most cutting-edge modern thought, which for Daniélou was reflective of the best ancient thought. This is contrasted against Bruckberger's solemn warning that the only hope for a "world wherein intellects have been so violated, hearts so debased, and bodies so trampled" was a theology that could help man regain his own dignity and raise his "intelligence to the highest disciplines, those which, instead of dividing man, can unite him in the search for, and possession of, the truth."[60]

For Bruckberger, scientific theology is central to this task and should not be renounced simply because a "physio-chemical" notion of science has been monopolized by the modern world. In this effort Aquinas is the great architect of the science of theology:

> With St. Thomas, theological style is not the sole matter at hand. More importantly still, there is the scientific value of his work. In Greek

---

a tumultuous public life, at times filled with private scandal, at other times publicly taking up his pen in open war against the French episcopate after the Second Vatican Council. For a partial, albeit incomplete, account of his life, see Bernadette and Bernard Chovelon, *Bruckberger: L'enfant terrible* (Paris: Éditions du Cerf, 2011). For some of Bruckberger's own auto-biographical reflections (prior to his final years, which reportedly included repentance for sins against his vows as a Dominican) and some relevant articles written during the 1970s, see Raymond-Léopold Bruckberger, *Tu finira sur l'échafaud: Mémoires* (Paris: Flammarion, 1978); *À l'heure où les ombres s'allongent* (Paris: Albin Michel, 1989); *Toute l'église en clameurs* (Paris: Flammarion, 1977).

[59] See Marie-Michel Labourdette, Marie-Joseph Nicolas, Raymond-Léopold Bruckberger, *Dialogue théologique: Pièces du débat entre "La Revue Thomiste" d'une part et les R.R. P.P. de Lubac, Daniélou, Bouillard, Fessard, von Balthasar, S.J., d'autre part* (Saint-Maximin: Les Arcades, 1947).

[60] Bruckberger, "A Theological Dialogue," 127 below.

temples as well as Romanesque and Gothic churches, in the Palace of Versailles and Baroque monuments, we see various expressions of the identical and invariable laws that constitute the universal code of architecture, at least as regards the elementary laws of gravity and resistance that a native applies instinctively when building his hut and that Mansart observed in designing the Versailles. And without the application of these laws, neither hut nor castle would ever exist.

The same is true for St. Thomas. His value does not consist so much in having constructed a magnificent theological edifice in an admirable style which is now, however, outdated. Rather, his value lies in the fact that, more than any other thinker, he made greater progress in theological knowledge, in its scientific systematization, to the point of having written the manual *par excellence* for the theologian, a text that will always be of use in order to purely and simply become a theologian, just as one goes to school in order to become an architect.[61]

Bruckberger's assessment is tempered by the sober awareness of "human malice and stupidity" which plagues a humanity "worn out as much from lies as it is from hardships and sorrow," and this sober appraisal, so divergent from that of Daniélou, concludes with the Gospel admonition that the "harvest is plenty, but the laborers few."[62] Bruckberger feared that ultimately the exchange would be a failure and that a "dialogue of the deaf" would ensue. As we shall see, this is indeed what happened. Thus, as we read the texts, we can ask: Why is it that one of the most important exchanges of the modern era, on the vital question of the relationship between history, truth, theology, and dogma, was never brought to its completion? A fresh examination of the exchanges reveals the need for historical revision.

In contrast with the soaring rhetoric of Bruckberger's words, the tone of Labourdette's article is all the more striking, polite and affirming to the point of being almost obsequious. Keying in on two recent book collections edited by the Fourvière Jesuits, *Sources Chretiennes* and *Théologie*, which he praises in no uncertain terms, describing them, for example, as a "wonderful achievement," and "magnificent enterprise" which "cannot be highly praised enough," and after reviewing Jean Moureaux's *Sens chrétien de l' homme* in the most-glowing terms and without registering any strong accusation, Labourdette nonetheless raises "grave concerns" over the two collections, which manifest a "common spirit." However, he stresses that their "positive and constructive design is more important than the defects which tarnish their aim."

---

61 Bruckberger, "A Theological Dialogue," 128 below.
62 Bruckberger, "A Theological Dialogue," 132 below.

Before continuing with what he senses to be the anti-Scholastic aim of the two projects, Labourdette recognizes the deficiencies often manifest in the Scholasticism of his day in a self-effacing passage where he admits that a developed theology always risks getting stuck in its own problems and questions:

> It is almost run-of-the-mill to note—and this is easily confirmed—that on many points the problematics involved in our theology have become [overly] academic [*scolaire*]. I mean, it is something learned and often remains bookish in character. Such theology indeed lends itself to reflection and real solutions, but nonetheless, it lacks a kind of dynamism [*activation*]. It is freighted, too hastily presuming itself to be completed and perfected. Only with difficulty does it escape the temptation to indolence and ease, merely resting on its past achievements. . . . Anyone who has had to teach theology will have had ample opportunity to experience this mental laziness, more the friend of formulas than of apprehension, more eager to rest on what has been achieved than to seek the first apperceptions of such truths so that one might then trace out anew the whole subsequent course of thought, doing so in a wholly personal way.[63]

Labourdette further states that given that *ressourcement* theology has not presented itself in too-literal a formulation and remains in some respects vague, he will not identify individual thinkers, but instead, wishes simply to discuss certain tendencies and a contemporary mentality. Moreover, he makes a point of saying that he is not questioning the whole thought of either de Lubac or Daniélou, which he praises, but instead, wishes to raise concerns only about specific aspects. Further, he mildly notes that the emphasis on patristic riches is accompanied by a depreciation of scholastic theology, but he fears that this rejection threatens to ruin the foundations of their own project, which "presupposes a previously-existing edifice." It is clear that Labourdette is deeply concerned that Daniélou's rejection of scholastic thought in order to make contact with Marxism and existentialism (the history and subjectivity they presuppose and focus on) is imprudent. Furthermore, he rejects the notion that these categories are foreign to Thomism: "it is a perfectly living way of thinking, one that is both ambitious and capable of entering into and understanding new problems, able to assimilate everything contained in the most modern of doctrines." However, he continues, "it has too much respect for the truth and is too concerned with its scientific rigor and with avoiding facile conformism for it to adorn itself immediately with ideas and 'categories' that it would not have first carefully examined and critiqued."[64] Labourdette is clearly concerned that modern thought should be carefully tested and approached with caution lest

---

[63] Labourdette, "Theology and its Sources," 136.
[64] Labourdette, "Theology and its Sources," 141n8 below.

wisdom be swept away in the "flood of impermanence." Moreover, modern thought must take care to avoid "the permanent temptation to judge all systems of intellectual expression first and, indeed, ultimately, in terms of the historical context and experiences of its author and the era in which he lived, not essentially in terms of their conformity with the reality of what is."

He continues that history is not the issue, which in the form of positive theology, Thomism also finds indispensable, as he argued in his article "Theology: Faith Seeking Understanding," but in fact, the real issue is the *philosophy of history* that Daniélou and the others seemed to be employing, a philosophy of history that risked entailing a "pseudo-philosophy," unknowingly driven by a historical relativism. In this philosophy the notion of speculative truth becomes suspect: "The very idea that our mind could, in its most-assured notions, come to grasp and identify timeless truth becomes, strictly speaking, unthinkable."[65] This leads to a critique of Bouillard's work, which is occupied by concerns that Labourdette claims to also share: "to show how historical methodology need not lead to a form of complete relativism."[66] Labourdette points out the inherent weakness of distinguishing absolute affirmations from relative formulations and argues that our mind cannot isolate them from one another. Even here, Labourdette's magnanimity is front and center as he extols Bouillard's "praiseworthy" attempt to avoid relativism. Thus, Labourdette makes it clear that it is not history that is at issue, but rather the general *ressourcement* methodology concerning the place of historical studies in theology, and he concludes by reiterating points which he made earlier, stating that this attempt to make contact with existentialism, Marxism, and other contemporary currents, as especially laid out in Daniélou's "Present Orientations," falls "into the most unfortunate kind of ready harmony, drawing immediate connections between the most superficial confluences [of thinkers and ideas]," and Labourdette makes clear that his response is simply a defensive maneuver: "the powerful thrust of irrational philosophies is the principle cause of the offensive taken against scholastic philosophy, which we seek to defend."[67]

The most surprising aspect of the debate is de Lubac's anonymous response, which even figures like Jean Daniélou and the Jesuit superiors found too harsh and polemical.[68] De Lubac avoided direct debate altogether,

---

65 Labourdette, "Theology and its Sources," 146 below.

66 Labourdette, "Theology and its Sources," 149 below.

67 Labourdette, "Theology and its Sources," 157 below.

68 Because of the structural changes made to this volume, this text must be read in Patricia Kelly's aforementioned work, which however, for the reasons adduced at the beginning of this introduction, must be approached with caution. For de Lubac's confirmation of his authorship of the anonymous response in a 1988 letter to the Italian historian of theology Antonio Russo, see Aidan Nichols, "Thomism," 10. For the disapproval of the polemical tone of the response, see Fouilloux, "Dialogue," 181.

casting aspersion on Labourdette's legitimate questioning and attempted to array the Society itself against the Dominicans, citing an unnamed high authority who encouraged a response. As Fouilloux has noted, the response constitutes a real tragedy, as this is the moment that a much-needed discussion could have and should have happened, as the Toulouse Dominican interlocutors presented themselves interested in a serious and genuine dialogue. The moment, however, was lost as Garrigou-Lagrange's intervention, as we shall see, took center stage and overshadowed this overture.

De Lubac's article eludes a close analysis, as it deliberately makes no attempt to further the discussion but instead casts aspersion on Labourdette's claims and motives, with de Lubac declaring himself a victim put on trial. Further, the author gives the impression that he wants nothing to do with the Dominican discussion, and claims he is only responding on the advice of "high authorities." The opening of the response captures the tone of the piece:

> Fr. Labourdette does not want us to profess "the essential historical relativism of all human expressions of divine truths." He does not want a Christian mindset that is "ashamed of its past." He does not want "theological wisdom to be swept away by the flood of impermanence." He does not want historical methodology to be weighed down by a "pseudo-philosophy" which "replaces the metaphysical notion of speculative truth with that of a more modest historical truth." He does not want us to "perpetually recast our conceptions of God," all under the pretext of critiquing "theological progress." He does not want a "nominalist philosophy" which, through a veritable "caricature of the life of the mind," professes the notion that "the only thing that human reason ... directly reaches is its concepts, which such nominalism holds are mere empty abstractions, logical frameworks whose value is wholly pragmatic in nature." He does not want us to deny that "the divine message is addressed also to our intellect." He does not want us to subscribe to "the complete emptying of the idea of speculative truth." He does not want us to say that speculative truth is "inaccessible for us, nor, to deny our mind, "in its most assured notions," the power of grasping, "an atemporal truth." He does not want metaphysics and theology to be judged, in the end, "according to the categories of aesthetics." He does not want us to expect "that a teaching would do nothing more than awaken in us the sense of the beautiful or lead us to an incommunicable experience." Finally, he does not want us to doubt that there are "definitive acquisitions in the domain of knowledge."[69]

After framing these questions, de Lubac quickly dismisses them by declaring:

---

[69] Anon. (Henri de Lubac et al.), "La théologie et ses sources: Réponse," *Recherches de science religieuse* 33 (1946): 385–86 (pp. 76–77 in *Dialogue théologique*).

[How] right he is! We certainly do not want any of this any more than he does, and there is nothing that would give anyone any reason to suspect that we do want it. And he does not cite a single text of ours that implies any of this. Moreover, while we are happy to tell him that we are in full agreement, we are suprised that he has invited us to explain ourselves.[70]

De Lubac roundly dismisses any notion of a common project or "tendencies" and declares that the warning of historical relativism is comical. Sadly, through such defensiveness, he squandered an opportunity to discuss what would continue to be one of the most pressing issues throughout the twentieth century (and to our present day): the relationship between history, theology, truth, and dogma.

The Thomists gathered around the *Revue thomiste*, including figures such as Jacques Maritain, were stunned by the response and felt chastened. Fouilloux writes that the major feature of the Response is the "denial of the debate in substance."[71] Marie-Joseph Nicolas, in a letter to de Lubac, wrote that Labourdette's article was simply "a fair and courageous expression of a wounded and anxious Thomism," declaring that "if there is a fundamentalist [*intégriste*] party, we are not it," but in a firm response, de Lubac accused Labourdette of firing a "parthian arrow" based on "imaginations" that portray his victims as "semi-heretics."[72] Although Labourdette had a much warmer and fraternal personal correspondence with Daniélou, amongst themselves the Jesuits accused the Dominicans of being intellectually second-rate, and de Lubac declared that their time would be better spent in choir, later accusing Labourdette of avoiding a face-to-face encounter on account of "timidity."[73] De Lubac wrote to Daniélou that there was nothing else to discuss with the Dominicans, "because we do not accept the imaginations of Labourdette and Garrigou. If the good fathers so wish, let them tilt at windmills. However, I do not accept my name being placed upon these windmills."[74]

Maritain, in his turn, wrote that de Lubac "seemed to me to be a superior mind, though accompanied by that intellectual arrogance (virtuously concealed) frequently found among the Fathers of his Society."[75] Moreover, he

---

70 De Lubac, "La théologie," 386.

71 Fouilloux, "Dialogue," 173.

72 Marie-Joseph Nicolas, Letter to Henri de Lubac, February 5, 1947, with a response on February 7 (ASJF), quoted in Fouilloux, "Dialogue," 180.

73 Nichols, "Thomism and the Nouvelle Théologie," 15.

74 Henri de Lubac, Letter to Jean Daniélou, February 7, 1947 (ASJF), quoted in Fouilloux, "Dialogue," 180-181.

75 Jacques Maritain, Letter to Charles Journet, Oct. 6, 1945 (AJRM), quoted in Fouilloux, "Dialogue," 164.

declared that the "Jesuits, the more intelligent they are, the more they bend to the era in which they live and adapt to its weaknesses."[76] Fouilloux provides a more charitable interpretation of de Lubac than Maritain, writing in the *Response*, that we see "a man of poor health and anxious temperament, naturally inclined to exaggerate the scope of such a case and its effects. His pessimism, admittedly not wholly unfounded, gives the '*Response*' much of the severe formality and harshness that he will be accused of."[77] For his part, de Lubac expresses his frustration even more stridently in private correspondence, writing that the issues "are at once annoying and disarming. One cannot discuss this with children, but they should not be entrusted with positions as directors of major doctrinal reviews.... These childish actions risk causing a great deal of damage."[78]

The exchange is almost predictable at this point, with the chastened Labourdette responding defensively in order to further explain his positions and methodology against de Lubac's criticism. In his response, "Criticism and Theology" (as well as in his own annotations added to his original article when it was republished in the volume *Dialogue théologique*), he spends a good deal of time arguing a point that virtually everyone now admits, which de Lubac continually denied, namely, that there was, at least on some broad level, a movement and common project shared among the *ressourcement* theologians, and therefore, as current proponents of the movement have noted, certain general "tendencies" can in fact be discerned.[79]

---

[76] Jacques Maritain, Letter to Charles Journet, June 24, 1945 (AJRM), quoted in Fouilloux, "Dialogue," 164.

[77] Fouilloux, "Dialogue," 175.

[78] Henri de Lubac, Letters to Bruno de Solages, Feb. 8 and 15, *Archives dominicaines de la Toulouse*, henceforth, ADT, quoted in Fouilloux, "Dialogue," 181–82.

[79] Jürgen Mettepenningen sees four central characteristics (it is French, open to the historical method, favoring positive theology, and anti-Neoscholastic) in *Nouvelle Théologie*, 7–13. For a treatment of the cultural and generational tendencies of the movement, see Kirwan, *Avant-garde*. David Grummet sees the movement as a "collection of ideas" and "tendencies" in "Nouvelle Théologie," in *Cambridge Dictionary of Christian Theology*, ed. Ian McFarland, David Fergusson, Karen Kilby, and Iain Torrance (Cambridge: Cambridge University Press, 2014), 348–49. Gabriel Flynn describes it as a "movement of renewal" comprised of a "host of new initiatives" in the introduction to *Ressourcement: A Movement for Renewal in Twentieth-Century Catholic Theology*, ed. Gabriel Flynn and Paul Murray (Oxford: Oxford University Press, 2012), 1–2. Hans Boersma repeatedly speaks of a "ressourcement movement," even with "key characteristics," in *Nouvelle Théologie and Sacramental Ontology: Return to Mystery* (Oxford: Oxford University Press, 2009), 134. Brian Daley writes that the Scholastic Msgr. Pietro Parente "was not entirely wrong" about the existence of a movement and outlines the "characteristics" and "basic convictions" of the *ressourcement* thinkers in "The *Nouvelle Théologie* and the Patristic Revival: Sources, Symbols and the Science of Theology," *International Journal of Systematic Theology* 7, no. 4 (2005): 363, 375.

Labourdette argues that these tendencies can be discerned in the two collections, *Théologie* and *Sources Chrétiennes*. He dismisses de Lubac's insinuation that he is unduly obsessed with heresy hunting, arguing instead, that legitimate concerns regarding history and relativism were at stake in the unifying aspects of these collections.[80] Furthermore, he claims that Thomism can be attentive to history and subjectivity, and nowhere does he indicate that these categories in and of themselves are to be avoided. In attempting to refocus the debate, now becoming deeply personal, Labourdette concludes by articulating a list of general norms that should be followed in any continued discussion.

Nicolas provided the *Dialogue théologique* volume with its conclusion, "Theological Progress and Fidelity to St. Thomas," therein declaring that they were "disappointed at having received a joke in response to our concerns."[81] He further defended the concept of speculative truth, as well as St. Thomas' own categories. To Nicolas' eyes, to the degree that contemporary thought scorns those categories, it poses a great danger:

> The abandonment of the central positions of St. Thomas's metaphysics would lead, little by little, to the ruin of the faith. Maybe we are wrong in feeling that St. Thomas is so absent from the new theology. Perhaps this reservation simply comes from the well-justified persuasion that our contemporary mentality is too impregnated with idealism, existentialism, or evolutionism for Thomistic language to be rendered understandable, even if it were expressed in language that is fashionable today. Perhaps one feels, in fact, that Thomism is too much the property of a particular sort of mind which is closed off to history, science, and to contemporary sentiments for it possibly to be used freely. Perhaps the need to Christianize certain intellectual subjects which hold an all-powerful sway over contemporary minds is judged to be far too urgent for us to spend time waiting until Thomism manages to integrate this into its metaphysics without denaturing the latter.[82]

Sadly expressing the difficulties involved, Nicolas notes that holding to the truth of Thomism necessarily puts one at odds with much of the modern world, which he believes is, nonetheless, fundamentally flawed, despite being assimilable on various points. To stress this point, we can once more cite Charles Journet's letter to Jacques Maritain, in which the former declares "in

---

80 In the case of the *Sources Chrétiennes* series, Labourdette's explicit concern was *not* with the publication of patristic works in translation but, rather, with the notes and introductions which accompanied these texts, voicing an anti-scholastic bias.

81 Nicolas, "Theological Progress and Fidelity to St. Thomas," 187 below. He is referring to a joke that is cited in our translation.

82 Nicolas, "Theological Progress and Fidelity to St. Thomas," 190 below.

this disintegration of the world, one seems a fool for trying to remain faithful to St. Thomas."[83] Labourdette wrote to Maritain and declared that the Jesuit response was "a bit of a declaration of war," and the Jesuits "seem convinced that no one will dare to speak out on behalf of Thomism."[84] For his own part, Nicolas stressed that Thomists take no joy in being so ostracized and long to participate in the categories that Daniélou's "Present Orientations" stressed, namely, engagement and incarnation:

> Perhaps the vivacity of our criticism bore the accent of the bitterness experienced when one feels so lonely in holding an intellectual outlook which we, however, feel it intellectually and morally impossible not to take, an outlook which we, in the end, believe holds the greatest promise for success, while modern thought increasingly unveils to the eyes of all the profound vices that corrupt it.[85]

In conclusion, Nicolas admitted "it is more difficult for us than for them to accept all intellectual outlooks which differ from our own." However, he insists that they cannot be accused of being haughty and overly self-confident: "We know how to recognize our errors and forever will do so." Though, he is also clear that the Thomists will continue to elaborate their convictions:

> While we strive never to confuse, on the one hand, the human mind's general aptitude for reaching certitude with, on the other, the truth of our own judgments, we will not be overly scrupulous in saying what we think, beseeching those who read us not to see in our criticism verdicts uttered by a judge or even appeals to a sacred tribunal but, simply, the free and frank expression of our sentiments.[86]

Nicholas concludes with the tone that Bruckberger took at the opening by declaring that they too seek to reach the needs of modern man and to "resolve the questions that every contemporary Christian thinker asks himself with anguish, doing so with the assistance of St. Thomas's thought."[87] By the spring of 1947, any hope of a fruitful dialogue had passed, but the Toulouse Dominicans sought an amicable face-to-face meeting with the Jesuits.

---

[83] Charles Journet, Letter to Jacques Maritain, August 9, 1945, *Archives Jacques et Raïssa Maritain* (Jacques and Raïssa Maritain Archives, Kolbsheim, France, henceforth, AJRM, quoted in Fouilloux, "Dialogue," 158.

[84] Michel Labourdette, Letter to Jacques Maritain, March 23, 1945 (AJRM), quoted in Fouilloux, "Dialogue," 159–60.

[85] Nicolas, "Theological Progress and Fidelity to St. Thomas," 191 below.

[86] Nicolas, "Theological Progress and Fidelity to St. Thomas," 191 below.

[87] Nicolas, "Theological Progress and Fidelity to St. Thomas," 192 below.

Bouillard wrote to de Lubac, declaring that the Dominicans "obviously have an inferiority complex faced with those who attacked them. They wish to meet with us, not so much to explain themselves as to receive a public testimony of esteem."[88] Fouilloux writes that, despite this, goodwill persisted in the Dominican camp and cites as proof their article "Closing Remarks Concerning Our Position," which Labourdette described in a letter to Maritain as "a text that is not at all polemical but which has the importance of wanting to define the burning questions somewhat," and he insists that he wants to free the debate from personal implications and insist on the freedom of different theological schools.[89] Roman Thomists felt that Labourdette was too soft and downplayed the relationship between the Magisterium and theology, with one declaring that Labourdette seemed to apologize simply for speaking clearly, and, on the other side, the Jesuits, likewise, were not satisfied, with de Lubac declaring it only a partial retraction.[90] Finally, Bruno de Solges, Rector of the Institut Catholique in Toulouse, organized a kind of Thomistic joint statement that de Lubac agreed to sign, but Chenu and Fessard were reluctant, as the former was convinced that Thomism needed to be rethought in terms of modern science and the latter fearing that they would bring ridicule upon themselves by signing it.[91] Ultimately, the Jesuits decided against any accord unless *Dialogue* was disavowed.

In mid-1947, the Dominicans were surprised that the Jesuit philosopher, Jean-Marie Le Blond, wrote an article in *Recherches* that seemed to restart the polemics on the question of analogy and its application to notional relativity.[92] As we shall see, the doctrine of analogy will be central, as both Bruno de Solages and Bouillard invoke the notion as the key to firmly grounding the disputed union of the formulation and affirmation. Le Blond's article is worth describing here, as he puts front-and-center the question of anthropology and in particular the doctrine of Pierre Rousselot, so central to the *nouveaux théologiens*, which posited that an intellectual drive toward the absolute precedes and orders a weak and more unstable conceptual

---

[88] Henri Bouillard, Letter to Henri de Lubac, May 4, 1947 (ASJF), quoted in Fouilloux, "Dialogue," 189.

[89] Marie-Michel Labourdette, Letter to Jacques Maritain, April 11 (ADT), quoted in Fouilloux, "Dialogue," 189–90.

[90] See Fouilloux, "Dialogue," 190.

[91] See Fouilloux, "Dialogue," 191.

[92] See Jean Marie Le Blond, 'L'Analogie de la vérité: Réflexion d'un philosophe sur une controverse théologique', RSR, 34 (1947), 129–41. An English translation exists in Kelly's volume, though, for the reasons adduced at the beginning of this introduction, it must be approached with caution. For Le Blond's intervention, see Hans Boersma, "Analogy of Truth: The Sacramental Epistemology of *Nouvelle Théologie*," in *Ressourcement: A Movement for Renewal in Twentieth-Century Catholic Theology*, 157–71.

knowledge.[93] (Moreover, the Dominican parties gathered in this volume sensed the background influence of Henri Bergson, whose theory of pre-conceptual intuition resembled aspects of the noetic presupposed by Le Blond and Bouillard, and Garrigou-Lagrange was quite insistent on the importance of bearing in mind Maurice Blondel's writings related to the nature of truth.[94]) He begins by invoking Aquinas on the analogy of being and insists on an equally present "analogy of truth":

> The thesis of the analogy of truth, in fact, does not impose itself to a lesser degree than that of the analogy of being. Truth is not univocal; there is, we have said, a subsistent Truth which is absolute, which is God Himself in His simplicity, God insofar as He knows Himself and knows all things in Himself. The counterpart of this assertion, which no Christian philosopher can question, is this, which no one will deny but from which we will not always frankly draw the consequences, namely, that all the other truths are complex and deficient, that they imitate simple truth, without being able to equal it in their multiplicity. They are, in a word, truths which are *analogous* to the first Truth.[95]

Le Blond continues by explaining the relationship of these complex and deficient truths with the simple truth of God himself within the anthropology inspired by Rousellot and Joseph Maréchal.[96] These truths are still true,

---

[93] For an overview of the importance of Rousselot on the Jesuit *nouvelle théologiens*, see Kirwan, *Avant-garde*, 76–90, 108–21; and Boersma, *Nouvelle Théologie and Sacramental Ontology*, 67–83; and for the influence of Rousselot on Chenu's development, see Carmelo Giuseppe Conticulo, "'De Contemplatione' (Angelicum, 1920) La Thèse inédite de doctorat du M.-D. Chenu," *Revue de sciences philosophiques et théologiques* 75 (1991): 362–422.

[94] For the clearest exposition of the Bergsonian notion of intuition, see Henri Bergson, *An Introduction to Metaphysics*, trans. T. E. Hulme (Indianapolis: Bobbs-Merrill Educational Publishing, 1980). Bergson would remain a regular intellectual foe for Garrigou-Lagrange. A strong Thomistic response to Bergson, dependent on Garrigou-Lagrange, can be found in English in Jacques Maritain, *Bergsonian Philosophy and Thomism*, ed. Ralph McInerny, trans. Mabelle L. Andison and J. Gordon Andison (Notre Dame, IN: University of Notre Dame Press, 2007); also see Maritain, *De Bergson à Thomas d'Aquin* (New York: Éditions de la Maison française, 1944). The various relevant works of Blondel will be cited at length by Garrigou-Lagrange in the essays collected in this volume. For accounts of his influence on figures involved in the debate here gathered, see the index entries "Blondelian" and "Blondel, Maurice" in Kirwan, *Avant-garde*; William L. Portier, "Twentieth-Century Catholic Theology and the Triumph of Maurice Blondel," *Communio* (English edition) 38 (Spring 2011): 103–37; Michael A. Conway, "Maurice Blondel and Ressourcement," in *Ressourcement: A Movement for Renewal in Twentieth-Century Catholic Theology*, 65–82; Peter J. Bernardi, "Maurice Blondel: Precursor of the Second Vatican Council," *Josephinum Journal of Theology* 22, nos. 1–2 (2015): 59–77.

[95] Le Blond, "L'Analogie," 130.

[96] On the work of Maréchal's "Transcendental Thomism" in the background of Le Blond as well, see McCool, *Nineteenth Century Scholasticism*, 257–59.

because, in grasping any unity of concepts and judgments, its tendency to the absolute is manifested to the mind. In fact, the positing of the absolute, the existence of limitless act, is implied in every judgment through the use of the verb "to be," whether "copulatively" or "existentially." This positing of the absolute, which precisely speaking gives our affirmations their own, proper character, constitutes the *form* of our knowing, in an affirmation that extends to infinity and whose various representations provide a limiting *matter*. It unveils the ideal and the spring of the mind in this fundamental, implicit affirmation of the absolute underlying all its acts.[97]

Le Blond further stresses the difference between absolute truth and human truth, writing that "relative to the absolute and, as a result, distinct from the absolute, human truth is . . . relative to that which is multiple and mutable."[98] Thus, truth here below is composite, resulting from the encounter of two elements, the drive [*visée*] towards the absolute gives to the truth its proper character and imprints the character of Subsistent Truth.[99] However, on the other hand the concrete situation, in time and space, a limiting and restrictive element that explains in human truth, no longer the character of truth, but instead its character *precisely as human*.[100] It is this second aspect which introduces historicity into knowledge, and "it is not contradictory to speak of successive aspects of the truth developing in time."[101] Each individual drive toward the absolute has an individual character on account of its unique reference: "Each era, each school, and even each man has an original way of striving for the absolute and of drawing up its image, doing so with tendencies and images which are convergent and analogous, though they ultimately remain differentiated by their points of departure."[102]

This is especially true for St. Thomas, who, according to Le Blond, is sometimes treated as a divine word whose historical character is lost, and Thomists frequently argue about the "mind of Thomas," demonstrating a "clumsy veneration" that seeks to place Thomas above time. Thus, he says, Thomists have made very little progress for centuries, arguing over the same texts in order to precisely determine what the mind of Thomas is on a whole host of points. Le Blond declares that it is the historians who have finally made progress toward an "objective and exact" knowledge of Thomas.[103] Of

---

97 Le Blond, "L'Analogie," 131.
98 Le Blond, "L'Analogie," 134.
99 Le Blond, "L'Analogie," 134–35.
100 Le Blond, "L'Analogie," 135.
101 Le Blond, "L'Analogie," 135.
102 Le Blond, "L'Analogie," 136.
103 Le Blond, "L'Analogie," 136.

course, Le Blond refers here to figures such as Gilson and Chenu, and he continues with a discussion of the former's work.[104]

Attempting to integrate his account of the analogy of truth into the analogy of proportionality, Le Blond likens knowledge to a bronze coin, of real but inferior value, and it would be chimerical to exchange this currency for the gold coin it represents, which "synthesizes" in itself all the riches and which only God can give us by communicating himself directly to us.[105] Le Blond finally gets to the all-important question of the definition of truth and declares it cannot be a total adequation to reality, but it is "a certain assimilation which always leaves a certain degree of ignorance."[106]

Le Blond concludes by warning that if this doctrine is not adopted, a definitive break with the modern world will occur. Indeed, he declares that the "most profound wishes of the Church" call for adapting herself not only to the language but also the mentality of distant peoples: "she is not afraid to see her theology translated, not only into foreign words, but even into foreign concepts."[107] Le Blond's final paragraph is worth partially quoting here, as it underscores the link between the question of truth and his Rousselot[108]-inspired anthropology, which was simultaneously being debated in de Lubac's *Surnaturel*:[109]

> It would represent the ignorance of analogy, the transcendence of divine truth, and the proper character of human science. It would be a sign of a hidden but very real victory of Cartesian rationalism and of Spinozist

---

[104] Concerning the affection felt by Gilson, himself a close associate of Chenu, for the *nouvelle théologie*, see "Correspondence Étienne Gilson—Michel Labourdette," ed. Henry Donneaud, *Revue thomiste* 94 (1994): 479–529; also, see Étienne Gilson and Henri de Lubac, *Letters of Etienne Gilson to Henri De Lubac*, trans. Mary Emily Hamilton (San Francisco: Ignatius Press, 1988).

[105] This is an analogy that the *nouveaux théologiens* drew heavily on from even their first years reading Rousselot, and de Lubac wrote to Yves de Montcheuil: "Because if it is true that Thomism's theory of the agent intellect, the phantasm, and the essence of things is now untenable, as you claim, and also that they constitute the most apparent part of the doctrine of Aquinas, then, on the other hand, it seems to me also true that we find explicitly in St Thomas certain principles even more fundamental. When these are drawn out, they overshadow the famous 'material essences', thus permitting a disciple of St Thomas to sacrifice them without being unfaithful to the master. Rousselot remarked in his thesis that if St Thomas held to the essences, it was because he was preoccupied with higher things. He does not take the trouble to verify the copper treasure that the world of his time thought was gold. . . . More and more I find in St. Thomas texts that open me to other perspectives." De Lubac, letter to Yves de Montcheuil, dated Thursday, Autumn 1924, ASJV, quoted in Kirwan, *Avant-garde*, 111.

[106] Le Blond, "L'Analogue," 139.

[107] Le Blond, "L'Analogie," 141.

[108] Along with Blondel and Bergson.

[109] Henri de Lubac, *Surnaturel: Études historiques* (Paris: Aubier, 1946).

univocity, no matter how venerable the clothing that covers them. Perhaps a theologian could manifest the intrusion of this rationalism in certain theories concerning a quasi-natural faith, where human logic leaves practically nothing for grace. In any case, it emerges in the confusion that some would like to establish between absolute and univocal, between relative and analogous. This represents a formidable danger for Christian philosophy, and it is fundamentally opposed to the spirit of St. Thomas. Truth has an absolute character, but it is not univocal. Our human truths, which are not purely relative, are only analogous to the divine truth.[110]

In response to Le Blond's article, Labourdette and Nicolas penned a lengthy article in *Revue thomiste*, "The Analogy of Truth and the Unity of Theological Science." After a five-page summary of Le Blond's arguments, Labourdette and Nicolas begin a lengthy discussion of the nature of truth and the philosophical and theological anthropology that underpin claims that one makes concerning these matters. They carefully distinguish logical truth (which will be the primary domain of their concerns) from the ontological truth of things (which seems to be the primary domain of Le Blond's focus on the analogy of truth). They develop the logical notion of speculative truth (as the adequation of the mind to reality, expressed precisely in judgments, the products of the second "operation" of the intellect) in human knowledge carefully but quickly moving toward the truth character of revealed data, as well as the knowledge articulated in theological science.[111]

Following these introductory points, Labourdette and Nicolas present a lengthy set of sub-distinctions concerning the various kinds of diversity to be found in human knowledge. They begin with the physical / biological distinctions that exist among human persons.[112] Although they depict racial diversity with perhaps an overly broad brush, their intention in this sub-section is quite clear: beyond questions of physical differentiation, there is immense differentiation within human culture and civilization. Moreover, human activity, precisely because it is incarnate, is stamped with the mark of historicity and temporal development (and backsliding). Nonetheless, they also assert that in the midst of all of this historical change, there are elements that enable one to affirm that the "entirety of the human condition"[113] is present in all men.

---

[110] Le Blond, "L'Analogie," 141.

[111] See Labourdette and Nicolas, "The Analogy of Truth and the Unity of Theological Science," 199–208 below.

[112] See Labourdette and Nicolas, "The Analogy of Truth and the Unity of Theological Science," 208–13 below.

[113] Labourdette and Nicolas, "The Analogy of Truth and the Unity of Theological Science," 213 below.

In the next section, they develop the Thomist school's noetics of science, reflecting directly on the epistemological question of the various degrees of truth involved in human knowledge, tracing out the differences between *per se nota* principles (known through the virtue of understanding), scientific judgments (which are known in an objectively illative manner, through the virtues of *scientia* and *sapientia*[114]), and opinions, noting how the careful drawing of distinctions can help to discern what is true from what is false in this final category of judgments.[115]

Continuing in this section, they discuss a point that is often not parsed carefully enough in this debate as a whole: the kind of "truth" which is found in conceptualization. Strictly speaking, this is not the same sense of truth as what is involved in judgments (where truth is most strictly found).[116] Here, in conceptualization, the mind has a kind of ontological truth through "fidelity" to the nature that is known, although often involving significant labors in order to arrive at a definition of what is known. Labourdette and Nicolas reject an epistemology akin to that of Henri Bergson, who proposed that conceptualization is, in fact, a product coming after a primordial, intuitive, non-conceptual contact with reality. Rather, over the course of a number of pages, they develop a theory of conceptual elaboration which bears witness to the way that the human mind must progress from the vague to the distinct, as well as the various ways that knowledge is marked by the abstractive character of human knowledge.[117] After discussing these points concerning conceptualization, Labourdette and Nicolas take up the question of the linguistic expression of what is known, discussing the way that history, culture, style, and genre all interact with our conceptualizations.[118]

Next, they take up the question of systematization. This particular point touches on the nerve of the whole debate that is raging around them at this time, for it is precisely the question concerning the nature of theological science, which is at the heart of the disagreements between the Dominican and Jesuit parties writing in the debate concerning the *nouvelle théologie*.

---

[114] On this topic, see the remarks made in Minerd, "Wisdom be Attentive," 1103–46.

[115] See Labourdette and Nicolas, "The Analogy of Truth and the Unity of Theological Science," 214–18 below.

[116] See the texts cited in note 217 in the systematic portion of this introduction.

[117] See Labourdette and Nicolas, "The Analogy of Truth and the Unity of Theological Science," 214–23 below. In the text itself, it is clear that they are relying upon Maritain's work in the *Degrees of Knowledge*. However, much of what they say about definition and the development of an initially-vague notion seems almost certainly to be a continuation of Garrigou-Lagrange's own reflections on these matters. Regarding the latter, see note 217 in the synthetic subsection of this introduction.

[118] Labourdette and Nicolas, "The Analogy of Truth and the Unity of Theological Science," 223–25 below.

Systems of thought, organizing *explanatory principles* and *explained conclusions*, are attempts aiming at scientific elaboration. The overall architecture of these systems will be dominated by their principles, which will determine their respective scopes, as well as their pliability in the face of new data.[119] Moreover, even within a given system of thought, various thinkers will bring to bear their own "mentalities," coloring one and the same overall conceptual content with various contingent factors that must be carefully disentangled with the tools of both history and systematic thought in hand.[120]

Labourdette and Nicolas draw their article to a close by reflecting on St. Thomas's place in the history of theology, whom they assert will necessarily be replaced if one were to attempt to "baptize" Hegel, Bergson, Kierkegaard, or Marx in a way analogous to the way that Aquinas purified and utilized Aristotelian thought, for according to Labourdette and Nicolas, the disparity between these modern thinkers' principles and those of St. Thomas is far too great for any true synthesis to be fashioned. To accept their principles would ultimately be to deny St. Thomas's. Aware that this assertion might seem a-historical, they protest that it is not at all such, for true progress is possible in human knowledge, just as it is in the applied arts:

> These are men [i.e., St. Thomas and Aristotle, along with other Fathers] who, in fact, discovered or decisively expressed this or that truth, placing their stamp upon it. But who thinks of the inventor of the plow? Nonetheless, the plow exists and has become a perfected machine whose principles have not changed. Certain ideas and methods are inventions that are more precious than the plow or than any other tool. And I know quite well that Aristotle and the whole of Greek thought itself seem to represent a rather partial view of the human mind concerning things when we think of the world of Hindu thought or even, having become so different from them, that of modern thought. Nonetheless, it is not for nothing that the Divine Truth was revealed and first taught in Hebrew and Greek concepts. Without a doubt, they were adapted to this task and prepared for by the Word who illuminates every man coming into this world. Without a doubt, they were, above all, flexed and rectified, thereby being given more truth, by this Divine Truth which had to be expressed in them. Plato and Aristotle are our masters, but how transformed are they by the Faith which found in them the concepts needed for its own human expression![121]

---

[119] See Labourdette and Nicolas, "The Analogy of Truth and the Unity of Theological Science," 226–28 below.

[120] See Labourdette and Nicolas, "The Analogy of Truth and the Unity of Theological Science," 228–31 below.

[121] Labourdette and Nicolas, "The Analogy of Truth and the Unity of Theological Science," 235 below.

They likewise address the seeming-imperialism of scholastic thought, which would strive to establish a single theological science. They acknowledge that no such unified theological science can ever be fully achieved. Nonetheless, they believe that the requirement that it be *scientific* in character will lead it to tend toward an increasingly unified form, explaining the objective content of faith, even while it may be inspired by non-objective factors involved in the theologian's personal experience of reality and, above all, of the mysteries through mystical experience. They acknowledge, moreover, that the encounter with new systems of thought (in the course of missionary activity) will lead to the refashioning of some points of Latin theology. However, this does not mean that cultures receiving Christian thought would ultimately need to fully recast the latter, thus leading to the abandonment of the heretofore accepted notional content of Christian dogmas. Moreover, they point out that Western philosophy was profoundly altered by Christianity, implying that the same would likewise happen to Eastern philosophy in its encounter with Christian truth.[122]

The article draws to a close with strong words written in an almost-prophetic tone:

> How can we fail to see that Thomism finds itself at a critical moment— and along with it, all the traditional theological schools, for none of them would survive its ruin unscathed, existing thereafter only in the form of scattered themes taken up and transformed into brand new intellectual constructions? Is it a gangue to be broken up so that Christian Dogma may be thereby freely extracted therefrom? Or, by contrast, does it remain its most perfect and perfectible scientific elaboration? In any case, if it could only survive as an "analogical" relic, then, in keeping with its most essential contention, it would be most appropriate for it to step aside and allow itself to be replaced.[123]

Though generally careful and measured in their responses and reactions to their Jesuit interlocutors, the Dominican Fathers at the *Revue thomiste* here bear witness to the profound concern that they feel. This sentiment will be matched upon the pen of their older confrere writing from Rome, to whose interventions we will now turn.

---

[122] Labourdette and Nicolas, "The Analogy of Truth and the Unity of Theological Science," 237 below.

[123] Labourdette and Nicolas, "The Analogy of Truth and the Unity of Theological Science," 239 below.

THE ROMAN RESPONSE

The Roman response was undertaken primarily by Garrigou-Lagrange. Of course, there were other theologians who opposed the various authors in question,[124] but he was the most prominent of the Roman theologians, and his response was, in the end, what came to characterize the entire affair. Just as we began the Toulouse section with an article on the nature of theology from their perspective, acting as an anchor and contextualizing their later articles, we have done the same here, including one written by him during the 1930s debates on the nature of theology.

The bulk of the affair involved eight articles (and a set of letters), six written by Garrigou-Lagrange, and two responses from the *nouvelle théologie* camp, one by the secular cleric and friend of the Jesuits, Bruno de Solages and the other by Bouillard himself. Of these eight articles, only the first has been remembered, and it is one of the most famous pieces of the twentieth century, "Where is the New Theology Headed?" The article has existed in English for over two decades, and it is often referred to as the "atom bomb" that dramatically escalated the affair.[125] The exchange unfolded in the following order:

1. Garrigou-Lagrange, "Where is the New Theology Headed?" (1946)
2. Bruno de Solages, "For the Honor of Theology: Fr. Garrigou-Lagrange's Misinterpretations" (1947)
3. Garrigou-Lagrange, "Truth and the Immutability of Dogma" (1947)
4. Garrigou-Lagrange, "Concerning Notions Consecrated by the Councils" (1947)
5. Garrigou-Lagrange—Maurice Blondel, "Correspondence" (1947)
6. Henri Bouillard, "Conciliar Notions and the Analogy of Truth" (1948)
7. Garrigou-Lagrange, "On the Need to Return to the Traditional Conception of Truth" (1948)
8. Garrigou-Lagrange, "The Immutability of Defined Truths, with Remarks on the Supernatural Order" (1948)

---

[124] See for example, Charles Boyer's articles "Nature pure et surnaturel dans le Surnaturel du Père de Lubac," *Gregorianum* 28 (1947): 379–95, and "Qu'est-ce que la théologie? Réflexions sur une controverse," *Gregorianum* 21 (1940): 255–66; Pietro Parente, "Nouve tendenze teologiche," *L'Osservatore Romano* (9–10 February 1942): 1; and for an early Anglophone critique see David Greenstock, "Thomism and the New Theology," *The Thomist* 13 (1950): 567–96.

[125] Reginald Garrigou-Lagrange, "La nouvelle théologie: où va-t-elle?" *Angelicum* 23 (1946): 126–47; English translations have existed for over two decades, with the first, widely circulated online, by the traditionalist publication *Catholic Family News* in 1998. That translation was refined and reprinted in a special issue of the *Josephinum Journal of Theology*, vol. 18, no. 1 (2011), which we have used here with some changes.

9. Garrigou-Lagrange, "Relativism and the Immutability of Dogma According to the [First] Vatican Council" (1949)

Garrigou-Lagrange does not engage in the open irenicism of the Toulouse Dominicans (who actually refused to publish "Where is the New Theology Headed?" in the *Revue thomiste* on account of the tense situation in France). However, his tone is much more measured than the bitter dismissal that characterizes Henri de Lubac's (anonymous) response. Indeed, throughout the entire exchange, he is nothing but polite and restrained.[126] His tone is never personal, and he takes care to note that he has had a long and cordial correspondence with Blondel over the years.[127] Despite this, his charge that *ressourcement* theology was leading back to the errors of theological modernism was enough to overshadow the Toulouse overture.[128] The first response to Garrigou-Lagrange came from Bruno de Solages in a wide-ranging piece that was emotional and accusatory and sought to defend each of the major *ressourcement* thinkers.[129] He made numerous charges, which we shall discuss below, accusing Garrigou-Lagrange of sloppiness and dishonesty.

---

126 Nichols, "Thomism," 12. For an account of the postwar situation in France, which highly favored the *ressourcement* thinkers, see Kirwan, *Avant-garde*, 204–51. This characteristic tone of Garrigou-Lagrange, which is never personal, is exemplified in an article not included by us in this sequence, though published immediately thereafter, Reginald Garrigou-Lagrange, "Le relativisme et l'immutabilité du dogme," *Angelicum* 27, no. 3 (Sept. 1950): 219–46. This text focuses on Hume, Kant, and Hegel. If any Catholic falls under a direct critique, it would be Antonio Rosmini and Anton Günther, and even then, these long-dead thinkers are mentioned only in passing.

127 For further details of this relationship, see *U potrazi za istinom: korespondencija Blondel-Garrigou-Lagrange*, ed. Hrvoje Lasic (Zagreb: Demetra, 2016); John Sullivan, "Forty Years Under the Cosh: Blondel and Garrigou-Lagrange," *New Blackfriars* 93 (2012): 58–70; Michael Kerlin, "Reginald Garrigou-Lagrange: Defending the Faith from *Pascendi dominici gregis* to *Humani Generis*," *U.S. Catholic Historian* 25, no. 1 (Winter 2007): 97–113.

128 However, because of certain lingering distortions concerning the history of this intervention, it is important to emphasize the fact that his *main* focus was the conclusion to Bouillard's volume. As Maritain wrote to Journet, following upon a meeting with Garrigou-Lagrange on June 2, 1946, during which the men spoke about the state of mind reigning then at the Holy Office:

> From what he told me, it appears that no public threat seems possible against the [general] tendencies [and] the articles of the review (this relieved me). His predominating concern is with Bouillard's book (let them do with it what they will). My own opinion is that the Pope should promulgate a positive document, enlightening minds concerning the nobility of speculative knowledge and the need for Catholic thought to be inspired by the wisdom of St. Thomas (Fouilloux, "Dialogue," 168–69).

129 See Bruno de Solages, "'Pour l'honneur de la théologie': le contre-sens du R. P. Garrigou-Lagrange," *Bulletin de littérature ecclésiastique* 48 (1947): 64–84.

Ultimately, de Solages's intervention did little to move the debate forward, and Garrigou-Lagrange responded with two articles in the same volume of *Angelicum*. Bouillard finally countered the first Garrigou-Lagrange article in 1948 with an excellent piece. His tone is measured, with an approach that is focused and clear, and the article gives a sense of what could have been possible if the debate had been successful. As we will discuss below, Bouillard provided a thorough defense of his positions, attempting to refute Garrigou-Lagrange's charge, and most importantly, clarifying his famous conclusion, the precise response for which the Thomists had been awaiting for several years. There is no doubt that the brief Garrigou-Bouillard exchange represents a highpoint in this whole affair. Both parties were neither personal nor excessively wide-ranging (as were the Toulouse thinkers at times), and most importantly, they attempted to address the arguments against them directly, without obfuscation or indignation. Garrigou-Lagrange was clear, as were the Toulouse Dominicans, that they were not accusing the Jesuits *themselves* of modernism, but, rather, only that they feared their theological methodology would ultimately imply results that revisited modernism. Although the Toulouse Dominicans were privately in full agreement with the substance of Garrigou-Lagrange's first article, they were careful not to use the word "modernism" because of the effect it would have on a French church already decidedly against them.

Garrigou-Lagrange continued his response with two articles in the same 1948 issue of *Angelicum*, and a final article in 1949. Thus, the debate ended before it was begun in full rigor. Due to the arguably-intemperate Jesuit response as well as Garrigou's invocation of modernism, the Jesuits were effectively silenced. Before we briefly peruse the high points in the debate, a brief note about Garrigou-Lagrange is in order, at least to explain why he took such a strident stance against Bouillard's conclusion.

If Garrigou-Lagrange's long life as a theologian can be summed up with one issue, it would be the defense of dogma and its immutability. This was a central preoccupation and directed many works in his expansive bibliography,[130] from his earliest work up to this late-life debate. Indeed, the kind of religious conversion he experienced after reading Ernest Hello's *Life, Science, and Art* was what prompted him to join the Dominicans, and this conversion involved the question of the immutable character of speculative truth. He later recounted:

> In an instant, I glimpsed that the doctrine of the Catholic Church was the absolute truth about God, about His intimate life, and about man in his origin and supernatural destiny. I saw in an instant that this was not a truth that is relative to the present state of our knowledge but, rather,

---

[130] See Benedetto Zorcolo, "Bibliografia del P. Garrigou-Lagrange," *Angelicum* 42 (1965): 200–72.

an absolute truth that will not pass away, though it will shine with ever-increasing radiance until we see God *facie ad faciem*. A ray of light made the Lord's words shine in my eyes: "Heaven and earth will pass away, but my words will not pass away." I understood that this truth must bear fruit like a grain of wheat in good soil. . . . *Gratia est semen gloriae*.[131]

Thus, he entered the Dominican Order as the Church was in the throes of the Modernist crisis, which challenged the very notion of dogma on both philosophical and historical grounds. His most important non-commentatorial works in speculative theology and philosophy, such as *Sens commun* (in English, *Thomistic Common Sense*), *De Revelatione* (in English, *On Divine Revelation*), *God, His Existence and His Nature*, along with his philosophical writings on the principle of finality, all have this defense in mind, at least peripherally, and the first of those books was written precisely as a response to the Catholic Modernist, Edouard Le Roy. *Thomistic Common Sense* defended the transhistorical character of language and its ability to support the immutability of dogma.

It was also during this period that Garrigou-Lagrange entered into a four-decade-long charitable personal correspondence with the philosopher Maurice Blondel. Although they had strong disagreements, he always held that Blondel was acting in good faith, in contrast to figures such as Alfred Loisy and George Tyrrell. He disagreed most strongly with Blondel's philosophy of history and the way he replaced the classical definition of truth, as the conformity of mind and reality in judgment, with the conformity of mind and life, believing that this gravely imperiled the absolute character of dogma. This preoccupation continued in the 1930s when he was forced to intervene in the affairs of Marie-Dominique Chenu and Louis Charlier over works that seemed to undermine the immutable character of dogma.[132] Thus, Garrigou-Lagrange's formative years during the Modernist crisis marked him as perpetually wary of a recurrent threat, and in the post-war decades of the 20s and 30s, Catholics were divided over whether the Modernist threat was in the past or just lurking beneath the surface, waiting to reappear. Thus, after the appearance of Bouillard's book, Garrigou-Lagrange's response had none of the complimentary or wide-ranging character that marked the Toulouse response. Rather, he went directly to the heart of the matter: to his eyes, Bouillard's sometimes-vague and unclear explanations (something the latter would himself later seem to admit) weakened the stability of the content of dogmatic propositions and would dangerously *lead* to modernism. Although he is perhaps less clear than Labourdette on this score, the concern is above

---

[131] Quoted in Marie-Rosaire Gagnebet, "L'oeuvre du P. Garrigou-Lagrange: itineraire intellectuel et spirituel vers Dieu," *Angelicum* 42 (1965): 9–10.
[132] See notes 34 above and 212 and 269 below.

all with Bouillard's *theological* explanation which, nonetheless, seemed to risk implying problems on the level of *De fide* requirements against modernism.

In the famed first article of the sequence, Garrigou-Lagrange goes immediately to Bouillard's claim that a theology that refuses to be contemporary would be a false theology, likewise challenging Bouillard's claim that the Council of Trent did not intend to canonize the notion of formal causality, which according to him is now obsolete and thus able to be replaced with another notion:

> If it is another notion, then it is no longer that *of formal cause:* Then it is also no longer *true* to say with the Council: "Sanctifying grace is the formal cause of justification." It is necessary to be content to say that grace was understood at the time of the Council of Trent as the formal cause of justification, but today it is necessary to define it *otherwise;* this *passé* definition is no longer "contemporary" and thus is *no longer true,* since a doctrine which is no longer contemporary, as was said, is a false doctrine.[133]

Garrigou-Lagrange continues by charging that Blondel's definition of truth is the source of the trouble:[134]

> We can see the danger of the new definition of truth, no longer the *adaequatio rei et intellectus* (adequation of intellect and reality) but *conformitas mentis et vitae* (the agreement of mind and life). When Maurice Blondel in 1906 proposed this substitution, he did not foresee all of the consequences for the faith. He himself would be perhaps terrified, or at least very troubled.[135] Which "life" is meant in this definition of: "*agreement of mind and life*"? It means human life. And so then, how can one avoid the Modernist definition: "Truth is no more immutable than man himself, since it evolved with him, in him, and through him."[136] We can understand why Pius X said of the Modernists, "They pervert the eternal concept of truth."[137]

---

133 Garrigou-Lagrange, "Where is the New Theology Headed?," 289 below.

134 For the influence of Blondel on the Fourvière Jesuits, see Chs. 2, 4, and 6 in Kirwan, *Avant-garde*; also Antonio Russo traces these influences and reproduces some of their correspondence in *Henri de Lubac* (Turnhout: Brepols, 1998).

135 Another theologian, whom we shall cite further on, invites us to say that at the time of the Council of Trent *transubstantiation* was conceived as the changing, the conversion of the substance of the bread into that of the Body of Christ, but that today it has come to be thought of as *transubstantiation, without this changing of substance,* meaning that the substance of the bread, which remains, becomes the efficacious sign of the Body of Christ. And this pretends to conserve *the Council's meaning!* (Footnote Garrigou-Lagrange's.)

136 Holy Office of Pius X, *Lamentabili*, no. 58 (Denzinger, no. 3458 [old no. 2058]).

137 Garrigou-Lagrange, "Where is the New Theology Headed?," 290–91 below.

For Garrigou-Lagrange, from "this principle, it emerges that the truth is always *in fieri* [in process], never immutable. Faith is the conformity of judgment, not with being and its necessary laws, but with life, which is constantly and forever evolving."[138] Thus, foundational doctrines such as original sin, hell, and the Real Presence of Christ in the Eucharist are all in danger of being swept away.

As mentioned above, de Solages responded to Garrigou-Lagrange in the April–June 1947 issue of the *Bulletin de littérature ecclésiastique*, the journal of the *Institut catholique* in Toulouse, and accused him of "outrageously violating" the elementary laws of historical and literary criticism and engaging in a dishonest examination in which he used Thomism as a "bludgeon to crush his opponents."[139]

First, by accusing Garrigou-Lagrange of irresponsibly using private texts, he is referring to the anonymous but influential mimeographed papers and books circulating in French Catholic circles most often associated with Teilhard de Chardin's thought.[140] De Solages declares that, given their private nature and questionable authenticity, he refuses to comment on them. He asks why Garrigou-Lagrange would use texts of an unknown origin and aim.

Second, de Solages accuses Garrigou-Lagrange of arbitrarily naming the adherents of the *nouvelle théologie* movement, and de Solages listed Bouillard, Blondel, de Lubac, Fessard, and Teilhard de Chardin, declaring that "none of these authors have, as far as I know, spoken of a 'new theology.' Moreover, they constitute an artificial block, arbitrarily constituted and singularly disparate."[141] Here, de Solages essentially takes up de Lubac's position in his response, namely, that there was no movement or group of *nouveaux théologiens*. At every point, he attempts to use St. Thomas to scold Garrigou-Lagrange, declaring: "Saint Thomas gives us here an admirable example. Living in a period when one was far from having the means at hand for knowing the history of philosophy and to unravel the different currents of thought involved therein, far from confusing Platonic and Aristotelian currents of thought, he always strove to distinguish them."[142]

Third, and most serious of all, is Garrigou-Lagrange's use of citations: "He is content to quote some sentences, often citing mere sentence fragments, from each of the authors he attacks. This is already poor methodology when one wants to judge the thought of an author. But this is nothing! These

---

[138] Garrigou-Lagrange, "Where is the New Theology Headed?," 298 below.
[139] de Solages, "Pour l'honneur," 66.
[140] de Solages, "Pour l'honneur," 67.
[141] de Solages, "Pour l'honneur," 68.
[142] de Solages, "Pour l'honneur," 69.

citations are inaccurate, detached from any context, and misinterpreted."[143] De Solages declares that also in this regard, Garrigou-Lagrange shows himself to be a "very bad disciple of St. Thomas."[144]

After this five-page introduction, de Solages then, in the next ten pages, treats individually de Lubac, Daniélou and Chenu (in the same section), Bouillard, and Blondel. Regarding de Lubac, de Solages castigates Garrigou in no uncertain terms for having quoted merely a single phrase from de Lubac's *Surnaturel* and accuses him of being totally unconcerned with understanding de Lubac's actual position.

In the section on Daniélou and Chenu, de Solages quotes an entire paragraph where Garrigou-Lagrange anonymously quotes passages on the relationship between spirituality and theology. This is a key issue for Garrigou-Lagrange, since some of the Modernists held that theology was merely the reflection of a spiritual experience, and the Dominican claims that Daniélou's formulation is excessively vague and potentially dangerous:

> Moreover, is this not the new definition of truth that is found in the new definition of theology: "*Theology is no more than a spirituality or religious experience which has found its intellectual expression.*" And so follow assertions such as: "If theology can help us to understand spirituality, spirituality will, in most cases, burst open our theological frameworks, and we shall be obliged to formulate different types of theology. . . . For to each great spirituality has corresponded a great theology." Does this mean that two theologies can be true, even if their main theses are contradictory and opposite? The answer will be "no" if one keeps to the traditional definition of truth. The answer will be "yes" if one adopts the new definition of truth, conceived not in relation to being and to immutable laws, but relative to different religious experiences. This idea brings us remarkably close to Modernism.[145]

De Solages charges that Garrigou-Lagrange quoted Daniélou (the author of the second, longer quote) anonymously, accusing him of taking the Jesuit out of context and ignoring the larger point in the selection. As regards the first quote from Chenu, he claims that Garrigou-Lagrange took the former out of context, and Chenu refers only to "theological systems," *per se*, rather than simply theology in general:

> It is not a question of *theology*, of theological *science*, but of *theologies*, that is to say, of *various theological systems*, partial, more-or-less perfect incarnations of theology or of theological science. Fr. Garrigou-

---

[143] de Solages, "Pour l'honneur," 69.
[144] de Solages, "Pour l'honneur," 69.
[145] Garrigou-Lagrange, "Where is the New Theology Headed?," 291 below.

Lagrange's definition reads: "*Theology* is none other than..." Fr. Chenu's phrase is "*a* theology." This underlines the fact that there are several "theologies," and therefore that it is a question of systems, as the immediate context proves abundantly, since it is a question of Bonaventurian, Augustinian or Scotist and Molinist, alongside Thomism.[146]

Regarding Bouillard and the famous claim that a theology that is not contemporary is false, de Solages tries to clarify that the former

> in no way affirms the monstrous notion that a theology that would have been true at one time becomes objectively false 'when the mind evolves,' but rather, that it will be *subjectively false*, meaning that it would be interpreted in a false sense by a mind that, as a result of its own evolution, would no longer give the same meaning to the various notions used by this theology.[147]

Regarding Bouillard's controversial attempt to square dogma and development with the notion of absolute affirmation,[148] de Solages insists that it can be understood in "another language, one that is more Thomist" and appeals to the notion of analogy, insisting that the "more superficial element" (the relative formulation) does not jeopardize the substantial orthodoxy of the theory, given that Bouillard insists that—and here de Solages's appeal remains as vague as Bouillard's conclusion—a notion of *equivalency* binds them together. Finally, with respect to his defense of Blondel, he accuses Garrigou-Lagrange of once again taking him out of context and failing to understand the philosopher's meaning.

Garrigou-Lagrange promptly responded to de Solages later in 1947 with two articles totaling thirty pages in *Angelicum*, "Truth and the Immutability of Dogma," in which he attempts a point by point refutation of de Solages's charges, and "Concerning Notions Consecrated by the Councils," in which he disputes that analogy can be used to ground his affirmation-formulation notion Thomistically, and he challenges Bouillard's claim that conciliar notions, like Trent's use of formal causality, can be abrogated.

Bouillard himself finally responded in 1948 with "Notions Conciliaires et l'Analogie de Vérité" [Conciliar Notions and the Analogy of Truth], a twenty-page essay in *Recherches de science religieuse*. He begins by denying

---

146 de Solages, "Pour l'honneur," 74.

147 de Solages, "Pour l'honneur," 75.

148 It should be noted that although Gardeil's first chapter of *Le donné révélé et la théologie* strives to show that there is something absolute in our affirmations, his purely Thomistic theory of judgment and truth is the same as that of Labourdette and Garrigou-Lagrange and not that of Bouillard, de Solages, or Le Blond.

any radical intentions, and he declares that he holds to the traditional definition of truth (*adequatio rei et intellectus*), recalling a passage from his famous conclusion that clearly shows he also holds that absolute affirmations not only pertain to dogmas but also to Scripture and Tradition as well as first principles and acquired truths:

> To avoid all equivocation, let us note that the absolute affirmations that we contrast with contingent representations include not only defined dogmas, that is to say propositions canonized by the Church, but also all that is contained explicitly or implicitly in Scripture and Tradition. Likewise, they include the invariant or the absolute of the human mind, first principles and acquired truths, all necessary for defining dogma. We contrast this set of invariants with what is contingent in theological conceptions. It is essential that we understand that these invariants do not subsist *alongside* (and independent of) such contingent conceptions. They are necessarily conceived and expressed *in them*. However, when they change, the new conceptions contain the same absolute relations, the same eternal affirmations.[149]

Bouillard goes on to declare that he refers only to "*certain technical notions*," which theologians have used to express divine truth, the permanence of which he has highlighted. Moreover, he writes that his historical work has been primarily concerned with the differences between theological systems rather than with the "profound and essential identity of their doctrinal teaching."[150] Furthermore, he declares that across concepts and systems, which have undergone modifications, the same truth always remains:

> The history of these notions is in fact dominated by a fundamental and constant affirmation: justification is a free gift of God. It is by grace that man is freed from sin and can accomplish good works. This thesis constitutes what one can call an invariant. We forever find it present in the evolving notions and systems. Most of all, in order to maintain its own integrity, it itself brings about the use of new notions and schemata.[151]

He continues by quoting from the conclusion to stress that he did indeed underscore the importance of divine truth in his work: "Thus the history of theology causes us to see the permanence of divine truth, and at the same time reveals to us what is contingent in the concepts and systems in which we receive it."[152] For Bouillard, it is the task of historical theology to "grasp"

---

[149] Bouillard, *Conversion et grâce*, 221.
[150] Bouillard, "Notions conciliaires," 253.
[151] Bouillard, *Conversion et grâce*, 216.
[152] Bouillard, *Conversion et grâce*, 219.

the absolute that lies at the heart of theological development. Thus, for Bouillard these absolute affirmations are the constant meaning that persists despite the changing formulations.

However, he concedes the possibility that formulas in his book could have been better stated ("ne soit pas entierement heureuse"), admitting that "the facts analyzed can be interpreted differently, provided that proof is given."

He then attempts to clarify another contentious sentence, which directly precedes the admonition about a theology that refuses to be contemporary: "When the mind evolves, an immutable truth is maintained only thanks to the simultaneous and correlative evolution of all the concepts, in which the same relationship is maintained."[153] To this Garrigou-Lagrange had responded: "how can '*an unchanging truth*' maintain itself if the two notions that are united by the verb *to be* are *essentially variable or changeable?*"[154] When he came to defend himself, Bouillard insists that he says the same thing in different words, adding the clarification that something immutable expresses itself differently according to the chosen system, and here he employs the notion of analogy that de Solages argued for earlier in the debate, but which Garrigou-Lagrange (as well as Labourdette and Nicolas) will challenge later on:

> This immutable thing is expressed in a different manner, depending on the system one chooses. This is the law of analogy which can be ignored by no Thomist. When one and the same revealed truth is expressed in different (e.g., Augustinian, Thomist, Suarezian, etc.) systems, the various notions which are used for translating this truth are neither "equivocal" (if they were, one would no longer be speaking about the same thing), nor "univocal" (for otherwise, all systems [of thought] would be identical) but, rather, "*analogous.*" In other words, they express the same reality in different ways.[155]

Bouillard draws to a close by arguing that his conclusion was not meant to articulate a general theory of development / evolution and permanence in theology and, therefore, should not be read in isolation from the rest of the book on which it depends. Furthermore, he argues that his famous claim about false theologies is being misunderstood:

> A theology which, by maintaining old technical notions among new technical notions, would not scrupulously *maintain relevance regarding truth* [*l'actualité du rapport de vérité*] and would make false assertions.

---

[153] Bouillard, *Conversion et* grâce, 219.
[154] Garrigou-Lagrange, "Where is the New Theology Headed," 288 below.
[155] Bouillard, "Notions conciliaires," 254.

INTRODUCTION: A DIALOGUE DELAYED 43

> It is all-too-clear that I have never meant that a theology that was true in the past would then become objectively false but, rather, simply that it would be misunderstood by a mind that would no longer give the same meaning to the concepts used.[156]

This of course is much different than what Bouillard had implied in his conclusion. He claims that he never intended to say anything other than what Garrigou-Lagrange himself said regarding Trent and Aristotle, namely, that the Council did not canonize the Aristotelian notion of form with all of its relations to other notions used in the Aristotelian system. Bouillard here seems to backtrack and attribute a strikingly mild intention to his conclusion:

> When speaking of 'formal cause' to a man who has no rudimentary knowledge of Aristotelian philosophy or scholastic theology, such a person will not understand. He will interpret the word 'form' as meaning the exterior figure of a thing, which has nothing to do with the thought of the Council of Trent. We are here dealing with technical terms which need to be explained. However, to explain them is to translate them into other terms that are equivalent to them.[157]

He concludes this section by once again appealing to his particular interpretation of the notion of analogy.

After defending his conclusion, Bouillard responds to Garrigou-Lagrange's three main points. First, Garrigou-Lagrange claimed there are certain notions, even technical notions, which have truly been consecrated by the Councils. After analyzing several key issues, Bouillard declares that his position is closer to Garrigou-Lagrange's than the latter seems to think. First, he accuses Garrigou-Lagrange of overstating the problem by citing almost the entire table of contents of Denzinger as an example of this issue. Moreover, he argues that Garrigou-Lagrange is confusing *human* and *technical* notions, further contradicting himself when he argues that the terms are technical but not Aristotelian:[158]

> The Aristotelian notion of form is technical when it is understood with its relations to other notions of the Aristotelian system (which is the only way to understand it correctly). Otherwise, it is no longer either

---

156 Bouillard, "Notions conciliaires," 256.
157 Bouillard, "Notions conciliaires," 257.
158 This is an argument that goes back to the section on dogmatic formulas in Garrigou-Lagrange's *Sens commun*, where he argues that such notions used in dogmatic formulas are rarely merely those of common sense. Rather, they are technical notions which, nonetheless, are accessible to common sense. See Garrigou-Lagrange, *Thomistic Common Sense*, 245–300.

technical, nor properly Aristotelian. There is a contradiction involved in writing that the Council has consecrated this technical notion without canonizing all its relations to the system [from which it was derived]. Either the Council of Trent consecrated a specific Aristotelian notion, or it has not consecrated a technical notion.[159]

Bouillard then goes on to analyze Trent on both the formal cause of justification as well as Transubstantiation, arguing on textual grounds that neither was consecrated by the Council. Maintaining that he and Garrigou-Lagrange are closer than the latter thinks, he concludes the section by saying:

> Summarizing, we can say that the Councils often *utilize* technical notions, sometimes as subjects of their propositions, sometimes as predicates. Some are philosophical in origin. In order to understand them, it is not always enough to refer to a very general metaphysic, to notions that are simply human. Sometimes at least, it is necessary to refer to the system from which they are drawn. But the Councils did not want to *consecrate* them as linked to this system.[160]

Bouillard attempts to refute a second argument, namely, that "one cannot, without modifying the meaning of the Council's teaching, renounce these notions or let them fall into obsolescence, substituting them with other so-called equivalent or analogous ones."[161] First, Bouillard states that he never claimed the notion of formal cause was "unstable" but only that it was contingent, which simply indicates that it is "non-necessary and means here that other notions (equivalent and analogous) can be used"[162] to designate the same reality. Bouillard then argues against Garrigou-Lagrange's contention that in theological development, for example between Augustine and Aquinas on the issue of the Real Presence and habitual grace, "there is only here a passage from the vague to the distinct for the same notion, not two different and analogous notions; it is the same notion becoming more explicit and distinct."[163] Bouillard tries to refute this claim, which would certainly undermine his theory of historical analogy, which he articulates in the following passage:

> To imagine that the Fathers of the Church had only vague notions, and that Saint Thomas alone knew how to express them in explicit form, would be to misunderstand the history of ideas, indeed, an error identical

---

[159] Bouillard, "Notions conciliaires," 260.
[160] Bouillard, "Notions conciliaires," 263.
[161] Bouillard, "Notions conciliaires," 258.
[162] Bouillard, "Notions conciliaires," 264.
[163] Bouillard, "Notions conciliaires," 264.

to the one that led to the assertion that philosophy begins with Descartes, art with the Renaissance, and political life with the French Revolution. Each thinker, like each period, has his own intelligibility. He must be understood for his own sake and not just as a transition to something else. Certainly, in the course of the history of ideas, progress takes place and notions become clearer. Although it then assumes a special character, such progress also takes place in theology (and there is no need to stop it in Saint Thomas). But sometimes new ways of thinking abandon precious elements of the past. The light cast on such-and-such a notion or problem leaves in the shadows what was perhaps clearer before. To imagine that Augustine's notions are vague whenever they do not exactly cover Thomist conceptions is to ignore the reality of history.[164]

The third and final charge of Garrigou-Lagrange that Bouillard challenges is his own notion of analogy and the former's contention that the meaning of certain conciliar proposals would become unknowable or uncertain even for the Church, leading to relativism. Bouillard argues that different councils have often expressed an identical truth in different terms. He provides this example:

> When a professor, catechist, or preacher teaches Christian doctrine, they need to explain what transubstantiation, formal cause, and hypostatic union mean. How can this be done if not by translating these terms into equivalent terms? Without a doubt, there is a risk of error, and indeed preachers or professors express themselves here or there in an inexact way. Father Garrigou-Lagrange himself, *salva reverentia*, does not always explain in a perfect way the texts of the Councils. The risk of error is inherent to the human mind. To do away with this risk, we would need to do away with human thought. However, man does not always make mistakes. We must not forget that the mind is an active power of discernment, able to grasp differences and relationships [*parentés*], contradictions and identities. It knows how to spot the permanence of essential elements under surface-level changes, or changes of meaning under identical terms. No theologian doubts his own thought, I believe, when he affirms, in spite of differences in the conception of the Eucharist in Augustine and St. Thomas, "the reality aimed at [*réalité visée*] always remains the same." Moreover, although the isolated individual can be wrong, the Church assisted by the Holy Spirit discerns with certainty. How often has one Council interpreted another Council, or one decision another decision, translating the doctrine in a different way, because intellectual needs demanded it![165]

---

164 Bouillard, "Notions conciliaires," 266.
165 Bouillard, "Notions conciliaires," 267–68.

Bouillard continues by declaring that he never claimed that

> absolute and immutable truth can *only* be expressed by different and successive notions but, rather, simply that it *can* be expressed through different and equivalent notions... and in addition, it is necessary to admit that the Church has the active power to distinguish equivalences from contradictions, what is essential from the accessory. Otherwise, one would deny its infallible doctrinal power.[166]

Bouillard's sober and thorough article represents a highpoint in the exchange and gives us a sense of what might have been possible had the discussion been allowed to play out. Due to the controversy that swelled from both de Lubac's response and Garrigou's accusation of a return to modernism, Bouillard was not permitted to respond, and the debate essentially concluded with three articles from Garrigou-Lagrange.

The first two articles were both published in the same 1948 issue of *Angelicum*, and the first, "On the Need to Return to the Traditional Conception of Truth," appears to have been written before he had read Bouillard's response and may well have been a response to de Solages's criticism. The second is a response to both Bouillard's aforementioned article and de Lubac's latest piece in *Recherches* on the *surnaturel* debate. The final article, published in 1949, seems to be the last major piece in the debate before *Humani generis* put an official end to the affair.

HISTORICAL CONCLUSIONS

A number of questions and observations emerge from a complete reading of this debate. It is obvious that, at least in the case of the Toulouse Dominicans, the myth of a "Thomist attack" is not easy to defend. In their writing, we find very little (arguably nothing) in the way of sarcasm, dismissal, evasion, or personal attacks, nor any calls for magisterial intervention. It is debatable whether this description applies even to Garrigou-Lagrange's more-strenuous articles. In any case, it would certainly be difficult to fault Labourdette and his confreres at any point for their generally magnanimous and irenic tone. Despite this, they indeed were committed Thomists, and their disagreement with Garrigou-Lagrange was of style and strategy rather than substance. Regarding the Roman response, Garrigou-Lagrange was direct and to the point, never responding with sarcasm or personal attacks. Although he insists that it is his right to charge that a certain theology will indeed lead to modernism, he might be faulted for not first seeking a clarification from Bouillard before employing such a charged word, thereby

---

[166] Bouillard, "Notions conciliaires," 268.

inflaming the situation.[167] However, it is difficult to deny that some of the formulations in Bouillard's conclusion are indeed vague and seem to allow for at least the possibility of a dangerous historicism.

On the Jesuit side, it is difficult to exonerate de Lubac from his responsibility for the breakdown of the discussion. As Fouilloux has remarked, clearly it was a discussion of the utmost importance that needed to happen. Not only did de Lubac scorn the Dominicans, but he dismissed their concerns, which he insisted were unfounded.

Although de Solages only elevated the temperature, Bouillard's sober and thoughtful piece gives us a taste of what could have been possible. With precision and reserve, he calmly attempted to answer Garrigou-Lagrange's charges, both clarifying himself as well as probing Garrigou-Lagrange's position for weak spots.

However, beyond these historical questions about "attacks" and "counterattacks," which primarily deal with a journalistic history of embittered attitudes and bruised egos, the central question remains: Were the Toulouse Dominicans correct in initiating the debate and raising the questions about truth, method, and dogma? Moreover, were they right to be concerned that the intellectual currents in the highly volatile climate of postwar France might indeed open the theological terrain to problematic and ultimately dangerous formulations about the relationship between history and truth? In short, were their fears justified?

In answering these questions, we have the benefit of clear hindsight, and given that, less than two decades after this exchange came to an abrupt halt, the Church underwent a deep crisis over precisely questions of truth, history, and dogma, we can say with confidence that indeed, regardless of their solutions, the Toulouse Dominicans were right to raise the issues and even to be concerned. The *nouveaux théologiens*' brisk dismissal of their concerns is all the more striking given how during the post-conciliar crisis they themselves diverged sharply on these questions. In the 1970s, Chenu sent de Lubac a copy of a long interview he had given, inscribed with the words, "Regarding a 'journey,' all the memories of which we have in common," and next to

---

167 The relationship between the *nouvelle théologie* and modernism is contested, and Boersma dismisses any connection between them, insisting that despite some "overlap," the two agendas were "fundamentally different" (*Nouvelle Théologie*, 17–21). Gerard Loughlin holds that George Tyrrell's thought was much closer to that of the *nouvelle théologie* and that Garrigou-Lagrange was correct that it "goes back to Modernism" ("Nouvelle Théologie: A Return to Modernism?," in *Ressourcement: A Movement for Renewal in Twentieth-Century Catholic Theology*, 36–51). Mettepenningen is more nuanced and claims that it did not "repeat" modernism but "developed its core ideas" in "Truth as Issue in a Second Modernist Crisis? The Clash between Recontextualization and Retrocontextualization in the French-Speaking Polemic of 1946–47," in *Theology and the Quest for Truth*, ed. Mathijs Lamberigts, et al. (Leuven: Peeters, 2006), 141.

Chenu's claims that Vatican II ushered in a Copernican revolution in the "axis of the faith," in that the Word of God is now found in "the existential fabric of the Church, in the life of the Church," rather than "reduced in a series of authoritative utterances," de Lubac simply scribbled, "absurd." In the paragraphs that follow, where Chenu expounds his theory of history, in which the Word of God is discerned not in propositions but, rather, in "events" or "signs of the times," and theology's role is to interpret these unfolding events, de Lubac has filled the margin with question marks punctuated by the word "superficial."[168]

To highlight with greater clarity how far Chenu had seemingly moved in denying the "trans-historical" underpinnings of language used to express the faith, he wrote:

> The Word of God both creates history and is interpreted within history. . . . Understanding of the unity of Word and event, in which the truth occurs, is a fundamental point of departure for theology. . . . Biblical truth . . . in keeping with the Hebraic mentality, does not directly affront that which is, but that which happens, that which one experiences. . . . Greek thought develops through a reflection on the substance of beings, and terminates in a philosophy of immutability and permanence. It ignores that which is proper to biblical thought: the dimension of time. . . . One must not establish a division between the act of the divine Word and the formulas in which it takes shape and which give it its intellectual content. But one also must not cede to a facile concordism in which the historical and existential character of the truth of salvation dissolves, and where the Word of God is absorbed into and neutralized by a theological "science." . . . The truth is a radically Christological concept. It should not be treated as the manifestation of the eternal essence of things. [!][169]

Thus, among devotees of Rousselot and Maréchal, there are widely divergent opinions about the status of dogma, and thus the value of conceptual formulations. Both Chenu and de Lubac[170] adopted Rousselot's general

---

[168] Kirwan, *Avant-garde*, 278–79.

[169] Marie-Dominique Chenu, "Vérité évangélique et métaphysique wolfienne à Vatican II," *Revue des Sciences Philosophiques et Théologiques* 57 (1973): 637–38, quoted in Thomas Joseph White, "The Precarity of Wisdom: Modern Dominican Theology, Perspectivalism, and the Tasks of Reconstruction," in *Ressourcement Thomism: Sacred Doctrine, the Sacraments, and the Moral Life: Essays in Honor of Romanus Cessario*, ed. Reinhard Hütter and Matthew Levering (Washington, DC: The Catholic University of America Press, 2011), 92–123. In his analysis, White draws substantially from Henri Donneaud, "La constitution dialectique de la théologie et de son histoire selon M.-D. Chenu," *Revue thomiste* 96, no. 1 (1996): 41–66.

[170] Concerning the relationship between the thought of de Lubac and Rousselot, see John M. McDermott, "De Lubac and Rousselot," *Gregorianum* 78, no. 4 (1997): 735–59.

anthropology early in their academic careers, but the former had a much more radical interpretation, making a sharp distinction between the dogmatic aspects of faith, which are defective, burdensome, and fragile, on the one hand, and the non-conceptual and mystical drive to understand the object of faith, God Himself, on the other: "Far from resting complacent in the social [and dogmatic] servitude of his faith, far from being content in a narrow security, the believer is allured by the mysterious object of that same faith, and within the limits of his power he strives for an understanding of the mystery of divine life."[171] Chenu writes regarding faith that it is

> not a conclusion; it is not a composition of ideas and concepts which permits us to grasp reality. Neither is it a proof; nor is it an explanation of the world, an argument from causality, an apologetic of creation. It is a look, a view. It is a dialogue between my soul and God concerning God himself. . . . I see myself and my own mysterious destiny, within the framework of the mysterious destiny of the world in the presence of the triune God.[172]

However, regarding de Lubac, in the end (as Aidan Nichols notes), he is closer to Garrigou-Lagrange on the question of revelation than is commonly known. In commenting on the first articles of *Dei Verbum*, de Lubac, although holding that words are secondary to the acts whose meaning they illuminate, nonetheless, defends against any depreciation of words. Quoting de Lubac, Nichols writes that de Lubac issues a warning:

> By, as he writes, "reaction against an 'intellectualist' thesis that would end up in 'atomizing' the truths of the faith, and in order not to reduce divine revelation to the 'series of words that explain it,'" people are now tempted to discount the word-aspect of revelation, and notably what he terms "the formulae in which the divine Word is embodied and which give it its intelligible content." Borrowing language from another *nouveaux théologien*, the Oratorian Louis Bouyer, de Lubac roundly castigates such a reaction as nothing less than "ceding to that permanent temptation of agnosticism which too often paralyses modern religious thought."[173]

---

[171] Chenu, "Les Yeux de la foi," quoted from the English translation, "The Eyes of Faith," in *Faith and Theology*, 9.

[172] Marie-Dominique Chenu, "L'Unité de la foi: Réalimse et formalisme," *La Vie spirituelle* (July–August 1937): 1–8; taken from the English translation, "The Unity of Faith," in Marie-Dominique Chenu, *Faith and Theology*, trans. Denis Hickey (New York: Macmillan, 1968), 2. The reader who is apprised of the general Thomist manner of speaking of the supernatural resolution of faith will sense certain points of continuity between that position and Chenu's remarks cited here, though his words are also marked by a kind of ambiguity regarding the objective content of the assent of faith.

[173] Aidan Nichols, "Garrigou-Lagrange and de Lubac on Divine Revelation," *Josephinum Journal of Theology* 18, no. 1 (2011): 109.

Regarding the Thomists and the relationship between history and conceptualization, contrary to popular belief, they did understand the importance of historical analysis, but they also distrusted its provisional and perspectival character and saw it as open to endless revision and shaped by this or that concrete context. Ambroise Gardeil, interestingly, an influence on both Garrigou-Lagrange and Chenu, illustrates the limitations of history and the importance of aligning history precisely with a historiography that respects the entirety of tradition with an analogy of riverine explorers:

> It might be helpful to compare the recent adventures of two geographers responsible for correcting the hydrography of a well-known river.... The first went to the mouth of the river, where it spread out in all its power, and he travelled methodically up each of the tributaries one by one. Meanwhile, he pointed out the exact position of the springs and ridgelines, measured the flow, and carefully noted the orientation of the streams. He returned on time, and his work has corrected previous maps on more than one point. It was a success. The second explorer set up camp straightaway at the watershed, and no one can describe the misfortunes that awaited him. Sometimes he followed a promising stream only to find himself interminably lost in the sand or in various caves, and other times he found himself in the middle of a nearby basin surrounded by the inconsistent flow of his river. He went this way and that, sometimes retracing his steps, across trails and dead-end paths, and his explorations were filled with endless hopes and disappointments. Finally, the time he had judged necessary to complete his mission had long since passed, and still he had not yet returned. They feared he would be found at the bottom of some great cliff. The rumor even spread that a message in a bottle, thrown into his beloved Congo to pass his discoveries on to history, came to land, in the flood of last September, in the wheat field of a peasant from Cairo.[174]

The difference of methods and the question of theological science itself represents perhaps the greatest of the open questions bequeathed to the Catholic intellectual world from the debates dating back to this tumultuous Francophone affair during the second half of the 1940s. Although not the only topic of importance leading up to the Second Vatican Council, it represents an issue of primary importance. Though unresolved, such speculative positions certainly were in the intellectual background among conciliar *periti*. We thus find ourselves at an interesting moment in the post-Vatican II Church. In the conciliar documents, we have clear *pastoral* (i.e., practical) directives concerning theological method, but the speculative elaboration

---

[174] Ambroise Gardeil, "La Reforme de la théologie catholique: idée d'une méthode régressive," *Revue thomiste* 11 (1903): 19, quoted in Kirwan, *Avant-garde*, 75–76.

remained unresolved as the Council Fathers faced the pressing desire to provide a practical program for ecclesiastical activity in the contemporary world. But paradoxically, matters remain unsettled and uncertain as regards the speculative questions of theological methodology, something clear before the eyes of all Catholics living in the midst of contemporary disputes. Thus, Vatican II punctuated a moment when speculative disputes, at that time unresolved, ceded to practical programs. Perhaps, in the post-Vatican II period, practical programs might inspire theologians to pick up the question of the speculative disputes once again, something of great importance, given the objective dependence of the practical upon the speculative.

The next section will present a systematic outline of the notion of theology that emerges from the articles that are brought together in this volume. It is intended to be a first sketch of the sort of discussions that are needed in order to engage productively in elaborating the fundamental positions that have been, and indeed still are, taken by various Catholic intellectual camps concerning these matters of theological methodology.

SYSTEMATIC OVERVIEW

As was recounted in our historical-textual introduction, the two streams of theological criticism—the articles in the *Revue thomiste* and the texts emanating from Rome in the pages of *Angelicum*, under the pen of Garrigou-Lagrange—are not unrelated to each other. The writers at the *Revue thomiste* were deeply dependent upon the older Roman Thomist, whether as his students, through the intermediary of others (such as the contemporaneous work of Fr. Gagnebet and that of Maritain, whose intellectual debt to Garrigou-Lagrange was significant), or merely through the general shared atmosphere of the Dominican Thomistic school, which provided a common vocabulary for their approach to philosophical and theological questions. However, as we also made clear in our historical introduction, there were strategic differences between the two groups, with the younger men being solicitous to keep guard against sounding as though they were calling for a Roman intervention.[175]

Nonetheless, despite this difference (one that, arguably, is but a nuance between the two streams of response / reaction), a close textual reading of the articles gathered in this volume bears witness to a shared body of doctrinal positions and concerns. Obviously, the younger men at the *Revue thomiste* were more explicitly concerned to dialogue with their Jesuit brethren, being openly interested in expanding and developing the Thomist notion of theological science, all the while maintaining their historical connections with the Thomist

---

[175] See "Correspondence Étienne Gilson—Michel Labourdette," 498n10, cited at length in note 196.

school upon which they depended. Their gaze was forward-looking without compromising on essential points of the overall noetic involved in the task of seeking some *intellectus fidei*. This is clear in Labourdette's own words:

> This does not imply, moreover, that the teachings of St. Thomas must be simply repeated word for word. It is all-too-true that it would thus remain inaccessible to many, and we would deprive ourselves of the wonderful and genuine progress resulting from later Christian (and non-Christian) thinkers. Nonetheless, it remains the case that these forms of progress, on pain of ruining their own foundations, presuppose the previously-existing edifice, building upon it, neither destroying nor replacing it. They represent expansions of a synthesis, not a total recovery seeking to build a new "representation" of the world according to the categories of modernity, condemning everything that has preceded it as being irredeemably outmoded. Yes, there are many things that have become outmoded, but what we cannot admit is that form of aging which, in fact, reaches down more deeply than the level of mere formulations: the idea that the entire worldview characteristic of a certain cultural milieu could also reach down into the very truths of theology. What we cannot admit is that theological wisdom would be swept away by the flood of impermanence and that its acquisitions could not be held as being definitive. Now, this does not mean that they are closed and no longer subject to further refinement but, rather, implies that they are capable of progressively assimilating new insights and reflections.[176]

For his part, the older Dominican, Garrigou-Lagrange, was far more focused in his concerns, almost exclusively concentrating on the immutable character of speculative truth, understood as *adaequatio intellectus et rei*, the adequation between the intellect (in the act of judging) and reality.[177]

---

[176] See Labourdette, "Theology and its Sources," 141–42 below.

[177] On the whole, we prefer "reality" to "thing," in order to account for the way, for example, that synderesis grasps truth *"per conformitatem ad rem."* For a brief discussion of this, as regards the speculatively-practical truth of synderesis, see Matthew Minerd, "A Note on *Synderesis*, Moral Science, and Knowledge of the Natural Law," *Lex Naturalis* 5 (2020): 47–48 and 53n17–21.

In one of the letters presented below in our volume, Blondel requests that Fr. Garrigou-Lagrange admit this point. Alas, this request was not responded to by the Dominican priest. For the best defense of the "adequation theory" of truth as Fr. Garrigou-Lagrange understands it, see Yves R. Simon, *Introduction to Metaphysics of Knowledge*, trans. Vukan Kuic and Richard J. Thompson (New York: Fordham University Press, 1990), 136–49. Also see John C. Cahalan, "The Problem of Thing and Object in Maritain," *The Thomist* 59, no. 1 (1995): 21–46; Jacques Maritain, *The Degrees of Knowledge*, 96–107. The central nucleus for all of these thinkers can be found in Reginald Garrigou-Lagrange, *Thomistic Common Sense*, 54–55, 105–6, 147n34, 156, 160n67, 281. The same theory of

The resonances in his mind were far more tuned into this single problem, and they awoke in him many of the concerns that had been at the center of his work from early in his writing career, which began in the wake of the encyclical *Pascendi dominici gregis*. The roots of these concerns dig down deeper, going back into the nineteenth century, with ecclesial responses concerning the idealism and historicism already being battled in the run up to the First Vatican Council and then in its wake,[178] and with particular proximity to Garrigou-Lagrange, in the work of his own mentor Marie-Benoît Schwalm, OP, who touched on many of these themes in the very first issues of the *Revue thomiste*.[179] In fact, as already noted in our historical discussion, Garrigou-Lagrange's concern during the crisis in the 1940s nearly wholly focuses on what he interprets as being a pragmatic theory of speculative truth operative in the writing of the lay philosopher, Maurice Blondel, and played out as a theory of doctrinal development in the infamous conclusion to *Conversion et grâce chez S. Thomas d'Aquin* by Henri Bouillard, SJ, discussed in the first portion of this introduction. These concerns had already been percolating in Garrigou-Lagrange's mind prior to the writing of "Where is the New Theology Headed?," as is attested in several articles from that period, namely, "Vérité et option libre selon M. Blondel"[180] in 1936 and "La notion pragmatiste de la vérité et ses consequences en théologie,"[181] as well as in his other theological and philosophical writings, dating from early in the twentieth century.[182]

---

speculative truth is echoed in Garrigou-Lagrange, "On the Immutability of Defined Truths, With Remarks on the Supernatural Order," 344 below.

178 Thus, the work of Alfred Vacant, the first editor of the famed *Dictionnaire théologie catholique*, remained an important touchpoint for him throughout his career. See Jean-Michel-Alfred Vacant, *Études théologiques sur les constitutions du Concile du Vatican*, vol. 2 (Paris: Delhomme et Briguet, 1895).

179 See Marie-Benoît Schwalm, "L'acte de foi, est-il raisonnable?," *Revue thomiste* 1 (old series) (1896): 36–63; "Les illusions de l'idéalisme et leurs dangers pour la foi," *Revue thomiste* 1 (old series) (1896): 413–41; "L'apologétique contemporaine," *Revue thomiste* 2 (1897): 62–92; "La crise et l'apologétique," *Revue thomiste* 2 (1897): 239–71; "La croyance naturelle et la science," *Revue thomiste* 2 (1897): 627–45; "Le dogmatisme du coeur et celui de l'esprit," *Revue thomiste* 3 (1898): 578–619.

180 See Reginald Garrigou-Lagrange, "Vérité et option libre selon M. Blondel," *Acta Pont. Acad. Rom. S. Thom.* (1936): 46–69.

181 See Reginald Garrigou-Lagrange, "La notion pragmatiste de la vérité et ses consequences en théologie," *Acta Pont. Acad. Rom. S. Thom.* (1943): 153–78.

182 See Reginald Garrigou-Lagrange, *God: His Existence and His Nature*, vol. 1, trans. Bede Rose (St. Louis, MO: B. Herder, 1949), 40–60, 331–37; *On Divine Revelation*, vol. 1, 238–48, 378n24 (a quite positive remark); 465n31, 664–65, 784–85. There are more indirect references in *The Sense of Mystery*, trans. Matthew K. Minerd (Steubenville, OH:

The articles gathered together in this volume bear witness to the close conceptual bonds linking the Toulouse and Roman responses to the *nouvelle théologie*, for both Labourdette as well as Garrigou-Lagrange voice particularly direct concerns regarding a latent theological relativism underlying the claims laid forth by the Jesuit fathers in general, along with a quite-proximate danger of such relativism in the brief account of doctrinal development presented by Bouillard and those who came to his defense, such as de Solages and Le Blond.[183] Moreover, on the conceptual level, these two Dominican streams (concerning the immutability of truth and dogma and concerning the nature of theology) converge inasmuch as the question of the immutability of notions (and of judgments based thereupon) functions as a presupposed substructure for the possibility of science as such.[184] At root, the very possibility of *scientia*, "science" in the Aristotelian sense laid out in the *Posterior analytics* and developed through later scholasticism,[185] demands that there be some immutable first principles, judgments that express *per se nota*, "self-evident," truths which stand firm as certain and fixed lights for the scientific discourse in question. On the basis of such truths, the entire structure of *scientia* is built, as a discourse aiming at *objectively inferential truths known precisely as new conclusions drawn from these first truths*. For the Thomists (and, in fact, for any of the traditional *scholae* broadly depending upon this Aristotelian noetic, itself

---

Emmaus Academic, 2017), 162n25; *The Order of Things: The Realism of the Principle of Finality*, trans. Matthew K. Minerd (Steubenville, OH: Emmaus Academic, 2020), 89, 254n2; Reginald Garrigou-Lagrange, *Thomistic Common Sense*, 124–25.

In his concerns, he was joined by other Thomists, even members of the Society of Jesus. See for example, Joseph de Tonquédec, *Immanence: Essai critique sur la doctrine de M. Maurice Blondel* (Paris: Beauchesne 1913); *Deux études sur "la Pensée" de M. M. Blondel* (Paris: Beauchesne, 1936). Also, see François-Xavier Maquart, *Elementa Philosophiae*, vol. 3 Critica (Paris: André Blot, 1938), 174–86 (*De doctrina cognitionis iuxta D. Blondel*). Moreover, Fr. Garrigou-Lagrange regularly cited a critique registered from outside of scholastic circles, by Émile Boutroux in *La science et la religion* (Paris: Flammarion, 1908), 296.

[183] See de Solages, "Pour l'honneur," 64–84; Le Blond, "L'analogie," 129–41. For Bouillard's response to Garrigou-Lagrange's, "Concerning Notions Consecrated by the Counsels," see Bouillard, "Notions conciliares et analogie de la vérité," 251–71.

[184] Labourdette draws this connection openly, stating that a pragmatic theory of truth would ultimately be a caricature of the mind's life, destroying the very notion of theology as a science. See Labourdette, "Theology and Its Sources," 147 below.

[185] It is clear, for example, that all the authors presuppose the elaborations that can be found in John of St. Thomas's *Ars logica*, elaborations which can be found in English in *The Material Logic of John of St. Thomas: Basic Treatises*, trans. Yves R. Simon, John J. Glanville, G. Donald Hollenhorst (Chicago: The University of Chicago Press, 1965), q. 24–27 (pp. 436–586).

developed from Platonic insights[186]), the very possibility of scientific discourse rests upon judgments which are not themselves deduced.

In theology, this "scientific structure" (a structure which, in fact, is sapiential as well, giving theology unique offices that a "mere" science does not have[187]) depends on first principles which are *per se nota* solely through faith (thus giving theology its status as a "subalternate science").[188] For the authors who all here to some degree depend on the Thomist line which includes John of St. Thomas, this state of affairs marks our "wayfaring theology" with a congenital deficiency: its knowledge of principles remains *non-evident*. Nonetheless, thanks to the supernatural attestation of God who reveals, the person who holds a truth on faith holds them as *certain*, even if such truths are not known *in an evidential manner*. (In fact, according to St. Thomas himself, they are known more certainly, in themselves, than are first principles which are known through reason.[189]) Obviously, this intellectual certitude is marked by its own unique character, which includes the supernaturalized movement of the will needed in order to fix the intellect in the judgments of faith.[190] Still, according to John of St. Thomas, such certitude

---

186 A point of continuity acknowledged by Aristotle in *Nicomachean Ethics*, trans. W. D. Ross and J. O. Urmson in *The Complete Works of Aristotle*, ed. Jonathan Barnes, vol. 2 (Princeton, NJ: Princeton University Press, 1995), bk. 1, ch. 4 (1095a14–13). And, as is obvious in the opening of the *Posterior analytics*, the whole of Aristotle's endeavor is to articulate his notion of ἐπιστήμη, "scientific knowledge," as an answer to the paradoxes discussed in Plato's *Meno*. See Aristotle, *Posterior Analytics*, trans. Jonathan Barnes in *The Complete Works of Aristotle*, vol. 1, bk. 1, ch. 1 (71a1–71b8).

187 Concerning the question of the sapiential nature of theology, see Minerd, "Wisdom be Attentive," 1103–46; Kieran Conley, *A Theology of Wisdom: A Study of St. Thomas* (Dubuque, IA: Priory, 1963); Mark P. Johnson, "God's Knowledge in Our Frail Mind: The Thomistic Model of Theology," *Angelicum* 76, no. 1 (1999): 25–45; Mark Johnson, "The Sapiential Character of *Sacra Doctrina* in the Thought of St. Thomas Aquinas," Ph.D. Diss. (University of Toronto, 1990); Francisco P. Muñiz, *The Work of Theology*, trans. John P. Reid (Washington, DC: Thomist Press, 1958).

188 For various discussions of this topic, see Marie-Dominique Chenu, *La Théologie comme science au XIIIe siècle*, 3rd ed. (Paris: Vrin, 1969), 67–92; Marie-Rosaire Gagnebet, "La nature de la théologie spéculative," 233n1 (a lengthy and informative note, full citation below in note 212); Antoninus de Carlensis, *Four Questions on the Subalternation of the Sciences*, trans. and ed. Steven J. Livesey (Philadelphia: American Philosophical Society, 1994); Egidio (Aegidius) Magrini, *Ioannis Duns Scoti doctrina de scientifica theologiae natura* (Rome: Antonianum, 1952), 22–25 (cited in Salm, "The Problem of Positive Theology," 10n8).

189 See *ST* II-II, q. 4, a. 8.

190 On the character of the assent of faith, see Reginald Garrigou-Lagrange, *The Theological Virtues*, vol. 1 *On Faith*, trans. Thomas à Kempis Reilly (St. Louis, MO: B. Herder, 1965), 298–315; also see Labourdette, "La vie théologale selon Thomas d'Aquin, L'affection dans la foi," cited in note 38 above. This point, along with its

suffices for one to have a discourse that is scientific, albeit in an *imperfect state*, so long as the truths of faith are not known through vision.[191]

Now, especially upon reading Labourdette's own insistent remarks,[192] it would seem that the whole debate, at least on the Toulouse side, should be situated on the level of theological reflection and discussion, that is, as something not calling into question the *de fide* convictions held by the interlocutors.[193] For his part, Garrigou-Lagrange's level of discourse is perhaps less

---

structural repercussions on theological knowledge, is acknowledged openly by Labourdette in "Theology: Faith Seeking Understanding," 97–98 below. The reader should bear in mind that the translation of *The Theological Virtues* is slightly idiosyncratic, altering the content and layout of the text on occasion, though it is still an overall faithful presentation of Fr. Garrigou-Lagrange's thought.

[191] See John of St. Thomas (Poinsot), *On Sacred Science: A Translation of Cursus theologicus I, Question 1, Disputation 2*, trans. John P. Doyle, ed. Victor M. Salas (South Bend, IN: St. Augustine's Press, 2020), disp. 2, a. 3, no. 6: "In the nature of a science there is not evidence, but only certitude. For Aristotle (1.2.71b10–12) in the definition of science does not posit evidence but certitude, when he says that 'to know scientifically is to know that the cause on account of which a thing exists is in fact the cause of that thing, and that it cannot come about that the thing be other than it is.' And the reason is that by certitude alone, even when evidence is absent, that habit is based upon an infallible connection and relates to an infallible truth; therefore, in this it is distinct from an opinionative habit which relates to a fallible and contingent truth and is, therefore, a habit which is subject to error, which is not to be a correct or virtuous habit of an intellectual kind. A habit, however, that proceeds infallibly and certainly perfects the intellect without any danger of error and without possible failure (*indefectibiliter*)." We would like to thank Dr. Victor Salas for providing us with this draft text, the last work of his great mentor Dr. John Doyle, one which has been long delayed. It will provide an excellent resource for those readers who must read John of St. Thomas's text in English.

[192] See Labourdette, "Closing Remarks Concerning our Position," 241–49 below; Labourdette and Nicolas, "Discussion Surrounding our 'Dialogue Théologique,'" 265–66 below.

[193] However, Étienne Fouilloux held that this claim of honest theological debate was a bit naïve given that even if the director of the *Revue thomiste* honestly thought such theological pluralism were permitted, the censors in Rome were not so broadminded. See Donneaud, "Correspondence Étienne Gilson-Michel Labourdette," 498n10. Fouilloux's claim, as reported by Donneaud, seems a bit absolutist, merely if we were to consider, by way of example, the various theories of sacramental causality (no small point of doctrine) permitted even in light of the Council of Trent's declarations. Despite the fact that certain theologians wanted to suggest that the *de fide* requirements of Trent and the later magisterium slid in the direction of those Thomists who held to a physical-instrumental-causality view of the matter, the Church clearly left room for a number of theories which were stamped with a much more moral-causal view of the sacraments, most famously the "intentional causal" theory of one-time-Cardinal Billot. See Ludwig Ott, *Fundamentals of Catholic Dogma*, 2nd ed., trans. Patrick Lynch, ed. James Canon Bastible (Rockford, IL: TAN, 1974), 330–32; Bernard Leeming, *Principles of Sacramental Theology* (London: Longmans, 1963), 295–97; Emmanuel Doronzo, *Tratatus dogmaticus de sacramentis in genere* (Milwaukee: Bruce, 1946), 161–97.

clearly stated. We believe that his concerns remain *theological* (and philosophical, to the degree that such philosophy is instrumentally involved in theological reasoning), even if he is quick to warn his interlocutors of the danger of falling into modernism. In fact, he readily asserts that he is not questioning the supernatural faith of Maurice Blondel, whose thought is profoundly involved in the controversy at issue in most of the *Angelicum* articles presented in this volume, as well as in Garrigou-Lagrange's earlier article, "Theology and the Life of Faith," included in the texts gathered here.[194] This would seem to mean that even for the older Dominican, whose critique falls most bluntly on the question concerning the nature of truth, the debate remains on the level of philosophy and of theology, not that of faith *per se*. Nonetheless, in the opening to his article, which recounts the theological vagaries of Anton Günther and the nineteenth century roots of intellectual trends leading up to the First Vatican Council, Garrigou-Lagrange cites a strong statement from Vacant approvingly:

> In order to fall under the Council's anathema and be guilty of heresy, it suffices that one claim that, on account of the progress of science, there is sometimes room to attribute *another meaning* to the dogmas proposed by the Church, one differing from the meaning that she once gave for them and, indeed, continues to give for them.[195]

And, still citing Vacant, Garrigou-Lagrange continues by stating that this claim is founded on "the nature of truth and of infallibility." If nothing else, the distinctions between theological assent (as well as, in a way, philosophical assent) and *de fide* assent are less rhetorically clear here. One can at least understand why Marie-Joseph Nicolas privately wrote his older confrere to tell him about the need being felt (at least in France in the pages of the *Revue thomiste*, if not in Rome) to carefully distinguish theological debate from authoritative intervention.[196]

---

194 See Garrigou-Lagrange, "Truth and the Immutability of Dogma," 305n2 below: "Thus, *a fortiori*, we do not question his personal faith, nor even the good that has been brought about by his philosophy for certain minds [*esprits*]. We recognize that his last works indicate a manifest intention to remedy issues which existed in his earlier writings and that they express thoughts having an undeniable loftiness"; Garrigou-Lagrange, "Correspondence," 372–73 below: "As we said in an article found in this same issue, we in no way question Monsieur Blondel's personal faith, nor the lofty elevation of his thought, which we have always recognized. Nonetheless, we have examined what can be deduced from certain assertions that he has made, along with what has, in fact, been deduced from them on a number of occasions."

195 See Garrigou-Lagrange, "Relativism and the Immutability of Dogma According to the [First] Vatican Council," 360–61 below; Vacant, *Études théologiques*, 286 (emphasis added).

196 See Henry Donneaud, "Correspondance Étienne Gilson-Michel Labourdette," 498n10: "The doctrinal crisis is grave, and we here find ourselves engaging in a difficult

In any case, Garrigou-Lagrange is quite clearly concerned with the way that philosophically explicated notions[197] are taken up for use in dogmatic formulas. Throughout his articles, one rightly senses that the older Dominican fears a return to modernism, and he does not fail to cite the 58th condemned proposition from the decree *Lamentabili sane exitu*: "Truth is no more immutable than man himself, since it evolved with him, in him, and through him."[198] Clearly, to his eyes, the danger was that a philsophico-theological position (whether held by Bouillard, Blondel, or others) was sufficiently proximate to faith to be closely connected to the danger of modernist errors concerning the nature of dogma and its development. Labourdette was not insensitive to this possibility, though, in his concluding reflections on the *Dialogue théologique*, he explicitly states that he has tried to avoid the term "Modernism" because of all of the meanings attached thereto.[199] However, one should recall, once more, Garrigou-Lagrange's own unequivocal statement that he too wishes to remain theological in scope:

> A theologian is not forbidden to say that, to his eyes, a given new position leads to heresy and even that it seems to him to be heretical. He only says this from the perspective of theological science and its

---

battle, one that is quite different from the one that you are undertaking in Rome. The vast majority is against us, and they are often the most active, the liveliest and, as far as can be judged, the most generous of Christians. There is one thing which we must absolutely avoid, on pain of losing all credibility: giving the impression that, in order to cut short debates, we feel the need to make recourse to Rome's authority. Of course, authority must be exercised, and perhaps it indeed usually ends up acting only all too late. However, it is not our role to warn it, in whatsoever manner. Others may have the duty to do so. Our role, for the sake of the truth, is to defend it solely by making use of our own intelligence and valid reasoning. When I say, 'We,' I am speaking of the *Revue thomiste*. In people's current state of mind, not only would we lead people who are disposed to hold St. Thomas's position to end up standing in opposition to us, but above all, setting all questions of tactics aside, it would be catastrophic if Thomism were only able to defend itself through recourse to authority. I believe that the mission of the *Revue thomiste* is to defend it by itself and solely by its own intrinsic force."

[197] But, not, *positions properly tied to any particular philosophical school*, a point which he held from the time that he wrote *Sens commun*. See Garrigou-Lagrange, *Thomistic Common Sense*, 245–300. An echo of his position can be found in Charles Journet, *The Mass: The Presence of the Sacrifice of the Cross*, trans. Victor Szczurek (South Bend, IN: St. Augustine's Press, 2008), 154.

[198] Holy Office of Pius X, *Lamentabili*, no. 58; Denzinger, no. 3458 [old no., 2058].

[199] See Labourdette, "Closing Remarks Concerning our Position," 249 below: "And I do not presume to suspect, *a priori*, that any contemporary Catholic theologians either do not accept this condemnation or knowingly take up this or that error drawn from among those that fall under this condemnation."

deductions, without *authoritatively* speaking like a judge in an ecclesiastical tribunal.[200]

Only a desire to claim that he has committed the sin of public dishonesty could justify the assertion that these words were deliberately false. Perhaps he was more direct in his accusations, but it would seem that, on the whole, he and his younger Dominican confreres shared similar concerns on this point.

The *shared* reaction of the two parties did not fall as much on Blondel as upon the rather hasty[201] account of doctrinal development presented by Henri Bouillard (and defended by Le Blond). In the conclusion of *Conversion et grâce*, Bouillard makes it clear that he is attempting to thereby explain the immutability of dogma in the midst of changes; however, even to the eyes of Labourdette, this *explanation*,[202] which would formally be on the level of theological reasoning using a particular philosophical theory of historical development, seemed unable to overcome the risk of falling into a kind of conceptual relativism.[203]

Both Labourdette and Garrigou-Lagrange find themselves particularly vexed by Bouillard's claim that the notion of formal causality,[204] used by the Council of Trent in the *Decree on Justification* in order to defend the entitative reality of created grace, merely belonged to an earlier era of speculation on the theology of grace:[205]

---

[200] See Garrigou-Lagrange, "Truth and the Immutability of Dogma," 316 below (emphasis added).

[201] The hastiness of the account, especially the infamous phrase, "A theology which is not contemporary [*actuelle*] would be a false theology," is admitted by someone like Joshua Brotherton, who is not overly critical of Bouillard in "Development(s) in the Theology of Revelation: From Francisco Marín-Sola to Joseph Ratzinger," *New Blackfriars* 97 (2016): 664n7: "These words can certainly be interpreted more charitably than they are by Garrigou, but they could have also been more carefully chosen."

[202] See Labourdette, "Theology and Its Sources," 149, annotation (o) below. Moreover, see ibid., 140n19, where Labourdette charitably attempts to read Bouillard as using words which in fact to not measure up to his real intentions and thought.

[203] See Labourdette, "Theology and Its Sources," 146, annotation (l) below: "I am critiquing him—and no response has been extended to me concerning this very matter—for falling for a pseudo-philosophy that is unconsciously inspired by the methodologies of history, to the point of no longer daring to conceive of the permanence of a *notion*." For his full discussion of this, see ibid., 149ff below.

[204] However, both streams, the older and the younger, note that there are many other notions as well which are used by the Church. Labourdette notes merely *person, nature, transubstantiation*, "and other precise terms." See Labourdette, "Theology and Its Sources," 152 below. For his part, Garrigou-Lagrange cites what would surely number far over fifty notions, given the somewhat bombastic list of notions enumerated in "Concerning Notions Consecrated by the Councils," 321–24 below.

[205] See Trent, *Decree on Justification*, ch. 7 (Denzinger, no. 1529 [799]): "Finally, the single formal cause [of justification] is 'the justice of God, not [that] by which He Himself is

It was certainly not the intention of the Council to canonize an Aristotelian concept, nor even a theological concept conceived under Aristotle's influence. It merely wished to affirm, against the Protestants, that justification is an interior renewal and not simply an imputation of Christ's merits, the remission of sins, or the favor of God. To this end, it made use of concepts which were common to the theology of the times. *However, others can be substituted for them without altering the meaning of its teaching. This is demonstrated by the fact that the Council itself much more often made use of equivalent notions derived from Scripture.*[206]

Ultimately, to Garrigou-Lagrange's eyes, the abandonment of the notion of formal causality would not merely spell doom for a particular dogmatic formulation concerning created grace but would ultimately undermine the whole apparatus of St. Thomas's own theology, which ubiquitously makes use of the notion of formal causality.[207] The claim would, in fact, apply to any of the classical scholastic schools which all utilize the notion of formal causality sketched out in a broadly Aristotelian sense as referring to the metaphysical principle which is constitutive or determinative of what something is. In short, if not properly nuanced, Bouillard's claim would seem to spell doom for Scotists, Suarezians, Bonaventurians, and Molinists in addition to Thomists, and Labourdette and Nicolas did not fear to point out this upshot.[208]

Moreover, although the notion of formal cause is not consecrated by the Church in its fully Aristotelian sense, with all of its systematic connections to the overall teaching of the Stagirite, it retains an organic connection to the basic, though critically refined, notion of "that which constitutes the being of something" (i.e., its "formal constitutive"). Thus, to Garrigou-Lagrange's eyes, to reject the notion of formal causality would place at risk the very notion of essence (or, perhaps we could even say, that which is *per se*, in rigorous contrast with what is *per accidens*), along with all the various philosophical principles that depend on the distinction of the essential from the non-essential.[209] And, looking upon the repercussions of the noetic proposed

---

just, but [that] by which He makes us just, namely, the justice that we have as a gift from Him and by which we are spiritually renewed."

206 Bouillard, *Conversion et grâce*, 221–22.

207 See Garrigou-Lagrange, "Truth and the Immutability of Dogma," 344 below.

208 See Labourdette and Nicolas, "The Analogy of Truth and the Unity of Theological Science," 239 below (and quoted above).

209 See Garrigou-Lagrange, "On the Immutability of Defined Truths, With Remarks on the Supernatural Order," 346 below: "To abandon the notion of formal cause (or, the notion of *the formal constitutive*) would be to abandon the notion of *essence*, as well as the *first principles* which presuppose this notion. It would be to fall into relativism, and

by Bouillard, Labourdette, who is often credited for being more measured than Garrigou-Lagrange in his response, did not fear to state his concerns boldly in his follow-up article, "Criticism in Theology: A Response," where he voices the concern that the *theological* position being staked out does potentially have dire consequences for matters of faith without, however, accusing the Jesuits of actually drawing this consequence (and thereby sinning against faith in the irreformable character of *De fide* truths):

> It is true that I said that certain assertions, *pushed to their consequences*, do not seem to me compatible with the Church's teachings. But these teachings—that is, the objective determination of the faith or of truths more or less close to faith—are *the very principles of theology*. What would theological discussion be, or theological criticism, if we did not have the right *to compare consequences with their principles*, to strive to show their disparity and thus to detect the *illogicality involved in the theological reasoning being proposed*? Does this challenge the theologian's personal faith and his intention to remain orthodox? This represents an entirely different domain, and I have in no way permitted myself to enter into it.[210]

It is not, however, as though the Dominicans were guilty of a kind of static view of history, unable to account for the reality of dogmatic development. In fact, even the Roman Thomism offered at the Angelicum at Garrigou-Lagrange's time was well aware of the need to acknowledge doctrinal development in more than a merely off-handed manner.[211] Thus, given how accessible many of the texts from this era are, it is troubling to see relatively recent studies which seem to deny this fact,[212] making stark claims which

---

the *Ecclesia docens* herself would fall into such relativism if she wished to follow down this path, which her discernment prevents her from taking.

By a necessity which is at once logical and metaphysical, whether or not one wishes, one erroneous denial would entail many others. . . ."

[210] Labourdette, "Criticism in Theology," 168–69 below (emphasis is Labourdette's).

[211] In fact, as will be discussed below, the closing of *Dei filius*, ch. 4, citing the well-known passage from Vincent of Lérins, invited all theologians to fashion some form of teaching concerning doctrinal development, while retaining the meaning of dogmas.

[212] See Dries Bosschaert, "A Great Deal of Controversy? A Case Study of Dondeyne, Grégoire, and Moeller Integrating Phenomenology and Existentialism in Louvain Neo-Thomism," in *So What's New About Scholasticism? How Neo-Thomism Helped Shape the Twentieth Century*, ed. Rajesh Heynickx and Stéphane Symons (Berlin / Boston: Walter de Guyter, 2018), 135: "At the same moment, also *Essai sur le problème théologique*, a work of the Louvain Dominican Louis Charlier, was placed on the index *for discrediting scholastic philosophy by acknowledging historicity in theology and recognizing dogmatic*

stand in contrast to the clear evidence in the pages of Roman professors like Garrigou-Lagrange, as well as his fellow professor Reginald Schultes.[213]

As is evidenced by a somewhat-jarring note placed at the end of his 1935 essay, "Theology and the Life of Faith," Garrigou-Lagrange found himself in the midst of a debate concerning the definability of theological conclusions, returning on occasion to critique the position concerning this matter articulated by his confrere teaching at Fribourg, Francisco Marín-Sola, who articulated a theory according to which theological *conclusions* could be defined as intrinsic developments of *de fide* revealed truths.[214] To the eyes of Garrigou-Lagrange (and, interestingly, to the eyes of the editors of the Reiser edition of John of St. Thomas's *Cursus theologicus*, which generally avoids any such editorial comment[215]), this involves an error of logic,

---

development" (emphasis added). The final words are, in particular, the most egregious historically and speculatively. For a better, albeit still-biased, presentation of this affair surrounding Charlier's work, see Mettepenningen, *Nouvelle Théologie, New Theology*, 61–69, esp. 68. Also, for a much richer appreciation of the various discussions surrounding development of dogma by thinkers in this era, see "Le Progrès de l'église dans l'intelligence de la foi," in Yves Congar, *La foi et la théologie*, 93–120.

For an articulation of the speculative concerns voiced by Charlier's fellow Dominicans, see Fr. Marie-Rosaire Gagnebet, "La nature de la théologie spéculative," *Revue thomiste* 45 (1939): 1–39, 213–55, 645–74, and Gagnebet, "Un essai sur le problème théologique," *Revue thomiste* 45 (1939): 108–45.

Likewise, in a recent article, Joshua Brotherton seems to present Garrigou-Lagrange along the stereotyped lines mentioned above, even if he acknowledges Garrigou-Lagrange's awareness of the occurrence of dogmatic development. See Brotherton, "Development(s) in the Theology of Revelation," 661–76.

[213] See Reginald-Marie Schultes, *Introductio in Historiam Dogmatum* (Paris: Lethielleux, 1922), 287–96; Garrigou-Lagrange, *The Theological Virtues*, vol. 1, *On Faith*, 125–49, and *On Divine Revelation*, vol. 1, 320–26. Moreover, one should consult the relevant work on the theological sub-treatise *De locis theologicis*, as set forth by Garrigou-Lagrange's forebears Gardeil and Berthier, as well as his student, Emmanuel Doronzo. See Joachim Joseph Berthier, *Tractatus de Locis Theologicis* (Turin: Marietti / New York: Benzinger, 1888); Ambroise Gardeil, *La notion du lieu théologique* (Paris: Lecoffre, 1908); "Lieux Théologiques," *Dictionnaire de théologie Catholique*, vol. 9.1, ed. Alfred Vacant et al. (Paris: Letouzey, 1926): cols. 712–47; Emmanuel Doronzo, *Theologia Dogmatica*, vol. 1 (Washington, DC: The Catholic University of America Press, 1966), 399–544.

[214] See Francisco Marín-Sola, *The Homogeneous Evolution of Catholic Dogma*, trans. Antonio T. Piño (Manilla: Santo Tomas University Press, 1988), 168–343. For a summary of the debate between Marín-Sola and Schultes (with the latter being close to Garrigou-Lagrange), see Labourdette, *La Foi*, 84–140. Also see Guy Mansini, "The Development of the Development of Doctrine in the Twentieth Century," *Angelicum* 93, no. 4 (2016): 785–822; from a slightly different, though related perspective, see Cyril Vollert, "Doctrinal Development: A Basic Theory," *Proceedings of the Catholic Theological Society of America* (1957): 45–74.

[215] See Joannis a Sancto Thoma, *Cursus Theologici*, vol. 1 (Paris: Society of St. John the Evangelist / Desclée et Socii, 1931), 361n1.

given the nature of objectively illative inferences, that is, the drawing of conclusions in which a new truth is stated, one which was only virtually, not formally, contained in the premises. No doubt, this assertion seems to split hairs, but the concern is to prevent something materially new from being added to the deposit of revelation. All of this was written in light of the First Vatican Council's closing statement of *Dei filius*, which simultaneously affirms the unchanging character of revelation, along with a notion of dogmatic development expressed in the famed maxim drawn from St. Vincent of Lérins:

> For the doctrine of faith that God has revealed has not been proposed like a philosophical system to be perfected by human ingenuity; rather, it has been committed to the spouse of Christ as a divine trust to be faithfully kept and infallibly declared. Hence also that meaning of the sacred dogmas is perpetually to be retained which our Holy Mother Church has once declared, and there must never be a deviation from that meaning on the specious ground and title of a more profound understanding. "Therefore, let there be growth and abundant progress in understanding, knowledge, and wisdom, in each and all, in individuals and in the whole Church at all times and in the progress of ages, but only within the proper limits, i.e., within the same dogma, the same meaning, the same judgment."[216]

Garrigou-Lagrange's concern in relation to Marín-Sola's erudite work is arguably liberating for dogmatic notions. By refusing to allow that *strictly theological conclusions* could be defined as something which is intrinsically *de fide*, one in fact protects revealed truth from becoming the servant of any school of theology—*even Thomistic theology*. Moreover, it opens space for theological debate, where claims of formal *infidelity* are not immediately necessary when errors are committed. One's theological *reasoning* can be invalid or unsound (on the level of *virtual revelation*) without thereby meaning that one volitionally does not affirm something that must be held *de fide* (on the level of *formal revelation*). If, in the 1940s, Garrigou-Lagrange does not emphasize this point as strongly as do his younger confreres, nonetheless, the point is certainly part and parcel of his own position.

However, what is the model, then, to be used for understanding how doctrine develops, something clearly implied in the second half of the selection just cited from *Dei filius* above? There can be no question as to what this model is for the older Dominican: the process of definition. Regularly throughout his writing, he refers to the process by which the mind passes from a vague concept to a distinct one as bearing witness to how conceptual content in fact

---

[216] First Vatican Council, *Dei filius*, ch. 4 (Denzinger, no. 3020 [old no., 1800]).

does develop without, however, implying that something formally new is drawn as a conclusion in the process of such intellectual elaboration.[217] The passage from vagueness to distinctness involves the "explicitation" of what is implicitly present in the notion in question, not the actualizing of something potentially and virtually contained within what was first known.

In short, such development ultimately takes place in the activity of the intellect's power to define things, the "first operation" of the intellect, not in its discursive "third operation" by which it draws out syllogistic inferences.[218]

---

[217] See Garrigou-Lagrange, *Thomistic Common Sense*, 229–45, 275–78; Garrigou-Lagrange, "On the Search for Definitions According to Aristotle and St. Thomas," in *Philosophizing in Faith: Essays on the Beginning and End of Wisdom*, ed. and trans. Matthew K. Minerd (Providence, RI: Cluny Media, 2019), 21–34; Garrigou-Lagrange, *The Sense of Mystery*, 15–26. For a critical assessment of Garrigou-Lagrange's position, see Guy Mansini, "The Historicity of Dogma and Common Sense," 111–38.

[218] As for the latent problem of "conceptualism" and how the second operation of the intellect is related to the first, this is not taken up by Garrigou-Lagrange directly. However, as regards the relationship between judgment and notions in the act of faith, see his comments on *ST* II-II, q. 1, a. 2 in *On Faith*, 84–90. For a lengthy consideration of the noetics of faith and theology generally developed in harmony with Fr. Garrigou-Lagrange, see Jean-Hervé Nicolas, *Dieu connu comme inconnu: Essai d'une critique de la connaissance théologique* (Paris: Desclée de Brouwer, 1966), 183–419.

Quite clearly, based on St. Thomas's theory of faith, the *revealed statements* expressed in judgments must, *in and through* the act of the supernaturalized judgment of faith, expand the natural notions instrumentally used for revelation, thus meaning that one can then return to these notions, which make up the termini of the judgment, finding them "expanded" by this act of supernaturalized judgment. For brief indications in this direction, see Jean-Hervé Nicolas, *Catholic Dogmatic Theology: A Synthesis*, vol. 1 *On the Trinitarian Mystery of God* (Washington, DC: The Catholic University of America Press, 2021), §167 (pp. 290–92).

This is something similar to what takes place in any case of analogy, even in the natural order. It is arguable that the "imperfect abstraction" spoken of by the followers of Cajetan concerning analogy would involve a sort of return by the intellect to its first act in the course of reasoning things out concerning the various relationships which exist among the analogates which are imperfectly subordinated to the analogous notion in question. The same is true concerning the relationship of a metaphorical term to its referent, a process of reference which cannot be fully explicated without understanding the reasoning which links together the various inferior notions. In any case, the second-intentional relationships of *superiority* and *inferiority* are fashioned by the first act of the intellect, giving rise for example to the famed predicables, but also to other second intentions as well. This topic is underappreciated by Thomists, given the paucity of texts in Aquinas himself. For indications concerning these matters, see Matthew K. Minerd, "Thomism and the Formal Object of Logic," *American Catholic Philosophical Quarterly* 93, no. 3 (2019): 411–44; Yves R. Simon, "On Order in Analogical Sets" in *Philosopher at Work*, ed. Anthony O. Simon (Lanham: Roman & Littlefield, 1999), 135–71; and for suggestive thoughts along these lines, see John Deely, "The Absence of Analogy," *The Review of Metaphysics* 55, no. 3 (Mar. 2002): 521–50. Historically, this involves the entire discussion of the *rationes*

The relationships of superiority and of inferiority implied in a definition (as properties of the *relationes rationis* known as *genus* and *species*[219]) are produced by this operation. By a kind of general, uncritical knowledge, we can have a vague notion of "man" or even of "subsistence." However, when we set forth a definition—Man: rational animal—we state again to ourselves a simple notion, albeit in a complex manner. This definition expresses—vitally within the depths of the soul—the nature of what we are discussing and thus enables us to pass from vague knowledge of this notion to distinct knowledge thereof. However, note well: it is one and the same notion which is expressed, with the vague concept being the guiding insight which directs us toward this ultimate definition.[220] There may well be a good deal of *dialectical reasoning* up to this point. In fact, Aristotle himself organizes his *Topics* around the idea of the so-called predicables, which are involved as second-intentional relations in any given definition. Such dialectical reasoning *reveals* the parts of a definition without, however, meaning that the definition would be a direct conclusion of this reasoning.[221] One either sees or does not see the distinct concept as expressing the vague one.[222]

The reader will here excuse a rather technical parenthesis, which addresses certain criticisms that have been registered against Garrigou-Lagrange's conception of dogmatic development and its relationship to "common sense." From early on in his academic career, Garrigou-Lagrange developed the Aristotelian notion of *intellectus*, the habit of first principles, in a way that made clear the profound implications of the claim that such principles are directly apprehended through the immediate correspondence of their terms to each other, without the intervention of further discursive scientific or sapiential elaboration. Following in the wake of the Thomist school,

---

involved in analogy. For an excellent study of various the treatment of this issue by various Dominican figures, see Dominic D'Ettore, *Analogy after Aquinas: Logical Problems, Thomistic Answers* (Washington, DC: The Catholic University of America Press, 2019).

For important citations from J.-H. Nicolas, Maritain, Gardeil, Charles Journet, and Édouard Hugon, see the translator's introduction to Garrigou-Lagrange, *On Divine Revelation*, 47n5.

219 See Minerd, "Thomism and the Formal Object of Logic," 436–41.

220 See the very interesting remarks in Garrigou-Lagrange, *The Sense of Mystery*, 23.

221 Granted, one can, for example, demonstrate a definition through formal cause from one given through a thing's efficient or final cause. See Garrigou-Lagrange, "On the Search for Definitions According to Aristotle and St. Thomas," 23–24.

222 Interesting developments on the logic involved in "topical" reasoning could be drawn from Louis-Marie Régis, *L'Opinion selon Aristote* (Paris: Vrin, 1935); Ambroise Gardeil, "La certitude probable," *Revue des Sciences philosophiques et théologiques* 5 (1911): 237–66, 441–85; Gardeil, "La topicité," *Revue des Sciences philosophiques et théologiques* 5 (1911): 750–57.

though here pushing it forward in its articulation, he saw quite powerfully that this state of affairs indicated that there was a primordial connection between our most basic apprehensions of reality and the philosophical rearticulation of these same principles.[223]

Recently, Guy Mansini published an important study concerning the relationship between history and the intellectual apprehensions possible for common sense (in the natural order) and Christian common sense (in the supernatural order of faith).[224] Mansini rightly notes that Garrigou-Lagrange is somewhat naïve in his account of the relationship between history and the grasping of supra-historical truths. However, a path forward is possible within the basic overall framework offered by Garrigou-Lagrange, though with important emendations, precisely for the reasons observed by Mansini, Congar, and others.

Too often, Thomistic discussions of "insight into first principles" (i.e., *intellectus*) seem to present a kind of automatic process, whereby the mind quickly sees the immediate connection of two *termini*, as though very little reflection were needed, let alone a great deal of historical elaboration and

---

[223] It is here that we see an interesting point, of no small importance in relation to what Labourdette says below in "Theology: Faith Seeking Understanding," namely how the insights of *intellectus precisely understood as "common sense"* differ from the re-articulations of this same data when considered from within the context of a given scientific or sapiential body of knowledge. *Intellectus* within the warp-and-woof of *sapiential* reasoning is part of a greater whole. It is indeed the most important part, but it no longer can be considered in isolation from the reasoning which considers the conclusions drawn therefrom (in forms of *scientia* and *sapientia*) as well as that which considers the intrinsic intelligibility of the principles themselves (in forms of *sapientia*)

As St. Thomas remarks in *ST* I-II q. 57, a. 2 (and as Cajetan draws into brilliant relief in his commentary on the same article), wisdom contains both science and *intellectus* / understanding by way of eminence. Cajetan remarks: "For wisdom makes use of *per se nota* principles by deducing conclusions, which is [an office] of science, and it judges, defends, and establishes that these very *per se nota* principles are true on the basis of their terms' meanings, something that understanding sees in an absolute manner [and not through a reflective, analytical judgment upon them]. And it has both [of these offices] through the resolution that it makes to the highest cause, containing these offices in a more eminent manner." Also, see Minerd, Wisdom be Attentive: The Noetic Structure of Sapiential Knowledge," 1103–46.

[224] See Mansini, "The Historicity of Dogma and Common Sense," 111–38. The comments that follow are not meant so much to be a direct response (and most especially not a critique) of Mansini but, rather, a refraction of his concerns through a lens that looks to provide a kind of "reverential" interpretation which bears witness to how Garrigou-Lagrange is just as much the heir to Schwalm, Gardeil, and others from the great figures of the Saulchoir as were Chenu and Congar. While the latter were thematically more sensitive about, and concerned with, the role played by historicity in knowledge, even Garrigou-Lagrange was not lacking in the primordial insights necessary for elaborating a full account of positive theology.

knowledge. Throughout his works, Garrigou-Lagrange could seem to present a sort of historically insensitive account of *intellectus*. Nonetheless, the authors of this introduction are convinced that a charitable interpretation of his texts bears witness to a foundational sensitivity to the question of historicity and development. In point of fact, this is quite clear in *Thomistic Common Sense*, which is ultimately concerned with explaining the true nature of dogmatic development.

As we have said, when discussing the phenomenon of dogmatic development, he has at hand a ready instrument for explanation: the process of definition—the passage from a vague ("confused") notion to a distinct one. Although certain definitions can be proven from other definitions—as in the case of proving a definition through material causality ("axe: a hard and sharp blade") from a definition through final causality ("axe: a device for chopping wood")—properly speaking, the process of defining is the work of what the Thomists refer to as the intellect's "first operation," that is, the process by which the mind expresses to itself more distinctly the reality that it already knows vaguely.[225] For this reason, there are even unique "*relationes rationis*" involved here, ready to be studied by the logician who considers all of the various logical relations formulated by the intellect as it defines, judges, and reasons about reality.[226] The process of defining is Garrigou-Lagrange's primary model for explaining the development of dogma,[227] though it could also be applied, with all due proportions maintained, to the articulation of first principles in philosophy, as well as the articulation of scientific, philosophical, and theological conclusions.[228] In fact, he refers to the development

[225] See Garrigou-Lagrange, *The Sense of Mystery*, 23: "At the end of this *venatio definitionis realis*, of this hunt for the definition (as Aristotle says in providing the rules for such a chase), *the vague concept*, which was THE GUIDING PRINCIPLE of the ascending and descending search, is itself recognized in *the distinct concept*, as a man who is half asleep recognizes himself when, fully awake, he looks at himself in a mirror. Thus, the search for the definition is the work of understanding [intelligence]—more a work of νοῦς than it is a work of discursive reason."

[226] See Minerd, "Thomism and the Formal Object of Logic," 411–44. For remarks about the need for some expansion of the Thomistic teaching on this point, see the translator remarks in Reginald Garrigou-Lagrange, *The Order of Things*, 232n12. Also, see note 218 in this introduction. For interesting connections between the Aristotelian doctrine of *nous* and this process of defining, see the texts cited in the previous two footnotes, as well as Robert Sokolowki, "Making Distinctions," in *Pictures, Quotations, and Distinctions: Fourteen Essays in Phenomenology* (Notre Dame, IN: University of Notre Dame Press, 1992), 55–91.

[227] See Garrigou-Lagrange, *Thomistic Common Sense*, 95–109, 241–55, 313–31; Garrigou-Lagrange, "Theology and the Life of Faith," 277–78 below. Schultes, *Introductio in Historiam Dogmatum*, 287–96.

[228] However, one must be *very* careful to distinguish, in both the natural and supernatural orders, knowledge of first principles from the knowledge of conclusions that are only

of Aristotelian and Thomistic philosophy as "the work of centuries,"[229] and in his essay "Theology and the Life of Faith" (included in this volume), he makes a remark that is pregnant with implications for further development toward an awareness of the importance of history for knowing the objective character of a given truth:

> Even were theology not to deduce *any* theological conclusions, properly so-called, but were only to explain, through a profound metaphysical analysis,[230] the subject and predicate *of revealed truths*, and even were it only to show *their subordination* in order to make us be better aware of the depth, riches, and elevation of the very teaching of the Savior, even in such a case, it would have considerable importance. And this is how theology prepares for the elaboration of increasingly explicit dogmatic formulations of one and the same dogma, that is, of one and the same assertion or revealed truth, before it is a question of deducing from it *other truths* through *objectively illative* reasoning.[231] This deepening of the meaning of a fundamental truth sometimes takes centuries, as with the deepening of this expression: "And the Word was made flesh."[232]

---

virtually contained in the former. The latter are *new truths*, known mediately through *objectively illative reasoning*, whereas the former can be known *either directly* or *indirectly* (through a sapiential, though objectively extrinsic, defense of these first principles). This is, however, a point of great technicality. For the position informing this introduction, see Minerd, "Wisdom be Attentive," 1103–46.

Note, also, that first *principles* are formed by the intellect's second operation, by which we fashion *judgments*. Still, the explicitation of subject and predicate involved in a given judgment involves the process of defining one's terms. In any case, Garrigou-Lagrange was not insensitive to the distinction between conceptualization and judgment.

229 See Garrigou-Lagrange, *Thomistic Common Sense*, 104.

230 [Tr. note: By "metaphysical," he merely means an analysis searching for the most essential definition (or at least what is closest thereto *quoad nos*) of a given reality.]

231 [Tr. note: The following explanatory remark is included by Fr. Garrigou-Lagrange:] We use the expression "*objectively illative* reasoning" for that form of reasoning which leads *to another [objectively new] truth*. For example, from the Divine Intelligence, we can deduce the Divine Freedom through this major premise: every intelligent being is free. By contrast, reasoning is only *explicative* (or at most *subjectively illative*) when it establishes the *equivalence* of two propositions in stating the *same truth*. For example, there is the *equivalence* of these two propositions: "You are Peter and upon this rock I will build my Church; and the gates of hell will not prevail over it" = "The successor of Peter, when he speaks *ex cathedra* to the universal Church, in a matter of faith and morals, cannot be deceived."

See, at the end of this article, an *appendix* concerning the question of knowing whether theological conclusions obtained by *objectively illative* reasoning with the aid of a *natural premise* (even when the latter is the major, that is to say the more universal premise) can be *defined* as *a dogma of faith* to be acknowledged under pain of heresy properly so called (and not only of error).

232 See Garrigou-Lagrange, "Theology and the Life of Faith," 277 below.

Now, the activity of *defining* is at once a psychological process by which the intellect gives birth to the *verbum mentis* (also referred to as the *conceptus* or, by later Thomists, the *species expressa intellecta*),[233] as well as something bespeaking a "becoming" (or, better, coming-to-be) in the order of objectivity (or "intentional" existence).[234] One of the great tasks of the mind is to trace along the objective implications of the sometimes-centuries-long process of articulating a definition, as well as a scientific middle term and the scientific demonstrations connected to it. Although, no doubt, a process of reflection dear to phenomenological analysis,[235] this kind of "re-enlivening" of knowledge is also well-expressed by the Thomist Fr. Jean-Hervé Nicolas:

> Theology is a science. That is, it is a form of knowledge aiming at objective certitude. By its nature, every science is the work of man and of reason—a difficult and lengthy work. It is so lengthy that a single human lifetime is insufficient for it to be brought to its completion.

[233] This would be the "virtual productivity" spoken of by the Thomist school, above all following in the wake of John of St. Thomas. This sort of elaborative-production is involved in intellection, memory, estimation / cogitation, and imagination. See the index entries for "concept," "internal sense," "phantasiari," "species expressa" in John Deely, *Intentionality and Semiotics: A Story of Mutual Fecundation* (Scranton and London: University of Scranton Press, 2007). Also see the discussion of this matter in Simon, *An Introduction to Metaphysics of Knowledge*, 39–158.

[234] This would be the very intentional being of the other as other that formally constitutes knowledge, above all in its speculative manifestation of pure objectivity (in distinction from practical reasoning's extrinsic informing of the will through prudence and art). See Reginald Garrigou-Lagrange, "*Cognoscens quodammodo fit vel est aliud a se* (On the Nature of Knowledge as Union with the Other as Other)," in *Philosophizing in Faith*, 63–78; Simon, *An Introduction to Metaphysics of Knowledge*, 1–38; John N. Deely, "The Immateriality of the Intentional as Such," *The New Scholasticism* 42 (1968): 293–306. This psychological-intentional duality is well discussed in Jacques Maritain, *The Degrees of Knowledge*, 127–36, 411–41.

[235] On this subject, there are points of interesting connection in relation to the theme of "sedimentation" in our knowledge, forever requiring us to recover the roots of our current articulation of knowledge, by considering the manifold presuppositions built into the conceptual notions and terms that we deploy. Failure to be sensitive to such sedimentation can turn scientific, philosophical, theological, and even moral reasoning into mere word games. Though only briefly mentioned on this or that occasion, this is a very important point in the thought of Msgr. Robert Sokolowski, who also as a professor pushed his young Thomist students to avoid falling into mere word play. See Robert Sokolowski, *The Formation of Husserl's Concept of Constitution* (The Hague: Martinus Nijhoff, 1964), 172, 182, 188, 212–13; *Husserlian Meditations* (Evanston, IL: Northwestern University Press, 1974), 42, 66; *Moral Action: A Phenomenological Study* (Bloomington, IN: Indiana University Press, 1985), 20, 35–36; *Introduction to Phenomenology* (Cambridge, UK: Cambridge University Press, 2000), 165–68. Sokolowski's remarks can be profitably read alongside Jacques Maritain, "Appendice 1: Sur le langue philosophique," cited in note 242 below.

Every science is slowly fashioned through the long effort of generations, and the generation that receives a given science from the preceding generations will leave it behind to the next generation unfinished and forever in the midst of being accomplished. Every science is the never-definitive terminus of a never-accomplished investigation. Moreover, he who today enters into the worksite cannot content himself with reaping the fruits of the investigation in progress. He must, on his own behalf, undertake it again for himself. Certainly, he does not do this by starting over as though nothing had been accomplished before he existed. Rather, he remakes this intellectual journey by personally reproducing the efforts undertaken by his predecessors, though not without critiquing them, all so that he might make their results his own. This is how things must be, because achieving scientific knowledge is not merely a matter of knowing only what others have discovered regarding some given object. We must retrieve it for ourselves, under their guidance, so that we may not merely know the conclusions reached by others but may know the reasons for those conclusions. We must make these reasons our own, as though we had discovered them ourselves.[236]

Here, on the pen of a Dominican who owed a debt of intellectual and filial piety to Garrigou-Lagrange[237] and who also approvingly cites the articles concerning the nature of theology written by Labourdette and Gagnebet, we find a firm affirmation of the close relationship between history, knowledge, and dogma. Though not developed with such force by Garrigou-Lagrange, the sentiment is nonetheless in line with the fundamental élan of important remarks which he makes.

St. Thomas used the notion of *intellectus* to unpack the implications of the obscure knowledge we have through the theological virtue of faith.[238] One central implication of this explanation is that our faith-knowledge is not discursively mediated through a middle term but, rather, is immediately grasped in and through the very propositions of faith. The formal motive for this judgment is not the intellectual light of reason illuminating the terms of the proposition and setting them forth as having an immediate, *per se* connection but, rather, is the supernatural authority of God who reveals (and who through grace capacitates the soul to assent to this supernatural truth which He reveals).[239] In and through the judgment in which the truths of

---

[236] Nicolas, *Catholic Dogmatic Theology: A Synthesis*, vol. 1, 2.

[237] See Jean-Hervé Nicolas, "In Memoriam: Le Père Garrigou-Lagrange," *Freiburger Zeitschrift für Philosophie und Theologie* 11 (1964): 390–95.

[238] For a full discussion of this, see the texts cited in note 38 above.

[239] Thus, too, one understands why a Thomist like Garrigou-Lagrange would be vociferously opposed to the notion of "discursive faith," which would ultimately resolve the

faith are expressed, natural concepts (e.g., person, substance, sign, society, rebirth, relation, etc.) take on a supernatural signification.[240] Although the more recondite and detailed articulations of the faith remain too technical for the "believer on the street," ultimately they can be rearticulated for such a believer by an able pedagogue.[241] (And we all remain such "believers on the street," for our supernatural faith has primacy here, not our technical theology.) Rhetoric and preaching have the role of making such truths (whether philosophical or *de fide*) known to all the faithful, who have the foundational capacity for grasping such *per se nota* truths (respectively through natural *intellectus* or supernatural faith).[242]

---

content of faith formally into the evidence had through naturally knowable truths, even were they the loftiest motives of credibility. See Garrigou-Lagrange, *On Divine Revelation*, 675–77, 696–97, and (especially) 731–75.

[240] See Nicolas, *Dieu connu comme inconnu*, 183–316. Also, see the citation regarding the "superanalogy of faith" found at the end of note 218 above. Although Garrigou-Lagrange does not explicitly articulate a doctrine concerning the superanalogy of faith, he is not unaware of the super-elevating of the natural notions used in the propositions in which faith is expressed. See Garrigou-Lagrange, *On Divine Revelation*, vol. 1, 311–16.

[241] This was the reason why Garrigou-Lagrange spoke of the notions used in faith-knowledge as being in *continuity* with common sense but not purely reducible thereto. See Garrigou-Lagrange, *Thomistic Common Sense*, 287–90. The idea of *directly* linking faith to common sense seemed, in his opinion, to risk falling into a modernist position akin to what one finds articulated in Pius X, *Pascendi dominici gregis*, nos. 11–13.

[242] Thus, Garrigou-Lagrange proposes preaching along the lines of Bossuet as providing this kind of contact between theological articulation and the fundamental grasp of *de fide* truths through supernatural faith, the root *habitus* of faith. (One might also think of the great Parisian preaching of Dominicans such as Jean-Baptiste Henri Lacordaire, Jacques-Marie-Louis Monsabré, or Marie-Albert Janvier.) See Garrigou-Lagrange, *Thomistic Common Sense*, 278–83 and 289.

Maritain made interesting (non-Straussian) remarks concerning esoteric and exoteric writing for communicating philosophical doctrines to non-philosophers. See Maritain, "Appendice 1: Sur le langue philosophique," in *Réflexions sur l'intelligence*, 3rd ed. (Paris: Desclée de Brouwer, 1930), 338: "I know of but one solution to this difficulty [concerning how to communicate such technical philosophical truths to intelligent non-philosophers]. In short, it is the same solution offered by the ancients: alongside the philosopher's properly scientific and demonstrative work written above all for experts, the philosopher rightly should present the fruits of his works to the educated public, to 'everyone,' though using an expositional style that henceforth will be that of the art of persuading ('dialectical' in the Aristotelian sense), a style aiming to beget within his listeners *true opinions*, rather than *science*. This was what led Plato and Aristotle to write their dialogues."

However, in the case of sacred rhetoric, the ultimate knowledge begotten is not opinion but, rather, the certitude of faith, which itself lays at the root of acquired theological cogitation. For interesting directions for further reflection in this vein, see Charles Journet, "Supernatural Rhetoric and Science," in *The Wisdom of Faith: An Introduction to Theology*, trans. R. F. Smith (Westminster, MD: The Newman Press, 1952), 33–40.

Rather than being "epistemologically strange,"[243] what Garrigou-Lagrange's account of common sense attempts to articulate is the following distinction of formal objects. (1) On the level of nature, there is a distinction between (a) common knowledge had through *intellectus* and (b) the intellectually scrutinized understanding of the knowledge had through *intellectus*, though illuminated by way of discursive reflection[244] (i.e. philosophical grasping of those truths first known by the "man on the street"). (2) On the level of grace, there is a similar distinction between (a) the knowledge of faith (which we could call Christian common sense, so long as we understand thereby the knowledge of the mysteries had by *all* through obscure faith and perfected through the gifts of understanding, knowledge, and wisdom[245]) and (b) technical theological reflection on the deposit of faith itself.[246]

Even if Garrigou-Lagrange's own language tends toward a kind of ahistoricism, as we have already cited above, he is not wholly indifferent to the role of history in the articulation of human knowledge. Again, to cite his words from above: Aristotelian and Thomistic philosophy are "the work of centuries," and in the domain of supernatural truth, the "deepening of the meaning of a fundamental truth sometimes takes centuries of reflection," as was true in the centuries of the first Ecumenical Councils. One need not set traditional Thomism against a sound *ressourcement*. A bit of fair, mutual understanding should allow bridges to be built between the Thomists gathered here in this volume and those thinkers who are more desirous of integrating historical reflection and positive theology into theological science.

Thus, according to Garrigou-Lagrange, such development applies to some of the most important notions of philosophy and theology. The progress is true—just as *Dei filius* calls for—without, however, implying a material expansion of the deposit of faith—as *Dei filius* also requires. The early Councils merely developed the *de fide* insight found, for example, in the words of the prologue of St. John's Gospel: "And the Word was made flesh."

---

[243] See Mansini, "The Historicity of Dogma and Common Sense," 124–26.

[244] This capital point is somewhat overlooked, though it is central for understanding how it is that *sapientia* formally-eminently contains *intellectus* (and *scientia*). See Minerd, "Wisdom Be Attentive," 1113–14, 1125, 1138–41. Also see the citation from Cajetan in note 223 above.

[245] See "The Offices of Wisdom, Supernatural and Natural," in Minerd, "Wisdom be Attentive," 1126–32.

[246] In the supernatural order, this is the true wisdom, not notional, theological wisdom. See Garrigou-Lagrange, *Thomistic Common Sense*, 310–19; also, Garrigou-Lagrange, "The Language of Spiritual Writers Compared with That of Theologians," in *The Three Ages of the Interior Life: Prelude of Eternal Life*, trans. Sister M. Timothea Doyle, vol. 2 (St. Louis, MO: B. Herder, 1948), 3–20.

This theme concerning dogmatic development was constant in Garrigou-Lagrange's writings, going back to his work in *Sens commun*. In the final edition of that work, he lays out the whole of his position with great clarity in a lengthy passage which is worth citing, in order to allow him to speak for himself:

> This notion of *subsistence*, thus given precision, is obviously already an explication of the rudimentary metaphysics that common sense professes (*in actu exercito*), without reflecting upon it. Common sense uses *subjects* and *attributes* without noting (*in actu signato*) what constitutes the subject as a subject. It employs the word *subsister*, applying it to the persons and to things and not to their parts, but it does not ask why. Someone like Aristotle will need to come and write chapter eight of the fifth book of the *Metaphysics* in order to extricate the metaphysics of *first substance* implicitly contained in the least phrase composed of a concrete subject, the verb *to be*, and a predicate. Everyone uses the principle of [non-]contradiction, but Aristotle needed to write the fourth book of the *Metaphysics* in order for it to be abstractly and rigorously formulated, in a way susceptible to being applied to all beings.—The same was true for the notion of *subsistence*. As an explication of a vague datum of common sense, it is accessible, to a degree, to the latter, though, to a degree, it exceeds it by its rigor and its precision. Were not quite lengthy debates between the Greeks and the Latins, between St. Basil and Pope St. Damasus, necessary before the formula "three persons" was admitted by the Greeks and that of "three subsistences" by the Latins? Were one to deny that the philosophical terms employed by developed dogmatic definitions exceed the strict limits of common sense, would this not be to wish to deny progress in our knowledge of dogma such as it is universally defined by Catholic theologians? Between the merely common-sense notion that the primitive Church had concerning the God-Man and the definition of the Second Council of Constantinople concerning the hypostatic union, there is all-too-obviously a passage from the implicit to the explicit.[247]

Granted, the older Dominican perhaps would not be the first to laud the growth in historical focus characteristic of so many disciplines in the nineteenth and twentieth centuries. By contrast, in an article published prior to the full outburst of the events surrounding the articles which make up the *Dialogue théologique*, Labourdette was indeed quite emphatic that the development of historical consciousness represented a natural and salutary deepening of theological methodology, not merely for "positive theology" concerning the sources of theological reflection but even for the scientific activity of speculative theology itself:

[247] Garrigou-Lagrange, *Thomistic Common Sense*, 276–77.

> Theology has become far too developed as a science for historical methodology, understood precisely in this self-critical sense, not to be something far more than a necessary supplement: it is an irreplaceable instrument for speculative reflection itself.[248]

However, immediately after these remarks, he is equally emphatic that the theologian must maintain himself or herself at the level of speculative reflection concerning the interrelations of the truths in question, not merely at the level of history, chronicling what various people have happened to think:

> This is because, however independent we may think that a given theological formulation is from historical contingencies, it always and inevitably is impacted by the circumstances that originally surrounded it: the preoccupations of the era, errors to be combatted, influences undergone, aspects that are primarily emphasized, the worldview and culture common in a given era, place, etc. . . . It will always be important to discern within an ensemble of notions and within a group of assertions their strict scientific scope, their permanent value, and the great halo of historical connections they have either with the context in which they originally were proposed or with other assertions that were common at that time but which did not have the same value. Such discernment requires an infinitely refined touch and a culture that is at once theological and historical. A mind that is too exclusively that of a historian will end up emphasizing, above all, the changes that it perceives, poorly grasping the formal difference which separates notions from facts, imperishable essences from the conditions of temporal existence, and ideas from their histories.[249]

And his closing words show that these concerns are nothing more than a restatement of the broader concern to maintain the scientific status of theology: "It will fall to the theologian, if he is well-informed, to take and use this idea, now understood more fully through historical reflection, though itself independent from the whole of history as regards that idea's own essential notes, *so that he may present his theological science in its permanence*" (emphasis added).

Obviously, as a subjective (and even as a sociological) reality, no science exists in a kind of pure state of one deduction after another, proceeding from complete scientific surety to complete scientific surety and permanence, lodged in a Platonic heaven.[250] This is all too obvious in the case of the phys-

---

[248] Labourdette, "Theology: Faith Seeking Understanding," 124 below.

[249] Labourdette, "Theology: Faith Seeking Understanding," 124 below.

[250] On this, Garrigou-Lagrange at times sounds like he does think that this is the case, given his concern to show the continuity between God's self-knowledge and our own theology, even in its wayfaring state.

ical sciences, wherein hypothesis and preliminary explanation remain quite necessary as the dialectical means for ascertaining what essential and what is not. Theology also will involve discovery and debate. Each theologian must rediscover, with the aid of tradition, the meaning and scope of the problems faced today in theology,[251] and in executing this task, it will primarily be a question of *argumentative strength*, not of declaration by authority.[252] In short, a theology which is distinct from (but vitally connected to) faith will call for debate and dialogue. With characteristic vigor, Bruckberger thunders this point in his introduction:

> Theology has neither laboratories nor test fields in which to give wing to its theories. However, there is free discussion. And who does not see that without this free discussion and dialogue, the *de iure* impunity of the theologian who is mistaken would be but a scientific fraud? Or would we instead need to appeal immedialy, each time, to the Magisterium, asking her to settle the debate by way of authority, which in the end would again be a mere cop-out [*une échappatoire*]? A theologian's honesty is measured by the intellectual effort he expends, illuminated by faith, and by the stubborn rigor of his reasoning. All the rest is [mere] literature.[253]

Moreover, as Labourdette indicates in a very important section of his essay on theological methodology, the passage from the assent of faith (formal revelation) to that of theological science (virtual revelation) requires more than a mere quick shift in one's focus. Developing suggestions found in Maritain and Yves Simon concerning the nature of facts within each domain of knowledge,[254] he lays out a careful analysis of the way that the

---

[251] This dynamic is well expressed by Marie-Joseph Nicolas's brother, Jean-Hervé Nicolas, who himself openly stands in line with the vision of theology held by Labourdette and Gagnebet. See the quote from Nicolas cited in note 236 above.

[252] Though, theology will always be marked by its foundation upon *de fide* truths, which are assented to on the basis of authority (formally the authority of God who supernaturally reveals, as a *conditio sine qua non* on the authority of the Church as objectively proposing a teaching). See *ST* I, q. 1, a. 8, ad 2. On the formal character of the assent of faith, see Garrigou-Lagrange, *De revelatione*, vol. 1, 427–81. This is a very important and lengthy article in this work by Fr. Garrigou-Lagrange.

[253] Bruckberger, "A Theological Dialogue," 129 below.

[254] In English, see Yves Simon, "Philosophers and Facts," in *The Great Dialogue of Nature and Space*, ed. Gerard J. Delacourt (New York: Magi Books, 1970), 139–62; Maritain, *Degrees of Knowledge*, 60–64; also see the insightful and lucid reflections in Michael D. Torre, "Yves R. Simon, Disciple of Maritain: The Idea of Fact and the Difference Between Science and Philosophy," in *Facts are Stubborn Things: Thomistic Perspectives in the Philosophies of Nature and Science*, ed. Matthew K. Minerd (Washington, DC: American Maritain Association, 2020), 19–39.

establishment of properly scientific-theological data shifts one's formal perspective from that of adherence to the revealed message (i.e., the formal perspective of infused supernatural faith) to that of *understanding what is revealed* (i.e., the formal perspective of virtual revelation):

> From this first acceptance by theology, the truths of faith present the mind with a different appearance than that of being mere objects of adherence. Henceforth considered in their intelligible virtualities, such data of faith become "theological data." The same truths which, on the one hand, are purely objects of faith, will come to find themselves now engaged in an intellectual activity which is that of knowledge's own investigation, striving to establish a science where they will play the role of being truths that are either explanatory or explained (i.e., by other data of faith). They are at once truths of faith and also *theological truths*.[255]

One can say that the seeds for such theology exist in every believer who seeks to understand what he or she holds on faith.[256] This attests to the "homogeneity" which links together faith and theology, even while the two remain formally distinct.[257] The life of faith and the life of theology must be

---

[255] Labourdette, "Theology: Faith Seeking Understanding," 109 below.

[256] For suggestive remarks concerning this, while bearing in mind the differences which came to separate these Dominican brothers, see Marie-Dominique Chenu, *Is Theology a Science?*, trans. Adrian Howell North Green-Armytage (New York: Hawthorn Books, 1959), 14–24. Particular care must be taken here to note that Chenu draws faith and theology close. No doubt, part of his concern here is a solicitude, felt by a number of thinkers, to make clear that the assent of theology is not merely concerned with drawing those conclusions which lay outside of the domain of faith, a real danger faced (and an error committed) by a simplistic understanding of virtual revelation. Labourdette himself felt the need to address this sort of error head on. See Labourdette, "Theology: Faith Seeking Understanding," 119 below: "The latter's function is not at all a kind of mere deduction of propositions laying outside of the revealed deposit. In that case, we would need to say that theology begins where faith comes to an end. On the contrary, it works on the datum of faith in its entirety, each of whose statements, at the same time that it is, under the light of faith, purely an object of adherence, becomes, under the theological light defined above, a theological truth, viewed in its connections with the others, in its intelligible virtualities, as truths that explain or truths that have been explained. And it strives, in this light, to lead this entire ensemble of truths to the perfect state of scientific knowledge."

For an outline of the point of terminology, "virtual revelation," see Reginald Garrigou-Lagrange, "Remarks Concerning the Metaphysical Character of St. Thomas's Moral Theology, in Particular as It Is Related to Prudence and Conscience," trans. Matthew K. Minerd, *Nova et Vetera* 17, no. 1 (2019): 261–66 ("Translator's Appendix 1: Concerning the Formal Object of Acquired Theology"); also see the further points of explanation offered in Minerd, "Wisdom Be Attentive," esp. 1108n13, 1120–25.

[257] See Gardeil, *Le donné révélé et la théologie*, 118–317; Garrigou-Lagrange, *De revelatione*, 19n1. For some discussion of this, see Mansini, *What is Dogma?*, 256.

INTRODUCTION: A DIALOGUE DELAYED 77

connected; in fact, they call for each other of their very natures. However, if one is not careful, this assertion comes with the danger of sliding from *scientific reflection*, with all its essential rigors, to a more accessible and popular form of exposition open to all believers. Without rejecting the place of pedagogical presentation, theology "on the march" of scientific research calls for a rigorous state of mind, no less than does any other intellectual discipline.[258]

All of this entails that theological investigation will involve many non-scientific *opinions* as theology strives to constitute itself and to develop.[259] However, this is not the same thing as holding that theology is constituted solely from "opinions," an assertion that one senses in the use of the terms "theological opinions" in ecclesiastical discussions even today, implying that only ecclesiastical authority can make theological conclusions binding.[260] A scientific theology is concerned not merely with opinions but, rather, with the objective connections between principles and conclusions (and likewise and foremost, to the degree that theology is a form of wisdom, with the objective

---

[258] See Labourdette, "Theology: Faith Seeking Understanding," 115 below. There also is the risk that one will not be clear enough about the distinction between theological development and dogmatic development. This kind of confusion was partially what led to the Indexing of the work by Louis Charlier in 1942. For a Thomistic response to Charlier, see Charles Boyer, "Qu'est-ce que la théologie: Réflexions sur une controverse," 255–66; also, see the important texts cited at length in note 269 below.

[259] See Labourdette, "Theology: Faith Seeking Understanding," 121 below; also, below, in Labourdette and Nicolas, "The Analogy of Truth and the Unity of Theological Science," see sections 3.1 ("The Various Degrees of Truth in Human Judgment"), 3.4 ("Conceptualization and Systematization") and 3.5 ("Mentalities"). Their position is an echo and development of what is found in John of St. Thomas, *Material Logic*, 586 (q. 27, a. 2 p.):

Finally, let us recall that the sciences, such as they exist factually in our minds, comprise not only demonstrations but also many opinions. These opinions are not elicited by the scientific *habitus*; inasmuch as they involve no scientific assent, they do not pertain to science. Because they are conversant with the same subject matters as sciences, they are expressed in the same disciplines, but the *habitus* that they generate are not the same.

[260] Such an outlook is expressed by Fr. Garrigou-Lagrange in "Theology and the Life of Faith," 270 below: "It suffices, some say, that we adhere to the fixity of faith and, for action, to the directions of ecclesiastical authority. As regards *theological opinions—whose ensemble*, they think, *constitutes theology!*—they are merely disputed questions to be investigated by the dedicated teams of laborers belonging to various religious orders. These groups and their doctrines all hold an equally probable certitude, allowing the mind complete freedom in choosing among them and even the possibility of choosing none of them. The vital questions would lie elsewhere."

A similar outlook is considered and critiqued in Labourdette, "Theology: Faith Seeking Understanding," 121 below; and, in particular, see the section "Authority in theology" in Labourdette, "Closing Remarks Concerning Our Position," 241–46 below. Also, for a critique of this kind of assertion in the work of Charlier, see the text of Boyer cited in note 258 above.

truth of the principles themselves, which are to be appreciated in their own formal luminosity[261]). For the writers at the *Revue thomiste*, this notion of theology was the central point of contention between the two parties:

> The full meaning of the debate opened here by this brief introduction[262] comes to light as soon as one considers the fact that it is concerned with the rigorously scientific character of theology, with the the bonds of formal causality that unite the principles of faith to the most minute of theological conclusions. We remain outside the domain of theology if we refuse to enter its process of drawing rational connections. Without this, one can have impressionism or sentimentality, but not science.[263]

And here, we have a point that marked a profound distinction between the two parties debating each other. Perhaps, as well, this difference explains why two faithful Catholic parties would manage to differ so profoundly regarding the very notion of dialogue. The primary dialogue desired by the Fourvière Jesuits was with the world of contemporary thought, whereas the Dominicans wished first to undertake a properly theological dialogue, within the household of Catholic faith. Indeed, for the latter party, the formal and dominating characteristic of theology is scientific and not *intrinsically apostolic*, seeking to speak the message of faith to the world. As Labourdette remarks in language that is honest and direct, if perhaps a bit heated:

> Although I refrained from saying it so bluntly, I also think that certain apologetic concerns, certain ways of making connections with "contemporary thought," reflect—objectively and despite whatever might be the personal intentions of the authors, something which I have never questioned, not for a single moment—an intolerable form of dalliance. This assessment can be debated. But is this criticism also entirely negative, and do we not have the right to think that theology would gain much by ridding itself of attitudes that, to the eyes of many unbelieving thinkers, seems like a vulgar inferiority complex?[264]

And responding to a Protestant reflection on *Dialogue théologique*, Labourdette and Nicolas emphasized the same point:

> Theology is not the science or art of "speaking to the world," above all to the world in its present character, to this or that man, or even to this or that class of men. However, this wholly apostolic science of speaking

---

[261] See Minerd, "Wisdom be Attentive," 1144–46.
[262] [Tr. note: That is, to the *Dialogue théologique* volume.]
[263] Bruckberger, "A Theological Dialogue," 129 below.
[264] Labourdette, "Criticism in Theology: A Response," 167 below.

to the world presupposes theology, which it must know in-depth, knowing even what it contains that is independent of this or that immediate apologetic necessity, in order to be able to adapt it and cast it into categories which lend themselves to such a task only partially and not in a fully adequate or "formal" manner. The term *kerygmatic* has rightly been proposed as a name for this kind of theology, which is wholly ordered to preaching and to the salvation of souls. It presupposes scientific theology.[265]

In fact, it was precisely this perceived background apologetic concern which lay underneath Labourdette's reaction to the publication of the first volumes in the *Sources Chrétiennes* and *Théologie* collections. While grateful for, and edified by, their content, he was nonetheless concerned to see what he interpreted as being an "overly apologetic inflection" of the volumes themselves, even those which were translations of ancient texts, for their introductions and notes seemed, to his eyes, to bear the marks of a particular theological enterprise that would seek to undermine scholastic theology—by which he did not mean a kind of "party-spirited" Thomism (or Suarezianism, etc. for that matter) but, rather, a theology that was scientific in its very noetic character.[266] Nonetheless, he makes broad room for a renewed use of the Fathers in such scientific theology, so long as such an enterprise is striven after in a spirit of continuity with the prior theological tradition, above all avoiding a mentality whose sole concern would be to study the Fathers with a non-systematic, predominantly-historical interpretive lens:

> Far from opposing the latter either to the breadth of tradition or to attempts at a renewed presentation (as though this could only be a dangerous undertaking for it), for our own part, we believe that Scholastic theology, precisely in the form given to it by St. Thomas, represents the truly *scientific* state of Christian thought. This implies no disdain for what came before it, a patrimony which can never be valued too highly, and surely the Thomistic synthesis will be the first to benefit from it. This does not imply, moreover, that the teachings of St. Thomas must be simply repeated word for word. It is all-too-true that it would thus remain inaccessible to many, and we would deprive ourselves of the wonderful and genuine progress resulting from later Christian (and non-Christian) thinkers. Nonetheless, it remains the case that, these forms of progress, on pain of ruining their own foundations, presup-

---

265 See Labourdette and Nicolas, "Discussion Surrounding our 'Dialogue Théologique,'" 257–58 below.

266 See Labourdette, "Criticism in Theology: A Response," 172 below. Also, regarding his particular concern with what he saw as an ulterior, antischolastic motivation in the works of the Jesuit Fathers, see Labourdette, "Theology and Its Sources," 134n2, as well as annotations (b), (c), and in particular (g) below.

pose the previously-existing edifice, building upon it, neither destroying nor replacing it. They represent expansions of a synthesis, not a total recovery seeking to build a new "representation" of the world according to the categories of modernity, condemning everything that has preceded it as being irredeemably outmoded. Yes, there are many things that have become outmoded, but what we cannot admit is that form of aging which, in fact, reaches down more deeply than the level of mere formulations: the idea that the entire worldview characteristic of a certain cultural milieu could also reach down into the very truths of theology. What we cannot admit is that theological wisdom would be swept away by the flood of impermanence and that its acquisitions could not be held as being definitive.[267]

This may be the best way to draw these brief systematic considerations to a close. The issues discussed in the texts which we have drawn together in this volume are rich and varied, not readily outlined in all of their details. In the texts cited and interpreted above, we can see that both Dominican streams of authorship share a great deal in the concerns which they voiced in the course of the 1940s debate with their Jesuit brothers in faith. Obviously, this debate was not a completely new affair. Setting aside the question of centuries of scholastic debates on the nature of theology among (and within) the various *scholae*, we can merely say that in the twentieth century the issue concerning the nature of theology had been boiling for some time already. There was the well-known controversy surrounding Chenu's *Une école de théologie: le Saulchoir* in the 1930s,[268] but just as inter-

---

[267] Labourdette, "Criticism in Theology: A Response," 142–43 below. See the numerous and lengthy notes connected to this text as well.

[268] Most famously in *Une école de théologie: le Saulchoir*. See Mettepenningen, *Nouvelle Théologie*, 48–57; Kirwan, *Avant-garde*, 174–76; Peddicord, *The Sacred Monster of Thomism*, 100–13.

Moreover, the 1930s gave rise to significant discussions concerning the nature of theology in the pages of the *Revue thomiste*. Arguably, the arc of this whole debate needs to be connected historically to this period (and, really, back into its earlier rumblings in the period when Fr. Marín-Sola wrote his work on the development of doctrine and Fr. Ambroise Gardeil published his works on theological methodology).

In any case, because the current volume hopes to stir up fraternal understanding between Thomists and those who are more sympathetic to the concerns voiced by the Jesuit fathers in the 1940s, it is useful to chronicle here the titles of the articles addressed in this 1935 issue of the *Revue thomiste*, in order to point readers in the direction of a longer historical arch reflecting the Thomist concerns regarding the nature of theology: "J. Messaut, 'Le rôle intellectuel de la théologie dans l'apostolat'; M.-M. Philipon, 'La théologie science suprême de la vie humaine'; F. Claverie, 'Théologie et conscience individuelle'; F. Valette, 'Théologie et action codifiée'; R. Garrigou-Lagrange, 'La théologie et la vie de la foi'; F. Valette, 'Religion et vie: Une théorie activiste de la sainteté'; H.-D. Simonin, 'La théologie thomiste de la foi et le développement du dogme'; M-.M. Gorce, 'Le méthode

estingly, there were the debates that arose surrounding the work of Louis Charlier and Jean-François Bonnefoy.[269]

The Dominican Fathers were concerned with what they thought to be a hasty readiness—for what, at least according to the Toulouse group, were obviously noble apologetic reasons—to do away with the theological gains of scholastic thought, including what was still perennial in the Baroque period of scholasticism, as well as in what came thereafter. Their attitude was quite different from what we find elaborated by their contemporary interlocutors, even within their own order. Though he was not directly involved in the debates chronicled in our current volume, the reflections of Yves Congar, recalling a discussion with Marie-Dominique Chenu, reveal a cast of mind that was developing, even within the Dominican Order, in quite a different direction from that of the two strands of thought we have gathered together in this volume. This new impulse would ultimately reign triumphant in the second half of the twentieth century:

> One day, chatting at the entrance of the old Saulchoir, [Chenu and I] found ourselves in profound accord—at once intellectual, vital and apostolic—on the idea of undertaking a 'liquidation of baroque theology.' This was a moment of intense and total spiritual union. We elaborated a plan and distributed the tasks among ourselves. I still have the dossier that was begun then. . . . It was not a question of producing something negative: the rejections were only the reverse aspects that were more positive. . . . What would a little later be called *"ressourcement"* was then at the heart of our efforts.[270]

Moreover:

> [Chenu and I] came to a deep agreement, both on this mission [of bringing to fruition in the Church what was good in modernism's

---

historique du maître de la théologie'; R-M. Gagnebet, 'Le naufrage doctrinal d'un adversaire de la théologie: le Père Laberthonnière.'"

269 See Henry Donneaud, "Un retour aux sources cache sous son contraire: Rosaire Gagnebet contre Louis Charlier sur la nature de la théologie spéculative," *Revue thomiste* 119 (2019): 577–612; Mettepenningen, *Nouvelle Théologie, New Theology*, 61–82; Jean-François Bonnefoy, *La Nature de la théologie selon saint Thomas d'Aquin* (Paris: Vrin, 1939); Louis Charlier, *Essai sur le problème théologique* (Thuillies: Ramgal, 1938); Marie-Rosaire Gagnebet, "La nature de la théologie spéculative," 1–39, 213–55, 645–74; Gagnebet, "Un essai sur le problème théologique," 108–45; Gagnebet, "Le problème actuel de la théologie et la science aristotélicienne d'après un ouvrage récent," *Divus thomas* 46 (1943): 237–70.

270 Janette Gray, "Marie-Dominique Chenu and Le Saulchoir: A Stream of Catholic Renewal," in *Ressourcement: A Movement for Renewal in Twentieth-Century Catholic Theology*, 209.

appeals and concerns] and on the necessity of "liquidating" Baroque theology.... We began a dossier on this theme.... Some months ago, at the beginning of [19]46, I said to Father Chenu that our dossier had become pointless, since the "Baroque theology" was being liquidated every day and the Jesuits were among its most ferocious liquidators.[271]

Wayfaring theology will forever involve debate and discussion,[272] but it is impossible to have such a discussion if we do not include the great voices from previous generations. One cannot be historically conscious without simultaneously being sensitive to traditional themes and voices from the past.[273] Although *ressourcement* has been nobly concerned with recovering the patrimony of Scriptures, the Fathers, and historical knowledge of medieval thought,[274] what is now needed, however, is a generous appreciation for the theological thought that came thereafter. There are no "flyover zones" in the history of the Church's life. Failure to have appreciation for *all* of the periods and locales of the Church's history dooms oneself to a kind of academic presentism that perhaps acknowledges past thinkers (in the words of Frs. Labourdette and Nicolas) "only in the form of scattered themes taken up and transformed into brand new intellectual constructions," while nonetheless failing to seek a true communion of minds with those who through *all* centuries of belief have sought out some *intellectus fidei*, some understanding of the faith.

Indeed, we hope that this will arouse discussion even within Thomistic circles. As is clear merely from the work of someone like Rosaire-Marie Gagnebet, a student of Garrigou-Lagrange (and someone warmly mentioned by *both* of the streams included in this volume), as well as the great Swiss theologian, Msgr.-then-Cardinal Charles Journet, the more-conservative Thomists of this era were capable of critiquing their own tradition, without for

---

[271] Christopher Ruddy, "Ressourcement and the Enduring Legacy of Post-Tridentine Theology," in *Ressourcement: A Movement for Renewal in Twentieth-Century Catholic Theology*, 185. See Kirwan, *Avant-garde*, 161–66.

[272] Though, a day will come when this *discursus* of *viatores* will cease in the presence of the dawning of Eternal Light, the Vision of God, to which the blessed will be subjectively adapted by the light of glory, and in that intuitively-seen radiance of the Deity, theological science will seize its object with the tranquil actuality of the participated eternity of the blessed.

[273] For suggestive reflections on this from a Thomistic perspective, see Serge-Thomas Bonino, "Antropologia della tradizione, Prospettive di metodo," in *Persona humana, Imago Dei et Christi in historia, Atti del Congresso Internazionale, Roma 6-8 settembre 2000*, vol. I, *Sentieri, Studi* 1999–2000, ed. Margherita Mari Rossi and Teodora Rossi (Rome: Angelicum, 2002), 99–109.

[274] And somewhat with a recovery of the sacred liturgy.

all that rejecting it as mere decadent baroque flotsam.²⁷⁵ It is our hope that such a bold spirit will inspire charitable discussions among Thomists, as well as between Thomists and the members of the *Communio* school of thought, which has benefitted so greatly from thinkers like de Lubac, von Balthasar, Daniélou, and others discussed and debated in the texts which we have gathered together here.

Writing in the 1940s, Msgr. Joseph Clifford Fenton attempted to put a positive spin on the state of American theology at that time. Doubtlessly, there were important works being written in his days, and with the coming decades, many influential figures would emerge upon the American scene, men of great erudition.²⁷⁶ Nonetheless, we must admit that the French theological scene of the first-half of the twentieth century was dazzlingly brilliant in comparison with the English-speaking scene at that time,²⁷⁷ and among the voices which were expressing themselves in that era, the Thomist school had adherents whose influence could be felt far and wide. In this volume, we wish merely to give voice to some of those authors so that their thought might be considered and retrieved as a positive acquisition in contemporary debates concerning theological methodology. In short, and with all the meaning suggested by each of the words that comprise the title of this introduction, our hope is that this volume will provide a resource that might enable, in charity, the taking up of "A Dialogue Delayed."

A TIMELINE

The following is a general timeline of the major articles related to this volume. Due to the rapidity of responses and post-war publication delays, one should take care not to draw conclusions regarding the dependence of one article on another except where clear internal or external criteria are available.

1. Garrigou-Lagrange, "La théologie et la vie de foi." *Revue thomiste* 40, NS 18 (1935): 492–514.
2. Labourdette, "La théologie, intelligence de la foi." *Revue thomiste* 46 (1946): 5–44.

---

275 See the text of Fr. Donneaud cited in note 269 above. The same could be said of all the authors cited herein, including Fr. Garrigou-Lagrange, all of whom were willing to critique, in charity, various members of their own *schola* concerning a variety of topics.

276 See Joseph Clifford Fenton, *The Concept of Sacred Theology*, ed. Cajetan Cuddy (Providence, RI: Cluny Media, 2018), 275–81.

277 Although they were looking to accomplish different ends, the well-known *American Catholic Encyclopedia*, published in the first decades of 1900, pales in comparison to the immense erudition found, for example, in the conservative *Dictionnaire théologie catholique*, which even today on certain topics remains an important touchpoint for researchers.

3. Daniélou, "Les orientations présentes de la pensée religieuse," *Études* (1946): 5–21.
4. Labourdette, "La théologie et ses sources" *Revue thomiste* 46 (1946): 353–71.
5. Jesuits (de Lubac), "Théologie et ses sources: Réponse," *Recherches de science religieuse* 33 (1946): 385–401.
6. Garrigou-Lagrange, "La nouvelle théologie ou va-t-elle?" *Angelicum* 23 (1946): 126–47.
7. Bruckberger, "Introduction" in *Dialogue théologique* (1947).
8. Labourdette, "La théologie et ses sources" (annotated version) in *Dialogue théologique* (1947).
9. Labourdette, "De la critique en Théologie, réponse" in *Dialogue théologique* (1947).
10. M.-J. Nicolas, "Le progrès de la théologie et la fidélité à saint Thomas" in *Dialogue théologique* (1947).
11. Labourdette, "Ferme propos," *Revue thomiste* 47 (1947): 5–19.
12. De Solages, "Autour d'une controverse," *Bulletin de littérature ecclésiastique* 48 (1947): 3–17.
13. De Solages, "Pour l'honneur de la théologie: le contre-sens du R. P. Garrigou Lagrange," *Bulletin de littérature ecclésiastique* 48 (1947): 64–84.
14. Garrigou-Lagrange, "Verité et immutabilité du dogme," *Angelicum* 24 (1947): 124–39.
15. Blondel and Garrigou-Lagrange, "Correspondence," *Angelicum* 24 (1947): 210–14.
16. Le Blond, L'analogie de vérité: Réflexion d'un philosophe sur une controverse théologique," *Recherches de science religieuse* 34 (1947): 129–41.
17. Garrigou-Lagrange, "Notions consacrées par la Concile," *Angelicum* 24 (1947): 217–31.
18. Labourdette and Nicolas, "L'analogie de la vérité et l'unité de la science théologique," *Revue thomiste* 47 (1947): 411–66.
19. Labourdette and M.-J. Nicolas, "Autour du 'Dialogue théologique,'" *Revue thomiste* 47 (1947): 577–85.
20. Bouillard, "Notions conciliaires et analogie de la vérite," *RSR* 3 (1948) 251–71.
21. Garrigou-Lagrange, "Nécessité de revenir à la conception traditionnelle de la vérité," *Angelicum* 25 (1948): 185–98.
22. Garrigou-Lagrange, "Immutabilité des vérités définies et la surnaturel," *Angelicum* 25 (1948): 285–98.
23. Garrigou-Lagrange, "L'immutabilité du dogme selon le Concile du Vatican, et le relativisme," *Angelicum* 26 (1949): 309–22.

TRANSLATION-RELATED COMMENTS

There are many people who provided generous assistance, for which we are grateful. First, we would like to thank Père Philippe-Marie Margelidon, OP, Director of the *Revue thomiste*, and Margherita Maria Rossi, at the *Angelicum* journal, for allowing for the translation and publication of the articles included here. Thanks also to Matthew Horwitz, the librarian at St. Patrick's Seminary, for helping to gather some of the original articles. Gratitude is owed to Cluny Media for use of the text of Fr. Garrigou-Lagrange's "Theology and the Life of Faith,"[278] to *Saint Anselm Journal* for allowing permission to use an earlier form of portions of this introduction,[279] and to *Josephinum Journal of Theology* for the use of their translation of "La nouvelle théologie où va-t-elle?"[280]

In general, scriptural references have been taken from the Revised Standard Version of the Bible. Where contextual or rhetorical concerns did not seem to allow this, we translated the text from the French provided by the author in question. All such citations from the Revised Standard Version are marked in the scriptural citation. For example, if a direct citation has been taken from Romans 6:1, it is cited as Rom 6:1 (RSV). Where needed, the Douay-Rheims version is used for translations of the Latin Vulgate. Such citations are marked with (DR). All direct citations from Denzinger are taken from the English translation provided in the forty-third edition published by Ignatius Press.

Our greatest thanks goes to John Martino, without whose diligent care this volume would not have been brought to press. Moreover, we sincerely thank the reviewers of the volume, whose warm recommendations have only served to improve the text. We also thank Aaron Weldon for his indispensable copy-editing work and likewise express our gratitude to the design and marketing team for creating so beautiful a volume in honor of these Thomist theologians who have become dear to our hearts.

Finally, we dedicate this volume to contemporary and future students of theology, whom we hope will take up this dialogue in a spirit of fraternal charity.

---

278 See Reginald Garrigou-Lagrange, "Theology and the Life of Faith," in *Philosophizing in Faith*, 421–43.

279 See Matthew K. Minerd, "*Humani Generis* and the Nature of Theology: A Stereoscopic View from Rome and Toulouse," *Saint Anselm Journal* 16, no. 2 (2021): 1–35.

280 Reginald Garrigou-Lagrange, OP, "Where is the New Theology Leading Us?" *Josephinum Journal of Theology* 18, no. 1 (2011): 63–78.

Part 1

The Toulouse Response:
Revue thomiste and *Dialogue Théologique*

1

Theology: Faith Seeking Understanding

Michel-Marie Labourdette, OP

> Ratio, fide illustrata, cum sedulo, pie et
> sobrie quareit, aliquam, Deo dante,
> mysteriorum intelligentiam, eamque
> fructuosissimam, assequitur.
> —Conc. Vatic., Sess. III, ch. 4

> If reason, illuminated by faith,
> inquires in a pious and sober manner,
> it attains, by God' grace, an understanding
> of the mysteries which is most fruitful.
> —Vatican I, *Dei filius*, ch. 4, Denz., no. 3016 [1796]

1. The word "theology" can be understood in a broad sense as designating every form of knowledge that is concerned with God: just as biology is the study of living beings, theology is the study of God, the study of divine things. However, we can know God in many ways. In particular, following upon the elaborations wrought during the Middle Ages, the Latin Catholic tradition distinguishes three broad domains for our knowledge of God, each requiring us to use the term "theology" in a completely different sense.

The first belongs solely to the natural order. That is, it abstracts from every form of positive revelation. What can we know about God? Does He exist? Are we able to know Him? If so, how can we conceive of Him? In being occupied with such questions, one does indeed engage in a form of theology, namely, *natural* theology.

The second kind of theology will be founded on the revelation that the same God makes concerning truths that exceed our mind's natural field of investigation. To believe that God has spoken to men, that He has revealed to them His intimate life, as well as the designs of His providence, and so forth, requires us to admit that we have a new and unexpected means for knowing God. This form of theology, which is the principal meaning for the very term "theology," is "*Theologia Sacra*," theology *tout court*.

A third kind of knowledge of divine things also traditionally bears the name "theology": *mystical theology*. The expression itself is equivocal, today tending to mean, "the theology of mysticism." When it is considered in these terms, it only designates one part of "Theologia Sacra." However, for a long time, the term retained its traditional sense, indicating "knowledge of the revealed God through mystical experience."

These distinctions are profound and must be understood aright.

A fundamental dogma of Christianity lies in the fact that the real destiny that God has given to humanity radically exceeds human nature. This destiny is *supernatural*. Solely on its own, human nature is not proportioned to it, and it requires new principles of spiritual activity.[1] A whole order of objects of knowledge and love that heretofore laid outside of man's grasp are now offered to him. Revelation opens up before the intellect an order of truths that it could not attain by itself, informing it about these new things. Therefore, here we have a rigorous distinction of spiritual lights differentiating natural knowledge (even that which is concerned with divine things) from knowledge founded on revelation made by God.[2]

The distinction between "sacred theology" and mystical theology will be a more delicate affair, though it is no less strict. Both of them are essentially Christian and presuppose revelation. Now, is not every kind of knowledge of the revealed God, properly speaking, "mystical," given that it rests on the interior light of faith? Certainly, the philosopher can freely define his terms. Still, he must specify those which he adopts if he wishes to give them a special meaning. In theology, terminological freedom itself is singularly restricted by a very elaborate tradition, as well as by the whole weight of history, which freights many of the terms that come down to us. If every kind of adherence to the mystery on account of an interior personal light or affective inclination is called mystical, we can use this term for pure and simple faith. However, in that case, its technical meaning is thereby singularly enlarged, and this will not be free from the grave danger of causing confusion. In truth, by its very means of knowing, what we are here calling mystical knowledge of God is essentially distinct from theology properly so called, even though they do

---

[1] Whatever one holds concerning "mere / pure" human nature, left to itself, it is certain that man called to a supernatural destiny is, as it were, a new creature, having different aspirations, needs, responsibilities, and aids. In order to understand him integrally, a new light is needed.

[2] See [First] Vatican Council, *Dei filius*, ch. 4: "The perpetual common belief of the Catholic Church has held and holds also this: there is a twofold order of knowledge, distinct not only in its principle but also in its object; in its principle, because in the one we know by natural reason, in the other by divine faith; in its object, because apart from what natural reason can attain, there are proposed to our belief mysteries that are hidden in God that can never be known unless they are revealed by God" (Denzinger, no. 3015 [old no., 1795]).

indeed have the same source, infused faith. In order to penetrate more fully the teaching that has been received from God, theology uses all the rational procedures at the intellect's disposal, all of its resources of knowledge with all of its greatly diversified methods, from notional analysis to historical methodology, as well as textual and documentary criticism. By contrast, mystical knowledge is intrinsically quite distant from all forms of logical discursion and will be an experiential knowledge of divine things through union with them, an essentially supernatural knowledge in the very means bringing about such knowledge, namely, the infused love of charity, as well as in its principle, namely, the inspiration of the Spirit of God currently active in the soul.

In this study, we will only be directly concerned with Theology properly so called, considering supernatural mystical knowledge and natural knowledge of God only on occasion and by way of comparison. As we said, this Theology finds its source in the revelation that God has made to us concerning what He is and what He has willed for our salvation. It is no longer the science of God such as He is manifested by His creatures but, instead, is the science of God such as He has *revealed* Himself through His personal intervention [in salvation history]. Here, faith will be the indispensable principle for this revelation, not as a point of departure that one would then leave behind but, rather, as a permanent source of light and truth. Faith is the only spiritual means for a truly living theology.

However, can this theology really be a science? What will be its structure and methodology? How can one define its status and inventory its domain?[3]

I. SOME GENERAL METHODOLOGICAL OBSERVATIONS[4]

2. *The general notion of science.* In St. Thomas's philosophy, the word "science" calls to mind a completely precise, though nuanced and

---

[3] The notion of theology has been the object of a number of recent studies and discussions. While attempting to draw profit from this or that study, our current reflections are not specifically written to carry on this discussion or to express something new. Rather, we have found that we must set forth, on our own behalf, how the traditional notion of Theology is to be understood today. This is the exposition that we have published here.

[4] Due to the fact that these notions are used with substantially different meanings in the logic used by St. Thomas, on the one hand, and in modern noetics, on the other, equivocations are not rare concerning the very notion of science and its various implications. Here, without considering in themselves questions which would require lengthy studies, we simply wish to specify what we mean when we speak of science, observation, explanation, and so forth. Obviously, the precise techniques to which these several points are connected already presuppose that one holds certain essential philosophical positions concerning the realism of the intellect, the value of concepts, the relationship of the intellect to being, the scope of the demonstrative syllogism, and so forth... Our perspective here is that of St. Thomas's philosophy.

complex, notion. Taken in a general sense, it characterizes a given, perfect state of intellectual knowledge, a form of knowledge wherein the mind attains things in their proper principles, in their *raisons d'être*, in what gives them their "necessity." And because such knowledge is a perfection, we use this term to designate the very knowledge that God has of Himself and of all things, thus speaking of the "Divine Science."

In the domain of human knowledge, the word "science" will simultaneously have a narrower scope and a greater complexity. Given that it must abstract the notions which it utilizes, our intellectual knowledge is essentially progressive in nature. Like every form of knowledge, it consists in the fact that things come to take on a new life in the mind according to an immaterial mode of existence, there taking on a new intelligible clarity, not as though they were sketched out like duplicates on a painting but, rather, as transparently presenting themselves to us. The immaterial possession that this presupposes attains a degree of perfection only through multiple procedures, through the recomposition of concepts, the separations and rapprochements that rule a great number of logical processes that are more or less complex and refined. Starting with a mass of initial knowledge, as of yet neither critiqued nor coordinated, the mind strives to attain the stability of complete certitude and perfect clarity. And given that this certitude is immediately found only for a certain number of first principles, all our other judgments will need to seek after such certitude in knowledge of the cause which makes the thing judged be what it is and not able to be anything else: its proper and necessary cause. This is what, on the level of human knowledge, is properly called "science": a certain form of knowledge through causes or reasons for being, *raisons d'être*.

Science is distinct from the grasping of first principles in that the judgment at which science terminates is not itself immediately evident. The relation between the two terms that it unites is seen to be true in light of a third term in which we can see the reason why the predicate term belongs to the subject. This middle term (which, in the perfect type of science, is the definition of the subject) is the essential element of scientific knowledge. We can say that inasmuch as knowledge is indeed scientific, it, so to speak, passes over into the middle term, which specifies such knowledge. Thus, the middle term is its *objective light*, the determining motive for its certitude.

Before providing this very general notion with those nuances which are utterly necessary, given the highly diversified state of our sciences, we should first emphasize two particularly important points.

In scientific demonstration, the middle term has its value as a middle only if it is first perceived in its immediate identification with the other terms, that is, if it is first perceived as playing its role as a *principle*. Grasping this is indispensable for scientific reasoning. This is why, even though scientific knowledge is distinct from immediately self-evident knowledge of principles, the former not only presupposes knowledge of the latter but, indeed, it is suspended to this fundamental intuition, not only in the sense that this intuition is part of scientific knowledge, but moreover, because such knowledge remains forever actualized by its illumination. It is entirely penetrated and vivified by it. It depends on it in its own proper certitude and its own proper clarity. Sufficient emphasis is not always placed on the fact that at the heart of every science, even one that is quite developed, a permanent place remains for this necessary *intuition of its principles*. It alone provides science with the means for escaping the menacing possibility of formalism coming from an overburdening logical apparatus which will overtake it if it loses contact with its living source. Even if they are attained and manifested through complex logical processes, such objects of intuition—the common principles which express the fundamental laws of being and, likewise, the definitions that are a given science's own proper principles—are never, properly speaking, dependent on such discursive reasoning. They are never "demonstrated." They are grasped.

Every human science is progressive and is acquired through personal labor. Therefore, knowledge of its conditions in its terminal and perfect state will never be sufficient by itself. It is important to analyze its *undertakings*, its movement as a whole. The ideal goal of every science is to come to explain a given datum.[5] To explain is to assign the *raison d'être*, the proper cause which provides full intelligibility to a truth that is still only formulated in a factual manner through observation. Obviously, this presupposes a prior phase of observation and research. Thus, every science, like every intellectual undertaking, begins with an acceptance of a given order of realities through the observation of a given datum. Its first task will be to investigate and critique it, meaning that it must examine the datum in question and formulate it in its own proper light. This will represent the phase of *observation*. Thereupon, the characteristic effort of science as such is to go out in *search of causes* (this is, in Thomistic vocabulary, the stage of scientific *discovery* [*invention*]), seeking to reduce the multiplicity of data so observed to the unity of a synthesis around explanatory notions, namely, causes. Thus, one will come to the stage of *explanation* (in Thomistic vocabulary, this is the stage of science in its constituted form, the definitive *judgment*, enabling the synthesis "*in via iudicii*").

3. *Different kinds of sciences and the various phases of science*. However, what we here have presented is an idealized schema. In order to have a concrete and adapted methodology at one's disposal, it is important that we understand the many nuances involved here.

---

5 Obviously, our perspective here is that of St. Thomas and Aristotle, holding that knowledge *precisely as such* has a purely *speculative* finality. The proper end of knowledge is not to enable one to live well but, rather, to enable one *to know* well.

And first of all, let us note that there are *various kinds of sciences*. When we wish to determine the general idea of science and provide a definition for it, we consider it in its pure state, according to its perfect typology, quite disengaged from the various, differentiated sciences with which we are familiar. Indeed, we actually have a great number of sciences, quite unequal in their perfection, realizing with considerable differences the schema that we have described. Jacques Maritain rightly notes in *The Degrees of Knowledge* that our science not only progresses in extent but also in its "internal noetic morphology." New disciplines are gradually disengaged from the substance of infra-scientific knowledge and progressively rise up to the level of science. Only gradually does their scientific character manifest itself.

The same author notes that according to Thomist logic, the notion of science finds its most typical natural realization in metaphysics. The description that one gives for it normally undergoes the attraction of this privileged realization. The other sciences, above all those of the "first degree of abstraction"—and even more so the "practical sciences"—present more or less profound deficiencies in relation to this ideal notion. By contrast, in the noetic of most modern thinkers, the idea of science is completely dominated and, as it were, attracted by the experimental sciences. According to contemporary terminology, something is "scientific" only if it is experimentally verifiable or [historically] established by irrefutable documents. Thus, "philosophy" is today contrasted to this so-called "positive" science. This perspective difference is the source of all-too-frequent equivocations—even, as we will see, in the case of theology. However, this also will enable us to extend the term "science" to disciplines to which the traditional schema no longer applies, except in a wholly different manner (for example, to history).[6]

In the *elaboration of science* (i.e., science "*in fieri*"), these two phases (observation and explanation) closely interpenetrate each other. A continual back-and-forth takes place from first observations to a fragmentary explanation, sometimes to a provisional explanation (i.e., a hypothesis), then from explanation to new observations. We certainly do not need to exhaust the field of observation before proceeding to our investigation into causes.

4. *Scientific observation.* These remarks lead us to an essential notion brought to light by Jacques Maritain.[7] Observation *is part of the science* which it furnishes with data. It is performed under that science's own proper light. It does

---

[6] In history, the tendency to strive after "explanation" is certainly not absent, but it is no longer the same kind of explanation [as in the other sciences]. That is, it is no longer an explanation through something's essence.

[7] See Jacques Maritain, *The Degrees of Knowledge*, trans. Gerald Phelan et al. (Notre Dame, IN: University of Notre Dame Press, 1999), pt. 1, ch. 1. Likewise, see Yves Simon, "La science modern de la nature et la philosophie," *Revue Néo-scolastique de philosophie* 49 (Feb. 1936): 64–77.

not fall to some common, prior form of knowledge. On the contrary, an absolute law of the logic of the sciences asserts that an observation, a "fact," is of interest to a science only as something seen under that science's own light and as critiqued by it. A brute fact is not a scientific fact. A single scientific observation is of infinitely greater value than many vague testimonies. In any case, it alone is immediately able to be assimilated into the science which is interested in this fact.

Likewise, brute facts or even scientific facts absolutely are not yet "metaphysical facts." They will only become such by being formulated in terms of being.—Any given fact concerning the past is not a historical fact. It will become such and be able to be assimilated by scientific history only by being critiqued and controlled by such historical knowledge. There are infinitely more real facts than those that are historical in the sense just defined; there are many pseudo-historical facts. Only a fact that is duly controlled by the methods of historical criticism will be able to be justly presented as belonging to historical *science*.— We will see that theology is not exempt from this law. For it too, observation of its data and of the various facts that are of interest to it are undertaken in its own, proper light. Whatever it has not previously examined and critiqued (through a *theological* critique), strictly speaking, still cannot be assimilated by it.

And we must not believe that basic observation and the scientific observational determination which is its fruit, would be something easy, a task that one can perform with ease. Granted, in metaphysics, very simple observations generally are sufficient. The difficulty lies in the research into causes and in the passage [from nominal and vague definitions] to real and distinct ones. However, in many sciences, observation by itself requires great labor and the employment of meticulous, refined methods. Merely think of all the experimental labor required in the natural sciences in order to discover a truly scientific fact. Likewise, think of all the meticulous work involved in historical criticism. With all its resources and with full awareness of the proper requirements of the science that it pursues—in short, *under this science's light*—what is applied to this task is intelligence, an intelligence which also has (above all when it is a question of unique observable facts) what contemporary language might call a "flair," something presupposing, beyond a given amount of imagination, a kind of instinctual connaturality which increases in the mind through the presence of a scientific *habitus* in relation to its object.[8]

---

8 These very brief, summary remarks find their full justification only in a complete [philosophical-theological] exposition of a doctrine taking everything into account. The reader can refer to the commentaries by St. Thomas and Cajetan on Aristotle's *Posterior Analytics* and to John of St. Thomas's *Ars Logica*. From the perspective of the more particular remarks that we have made, it would be appropriate for one to develop the doctrine contained in the following texts: Aristotle, *Posterior Analytics*, bk. 2, chs. 1 and 2 (on the four scientific questions and their interrelations), along with the commentaries by St. Thomas and Cajetan on these passages. Likewise, see Gaetano San Severino, *Philosophiae*

II. FAITH AND ITS OBJECT

5. *The light of faith*. The "subject" which our theology strives to study is God. As we have said, it is not God as He is manifested to our reason through His creatures but, rather, such as He has revealed Himself, that is, such as He knows Himself, such as He is in Himself. And, secondarily, this revelation, while always referring to God, will also be all of His works inasmuch as this revelation illuminates us regarding them: creation and creatures' ascent to God, as well as the providential economy in which all the things that God wills are inscribed: the Incarnation, the Redemption through the Cross, the Church, the Sacraments, and so forth....

All this constitutes a strictly supernatural object for our minds: God's intimate life and the ways it is participated in by creatures. Such an object will be a "datum" for us only if we are elevated to know it by a light that is proportioned to it. No more than a sense power could grasp an idea, our reason, left to itself, cannot enter into the secrets of the Divine Being. And in order for us to have authentic knowledge here, it will not be enough for us to merely have, in human terms, an external presentation of these mysteries which exceed our reason. We would stand before such knowledge like the archeologist who discovers a tablet covered in still-undecipherable characters: he sees the writing quite well enough, but it remains utterly meaningless for him. Supernatural revelation implies an interior aid given to our mind, a grace-given illumination that elevates it to a superior level of knowledge. In truth, the only created light that is adequately proportioned to this Object, the Divine Being in itself, is the light of the Beatific Vision, the "light of glory." God will then present Himself "to be discovered." We will see Him face-to-face, "as He is," in accord with what is promised in Scripture. And in this light, our knowledge of God and even our very theology, which our mind constructs to its own measure (in the way that we will come to discuss in what follows below), will reach its perfect state, that of full evidence and complete clarity.

Here-below, we are presented with the same supernatural Object through God's revelation. However, it is not seen directly but, rather, is described to us by God Himself. God gives us His testimony concerning it. Revelation's mode of expression is quite different from vision. In relation to

---

Christianae cum antiqua et nova comparatae, [vol. 1 (Naples: Apud Officinam Bibliothecae Catholicae Scriptorum, 1873)], 166–86, and more specifically, the invaluable elucidations provided by Jacques Maritain in the first part of *The Degrees of Knowledge*.

[Tr. note: The reference to San Severino is to "vol. 3," which does not correspond to the section devoted to logic in the edition consulted to fill out this citation. The pagination given corresponds to the beginning of the 3rd part of the logic, devoted to methodology. However, this ends in the middle of the particular section. See pp. 166–209 for the complete section "*methodologia*."]

the state of glory, our current state is a kind of apprenticeship, an initiation: before knowing what God is, we must begin by believing in Him. To the ensemble of statements through which God makes Himself known to humanity, constituting objective revelation, there is added, in the mind of those "who hear the word of the Father," the grace of light and adherence that we call supernatural faith, infused faith.[9]

This light is essentially supernatural. It is so not only because God is the one who gives it or because the statements in which it is formulated also come from God. It is supernatural in itself and by the nature of the knowledge that it procures precisely because the proper object that it attains in these statements is God in His intimate life and because the motive by which it enables one to adhere to them is the very testimony of God—a testimony which is not perceived by reasoning based, for example, on the observation of miracles (thus remaining wholly in the natural order) but, rather, is perceived *by faith itself* as something included in the presentation of the supernatural object. The motive of divine faith is neither rationally seen nor deduced. This motive is itself supernaturally believed. Faith is altogether supernatural in both its object and its motive. And if it is perfectly true that revelation does not lack testimony which it can offer before the eyes of reason and indeed, much to the contrary, offers reason the most solid [motives of] credibility, it is no less certainly true that, in the theology of St. Thomas, the only sufficient motive for a supernatural and infallible adherence is itself supernatural as well.

We must not allow ourselves to be deceived by the use of the word "light" in describing faith. We most certainly are still here concerned with *faith*, not evidence, and therefore with something totally different than a scientific light. Faith neither reasons nor proves. It adheres to the truth of what God tells us about Himself and His works, doing so under the impulse of the will, moved by Him, on account of the Divine Veracity. This role played by the will in the act of faith is essential. Faith is not the simple profession of particular ways of looking at things, the intellectual acceptance of particular ideas; it indispensably presupposes the engagement of the free will, a personal acceptance. The Divine Object is not presented to us clearly enough for the sight of it alone to suffice for discovering its truth. We must have a relationship with Him who proposes it to us, and this cannot be brought about without an affective motion of confidence in this incomparable Witness. Certainly, this testimony is proposed to the intellect, and the intellect will be the essential dwelling place for the supernatural virtue which will enable it to grasp this

---

9 See [First] Vatican Council, *Dei filius*, ch. 3: "Though the assent of faith is by no means a blind impulse of the mind, still, no man can 'assent to the Gospel message,' as is necessary to obtain salvation, 'Without the illumination and inspiration of the Holy Spirit, who gives to all delight in assenting to the truth and believing it'" (Denzinger, no. 3010 [old no. 1791]).

testimony at the same time as it grasps the objects whose truth it affirms. However, its adherence to this truth is definitively explained only through the will's own free choice, itself supernaturally elevated and bearing the mind to faith by an initial love which is both a desire for the beatitude thus announced and a form of confidence in Him who announces it. If, through adherence to revealed truth, faith is found at the foundation of every form of progress undergone by our supernatural knowledge of God prior to the Beatific Vision, through this first engagement of our personal freedom, it also lies at the foundation of this profound and intimate life of supernatural affections which the other virtues will come to constitute and develop, though, it will include in itself the very first movement of these other virtues.[10] It is in continuity with this first impulse, surpassing it without suppressing it, that the will, receiving yet again from God the virtues of hope and charity, will be borne toward Him with all its weight and, through an inevitable reverberation, will come to affirm and animate the very adherence of faith as well as its supernatural penetration.

However, what does faith bring about in the intellect itself? Its precise role is to secure it, making the intellect hold as absolutely certain a given ensemble of supernatural truths which our science and experience could not reach or verify on their own. Without faith, the very terms in which these truths are formulated for us would be directly intelligible for us only in their natural signification, in their signification in the language of created being, which is our own, in accord with its categories, like the archeologist looking upon the undecipherable tablet and seeing only the characters without grasping their meaning. However, illuminated by the light of faith, these terms take on *a supernatural signifying value* when they are set before the believer's mind. Instead of only bearing the mind to their natural significate, they lead it to their supernatural significate, functioning as the means for a knowledge that terminates in the divine reality in its very character as something

---

10 One of the difficulties involved in our analyses, requiring us to carefully distinguish what we must not confuse, is the fact that they force us to sometimes seem to forget elements that are not of immediate concern for our study. This is to be feared in the definition of our supernatural knowledge had through faith. If our attention turns too exclusively either to its intellectual side or to its volitional element, we risk inflecting research toward concerns that are correct but partial and, perhaps, not well-enough aware of their limitations. The very aim of the current article will require us to insist much more on the intellectual character of faith than on the indispensable role played by the will in its constitution and progress. Bear in mind that this emphasis is not due to some kind of disregard for this volitional side or due to a lack of esteem for its importance but, rather, flows from methodological necessities facing us here. On the contrary, we think that it is through this first and essential dependence [upon the will] that love renders faith amenable, through the intervention of the other virtues and the gifts of the Holy Spirit, to its full fructification in mystical, experiential knowledge of the Triune God.

reserved and naturally unknowable by every creature. This adds absolutely nothing to their conceptual content but quite precisely enables these terms, united by the verb *to be*, which expresses our adherence, to truly become for our mind the formal means for attaining the supernatural, Divine Reality. As regards every natural form of knowledge that is not a simple logical or grammatical reflection on the statement itself, we can truly say, with St. Thomas, that it does not terminate in the statement but, rather, in the signified reality: *non terminatur ad enuntiabile, sed ad rem*.[11] However, for faith, we have this new sense that the reality in question is nothing other than the Supernatural God such as He knows Himself and is not naturally accessible to any created knowledge. Infused faith enables our knowledge to truly attain its *terminus* in this reality. This is why, properly speaking, the term "faith" is used equivocally when applied to supernatural faith and to a human form of faith by which one would assent to a revealed truth on account of its natural credibility or for any other motive [than revelation by God who reveals supernaturally] (for example, the heretic's human faith). These are not at all the same kinds of knowledge, even though the truth might be expressed on both sides in completely identical terms.

What grandeur and poverty are involved in our formulas of faith! Marked with the infirmity of human language, they are the infinitely deficient translation of a Reality which exceeds them on all sides. They are an inferior kind of packaging given to a supernatural knowledge that will find its true proportion only in the face-to-face knowledge experienced in the Beatific Vision. Consequently, they are, for the whole of our supernatural life, the principle of an infirmity characteristic of the time of trial that we now are passing through. However, let us not overlook their grandeur: they *truly* lead our mind to this Sovereign Reality which exceeds them; this is what they *conform* it to; this Object is what our intellect is assimilated to through them. Thanks to them, this relation of indisputable conformity, speculative truth, is established between us and this Object. Through them, this inaccessible Reality is validly expressed within us. It enters into the domain of our superelevated reason, penetrates it, and dwells within it—yes, according to the particular modality of reason, but in a way which still fully realizes the very notion of speculative truth. Our conceptual statements become *expressions* of it. Yes, they are deficient because they are human, but nonetheless, they are purely and simply valid, objectively conformed, despite their poverty, to what *is* in God, to *what God is*.

6. *The object of faith within the Church*. Nonetheless, our faith does not rest upon a direct revelation, made to us in the form of a private revelation. Rather, it remains in contact with a public revelation which was a temporal

---

[11] *ST* II-II, q. 1, a. 2, ad 2.

event (or, rather, an ensemble of temporal events, for it took place over a long period of time and developed in an extremely slow and progressive fashion). *What* God said is not directly infused by Him into our intellect. It is *transmitted* to it, through the divinely instituted living body that is the Church. The Church has received the objective deposit of divine revelation; it falls to her to propose it to all generations and to each human intellect. The very life of the Church assures the continuity of this deposit. We do not need to reestablish a connection to it as to a dead letter that is so distant from us in its written form that we would forever remain anxious concerning the exactness of the historical and archaeological means by which we would reestablish such a connection. No, in the Church today, the living Church, we find it preserved, illuminated, and infallibly proposed. She holds the treasure of the Sacred Scriptures. She is utterly enriched by the great memory of Tradition. It is only through her that we arrive at this treasure as a source of faith.

Nonetheless, we should not believe that the Church's authority is the true and fundamental motive for our supernatural adherence. This infallible authority is needed for an authentic [objective] *presentation* of the revealed truth in various times and places, indeed, here, with the great distance separating us from the divine intervention by which revelation was made. Rather, what motivates our adherence and what, consequently, characterizes it as a form of knowledge is supernatural divine revelation itself, rendering testimony to itself in the believer's own mind. The Church's mediation is the indispensable condition for us to have an authentic encounter with the revealed truth. We only receive it through this intermediary, and the latter must indeed be indisputable in the very order of truth and, therefore, infallible. She cannot take the place of revelation nor substitute herself for the Testimony of God who reveals, on which the entire order of faith rests. Thanks to the Church, continuity is established between our minds and this Divine Testimony. We truly are "in her tutelage," receiving the truth from her. Through faith, our minds directly open out upon the mystery of God and are nourished upon it.

By offering a *Credo* which she has largely formulated herself, guaranteeing its fundamental identity with precisely what God revealed, the Church does not offer reason an unintelligible book of spells to be accepted submissively by faith. This kind of ascetic and, perhaps, meritorious exercise does not at all reflect the essential process of the life of faith. Certainly, this life includes submission ("*obseqium fidei*"), but we would betray it were we to define it *essentially* as a form of obedience. It is truly and essentially, indeed before all else, a form of *knowledge*, a conformation of the superelevated mind to the divine mystery. In this way, it is theological and is the nourishing root of our entire supernatural life. To the degree that it is possible for us prior to the Beatific Vision, it enables us to enter into the very knowledge that God has of Himself.

We have spoken of the "*Credo.*" This introduces an essential point for understanding what our faith is, as well as what our theology will be. It suffices to have been in contact with the sources of revelation such as they are preserved by the Church in their richness and diversity in order to realize that, while all the statements that they contain, to the degree that they are revealed, have exactly the same authority and certitude (since they are attained under the same motive) precisely as forms of knowledge, they nonetheless do not have the same "interest," the same value in our theological life. The very way in which revelation was made, the slow and progressive pedagogy which it followed in order to gradually enter into man's mind and heart, means that its essential object was proposed alongside other truths, whether natural or wholly contingent. The fact that the latter happened to be included within revelation is accidental in character. They do not exist in revelation for their own sake but, rather, are there in order to serve the revelation of faith's essential object. As St. Thomas tells us, this object of faith is, in substance, that Reality who will be our beatitude when we see Him [in glory].[12] To use the same example as he does: if divine inspiration guarantees that Abraham had two sons, this does not suffer any more doubt for a believer than does man's vocation to salvation; however, whereas the latter truth is essential to the object of faith, which would be incomplete without it, the former has only a factual connection to it. Man's vocation to supernatural beatitude is part of the very *substance* of faith.

This "substance" of the object of faith is not an indistinct, uniformly obscure (or uniformly illuminated) object. It is an organic whole, in which we can discern a certain number of fundamental truths—or, let us say with St. Thomas and the whole language of Christian discourse, "a certain number of *articles.*" These articles are the more explicit formulations which are rendered necessary by a specific obscurity existing in the essential object of faith, a specific account of the mystery. And they are what is presented in summary fashion to us in the Creed organized and defined by the Church. What we said above concerning the formulas of faith must be understood in particular for the articles of faith. In them, we find in full form this supernatural value and worth for our theological life, a value elevating us to divine knowledge. There, we find our spirit's true and profound nourishment. Now, it falls to the Church to define these formulas, to fix their true meaning, and to explain them authentically. Thus, they appeal to her *authority*, and from this perspective, they become *dogmas*. The notion of dogma is not exactly the same as that of an article of faith. The former places the accent on another note, that of the Church's own definition and universal proposition of that truth. A newly defined dogma is not necessarily a new article of faith. It can be a

---

[12] See *ST* II-II, q. 1, a. 8.

new aspect of an already-formulated article and can even be a less essential truth. However, the two notions are close neighbors and must not be separated. If we focus on the fact that a given definition has a particular formula as its object and insist on the authoritative character and precise obligation connected to dogmatic formulas (as though faith were first and foremost a form of obedience), we risk placing in the shadows dogma's own proper value as a supernatural truth and as part of the Christian life. Nonetheless, we must conversely take care not to overlook the immense benefit which we draw for our spirit, even from the perspective of its theological life, from a more precise formulation of the faith. The object of faith acts within our soul as a *truth* and not in virtue of a blind act of acceptance, and our mind is elevated so that it may be conformed, in the order of supernatural truth, to the divine being precisely through notions whose deficiency comes from their inferior character [as statements by finite creatures], not from their precision. To be able to say with the full certitude of divine faith that the Son is *consubstantial* to the Father does not do away with the mystery but, rather, for this faith in men's minds, represents a true and important form of progress in comparison to the prior, unformulated state in which the same truth assuredly was believed, though without being distinctly specified.

This last example introduces a new consideration: progress in the further elaboration of the faith. Through its presence in the Church, the object of our faith entered into history. By the very force of things, it has taken on a new "dimension." The history of *revelation*, properly so called, came to its completion with Christ and the Apostles, in whose teaching it found its consummation. Incomplete for millennia, taken up in certain periods and progressively brought to its completion, it thus has reached its goal. Henceforth, revelation is closed, becoming part of the past, no longer having a history.[13] However, another history then begins. The revealed object was entrusted to the Church. It has entered into her life and will forever be present in her, not as a kind of memory handed on from generation to generation but, rather, as an ever-active yeast within the dough of humanity, as an ensemble of truths, ever-announced yet ever-new. The Church possesses these truths and preaches them. She proposes them and adapts their formulas to the intellectual needs of human groups as individuals and as different generations. She preserves and explains. She defines. And after the history of revelation, which came to its close with the death of the last Apostle, what began was the life (and, consequently, the history) of dogma. The object of faith gradually becomes more dogmatically explicit, in accord with the Church's own progressive awareness

---

13 See the proposition condemned by the Decree *Lamentabili*: "Revelation, constituting the object of the Catholic faith, was not completed with the apostles" (Denziger, no. 3421 [old no. 2021]).

of it. The divine truth in the Church preserves itself only by living, though living after the manner of an organism which retains its identity, even throughout its most considerable developments. No more revealed truth exists today than did in the 2nd century of the Church. However, the revealed truth is more distinctly known and more explicitly proposed: *eadem fides magis exposita*.[14] The true author of this progress most assuredly is the Church, infallibly assisted by the Holy Spirit. Just as it falls to her to formulate and order the Creedal expression of the faith,[15] it will fall to her, through the course of the ages, to render explicit a given aspect of the faith that remains implicit when she finds that reason has run into an obscurity, into a specific mystery, which St. Thomas presents as the motive for the distinction of the articles of the Creed. However, various occasions give rise to such development. Perhaps the most profound one, though less visible than the others because its activity takes place continuously, is the very development of civilization and culture. Such progress cannot take place without new questions being posed concerning the meaning and scope of the divine teachings, and the Church responds to them through her ordinary Magisterium well before having recourse to the solemn exercise of her teaching power. "Every civilizational fact can be the point of departure for doctrinal development [*mouvement*] in the Church."[16] And in its own turn, this doctrinal development [*mouvement*] can be the occasion for an increasingly distinct formulation of a given truth of faith. As has often been noted, the most ordinary thing occasioning this is heresy, and St. Augustine teaches that if God permits heresy, He does so because He draws this great good from it: "Obviously, the disapproval of heretics makes what your Church thinks and what sound doctrine holds *stand out boldly*."[17] A truth already present in the revealed deposit but still latent in the Church's awareness is thus elevated to explicit precision.

Therefore, we can indeed say that the presentation of the revealed truths to the human intellect arouses intense mental activity. In fact, our intellect cannot remain indifferent to statements whose truth is solely guaranteed by faith (though with their intelligibility also being offered to it), statements which, moreover, are concerned with the most nourishing objects the mind can have, those which are the most "interesting" for it, indeed, the most decisive objects for human life. It will exert its full strength in developing this intelligibility. Returning to the words of classical theological terminology, we can say that the believer will seek to understand through his intellect what

---

[14] *ST* II-II, q. 1, a. 10, ad 2.

[15] See *ST* II-II, q. 1, a. 10.

[16] Ferdinand Cavallera, "A propos de la vie du Dogme," *Bulletin de Littérature Ecclésiastique* (April–June 1942): 69.

[17] Augustine, *Confessions*, bk. 7, ch. 19, no. 25.

he already holds through authority. In other words, he will go out in search for the "*intellectus fidei*."

III. THEOLOGY
A. The Structure of Theology

7. *The birth and structure of theology.* Thus will theology begin. How will this "understanding of the faith" come to birth and develop?

Will this come about through the exercise of the virtue of faith itself? Impossible. For faith does not reason, nor does it analyze nor make one "understand." It adheres.

Will this come about though a simple application of a purely rational light (the light of the first principles) to the data of faith, along with definite logical methods? No more can this be the case, for it would have no proportion to the data of faith. One would merely erect a chimerical metaphysics of the sacred, wholly dependent on its own proper rational categories and, at the very most, proportioned to the natural, human faith spoken of above.

Instead, this will be brought about through supernatural faith *placing in its service* all of our intellectual resources with the goal of bringing, as far as is possible, the intelligibility of the truths of faith to the perfect state of knowledge which we call science. Such is the role and ambition of Theology. This discipline's structure and various functions require great delicacy in order to be grasped in a fully precise manner. I would like to briefly define its elementary procedures and proper light.

Its datum, the theological datum, is the very same as faith's: the revealed God, that is, "materially," the ensemble of supernatural truths guaranteed by God and transmitted by the Church. This ensemble has its value as data for a discipline aiming to be a science only by being attained through faith, a living faith, the theologian's infused faith. Faith alone provides the certitude of the principles serving as the foundation upon which theology will construct itself (on the logical model of subalternation). Without this faith and its permanent adherence, no theology is possible, and all that one could then have would be a purely natural explanation, a wholly human commentary concerning historical and theoretical truths (as would be had, for example, in a theology of Islam or of Buddhism). To suppress infused faith is to suppress every form of *theological science*, allowing it to nod off into the somnolence of an overly formal scientific development, eluding its own light and instincts. To do so would lead one to lose contact with the living source of theological knowledge, like a science that would suffocate its very life-breath, the profound intuition of its principles.[18]

---

[18] See p. 93 above.

However, if this light of faith is absolutely indispensable for the birth of theology and for all of its development, it does not suffice for explaining it, for once again, faith's light does not have a scientific character. Now, the objective light characteristic of theological science will emerge *from the first acceptance of the data of faith with a view to then intellectually elaborating it*. (The *habitus* of theology, specified by this light, will be born emerge only after the first such acts and will then develop.) Therefore, what is this objective light?

It is exactly this: concepts and propositions that, through faith, were solely held as being guaranteed by God, solely as objects of adherence, are now considered as objects of an intellectual activity that introduces (under faith and its irradiation) a rational consideration with the aim of explaining these concepts' own, proper intelligibility, manifesting how these propositions are interconnected, becoming aware of the temporal and historical conditions involved in their revelation to man and in the progress undergone throughout their successive formulations, grouping certain ones around those which explain them, manifesting through reasoning all of their intelligible implications, and so forth. . . . In short, they are now considered as being engaged in the characteristic activity of the human mind striving after *knowledge*.[19]

Here we have a new kind of intellectual light. It is no longer that of faith, for rational consideration and inference are mixed in with it. It is not that of reason alone, for without the influence of faith upon it, not only does every form of certitude disappear but also all of theology's notions and propositions lose their formal representative value concerning the supernatural divine reality. The intellect is here stimulated by the intelligible virtualities of essentially supernatural truths (and objects of faith), giving rise in it to an appropriate type of consideration. In other words, the truths of faith play the role of principles in theology.[20]

---

[19] "*Inasmuch as it is scientific in* character, our knowledge of God makes use of the Deity, so to speak, as a cause of those things it knows to belong to God; *inasmuch as this knowledge is faith*, it uses the Deity as Him who testifies to this knowledge." (Cajetan, in *ST* II-II, q. 1. a. 1, no. 8).

[20] We can characterize the essential activity of this new discipline by means of the following logical schema. According to Thomism's Aristotelian vocabulary, in a scientific demonstration, the middle term is attained by two *habitus*. Inasmuch as it is part of the principles (an attribution of the definition to the defined, to the subject), it is known by the *habitus* of principles, to which every form of immediate knowledge falls. Inasmuch as it explains the attribution of the predicate to the subject on account of being a cause, it is known by the scientific *habitus* and is reached through its radiation in the (mediate) conclusion which it guarantees. However, its entire explanatory value depends on the fact that it is held under the light (and, as it were, within the extension) of one's grasp of principles. This also holds true in theology. However, here, the *habitus* of principles is, precisely speaking, the *habitus* of infused faith, which clearly plays an essential and

A science suffers from infirmity when one only has faith in one's principles, not evidential knowledge. Here we see the greatest weakness befalling our theology, indeed, its congenital infirmity. It finds itself to be in a diminished state. Thus, it naturally aspires to the glorious state in which its principles will themselves be *known* in a better light. Then, they will no longer be furnished by faith, by a form of knowledge having the character of belief, but rather, will be a perfect form of knowledge, the very knowledge [*science*] of God which the beatified mind draws upon in the vision of the Divine Essence. Thus, this humanly elaborated theology will depend on it, holding from it its own original light. To use the technical term, theology will be subalternated to that knowledge. It will be wholly penetrated by evidence, wholly traversed by this great, luminous current which will illuminate its principles. It will not know the danger of drawing back from it, of becoming merely an artificial construction.

Here-below, it is brought into continuity with this blessed science through faith. It must remain wholly penetrated by supernatural faith, faithful to its still-obscure light, though a light superior to every other. In this light, it finds its spiritual environment and the wellspring whence it ever pours forth. Theology still must beware of the danger of sometimes throwing itself into certain clarities that are too readily available and too immediately satisfying for the reasoning mind. If it loses the *sense of mystery*, it runs the grave risk of deploying its energies in a purely rational technique, in a wholly natural form of investigation, whose objective measure no longer is this intelligibility-appeal presented *within faith* by an essentially supernatural truth but, rather, gives way to a measure that is solely founded on the light of rational principles. By following this path, theology deteriorates into nothing more than the aforementioned extrinsic application of rational considerations to the deposit of faith. It loses its original light and its entire proper scientific consistency.

8. Developments in theology: complexity and unity. It is important that we understand that in our intellectual awareness' first grasp of the deposit of faith, *no longer in view of adhering to it but, rather, in view of understanding it* (*intellectus fidei*), we find, in embryo, the whole of theology, with all the various lines of reflection that it will follow, coming to explicitly manifest their requirements and own proper structure only in an established body of doctrine: a critical investigation of the data in order to determine what is

---

actual role in every theological elaboration. Therefore, the light of theology will be supernatural in its origin and natural in its substance. It is radically the light of faith and substantially the light of science. However, theology is so profoundly rooted in faith that it constitutes a science that is wholly set apart and superior to every other, not only through its object, but also through its certitude, even though it finds itself in a very imperfect state here-below.

truly revealed or to what point a given statement benefits from the authority of revelation (*an sit revelatum*); historical reflection on the presentation of revelation and its concrete development (*quomodo revelatum est*); and speculative reflection in view of setting forth the proper intelligibility of revealed truths in their interconnections and their implications, as well as in view of constituting their scientific synthesis (*quid sit quod revelatum est*). In the work of investigating a given datum, the methodologies of each of the two others are necessarily mixed in as well. First, there is criticism of facts, texts, and notions. Then, we have historical reflection on the past history of the data of faith currently proposed by the Church and on its concrete presentation in time as well as its development. As a whole, such reflection provides an enormous service in determining what is revealed and in understanding it, but its immediate goal is to grasp how the Church's contemporary faith was itself revealed, as well as the nature of the progress through which it was elaborated without adulteration or change in meaning. Speculative reflection, which benefits from all of this work, while also serving in this very work, strives to understand what the revealed realities are in themselves (through analogy, while remaining within the mystery). Normally, if it arises from charity and is brought to its completion there, it will lead to this ultimate fruit of theological activity: (theological) contemplation. The term "Speculative Theology" is used for this last type of reflection and for the body of doctrine to which it leads. For the other two (though not sometimes without imprecision), the term "Positive Theology" is used.

Considering the overall arrangement of the discipline thus constituted, positive theology emerges as being *logically* prior, above all in its first work: the theological observation of the revealed datum currently presented by the Church. *Logically speaking*, speculative theology is a terminal activity, a crowning achievement. However, we know[21] that in a science still in the midst of being elaborated—and theology will always find itself in such a state herebelow, more or less so depending on the treatises in question—there is a continual back-and-forth between observation, on the one hand, and investigation into causes and explanations, on the other. We do not need to completely traverse the entire field of positive theology in its multiple developments in order to then begin our reflection on the intelligibility of the revealed datum as well as on the possibility of developing it into a science. This reflection begins with the first acceptance of this revealed datum, and this acceptance presupposes only that it be actually proposed by the Church and that one have the light of faith. At the same time, historical and critical reflection will develop themselves along with their own proper methodologies. If both remain theological, each will benefit from the other's progress.

---

21 See p. 94 above.

Therefore, theological wisdom is a complex discipline. The particularities of its object (one that is strictly supernatural: God such as He is in Himself) and those befalling its state (it receives its principles in human statements guaranteed by the light of *faith*, presenting them in the context of a given *history*) require theology to have functions that are carefully differentiated in their methods. We have briefly characterized the two principal ones: positive theology and speculative theology. They are not the only ones, and we can immediately note another: theology must heed how its supernatural object presents itself to the eyes of reason alone, highlighting to reason *the credibility* of this object. This new development, Apologetics, belongs to theology itself, for it alone is qualified to reflexively grasp the true proportions of its object and to present them to the intellect.[22]

Moreover, in order to understand the complexity of speculative theology itself, one merely needs to consider the immense breadth of its domain. The scientific synthesis built up by it will embrace within the universal extension of its secondary object (the way that the divine life is participated in by His works) objects of knowledge which, when studied in the light of our reason, require reason to develop fundamentally different disciplines. The theological synthesis will pass from the level of metaphysical consideration and vocabulary to that of psychology or to that of morality. The use it will make of sciences that are already constituted (moreover, in many cases furnishing them with the opportunity to undergo development through such use) will not prevent it from entering into their own proper ends in their meticulous procedures, taking over their methods for its own use as well as their own ways of responding to their own particular objects. It will develop an entire psychology and an entire morality.

Nonetheless, none of these differentiations will break up its scientific unity. In theology, all of these partial objects are offered to our mind under one and the same illumination, where it develops into a stable and scientific form of knowledge the intelligibility that revelation enables our mind to grasp in these objects. All these various, relatively autonomous methodologies, each in its own domain, are in turn utilized for the same end and in the service of the same intellectual research, though none is adequate to everything that the revealed deposit invites us "to know." These various investigations ultimately remain under one and the same light, which we have described as being rooted

---

[22] On this notion of Apologetics, holding that it is a part of fundamental theology, see Ambroise Gardeil, *La crédibilité et l'apologétique*, 2nd ed. (Paris: Lecoffre, 1912); Reginald Garrigou-Lagrange, *On Divine Revelation*, 2 vols., trans. Matthew K. Minerd (Steubenville, Ohio: Emmaus Academic, 2022).—Note, from Fr. Gardeil, this final profession made in the preface to *La structure de l'âme et l'expérience mystique* (Paris: 1927): "Apologetics is a task of theology. . . . The Apologetic task of theology. . . , itself founded on faith, therefore is indeed a work of faith, despite its rational texture."

in faith, enabling us to reach something deeper in things than their own physical or metaphysical necessity: the necessity that they have *as objects of God's knowledge* [*science*], to which we are truly assimilated by theology.

B. The Work of Theology
Theological Observation

9. *The observation of theological data.* A science observes its data in its own light. In other words, the characteristic light of this science dawns with this observation and already guides the mind's reflection upon it. Theology is not exempt from this law. It must consider its data and place them on its own level.

However, does not faith sufficiently perform this task for us? Precisely speaking, no. From this first acceptance by theology, the truths of faith present the mind with a different appearance than that of being mere objects of adherence. Henceforth considered in their intelligible virtualities, such data of faith become "theological data." The same truths which, on the one hand, are purely objects of faith, will come to find themselves now engaged in an intellectual activity, which is that of knowledge's own investigation, striving to establish a science where they will play the role of being truths that are either explanatory or explained (i.e., by other data of faith). They are at once truths of faith and also *theological truths.*

This activity will embrace a number of moments in its development. 1° First, there will be the initial phase which is prior to any constituted theology, while simultaneously being the very seed of theology itself: the acceptance of an actual datum of faith, no longer from the perspective of adherence but, instead, from the perspective of intellection (*intellectus fidei*). 2° Then, there will be the entire critical effort striving to determine more precisely what is revealed, in what circumstances, according to what progress, and so forth. Logically speaking, in the ensemble of theological science's activities, this critical research comes first. In point of fact, however, given that it is generally reflexive, it will only slowly develop, following upon many doctrinal elaborations, in the form of a "return to the sources." Thus, it uses everything that has already been acquired by positive theology (for critiquing facts and texts) and speculative theology (for notional criticism), both critiques remaining entirely theological. We are not here faced with a confusion of levels and methods. Rather, what we have is a correct sense for the interpenetration of theology's various functions *at this stage.*

Revealed data are proposed by and in the Church. But how are we to completely recognize what the Church proposes as being something *de fide*? Nothing is more common than an undue over-expansion [*majoration*] of the Church's teachings. And while theology's goal throughout its entire scientific activity does not lay in the work of distinguishing what is *De fide* from what is not (for, instead, its task is to "understand" what the faith teaches us, "*intellectus fidei*"), this discernment nonetheless is one of its first preoccupations. It is one of the primordial goals of positive theology, which must discern and weigh out "*auctoritas.*" Here, a theological critique of the proposal of the object of faith will need to be established, rigorously applying the rules of the methodology that has received the name "*De locis theologicis.*"

This criticism takes us so far that it will subsequently lead to a magnificent development in positive theology, an entire *historical theology* ordered to the same ultimate goal of understanding the faith, though constructed with its own proper methods, finding its methodological inspiration in the historical sciences, and theological reflection no longer will be able to manage any of its tasks without it. Indeed, it happens that in the documents serving as the sources for the most authentic data of faith, we find this data mixed together with a conception of the world (or even an imagery) which we must not allow to deceive us. Certainly, speculative theological criticism will play its own role in this matter (for example, detecting certain anthropomorphisms in order to distinguish analogies of proper proportionality from the purely metaphoric analogies so frequently encountered in the Bible). This discernment is what was lacking in the desert monk spoken of by Cassian, tenaciously holding on to the idea that the God spoken of in Genesis was a white-bearded old man. However, historical-theological criticism will above all be needed in order to determine the exact scope of certain teachings by taking into account influences of this kind, which influenced their formation: the dominating preoccupation of given texts, their literary genre, and so forth.

In this way, through an infinitely strenuous labor, we have the development of the three great parts that can be assigned to organized positive theology.— 1° Positive theology concerning scriptural documents: quite clearly, revelation is proposed in Scripture (in particular in the Old Testament) in the context of a popular conception of the world which is not the same as the outlook elaborated by the most certain data of our sciences—indeed, such a scientific perspective would only have been possible if God had simultaneously wished, at the same time, to reveal purely scientific truths, something which would be, however, completely contrary to the normal workings of His Providential economy. Infinitely progressive in its nature, revelation finds itself engaged in the concrete becoming of a people, adapted to its various levels of culture. In fact, it used a great variety of literary genres, concerned only that they be compatible with the divine truth. Some of these genres (e.g., apocalyptic writings), flourishing in a given era and adapted to a given culture, can be mysterious and confusing for other eras. Thus, textual, literary, and historical criticism, as well as a theological criticism using all the other forms of criticism, under the Church's supervision, clearly are indispensable: we must fashion a positive biblical theology organized according to its own requirements and its own proper methods.—2° A positive theology of the witnesses to tradition. First of all, there is Tradition, properly speaking, a source of faith prior to Scripture and broader than it, having come to its close with the death of the last Apostle. By definition, it is unwritten. However, the documents of the first Christian centuries and Patristic writings form a "tradition-transmission" in which we hear the echo of this Tradition and a testimony to what the Church's faith was at her beginnings. Interpretive difficulties analogous to those which are encountered in the exegesis of the Holy Books are found again here in the study of these ancient documents. They are almost always texts written for some particular circumstance, highlighting only one part of the traditional teaching, according to the given necessities of the moment, and the goal of historical investigations is to enable us to reconstruct them. Here again, we stand in need of a positive theology, here focused on the writings of the Fathers of the Church.—3° Positive theology concerning the teachings of the ecclesiastical magisterium. Most [of the Church's] official documents are also texts pertaining to certain circumstances. Their general intent is to highlight some aspect of doctrine which has been misunderstood. Usually, they are responses, not expositions. Clearly, they can be understood only if one takes the trouble to understand what they are responding to and what circumstances gave birth to the question at hand. Here too, we find ourselves faced with an immense part of positive theology which must be developed: positive theology concerned with ecclesiastical documents ("symbolic" theology).

In these various parts, positive theology uses the results of exegesis and history. It constitutes itself into a discipline whose organization is not that of a speculative theological synthesis. It will not consist in grouping a certain number of texts or documents in connection with the particular needs of the various assertions made in systematic theology. Positive theology can be used like this; however, in order to be valid and secure, such use of positive theology's data presupposes that such positive theology has already been constituted in its own proper dimensions, and within these dimensions, it is closely bound to the concrete development of revelation and to the progress undergone by dogmatic formulas. And if we in no way need to await the completion of such work in order to indulge in speculative theology (which most often finds sufficient data for its essential treaties by turning to the common data of faith which are utterly simple and most secure, such as they are proposed by the Church in our own days), it provides a great benefit, both in terms of verification and of enrichment, namely, the benefit of being aware of the solidity of the treatises that have already been substantially constituted, now reflecting on them anew, with such knowledge as is afforded by positive theology.

By undertaking as *integral* a study as is possible concerning these immense domains of positive theology, we already are able to draw the great advantage of preserving the theologian against certain temptations to narrow-mindedness and hardening. A given controversy, at a particular time and place, does not necessarily emphasize what is most important, intrinsically speaking. Many contingencies can place in the foreground of theological preoccupation certain points of doctrine which in themselves are less essential and, in fact, sometimes even quite secondary. Indeed, the doctrinal ferment thus aroused can itself result in an intervention by the Magisterium which, in its own turn, placed this particular point in a brighter light. Too rapid a study of historical theology can lead one to overestimate the place in Christian doctrine rightfully assigned to data thus set in the foreground by the accidents of history. Such a perspectival error, which is certainly not just something deceptively dreamed up by some people, finds an excellent corrective in a more-open and more-integral knowledge of all the various witnesses that tradition has transmitted to us.

10. *The observation of facts and of data which are of interest to theology.* The revealed datum is the only *formal source* for theological science. However, since theology is a form of wisdom, using not only all the resources of our reason but also standing in need of all of our knowledge in order to better understand divine revelation, it finds indispensable ancillary information in many disciplines. Because its proper object, in every one of its domains, finds itself engaged in history and in the various activities and achievements of human life (merely consider, for example, the whole of moral theology), theology has the duty of observing and gathering the facts and data that can be of assistance in understanding its object, in whatever domain that such facts may present themselves. In this way, just as every important form of progress in the order of science or civilization can furnish an occasion for a more explicit formulation of a dogma, so too it can, *a fortiori*, furnish an occasion for progress in theological elaboration.[23] Certainly, here too, theology will be able to assimilate these data, doing so *in its own proper light, by critiquing them* in a rigorous manner in accord with its own principles, using them as a means for more fully understanding everything contained in revelation.

Progress in medicine and experimental psychology have enabled us to understand with the greatest of nuances the complex characteristics of the human activity that grace supernaturalizes, as well as the reverberations that certain mystical states have on the body. We can no longer write treatises on demonology in the style of 16th and 17th century works devoted to such matters nor treat of diabolic possession as did authors from that era.[24]

---

23 See p. 102–3 above.

24 See the all-too-brief but excellent little book by Joseph de Tonquédec, *Les maladies nerveuses ou mentales et les manifestations diaboliques* (Paris: Beauchesne, 1938).

Here, history is particularly informative: the history of societies, of doctrines, of civilizations, and of cultures. We do not give to a treatise on the Church the accent and formulas that would have been employed by a 1st-century Christian, living with the conviction that the Parousia was immanent. This event's delay, leading to a more profound understanding of what the Lord meant when He said that neither its day nor its hour are known, led to progress for Christian awareness and thought. Likewise, if we are commenting on the Church, we must take into account *facts* like the Greek Schism, the Great Western Schism, and the Reformation. They require us to be even clearer in our theological explanations concerning the exact nature of the assistance that the Savior promised to give His Church. In the same order of ideas, it is clear that after the awakening of the European nationalities, Leo XIII spoke about the powers of the Roman Pontiff with more-explicit distinctions than those that were employed by Boniface VIII. Therefore, we must admit that the important facts of history provide instruction for theology and that her observations also must take such matters into account. This does not provide theology with a formal source which would be added to the revealed deposit but, instead, furnishes an invaluable means for explication. The discovery of America furnished the occasion for new developments in international morality (e.g., in Francisco de Vitoria) and since then has acutely posed a problem which has been made even more urgent with the discovery (or quasi-discovery) of the great Indian and Chinese civilizations, namely, the problem concerning the salvation of non-believers and how to understand the nature of implicit faith.

We could easily come up with more examples like this. It is more important, however, to draw from them the precise lesson they teach us. Nothing highlights this lesson more than does knowledge of the "crises" through which Christian thought has passed. Without going all the way back to Origenism and the very first crisis provoked by more profound contacts with Greek thought, the history of theology (or, more broadly, that of Christian thought) offers a great number of telling examples. They immediately reveal the *benefit* that theology draws from a broad contact with culture, with all aspects of intellectual life and of human life, as well as the *danger* that this contact can easily introduce.

The progressive introduction of Aristotle into scholastic thought is a capital fact in the history of theology and the example of a crisis (whose full acuity we do not perhaps realize) which, happily resolved, led to magnificent progress thanks to St. Albert and St. Thomas.—Later on, it came to represent an outlook concerning the physical world which to most minds (and even to some theologians) was one with the Christian teaching, an outlook which the great scientific developments of the 16th century brought to ruin. Galileo remains the witness and the symbol of the gravity of this crisis. In place of the idea of an earth necessarily occupying the center of the universe (and above all bearing the prodigious sense that the drama of sin, the Incarnation, and Redemption unfolded upon it), these scientific developments gradually came to substitute the idea of an unremarkable planet, a rather secondary part of a solar system which itself is lost in the immense expanses of nebulas. Through this change, an ensemble of concrete views and conceptions came crashing down, outlooks that had given many dogmas of the Catholic *Credo* a framework that seemed completely natural. The new outlook certainly was not contrary to the faith, as theology thereafter showed, and Christian thought has perfectly assimilated this datum whose appearance was, at first, scandalous. Nonetheless, this conflict is very instructive concerning the duties and difficulties involved in a theology that wishes to be at once solid and well-informed.

Remaining in the domain of thought itself, one of the great facts (and doubtlessly, the greatest fact of the last century and our present one) is development in the domains of methodology and the historical sciences. Is it an exaggeration to believe that here too an entire outlook concerning the world's history is in the midst of collapsing, somewhat akin to how the ancient conception of the solar system came crashing down? At the very least, we must admit that the horizons of this history, along with its broad outlines, have significantly changed and that Christian thought is led to conceive with greater nuance the providential economy of God's supernatural education and of the salvation of humanity. It must look upon this as furnishing an opportunity to achieve new progress. It is clear that the theology of the creation of man and that of original sin cannot be disinterested in the discoveries of prehistory and that, given the knowledge that we have today concerning primitive civilizations, however fragmentary such knowledge may be, we can no longer have the same historical perspective and chronology as what is found in [Bossuet's] "Discourse on Universal History."

Theology must remain attentive to all of this. These new facts and data raise questions that cannot be indifferently left unanswered. The modernist crisis, at once the fruit of the legitimate expansion of critical studies and of an aberrant philosophy, made this fact quite clear. Nonetheless, however beneficial this observation may be, it is not lacking in its own danger. The benefit that can be drawn from it is what we have already tried to emphasize: a more profound or renewed understanding of a point of traditional doctrine. The danger is that of an insufficient *theological critique*, a premature assimilation of a given fact which has not yet been sufficiently sized-up by theology for want of adequate examination by it *in theology's own proper light* and *according to the analogy of faith*. This will bear fruit in an inconsistent intellectual liberalism or a superficial and ephemeral harmonizing. Here again we have an absolutely necessary application of the principle of scientific observation: any given fact, whether scientific or historical, is not yet a theological datum. It will be such, thus being for theology a datum that is assimilable or even a problem that can be resolved, only if it is examined and critiqued in theology's own light, grasped and formulated in all the proportions which it thus takes on in this light. Such a critique presupposes a living theology, fully in possession of all of its principles. It is not by sacrificing these principles or by trivializing traditional positions that this assimilation will be brought about. It has been justly written, of doctrines and organisms alike: "Assimilation is possible only if the organism is whole and intact."[25]

And, let us repeat: theology must remain in contact not only with the scientific and historical disciplines but, indeed, with *the entire universe of culture*. This too will come with its own dangers: one can easily slide from a strictly scientific form of reflection, necessarily requiring precise techniques, to an amateur form of reflection which is more accessible and less demanding. Theology must inflexibly retain the lofty level of its scientific effort. (Obviously, this does not exclude the choice of a genre of *expression* adapted no longer to the finalities of science but, instead, to those of a form of teaching concerned with providing a path for minds that are more or less prepared. No, indeed, it calls for such a pedagogical form, though it is important to heed the fact that it no longer lays within the order of rigorous research but, instead, in that of *exposition*.) However, precisely by holding to this lofty line of conduct, theology must make sure it remains human and living, and for this to be so it is infinitely important that it not become enclosed within a scholarly problematic, having become more or less bookish. Theology is not a study undertaken by detached bureaucrats. Life itself will set before it, *if theology observes it*, questions which, requiring it to rethink some traditional teaching, will lead it to develop some new aspect of the inexhaustible riches of its object.

This necessity is particularly urgent for the entire *moral part* of theological reflection. In every moral discipline, experience plays a fundamental role, and just because a form of knowledge is theological, this does not mean that experience thereby is useless. Like other forms of human knowledge, experience will be critiqued, elevated, and taken up under a loftier light, that of revelation. Nonetheless, experience is indispensable for a profound knowledge of man, as well as his individual and social activity. Everything that reveals man, whether in his loftiest spiritual activities, or in the physical conditioning of his supernatural life itself, will be information for an attentive theology. Personal experience, which is necessarily restricted at once by the circle wherein it takes place and by the qualities of the observational powers of him who amasses it, will be supplemented by the vaster and more penetrating

---

[25] Jacques Maritain, *Le Docteur angélique* [Paris: Desclée de Brouwer, 1920], 111.

experience of man which is contained in great human, philosophical, or even literary works as soon as they attain a certain density. Many of these works, although they are perhaps, in themselves, rather remote from every kind of theological consideration (and despite their sometimes-enormous deficiencies and errors from the perspective of moral rules), are extremely revelatory concerning the human heart, bringing to light particular dimensions thereof, for their authors were exceptionally clairvoyant: Montaigne, Pascal, Stendhal, Dostoyevsky, Nietzsche, etc. Without speaking of the wholly desirable benefit that the presence of a more efficacious theology can bring to culture and to human life, this knowledge is, for theology itself, a source of sometimes-unforeseen questions, hence providing an invaluable *ferment*.

Theological Explanation

11. *The task falling to speculative theology.*[26] The observation of theological data and the establishment of a positive and historical theology, as well as the observation of the progress of doctrines and cultures, provide an immense field of activity in which theology has experienced remarkable efflorescence during the last few centuries. However, this is far from the whole of theology, which will exercise its superior, terminal, and properly scientific (in St. Thomas's sense of the word) function only through an effort that is oriented toward the ultimate question: what are the revealed realities in themselves? After having observed and amassed an ensemble of data, it is important to pass on to the investigation into causes. Then, once these causes are known, making use of the procedure of analogy, which plays an essential role here, we must pass on to explanation, connecting to these causes all the data that depend upon them. And contemplation will be achieved precisely by connecting all these matters to what we thus know about the most profound character of the Divine Being (the Trinity of Persons in the unity of His Essence) or about His most fundamental Providential decrees, thus having in such contemplation the characteristic fruit of theological wisdom.[27]

12. *The investigation undertaken by theological explanation.* Once he possesses all of his essential data, the speculative theologian's first task—one that is neither the least lengthy nor the least delicate among the tasks facing

---

[26] In the sections that follow, what we say should be considered in parallel with questions already treated in the *Revue Thomiste* by Fr. Gagnebet (1938). We await from him a work which will develop, illustrate, and draw up in final form the essential positions taken up in his articles, to which we owe a great debt.

[Tr. note: See Marie-Rosaire Gagnebet, "La nature de la théologie spéculative," *Revue thomiste* 44 (1938): 1–39, 213–55, 645–74; "Un essai sur le problème théologique," *Revue thomiste* 45 (1939): 108–45.]

[27] "Theological" contemplation, not, of course, "infused" contemplation.

him—is precisely that which, in his science, corresponds to the "investigation into causes," that is, the slow work of "theological discovery."

Here, the theologian is faced with the task of examining and inventorying the data of theology, no longer aiming to specify what is and is not revealed, what participates more or less distantly in the authority of revelation—this is, on the whole, a task falling to positive theology—but rather, aiming to *explain* this data, establishing it as a body of scientific doctrine, that is, as an organic grouping of notions enabling the best possible intellectual assimilation of Revealed Reality. Here, the theologian is no longer tasked with discerning his data from the perspective of formulas but, rather, looks on them precisely as *realities* [*choses*], distinguishing what is accidental from what is necessary, properties from essential qualifications, and effects from causes.

As was his wont, St. Thomas borrowed the logical instruments for this investigation from Aristotle. Such instruments would first of all include the *procedures of dialectic* (the "Topics," no longer in Cano or Cicero's sense of the term, as we find in the *De locis theologicis*,[28] but rather, in Aristotle's sense, which differs significantly from how they spoke of this branch of logic), its discussions and investigations leading to common or probable explanations until, at last, it discovers the true cause for the matter under investigation (i.e., the necessary middle term). Then, there will be the particularly important procedures involved in *the investigation into definitions*, matters which are developed and examined in detail in the second book of the *Posterior Analytics*.[29] This analysis's goal is to take our at-first-vague, non-critical, and non-explicit notions of the first datum grasped, and bring them to the state of having real and distinct definitions expressing these notions.

However, besides this entire logical apparatus, this speculative function of theology will henceforth make use of that great instrument of thought: *the analogy of proper proportionality*, which is utterly distinct from merely metaphorical analogy as well as from a mere comparison of things. Thanks to the virtue of faith, analogy properly so called has a completely different scope in theology from what it has in Metaphysics, even though, as an instrument of knowledge, it takes on exactly the same shape and is subject to the same imperfections. As we said above,[30] by faith we not only adhere to truths that surpass our own abilities (this would already be true for the case of an acquired, human faith),

---

[28] Albert Lang has shown quite well that Melchior Cano depended much more on Cicero (through the intermediary of Rodolphos Agricola) than on Aristotle. See Albert Lang, *Die Loci Theologici des Melchior Cano und die Methode des dogmatischen Beweises* (München: Verlag J. Kösel und F. Pustet, 1925).

[29] It is clear that, according to St. Thomas, the integral methodology of theology is not at all reduced to a form of "Topics" in the Aristotelian sense but, rather, uses the whole of the "Analytics."

[30] See pp. 98–99 above.

but beyond this, the notions that express them, united by the copula which articulates our adherence, take on *a formal signifying value concerning the supernatural divine reality*. They cease to tell our mind only what is contained in their natural sense. Or rather (for the difference is not at all of the order of conceptual content formed by the first act of the intellect alone [*la différence n'est nullement de l'ordre du contenu conceptuel*]), they no longer solely lead our mind to the natural realities which they normally represent by themselves; now, they bear it onward, as it were, to the true terminus which it reaches in the Supernatural Divine Reality. This will also fall to theology inasmuch as it remains in continuity with infused faith, and moreover, it is only on this condition and to this degree that it will remain a science. Without faith and without this superelevation, not only does theology no longer have certitude; it quite literally no longer has an object. For what theology also claims to make us reach is indeed God such as He is in Himself, God considered from the perspective of His Deity. This is its proper object, its "formal object."

This is why our analyses of the analogical content of the notions of person and nature undertaken in order to represent the Divine Nature to ourselves are not empty mental games but, rather, provide us with a "very fruitful" entrance into the mystery of God. To develop the theory of the production of the [intellectual] word and of the spiration of love in order to clarify the revealed notions concerning the Trinitarian Processions is to develop an analogy properly so called, one that enables us *to know* and contemplate what the intimate life of God is in itself—doing so quite imperfectly and in a way requiring us to deny all the created conditions befalling our manner of conceptualizing this notion. This does not at all make the analogy thus developed, as well as the explanation that it enables, enter into the domain of faith (unless it also happens to be revealed on its own behalf). However, it does make it enter into the domain of *theological science*, which is indeed a much loftier domain than that of mere opinion.

13. *Theological explanation*. Having thus analyzed and critiqued the notions at hand, and, to the degree it is possible, having determined them in their essential content, we still must pass on to the task of explanation by effectively connecting to the notion of the subject (whether it be the central subject of the science or its partial, secondary subjects) everything that depends upon it. Here, we are not concerned with discovering new truths but, rather, with taking up given statements (which were already formulated on the level of an already more-or-less probable and more-or-less assured factual knowledge) and now elevating them to the level of perfect, scientific knowledge by connecting them to the *cause* which explains them and manifests their necessity. This is the decisive stage of *theological demonstration*.

On this subject, there are certain prevailing confusions, which Fr. Gagnebet has happily noted. These truths, which theological demonstration connects to given prior ones, are perhaps ones that were already themselves revealed. However, as an object of faith, they were not at all believed on account of the connection grasped by the intellect. The Gospel suffices as our testimony to the fact that Christ has a human will. However, this datum finds its explanation in a loftier notion as soon as it has been analyzed with sufficient precision: the fact that Christ had a perfect human nature. Viewed as depending on this principle, the existence of a human will in Christ is a theological truth. As something already revealed by itself, it was and remains a truth of faith. However, in other cases, the statement thus connected by a necessary middle term to a truth of faith is something that has not been revealed. Such is the case in the analysis of a revealed notion when the mind grasps something required by that notion, having no other reason to hold this new truth with certitude except in view of this inference. In order to express the fact that the theological inference attaining them is the only reason that they are admitted, modern theological vocabulary designates these statements by using the term "theological conclusion" in the strict sense.

Strictly from the perspective of "*auctoritas*" ([i.e.,] from the perspective of positive theology) this difference is considerable, but it remains accidental from the perspective of speculative theology. The latter's function is not at all a kind of mere deduction of propositions lying outside of the revealed deposit. In that case, we would need to say that theology begins where faith comes to an end. On the contrary, it works on the datum of faith in its entirety, each of whose statements, at the same time that it is, under the light of faith, purely an object of adherence, becomes, under the theological light defined above, a theological truth, viewed in its connections with the others, in its intelligible virtualities, as truths that explain or truths that have been explained. And it strives, in this light, to lead this entire ensemble of truths to the perfect state of scientific knowledge.

The essential logical procedure here is *demonstration*, such as St. Thomas himself analyzed in his commentaries on Aristotle's *Posterior Analytics*. In no way is demonstration an instrument of discovery (a confusion which for many minds seems to remain connected to the term "deduction"). Rather, it is the connection of an already-known proposition (of an infra-scientific form of knowledge) to the principles which manifest its *raison d'être* and, by that very fact, its necessity. According to St. Thomas's vocabulary, its end is judgment (*iudicium*) not discovery (*inventio*). Whether the proposition thus connected as a conclusion to a revealed principle already is a truth of faith held by revelation or is one that has been learned in a completely different manner, the process remains the same: it is a purely scientific procedure using inference and in no way *as such*, authority. The latter is involved in the processes of speculative theology in order to assure its principles but not at all in order to then demonstrate its conclusions.

Nonetheless, it remains the case that if speculative theology as such does not appeal to authority in order to "demonstrate" its conclusions, the theologian himself is quite interested in knowing whether, at the same time that these conclusions are placed before his mind as being connected to truths of faith through a necessary middle term, they also are revealed elsewhere, or at least, already "authorized" either by some important tradition, by the common assent of theologians, or by some indication expressed by the Magisterium. This is why he will be led to add to his own theological undertaking the results of positive theology concerning the same point by invoking Scripture and Tradition. Left to their own concerns and their own proper dimensions, speculative theology and positive theology develop into distinct treatises, having completely different appearances and organizations, just as they have two different methodologies.[31] However, an integral theological culture requires us to know how to unite them.

14. *Theological Synthesis*. Taken as a whole, speculative theology aims at as definitive a scientific synthesis as possible, just as it strives to attain a definitive explanation in each of its demonstrations. This was the essential effort undertaken by the authors of the "Theological Summas." However, theology will never be perfect nor ever fully achieved here-below.

As we already noted above,[32] in the sciences, there often are provisional explanations based on first observations. Such explanations are commonly called "hypotheses," meaning an apparent explanation that still must be confronted with all the available data in order to verify whether or not it is confirmed or broken by them. A generalized hypothesis will form an explanatory theory confirmed by a certain number of facts or reasons, although it will not yet be grasped as being *necessarily the only explanatory principle*.

Speculative theology also has its own hypotheses and theories. In the vast field of theological investigation (the domain of the "investigation into causes"), wide latitude is provided for this mental effort, as well as for the use of opinion and probable knowledge. However, hypothetical elements which are more or less proximate to scientific knowledge will inevitably enter into the very systematization of theological science, such as it is found in this theologian or that School. Not everything in such systematizations is definitive. It is possible that notions which are not sized up according to their true dimensions can come to be offered to faith as an instrument of explication. Along these lines, theological views that were imprudently associated with Aristotelian physics (e.g., concerning the localization of heaven and hell) obviously need to be revised. Of even greater importance, it can happen that,

---

[31] See Ferdinand Cavallera, "La théologie positive," *Bulletin de litterature ecclesiastique*, (Jan. 1925): 20–42.

[32] See p. 94 above.

within the most profound perspective commanding a given synthetic organization, some less-essential perspective may have been chosen [as a guiding principle for that synthesis's outlook], leading to the production of distortions in the very systematization itself because of one's desire to remain faithful to a restricted intuition or to an impoverishing technique. Hence, *a number of great theological syntheses* in fact exist, and they are notably different from each other in their overall élan, their general spirit, and in a significant number of their conclusions.

Merely because the word "system"—a word that, alas, is equivocal—is used for such syntheses, it would be quite inexact to think of them as being so many broad hypotheses, constructed out of theologians' "opinions." In truth, each of these systems claims to present the whole of theological science, along with hypothetical prolongations, doing so with varying degrees of success. In *speculative* theology, the criterion of the *scientific* state of an ensemble of explanations can be neither the agreement of all theologians regarding them nor even the number of more-or-less important votes cast on their behalf. Such considerations, which are in fact quite necessary, fall to positive theology, which aims at describing a given teaching from the perspective of "*auctoritas*." However, it will add authority's own guarantee to an explanation, whose own proper means of proof are different, and which reaches its scientific state by different paths.

On this point, many good minds are in the grip of a tenacious prejudice, one that is even fed by the terminology used in the logic of the sciences which itself has become "positivist," as well as by the idea commonly held today that "science" is opposed to "philosophy." By giving itself an object that is unknowable (from the perspective of reason), speculative theology would supposedly be the domain of that which is subject to opinion, where certitude could only be had through external consecration expressed by an "authority." From this perspective, it would seem that on all the points of doctrine where theologians are not in agreement, we could only speak of opinion and not of certitude. Consequently, we could speak not of demonstration but of hypothesis, not of science but of "systems." Now, it is in fact the case that what definitively removes a theological truth from discussion by theologians is hardly ever an argument but, rather, is an intervention by the Magisterium (whose customary practice, moreover, is to enter as little as possible into traditionally debated questions). Only one step—indeed, one that is often taken—separates this factual point from the conclusion that one can hold as "certain" in theology only what the Magisterium has more or less explicitly pronounced to be so.

This represents the confusion of the certitude of authority with that of science, as well as the confusion of the characteristic intellectual movement of faith with that of science properly so called. Now, theological science is not faith. Yes, it is rooted in faith and is entirely nourished by its light and fixed upon its object. However, what characterizes it as a science is the fact that it has recourse to properly intellectual procedures and determines its conclusions in the evidence of the explanatory activity of connecting [principles and conclusions]. It is not imposed by authority but, rather, is grasped by the intellect.

Certainly, in contrast to what takes place in human sciences, *authority does play an utterly important role in theology*. However, this is because faith assures theology's principles. If it then intervenes [in theological questions], by the same token (and to the degree that it makes some pronouncement) it makes the truth that belongs to the domain of pure science (as the conclusion of a demonstrative syllogism) depart from that domain in order to connect it to what must be held to be true on behalf of faith's own requirements—if not always on behalf of the theological virtue of faith, at least on behalf of a particularly weighty and well-placed faith, since it is given to the Church's Magisterium. I do not say that intervention by authority makes the truth that it imposes pass out of the domain of theological *consideration*, for this domain covers the same domain as faith. I say that from the perspective of the assent that we must give to it, it draws this truth back from an adherence which would be solely determined by the intellectual grasping of an evident connection (i.e., scientific adherence) so as to place it on the level of those truths which are admitted because they are taught by a competent authority.

Disagreement is no longer permitted concerning these latter: authority has intervened with sufficient clarity. Concerning the former, disagreement could be avoided solely by force of the evidence involved. And everyone knows that in theology, as in philosophy, indeed for analogous reasons, evidence does not present itself in the same way as it does in mathematics, and to St. Thomas's eyes this does not prevent either theology or philosophy from being true *sciences*. Above the domain where we find likelihoods and probabilities, where we can establish only opinions, and below, where an authoritative intervention removes a truth from discussions by requiring us to adhere to it in way that is more or less immediately and explicitly connected to faith, there is the utterly vast domain of theological science, where the intelligibility of the truths of faith, with increasing penetration, is led to the state of science properly so called solely by the intellect's own labor and by its own proper means.

The outlooks that we find ourselves fighting against profoundly underrate the powers of the human intellect and cast suspicion on everything that is a "conceptual construction." These attitudes are connected with quite different currents of thought than those animating St. Thomas's own and, indeed, clash with what quite obviously was his constant practice as a theologian. Thus, the problem must be transferred to philosophy's terrain and, most especially, that of the critique of knowledge. It lies outside of our present concerns to enter into that issue in this article, for we here presuppose a position which accepts St. Thomas's principles.

This difference of philosophical outlooks, which—without always being explicit, is profound—is not the only motive for the low esteem many have for the great theological syntheses and, along with them, for speculative theology itself. Many join to it a desire that testifies to their Christian sense and their zeal for God's House: does not speculative theology run the risk of incorporating a "philosophical system" into Christian doctrine? Will this not involve (and compromise) the faith in our speculations? Given that all philosophies remain human, with none of them being imposed upon revelation (which exceeds them and remains perfectly "free"), revealed truths, on account of their infinite transcendence, could perhaps be expressible to our minds in the vocabulary of wholly divergent or even incommensurable systems, like different geometries. For example, they could be expressed in line with a philosophy that acknowledges the principle of identity just as much as in line with one that does not recognize it.

Such an outlook completely misunderstands the proper nature of theology and the character of its light, as we have tried to analyze it up to this point. In point of fact, what theology claims to offer to faith as *an instrument of scientific explanation* is not the doctrine of this or that author—Aristotle, Plato, Confucius, or Shankara—but, rather, those notions which best assure us of attaining *definitive truths* and imperishable values, whose scope is not temporal or relative but, instead, supra-temporal. "When I have indeed known the truth," said Montaigne, "It is no more known as something held by Plato than as something known by me." What theology wishes to use (and, moreover, what the Church likewise uses in the more precise formulations of her dogmas) are not truth values that are relative to a given author or to a given time. Rather, she wishes to use absolute truth values, by which one reaches a particular, unchangeable aspect of reality. Here, the fact that such truth values do indeed exist is still a philosophical problem whose resolution depends on the notion that one forms for oneself concerning the intellect and its scope, as well as concerning the unity and permanence of human *nature*.

15. *The history of theology.* It at least remains quite certain that speculative theology's task is altogether formidable. And we would be far too optimistic toward human nature and human intelligence were we to think that theology could be carried out without "accidents" or that every theology would be perfectly faithful. This is obviously not believable *a priori*, and the history of theological thought abundantly illustrates the need for such reserve in these matters. The exceptional value of St. Thomas lies precisely in the fact that he attained, for a considerable and truly amazing number of data, a maximum degree of impersonality, atemporality, and absolute certitude. Still, we must not dogmatically maintain that this is necessarily the case for all of his assertions. Quite clearly, some of them are invalid precisely because the notions that served in their formulation and justification did not have this absolute truth value but, instead, in fact depended on the outlook of a given author or era. Here, we clearly see the great benefit that must indeed accrue to theology through a profound knowledge of its own history and of the history of doctrines. We no longer are speaking of the use of history in constituting a positive theology but rather, of the knowledge that an already-evolved and long-established science indispensably must have concerning its own past. Theology has become far too developed as a science for historical methodology, understood precisely in this self-critical sense, not to be something far more than a necessary supplement: it is an irreplaceable instrument for speculative reflection itself.

This is because, however independent we may think that a given theological formulation is from historical contingencies, it always and inevitably is impacted by the circumstances that originally surrounded it: the preoccupations of its era, errors to be combatted, influences undergone, aspects that are primarily emphasized, the worldview and culture common in a given era, place, etc. . . . It will always be important to discern within an ensemble of notions and within a group of assertions their strict scientific scope, their permanent value, and the great halo of historical connections they have either with the context in which they originally were proposed or with other assertions that were common at that time but which did not have the same value. Such discernment requires an infinitely refined touch and a culture that is at once theological and historical. A mind that is too exclusively that of an historian will end up emphasizing, above all, the changes that it perceives, poorly grasping the formal difference which separates notions from facts, imperishable essences from the conditions of temporal existence, and ideas from their histories. It will fall to the theologian, if he is well-informed, to take and use this idea, now understood more fully through historical reflection, though itself independent from the whole of history as regards that idea's own essential notes, so that he may present his theological science in its permanence.

CONCLUSION

16. *Theology is a science of reality.* Through all its entire scientific activity, it is neither a form of grammar, nor of exegesis, nor of logic. What it claims to know are neither texts, nor words, nor an organization of concepts but, rather, God. Its state here-below often requires it to use the science of words, that of texts, and that of concepts. It never does so in order to tarry there, whatever benefit it may draw from them. It forever stretches out toward a better fruit: *the understanding of the things of faith*, the knowledge of *things* divine.

On several occasions, we have used the expression, "theological contemplation." So long as theology does not forget its most profound orientation, its labor will indeed lead to a form of contemplation. It realizes to the highest degree what St. Thomas teaches concerning the intellectual *virtues*: "They perfect [man] in the contemplative life, which is not ordered further on to another form of life, whereas the active life is ordered to it."[33] And again: "They are a kind of draft sketch [*inchoatio*] of perfect beatitude, which consists in the contemplation of the truth."[34] Undoubtedly, this is not yet "infused contemplation" but, rather, is the analogical realization of the notion of contemplation that is found at the terminus of every true form of *wisdom* as soon as it is inspired by love and leads to it.

Moreover, if there is indeed a form of contemplation that is in some way "terminal," being a kind of fruit in relation to the work of theological speculation, it is clear that in relation to the supernatural knowledge established in us through faith and in which theology itself is rooted, such theological contemplation cannot be fully "terminal," and, far from being satiating, if it is true, it opens up the desire for a superior form of knowledge and itself feels the need to give way to infused contemplation or, at least, to be crowned therein, letting itself be directed by it. Then, the believer's mind will have a new "understanding of the faith," though one that is directed solely by the Holy Spirit.

---

33 *In* III *Sent.*, d. 33, q. 2, a. 2, qla 2.
34 *ST* I-II, q. 57, a. 1, ad 2.

2

A Theological Dialogue
Raymond-Léopold Bruckberger, OP

In an age such as ours, when war and politics have set up hatred and lies as necessities, it would be good to raise man's intelligence to the highest disciplines, those which, instead of dividing man, can unite him in the search for, and possession of, the truth. Spiritual goods do not allow for envy, for they abound more fully through communication to others. In a world wherein intellects have been so violated, hearts so debased, and bodies so trampled, it is perhaps not fanciful to imagine that theology should also take up responsibility for man's misfortune and help him maintain his first dignity, namely, his ability to strive to understand his own destiny so that he may live in accord with it.

Theology is a science. However, because it is the loftiest of the sciences, it is a form of wisdom, that wisdom which is spoken of by the Scriptures, a wisdom which stands at the crossroads, calling out to those who wish to drink from her consoling cup. Theology is a science, but since it is subalternated to the vision had by the blessed in Paradise, its lights are loftier than those of human understanding. Like the angels in heaven, theology speaks of God and with God; and marked with the infirmities befalling human language, it continues here-below the same dialogue that is being held among the elect in glory. The "Dialogues of the Dead" by Lucien or Fénelon are only literary fantasies, whereas, for the believer, God speaks in a language that is truly accessible in the treasury of Revelation and dogma, and this enables us to apply the understanding of our faith to this supernatural revelation and to systematize its concepts, thereby fulfilling a need felt by our human reason.

If, as it has been said, civilization is born of dialogue, indeed if its very characteristic trait is the fact that it is such a dialogue, theology can and must provide human civilization with the most concentrated form of dialogue, that dialogue which is most freighted with those truths which bring peace and the greatest reconciliation among men. If theologians were altogether equal to their task—that is, if they profoundly understood the data of revelation and the human condition, while also knowing how to speak to their fellow men—theology would then introduce a maternal serenity into the dialogue of civilization.

In any case, the reality is that this is what theology must be: a maternal wisdom for man's restless spirit. And if it fails to be such, we cannot simply resign ourselves to this state of affairs.

In recommending St. Thomas as the teacher *par excellence* of Catholic theology, the Sovereign Pontiffs surely did not intend to bind up modern understanding within a straightjacket. We are always a little embarassed when we give praise to St. Thomas, and Albert the Great's own words concerning St. Thomas come to mind: "It is not for the dead to praise the living." For the good that nourishes the human intellect is the truth, and a doctrine has vitality not through its timeliness in publication but, rather, through its truth value.

St. Thomas is a universe of the mind, harmonious and solidly organic. We believe that, on the whole, he carried theological investigation to its loftiest scientific perfection. We do not say that he cannot be surpassed. He does not mark an endpoint. However, precisely because his work exists upon the *scientific* level of knowledge, this work must first be understood and carried on if theological science wishes to make forward progress—just as no physicist has ever dreamt of neglecting the discoveries acquired by prior thinkers, even though he all the while assesses the truth of such past findings. However, in the scientific order, what is proven is acquired. Otherwise, we would still be standing alongside Archimedes. We refuse, indeed absolutely, to accept this sort of intellectual backsliding.

When one speaks of St. Thomas as though he were like an obsolete style of architecture, one has every right to attempt a theological exposé in French, for example, in another language and a different turn of phrase from that deployed in the *Summa*. We do not reconstruct cathedrals—though, for all that, neither do we despise them. However, with St. Thomas, theological style is not the sole matter at hand. More importantly still, there is the scientific value of his work. In Greek temples as well as Romanesque and Gothic churches, in the Palace of Versailles and Baroque monuments, we see various expressions of the identical and invariable laws that constitute the universal code of architecture, at least as regards the elementary laws of gravity and resistance that a native applies instinctively when building his hut and that Mansart observed in designing the Palace of Versailles. And without the application of these laws, neither hut nor castle would ever exist.

The same is true for St. Thomas. His value does not consist so much in having constructed a magnificent theological edifice in an admirable style which is now, however, outdated. Rather, his value lies in the fact that, more than any other thinker, he made greater progress in theological knowledge, in its scientific systematization, to the point of having written the manual *par excellence* for the theologian, a text that will always be of use in order to purely and simply become a theologian, just as one goes to school in order to become an architect.

The full meaning of the debate opened here by this brief introduction[1] comes to light as soon as one considers the fact that it is concerned with the rigorously scientific character of theology, with the the bonds of formal causality that unite the principles of faith to the most minute of theological conclusions. We remain outside the domain of theology if we refuse to enter its process of drawing rational connections. Without this, one can have impressionism or semtimentality, but not science.

All the same, we cannot renounce this characterization of theology as a science on the pretext that our contemporaries have more or less monopolized science in the physio-chemical order, where man's intellect, despite everything, dominates its object from on high. Still, a theologian could draw wonderful lessons from scientists as regards their respect for their object, their modesty, their humility, as well as their gratitude towards the researchers who came before them and towards their masters. The theologian's respect for his object is his personal devotion to God. However, in the end, this is not something subject to verification. Indeed, we have no example of a theologian being struck down by God for an inconsistent conclusion. However, from ancient Icarus to modern test pilots, matter quickly takes its revenge on a wrong calculation.

It is the honor and burden of the mind that it be sensitive to error. Theology has neither laboratories nor test fields in which to give wing to its theories. However, there is free discussion. And who does not see that without this free discussion and dialogue, the *de iure* impunity of the theologian who is mistaken would be but a scientific fraud? Or would we instead need to appeal immedidaly, each time, to the Magisterium, asking her to settle the debate by way of authority, which in the end would again be a mere cop-out? A theologian's honesty is measured by the intellectual effort he expends, illuminated by faith, and by the stubborn rigor of his reasoning. All the rest is [mere] literature.

That being said, theology does not depend on St. Thomas's authority, just as the law of gravity does not depend on Newton who discovered it. If someone were a Thomist only as a matter of [ecclesiastical] discipline, we could say that he misunderstands what Thomism is. Our dedication to St. Thomas is subject to a more exacting law, the law of logical necessity. Indeed, it is exasperating to continually hear the repeated remark that the Church did not canonize Aristotelianism when she canonized Saint Thomas. Neither did she canonize the syllogism. However, when someone chooses to cast the syllogism into the sawmill, he is nothing more than a witless fool, for the syllogism is the natural form of reasoning in its exercise of understanding.

---

1 [Tr. note: That is, to the *Dialogue théologique* volume.]

Theology is not Revelation. It illuminates Revelation, systematizes its data, extends its consequences, and puts it in contact with all that is of interest to the mind. Theology is—or, at least, should be—the permanent and universal presence of Revelation in culture. Revelation was given once and for all and now has come to a close. However, it is characteristic of the things of the mind that they be forever active. Likewise, the conditions in which this supernatural Revelation was made will never change. It is forever true that the supreme good for everyone who comes into the world is found in knowing, loving, and serving God, thus meriting eternal happiness. It is forever true that the intimate knowledge of God exceeds the natural powers of the human intellect and that we stand in need of Revelation, on the one hand, and the gift of faith, on the other. However, it is forever true that most men are hindered in the pursuit of divine truth either because of their inability to undertake metaphysical reflection, the concerns involved in day-to-day life, or because of their mental laziness. It is also forever true that human passions in general stand in conflict with the divine truth. And it is increasingly true that our contemporaries do not have the time to be concerned with God. Hence, Revelation brings an appreciable benefit to mankind, and there is an immense need that there be a theology continuously connecting man and divine Revelation, through a teaching that respects the latter while accommodating itself to the former.

There is only one Revelation, and as long as theology is to be scientific and rationally legitimate, there can be only one theology. Nothing can bewilder it, so long as it remains divine Revelation itself exercising all of its virtualities and intellectual fecundity and, consequently, in all the details of taking up a position. In the debate that follows, there will be discussion, for example, concerning two contemporary philosophies, existentialism and Marxism. We find in an article from fifteen years ago several pertinent lines written by a thinker who has always been held to be extremely faithful to the spirit and letter of St. Thomas:

> To the question, "Why do the necessities of laws, the objects of science, not extend to each of the particular events which unfold here-below," we must answer: The world of existence in act and in concrete reality is not the world of mere intelligible necessities. Essences or natures are indeed in existent reality, from which they (or their substitutes) are drawn forth by our mind; however, they do not exist there in a pure state. Every existent thing has its nature or its essence. However, the existential position of things is not implied in their nature, and they undergo mutual encounters which themselves are not natures and are not required by anything inscribed, in advance, within any nature. Existent reality is thus composed of *nature* and *adventure*, and this is why it has a direction in time and constitutes, by its duration, a *history*

(which is irreversible). History must have these two elements. A world of pure natures would not budge in time. Platonic forms have no history. No more would a world of pure change have an orienation. There is no history for thermodynamic equilibrium. (Jaques Maritain, *Philosophie et science expériementale*).[2]

We think that the theology of St. Thomas is the most perfect theology of adventure and, simultaneously, of natures and essences, thereby having a just and complete sense of history. While it has become conventional to point out how Marxism cannot overcome the difficulty involved in the fact that history is made by man while the latter is himself simultaneously the product of history, in point of fact, man's nature is above history. It gives him direction, just as it defines his existence.

And to continue in line with our present subject, theology also can and must have its adventures. It has its own history precisely because it has a complex but rigorously defined essence which ranks it as being the supreme degree of human scientific knowledge. Only strong natures undertake great adventures, and from this perspective, we can foresee wonderful developments in St. Thomas's teaching, provided that our Good God gives the next generation of Thomists an intellectual constitution which is as strong as their theology.

"Man does not live on bread alone, but on the word of God." The horrendous famine that ravages part of Europe today gives a tragic sense to these words of Christ and, perhaps, makes this debate seem absurd. Newspapers tell us that while granaries in America are full of enough wheat to feed entire nations, thousands of children are starving in Romania. The problem is not only that of transport but also that of human malice and stupidity. When one believes the truth of salvation extended to all contained in the Word of God, and when one knows that theology has the formidable and permanent duty of irrigating the whole of human culture and indeed all human cultures, of assimilating and making available to intellects that starve for their own good, namely, the truth of salvation, and when one knows, through faith in what the Popes teach, as well as on the basis of one's own study, that St. Thomas is precisely the master who most properly enlivens man's intellectual nature and nourishes it with the milk and honey of revealed truth, then there is no pride involved in calling oneself a theologian nor insolence in calling oneself a Thomist. Rather, one should experience heart-rending shame and distress upon seeing how little has been done, as well as everything that remains to be done in order that theology might take up the

---

2 [Tr. note: This can be found in Jacques Maritain, *The Degrees of Knowledge*, trans. Gerald B. Phelan et al. (Notre Dame, IN: University of Notre Dame Press, 1995), 29. The translation above is our own, from Fr. Bruckberger's text.]

position that is rightfully hers in the intelletual world, that of being the supreme wisdom which nourishes man, the supreme and maternal wisdom which brings support to the starvation which men experience for the truth, a starvation which kills souls as little children die on the frozen plains.

Thus, let nobody see arrogance here in the debate which we are introducing. Though limited by personal circumstances, it is important, for it calls into question the scientific nature of theology and, thereby, its power both of continuity and of assimilation. This debate can at times resemble a dialogue between the deaf. However, neither of its parties are deaf, and perhaps the great excuse for our quarrels lies in the fact that each of our sides is attentive, with all of our strength, to the distress calls sounding forth from a humanity who is worn out as much from lies as it is from hardships and sorrows.

If at that age when great vocations and ardent fidelities emerge some ardent youths meditate on these pages and receive from them some taste and ambition for the task of theology, this exhausting labor in service to the divine truth, both will be well rewarded. For in an age of horrible famines—both material and spiritual—the words of the Gospel resound with an ominous tone: "The harvest is plenty, but the laborers few."

3
Theology and Its Sources
Michel-Marie Labourdette, OP

Among[a] the many works that encourage Christian thought to return to its sources and increase its historical consciousness, few have been more interesting or more promising than the collection *Sources Chrétiennes*, under the direction of Henri de Lubac and Jean Daniélou. Ten volumes in this series have already been published, presenting translations of works that are particularly representative of the Greek tradition, accompanied by careful, extensive introductions and suggestive annotations. On its own, this first set of texts constitutes a quite wonderful achievement. Although publishing difficulties have prevented them from providing accompanying original texts, they have promised to provide us with these as soon as possible. May this indispensable compliment not be too long in coming![1]

(a) This piece occupied a modest place in the *Revue thomiste*. Offprints of it, followed by a piece written by Marie-Joseph Nicolas concerning the theology of the Church, were made, as we have done for other articles and critical reviews that are a somewhat long in the *Revue*, with the usual number of such offprints being twenty-five, with twenty going to the author and five to the editor of the *Revue*. Because there were two authors, fifty offprints were made, and we sent them to some interested parties and friends. However, their distribution did not exceed thirty-five copies. Our opponents call this a "call to arms" [*brochure de combat*] disseminated in "an unusual way." See "La Théologie et ses sources, Réponse," in *Dialogue théologique* (Saint-Maximin: Les Arcades, 1947), 94 (hereafter cited as "Résponse"). It is true that this offprint was published before the issue of the *Revue* to which it belonged and, in particular, before this booklet was distributed in France. The Reverend Fathers are not obliged to know that my preceding article ("La Théologie, intelligence de la Foi"), which attacked no one, was published in the same conditions and even more urgency [*précocité*]. Here again, I pushed the publication forward because I wanted to let Fr. Daniélou know as soon as possible that his article in *Études*, which every day sounds forth new echoes, has been noted by those for whom he manifested such apparent disdain. (1947)

1 *Sources Chrétiennes*, Editions du Cerf, Paris. Up to today, we have received ten volumes:

Gregory of Nyssa, *Contemplation sur la vie de Moïse*, intr. and trans. Jean Daniélou, S.J.
Clement of Alexandria, *Protreptique*, intr. and trans., Claude Mondesert, S.J.
Athenagoras, *Supplique au sujet des chrétiens*, intr. and trans. Gustave Bardy
Nicolas Cabasilas, *Explication de la divine liturgie*, intr. and trans. Severien Salaville, A.A.

A recent notice gives us hope that significant developments, if realized, will make this magnificent enterprise a unique work which cannot be praised highly enough. The collection will also present works from the Christian West, as well as certain non-Christian works considered as being "sources" on account of their importance for theological development and reflection. Our current discussion here covers only the first ten volumes, and it is possible that the wider scope promised to us through an expanded team of collaborators on this project will amend these characteristics and, by helping to balance it out, enrich the spirit and identity of the project which has already been so clearly established, above all in those works which have the very directors of the collection as their authors.

Although this enterprise is reminiscent of the collection of classical studies undertaken by Guillaume Budé, it differs from the latter in two ways. First and of lesser importance, many of the works are not, precisely speaking, critical editions but, instead, carefully curated working texts. Although we greatly desire full scientific rigor, we will not reproach the directors for this state of affairs. Rather, we are grateful that they did not feel obliged to wait for the outcome of lengthy scientific labors in order to place in our hands such precious texts, which are based on substantially guaranteed contemporary editions. Second, the collection is clearly oriented by a common spirit and intention aiming to directly support certain theological positions, and this aim animates several introductions and commentaries. This spirit, as well as the theological positions that we will discuss in this article, express something quite different than a merely historical concern with presenting ancient authors to the reading public.[2(b)]

Diadochos of Photiki, *Cent chapitres sur la perfection spirituelle*, intr. and trans. Édouard des Places, S.J.
Gregory of Nyssa, *La création de l'homme*, intr. and trans. Jean Laplace, S.J., notes by Jean Daniélou, S.J.
Origen, *Homélies sur la Genèse*, intr. Henri de Lubac, S.J., trans. Louis Doutreleau, S.J.
Niketas Stethatos, *Le paradis spiritual*, text, trans, and comm. Marie Chalendard
Maximus the Confessor, *Centuries sur la charité*, intr. and trans. Joseph Pégon, S.J.
Ignatius of Antioch, *Lettres*, text, intr, trans, and notes by Thomas Camelot, O.P.

2 Fr. Daniélou characterizes the intention of the collection very well by contrasting it to the one which was formerly directed by Hemmer and Lejay: "For the earlier series, the primary goal was to publish historical documents, witnesses to the faith of the ancients. The new series holds that we can ask even more of the Fathers. They are not merely true witnesses to a past state of affairs; they are also the most up-to-date nourishment for contemporary men, because here we find precisely a number of *categories that are the categories of contemporary thought, categories which scholastic theology had lost*" [emphasis Labourdette's]. "Les orientations présentes de la pensée religieuse," *Études* 249 (April 1946): 10. This intention, strongly illustrated in Daniélou's introduction to the

Other journals have discussed (or will do so) the technical qualities or defects of these translations. They will recognize the critical value of the edited texts, as well as the historical truth of their introductions and commentaries. Although we are not uninterested in this, we would like to stress the great riches offered to speculative theology by these texts, many of which are venerable and the product of human reflection on the truths of the faith. Although we shall examine several of them later on, our primary concern will be with the overall plan of the project rather than with the details of its particular volumes. This will enable us to tackle some more general problems which we think are more pressing for contemporary theology.

Indeed, our discussion should not separate the collection *Sources Chrétienne* from the recent *Théologie* collection (Éditions Montaigne) directed by the Jesuits of Fourvière. Frs. de Lubac and Daniélou are so profoundly engaged in this project that here too they seem to be its organizers.[3(c)] There

---

first volume, happily, does not appear in several others which have striven solely after the greatest exactitude and remain models of honest work which are not directed or underpinned by any ulterior motive.

(b) I highlight the character of *Sources Chrétiennes* because it is interesting, not because it scandalizes me. My sole critique is that its aim (in itself excellent) to provide texts written by ancient authors is not unalloyed but, rather, is inflected by an apologetic concern of adaptation to contemporary tastes, toward the choice of the best works for manifesting the contemporary insufficiency of scholastic theology. What I have called the "ulterior motive" of the collection was, in fact, declared by Fr. Daniélou in a way that we are entitled to called "authoritative" given that he, with Fr. de Lubac, is the *director* of the collection *Sources Chrétiennes*. Let the reader take note of each of the precise criticisms leveled against me: he will note the same deformation. (1947)

3 The collection *Théologie* (Editions Montaigne, Paris) currently contains eight volumes:

Henri Bouillard, *Conversion et grâce in St. Thomas Aquinas. Étude historique*.
Jean Daniélou, *Platonisme et Théologie mystique. Essai sur la doctrine spirituelle de saint Grégoire de Nysse*.
Henri de Lubac, *Corpus mysticum. L'Eucharistie et l'église au moyen-age*.
Claude Montdésert, *Clément d'Alexandrie. Introduction à sa pensée religieuse à partir de l'écriture*.
Gaston Fessard, *Autorité et bien commun*.
Jean Mouroux, *Sens chrétien de l'homme*.
Maurice Pontet, *L'exégèse de saint Augustin, prédicateur*.
Henri de Lubac, *Surnaturel. Études historique*.

(c) The response article protests: "Thus, in order to understand the hidden meaning of innocent translations of the Fathers, they should be interpreted on the basis of a collection of theological studies" ("Réponse," 78). I respond to this as follows. 1. In order to understand the "hidden meaning" of the collections *Sources Chrétiennes*, I have no need of another collection, for the express declaration of its director suffices (see previous note). 2. Merely from the list of published volumes, any reader can see how far the shared society of authors and subjects between these two collections goes: Fr. Daniélou, who

are parallels between the two collections, which share a common spirit, and although we feel that we must register some grave reservations concerning them, they manifest a positive and constructive design which is more important than the defects which tarnish their aim. It presents a theology which is more conscious, at once, of its rich sources, the diversity of its historical expressions, the conditions of its historical development, and the most pressing and contemporary of human realities. Let us state up front our full agreement and complete sympathy with these aims.(d)

* * * * *

What is most striking to us when we read these ancient texts (which, in the collection *Sources Chrétiennes*, stand out all the better by being highlighted by the translator's annotations) is the fact that most of our problems are found in said annotations. However, these problems are caught up at a point where nothing yet has been fixed in too literal a formulation. It is almost run-of-the-mill to note—and this is easily confirmed—that on many points the problematics involved in our theology have become [overly] academic. I mean, it is something learned and often remains bookish in character. Such theology indeed lends itself to reflection and real solutions, but nonetheless, it lacks a kind of dynamism. It is freighted, too hastily presuming itself to be completed and perfected. Only with difficulty does it escape the temptation to indolence and ease, merely resting on its past achievements. And, in my opinion, this observation applies beyond the teaching coming from the historical *scholae* in Catholic theology [*l'enseignement des Ecoles*]. There is a certain way, indeed one that is authentic and solid, of posing theological problems—even with reference to scriptural sources or concerns with contemporary life—which ultimately does not extricate itself from the received problematics, precisely because the questions themselves are formulated in accord with traditional categories, which have not been handled in such a way as to fully restore the value of intuition [into the very problem

---

in *Sources Chrétiennes* presented a volume of Saint Gregory of Nyssa and annotated a second of the same Doctor, published in the *Théologie* collection a lengthy work on the same Father. Fr. Mondésert, who translated the first *Protreptic* of Clement of Alexandria, published in the second a study on Clement. Fr. de Lubac, who in *Sources Chrétiennes* pled for the symbolic exegesis of Origen, published in *Théologie* a volume (*Corpus Mysticum*) wherein he highlighted indulgently [*avec complaisance*] the impoverishment involved for theological reflection by the way that the symbolic methodology of the Fathers was replaced by that of "dialectic" and "*ratio*" (by which scholastic theology was constituted). And, moreover, the close connection between the two collections was made by Fr. Daniélou himself in *Études* ("Les orientations présentes," 10). (1947)

(d) We ask that this declaration be read as bearing witness quite openly to something more than a mere empty formula. No, it represents the exact expression of our thought. (1947)

at hand]. Anyone who has had to teach theology will have had ample opportunity to experience this mental laziness, more the friend of formulas than of apprehension, more eager to rest on what has been achieved than to seek the first apperceptions of such truths so that one might then trace out anew the whole subsequent course of thought, doing so in a wholly personal way.

This is why it is so excellent a practice, solely from the perspective of speculative theology, to experience a set of problems which are quite different from those with which we are accustomed. For Latin theology, this is the case with the most important works of the Greek tradition. No doubt, the editors of this invaluable collection intend to "shock" those who read the volumes, and we thank them for having so quickly offered us so rich an assortment of readings for our meditation. We do not think that the theological wisdom of St. Thomas will be shattered by this shock[4] or that, confronted with other types of genuinely Christian reflection, it will be dispossessed of its place in the Church. If this comparison is indeed made, we do not believe that it must lead one to profess that all human expressions of divine truths are, by their very essence, relative in nature, implying that for every human expression of that which is divine (except, without a doubt, the formulas of faith) one would need to seek out a truth that expresses the ineffable realities of man's experiences, not one that is found in conformity with what actually exists in God or in supernaturalized man.

Truth be told, this poses before us the entire problem of theology and its claim to be constituted as a form of knowledge *properly so called*. In another article, we have discussed how we believe that this problem must be resolved.[5] One of the most significant challenges to this resolution is found more in the contemporary "mentality" than in explicitly formulated theories. By this very way of posing the problem, we thus go beyond the expressions that can be found in the books that furnish us with the occasion for taking up this discussion. Let it be understood, however, that our precise goal is to illuminate, by way of opposition, these various solutions which we will be striving to bring to their most explicit formulation; however, we do not attribute to anyone, precisely in the form in which we will present it, the theory that we here are opposing. And even though a number of its tendencies seem to us to converge toward this end—so much so that, instead of remaining an ideal solution, it receives from it an "overall truth"—we would believe ourselves to be placing tendencies on trial were we to attribute this end to

---

[4] For many, it is a settled matter, and Maurice de Gandillac in the 3rd issue of *Dieu vivant* definitively endorses the death of Neo-thomism, in fact, doing so by relying on the verdict delivered by Fr. Hans Urs von Balthasar. It would be futile to plead against his judgment. Just as movement is proven by walking, life must be manifested by its fruits, and to put it mildly, we would indeed be half-dead [*agonisants*] if we did not accept the challenge.

[5] See Michel Labourdette, "Theology: Faith Seeking Understanding," in this volume.

someone in the absence of texts which formally declare on the matter or on the basis of a group of lines taken out of context.[6(e)]

* * * * *

However, before registering any words of criticism, we would like to note the great achievement that we ourselves see in Jean Mouroux's book, *The Meaning of Man*, the sixth volume in the *Théologie* collection. Our intention is not to exclude this beautiful text from what we called the "spirit" of this collection, and it would not be overly difficult to show how it fits into it, indeed corresponding to its best ambitions. However, it seems to us that it quite precisely represents what is excellent in this spirit, without manifesting the questionable aspects found in certain other works animated by this same spirit.[(f)]

Mouroux's intention was to write neither a scholarly book nor a theological exposition whose technical character would have made it difficult for the uninitiated. He remarks, "This book's only desire is to be a testimony." However, do not let this modesty deceive us. It is true that Mouroux's approach does not limit itself to the level of scientific analysis but rather, functions as, in his own words, "a lengthy theological reflection." Nonetheless, this reflection is nourished and filled throughout by the living sources of Christian thought, especially the Word of God and, above all, St. Paul. His command of these matters would have been impossible without meticulous study, giving him long familiarity with the matters he discusses.

An analysis of this book would be materially easy; it is clear and progresses along distinctly established lines. For as nuanced as they are, the author's views are neither vague nor concealed. However, an analysis would ultimately fail to capture both the richness of what he develops, as well as

---

6 This article is concerned with the collection *Sources Chrétiennes* and *Théologie* as wholes. (We will return later to the most characteristic volumes in this series.) Now, this generality might itself lead one to believe that throughout our remarks we are questioning, in all these pages, the personal thought of Frs. de Lubac and Daniélou, who direct the first series and are the most representative collaborators in the second. However, this is not our aim, or at least when it is, we will make this clear. Frs. de Lubac and Daniélou know quite well what they intend to say and do not stand in need of interpreters. If, however, it seems to them that, while going beyond their thought, we nonetheless take aim at them again, we will always be quite happy to receive their corrections and adjustments. This could provide an opportunity to prevent their readers from falling into certain misunderstandings, some of which are dangerous.

(e) I explain later on, at the end of my *Reply*, the meaning of this point, which is not at all what has been attributed to me. (1947)

(f) I did not praise the intentions [*propos*] of the *Théologie* collection only in the abstract. It represents one of its excellent accomplishments. And I contrasted nothing that I praised in Mouroux's text with the aims of the collection. To the contrary, I said that it corresponded to these aims. (1947)

what seems most novel and indeed deserving of praise in his work, namely, his method, along with a concentrated fervor bearing witness to the lengthy, meditative maturation of his thought, as well as to the profound generosity of his Christian spirit. Nonetheless, let us provide a broad outlines of the text.

The work, dedicated to the subject of man, is divided into three unequal parts: first, *temporal values* (ch. 1, The Temporal; ch. 2, The Universe); then, in three chapters, *bodily values* (ch. 3, The Grandeur of the Body; ch. 4, The Misery of the Body; ch. 5, The Redemption of the Body); and finally, at greater length, *spiritual values* (ch. 6, The Human Person; ch. 7, Spiritual Freedom; ch. 8, Christian Freedom; ch. 9, Love; ch. 10, Charity). Despite its appearances, this last part seems to be the most novel—not on account of its subject, for it is concerned with eternal problems, but rather, because of its synthetic method, joining together speculative reflection and history, the most traditional teachings and the most cherished insights drawn from contemporary thought. A conclusion, whose proper subject is without a doubt too quickly touched upon, presents man as a *sacred being*.

Mouroux does not misuse his notes and references, though a number of them are quite useful and subtly testify to an erudition which does not weigh down and limit his own thought, and the reader of his volume will draw great benefit from internalizing this erudition in his own turn. Indeed, the author unites deep knowledge of the documents of the Christian tradition (Patristic literature, liturgy, and conciliar teachings) to contemporary currents of thought [*information nouvelle*]. The various problems that he poses are addressed from within the framework whence most of our contemporaries draw the most common data of the modern sciences, philosophy, and literature. We do not get a sense that Mouroux is a specialist—clearly his specialty is theological reflection—but we appreciate this openness to such cultural currents, something which has genuine worth, and he does not rush to the first mirage of novelty so that he can then proclaim his agreement. Rather, he is concerned not to lose any positive acquisition, while at the same time taking care not to connect the presentation of eternal truth to forms of expression that come from an outdated culture which, instead of opening the way to understanding, only serve to set up obstacles to the contemporary mind. Even more than in the first chapters (which seem to be the most recently written ones, though to our eyes, the least profound in the volume, even though they are full of very interesting suggestions), we believe that this work contains commendable studies on the individual, freedom, and love.

All of this presents a theology at once of great beauty and full of life, and if its author expresses such depth in so effortless a manner, we have no doubt that this is due to his mastery of speculative theology. He handles it with an utterly correct sense of things and with constant exactitude. Whether discussing the union of soul and body, the person considered in his subsistence or in his openness to God, the historical situation of man between the first and second Adam, original sin and the forces left to fallen nature, natural love of God and the love of charity, or the problem of selfless love, Mouroux's mastery is undeniable. We do not say that we accept all his assertions. This would, in any case, represent thin praise. The theological reflection presented here is too personal for the author not to present original insights which call for further examination, and we will not fail to thank him even when it seems that a different solution must be sought out. However, what we appreciate most is the fact that when he innovates—or at least, when he sheds greater light on some aspect of a topic which normally receives less emphasis [by others], ultimately founded on theological themes which are at once wholly classical and nonetheless profoundly assimilated—he nonetheless is always judicious, fully aware of what he is doing, conscious of the positions that he is abandoning, and forever serious in weighing out what is at stake in them. For example, many theologians will perhaps not be comfortable with his treatment of original sin and the state of fallen nature.[7] However, we do not think that anyone could blame him either for disregarding or failing to carefully consider certain aspects of the problem. This gives his work a solidity which, in such a text, could have been inflected toward much simpler arguments, given the work's apologetic aims (by which I mean that its obvious end is to find a reading among minds which have been penetrated by the spirit of modern culture). Mouroux provides us with a proof that Christian thought can enter contemporary discussions without the spirit of resignation, shame for her past, as well as without a sense of superiority, and, in all frankness and loyalty, awareness that she has much to learn, for she remains forever young. He shows us that theological thought can remain wholly precise and retain the richness of its traditional acquisitions by seeking to formulate this thought in a new manner. We will forever be grateful to the *Théologie* collection for presenting us with works of this caliber.

* * * * *

Moreover, nothing that it presents to us is without value, as we will have the occasion to say, at least in future reviews. However, we regret to see that, in several of these volumes, the emphasis upon the riches of the patristic tradition, along with the editors' efforts to find more contemporary formulations [for the theological matters at hand], is accompanied by an obvious depreciation of scholastic theology.[(g)] Far from opposing the latter either to the

---

[7] We do not feel such concerns, however, for the author seems to maintain quite correctly the equilibrium (which is, in fact, somewhat "paradoxical") between the opposed exaggerations of Jansenism and of naturalistic humanism.

[(g)] I am made to say: "But, let one not claim today still to search in these remote times for some directly-assimilable intellectual nourishment. In so doing, one would manifest

breadth of tradition or to attempts at a renewed presentation (as though this could only be a dangerous undertaking for it), for our own part, we believe that scholastic theology, precisely in the form given to it by St. Thomas, represents the truly *scientific* state of Christian thought. This implies no disdain for what came before it, a patrimony which can never be valued too highly, and surely the Thomistic synthesis will be the first to benefit from it. This does not imply, moreover, that the teachings of St. Thomas must be simply repeated word for word. It is all-too-true that it would thus remain inaccessible to many, and we would deprive ourselves of the wonderful and genuine progress resulting from later Christian (and non-Christian) thinkers.[8(h)(i)]

'an evident devaluing' of the work that followed them" ("Réponse," 84). What has not been cited from me? In short, the text where we lament the fact that, quite unnecessarily, this devaluing *accompanies* the highlighting of patristic riches (and certainly, with the goal of nourishing us upon them, with making us directly assimilate them). We are made to say that the mere showcasing of the Fathers constitutes a devaluing of scholasticism. (1947)

8 The question concerning the progress of theology and its adaptation to new data arises, therefore, in our opinion, in a completely different manner than the way Fr. Daniélou states: "To these two abysses, historicity and subjectivity, we must add something shared by Marxism and existentialism: their clear perception of our coexistence, the way each of our lives causes reverberations in the lives of others. Therefore, these two abysses require theological thought to broaden itself. *Indeed, these categories are quite obviously foreign to scholastic theology*. Its world is the *immobile world of Greek thought*, where its mission was to incarnate the Christian message. This conception retains a lasting and ever-valuable truth, *at the very least* because it consists in affirming that the decision of human freedom and its transformation of life's conditions do not represent an absolute beginning; man's freedom is not a form of self-creation, but rather, a response to a vocation from God, which is expressed by the world of essences. However, scholastic theology *makes no room for history*. And, on the other hand, by placing reality in essences more than in subjects, it neglects the dramatic world of persons—concrete universals that transcend every essence and are distinguished only by their existence, that is, no longer according to the intelligible and intellection, but rather, according to value and love, or hate." Daniélou, "Les orientations présentes," 14, emphasis Labourdette's.

Scholasticism does not stand before modern thought as a closed system built upon "categories" which are irredeemably closed off from assimilating any new data. Its permanence is not that of a completed construction that has seen its day and whose scope, consequently, would remain limited strictly to problems historically considered, to solutions already given and to formulations that remain forever fixed. On the contrary, we believe that it is a perfectly living way of thinking, one that is both ambitious and capable of entering into and understanding new problems, able to assimilate everything contained in the most modern of doctrines. However, it has too much respect for the truth and is too concerned with its scientific rigor and with avoiding facile conformism for it to adorn itself immediately with ideas and "categories" that it would not have first carefully examined and critiqued. Without a doubt, this was the restoration that Leo XIII wanted, and if it did not meet his hopes, this is doubtlessly because such a restoration would have needed to find more numerous and better laborers, not because scholastic theology is a mode of thought that is henceforth *exhausted*. (See note *i* as well.)

Nonetheless, it remains the case that these forms of progress, on pain of ruining their own foundations, presuppose the previously-existing edifice, building upon it, neither destroying nor replacing it. They represent expansions of a synthesis, not a total recovery seeking to build a new "representation" of the world according to the categories of modernity, judging everything that

Daniélou is free to devote himself to "dramatic" theology, which is quite legitimate for the specific aim, not of developing the divine message on the level of speculative truth, but rather that of making certain concrete data of the situation of the Christian in this world "sensible to the heart." We will applaud his success. Moreover, no less than he, do we desire the development of historical theology and, just as much as he does, desire that speculative theology appropriate for itself a sense of history. Far from believing it to be incapable of doing this, we think that marvelous developments are possible in this venture, because it has, in this respect, virtualities that many do not seem to suspect. It is also equally clear that theology must draw closer to culture and indeed remain in contact with various cultures, anxious to learn everything that they reveal concerning man, his historical situation, and his existential dimensions. But theology must not lose its primordial concern with remaining the rigorous scientific expression of Christian thought concerned with focusing on the truths of the faith. This is what St. Thomas calls us to, both by his example and by his doctrine. The enlargement desired by Daniélou—according to his own expressions—would ultimately end in an infinitely deplorable loss: the loss of that achievement in which we find our most precious intellectual treasure and the reduction of scholastic thought to the state of being nothing more than a historical witness to a bygone era (no doubt, a permanent witness, though akin to a statue in a museum). Thomism also claims to be alive, no less than do existentialism, Marxism, or the evolutionism of Fr. Teilhard de Chardin.

(h) Here again our thought is skillfully deformed: "Fr. Labourdette professes to have 'no disdain,' he assures us, for the first twelve centuries of Christian thought." Let us note already that the ridiculousness of this phrase comes entirely from the adjustment made to an assertion which here only has two words cited from it. We said: "*this* (i.e., the affirmation of the scientific character of scholastic theology) does not imply any disdain for what preceded it (i.e., a still-prescientific theology)." The response article continues: "However, he hardly seems to appreciate them, except only insofar as the Thomist synthesis has drained them of their substance. Since this synthesis represents the 'truly *scientific* state of Christian thought,' why linger in its pre-scientific state?" See "*Réponse*," 84. We do not deny the dialectical procedure consisting in undertaking a *reductio ad absurdum* on the basis of our propositions. Still, one should not have the appearance of charging us with having said it ourselves and, instead, should show that absurdity follows from what we had truly written. Now, what we wrote was: "[it] can never be valued too highly, and surely the Thomistic synthesis will be the first to benefit from it." This is precisely the opposite [of what is imputed to our words], for it is clear that the benefit will consist in integrating new elements that the synthesis has not yet absorbed, and I believe this is in fact the case for many texts from the Greek tradition. (1947)

(i) We are reproached for claiming that Daniélou said that scholastic philosophy is a mode of thought that is now *exhausted*, but did he not say that it is foreign to contemporary categories of thought? How can it continue to bear fruit in a world that is no longer "the immobile world of Greek thought, where its mission was to incarnate the Christian message?" (1947)

has preceded it as being irredeemably outmoded. Yes, there are many things that have become outmoded, but what we cannot admit is that form of aging which, in fact, reaches down more deeply than the level of mere formulations: the idea that the entire worldview characteristic of a certain cultural milieu could also reach down into the very truths of theology. What we cannot admit is that theological wisdom would be swept away by the flood of impermanence⁽ʲ⁾ and that its acquisitions could not be held as being definitive. Now, this does not mean that they are closed and no longer subject to further refinement but, rather, implies that they are capable of progressively assimilating new insights and reflections. I know quite well that this conception poses problems, indeed, more than we can address in this simple article. We will have the opportunity to return to it, especially to the splendid efforts of missionary theology. However, is careful enough attention given to the fact that the greatest difficulties hold true just as much against dogmatic formulations themselves as they do against the idea of theological *knowledge*, which, yes, is incomplete and forever perfectible, but nonetheless has its own kind of stability as well: indeed, certitude in its central teachings, possessing an indefectible truth, and in a good number of other positions, a knowledge which it affirms with increasing probability?

* * * * *

Contemporary thought experiences the permanent temptation to judge all systems of intellectual expression first and, indeed, ultimately, in terms of the historical context and experiences of its author and the era in which he lived, not essentially in terms of their conformity with the reality of what is. (For it is asked: how can we reach it?) It is said that the mystery of subjectivity is of greater interest to it than is impersonal truth. What is above all looked for in a given work is its meaning and the scope of its "witness," its sincerity and depth of *experience,* along with the vibrating energy with which it remains charged. Hence, its logical coherence, along with the properly intellectual (or so-called "conceptual") meaning of the analyses or syntheses it presents, seems to be secondary. No longer will we need to speak of our concepts being analogical in character but, instead, will find that we must say

---

(j) Astonishment is expressed at the fact that we felt the need to reject the claim that wisdom would be carried away by the flood of impermanence: "Nothing warrants anyone of suspecting that we desire this, and none of our texts are quoted supporting this claim" ("*Réponse,*" 76). I did, however, quote texts from Fr. Bouillard, among others, that bear clear witness to this: "When the mind evolves, an immutable truth is maintained only thanks to the simultaneous and correlative evolution of *all* the concepts, in which the same relationship is maintained. A theology that would not be contemporary would be a false theology" (cited on 150–51 below). This is a remarkable claim [*idée*] concerning the permanence of theological assertions, namely, that *all* their notions are perpetually recast, to the point that their content in one given era will be regarded as false in a later one. (1947)

that they are symbolic, judging them in terms of how they express the "living" reality in man—expressions which, as soon as they take on their logical signification, appear so impoverished, desiccated, and reified in comparison with the experience from which they flow forth, like what one might perhaps call waste-products rather than fruits. How can life be enclosed within concepts? Above all, how can we enclose within them this kind of life which exists in a relationship with God, culminating in the obscure awareness of a mysterious contact which we claim is grounded upon a true experience? Beyond the truth that is transmitted by clear teaching, does there not exist one that is more precious, namely, the truth testified to by spiritual experience? And must we not turn our attention this way, if we are to discover the meaning of great intellectual works, at least those whose object is knowledge of man and of God?[9]

It seems to me that two kinds of habits of the modern mind provide this temptation with a unique source of power. One is born of training in the historical disciplines, something which is of infinite value. We need not emphasize the fact that we believe that the progress undergone in the latter represents an invaluable gain for human knowledge.[10(k)] Thanks to such studies, we have

---

[9] Speaking of the demands that one finds in "contemporary theology," Daniélou writes in the article already cited: "it must treat of God as God, *not as an object* but as the Subject par excellence who manifests Himself whenever and however He wishes and, consequently, must above all be permeated with the spirit of religion" ("Les orientations présentes," 7, emphasis Labourdette's). We are quite fine with the fact that Fr. Daniélou speaks using a different vocabulary than our own, though we still lament the fact he so clearly is anxious to enter into the vocabulary of contemporary philosophy without ourselves benefitting from the same effort at [intellectual] sympathy. However, does he not know that the notion of *object*, in theological language, excludes neither the "spirit of religion," nor, as he says later on, "the sense of mystery," ("Les orientations présentes," 16), and that to say that our intellect has as its *objects* the very *mysteries* of faith is not only an expression of this "rationalized theology," namely, "neo-Thomism," but, indeed, is an expression consecrated by the solemn teaching of the [First] Vatican Council in statements which certainly have neither the intent nor the result of emptying the mystery of its meaning, even if they do not refer to Kierkegaard's categories: "The perpetual common belief of the Catholic Church has held and holds also this: there is a twofold order of knowledge, distinct not only in its principle but also in its object; in its principle, because in the one we know by natural reason, in the other by divine faith; in its object, because apart from what natural reason can attain, there are proposed to our belief mysteries that are hidden in God that can never be known unless they are revealed by God" (Vatican I, *Dei filius*, ch. 4; Denzinger, no. 1795 [3015]).

[10] We are far from agreeing with the judgment of Fr. Daniélou: "The notion of history is foreign to Thomism" ("Les orientations présentes," 10). If one wishes to speak of the use of critical methods, we will admit that the historical preoccupation, properly so-called, was not awakened in modern thought until well after St. Thomas. We do not think that the idea of *evolution*, for example, is in itself foreign to a Thomistic outlook concerning the world and its becoming, which command St. Thomas's philosophy and theology. It

become increasingly aware of an authentic "dimension" of man and of human things. There is nothing human—and certainly not even the most impersonal ideas or sciences—which fails to bear the mark of this spatio-temporal engagement and which, consequently, fails to be infinitely better known when its essential structure has been penetrated by tracing out its progress—a genesis that so often is slow and groping, a successive formation taking shape through the most unexpected of detours. Fr. [Marie-Joseph] Lagrange liked to recall the words of Aristotle: "the best means for understanding is to consider things in their origin and follow their development."[11] That is why we whole-heartedly applaud the historical accuracy of the collections under discussion here, and we congratulate their authors for the substantial contribution which they have made through their work, indeed placing us in their debt. We will mention once again the high opinion we have for such fine studies as those, for example, written by Fr. Daniélou[12] and Fr. von Balthasar[13] on Gregory of Nyssa, along with the questions that they raise for our reflection.

Nonetheless, historical methodology is one thing, and the philosophy with which it is often unwittingly weighed down, constituting a pseudo-

---

is true, however, that this idea, as it has become familiar to us (much more often as a myth than as a precise notion), stands outside St. Thomas's own personal perspectives. However, if one understands the term "history" as referring to the sense for events which occur, the meaning of that which is a *de facto* economy, one need only skim through the *Summa* with a superficial glance in order to see clearly how history, and with it the whole historical development of humanity, fits into it in the *Tertia Pars*. Is it not St. Thomas who maintains quite precisely the perfectly "historical" character of the Incarnation, which no *a priori* reason requires but, rather, exists only as part of the providential economy involving the concrete becoming of a *sinful* and redeemed humanity? (See note *k* as well.)

(k) "Why be so indignant at hearing it said that, historically considered, (the work of St. Thomas) lacks a certain sense of history?" See "Réponse," 87. Fr. Daniélou did not say that the work of St. Thomas, historically considered, lacks a certain sense of history, which I would not have contested in any way, for I indeed admit this fact. Rather, he said, and I quoted him literally, "that the notion of history is foreign to Thomism." This is what I criticized. He has the right to say that he was mistaken or that his expression exceeded his thought—here, it would be by much!—but he has no right to replace his previous assertions with a new one so that he can claim to have been unjustly attacked. A basic honesty is at stake here. (Besides, I do not question him personally, because I have good reason to believe he did not compose the anonymous response. I speak only about the method of its composer.) (1947)

11 Aristotle, *Politics*, 1.1.2.

12 See Daniélou's introduction in *La Vie de Moïse* and the annotation in *La Création de l'homme* by St. Gregory of Nyssa in *Sources Chrétiennes;* also see, by the same author, *Platonisme et Théologique Mystique* in the *Théologie* collection (Paris: Aubier, 1944).

13 Hans Urs von Balthasar, *Presence et Pensée: Essai sur la philosophie religieuse de Grégoire de Nysse* (Beauchesne: Paris, 1942). Also, see the work in *Sources Chrétiennes* by Claude Mondésert on Clement of Alexandria.

philosophy that many believe to be provided by history itself, is another matter altogether. Great care must be taken in order to maintain the intellectual purity required by a highly specialized methodology. We have been burdened with pseudo-metaphysical assertions elaborated by physicists and biologists who here apply to metaphysical problems methodologies which have indeed produced excellent results in biology and physics but which, upon application to philosophy, result only in poverty. (Such pseudo-metaphysics remains a way of doing metaphysics rather than of denying it, a way of speaking about it without getting into its details.) Is not methodological autonomy demanded by the very laws that rule the pursuit of true knowledge? Certainly, historical awareness offers ample matter for philosophical reflection. Indeed, the philosophy of human activity and of culture cannot do without it. However, if it is true that this philosophy presupposes the rigorous use of historical methodologies, this must come after it, as a kind of reflection which is rather different in character, indeed proceeding from completely different principles. The pseudo-philosophy which unknowingly is inspired by historical methodologies is "relativism," in the strong sense of the term, indicating a theory, or even more so, an intellectual attitude that replaces the metaphysical notion of speculative truth with the more modest notion of historical truth, as the more or less complete expression of the mentality and experience of an era or group of men. The very idea that our mind could, in its most-assured notions, come to grasp and identify timeless truth becomes, strictly speaking, unthinkable.[1] The idea that this truth could represent a definitive gain for human understanding and could be transmitted to distant men separated by time and culture seems absurd. If humanity only progresses by going beyond itself, is it not contrary to the very movement of life to ascribe an absolute intellectual value to statements which bear the clear mark of the era in which they were formulated, the cultural milieu wherein they were born? Is this not just like the adult who wishes to wear the clothes which were adequate for him in his childhood?

However, in that case, we must renounce any notion of a valid and universal teaching, any function of the permanent Magisterium, and along with the notions of acquisition or gain, the very notion of progress vanishes. In any case, intellectual progress quite clearly cannot be conceived as being an unwavering, linear ascent. Like civilization, thought experiences tragic

---

[1] The response article proclaims its agreement and is indignant that we would have judged it good to recall such elementary truths. However, in my opinion, this exercise in recollection is fully justified by the text cited further on from Fr. Bouillard, to which these paragraphs serve as an introduction. I am critiquing him—and no response has been extended to me concerning this very matter—for falling for a pseudo-philosophy that is unconsciously inspired by the methodologies of history, to the point of no longer daring to conceive of the permanence of a *notion*. (1947)

periods of regression. However, how can one claim that nothing remains of all that the mind had previously gained, and that everything that was previously formulated, if it still has the value of furnishing an example for what we must do when faced with new problems, cannot have any value as furnishing an objective teaching? We strongly agree with Fr. de Lubac[14(m)(n)] that the differences between theology and dogma are quite evident and that progress in theology cannot be likened unto that of dogma. Still, how can one fail to see that the arguments adduced in order to combat assurance in theological progress, in the interest of defending the claim that our notions concerning God in accord with the diversity of times and of cultures, would retain all their force even were they applied to claims that would reduce to unacceptable proportions the progress of dogma itself within the Church? This is because the most fundamental of these arguments (illustrated by the interpretation of history, but ultimately coming from views other than historical knowledge) is the depreciation of the intellect, the postulate common to any nominalist philosophy, holding that our reason, when it has knowledge that is clear and expressible, attains nothing but notions, themselves being empty abstractions, logical frameworks whose value is wholly pragmatic. We do not agree that such a caricature of the life of the mind, one that in fact destroys the notion of theology as a science, is better adapted to the idea of dogma proposed by the Church, an idea which enables us to render account of the place which *truth-values* hold in Revelation and in Catholic preaching. Moreover, it suffices that one consider what this would mean in relation to the notion of *orthodoxy*, something which is still quite capital, not only in the Church's teaching, but also in her practice and life. It is commonplace to accuse the Roman Church of intransigence regarding dogmatic questions. However, does this constant character of her practice evade the corrective action of the Divine Spirit who animates her? Is it only the merely human weight of a certain form of culture, and does it, in fact, distort the essential mystery of the Christian life? We readily agree that the very idea of orthodoxy

---

14 Henri de Lubac, *Surnaturel* (Paris: Aubier, 1946), forward (p. 5). Having been received just recently, this book will be reviewed later. *Corpus Mysticum*, by the same author is analyzed and appreciated by Marie-Joseph Nicolas below [in this issue of *Revue thomiste*]. It is one of the most remarkable books of the collection, but while its beauty enriches it, it also accentuates its reactionary character against the speculative theology elaborated by St. Thomas. See annotation (n) below.

(m) Further on, in my reply (p. 176 below), I explain the scope of this citation. (1947)

(n) Fr. de Lubac has misread this note. He reads the last sentence in it as referring to his text *Surnaturel* and is triumphant in showing that it does not apply to it. See "Réponse," 80. Every reader will immediately see that this phrase logically and grammatically refers to *Corpus Mysticum*, and I believe that the evaluation expressed therein is perfectly valid. (1947)

and the practical attitude that it commands are often quite improperly extended by Christian thinkers to assertions which do not belong to the revealed teaching that has been transmitted by the Church, thus giving rise to the deplorable habit of wanting to resolve questions by appealing to authority rather than through serene discussion, and we have no sympathy for this form of argumentation. Nonetheless, the fact remains that the divine message is addressed to our intellect, meaning that this message consequently presupposes it, and that, even in its distinct and expressible [*formulable*] knowledge, there must be enough [surety] in order to make possible the solemn affirmation required by Pope Pius X:

> Thus, I hold steadfastly and shall continue to hold to my last breath the faith of the Fathers in the *sure charism of truth* that is, has been, and always will be "*in the succession of the bishops from the Apostles*," not so that what seems better or more suited according to the culture of each age should be held, but so that the absolute and immutable truth, which from the beginning was preached by the apostles, "should *never be believed, never be understood, in a different way*."[15]

As holds true in every other field of knowledge, we believe that it is infinitely valuable in theology to know the minute historical details of its notions and doctrines, even those which are now taught with the greatest of theological certitude.[16] Often, through this means, we can draw a distinction between the permanent intelligible content of an idea and a host of contingent aims that have been more or less profoundly associated with it through the course of history, in accord with various cultural milieux, in line with this or that worldview of a particular era or thinker, wherein this idea may have been embedded within a vast referential network, which often can be disentangled only with difficulty. No theological synthesis can fail to provide immense gains for our understanding by offering more precise knowledge concerning the time when it was born and the cultural milieu that gave rise to it and circumscribe it. However, if it is true that intellectual activity is a form of life and that, in the midst an entire subjective conditioning of logical relations, it reaches extra-mental reality through the concept which actualizes this life (and it is quite obvious this question does not fall within the purview of history), every idea expressed is of interest because of something very different from its historical characteristics, calling for a different kind of appreciation: appreciation for its truth, pure and simple. Here, we have a judgment that

---

15 Denzinger, no. 3549 [old no. 2147].

16 This is why we wish, a *priori*, that studies like those by Fr. de Lubac will multiply in number. Their great usefulness is all too obvious, and they will be of use all the more to the degree that they are not too hasty, too partial, or too committed to a "thesis."

does not fall to history, even though it is often made only by those who have exact knowledge concerning history, and this judgment refers to criteria belonging to a different order.

The question we are here discussing is found in Fr. Henri Bouillard's recent volume, the first in the *Théologie* collection.[17] This work's conclusion is animated by a preoccupation similar to our own: to show how historical methodology need not lead to a form of complete relativism.[o] Within theological development, Bouillard affirms the permanence not only of "defined dogmas, that is, those propositions which have been canonized by the Church, but also everything that is contained explicitly or implicitly in Scripture and Tradition." And, moreover, he adds to these: "the invariant or absolute of the human mind, those first principles and acquired truths which are all necessary in order for dogma to be thinkable."[18] However, truth be told, we do not fully understand the explanation he provides, which consists in distinguishing a set of absolute affirmations from the notional or notional systems in which these affirmations come to be incarnated. Said notions are the domain of "representation," which is necessarily intrinsically affected by temporality in a way that entails that this domain is radically contingent in nature. Now, these two elements are not separate, and our mind cannot isolate them from one another. We do not reach absolute affirmations alongside, or as something above, the overall representation that we form for ourselves. In other words, we can reach and think these affirmations only in such notions.[19] When the latter change—and they cannot fail to change—what is established along wholly new lines is the entire system of representation, though translating, in this new system's own manner, the same eternal affirmations, by means of this system's own [conceptual] relationships.

This laborious explanation testifies to a praiseworthy attempt to avoid relativism, but we are not sure that Bouillard is successful, and to our eyes, some of his formulas manifest his failure all too clearly. If these two elements interpenetrate each other, so much so that we attain the first only in and through the second—because such is "the law of incarnation,"[20]—how can

---

17 See Henri Bouillard, *Conversion et grâce chez saint Thomas d'Aquin* (Paris: Aubier, 1944).

(o) I emphasize, however, that my "negative criticism," recognized and maintained Fr. Bouillard's intentions [*propos*]. What I contested was the value of his explanations. (1947)

18 Bouillard, *Conversion*, 221.

19 "It is essential to understand that these invariants do not remain *alongside* and independent of contingent conceptions. They are conceived and expressed *within them*. But when they change, the new conceptions contain the same absolute relations, the same eternal affirmations" (Bouillard, *Conversion*, 221). By what miracle, and with what guarantee, is this so if these elements are inseparable for the mind?

20 Bouillard, *Conversion*, 220.

we distinguish them? The only way we will be able to do so will be through our "notions," taking place in our "representation"[21] and, therefore, as something which is obsolete like them. Thus, we will find it impossible to specify what truths are taught to us by faith, as well as those "acquired truths which are all necessary in order for dogma to be thinkable." If we could specify them, they would form an ensemble of enduring affirmations set *alongside* and *above* our passing representations. Will we entrust to the Church, who is divinely assisted, the task of clarifying, within a system of representations, which conceptual relations safeguard "the eternal affirmations" and which compromise it? However, is the Church charged with the task of guaranteeing for us, in addition to "defined dogma," "those first principles and acquired truths which are all necessary in order for dogma to be thinkable"?

In the explanation offered by Bouillard, the very idea of truth is quite contradictory, and although this would possibly not be disturbing for a Hegelian conception of history, it is dangerous not only for theology but also for the Christian faith. The same notions would need to have actual solidity as the means enabling us to reach and think of eternal affirmations (by which they are *true today*) and, at the same time, an instability which requires them to give way to other truths which are essentially different, by which they become *false for another era* or for a mentality which has a different "representation." Therefore, not by way of distraction, as we had at first thought, but instead by the very exigencies, perhaps obscure, of a profound logic, after having defined the schemata proper to St. Thomas's theology in opposition to those formed by modern theology,[22] Bouillard is led to say, three pages

---

[21] "Christian truth never remains in a pure state. I do not mean by this that it inevitably presents itself as being mixed with error but, rather, only that it is *always* embedded within contingent notions and schemata that determine its rational structure. *It cannot be isolated from them.* It cannot free itself from a system of notions except by passing into another. . . . The truth is never accessible outside of all contingent notions. This is the law of incarnation" (Bouillard, *Conversion*, 220, emphasis Labourdette's).

Fr. Bouillard's formulas here doubtlessly go beyond what he actually thinks, for he is indeed required four pages later to make allusion to the possibility that we could separate absolute truth and contingent notions from each other: "In order for theology to continue to provide meaning to the mind, to fertilize it and progress with it, it must also renounce these notions. Unfortunately, it is not always easy to *separate* them, without error, from the absolute truth which they cover over [*recouvre*]" (*Conversion*, 224). But is not "to separate" to set apart? When we mentally separate things, do we not "think them independent of each other" ["*penser indépendamment*"], thus violating "the law of incarnation," which is dear to Fr. Bouillard?

[22] "We can see how St. Thomas conceived and expressed Christian truth according to notions and schemata borrowed from Aristotle. He was simply following the craze of his age. When we compare his theory to that of the Fathers or to modern theology, which has been influenced by him, we will notice what is contingent in the conceptions and systems in which the divine Word is successively incarnated" (Bouillard, *Conversion*, 216).

later: "When the mind evolves, an immutable truth is maintained only thanks to the simultaneous and correlative evolution of *all* the notions, maintaining their inter-relationship. *A theology that would not be contemporary would be a false theology.*"[23] This means, at least for those who are naïve enough to still believe in logic, that the notions in which St. Thomas expressed his theology of grace constitute a theology that was true for his time, but today is false.

Then Bouillard raises the question concerning *the notions implied in conciliar definitions.* When the Council of Trent used the notion of formal causality against the Protestants, did it not thereby incorporate this notion into the dogma it declared?

> By no means. It was certainly not the intention of the Council to canonize an Aristotelian notion, nor even a theological notion conceived under Aristotle's influence. It merely wanted to affirm, against the Protestants, that justification is an interior renewal and not simply an imputation of Christ's merits, the remission of sins, or the favor of God. To this end, it made use of notions that were common to the theology of that era. However, others can be substituted for them without altering the meaning of its teaching. This is demonstrated by the fact that the Council itself much more often made use of equivalent notions derived from Scripture.[24]

However, are the "interior renewal" (which is affirmed) and "the imputation of the merits of Christ" (which is ruled out as being insufficient by itself) not themselves *notions*? Would we find there, by chance, in a pure state, one these "eternal affirmations" that Bouillard assures us exist, though they are only accessible in notions, in an essentially temporal and alterable representation? And if these expressions are indeed still notions, do they escape the fate befalling all other notions which, although true for a time according to the system containing them, are false later on when the mind's evolution comes to force the system of representation to change? If at least this affirmation of renewal remains permanent, or "irreformable," why not that of the statement holding that sanctifying grace is the unique formal cause of justification, "*unica formalis causa*"? We willingly agree with Bouillard that the Council of Trent intended to canonize neither Aristotle, nor his philosophy, nor this or that notion precisely as Aristotelian, any more than it intended to canonize Thomistic notions precisely as Thomistic. However, if it is true that the human intellect reaches the universal and that this is something other than a merely shared name, if the concept refers essentially to an objective reality which, in its essential notes, is independent from temporal existence, then a notion

23 Bouillard, *Conversion*, 219, (emphasis mine).
24 Bouillard, *Conversion*, 221–22.

contains something other than a reference to the author who expressed it, something other than the contingent modalities of its formulation, namely, an element which is perfectly timeless because it expresses an essential necessity. Here, we can draw a distinction between what a Council uses (for the divine truth is expressed to us in a language which is indeed *human*) and what it does not consecrate. In this regard, a notion is no more Aristotelian or Thomist than it is French, German, or Greek. It is purely and simply *human*. Is not this distinction one of these "acquired truths necessary in order for dogma to be thinkable"? And I know quite well that distinguishing the essential contents of an idea from its contingent connotations is often a difficult affair and that these lines of distinction can be poorly drawn. That is why the Church exercises her wisdom with such great mercy, avoiding, as much as possible, in her dogmatic formulas, words and notions which are at the center of [theological and philosophical] controversies. However, she does not always avoid making use of them and has made her own various words and notions: person, nature, transubstantiation, and other precise terms. None of them are subordinated either to Aristotle, Athanasius, or Augustine, but instead, they come from the need to express divine things in human language. Here in the full light of day, we can see the benefits proper to historical methodology, whose services we appreciate no less than does Fr. Bouillard himself, though they certainly are not ordered to the resolution of the [philosophical] problem concerning [the nature of] universals. Yes, it's true, this brings us back to ancient debates concerning [the distinction and relationships between] nature and the individual, existence and essence, and the abstract and the concrete. We believe that these problems are still raised today, with the same necessity as in past days, and that there has been no change in how they must be answered. Granted, these debates are not popular today, but the categories of old and new are not a criterion in metaphysics. We are sensitive to the apologetic intentions[25] of many of the collaborators in the *Théologie* series; however, we believe that it is important to maintain, above all else, *truth*-values and that conformism of any kind serves truth poorly.[26(p)(q)]

25 As regards the schemata used by medieval thinkers, schemata which according to Bouillard have become unusable, he writes: "They served in their era by transmitting the mystery and, as such, are venerable. But like an old-fashioned garment or an outdated tool, they hamper the process of theological reflection. They *prevent those who do not understand them anymore* from grasping the exact meaning of Christian doctrine" (*Conversion*, 224, emphasis Labourdette's). Therefore, do they not hamper those who understand them? And is it not precisely the task of the theologian to explain them?

26 We will pause only briefly to make remarks concerning the book by Fr. Fessard, *Autorité et Bien Commun* (Paris: Aubier, 1946). Its proper subject is too distant from our present considerations. However, his methodology is relevant, given his explicit concern to undertake a more complete adaptation to the needs of contemporary understanding: "For long, philosophers have held that the notion of the common good is the keystone

THEOLOGY AND ITS SOURCES 153

* * * * *

Another habit of the modern mind reinforces the relativism easily professed by the historian with regard to systems of ideas: the habit of interpreting the term "conceptual" not so much from the perspective of its objective significate (that upon which, logically, it claims to measure itself) but, instead, first and foremost from the perspective of the subjective life it translates.⁽ʳ⁾ Everyone knows the emphasis given to this method by the Freudian doctrine concerning dreams. Roland Dalbiez has admirably analyzed this topic in his already-classic work *Le Méthode psychoanalytique et la doctrine freudienne*.[27] Certainly, without drawing any comparison between psychoanalytic techniques and a form of reflection which is dependent on many other influences and is applied to another matter, we belief that this rapprochement

---

of every social structure. Then, when citizens became aware of the rights which are the privilege of human nature, it was dethroned and returned to the shadows. Today, it is beginning to emerge from the oblivion into which it had fallen. However, those same jurists, philosophers, and theologians who bestow on it new honors *typically clothe it only with the garments of the thirteenth century, a vesture which make its advancement difficult* (*Autorité et Bien Commun*, 8, emphasis Labourdette's). We see that this clothing metaphor, already famous at the beginning of the century, itself retains its currency. We have encountered it in the writings of Fr. Bouillard. Is there any need to emphasize its impertinence as regards the question of assessing the permanence or decrepitude [*caducité*] of those notions which are essential to St. Thomas's theology? (See note q as well.)

(p) It is regrettable that the response article, while accusing me of having raised, wholly unprovoked and without any precise analysis, the problem of historical and doctrinal relativism, does not speak of the objections made to Fr. Bouillard's texts. In all honesty, were we wrong to consider this book as representative of the spirit of a New Theology? (1947)

(q) Now, here is the response made to the criticism which we raised: "Our aim here is not to reject the traditional notion of the Common Good as though it were outdated clothing; quite to the contrary, we look to restore its value. The whole work attests to this fact." Now, we do not accuse Fr. Fessard of wanting to reject the notion of the common good but, rather, the philosophy in which it took shape in the thought of St. Thomas, the "garb of the middle ages" that stands in the way of its advancement. (1947)

(r) In response to our assertion, our critics write: "Again, what they have in their targets is a ruinous historical relativism that threatens the very idea of truth, fearing that certain historical studies are less interested in 'the objective significate' of the thought they analyze than the 'subjective life' that this thought manifests" ("*Réponse*," 89). Here, two tendencies find themselves blocked together, though they are carefully distinguished in our study, the first of which we might call *historical relativism*, which we analyzed at some length, first doing so in general, in the way that the contemporary mentality has a tendency to introduce it into theology (pp. 144–49 above), then in the characteristic form that it takes on in Fr. Bouillard's book (pp. 149–52 above). The second tendency is *subjectivist relativism*, which we briefly analyze as being a simple reinforcement of historical relativism, as exemplified in Fr. Daniélou's account of a book by Gilson. (1947)

27 Roland Dalbiez, *Méthode psychoanalytique et la doctrine freudiene*, vol. 1. ch. 2, (Paris: Desclée de Brouwer, 1936), 51–201.

is enlightening. What is of interest in dreams is not their objective meaning, which is usually incoherent, thus sufficing by itself to denounce the vanity of the idea that they represent an expression of the truth. This interest must not be looked for "from the front" but, so to speak, *a tergo* [from behind], on the side of its subjective causes, in the life of the instincts and affections which are symbolically projected within the dream. Surely, many contemporary minds experience the profound tendency to consider every conceptual or imaginative expression as being, first and foremost, something that symbolizes our interior life and experience:[(s)] a more-or-less-rich and more-or-less-authentic experience, concerning which one will need to ask oneself whether the symbolic expression is a valid witness to it instead of remaining merely a verbal amplification thereof.

Thus, the idea of speculative truth, which of itself expresses a relationship of conformity between one's statement and things, will find itself bent in a very different direction: that of one's sincerity in this testimony and its expression, as well as in the direction of authenticity in the formation of one's experience. The interest of a philosophy or theological synthesis will no longer be its overall meaning, considered in the coherence of its assertions, or in its teaching value for transmitting permanent truths. From this perspective, is not every system of ideas subject to aging and death? Its interest, if it was a great and truly human philosophy, if it was an authentic theology, is first and foremost found in the inner experience from which it emanates, in the "spirituality" from which it arises and draws its true value.[28]

(s) One speaks here "of a brilliant tirade in which the virtuosity of its author finds a way to appeal to the Freudian doctrine of dreams and to the psychoanalytic method, in which it is only a question of providing an illuminating rapprochement." One should reread our text and tell us whether it wouldn't have been more "illuminating" to likewise cite this sentence: "Surely, many contemporary minds experience the profound tendency to consider every conceptual or imaginative expression as being, first and foremost, something that symbolizes our interior life and experience." All readers would have understood the purpose of bringing to light the deep constants of contemporary psychological trends. Every reader would have also seen that we are not here denouncing any of the Reverend Fathers but, instead, have our sights set upon one of the categories of modern thought to which there is an attendant tendency—one that is quite widespread among contemporary theologians (and not only among them)—to hold that theology is only the conceptual expression of a given spirituality. (1947)

28 In his review of a little book by Etienne Gilson, *Théologie et Histoire de la Spiritualité* (Paris: Vrin, 1943), Fr. Daniélou writes: "It is true that theology has a right to give us principles, whereas history provides facts, but, still, we must be careful not to apply the principles of this or that theological school indiscriminately to any given spirituality. It is clear, for example, that the relationship between contemplation and action in the philosophy of St. Thomas can in no way account for spiritualties like that of St. Francis or St. Ignatius. Consequently, if theology can help us understand spirituality, spirituality in turn will, in many cases, burst our theological frameworks and force us to conceive of

We would not dream of denying that theoretical elaboration can be influenced by the "spiritual climate" within which this theology is constructed. Even less would we deny the influence which various experiences have exercised upon the orientation of different theological syntheses. (Here, we have an all-too-evident datum which is dear to the historian of doctrines and valuable for theological reflection itself.) However, what we cannot admit, from such an outlook, is the complete evacuation of the *idea of speculative truth*. And if someone were to ask us whether we believe that the truth is something accessible to us, we would have the naivety to respond, "Yes." We hold that [speculative] truth is the conformity of the knowing intellect with a reality which is something given to it, something which in no way is a "construct." It is true that, for us [humans], this conformity is brought about through impoverishing categories, given that they are the fruit of an activity which is abstractive in nature; however, we

---

various types of theology. This is one of the great benefits we can expect from the development of spiritual theology. If Gilson did not speak about it, his whole work gives evidence of it, showing us that to each great spirituality there corresponded a great theology, and that St. Augustine, St. Bernard, St. Thomas, and St. Bonaventure each had a theology drawn from their spirituality" (*Révue du Moyen-Age Latin* 1, Jan.-Mars. 1945, 65).

We are not in the position here to set out Gilson's authentic thought; however, we are grateful to him for having spoken with more nuance. We do not think that his very fine studies, referred to by Fr. Daniélou, studies which to our eyes seem methodologically excellent from the perspective of the history of Christian thought, entail such a simple conception, even to the slightest degree. Great benefit can be drawn from understanding a theological synthesis, appreciating its profound orientations, and grasping the spiritual climate in which it was elaborated, as well as what experience and fundamental intuition it responds to. However, when this passes over to the level of intellectual formation, this fact in no way prevents this theology from being appraised in light of perspectives coming from outside of the spirituality from which it emanated. This elaboration is not automatic and infallible, and the assertions it contains do indeed claim to be measured on an objective reality. It therefore raises the question of speculative truth. Shall we say that in the theological order two systems of contradictory statements can be true at the same time? Certainly, it is valuable to understand the source of their various tones and, perhaps, the source of the distortion undergone in the rational development of one of them. However, it necessarily follows that if one assertion is true and that another rationally contradicts it, then the second is not. And it is clear, precisely because an entire work of analysis and synthesis has presided over this elaboration, that the unfavorable judgment made concerning one or another of his statements does not disqualify, for all that, the spiritual experience of the theologian: the latter may very well have been—and forever be—perfectly authentic. And if it were true that St. Thomas's theology cannot account for the experiences to which Fr. Daniélou refers, we would simply need to conclude from this that it has not, in this regard, attained the universality required by a true science, thereby remaining too narrow. However, we are still waiting for this to be demonstrated to us.

believe that, by means of these categories, things are reached by an authentic intellectual intuition.

In other words, we hold that Saint Thomas's philosophical explanation of the problem of knowledge presents us with a timeless truth. It is valid, not precisely because we have received it or because we have been given the mission to defend it as an expression of orthodoxy, but instead, because we believe that we grasp within it a permanent truth, something much more *living* than contemporary theories—from which, however, we also certainly drawn instruction for ourselves, for we grasp their value, alongside (at least to our eyes) their defects. Without a doubt, greater respect is found, I believe, not only for the truth, but also for various teachings, when we frankly recognize a disagreement which allows for sincere discussion, than when we have the constant disposition—however well-intentioned it may be—to take advantage of the smallest convergences in order to affirm an agreement [between various thinkers] which would be at once substantial and miraculous.

On this point, despite the esteem that we have for the apostolic intention of his work and the high value of much of his research,[29] we find ourselves asking whether Fr. Daniélou, in the somewhat-cavalier manner that, thanks to the efforts of Fr. Teilhard de Chardin, he looks to annex to contemporary theology the benefits of Marxist reflection, existentialism, etc.,[(t)] does not fall into the most unfortunate kind of ready harmony [*concordisme*], drawing immediate connections between [*homologuant*] the most

---

29 This is why we excuse ourselves for giving so much importance to an article written, as a matter of fact, for "the general public" and which possibly belongs—Alas!—to that genre, flourishing so vigorously today: *propaganda*. However, this article contains such stances and so naïve [*ingénu*] a disdain for contemporary Thomism that the *Revue thomiste* was forced to stand up and respond. For example, see Daniélou, "Les orientations présentes," 6–7: "Faced with the danger of agnosticism, neo-Thomism again blamed theological rationalism.... There was need of warding off the dangers created by modernism. Neo-Thomism and the Biblical Commission provided guardrails, but guardrails obviously are not answers." And even more than its particular assertions, the article's tone bears witness to his assuredly low estimation concerning a mode of thought he considers to be obsolete, though it is one that we consider to be forever valid, one to which the *Revue thomiste* seeks to be wholeheartedly faithful.

(t) Here, I correct this unfortunate editorial lapse, both elliptical and embarrassing. The very quotation I used in the reference shows quite clearly that I had no intention of making Teilhard du Chardin into an existentialist! I was concerned with the way that Fr. Daniélou uses him on behalf of the annexation of *Marxism*. [*C'est pour l'annexation du marxisme que le P. Daniélou l'utilise.*] (The response article, with more skill than honesty, replaces this word with an ellipsis.) I only wanted to say that I thought that, as regards existentialism, Fr. Daniélou is up to the task by himself. I ask pardon for this incorrect wording and ask that it be read as stating: "thanks to the efforts of Teilhard de Chardin, the benefit of Marxist reflection, and, *through personal efforts that I believe are* illusory, such as existentialist reflection, etc...." (1947)

superficial confluences [of thinkers and ideas].[30] Frs. de Lubac and Daniélou seem to enjoy placing into question positions which are all-too-easily taken for granted. And in this regard, we ourselves share, to a large degree, in their outlook. The Church draws great benefit from this kind of critical spirit. Through her whole host of institutions, she possesses such great power for conservation and "tradition" that we must rejoice to see, at the same time, this kind of constant concern for *verification* exercised within her very bosom and, to our eyes, with such fidelity to her true spirit. We have enough confidence in the Church's truth to believe that she has no need of our deceptions and that many of our "prudent" concerns are, in fact, forms of cowardice. However, precisely what we are looking for is a critical spirit when we see Fr. Daniélou's eagerness lead him to make so many data drawn from modern philosophy, indeed, things still remaining quite equivocal, converge toward a renewed theology.

* * * * *

Without a doubt, the powerful thrust of irrational philosophies is the principle cause of the offensive undertaken against scholastic philosophy unfolding before our eyes. It is not the only one; or, rather, the experience that gave birth to it is also expressed in other domains. Far be it from us to deny that this experience has value and that it can be assimilated into theological thought. Indeed, we feel its human meaning. However, we believe that the categories in which it is expressed must not elude criticism, and we refuse to see theological thought assimilated by it, in accord with formulas that are eminently contestable. It is easy to note that in our day philosophy has often descended to the level of literature, and thus we ourselves have been led to appreciate it according to the same standards as those holding for poetry and art. I am quite well-aware of how, to many, it seems naïve to say that philosophy could be conceived as being an exact science concerned with technical rigor and precision. I admit that this conception has been compromised by the Cartesian idea of unified knowledge spread out upon a [single] level of immediate clarity, along the lines of the type of knowledge found in mathematics. This conception, preserved by classical rationalists, is also opposed, to the greatest degree, to St. Thomas's view of the matter. Likewise, far be it from us to agree, for example, with the claims made by

---

[30] "It is deserving of note that the dogma of original sin quite precisely places us in the presence of these two abysses: that of history and of the goodness of the world, and that of freedom and the absurdity of the world, which, as we have just seen, are precisely the abysses that Marxism and existentialism open up before us. We see that the Christian mystery is the place where the conflict of modern thought finds its supreme expression and, therefore, that to be present to our time, theology need only pursue its own requirements to the fullest, holding at once to St. Irenaeus and St. Augustine, to Fr. Teilhard and Kierkegaard" (Daniélou, "Les orientations,"16).

Julien Benda,[31] and we appreciate neither his often very-curt judgments concerning our great masters in contemporary literature, nor his idea of "philosophy," which is wholly traced out along the lines of sciences that, in fact, belong to a different level of knowledge. In truth, this represents an oversimplified form of philosophy, despite its demands for precision. Nonetheless, bearing in mind these [qualifying] remarks, we are grateful to him for pleading for clarity and rigor, for denouncing the use of a vocabulary which floats upon the surface of a cultivated equivocation, and for recalling the basic distinction which exists between genres. This distinction does not represent an arbitrary classification but, rather, is the expression of spiritual activities that fundamentally differ from each other through the very principles and criteria to which they refer.[u]

No more than metaphysics, theology is not amenable to being judged in accord with the categories of aesthetics. I do not mean in its expressions but, rather, in the value of the universality and permanence of the truths that it defines. This flawed but brilliant and superficial page, written by a most distinguished author, provides a good example. Although it does not belong to one of the works of the two collections that we have discussed, it finds a natural place in our discussions here:

> In a present so ambiguous, between a death that is being consummated and a life that is being born, what can the theologian do? What ought he to do? His first move will be to return once more to the past. This

---

[31] Julien Benda, "De la mobilité de la pensée selon une philosophie contemporaine," *Revue de Métaphysique et de Morale* (Juillet 1945): 161–202.

[u] We again note this passage: "concerning this matter, the reference (following Benda) to 'the powerful thrust of irrational philosophies,' introduces a touch of humor into this allegation." If Benda, alerted to this strange reference, rushes to read our text, he will see that he is neither accused of drawing irrational philosophies in his wake nor even with denouncing their thrust, but instead, is simply praised for reminding everyone of [the importance of] precision and the drawing of distinction among genres.

This way of citing us raises much greater concerns for us—we must acknowledge this fact—regarding the attention with which we have been read, than whatever concerns we might have regarding our critics' benevolence. Nonetheless, a note proves to us that some portion of our thought has been retained: "Let us likewise note that there is some arbitrariness involved in claiming for the same theory both the characteristic of rigorous scientific methodological sophistication as well as a perpetual openness and extreme plasticity." We do not believe that scientific theology is something closed [and complete]. Instead, we think that it can be revised, indeed frequently, not in order to replace an idea that was fashionable in the thirteenth century with one that is fashionable in the twentieth century but, rather, in order to benefit from the informative labor and reflection undertaken through the centuries, forever striving to attain a greater amount of truth. More than the rights of St. Thomas's teaching, what we uphold are the rights of theology as a science. (1947)

return will be beneficial but only on one condition: that he understand well that history, far from dispensing us from creative effort, imposes it on us. Our artists, and in particular our architects, all acknowledge this. A Greek temple, a Romanesque church, a Gothic cathedral all merit our admiration, because they are witnesses to a beauty and truth that are incarnate in time. But to reproduce them now in our present day would constitute an anachronism, all the more appalling to the extent the copies were more minutely exact. The intent to revive them, to adapt them to the needs of the time, would be even worse. Such an effort could only beget horrors. All attempts at "adaptation" to current tastes are doomed to the same fate. No more than architecture does theology escape this universal law. In neo-Greek style, the column of antiquity loses its original qualities of simplicity and becomes an intolerable imitation. And the same may be said of Saint Thomas: "A great and estimable doctor, renowned, authoritative, canonized, and very much dead and buried" (Péguy). We should not imagine that there are other estimable figures who in our eyes are better capable of withstanding such treatment! We have turned our gaze on a more distant past, but we have not done so in the belief that, in order to give life to a languishing system of thought, it would suffice to exhume the "Greek Fathers" and adapt them for better or worse to the needs of the modern soul. We are not ingenious enough to prefer a "neopatristic" theology to a "neoscholastic" theology! There is never a historical situation that is absolutely similar to any of the ones that preceded it in time. Thus, there is no historical situation that can furnish us with its own solutions as a kind of master key capable of resolving all the problems that plague us today.[32(v)]

But can we be so certain that a historical period necessarily knows only particular problems and always refuses to rise to those that are simply human,

---

[32] Hans Urs von Balthasar, *Presence and Thought: Essay on the Religious Philosophy of Gregory of Nyssa*, trans. Mark Sebanc (San Francisco: Ignatius Press, 1995), 9–10.

(v) One can see in "Réponse" the complaint our citation suggests ("Réponse," 80). Now, we maintain that this text contains exactly what we critique in it. The fact that he likens the Fathers to St. Thomas does not reassure us at all. It is not only opposed to the adapting of an old doctrine to the tastes of the day but is also opposed to its "exhumation." The comparison between theology and architecture is inadmissible, for it forbids us from returning to ancient thought, as we have suggested, on the pretext that no historical situation is absolutely similar to any of those which preceded it, as if thought has never ascended, and could not still ascend, to that which is eternally human [*à de l'éternellement humain*], to that which is timeless. This justifies our protest: "For our part, we believe that definitive intellectual acquisitions take place in the domain of [human] knowledge." Any theology worthy of the name tends, with more or less success, towards such acquisitions. As regards the burial of St. Thomas, it would take no less than all the resources of figurative exegesis in order to exonerate Fr. von Balthasar for having so readily proclaimed it following Péguy (whom we love for other reasons, though we do not hold that he is a significant authority in this debate). (1947)

problems whose data and solutions will reach up to the level of universal truth? And while it is indeed the case that truth and beauty converge and are really identical in being, expressing for us riches that are found in being but that are not sufficiently explicit in our own first knowledge thereof, nonetheless, precisely speaking, the notions of truth and beauty have different meanings, thereby calling for different spiritual activities on our part and, thus, fundamentally different attitudes. We expect a teaching to do something more for us than merely to awaken within ourselves a sense of beauty or merely to expose us to what is, in the end, an incommunicable experience. If it does this as well, we will be all the more indebted to such a teaching. However, its first responsibility is to raise us up to perceive—certainly, yes, with our own personal and living intelligence—truths that others have perceived before us, truths that have the same value for us as it had for them. We should not look upon theology as though it were a series of museum displays that, in the end, only function as an invitation for us to do something similar in our own era. For our part, we believe that definitive intellectual acquisitions are found in the domain of [human] knowledge. Nonetheless, no matter how much one might believe that something represents a form of progress, not all cases of apparent advance have in fact represented true steps forward. Many illusions and regressions can be found in the history of thought, but those cases of progress that have been tested and proven by time are to be counted among the most valuable riches that our culture has bequeathed to us. And if St. Thomas is so dear to us, this is because, to our eyes, he is the theologian who best introduces us—at once with the greatest of self-effacement and true boldness—to "a most-fruitful understanding of the mysteries," something which, according to the [First] Vatican Council, constitutes the very nature of theology (Denz. 3016).

4
Criticism in Theology: A Response
Michel-Marie Labourdette, OP

[Prefatory note in the volume *Dialogue théologique*:] The solemn and public character of the response [that, in the volume *Dialogue théologique*, directly precedes this essay[1]] did not permit us to wait for the next issue of the *Revue thomiste* [in order to respond in turn]. Given that the response by the Jesuit fathers was not signed, we believe that each person we critiqued, even if only in passing, takes full responsibility for the response. Therefore, we have named Frs. de Lubac, Daniélou, Bouillard, Fessard, and von Balthasar. If, here and there, we happen to single out one of them—for example, Fr. de Lubac—the reader should understand this as being solely a stylistic device, bearing in mind that we do not mean to split them up.

* * * * *

The most recent issue of *Recherches de science de religieuse* in 1946 presented a collective response to the criticisms I formulated in the *Revue thomiste* (May–August 1946) regarding certain orientations in the collections *Sources Chrétiennes* and *Théologie*. The authors did not sign their names to the work, intending thereby to show that the article was written as a shared enterprise, aimed at what they consider to be an act of aggression. I need only remind you of their names—Frs. de Lubac, Daniélou, Bouillard, Fessard, and von Balthasar—in order for you to see that we are dealing with a formidable contingent. The fact that this opposition is so capable a group renders it quite unlikely that we intended for our earlier article to be a "summary execution" of these men.

I would like to begin by thanking my critics for giving me this opportunity to explain myself more fully. All this discussion, they say, has been "uneven"[2] [*en porte à faux*], or so they would have us believe. However, we believe that it is quite easy to show that this state of affairs has arisen solely

---

1 [Tr. note: The response penned by the Jesuit fathers can be found as "Response to 'The Sources of Theology'" in *Ressourcement Theology: A Sourcebook*, ed. and trans. Patricia Kelly (New York: Bloomsbury, 2020), 73–82.]

2 *Dialogue théologique*, 94.

because they have shifted the focus of the debate and that it could be—that it can without a doubt always be—the starting point of very useful clarifications, not only concerning our respective positions (which after all are not so very important) but, moreover, concerning much broader questions pertaining to theological methodology. In any case, I believe that this is the only real matter of interest to be considered, and it alone provides my most worthwhile excuse for continuing to speak about these matters to our readers. I would have preferred for these discussions to remain solely on this ground. Thus, I apologize for needing to begin by explaining certain grievances which have no bearing in this present intellectual debate. Indeed, personally, I would normally not allow myself to introduce them into a theological discussion.

I. AN ENORMOUS EXTRAPOLATION

The great reproach registered against me is that I followed a deplorable methodology that supposedly had as its essential principle—or its result—the constant exercise of "extrapolation." I will elaborate on this further on. However, I would first like to point out that, in their own self-defense, the five aforementioned authors commit all kinds of utterly unpardonable extrapolations: not one that, remaining within the field of ideas, erroneously universalizes, mixing together two different levels of knowledge, without respecting the differentiation of various noetics, but rather, a form of extrapolation that makes a debate over ideas into a personal affair, implying that a theological discussion in fact involves some kind of rivalry between religious orders and attempting to explain a purely doctrinal position in terms of machinations and the designs of who-knows-what sort of intra-ecclesiastical "politics." I am quite obliged to address these insinuations, which surely are the saddest part of this *Response*, sad not so much for me but for those who come to reflect on the "mores" [*moeurs*] involved in theological controversy.

1° They speak (granted, in very veiled words) of conversations held in certain circles close to us, of private correspondences (!), and of the "unusual" publication of our booklet prior to the publication of the volume of our *Revue* in which this article was to belong,[3] thus looking to insinuate that we are, if not the organizers of a "larger plan," at least the accomplices or the implementors thereof.[4] What lies underneath these insinuations? Do they know much more about these matters than do we? And thus, are they sure

---

[3] How can one use the expression "a call to arms" [*brochure de combat*] for a simple off-print that had a distribution of only 35 copies?—See note (a) in the previous article.

[4] "La Théologie et ses sources, Réponse," in *Dialogue théologique* (Saint-Maximin: Les Arcades, 1947), 94.

concerning machinations that we have the honor of being unaware of? If so, then why mix us up in these affairs? Or, perhaps they voice suspicions and are referring to certain agitations that we have in fact encountered, and in that case, I can tell them that they may well be astonished (at least in the state of mind they manifest in their writing) if they knew what we actually think regarding these agitations. We respect the Magisterium too much to muddle it up with our quarrels. It falls to it alone to assess whether it needs to intervene. I have had the occasion to write to one of our interlocutors and to convey to him that our specific intention was to place the debate on the field of fair and public discussion oriented toward clear explanations, believing that nothing was better suited to removing it from the atmosphere of covert suspicions and denunciations, which, alas, all-too-often ends up bogging down theological controversies. Would they have prefered us to circulate anonymous papers, like those with which France is currently awash? We do not condemn anyone, and it is too easy to return an anathema against him who levels it without authority. We have remained solely on the field of ideas, and our adversaries were the ones who left it by resorting to methods that, to say the least, are uniquely suited for lowering the level of this debate.

2° The *Response* does not fear to expand this debate into a rivalry between religious orders. I have "attacked a certain number of Jesuit theologians"! (I wanted to take up anew the "disputes of another age"!) This group is the one who responds to me, but they let me know—and I understand all too well the trouble I have gotten myself into!—that they have the support of the censors and superiors of the Society of Jesus, "without whom [they] do not publish a single line."[5] Did I have the slightest intention of accusing the Society along with its censors and superiors? I have the most sincere admiration for it, its saints, its great spiritual writers, certain theologians, apostles, and missionaries, and I am well aware of the great loss the Church would suffer if the Jesuits were to disappear. Merely in terms of Catholic publications at present, and only in France, this would lead to the disappearance of a great share of the best works being put into print. Indeed, for Thomism itself, this would involve the absence of studies of the highest quality, such as, merely to give one example, Fr. Joseph de Finance's recent book, "*Être et agir.*"

But such a thought never crossed my mind! I do not think the authors I have named would engage the Society in this dispute any more than I would engage the Order of St. Dominic, which, even if I wished to do so, certainly does not lend itself to such mobilization. I have mentioned neither the name of my order nor the province to which I belong, nor the name of the house of studies where I reside, nor even the name of the *Revue thomiste*,

---

[5] "La Théologie et ses sources, Réponse," 95.

whose editorial board, granted, is homogenous enough for its members to recognize themselves in the idea I have defended, though, nonetheless, theologians and philosohers who are entirely indepedent collaborate in its work as well.

Moreover, is it not common knowledge that the collection *Sources Chrétiennes*, directed by Frs. de Lubac and Daniélou, is edited by a team that has connections to our own Dominican brotherhood and, moreover, that for our own part, we feel frank admiration for its inventive spirit and energy, even though, with good reason, I did not think it would feel that it was being persecuted merely because we would exercise our free right to register criticism concerning this or that publication in the collection?

3° In connection with the first insinuation (still not about my person, "we want to say," but about my "environment") and through an "overreach" [*dépassement*] that is no more forgiveable, the authors of the *Response* come to speak of the resurrection of "fundamentalism" ["*intégrisme*"]. If this involves specific facts or attitudes, let them tell us about them! Otherwise, we are entitled to assume that this game of labels is akin to that played by parties who mutual accuse each other of being "fascists" and "communists." May God grant that the example offered here by the Reverend Fathers not be followed and that these *mores* [*moeurs*] not be introduced into theological controversy! If a fundamentalist party exists, we are not members of it. We belong to no party, for we refuse to consider Thomism as being a party.

4° The *Response* presents an entirely dramatized account of my critical intervention. It seems that I consider myself a "judge" charging a defendent upon the stand or an "examiner" bullying timid defendants. Is it not enough to repeat that the defendants in question are Frs. de Lubac, Daniélou, Fessard, and von Balthasar, all who have been well-known for some time as the authors of important and justly-praised works, which have recieved the most complimentary [*flatteuses*] reviews in most journals? For heaven's sake, next to them, who am I! I did not think that my position as director of the *Revue thomiste* could make an impression on them and arouse such feelings of "persecution."

5° Finally, should we not mention, in a debate that could have remained entirely objective, the constant shift (extrapolation, as they say) towards arguments that engage circumstances or personal qualities (or, alas, even flaws!)? Below, we will discuss how it is that we conceive of the role to be played by criticism in theology, a modest role, perhaps, but how necessary indeed. We are also asked to produce "works" ourselves. This is our desire and our ambition. We are striving to do so with our own resources, but none of us thinks we have rendered the Church services that would equal those, for example, of Fr. de Lubac. (I say this without a hint of irony.) Leave it to others to tell us again and again that our means are poor and results nonexistent.[6]

Once again, I ask pardon of our readers for this kind of controversy, which we greatly desired to spare them, given that it is fruitless and, really, uncalled for. I did not desire for the debate to be lowered to the level of polemics, but I am obliged to raise it and give my response. My excuse will be that often made by the great Cajetan after certain debates: "*Stultus fui: Durandus me coegit. I was foolish: Durandus forced me to it.*"

II. CRITICISM IN THEOLOGY

Let us attempt to elevate this debate. We have yet to explain ourselves or to respond to some severe criticisms raised against us. At the very least, this response will be on the level of ideas and made in the hope of a reaching a result belonging to a more universal order of things. It will not be useless to reflect on certain general principles that underlie the legitimacy of criticism in theology as well as on the qualities or disadvantages of certain methodologies that, in the present case, are called into question.

A. The Legitimacy and Meaning of Criticism

The article for which I am being critiqued was presented as being a *critical study*. This type of work is nothing new, and while it requires as much seriousness as any other, I do not think that its general utility is questionable. Still, we must recognize its own particular requirements.

1° By its very nature, a critical study involves the *assessment* [*appréciation*] of certain doctrines. If the critic desires to perform something other than a mere review of the information, he must take a position and begin a debate that, perhaps, will call for discussion. One may think that many discussions are useless, but isn't this true for all kinds of works? Were criticism only to inspire authors to do the best they can and to overcome facile mediocrity, it would deserve to be cultivated. However, how can someone undertake such a task without expressing and defending his own

---

[6] Allow me to address but one point, for it is indicative of the tone of the *Response*, showing how its authors interpreted what I meant by stating my desire for greater rigor in thought and greater care to be exercised in the specifying of terms. They pretend to believe that I was proposing myself as a model and add that I do not hold a monopoly in this kind of rigor and that, moreover, when understood along the lines that I seemed to conceive of it, such rigor is, rather, a form of illusion and the mark of an unfortunate confusion. However, I am ready to say, just as much as they are, they all have what it takes to be more rigorous, more profound, and more precise than I. I will even use superlatives here for them, for I refuse to get involved in this ridiculous competition.

thought? Does the fact that one defends it and continues to manifest its firm foundations necessarily imply the desire to "impose" it?

The Reverend Fathers have, in fact, resorted to raising a protest which is all too easy to make. (And why do so in this tone?) It seems that I gave in to the temptation to "monopolize the truth in its contents, as well as in its very form."[7] On the other hand, they will never consent to "reduce the boundaries of orthodoxy to that of (their) personal thought in its most systematic expression."[8] We thank them for this. However, do I really need to point out the quite-obvious fact that I don't claim to be infallible? None of the editors of the *Revue thomiste*, and especially I myself, refuses, in turn, to be subjected to criticism. I agree to be measured with the same measure that I use and will be convinced of my errors when I am mistaken! If my interpretation was not accurate, perhaps it was at least a beginning. If I am guilty of some confusion, perhaps many others have fallen into the same confusion. Isn't this simply an opportunity to explain one's reasoning? Has the dramatization presented by the Reverend Fathers become a hallucination, leading them to look upon me as though I were clad in a judge's robe?

2° Not only did I express my thoughts on points pertinent to my opponents' work, but, moreover, it seems I did it with "negative critiques."[9] What does this mean? If I understand things aright, a critique remains negative when it is systematically destructive, remaining unconcerned with discerning the true from the false or the good from the bad. Its only aim is to contradict without any concern to direct the mind towards solutions, or at least toward principles of solution, which will be brought to light by the discussion itself. Now, does this describe our critique? I don't believe it does.

We expressed our admiration for Jean Moroux's book, *The Meaning of Man*. I could have been tempted to contrast this book with the "spirit" of the *Théologie* collection, but on the contrary, I expressly noted that it obviously belongs to it and offers a model of what it might give us if its intention, which is indeed excellent in the positive claims that it makes, were not vitiated, in several other volumes, by a visible tendency to depreciate scholastic theology. Certainly, this is my personal thought, but why should I be forbidden to express it, if I justify it (as I believe I have done)? I did not attempt to define the authors' intentions, which I certainly do not know, but rather what, objectively, appears to a reader of the first volumes as being the general plan of the collection: "a positive and constructive design which is more important than the defects that tarnish their aim. It presents a theology that is more conscious, at once, of its rich sources, of the diversity of its historical expres-

---

[7] "La Théologie et ses sources, Réponse," 92.
[8] "La Théologie et ses sources, Réponse," 97.
[9] "La Théologie et ses sources, Réponse," 93.

sions, of the conditions of its historical development, and the most pressing and contemporary of human realities. Let us state up front our full agreement and complete sympathy with these aims." Do we not see such "entirely negative criticism" wholly on the side of a "response," which holds that these were empty praises, choosing, instead, to focus on my reservations—which I myself, however, declared to be secondary (pp. 135–36 above)—as though they alone had determined the reflexive response of a wounded sensitivity?

The Response speaks (*Dialogue théologique*, p. 86) of my "scandal at the thought that, in contrast to the Budé collection of classical texts, someone might dare to try to give life, in some way, to the writings of Christian antiquity." My text makes no such claim. I appreciate this design, and I praised it. In my opinion, the benefit and timeliness of the *Sources Chrétiennes* collection are obvious. Did I hide this opinion? Here again, why was it necessary to pass over my praises and mention only my reservations? The critique that seemed unacceptable had none of the meaning given to it in the response. I said, and do indeed think, that we can never value ancient Christian texts highly enough. I see no drawback in translating texts in order to "highlight" them by "bringing them to life" or by understanding them from within. I only expressed my reservation on one specific point involved in the orientation of *Sources Chrétiennes*, namely, the desire to emphasize, above all, "categories that are those of contemporary thought, which scholastic theology had lost." This "ulterior motive," which is already quite noticeable in several volumes, happened to be formulated in express terms by one of the directors of the collection, Fr. Daniélou. Did I not have the right to question it and prefer either a pure historical methodology or less preoccupation with finding ready harmony [*concordisme*] with contemporary thought. How does this remark go beyond the rights of criticism and render "entirely negative" an overall assessment that is, in fact, substantially positive?

Although I refrained from saying it so bluntly, I also think that certain apologetic concerns, certain ways of making connections with "contemporary thought," reflect—objectively and despite whatever might be the personal intentions of the authors, something I have never questioned, not for a single moment—an intolerable form of dalliance. This assessment can be debated. But is this criticism also entirely negative, and do we not have the right to think that theology would gain much by ridding itself of attitudes that, to the eyes of many unbelieving thinkers, seems like a vulgar inferiority complex?

Supposedly, my bias to criticize at any cost led me to present reflections regarding the "clothing metaphor," which contradicted earlier statements made by the *Revue thomiste*. I persist in thinking—for they do not even bother to point out my error—that this metaphor is objectionable, not because it is utterly incapable of having an acceptable meaning, but rather, because it is so freighted with historical connections (given how it has been used over the course of the last fifty years) that it today calls to mind the most questionable ideas[10] I have already written about why the ideas of Fr. Bouillard clearly seem questionable to me, giving this metaphor an unacceptable sense. I noted it in the preface by Fr. Fessard, where I believe it has a similar meaning in relation to the *Thomistic* notion of the common good. It is not without paradox that this book presents itself as being dedicated to "restoring the value" of this notion, written by a convinced Thomist, whereas the entire effort expended in the work aims to ground the notions that he proposes by placing them on the foundation of a fully Hegelian dialectic, thereby giving them new meaning. In no way do I deny Fr. Fessard the right to not be a Thomist, but I reserve the right to critique his effort in the pages of the *Revue thomiste*, doing so from the Thomistic perspective, and to say that the use of this metaphor represents a cavalier way of casting aside St. Thomas's authority in *theology*.[11]

3° I finally arrive at a capital point: I am essentially being accused of *litigating matters of orthodoxy*. What is the basis for this reproach?

I will not go back over the insulting insinuations, which I will leave to my readers to classify (conversations in circles close to us, correspondence, etc. . . .). If this were the only thing one could think of, then I would deny them outright, though not without strongly protesting against the publicity given to such suspicions.

Could this claim be founded on the tone I used, in which my opponents heard the desire to "impose" my own outlook? I have already explained myself concerning this accusation, and I must reiterate that such sensitivity surprises me. I believed myself far too puny, especially in comparison with the authors I criticized, to think I would be given an authority other than that which properly belongs to my arguments.

Therefore, this claim can only be founded on the arguments presented. But, in that case, our plaintiff's protest rests on an enormous misunderstanding.

It is true I said that certain assertions, *pushed to their consequences*, do not seem to me compatible with the Church's teachings. But these teachings—that is, the objective determination of the faith or of truths more or less close to faith—are *the very principles of theology*. What would theological discussion or theological criticism be if we did not have the right *to compare consequences with their principles*, to strive to show their disparity and thus to detect the *illogicality involved in the theological reasoning being proposed*? Does this challenge the theologian's personal faith and his intention to remain

---

[10] See "La Théologie et ses sources, Réponse," 85n1. My own assessment can be found in the words of another author who is completely uninvolved in the present discussion, writing in 1930: "To judge that Thomism was a garment worn in the thirteenth century but now is out of fashion, as though the value of metaphysics were time-dependent, represents a truly barbaric way of thinking." (Jacques Maritain, *Le Docteur Angélique*, 14).

[11] If this study was not theological, why would it be in the *Théologie* collection?

orthodox? This represents an entirely different domain, and I have in no way permitted myself to go there.

I said, and continue to think, until the contrary is shown to me, that the way Fr. Bouillard explains the progress of theology, as well as the permanence of dogmatic formulas, is incompatible with the demands of the latter. However, I also said, and am convinced, that he believes that he sees this compatibility, and his intent was even to escape the very relativism that, in my opinion is implied by the formulas he uses (p. 149 above). All I want is to be convinced that I have made a mistake. If his explanations are victorious, it will bolster the clarity of his own formulations and will be of aid to myself as well. But God forbid I should think—or even more so, insinuate—that any of the Frs. de Lubac, Daniélou, Bouillard, Fessard, von Balthasar, or anyone else, intend to reject Catholic orthodoxy! I affirm that I very clearly think the opposite is the case and that, in my opinion, any unprejudiced mind considering their works will admire the Christian spirit and apostolic zeal animating them and will surely only be able to find its wellsprings in a living faith. May God grant that we may emulate them in this!

This conception of criticism is not unusual. What do we reproach a philosopher for if not for having poorly observed, poorly reflected upon, or poorly reasoned, and consequently, for presenting conclusions that can be denounced for their inconsistency or illogicality? Does this call into question the soundness of his mind or, *a fortiori*, his mental health?

Instead of debating my "errors," the Fathers, invoking this time all the "censors" and "superiors" of the Society, ask me if I consider them all to be so blind as to not realize that they would, in fact, bring about dogmatic devastation?[12] But what would they say of a philosopher who would simply reply to any criticism of his ideas that if his opponent were right, he himself would have been intelligent enough to see his error? Can we not reject an opinion without implicitly considering its author blind or unintelligent? In truth, this represents quite a unique conception of the life of the mind, its complexity, the difficulties it encounters, and the thousands of occasions for it to fall into error. Or would this not be to fall into that *subjectivism* for which I am critiqued so much for having spoken of, a subjectivism which ultimately shows itself to be incapable of considering a set of objective statements independently of the qualities or defects of its author?

4° Perhaps it would remain to be seen whether criticism thus conceived is actually *useful*, useful precisely inasmuch as it is *demanding*. But here we encounter, under our opponents' pen, a confession which is not lacking in ingenuity: "*Securi loquebamur.*"[13] Were they then forgetting the point they

---

12 See "La Théologie et ses sources, Réponse," 95.
13 "La Théologie et ses sources, Réponse," 83.

quite rightly make further on, that "the first rigor to be exercised in dogmatic matters is a rigor against oneself"[14]?

Yes, we believe that the security of approval and praise numbs this requirement and rigor and that one of the important roles played by criticism is that of requiring an author to preserve and exercise it. It is certainly less compromising and more comfortable—especially when speaking about works by a person so widely lauded [*aussi flatteusement connu*] as Fr. de Lubac, for example—to use only holy water and express only admiration, which indeed is justified in many ways. But were we merely to limit ourselves to expressing praise, would we really render any service, even to his thought and to the quality of his works? I doubt it.

Just as our criticism does not intend to be completely "negative," to no less degree does it mean to express some bias, especially one that would be personal. We do not feel the slightest pain in proclaiming that Fr. de Lubac wrote an admirable book on Proudhon, indeed, one that perhaps he alone could ever have written. However, we do not believe we are dispensed from saying with no less force that *Corpus Mysticum*,[15] under the guise of presenting a historical account, introduces points concerning the role played by "*ratio*," reason, in theology and scholastic methodology that are contestable and tend *of themselves*—once again, we are not placing motives on trial!—to depreciate St. Thomas "in a matter in which he is the doctor." We will also say that *Surnaturel*, alongside solid historical studies, presents summary and hasty generalizations,[16] wishing, out of an allegedly "historical" concern, to lead us back to a St. Thomas, whom he sees through the lenses of a very contemporary school of thought, which has drawn significant inspiration from the ideas of Maurice Blondel. He is free to defend himself against such criticism, but why should he be content with being indignant about it?

5° We will summarize the intention of the critical studies published in the *Revue thomiste* by saying that our aim is *to render services, not judgments*

---

14 "La Théologie et ses sources, Réponse," 97.

15 I note here a misreading that would lead us to doubt the attention with which we have been read. Fr. de Lubac refers ("La Théologie et ses sources, Réponse," 80) to an assessment I made concerning his book *Surnaturel* that, in fact, was expressly directed against *Corpus Mysticum*: "A book that also accentuates the reactionary character (of the *Théologie* collection) against the speculative theology elaborated by St. Thomas" (p. 147n14 above). It seems Fr. de Lubac is not upset for giving the impression that we did not read his books before commenting on them. What, then, should we think about the indignations he registers against our "methodologies" [*procédés*]?

16 Fr. Jacques de Blic, who does not publish "a line without the approval [*en dehors des*] of the censors and superiors of the Society" has recently noted an example of this in "Quelque vieux textes sur la notion de l'ordre surnaturel," *Mélanges de science religieuse* (1946): 359[–62].

(Péguy). We are not infallible, nor do we believe ourselves to be so. If we stake out clear positions, rather than wandering around in doubts, we in no way do so in a spirit of imposing them on anybody. Anyone who wants to contradict us has at his disposal the same types of arguments as do we. If there are "parties" (even here!), we do not belong to any of them, for we refuse to consider Thomism as being a party, or a church, or *a fortiori*, a chapel. If it happens that we compare an author's conclusion with what seems to us to be the requirements of objective determinations of the faith, this is because theological argumentation could not abandon this kind of reasoning without thereby itself vanishing. However, our reasoning has no other authority than itself, and it stands freely in the open for anyone to show that we are wrong. And such debates must in no way involve personal accusations, nor claims concerning the quality of their interlocutors' faith, nor their intention to defend Catholic orthodoxy! It took no less than so huge a misunderstanding by our opponents to make us judge it useful to proclaim this obvious fact.

We are entitled to ask more of the critique registered against us. It would be a major reproach to say that it is aggressive or systematically negative. In order to avoid the appearance of attributing any superiority to ourselves—on what grounds?—we will not speak of "benevolence"; however, we will speak of "sympathy," something that we do not think that we have lacked.

B. On the Methodology to Be Used in Criticism

The grievances we have raised so far lie at the roots of the most serious misunderstandings, at least those that have done the most to displace this discussion and to lead it into a domain we wish we had not been forced to enter. Nonetheless, one of the most specific criticisms raised, one I would most willingly accept if it were supported by arguments and not mere indignation, is that of having followed a seriously flawed methodology. However, I am sorry that I am not convinced by the swift pages[17] dedicated to this subject, indeed pages that manifest unbridled imagination. They would make even those who are more convinced than we are skeptical concerning the scope of so many brilliant psychological reconstructions in history!

My "most unusual methodology [*procédé*]," the one "woven throughout" my entire critical study is, it seems, "the method of overreaching."[18] I believe this is what is called later my "boldness in extrapolation." Here is how it is reconstructed. [The authors of the *Response* claim that] after having forged a heretical monster on account of my "preoccupations" [*prévention d'esprit*], I looked for traces of it in the most diverse writings "without bothering to

---

17 See "La Théologie et ses sources, Réponse," 77–79.
18 "La Théologie et ses sources, Réponse," 82.

analyze any of them"—nor even, perhaps, to read them?[19]—commenting on them in light of one another. As a result, I was led—such was the "slope" that did not fail to lead me into the "abyss"—even to the point of supposing "ulterior motives," even where I could not see anything objectionable.

Do I need to say that, in my opinion, a study animated by such a spirit does not even have the right to be discussed? Do they impute this spirit to me so that they may dispense themselves of the need to engage in a discussion? It would seem so from reading the pleasant presentation that is then sketched out—in broad strokes, rest assured!—concerning the "results" to which this methodology led me.

But I must first explain myself concerning this very methodology, whose origins and development my opponents wanted to present from its roots (and from within?), and since they seem willing to be interested in the approach guiding my work, I will simply explain it to them.

During the years of silence that the war and occupation imposed on the *Revue thomiste*, we received relatively few books. The announcement of the *Sources Chrétiennes* collection seemed to me to be a considerable event. I followed it book by book without yet having any definite plans for review, allowing myself, to the contrary, to take in the incomparable charm of these ancient texts, along with the new-found freshness and savor of their Christian sentiment. I felt a fundamental appreciation for the founders of this collection, along with the warmest gratitude. I have not withdrawn any of these sentiments. This doesn't mean, however, that I didn't have my reservations. I will unequivocally confess that even the introduction of the first volume[20] seemed to me so evidently written *with an aim to please*, so concerned with being in close connection with "contemporary categories," and in this way, from the outset, with orienting the reader's mind towards something other than merely providing a nourishing contact with an admirable text, that I was sorry to see this overly "apologetic" inflection. To my eyes, this seems be a danger for the collection. The drawback to these kinds of accommodations is that what they render very contemporary for today begins, in but a day, to show its age by the very same token.

I did not feel less hesitant upon the subsequent publishing of Fr. de Lubac's introduction to Origen's *Homilies*. This plea for reinvigorating figurative exegesis did not persuade me that it was wise to seek from the Greek Fathers, among all the many riches that they offer us, something that, in my opinion, is less excellent in their thought [*ce que... ils ont eu de moins bon*]. Again, this is a point we can debate, so why raise one's arms in the air as though one were being attacked?

---

19 See "La Théologie et ses sources, Réponse," 81.

20 St. Gregory of Nyssa, *Vie de Möise*, intro., trans., and notes by Jean Daniélou.

Thus, little by little, a body of data was amassed, not new, of course, but brought up to date with the latest developments, which seemed to me to pose a much larger problem having a more general scope, one that possibly was even decisive for Christian thought: the relationship between our developed theology, which is indeed perhaps too fixed, and its sources. And I confess that this problem seemed to me even more interesting than the particular data that gave it a renewed urgency.

In the meanwhile, the *Théologie* collection was beginning to appear. The first volume, written by Fr. Bouillard, on the occasion of a particular point, though one of very great importance (for it concerns the very way that we must conceive of grace), devoted an entire conclusion to the general problem of the development of Christian thought. At the very least, his response seemed, to my eyes, obscure and confused, though clear in the assertion that since the historical position of St. Thomas differed fundamentally from that of modern theology it was now false.[21]

The second volume, written by Fr. Daniélou, after the disappointment caused by a title that was broader than the actual object of the book (the truth would have been better served by swapping the title and subtitle), gave the reader more substantial satisfaction, in my opinion, than the slightly limited study by Fr. von Balthasar also on Gregory of Nyssa. Fr. Daniélou at least approached, frankly and in a most interesting way, a problem that had already been posed elsewhere by, among others, Fr. Arnou, S.J. and Fr. Festugière, O.P. Contrary to these thinkers, Fr. Daniélou wanted to show that literal Platonic formulations, or more profoundly, schemata, had been, in reality, so deeply rethought and taken up again on a new plane by Gregory that they are, as far as he is concerned, purely and simply Christian. Far from having been a burden for the thought of the great Doctor, remaining like a defect in his formulations, they were quite successful in expressing an essentially Christian experience. I have no grounds for taking sides in this debate. However, without deciding whether he was right or wrong concerning this particular point, I noticed that in his reasoning, Fr. Daniélou greatly diminished the importance of conceptual constructions in order to be, above all, attentive to the authenticity of experience and of spirituality, which gave formulations their true value, using with a kind of pleasure the word "symbolism" to describe this claim.

Moreover, how can we fail to read this work alongside the two volumes in the *Sources* collection that translate texts of St. Gregory of Nyssa, the first entirely presented by Fr. Daniélou and the second annotated by him? How is it improper for us to compare books by the same author? And does the mere fact that they belong to different collections mean that we have no right to

---

21 See "Theology and its Sources," pp. 150–51 (above).

speak about them together? ("Thus, in order to understand the hidden meaning of innocent translations of the Fathers, they would need to be interpreted in light of a collection of theological studies."[22])

Shortly thereafter, a third volume appeared in the *Théologie* collection. It was by Fr. de Lubac and strove to provide a historical account of the ancient meaning of the expression *Corpus Mysticum*. So greatly did the supple talent of its author animate the work that it remained unburdened by the austerity of its unabashed erudition. However, under the apparent delimitation of its precise object, what problems his book raises! It implies nothing less than a radical alteration in the methodologies of theological reflection. Moreover, such observations are perfectly assured, but they are not delivered here merely at the stage of observation. The author connects the discussion with some of his cherished ideas, in particular all those concerned with the role played by symbolism in ancient thought. In the age of scholasticism, [we are told,] it happened that theology became *rationalist*. Interests shifted to new problems, resulting in considerable impoverishment. Thomism, which doubtlessly was one of the most successful fruits of this new method, was itself only a beginning, later far surpassed in the line of such rationalist desiccation. Let him who can conclude from Fr. de Lubac's presentation that this development brought substantial progress along with it. The obvious meaning—not of all of the erudition with which this book abounds, but of the idea, the historico-theological position that underlies it—is, much rather, that this was the source of a great misfortune. Not total misfortune, of course. Fr. de Lubac is not a personal enemy of St. Thomas—far from it! His declarations on this point are not only sincere (which we have no right to doubt); they are well-founded. However, his admiration is accompanied by the greatest of sorrow. Fr. de Lubac maintains an active nostalgia for the Patristic age and its methodologies, which he, in fact, excels in sharing. He has an absolute right to hold this opinion, but do we not also have the right to tell him that we see things differently? Do we not have the right to tell him that the historical arc he presents to us concerning the development of Christian thought seems, to our eyes, partially skewed, obscuring the profound meaning of the progressive constitution of theology as a science, properly so called? Do we not have the right, indeed an elementary right belonging to criticism, to see the continuity that exists between, on the one hand, this book and, on the other, the argument he offers on behalf of symbolic exegesis in the volume of the *Sources Chrétiennes* collection dedicated to Origen? Here again, the two collections meet again. Where is our "overreaching"? Where is our "extrapolation"?

Perhaps it is now clear why we thought we should speak about the *Sources Chrétiennes* and *Théologie* collections in one and the same critical

---

[22] "La Théologie et ses sources, Réponse," 78.

study. It is purely and simply *false* to say that I began by seeing "a heretical monster appear before my eyes"—maybe with the sole aim of attacking Jesuit theologians?—and that I searched in disparate and unconnected books, without "analyzing any of them," looking for anything that could give some plausibility to my naïve bogeyman.

But I will go even further with the explanations I never thought I would need to provide. Nowhere did I say that I wanted to present a simple review of the two collections that I mentioned. I was writing *a critical overview [une chronique] dedicated to the problem posed by the relationship between theology and its sources, the problem concerning the very progress of this theology and, thereby, the problem concerning its permanence.* Ideas expressed elsewhere thus entered into the scope of my study. In particular, the most recent *Revue du moyen-âge latin* came to my attention. With my attention piqued by the problem that Fr. Daniélou himself led me to pose with greater acuity concerning the relationship between spirituality or experience and theological expression, how could I fail to note the review of Gilson's small book written by Fr. Daniélou in that issue? What prevented me from using this text? I have always believed that the best interpretation of an author should be sought out from that author himself when, by chance, he has explained himself in other places than the particular works being given more specific consideration at a given time. In order to be true to the proper nature of a review, must we avoid speaking of the author's true thought? I do not mind the expression being less controlled and the writing quicker, but does this mean we must pay no attention to it?[23] That would be quite a unique conception of criticism!

This is how most texts spoken of in my critical study came together. (I shall speak of the others later). Their authors did not share merely a "family resemblance,"[24] something which, by the way, is true, though it is only of secondary interest to me. What was more, they objectively converged toward the same problem—treated here in passing, albeit in express terms, and there more fully, sometimes alongside Patristic studies and at other times alongside studies of St. Thomas or his predecessors. In short, it was the problem of theology itself, considered in its development, in its relationship with its sources, whether historical or subjective. Did we not have the right to discuss the ideas

---

23 I said that the terms Fr. Daniélou uses in this note concerning the relationship between spirituality and theological expression imply relativism in the latter, which would find its true measure in the former, likewise commenting that such relativism leads to subjectivism. The author's statements to the contrary are sufficient to convince me that he professes neither relativism nor subjectivism. I gladly acknowledge this, but I still have the right both to think and to say that the explanation that he offers is quite insufficient. I am delighted to have given him the opportunity to dispel such an equivocation, which doubtlessly would have caused him grief first of all.

24 "La Théologie et ses sources, Réponse," 78.

expressed on this point by various authors? The anathema launched against the "overall presentation"—a considerable argument: it is comparable to a "synthetic portrait"!—does not convince me that it was illegitimate. I remain persuaded that this methodology is perfectly suitable and presents serious advantages, despite the fact that it does have certain drawbacks. But isn't this true of every methodology? Which one would suffice on its own without continuous mental vigilance?

So, what remains is the way I used it. I will write neither a panegyric nor even a complete apology on behalf of this point. I recognize that, despite my intentions, as well as the precautions I believed I had taken, a given remark addressed to one of the authors unduly spills over upon the others. I will gladly take note of their protest and pass it on to my readers. I do not contradict myself in doing so, for I asked for it (p. 138n6 above). However, I should consider myself satisfied by the very way that this protest is made, since the five authors whom I named collectively defend all the passages of each of the authors where I raised a criticism! Can this fail to surprise: such solidarity, not only in protest, but in ideas, at the very moment when these authors solemnly proclaim their independence? I was prepared to say that I was wrong for having cited Fr. de Lubac (on p. 147 above) and for failing to specify that the further, much more general, discussion following that citation was not aimed at him. Moreover, it is not very difficult to see that this further discussion simply serves as a leadup to my critique of Fr. Bouillard's book. But now, by the very form of the *Response*, Fr. de Lubac seems to endorse Fr. Bouillard's ideas. If this is true, I will say, therefore, that without having targeted him, my criticism nonetheless also hit him, for I continue to believe that this critique remains valid against a system of ideas that alone would explain Fr. Bouillard's assertions. He speaks of "overreaching" and of "extrapolation." Improper overreaching would consist in attributing to the author the conscious acceptance of this system of ideas. I took great care not to level such a charge, but since when does the critic not have the right to assess a set of assertions and to point out their *objective* implications and consequences? I deny that the least amount of extrapolation was involved here. Rather, this represents an elementary methodology involved in any discussion. Getting indignant does not resolve the question, and no more does a broad declaration of contrary principles serve to resolve it either.[25] The only valid response is to discuss my arguments.

---

[25] This declaration of principles resolves only a personal problem I never posed, namely, that of Fr. Bouillard's intentions and those of his personal philosophy. I only spoke about his published statements and tried to spell out the philosophy objectively implied by these declarations. I did so without claiming any infallibility.

III. WHAT IS AT STAKE IN THIS DEBATE

However, it is very clear that the debate goes deeper still and engages questions which are more serious than those of methodology or even of the meaning of criticism in theology.

The *Response* speaks about my "preoccupation of mind" and "grave concerns." Well, yes! Doubtlessly, I have them in a different sense than they think, but I must admit the claim is true. The work of reflection that I have described thus far, even using the method of "overall presentation," would not have reached the text of my critical study in the form in which it was read [by them]. Another current of reflection, this one charged with concern and anger, brought with itself more tumultuous waters. My work was already mostly composed (and in a wholly different tone) when Fr. Daniélou's article was published in the April 1946 issue of *Études*, "Les orientations présentes de la pensée religieuse." In this exposé—which, in a delightful understatement, the *Response* calls, "a wide-ranging piece with formulas that are sometimes rapid in character"[26]—I read, "faced with the danger of agnosticism, Neo-thomism has again accused theological rationalism."[27] (Will Fr. de Lubac perhaps tell me that it should be understood that he has "indicted" it and that I should be grateful to the author for this great praise?) A little further on, I read, "There was need of warding off the dangers created by modernism. Neo-Thomism and the Biblical Commission provided guardrails, but guardrails obviously are not answers."[28]

Alongside these disdainful appraisals, I saw spreading forth that same desire to be pleasing and the intention to attract others that I noted above in connection with the same author's introduction to St. Gregory of Nyssa's *The Life of Moses*: "theological speculations separated from action and engagement have run their course."[29] Like Marxism or existentialism, we would have a "thought engaged in life [*une pensée engagée*]."—Without in any way renouncing either action or life, do we not have the right both to consider and to say that neglect of the speculative finality of knowledge as such would represent a great loss for Christian thought and that agreement with existentialism and Marxism on this specific point would be lamentable. Do we not have the right to fear this kind of *intellectual engagement*? Several times, the same author criticizes Thomism and scholastic thought for being too closed off from history.[30] And, obviously, by

---

26 "La Théologie et ses sources, Réponse," 81.

27 Daniélou, "Les orientations présentes de la pensée religieuse," *Études 249* (April 1946): 6.

28 Daniélou, "Les orientations présentes," 6–7.

29 Daniélou, "Les orientations présentes," 7.

30 The *Response* states in summary: "Why be so outraged upon hearing that, historically considered, it (St. Thomas's *oeuvre*) lacks a certain sense of history?" (*Dialogue*

this he means that reflection on history will only be integrated into contemporary Christian thought by utilizing a philosophy that wholly differs from Thomism. We have the right to hold that Thomism can be something more for us than a mere historical datum, an object of scholarship, and that, considered in its present life, it has something to offer to this reflection on history.

This instructive reading even taught me that scholastic theology (and, therefore, Thomistic thought), fixed as it is in the "immobile world of Greek thought," puts "reality in essences more than in subjects," and thereby "ignores the dramatic world of persons."[31] But its great sin is that it treats God as an "object," whereas He is "the subject par excellence."[32]

---

théologique, p. 87). Such a moderate and, in fact, unquestionable affirmation is, in no way, the source of my "outrage." Rather, my outrage is aimed at claims that are quite different: "the notion of history is *foreign* to *Thomism*" (Daniélou, "Les orientations présentes," 10); "*Scholastic theology* is foreign to these categories. The world which is its own is the immobile world of Greek thought. . . . Moreover, it makes *no room* for history" (Daniélou, "Les orientations présentes," 14, text cited in whole, above, p. 141n8 above). "To lack a certain sense of history" and to be entirely "foreign" to it, making "no room" for it, are by no means the same thing. Moreover, Thomism is not only for us "the work of St. Thomas . . . historically considered." It is a living doctrine that extends to truths that St. Thomas did not see, a doctrine that, of course, is also stripped of much adventitious data, outmoded conceptions, and forms of narrowness all inevitably connected to a number historical influences and to the state of medieval culture and science. We believe that Thomism is perfectly open to the notion of history and that starting points for this sort of reflection are not lacking, even in the work of St. Thomas himself, "historically considered." With the method of alternative theses and skillful retreats one can distort all discussions and then solemnly declare that discussion is "uneven" [*en porte à faux*]. Is this fully honest?

31 Daniélou, "Les orientations présentes," 14.

32 Daniélou, "Les orientations présentes," 7 and 16. Nowhere have I ever said that one is forbidden to be interested in "subjective life" (*Dialogue théologique*, 89n1). I believe quite the opposite, but I said that this very legitimate interest tends, in modern thought, to detract from, or overshadow, the consideration of timeless truth. On the other hand, the *Response* registers against me, on this point, a critique that would lead me to believe that, once again, its authors have been careless in reading me. I recalled that to consider God as an *object* is not something specific to this rationalized Thomistic theology but, rather, constitutes an attitude and vocabulary consecrated by the [First] Vatican Council. In that regard, they speak of "a war of words" and exclaim: "doesn't everyone, however, see at first sight that the meaning is not the same for both sides?" (*Dialogue théologique*, 94n2). Everyone? I do not know. But at least for my own part, I had seen it quite clearly and I say so in this very text: "We are quite fine with the fact that Fr. Daniélou speaks using a different vocabulary than our own" (p. 144n9 above). And our criticism meant that one is not free in theology to assign meanings to words willy-nilly. Moreover, it meant that if traditional theology is critiqued for treating God as an object, either it was actually understood in a different sense than what it itself intends, meaning that one thus committed a deplorable equivocation, or it was understood in the same sense as it itself intends, meaning that the Vatican Council was also in one's crosshairs. True, "there are many ways to be wrong." However, thoughtlessness or clever tactics cumulatively add much to this end [*en cumule beaucoup*].

Did they think these assertions would leave us indifferent, we who profess Thomism and do not hide the fact that we still have some interest in "theoretical speculations separated from (and uninterested in) action"? Should we thank the author for the sympathy he showed us and accept the brilliant future prospects that he traced out for Thomism? [It seems that we are told:] who has not understood, as we have, that Thomism doubtlessly played an honorable role in the past, but it was incapable of handling present difficulties, indeed, perhaps even of being aware of them? It would be a beautiful museum piece, covered with the most flattering, though archaic, labels, ones which, however, are though as unsuited to the current demands of the mind [*esprit*] as the heavy armor of the knights of old would be in our modern wars. Shall we say that these ideas were foreign to those that arose for us upon reading the other books by Fr. Daniélou, Fr. Bouillard's "conclusion," and the preface written by Fr. von Balthasar? Who does not see their convergence?

I do not attribute to all these authors all the ideas held by each of them individually. I do not suspect any kind of prior agreement. Rather, I am concerned with how the ideas expressed, as well as the expressions themselves, *objectively converge* towards a cluster of ideas: that Thomism is not fit for contemporary difficulties; that scholastic theology has had its day; that we must ask others, modern thinkers, for the philosophy faith needs in order for theological explanation to be possible; that, therefore, theology has never reached the state of science properly so called; and that what is needed here is a new theology.

I now believe I have said enough to bring the scope of the debate out into broad daylight. I have been critiqued for going beyond, in my Critical Study, the books that make up the *Sources Chrétiennes* and *Théologie* collections, and my critics obviously would have preferred me to present these different volumes one by one, a methodology that would have led me to treat, all at once, quite diverse subjects (or rather, would have prevented me from presenting them all at once). And, yes, it is true that this would have been much less offensive. However, what would have been striking was how a number of them—and we must say, indeed, those that are most significant among them—converge in their concerns. Therefore, I decided to focus my examination on this point of convergence. For that reason, I did not confine myself to the two collections I mentioned. The article by Fr. Daniélou—are not its echoes and repercussions well known?—fell directly within the scope of my study.

IV. CONCLUSION

I believe that the clarifications being demanded from me could very well have been found by carefully reading my Critical Study. However, if I can hope that this reply will be read more fully, then I will provide more explicit ones.

I have not spoken in the name of any authority, nor have I received any directives. I have no other purpose than to bring to light, with a view to discussing them in the open, ideas in circulation and cropping up in some texts. My object has not been to determine the exact thought of each of the Frs. de Lubac, Daniélou, Bouillard, Fessard, and von Balthasar. When they take their place in the tale of history, future writers will be charged with doing so. However, be that as it may, I was not charged with undertaking any fact-finding mission into any of them. Reflecting on publications in which they themselves pose the same question, I have posed this important problem concerning how theology is related to its sources, be they historical or subjective, as well as that concerning its permanent value in its scientific formulation. I tried to bring to light those principles which, in my opinion, command this debate and to define, by contrast, doctrinal positions which I necessarily formulated in the most explicit terms possible. Thus, knowing full well what I was doing, I took care to inform them that I was not attributing these positions precisely as such to anyone.

What direction was taken in the discussion with the authors whom I attacked? Very precisely that of saying that each of them, in various forms and with more or less commitment, had expressed, in the very writings that I cited at length,[33] ideas which could only find their true consequences or principles in the false positions that I was fighting. No extrapolation is involved here. Rather, it is nothing other than that process that is essential to any discussion of ideas: *objectively* showing the logical implications of an assertion. The logic of these implications is what needs to be discussed. Instead of this, we were presented with a common, solemn declaration of the principles that the authors *profess*, something I have never called into question.

Since it is desired that I explain myself on each point, I wished to say the following, and I will maintain it until the opposite is shown to be true:

1° That the *Sources Chrétiennes* and *Théologie* collections complement each other in a common effort, which has a substantially excellent intention. I am not the only one to draw this connection, for Fr. Daniélou himself drew

---

[33] In citing them, I did not take gleanings from here and there, drawing on expressions which were detached from their immediate context, as is done in the "Response." I gave precise references. For *Corpus Mysticum*, the citations were made by Fr. Marie-Joseph Nicolas in the critical overview [*chronique*] which followed by own in *Revue thomiste* 46 (1946): 383–88.

[34] Daniélou, "Les orientations présentes," 10.

it in the April 1946 issue of *Études*.[34] This was already externally and superficially apparent given that the two directors of the former gave to the latter "important works" (Daniélou, loc. cit.), which to this point in time represent the most significant volumes in the latter collection.

2° That the intention of the *Sources Chrétiennes* collection, such as it was explicitly defined by its directors, is inflected toward an orientation that I criticize without, for all that, ceasing to heap great praise upon this same intention, as well as its realization. This orientation, I repeat, consists in wanting to bring to light, most of all, "those categories which are those of contemporary thought, categories which scholastic theology had lost,"[35] something which amounts to wanting to show the present inadequacy of scholastic theology. I have the right to prefer that one "give life" to the writings of the Fathers with a less restrictive concern and to think that this very concern is characteristic of a shared spirit and common mentality.

3° That the way Fr. Daniélou, in his article in *Études*, speaks of Thomism and scholastic theology in general ranks both of them as belonging to a stage of now-outdated Christian thought, a fact that explains their inability to assimilate new categories, in particular, those of history and subjective experience, which is expressed by existentialism.

4° That the way Fr. Daniélou himself, in a text I cited at length, speaks of the relations between theological systems and various spiritualities leads him to look to measure theological expressions not by the objects that they wish to propose but, rather, by the theologian's religious experience, a claim that inflects the very notion of speculative truth, which is classically defined as being conformity with the object, turning it, instead, towards the idea that truth is found in conformity with subjective life. I am delighted to know that Fr. Daniélou thinks the opposite, especially since he wrote me [to tell me so] (and in a different tone, thanks be to God, than that of the collective *Response*), and I duly note this. Nonetheless, I maintain that his formulas can be objectively explained only by inflecting the claim in that direction.

5° That the two books by Fr. de Lubac, *Corpus Mysticum* in the *Théologie* collection and *Introduction aux homélies d'Origène* in *Sources Chrétiennes*, are connected with the same concern that I already discussed, the first volume by presenting the introduction of dialectic into theological reflection (the very thing that gave birth to scholastic theology) as though it were an impoverishment, the second one also by arguing for a return to symbolism, though this time in exegesis. I do not denounce any heresy, nor do I even denounce any excessive claim. I only say that this is debatable and that, objectively, these assertions go in the same direction as those that I already noted and that Fr. Daniélou himself willingly highlighted. I say, "in the same

---

35 Daniélou, "Les orientations présentes," 10.

direction," but without themselves going as far, by a long shot. If, in spite of my explicit warning, other ideas have been attributed to Fr. de Lubac solely on the basis of my Critical Study, I object to this and publicly retract everything that could have led to it.

6° That Fr. Bouillard's book, which opens the *Théologie* collection, presents in its conclusion a general theory of the development of theology that, in spite of its declared intentions, leads to the denial of the permanent value of theological science and even of dogmatic formulas. Since the *Response* makes no allusion to this discussion, despite the fact that it is lengthy, I am content to refer the readers to pages 149–52 above of the present edition of this debate.

7° That Fr. Fessard's preface to a book in which he wants to provide the foundations for an essential theological notion in a way that is valuable for our contemporaries, by utilizing a dialectic that is entirely Hegelian, casually casts aside St. Thomas's justification for this notion by appealing to a "clothing metaphor." The obvious meaning of the book is that Christian doctrine today will only find its explanatory instrument in a metaphysics that is not that of St. Thomas—in this case, in a Hegelian metaphysics. I do not denounce a heresy in this, but here in the *Revue thomiste*, I do defend the position of St. Thomas—and it just so happens that in the same volume this position is marvelously highlighted by Jacques Maritain.[36]

8° That Fr. von Balthasar, in the introduction to his book on St. Gregory of Nyssa, *Presence and Thought*, says that the present task of theology will involve refashioning it for our times, indeed, in a completely new way, the very thing done by the Greek Fathers or by St. Thomas for their times. I have by no means attributed to Fr. von Balthasar all the ideas expressed by other authors concerning the Fathers, and the fact that he puts the Greek Fathers in the same category as St. Thomas (minus the insolence) does not reassure me. What worries me in this text is his very conception of theological tradition and its meaning, concerning which the *Response* gives an answer that is as unexpected as it is soothing. (I note that, as regards the assessment of contemporary Thomism, an author who is entirely unengaged in our controversy, and with good reason, understood it in the same sense as I have, in fact, in order to approve it, namely, Maurice de Gandillac in the third volume of *Dieu Vivant*.[37])

9° That the article by Fr. Daniélou in *Études* considerably increased the evidence that these various works objectively converge towards a new con-

---

36 [Tr. note: This is likely referring to Jacques Maritain, "La personne et le bien commun," *Revue thomiste* 46 (1946): 237–78.]

37 Maurice de Gandillac, "À propos de Grégoire de Nysse," *Dieu Vivant* 3 (1945): 123–34.

ception of scholastic theology.

The Reverend Fathers invite us to renounce this type of discussion in order to dedicate ourselves to the magnificent tasks proposed recently by His Holiness Pope Pius XII. We have no trouble in joining them in this desire, and we will be happy to do our part in helping them. However, we do not believe that all these discussions are sterile, at least if we can abstain from lowering them to personal polemics. And if it is true, as the Holy Father also assures us, that a kind of "new theology" is currently spreading in minds, leading them astray, then it is quite a fine task, indeed, namely, that of combating this theology in order to better emphasize the permanent fruitfulness of traditional theology. All we ask is that we might fight this battle with them in brotherhood.

POST-SCRIPT [BY FR. MARIE-JOSEPH NICOLAS]

Since my lengthy analysis of Fr. De Lubac's *Corpus Mysticum* was called into question quite briefly and summarily,[38] I believe it necessary that I respond, at least briefly. "The only thing for which we reproach Fr. de Lubac" in this beautiful book, which we cited in abundance and admired, "is the fact that he looks upon the forgetting of Eucharistic symbolism as though it were the necessary consequence of the scientific form taken on by theology in the Middle Ages, holding that this scientific form represents the expression of an outdated mentality that is perhaps less accessible to minds of today, though, which in any case, is less traditional than the symbolic mentality of the Fathers." Certainly, I could have been mistaken in my interpretation of the chapter entitled "From Symbolism to Dialectic."[39] And possibly I had a poor grasp of his supple and brilliant thought, which I, nonetheless, was pleased to follow very closely. He is the one who speaks of scholasticism as being a form of "Christian rationalism"[40] and of those "syntheses which are more scientific than religious"[41] which replaced Patristic theology at that privileged moment of intellectual history [*l'histoire de l'esprit*], when "intellectual research and spiritual tension coincided, participating in the same impulse and drawing the same curve."[42] He is the one who exclaims, in expressing his conclusion concerning the replacement

---

38 See "La Théologie et ses sources, Réponse," 97.

39 Henri de Lubac, *Corpus Mysticum: The Church and the Eucharist in Middle Ages*, trans. by Gemma Simmons (South Bend: University of Notre Dame Press, 2007), 221–47. [Tr. note: Other direct citations come from the French.]

40 de Lubac, *Corpus Mysticum*, 273.

41 de Lubac, *Corpus Mysticum*, 298.

42 de Lubac, *Corpus Mysticum*, 268.

of "the dialectic of sign and thing" by that "of substance and accident and of quantity as a vice-substance[43]": "What ravages have thus been caused now by the very heresy that has been conquered! What unfortunate men, we might say by returning to a phrase from Pascal, who led the defenders of the faith to turn away from the core of religion so as to direct all speculation concerning the Eucharist to external apologetic problems!"[44]

Moreover, we have not dramatized this interpretation of theological progress. When I wrote, "The life of the mind may indeed be a form of life, but it does not develop in the way that a vegetable or animal does, renewing itself by making its successive forms pass through the indefinitely repeated cycle of birth, youth, maturity, and aging," I certainly did not say that Fr. de Lubac had written this. I will even say: it is because I know he cannot hold such a position that I raised it to him as an objection because of how it lays in line with texts like the following:

> No two great thinkers, no two great mystics, can pose essential problems in the same terms. Each of them, even within one and the same doctrinal or spiritual tradition, communicates to us the sentiment—if we know how to question it—concerning the perpetual discovery that is necessarily the life of the mind, along with, as it were, the way that its frontiers must perpetually be shifted. None of them passes without his action remaining inscribed upon the very regions where we believe ourselves to be in the presence of eternal categories. Happier than the greatest captains and the greatest builders of empires, they manage to make us forget the previous state of the spiritual world that they have managed to recast. But also, through the inevitable vengeance of things, as soon as their work, in turn, is "outdated," it is immediately misunderstood. We lack the imagination, even if the text is still between our hands, to reconstruct their mental universe. In order to do so we would need to support ourselves upon the very thing that, deep down within ourselves, has just been reconstructed.[45]

It seems to me that critiques like those I have allowed myself to perform have the benefit of provoking very useful explanations and clarifications. How

---

43 [Tr. note: This, language, of later scholastic provenance, refers to the way that quantity functions in place of substance as the foundation for the other accidents in the appearances of bread in the Eucharist. See *ST* III, q. 77, a. 1, along with Cajetan's commentary on this. Also see Reginald Garrigou-Lagrange, *De Eucharistia* (Turin: Berruti, 1948), 161: "In commenting on this article, Cajetan notes that the bread's quantity hence comes to play the role of substance (*quantitas panis fit vice-substantia*); that is, it takes on the mode, power, and property of substance."]

44 de Lubac, *Corpus Mysticum*, 279.

45 de Lubac, *Corpus Mysticum*, 268–69.

could one not grasp the profound sympathy of phrases such as these: "Why spoil his magnificent effort of openness and 'theological reinvention' through a perpetual fear concerning the 'fixity' of the truth?"

We should add, I have not, for one second, heard criticism of Fr. de Lubac for having spoken of St. Thomas so little in a matter in which he is the doctor. On the contrary, I thought it necessary to explain why I believed that St. Thomas's theology was attacked in a historical study aimed directly at the High Middle Ages.

5

Theological Progress and Fidelity to St. Thomas

Marie-Joseph Nicolas, OP

But let us now set aside our critical study. Every reader having before himself the *Response* written in answer to it will judge the complaints we provoked, as well as those that we ourselves raised in our turn. Let us turn to the explanations given to us. We would insult the Reverend Fathers were we to think that these summary pages provided a complete presentation of their thought. In fact, they have told us that they plan a series of studies in theology and history, and we are sincerely delighted to have provoked this project. Slightly disappointed at having received a joke in response to our concerns—the tale of the wise man who felt that to affirm three persons in God represented a tendency to affirm four[1]—we will leave this story aside so that we may ask ourselves what position they ultimately hold regarding both Saint Thomas and theology itself.

Let us begin by seeing what the Thomistic fidelity of the Reverend Fathers will not be.

It will not exclude the study of the first twelve centuries of Christian thought. Nor will this study be limited solely to historical studies concerning the genesis of Saint Thomas's thought. In these remote times, one will seek out any Christian food that can be directly assimilated. One will take up the progress made in later centuries without fear of bringing about, in certain cases, a "recasting," for St. Thomas's synthesis is not definitive, nor its categories eternal. More work lies ahead than merely placing some adornments upon it and drawing some conclusions from it.

---

1 [Tr. note: In their response, the Jesuit fathers told a tale that came to their minds in the face of Fr. Labourdette's concerns regarding the tendency he saw in their writings: "One day, a wise man said to his friend in a delicate situation, 'Oh unhappy man, beware of carelessly proclaiming that there are three persons in God! If you exaggerate but a little, you will come to say that there are four persons in Him. And, in fact, in speaking of three, do you not already manifest some tendency to posit four in Him? Why cast forth the highest number all at once? Say, instead, simply that there are two persons in Him. This is incontestable, and here at this universally reassuring golden mean, you will have the advantage of not advancing toward the very edges of the truth, where one finds oneself in such close proximity to error'" (*Dialogue théologique*, 82).]

Our authors continue: By assimilating the tradition for his own part, St. Thomas does not exhaust all of the nourishment that can be drawn from it. Even after him, we must return to the past. Likewise, later progress should not confine itself merely to making additions to what has been received.

"Scientific systematization" carries the risk of causing impoverishment and partiality. The same can be said concerning the fact that something was conceived in a given century when many of our means of knowledge were lacking, in particular, a kind of sense for history. In order to remain a living theology, Thomism must expand. It must integrate into itself a number of more concrete elements that have been overlooked in its efforts at systematization, elements that, moreover, are not opposed to it. Theological progress is not a straight line always passing from one conclusion to the next. The law of the mind is that it only truly progresses and deepens its knowledge by a rhythm that periodically refers back to the origins of its thought. By returning to St. Thomas's sources we will enable ourselves to discover, in his own thought, virtualities destined for enabling wonderful developments. Like Sacred Scripture, the Fathers are perpetually replenishing wellsprings, pouring forth even today.

Now, with the exception of a few expressions, we are in agreement with our critics on all of these points, which they seem to hold as though it were opposed to our own position. Moreover, they recognize that we have said—or even better, practiced—analogous things. Nonetheless, let us not exaggerate the scope of this agreement concerning *what Thomism must not be*. We would like to see *what is left of St. Thomas*, and without a doubt this will bring our disagreement more clearly to light. In their *Response*, what do our critics say about the permanent value of Thomism? We learn that they do not hold that Thomistic thought is "exhausted." They do not say, "We cannot there find any principle, any 'toothing stone,'[2] open to new constructions." However, only one positive aspect of the Thomistic system is questioned, and moreover, it is the most apposite for the group of problems discussed: *St. Thomas's intellectualism*. Rightly enough, our authors distinguish between intellectualism considered as a doctrine that accords the highest ontological value to intellectual activity (and they declare themselves divided on this point) and intellectualism considered as a doctrine that accords the intellect the *power of grasping* the truth, loudly professing this intellectualism, though on the condition that it be rightly understood:

> There can be, in theology, a kind of intellectualism, against which we don't hesitate to take a position. It is that which would tend to make

---

2 [Tr. note: In architecture, a "toothing stone" (*pierre d'attente*) is a projection from a wall that allows future construction to be built in continuity with the foundation of the older construction.]

Christian Revelation into the communication of a *system of ideas*, whereas it is first of all and forever the manifestation of a person, of Truth personified. Christ is simultaneously the bearer and the object of the divine message. The Word of God in its unique and definitive fullness is the Word made flesh. This does not mean that Revelation would not need to be expressed in concepts, nor that the course of time does not require this conceptual expression to be clarified or amplified, nor that we can only expect it to give us aid in the practical order, without the value of truth properly so-called. To those who in virtue of some scruple or a misguided reflection would be led to doubt the human intellect's ability to grasp the truth, the Incarnation of the Word brings, on the contrary, new motives for confidence. However, it follows that Catholic Truth will always exceed its conceptual expression and, *a fortiori*, its scientific formulation in an organized system. This is what Christian thinkers of all times have instinctively felt. This is what allowed someone like St. Bonaventure and St. Thomas, without renouncing their differences, to understand each other, even through something other than merely a spirit of charity.[3]

Let our critics rest reassured! This page which we just cited does not reveal to our eyes any abyss of murky complications. We do not ourselves confess the kind of intellectualism just laid forth in this critique. We simply remain unsatisfied and want more.

To shed some light on the debate, this is the question we should ask: Do you believe that the metaphysics of St. Thomas is *true*—and not only as a kind of hypothesis or as an expression of a mentality but, rather, objectively and in the nature of things? And the second question would be this: Do you at least believe that effort must be expended by Christian thinkers in order to grasp it, so that, thanks to it, the faith could be articulated in the most complete and most universal theology?

Yes, certainly, Revelation is essentially the revelation of a Person, though of a Person who has spoken and who has, therefore, expressed concepts enabling the analogical grasping of that reality which is ineffable and infinite, concepts that, granted, are profoundly engaged in the concrete whole that is made up of images, feelings, experiences, examples, and general environments, though ones that the Church has a mission to draw forth and specify, not without having recourse to philosophical reflection and, consequently, to other concepts that do not directly come from the Word of God, though she guarantees their ability to explain the Word of Christ to the human intellect. We are profoundly persuaded that these concepts, even those that the Church has thus fixed and guaranteed, are simultaneously *true* and yet also insufficient for expressing everything, not only concerning the Divine Reality

---

3 "La Théologie et ses sources, Réponse," 90–91.

but even concerning the real content of the living Word of Christ. We also say that this insufficiency is the cause of the one-sided character of all theological thought, even that of St. Thomas.

However, we do not think that two contradictory theological theses can be simultaneously true, except in those aspects where they mutually complement each other and do not stand in opposition. While willingly admitting the need to revise St. Thomas's theses, we think that, given how his general viewpoint represents the most essential one, his fundamental theses are true and that his synthesis represents the foundational synthesis needed for all solid theological construction. However, if a *truth* coming from elsewhere could not be integrated into this synthesis without the need to modify its essential data, we would salute this new theology and would frankly leave our Master behind rather than renounce the truth, the meaning and infinite breadth of which he himself teaches us above all.

We do not believe that one and the same truth, however infinite and elevated above all our concepts it may be, could also be truly expressed by means of a fundamentally different metaphysics. Certainly, all the various philosophies used by Christians contain shared truths, and although it would perhaps be too optimistic to attribute this fact to perceptions arising from common sense (for the latter is not the most widespread thing in the world), they are perhaps, rather, discovered precisely in virtue of *what is required by faith, which seeks out an intellectual world in which her lungs may find breathable air*. However, this "*philosophia perennis*," this minimum common datum of Christian philosophy is not enough for a perfect theology. Was not Saint Thomas's particular glory and historical significance the fact that he traced out the essential lines of Christian metaphysics?

Let's discuss this frankly, for ambiguity in this matter is not good. What would cause us the greatest concern would be if we felt that one were placing in question the very possibility and objective existence of a Christian metaphysics and, thereby, that of a scientifically elaborated theology, one which is never finished in its task of integrating new knowledge and new perspectives, along the way freeing itself from what "was neither gold, nor silver, but rather, straw."

Nonetheless, in response to anyone who would dare deprive St. Thomas of the glorious role that we recognize for him, we would not fear to oppose those reasons and intellectual possibilities that we have at our disposal, certainly not in defense of some kind of family property or even of one of our long-established and dear habits of thought, but instead, we would do so out of the conviction that the abandonment of the central positions of St. Thomas's metaphysics would lead, little by little, to the ruin of the faith. Maybe we are wrong in feeling that St. Thomas is so absent from the new theology. Perhaps this reservation simply comes from the well-justified persuasion that our contemporary mentality is too impregnated with idealism, existentialism, or evolutionism for Thomistic language to be rendered understandable, even if it were expressed in language that is fashionable today. Perhaps one feels, in fact, that Thomism is too much the property of a particular sort of mind that is closed off to history, science, and contemporary sentiments for it possibly to be used freely. Perhaps the need to Christianize certain intellectual subjects that hold an all-powerful sway over contemporary minds is judged to be far too urgent for us to spend time waiting until Thomism manages to integrate this into its metaphysics without denaturing the latter.

All this is possible. We also believe there's something more. Thomistic metaphysics cannot be true without being simultaneously convinced that modern thought is fundamentally flawed and that, however assimilable it may be on a number of points, it remains fundamentally opposed to Thomism. For men who, justifiably, are profoundly men of their times, this opposition to modern thought is bitter indeed. It is likewise such for us, who are not at all "displaced persons" [*émigrés*] and who dream, like our brothers, of engagement and incarnation. Perhaps the vivacity of our criticism bore the accent of the bitterness experienced when one feels so lonely in holding an intellectual outlook that we, however, feel intellectually and morally impossible not to take, an outlook that we, in the end, believe holds the greatest promise for success, while modern thought increasingly unveils before all our eyes all the profound vices that corrupt it.

We do indeed think our opponents are happy to see us remain faithful to Thomistic thought. Without a doubt, they will not be less liberal toward us than toward others. Even if this were necessary (though the opposite is what, in fact, is needed) for winning souls for the faith, they would not fail to flatter us. However, it is more difficult for us than for them to accept all intellectual outlooks that differ from our own. When considering matters from the perspective of faith, we are no haughtier than they. We will never confuse Thomist metaphysics with the Church's defined dogmas, nor even with her ordinary teaching. However, we think other certainties than those of faith exist and that merely because a position is not condemnable does not, however, mean it is above criticism. Intellectualism, which without confusing its system with dogma knows how to speak with assurance and how to affirm (and therefore to deny), has a kind of unpleasant savor about it. We mourn the wounds we could inflict and the irritation we might cause. However, let it be known that we are not guilty of excessive self-confidence. We know how to recognize our errors and forever will do so. Believing in the truth does indeed sometimes communicate a bit too much assurance to one's words. While we strive never to confuse, on the one hand, the human mind's general aptitude for reaching certitude with, on the other, the truth of our own judgments, we will not be overly scrupulous in saying what we think, beseeching those who read us not to see in our criticism verdicts uttered by a judge or even appeals to a sacred tribunal but, simply, the free and frank expression of our sentiments. Moreover, we know quite well that our most useful work will be to prove the possibility of movement by walking and to resolve the questions that every contemporary Christian thinker asks himself with anguish, doing so with the assistance of St. Thomas's thought.

6

The Analogy of Truth and the Unity of Theological Science

Michel-Marie Labourdette, OP,
and Marie-Joseph Nicolas, OP

In an article entitled, "L'analogie de la vérité: Réflexions d'un philosophe sur une controverse théologique," Fr. Jean-Marie Le Blond, S.J., returned, in *Recherches de Science Religieuse* (34, no. 2, 1947, pp. 129–41), to one of the points lying at the heart of the debate that recently found its first expression in the texts gathered together in our *Dialogue théologique*. He does not name any of us, nor does he cite any of our comments, instead only referring to "the debate which recently has opened up." However, he claims to show that the omission of "elementary points, admitted by all," and for the most part expressly taught by St. Thomas himself, led us to form "premature judgments and summary condemnations."[1] By issuing this reminder, he intends not only to justify the expressions placed into question in our controversy (in particular, those of Fr. Bouillard) but even to launch the accusation that we are unconscious rationalists, forgetful of the supernatural character of faith, opposed to the contemporary missionary directives of the Church, and, in any case, guilty (like Spinoza) of univocity, as it were, serene dogmatists who argue on behalf of the permanence and timeless character of Thomist philosophy and would have there be but one, single theology.[2] Needless to say, we feel no more accused of not submitting to the Church—for this would be implied in the accusation, as well as a humiliating mental vice—than we ourselves had the desire to make the accusation of heterodoxy against those who themselves hold a new theology.

Nobody desires more than we do to remain on the level of serene exchanges of opinions concerning a discussion that has all-too-quickly turned into a polemic. Indeed, our intention is to renounce the latter. However, Fr. Le Blond's response has the advantage of posing the question in a way that provides us with too apt an occasion for adding precision to the ideas that we defend for us not to seize the opportunity to present a general

---

[1] Le Blond, "L'analogie de la verité," 129.
[2] Le Blond, "L'analogie de la verité," 138–41.

statement of our position. Indeed, like Msgr. de Solages[3] before us, he places the entire weight of the debate upon the *analogical character of truth*.

We will first present a summary of this article, which was well-written, despite the fact that it is too influenced by its author's desire to justify one by one the expressions that were implicated in "Theology and Its Sources" concerning the relativity and invariability of conceptual expressions of the truth, the relations between "contemporary relevance [*actualité*]" and "truth," the inseparability of what is unchanging and what is mutable [in our conceptual expressions of the truth] etc.... After this summary, we will then examine, on its own terms, the problem thus raised.

I. THE ANALOGY OF TRUTH AND THE DIVERSITY OF SYSTEMS, ACCORDING TO FR. LE BLOND

Fr. Le Blond's argument is based on an application of the common doctrine of the analogy of being to another transcendental, namely, *truth*.

Only the Divine Truth is perfect, "absolutely absolute."[4] "All other truths are complex and deficient. *They imitate the simple truth, but in their multiplicity, they cannot equal it.* They are, in a word, truths that are analogous to the First Truth."[5] Thus, just as the multiplicity of creatures imitates the simplicity of the Divine Infinite without any of these fragmentary images on its own and without the contribution of others, being able to claim that it is the perfect image, so too the multiplicity of truths imitates the Simple, Infinite, Eternal Truth, which infinitely surpasses each of these truths.

Consequently:

> In order to safeguard the transcendence of Divine Truth and to avoid any danger of ontologism or proud rationalism, [we must] here-below maintain an unbridgeable divide between our judgments and human systematizations—even if it is the clearest and best constructed system—and the Subsistent Truth ... [t]he best human system ... will never be the best possible, *quo verior cogitari nequit*, a claim that, in the order of truth, as well as in that of perfection and being, remains the divine prerogative.... Thus, it does not seem very reasonable to speak of an absolute system, a unique system. The Thomistic synthesis itself—a sure synthesis, consecrated by the use made of it by the Church, prescribed by her for the formation of her clerics, and moreover a

---

[3] See Bruno de Solages, "Autour d'une controverse," *Bulletin de littérature ecclésiastique* 48 (1947): 3–17.

[4] Le Blond, "L'analogie de la verité," 132.

[5] Le Blond, "L'analogie de la verité," 130. The emphasis is ours (Frs. Labourdette and Nicolas).

singularly open synthesis—cannot equal Subsisting Truth and does not express all its riches. In fact, alongside it and below it, in the Middle Ages, for example, there were other syntheses, those of Saint Bonaventure, Blessed Duns Scotus, and Francisco Suárez, syntheses that were perhaps less firm and less well-constructed, though complementary rather than opposed to it. They too are part of the treasury of Christianity, expressing aspects of it that Thomism is aware of, though it does not illuminate them as brightly. In the future, too, other attempts will be ranked alongside it as well, all continuing man's asymptotic endeavor to approach the absolute, which we hope to possess in the next life. As powerful as it is, Thomism forever remains one system, a unified multiplicity, irreducibly different from absolute simplicity.[6]

As is clear, Fr. Le Blond, a bit too much a philosopher, does not even maintain the distinction between theological *science* and a theological *system*, a distinction held so firmly by Fr. Chenu, as Mgr. de Solages emphasized in his "Pour l'honneur de la théologie."[7] In his opinion, every intellectual construction, precisely because it is a "unified multiplicity," is a *system*.

Therefore, every human judgment is relative to the absolute. However, it is not itself absolute. Nonetheless, it is true, in the analogical sense of the word "true." What it has in the way of truth in itself, that which *tends toward the absolute*, is the given way it participates in the Divine Truth, namely, as an *affirmation*. Given that the multiple and changing matter underlying this affirmation *limits* the latter, as essence limits the act of existence: "The absolute character of our truths comes not so much from the representations to which they are applied as from the affirmation itself. These representations cannot entirely restrain it within their limits; rather, the assertion goes beyond them and stretches forth toward the absolute."[8]

Here, we recognize the formulas used by Fr. Bouillard concerning *affirmations*, which can remain self-identical, while *the notions* united in such an affirmation would change. However, the author wishes to show, through an application of the theory of analogy, how the truth can be affirmed in an absolute way through such relative and replaceable representations. Just as a created being is constituted by the union of a finite essence with the act of existence, which participates in the Pure Act that is God, though in a way that is limited by this essence that receives it, so too, a created truth is constituted by the affirmation-representation complex, wherein the verb *to be* affirmed by the act of judgment, participating in Subsisting Truth and striving

---

6 Le Blond, "L'analogie de la verité," 132–34.

7 Bruno de Solages, "Pour l'honneur de la Théologie. Les contre-sens du R.P. Garrigou-Lagrange," *Bulletin de Littérature Ecclésiastique* 48 (1947): 65–84.

8 Le Blond, "L'analogie de la verité," 134.

to reach it, plays the role of the act of existence, whereas the representations connected to each other by the verb *to be* would play the role of essence.

Have we understood this aright? And has our effort of analysis gone beyond an outlook which, at the very least, finds us outside of the original intention to remain content with elementary notions that are admitted by all? Let us retain at least this: by its act of affirming, the human mind tends toward absolute truth [*l'absolu de la vérité*]. However, *what it affirms* is irremediably affected by all the relativity implied in finite, deficient representations. Therefore, let us return, as the author himself does at this point of his exposition, to this element of relativity involved in human truths, namely, our "representative," "conceptual," and "fragmentary" way of grasping the truth, as well as our thought's dependence on language, concerning which the author indeed does not hesitate to say: "Our thought . . . is expressed by composing and dividing *the schemata imposed by various languages*, schemata which do not remain wholly external to thought itself."[9]

"This is the truth that we can reach in our present state: an endeavor towards the absolute, an affirmation of this absolute, but ultimately a human endeavor and affirmation, limited by the human condition, having a given ancestry, situated in a particular environment, coming at this or that time in the history of the world and of ideas.[10] Therefore, one can quite rightly speak "of successive aspects of the truth."[11] The truth is not studied outside of history. This is so much the case that we can say that "contemporary relevance [*actualité*] contributes to defining the truth,"[12] certainly not in Fr. Bouillard's sense, meaning that the truth would change alongside the mind's development, but rather, that we cannot fully know human truths without considering contemporary relevance (i.e., the relative aspect of human statements). Nonetheless, we do not believe that Fr. Le Blond here wishes to limit himself to saying that, given the fact that we cannot study objective, unchanging truth without being assisted by thinkers who predate us and guide us, we must historically study such thinkers in order to understand them, so that thereafter, or by means of such study, we would then attempt to see the truth as it is in itself. For indeed, I too, thinking today, find myself to be "in a situation," and all of my insights are affected by this fact. "Each era, each school, and even each man has his own original way of tending to the absolute and of drawing an image of it, convergent tendencies and images which are *analogous* but which remain differentiated by their starting points."[13]

9 Le Blond, "L'analogie de la verité," 134.
10 Le Blond, "L'analogie de la verité," 135.
11 Le Blond, "L'analogie de la verité," 135.
12 Le Blond, "L'analogie de la verité," 135.
13 Le Blond, "L'analogie de la verité," 136.

However great St. Thomas might have been, He was a man of his own time as well. He too is dated. He can only be understood historically, and thus in studying him, what one will grasp is not the truth but, rather, the Thomistic manner of grasping and expressing it. In point of fact, it is not clear whether such Thomistic truth has heretofore been truly grasped. Many have wrongly presented it as though it were supra-temporal, and throughout the centuries, there has hardly been any progress in coming to understand this thought: "Granted, in the last twenty years, objective and exact knowledge of the Thomism of Saint Thomas has made progress"[14]; "a work which has, in fact, only now begun to take shape."[15] Though, fortunately, this fact does not prevent the author from presenting the whole of his own study as though it were an expression of St. Thomas's teaching concerning truth and analogy—even before a full examination of medieval manuscripts has been completed.

However, in any case, it is impossible to consider, on its own, *the invariant* [aspect] of human truths in order to thereby establish an absolute and unique system. The tendency toward a single theology embracing all systems by finding a place for what is true in each of them represents a pretense that is wholly suffused with modern rationalism's own tendency to seek out a single Science.—For the record, let us repeat once more that this assertion excludes the possibility of there being any distinction between a theological science and particular systems. Theological science, in St. Thomas's sense, no longer exists.

The clear upshot of all of this is the fact that the Church must adapt her teaching not only to various languages but even to various concepts, and if she wishes to do away with the gulf that exists between her seminaries and the world of learning [*l'Université*], she must "make it relevant" ["*actualiser*"] by truly taking up the "situation" of contemporary thinkers. In any case, since [such a particular situation] is needed and will ultimately affect the pure truth expressed therein, is not the most "just" and the most "true" one (humanly speaking) the one that imposes itself upon us in our present circumstances?

Granted, we have added this last point to Fr. Le Blond's own considerations, though we find ourselves to be impelled toward it by the very movement that he impresses upon us. . . . And we will allow ourselves to be impelled even along still. Indeed, is it not clear that if we are destined to continually affirm the absolute without ever grasping it, we will find more satisfying results by remaining content to study history and the various forms of truth found in human minds through the passage of the ages than with searching for the truth in itself and for its own sake? In order to arrive at the synthesis that the human mind, in its incorrigibly "systematic" bent, ever seeks, we will even be tempted to consider the "situations" in which man

---

[14] Le Blond, "L'analogie de la verité," 136.
[15] Le Blond, "L'analogie de la verité," 136.

successively finds himself from generation to generation and there see something more than an "analogy": [perhaps] intellectual filiation, progress, and a form of ascent, with superior forms absorbing inferior ones, or, at least, a dialectic in which our mind's "drive toward the absolute" could push forward, closer and closer to its goal, proceeding from one opposed thing to another?

Again, we are saying something more than Fr. Le Blond himself, drawn along by the very élan impressed upon us by his thought. There are minds who will abandon the idea of a unified theology only to then replace it with a systematic interpretation of the history or "genealogy" of theologies. Would it not be completely normal for someone who adopts the "situation" of a modern thinker (who is much more concerned with seeking out a philosophy of the human mind than a philosophy of reality) to establish a theology of the Christian mind in place of a theology whose concern is with reality itself?[16]

---

[16] We have not included in our exposition a rather-astonishing paragraph written by the author. This paragraph is striking because, by itself, it would seem to nullify so much of the efforts he expended in order to maintain at least the analogical character of human truth. Moreover, the profound agnosticism it contains is attributed to St. Thomas:

> As far as sensible beings themselves are concerned, . . . their specific, substantial differences remain unknown to us. This modest assertion—expressing something quite different from what we see in the serene dogmatism of some contemporary scholastics—means that most of our concepts do not have, at their root, properly speaking, an intuition of nature, but rather, a group of schemata, a collection of sensible representations whose intersection enables us to establish a kind of provisional label by which we designate the quiddity. In this case, the *quiddity*, as the name implies, designates a kind of questioning of a substance rather than a true understanding thereof: the existence of this substance is posed without the nature being grasped. This is the ultimate source of the precarious, reformable character of many of our definitions, and their connection either with the metaphor (a connection which, most of the time, is not entirely broken), or with extrinsic methods of classification (Le Blond, "L'analogie de la verité," 139–40).

We admit that these remarks contain a truth. However, let us immediately note that for St. Thomas, all of our knowledge is based on our knowledge of sensible beings and depends upon it. Indeed, in reading these lines, one would think that St. Thomas himself fell into the nominalism denounced by Emmanuel Mounier:

> Must we, for all that, consider every dogmatic formula, every conceptual definition, as being a mere sign placed upon an unknowable reality, a symbol rebelling against every form of content that could be elucidated? The modernist critique tended toward this kind of nominalism, which annulled the entire continuity of the faith (*Esprit* (Sept. 1947), 440–41; see the discussion of Mounier's observations in "Discussion Surrounding our 'Dialogue Théologique,'" p. 263–64 above).

Fortunately, the author emphasizes, in a note, "according to Saint Thomas, this concerns the specific quiddity, not more general concepts" (Le Blond, "L'analogie de la verité," 140n1). Therefore, we are reassured that all our concepts of being, substance, cause, movement, end, person, etc. (in the end, all our metaphysical concepts) have true adequation to reality. And even though we can only form analogical concepts concerning

It is now our turn to consider a problem of the greatest importance, as much for the formulation of dogmas as it is for the missionary apostolate, as well as for the possible idea one can fashion for oneself concerning the nature of theological science.

II. THE SPECIFIC UNITY OF THE HUMAN MIND AND OF HUMAN TRUTH

However, we now find ourselves faced with an immense subject, indeed, one that is quite difficult to fully get our arms around. We do not at all believe that "certain elementary notions admitted by all" could suffice for us. When St. Thomas, in his famous *quarta via*, declares that all things are more or less beautiful, noble, and *true*, he does not furnish any explanation concerning this last point. Therefore, is truth susceptible to grades of more and less? In other words, is this a concept which is analogically realized through a participation that is more or less proximate to the Absolute Divine Truth? Yes, certainly, but it is important to carefully consider in what sense this is the case, before too hastily drawing consequences from it.

I. Logical Truth and Ontological Truth

Let us begin by distinguishing *ontological truth* from *logical truth*. Fr. Le Blond does not do so, though, he does say in one place: "Obviously, were there no mind, there would be no truth."[17] This statement is true, for truth is a relationship between mind and being, a relation which is called "adequation." Created beings are *true* in relation to the Divine Mind, the source of every created being, since the [Divine] Idea presides over the creative action. This means that it corresponds to the idea that God has of it; its entire essence is to be this correspondence [*cette réponse*]. A given being's truth is to be as God thinks it. Here, greater or lesser truth can only be thought of in terms of greater or lesser being, inasmuch as it depends on the Divine Intelligence, which is fully and completely expressed only in the Divine Word.

---

spiritual realities, Fr. Le Blond will surely not deny that we often can, through such concepts, successfully reach their essential realities (and not only a collection of phenomena tagged by a word or an image) as, for example, when we speak about our soul and about moral realities. After this, it is all too obvious that we can define the specific essences of beings that surround us. However, I do not believe that this "modest affirmation" would be "quite different from the serene dogmatism of certain contemporary scholastics," at least of those who affirm the permanence of St. Thomas's metaphysics. Therefore, here again, in order to explain the element of relativity involved in human knowledge, we must limit ourselves solely to the analogical aspect of the concept of truth when it is applied to the human mind.

17 Le Blond, "L'analogie de la verité," 134n1.

Logical truth is the truth that characterizes the mind in its relation to being; it is the adequation of our thought with things. Between human thought and the Divine Thought (which we also say is true) only an analogy exists, not univocity, despite the fact that we use the same words to refer to each. Nonetheless, there is knowledge of *the same thing*, of the *same* (ontological) *truth*. Neglect of this elementary point has important consequences here. Between the Divine Mind and our own, *there is the mediation of things*. In these things, our mind finds the principle of the truth which properly is its own: "The truth of our intellect is taken in accord with its conformity to its principle, namely *things*, from which it receives its knowledge" (*ST* I, q. 16, a. 5, ad 2).

The thing is measured by the Divine Idea, wherein it finds its ontological truth. However, in its own turn, it measures the representation that we make of it, in which our mind finds its logical truth. And, of course, the thing exists in the Divine Mind in a completely different way than it does in our own. Properly speaking, only an infinitely distant analogy exists between the way it is known by God, who causes and measures it, and the way that we, who are measured by it, know this same reality. And likewise, an infinitely distant analogy here again exists between the truth of angelic knowledge and the truth of the divine knowledge, even though this angelic knowledge comes from a participation in this divine knowledge and not from things. And just as things have more ontological truth to the degree that they have more being (and in this sense, we can say that they are more or less true, in accordance with the ascending dialectic of the *quarta via*), so too created minds [*esprits*] realize in their knowledge a more or less perfect logical truth through which they likewise draw more or less close to the only Perfect Truth, the Sovereign, Uncreated Truth—though, ever remaining infinitely distance from it. In angelic truth, there is more truth than what is found in human truth, while being infinitely less than that which is found in the Divine Truth.

2. Human Logical Truth

However, this overview only teaches us that, on the scale of intellects (i.e., human, angelic, and divine), truth is only realized analogically, that is, in a way that is at once proportionally the same and essentially different. We still must ask what this truth is in each of them. In particular, let us study the case of the human mind. If we have understood him correctly, Fr. Le Blond believes that he can account for human truth by means of this proportion: our affirmation, participating in the Divine Truth, is related to the notional representation[s] with which it is concerned, while being simultaneously limited by it, as existence, which participates in Pure Act, is related to essence, which that existence realizes while being limited by it. Truth has a value for our mind through this affirmation (because it is a drive for the absolute); it is limited and precarious on account of the notions with which this affirmation is concerned. Therefore, the value of our truth is entirely found in this drive for the Divine Absolute, in this participation in the Divine Truth. This analogical resemblance is what measures it. Thus, we see why nothing is completely absolute; we can always say: there is more truth.

Is this presentation exact? Alas, it forgets but one thing: the object! St. Thomas said to us, "The truth of our intellect is taken in accord with its conformity *to its principle*, namely *things*, from which it receives its knowledge." And, yes, this is one of his elementary teachings. *The affirmation of human truth is directly measured by the object that founds it*.[18] Granted, instead of grasping, in a single gaze, the whole of intelligible reality (as is the case for pure spirits), the human mind only grasps piecemeal that which bestows full intelligibility on each known element, recomposing it in an ever-incomplete manner, arriving at knowledge "from within" through knowledge coming "from without," and therefore arriving at what is more certain and more true (ontologically speaking) through what is less certain and less true. And this is why (logical) human truth reaches its perfection only after lengthy efforts. Nonetheless, the fact remains that this relation to the object is essential.[19]

Now, what the human mind forms concerning the objects it knows are concepts that have the ambition of being valid for all men. Below, we will come to speak about all the various elements that come along to limit this ambition. There, we will insist on the differences and variations that follow therefrom.

Here, however, we are speaking about the normal activity of the intellect as such. For *things* that are within its scope, it forms concepts that enable it then to fashion affirmations or negations whose own, proper truth is measured *by these things*. It is certainly the case that God knows them in a different way than we do and that the Divine Mind's truth is infinitely superior to our

---

18 Given that it stands outside of our purposes here, we are setting aside the case of *practical truth*, by which the human intellect, by contrast, measures the actions that it directs or to the works for which it provides the *idea*. In our exposition here, we are only concerned with the truth pertaining to the speculative intellect.

19 What we write here seems, to our eyes, to be connected to a frankly realistic theory of knowledge. He who would conceive of our representations, our concepts, as being a kind of "copy" of reality and would define truth as being a mere intra-mental relation which more or less approaches the Divine Absolute, could indeed suppose that our concepts are themselves only "analogical likenesses" of the elusive reality which the external object would be. Moreover, this would require us to renounce the claim that we have any kind of direct knowledge. However, if a concept has no other content, no other "essence," than the intelligibility of the object which it makes known, if it is wholly one with the object in the intelligible order, if, in a word, it enables us to directly reach reality, it is impossible that it would not contain its immediate significate (which can indeed be very partial), moreover passing (subjectively speaking) from extreme vagueness to the most precise distinction. This is what leads to the diversity found in human conceptions, as well as the difficulty involved in trying to arrive at a broad possession of the truth.

mind's own truth. However, we do not read the truth of things in Him, with each of us only forming various but analogically true conceptions of such things. What we know directly is not the Divine Truth. Rather, we directly know things, doing so with our human intellects. We form more or less universal concepts of these realities, grasping them either in their accidental and common elements, or in properties, which reveal an essence that, in fact, still remains hidden, or in generic essential elements, or (granted, more rarely) in their specific difference. These concepts enable men to have a certain number of common truths, not only *de facto* truths but *de iure* ones, enabling, as well, the establishment of human sciences that hold for all men.

However, all beings are not within our grasp in this way, for our intellectual knowledge comes from our senses. A whole other order of realities exists, those that are purely spiritual, as well as God Himself, attained only *by way of analogy with the realities we first directly know*. These latter realities stand before our reflection as the bearers of perfections that they themselves do not exhaust, perfections that they, on the contrary, exhibit in an inferior and limited condition, implying that they have their cause in a Being wherein this perfection is fully realized. On the basis of the first object thus directly known and conceived as an inferior analogate of a perfection that is realized in other modes, we form an analogous concept of this perfection. And it is thanks to this analogous concept that we affirm the realization of this perfection in God, as in its Cause, in an eminent manner, for which none of the created conditions of the inferior analogates hold. This philosophy can indeed be contested; it obviously depends on realist premises. However, our goal here is not to justify it but, rather, [1] to recall that it underlies the entire Thomist treatise concerning the existence of God and His attributes and [2] to see how it requires us to understand [the notion of] *human truth*.

Thus, we form a certain number of negative and affirmative judgments concerning God. We affirm that He exists. We deny He has any imperfections that creatures have: He is not composite; He does not change; He is not finite; He is not multiple; and so forth.... We affirm that the perfections with which He has endowed creatures are also realized in Him, though in a way that eludes us: He is true; He is good; He is intelligent; He loves; He is omnipotent; and so forth.... What provides the measure for the *logical truth proper to* these judgments that we say are *true*? It is not measured *directly* upon the truth of the Divine Intelligence, precisely because the latter does not directly fall under our knowledge. They are all judgments that are *conclusions*. Therefore, they presuppose the prior, human, logical truth of affirmations that are directly concerned with created realities, and by way of analogy with these realities, we then demonstrate what the human mind can know concerning God. The truth in question is forever human in character. It is all too evident that God knows Himself in a different way than how we know Him and that the truth of the knowledge that He has of Himself is completely different from the truth expressed in the knowledge that we have concerning Him. However, this in no way invalidates the fact that everything that we say about Him is necessarily subject to the laws and exigencies of *human* logical truth.

3. The Unity of the Human Mind

Fr. Le Blond appealed to the analogy of being in order to explain the analogy of truth: composed of essence and existence, various creatures realize being only analogically in relation to the Divine Being. At the same time, various created truths, composed of affirmations, tending dynamically toward the absolute, and of fragmented representations, only analogically reflect the Divine Truth. However, the analogy of being in no way implies that created beings, which are analogous to the Divine Being, would all be analogous to each other: otherwise, no two of them would *univocally* possess the same essence. I do not know whether Fr. Le Blond would accept such a form of nominalism, but I am sure his historical probity will not allow him to claim that St. Thomas held such a doctrine. Yes or no: are there beings that univocally realize one and the same essence? They will certainly all be analogous to the Divine Being, but this will be according to the same analogy, and they will remain univocal in relation to each other. And similarly, the fact that the truth of the human mind is only an analogous reflection of the truth of the Divine Mind—so that each time a man's mind rises upward to affirm a truth or to deny an error, it here finds itself, in its own, infinitely deficient manner, similar to the Divine Mind, Perfect Truth—in no way implies that human truths would be purely analogous in relation to each other, thereby being mutually incommensurable. Or, rather, this would be implied only if the human mind *were not a single nature having a specific unity*.

Therefore, we must ask whether the human mind is one, univocally one, *specifically one*. Do men only analogically participate in human nature or, rather, is this nature *specifically the same* in each of them? (And even if the latter is true, we should note well that this leaves open an immense field for individual differences.) In the end, this is what the debate comes down to, at least in the form given to it by Fr. Le Blond. *If the human mind is one, specifically one, its own human manner of being adequate to reality, of being true, and of being analogous to the Divine Mind, will also be univocally one.* We have never desired to deny or place in doubt the fact that *logical truth*, such as it is realized in the human intellect, only presents an infinitely distant analogy with Truth such as it is realized in the Divine Intellect. This is not the issue here. Rather, what is at stake is whether the *human* mind has a nature that is specifically one and, consequently, whether its own way of being true and of affirming the truth is specifically one. This is what we are accused of overlooking, thereby failing to accept the "human condition."

It is because we advocate on behalf of this unity (which exists in the midst of the diversities that we will speak of below) that we maintain that human truth concerning God does indeed have a unity, one toward which theological science itself tends. In comparison with the Divine Truth, our concepts are terribly deficient. However, if they are formed with precision, they hold true for all men. The analogous concepts in which we conceive this Truth are no less human than are univocal concepts. Ideally speaking, there is only one perfect and adequate *human* way of conceptually representing the Divine Truth to oneself, and thought's own efforts are undertaken precisely so that one may elevate oneself to these conceptual heights.

4. Revealed Truths

Does the fact that the supernatural divine truth is *revealed* change the situation of the human mind in relation to it? This question leads us to another consideration, one that is of capital importance in the subject facing us, indeed, a question that one runs the risk of forgetting when one intervenes solely as a philosopher in a debate concerning the nature of theology. The *datum* that the theologian analyzes and explains is not the Divine Essence (concerning which he could form only necessarily-impotent concepts). Rather, his datum is a *revelation that is made in human concepts*, in statements whose truth—which is supernatural and guaranteed by God—is a truth *that has the typical form belonging to human, logical truth*. The Divine Truth that measures theological science is a truth that is already translated and expressed in human concepts and language by God, indeed, by *God alone*. God alone reveals, and He reveals by speaking. The Church does not reveal and, *a fortiori*, nor does the theologian. The Church preserves and transmits by clarifying and adapting, though doing so by preserving the *same* supernatural *meaning* entrusted to her in human formulas, by preserving *the same truth*: eodem sensu, eademque sententia. Here, we have human statements that speak to us of the mysteries that are found in God. God is the one who guarantees these statements' relationship with the mysteries themselves. It is His revelation, something we cannot grasp on our own. And this is why the only thing in our mind that can respond to this revelation is an assent of *faith*: the motive of our assent of faith is the authority of God who reveals, leading us to believe *what God has told us* about Himself and about what He has providentially arranged for our salvation. An essentially supernatural light is what enables us to assent in this way, enabling our superelevated mind to attain its object: not the formula, but rather, the supernatural reality expressed by that formula. However, it attains it by means of the formula, and the latter alone is what *expresses*, in a way that is valid for man, the truth to which the intellect adheres. All of the statements that were progressively revealed up to the death of the last Apostle—statements organized into a *Credo*, which is not a philosophy but, rather, the Word of God made present to humanity in its own language—are all entrusted to the Church. How does Fr. Le Blond conceive of its simultaneous development and permanence? Will it suffice to say that the human concepts used in these revealed statements by God, who has translated the Divine Truth by means of such concepts, would then be replaced by other concepts, ones that are only analogous to the first ones, a claim that would quite exactly mean, in technical scholastic language, concepts that are proportionally alike but *essentially different*? Does the permanence involved here only hold for the *affirmation*, conceived of as being a drive for the absolute, independent of *what it* expresses, independent of the "notions" with which it is concerned? If this affirmation suffices, then, through the course of the ages and in different cultural milieus, one will slip underneath it *meanings* that are only analogous to each other—that is, meanings that are proportionally alike but essentially different.

Now, continuing to voice our concerns as theologians, we will say that such an outlook—one to which Fr. Le Blond's theory would lead us if it were pushed to its logical conclusions—is manifestly incompatible with the clearest and most solemn affirmations pronounced by the Ecclesiastical Magisterium from the [First] Vatican Council to the anti-modernist documents.[20]

We can never emphasize too greatly, in relation to the transcendent divine reality, the congenital deficiency that befalls the human statements in which the object of faith is offered to us. Indeed, a calling to another kind of knowledge is grafted upon it, knowledge that is essentially obscure: mystical knowledge of the Supernatural God Himself, a knowledge had by means of love. Indeed, we must go even further still. In order to express His mysteries in human language, God had to choose one or several particular human languages. Let us not Platonize concerning "human language" any more than we do for man in general. By revealing in this way, He made use of the possibilities inherent in this language, be it Hebrew or Greek, elevating it to an even loftier purity and truth; however, He also accepted its own, proper limitations. It is possible that in order to express this or that mystery, another cultural genius—and, consequently, another language (India or China here comes to mind)—would have offered Him other resources. However, what He has already done is not to be refashioned—and, in any case, He alone could refashion it. Just as, upon choosing to become incarnate, the Word of God took on a human nature that was necessarily individual, thus meaning that Christ is and forever remains a Jewish craftsman who lived at a precise

---

[20] Must we repeat what we explained in our volume *Dialogue théologique*, namely, that we do not intend, by this *theological argument*, to say or insinuate that Fr. Le Blond would not fully accept the documents of the Magisterium? It is precisely because he accepts them that this argument seems to us to have all of its power. It falls to him to show that his conception of human truth does not in any way entail these consequences.

historical moment, in a quite determinate cultural milieu, expressing Himself in the language of His own time and not even in the language of Greece or of Rome, which was so much more universal in His era (and we know, nonetheless, that the Incarnation involves all of human nature precisely because this nature is *one*), so too the Word of God expressing Himself in a human fashion was in fact spoken in Hebrew and in Greek, and from the death of the last Apostle, this revelation, which must be conveyed to the ends of the earth up until the end of time, is closed as a *revelation* properly so called. Consequently, whatever language into which it happens to be translated, whatever the cultural milieu that it will impregnate, whatever development humanity will undergo through the course of millions of years—if it still remains after millions of years—and however this revelation comes to be expressed, such expressions will need to remain entirely consistent with these Hebraic and Greek expressions, conveying *the same meaning* and the same *humanly formulated truth* that was so formed by God alone. Some might feel it is unfortunate that God did not wait for the complete "planetization of humanity" before bringing His revelation to its completion; but, once again, we need not, under the pretext of a historical spirit, refashion history.[21]

5. Theological Truth

By maintaining the debate upon this terrain, we neither identify nor confuse theology and dogma with each other. However, the idea that one fashions concerning theology *wholly depends on the idea one has concerning the nature of faith and dogmas.* Theology is not a "philosophy of dogma"; it is not, as it were, the external application of philosophy or of a philosophical system to the revealed deposit. It has its own, original light. It responds to the intelligibility appeal that the believer's mind experiences in the divine affirmation as soon as one passes on from simple adherence, now considering the Divine Word *in order to seek to understand it. Fides quaerit intellectum.* This intelligibility is

---

[21] Fr. Daniélou, in an otherwise truly remarkable article, "La pensee chrétienne," *Nouvelle revue théologique* 69 (Nov. 1947): 930–40, remarked that "the *memra*, the Hebraic word, is something completely different from the Greek *Logos* by which it was transcribed. And thus, the Christian *logos* is a new category, which is the biblical datum refracted into a cultural reality which gives it new harmonics" (p. 933). Or, more generally: "We are [only now] barely discovering, by turning back to knowledge of the Bible, how much our Western Christian thought is a Hellenized revelation." And in saying this, he is quite correct. However, he cannot purely and simply conclude, "Thus, the incarnation of Christian thought will be brought about in other great cultures, the unique message of Christ being thus refracted into these various forms, with each of them manifesting more aspects of this message." [This cannot be true in an unqualified sense,] for there neither was nor will be a Christian *revelation* in other cultures, and all of them, if they are to know the Supernatural Truth, are dependent upon the "Greek" concepts in which God was pleased to "recount" it to us.

what the theologian strives to bring to the humanly perfect state of knowledge that we call science (in a sense that differs, we must repeat, from the modern use of the term "science" in contrast to philosophy).

Undoubtedly, the theologian's essential desire is to know God. He strives to understand, to the degree that it is possible, what supernatural realities are in themselves; however, he can do so only by referring to *the teaching that has been revealed by God*, to the statements that express revelation in human language, so as to grasp, as fully as possible, the content that is intelligible for us, as well as its implications. What he studies are these divine truths, which have already been humanized in their formulation. Their meaning is what he analyzes and explains. *And our theology is measured by them, not by the truth of the Divine Mind.* The theologian does not see God. He does not benefit from any new revelation. What he strives to attain is the fullest knowledge that can be had concerning God by *the human mind*—and we do not cease to proclaim this mind's *unity of nature*, even in the midst of all its historically diverse forms—striving to do so by means of these truths that are already formulated in human language. This is why we advocate on behalf of the unity of theological science. In no way do we deny the existence and (necessarily unequal) value of various theological syntheses and systems. We only say that, to the degree that they are different, each of them represents a more or less successful effort in reaching the state of science, in elevating theology to the human unity that is its congenital ambition. And this certainly does not mean each of these systems, or even theological science itself, strives to make itself equal to the truth of the Divine Mind. Rather, it means that they strive to reach the best possible state of formulation for *human* truth concerning God on the basis of what His own revelation teaches us. In no way does it aspire to become dogma! It will always remain something human whose value will depend at once on faith and on the quality of the human reflection involved in theological knowledge. It will forever be nothing but an infinitely distant analogy of the Divine Truth, and I am not aware of any scholastic theologian who has ever dreamt of the contrary! He knows it remains human, that is, poor and deficient, a shadow of the Divine Truth more than a reflection of it. However, he quite precisely thinks it aspires to have worth *for the human mind as such*, that is, for all men and for all times.

III. THE VARIOUS DIVERSITIES BEFALLING THE HUMAN MIND AND HUMAN TRUTHS

In order to show the fundamental unity of human speculative truth, we appealed to the specific unity of the human mind, which implies the specific community of laws which make up its adequation to reality. The truth of our conceptions is not measured directly in relation to the divine truth, more or less approached in the utterly distant analogy that we maintain with it. Rather, it is measured in relation to the requirements of *the human mind* in its taking possession of its object.

However, it would imply a rather superficial and partial understanding of Thomist thought if one were to believe that its conception of the characteristics of human truth is confined to this "serene dogmatism." Perhaps it has emphasized this unity precisely because it has felt its full worth: is this not one of the values it has the mission of preserving?[22] Nonetheless, Thomism remains perfectly aware of the manifold variations befalling the human mind, and for our own part, we believe that it has, in its own principles, sufficient resources for explaining these variations, indeed more profoundly than they can be explained by a more empirical philosophy with a less ontological focus.

A. Individual, Racial, Cultural, and Historical Diversities

Quite appropriately, in relation to the analogy of being, Fr. Le Blond recalls to us the composition of essence and existence, as well as essence's character as the limiting component in this composition. Act is only limited through potency. Being is limited by an "ability to be," and this is what enables it to be multiplied: unreceived existence is unique; it unfolds in fullness everything that existence on its own can be when it is not limited to this or that partial realization.

However, potentiality can enter more or less distantly into the composition of a created being. It is always there from the perspective of the created being's essence. However, this essence can be a pure form. In that case, it is simple, and here all multiplicity is impossible precisely on the level of the degree of existence and of the divine resemblance represented by this essence. Given that such an essence is only a form, every differentiation involves specific differentiation. This is why St. Thomas taught that each pure spirit, each angel, is a species, a species that cannot have multiple individuals. The form cannot be multiplied in individuals precisely because it is not "received," because no capacity limits it to a particular realization that, not exhausting its own, proper virtualities, would enable it to be realized elsewhere in a different manner. In other words, the angel does not participate in its nature according to a certain receptive capacity. It only participates in existence.

---

22 It may be advisable to recall that the danger of forgetting this is not a fanciful fear if it is true that, as Pius XI said poignantly with regard to racism and the Jewish situation: "We have forgotten the doctrine of the universals." Let us add that, in speaking here of "Thomist thought," I do not intend to exclude Scholastics who did not belong to the historical Thomist school. On these great questions, the whole of scholastic thought is unanimous in agreement, with more or less profound nuances. We say, "Thomist," because this is properly speaking the perspective that we ourselves take in our justification and explanation concerning these matters.

However, it fully realizes, in a necessarily unique realization, the degree of existence and of participation in God that defines it.

The case is completely different for creatures engaged in the conditions of material existence.[23] Matter enters into the very essence of such beings. Here, we no longer have a pure form. In such creatures, the form itself is only an act that is limited to a receptive capacity, and the matter-form composite is a limiting potency in relation to existence. It determines the degree of being in accord with which existence will be participated in. Consequently, every material species is indefinitely susceptible to plurality, able to be multiplied into distinct individuals. Each of these individuals not only (like every created being) participates in existence, which it does not have of itself, but moreover, even participates in its own, nature, its proper form. It does not exhaust this form's virtualities. It presents only one particular realization of it, certainly retaining the same formal principles, univocally and specifically possessing the same form, but doing so in a realization that cannot deploy all of its virtualities. It belongs to the community of a given species. As an individual, it is a more or less successful realization of the nature that characterizes it. This nature is realized nowhere—except in its Divine Idea—in its ideal purity, in its exhaustive fullness. Here, we have the realist, though anti-Platonic, solution to the problem of the universals.

This is the case that applies to man. Certainly, his soul is spiritual. Nonetheless, it is the form informing a matter, with which it composes a single being, a single substance.[24]

Here, we meet up with the Thomist explanation of individuation by matter. We will not set it forth at greater length. We merely need to draw from it consequences that often are not given sufficient consideration. Based on the fact that the soul, even the spiritual soul, is individuated only on account of its relationship to the body, we must wholly avoid concluding that one man differs from another only through his body and bodily dispositions. The soul is individualized in order to make this body a single being. It is

---

23 Obviously, we are here speaking of "matter" in the precise sense that this word has in the philosophy of nature, a resolutely ontological sense that is completely different from the meaning that the word has for modern scientists seeking to identify the observable physical constitution of material being, often with the aid of mathematical symbols.

24 A theologian cannot fail to note here the formulas of the Ecumenical Council of Vienne: "Furthermore, with the approval of the holy council, we reject as erroneous and contrary to the truth of the Catholic faith any doctrine or opinion that rashly asserts that the substance of the rational and intellectual soul is not truly and of itself the form of the human body or that calls this into doubt. In order that the truth of the pure faith may be known to all and the path to error barred, we define that from now on whoever presumes to assert, defend, or obstinately hold that the rational and intellectual soul is not of itself and essentially the form of the human body is to be censured as a heretic" (Denzinger, no. 902 [old no. 481]).

wholly itself individualized, according to all of its powers, even those that are *spiritual*, thus being substantially distinct from all other individual human souls. The unity that remains, the unity we insisted on so strongly in our previous section, is purely formal. It is the community of [intelligible] notes that make up the species. Each person realizes the human species, but none exhaust it, none is the Ideal Man, fully exhausting all of the virtualities of humanity.[25] The individuation of the human spirit and its realization in a multitude of beings who are truly distinct and different from one another are of such a nature as to reverberate over the unity of human truth.

In[26] this sense, it is true to say that the species exceeds each of its individuals: it is the form that each one strives (metaphysically speaking) to realize as fully as possible. However, because this is impossible, it has an inclination to transmit itself, by means of generation, to other individuals, who will prolong its existential realization beyond its own life, each of them taking up anew for himself the temporal adventure of human existence. In this sense, one can speak of a great, species-wide life that, beginning with the first individuals of that species, is then pursued throughout subsequent generations.[27] This successive realization of the species involves successes and failures, as well as many average and mediocre realizations.

This multiplied instantiation [*plurification*] of the species is not a fragmentation into individuals without anything in common except for their

---

[25] A logician will here note the possible equivocation befalling the word "accidental." In the logical sense of the term, it is perfectly correct to say that individual differences do not reach *the essence*, the pure, essential definition of man, thus meaning that such differences remain accidental. However, it would be completely false to conclude that, metaphysically speaking, they only pertain to *accidents* in contrast to *substance*. These differences first and foremost attain the substance itself, according to its effective realization. What makes Paul distinct from Peter is accidental to the human species, without which they would not have the same nature. However, Paul's difference from Peter is substantial in nature. It remains true that an unconscious Platonism remains the temptation and danger experienced by realism in opposition to nominalism. The Anselmian speculations on original sin, *a sin of nature*, remain a telling historical witness to this fact.

[26] [Tr. note: We reproduce these next few paragraphs, somewhat naïve and dated, without approving of any possible negative applications of them. As the context makes clear, Frs. Labourdette and Nicolas *themselves* distance their words from *any* racism. They merely intend to begin this discussion of differentiation by considering the level of biological diversification within one species. For a recent study of the hard-scientific and social-scientific literature taking this question seriously, in the face of opposing trends, while attempting to avoid falling into reactionary excesses, see Charles Murray, *Human Diversity: The Biology of Gender, Race, and Class* (New York: Twelve / Hachette, 2020).]

[27] Here, we cannot take up the problem posed by the theory of the biological evolution of one species from another. On this point, the reader can find invaluable remarks made by Jacques Maritain in this very periodical, in his article, "Coopération philosophique et justice intellectuelle," *Revue thomiste* 46, nos. 3–4 (1946): 442–43.

essential nature. It is a well-established fact of experience that sub-specific groups exist within this proliferation, gathered together, nonetheless, through a certain number of common characteristics. However obscure it might remain, biologically speaking, in its true amplitude and proper causes, the notion of *race* obviously designates an important fact discovered upon observations, one that prehistorical discoveries confirm in a striking manner. The ideas of heredity and kinship lead us to conceive of the same reality. By taking individuation in an obviously analogical sense, one can speak of "collective individuation," that is, within a given species, the establishment of more or less numerous racial groups. It is true that categories taken from a solely biological perspective (indeed, ones that even in that domain are insufficiently precise) are quite inadequately applied to a given human fact. Nonetheless, already on this level, whatever might be the case for the intermingling of the various races within humanity itself (leaving this word open to all the possible fluctuations it involves), we must say that for racial groups, as for individuals, none of them represents humanity in its ideal form; each of them represents a particular, non-exhaustive realization of it. And just as, in the case of individuals, we spoke of successes and failures, so too we must speak of these in the cases of racial realizations. Of course, we do not mean that they would not have the same human nature—and, consequently, the same essential dignity. Rather, we mean quite precisely that all the various races do not represent the same successes. History makes known races that are better endowed, and among those that reveal themselves as being the best endowed, to judge them as a whole, their talents still are quite diverse, with aptitudes turned toward quite different sorts of human realizations.[28]

However, with such obviously inferior concepts, how far still do we remain from the true fact of human experience! These biological differentiations are only a doubtlessly rather distant substructure of the diversifications of human history. In order to understand the latter, we must have recourse to other notions. Because man is an incarnate spirit, not a pure one, he does not possess the intuitive intelligence that pure spirits enjoy. His intelligence is discursive, *reason*. And because he is rational, he only attains his full development gradually, with the aid of other men. He needs them, even for what is most human and most personal in him! Precisely so that he may receive this, a type of characteristically human community comes to be formed: the social community, properly so called. This is something completely different from community of species or race. It is a society organized in view of human

---

28 Here, we doubtlessly find the element of truth that was able to bolster the great error of racism. It is an error because it has misunderstood, on the one hand, the weight of the primordial and foundational *unity* of the specific nature, and on the other hand, the transcendence of the human *person* and his destiny in relation to all *individual* and communal conditions.

life. Consequently, the individual man finds himself caught up within the framework of human realizations that ultimately surpass him. If we reflect on his malleability, within the relatively lengthy time that is needed in order for him to become a man, the meaning of the influence of a human environment over the various members of a group becomes clear. It is an influence that is more or less overcome by particularly powerful personalities, but it remains ever-active in some way. A family, a city, or a social and political organization: all of this, understood in its most human sense, must be essentially ordered to elevate man toward the fullest realization of humanity, where he comes into contact with the loftiest and most universal values. Nonetheless, how greatly, and in how many other ways, is it freighted with psychological and moral pressures, as well as various forms of social determinism! Thus, human groups form with more or less homogenous characteristics under the influence of an ensemble of circumstances, thereby coming to be profoundly different from other groups. In this way, various civilizations and cultures come to be constituted, each tending toward the greatest human truth, though inevitably individuated, characterized in space and time.

Here too, we must say that no civilizations exhaust the virtualities contained in human nature. None of them ever bring it to its full perfection. However, some are more successful at this than are others. And if it is true that each civilization can learn much from others, thereby rectifying its own deficiencies, there are some that have managed to more fully express permanent elements of man and of thought.

Finally, let us add to this all-too-brief reminder of truths that call for many further developments one final point: in contrast to pure spirits, indeed because he is engaged in the conditions of material existence, man lives and acts *in time*. He only comes to self-realization gradually and progressively. Thus, all human realities are marked by temporality. Human life is not only an individual reality whose arc is immediately evident: infancy, youth, maturity, old-age, death. It is also a social reality, one of the central conditions involved in the realization of humanity. This is what gives history its reality and its profound human significance, without implying either that it is necessary—a whole cluster of contingencies are united therein to natural necessities, and freedom is at work in history alongside many blind forces, which are more or less deterministic and more or less discernable—or that it has a *de facto* orientation toward progress or decadence.

If at least from the perspective of biology, the arc of individual evolution is simple, by contrast the evolution of humanity, with all the differentiations we described above, will necessarily be quite serpentine. In this case, the curve of evolution is a slow conquest of man by himself: here knowing successes, there failures, sometimes, through the confluence of favorable circumstances, marvelous efflorescence, and sometimes, through the overpowering strength of the forces of dissolution, terrible periods of decay. Indeed, while the destiny of a group is to tend, by its own means, to the best realization of what it is to be human, nonetheless, many forces at work in history, starting with sin, tend, instead, toward the dissolution of human society and to its degradation into infra-human patterns, rather than toward the perfect realization of humanity. Doubtlessly, in the course of such evolution, something is gained, a kind of human experience, an ever-more-penetrating *prise de conscience* of man himself and of his "situation" in the world. Ethnology is a science that today is sufficiently developed so as to enable philosophical reflection to understand to what extent man changes while remaining within a fundamentally immutable nature, how much a primitive person differs in how he considers the world, how he imagines things and life itself, in contrast to how these things are considered by a man who is the heir to a long history of civilization and culture. Moreover, this does not represent a value judgment, for this evolution is not inevitably progressive, except along the lines of technique, whether of art or of science, but in no way on the level of pure intelligence, moral conscience, and the loftiest human values.

However, it remains the case that, after taking into account all of these differentiating factors, one can consider things from the opposite perspective and show under this incredible multiplicity the extent to which man always and everywhere remains the same, each bearing within himself, "the entirety of the human condition." The difficulty is found not in holding one of these two complementary truths but, rather, in not forgetting the one in favor of the other and in knowing, on the contrary, how to unite them if one wishes to philosophize concerning history.

B. Diversity in the Ways We Attain and Express the Truth

What we just said concerning the differentiations found in the human mind [*esprit*] right in the midst of the same specific nature already enables us to glimpse in what sense and for what reasons various human minds, considering one and the same objective truth, can form for themselves representations that are not identical with each other without, however, thereby excluding one another. There is no such thing as Human-Mind-as-Such. There are only *given* human minds, particular realizations of the same spiritual nature. This multiplicity is only due to matter, and the mode of knowledge proper to such a spiritual nature is affected by its condition: the human mind composes and divides, after first having "abstracted" [what it knows from sense experience, elaborated by the "internal senses," which furnish the objective instrument of human cognition]. This presupposes a kind of "slicing up" of reality so as to arrive at a mental "recomposition," an "order" that reproduces the unity of reality, thanks to a series of rationate relations [i.e., *relationes rationis*]. These successive and complicated operations of the mind, slowly reaching their result, are not performed without the possibilities of error or of some shortcoming appearing at each step along the way.

The mental expression of a truth, which by its very nature cannot be obtained all at once, "*tota simul*," will by its very essence be susceptible to admixtures [*mélanges*], to progress as well, and indeed, to greater or lesser perfection. From one mind to the next, from one generation or group of minds to the next, it will be able to vary without absolutely falling into contradiction. However, this in no way prevents there from being an ultimate object for the whole of philosophical research, a universal truth, though human in character, a truth whose essential elements at least can be (or one day will be able to be) considered, without falling into a naïve dogmatism, to have been attained, indeed, definitively.

And this bodily condition of mind [*esprit*] in man involves not only this abstractive and successive mode of knowledge but, also, as we have said, involves "individuation," the multiplication and temporal succession of human intellects (which, as such, would tend toward unity and fullness). Thus, it also seems essential that truth, precisely to the degree it is possible for man, will be affected by these individuating conditions that come to characterize and limit our intellectual nature. The truth—which is a mind's relation with being—whose typical form varies with the nature of this mind, will be found in man bearing the mark of both his essential unity and his necessarily multiple and changing character. This can be deduced *a priori* from his nature. However, we would like to show this in greater detail by examining the various acts by which, in the concrete conditions of life, the human mind grasps the truth, along with the conditioning which these acts cannot avoid.

1. The Various Degrees of Truth in Human Judgment

It is far too vague to merely speak of "human truth," that is, of the truth of human knowledge. For man, conceiving is one thing and judging another. Now, the mind's truth formally exists *in judgment*. It is in the affirmation of an object of thought as existing, as *real*, that the mind's truth is simultaneously affirmed. To say, "This is," (or, "this is such") is the same as saying, "It is true that this is" (or "is such"), which ultimately implies: the thought that I now form concerning this object is conformed to reality. Logical truth is, by definition, self-aware and self-affirmative. Its difference from ontological truth is found in this fact. Consequently, a judgment is more or less immediately true to the degree that its truth comes to light more or less immediately in the mere combining of that judgment's terms. There are judgments whose truth I see through the mediation of other judgments, which step-by-step bring me to evidential knowledge, to immediate vision of the object.

These non-immediate judgments, which are conclusions, the fruits of reasoning, are themselves more or less perfect, with a truth that is more or less immediately grasped and affirmed inasmuch as my mind, through its power of deduction or through long habit, more quickly and more synthetically perceives all the "reasons" involved, that is, the intermediary propositions that lead it to its conclusion. Our judgments are by far not equally radiant with the truth, for they are not all scientific in character. Some are "opinions" or "hypotheses." Certainly, they either are or are not materially conformed to the truth. However, this conformity is not always visible merely by combining their terms, nor seen in necessary reasons. And how many "conclusive" propositions are said to be such, wrongly, on the basis of quite correct principles! One can hold truths whose consequences have not yet been clearly perceived, though they nonetheless continue to press upon one's thought, with dimly-perceived implications, even while the same person explicitly denies such implications or even professes positions that contradict them. Therefore, in one and the same knowing subject, a false judgment can coexist alongside true judgments that logically undermine it. Perfect "coherence" within one and the same mind is obtained only rarely, though it remains the condition for perfect human truth. Therefore, one can quite well say that, concerning every object, there is a perfectly and essentially true judgment that the mind seeks to form, one that can be called "the truest possible" (in terms of the kind of truth that belongs to what the *human mind* can obtain, a truth that in no way equals the Divine Truth, which is infinitely truer than this).[29]

It is likewise clear that even judgments that cannot be called purely and simply true are often far from being entirely false. They occasionally hold true in what they affirm and not in what they deny. They are false in their universality, while remaining valid in this or that category of case whose particularity and proper character [*raison propre*] still evade our insight. When we discuss something "sympathetically," do we not essentially "distinguish" the terms at stake, specifying their various possible senses in order to retain the only sense that alone would enable the given judgment to be true? Many opinions could be true "in a certain sense," which is not always explicitly

---

29 One might wonder whether this "more or less" to which the concept of the truth is susceptible when it is applied to our judgments is the sign of an analogy. . . . However, even when this would indeed be the case—and we believe that between the truth of opinion and that of a scientific assertion there exists the same kind of analogy as that which exists between virtue properly so called and the mere disposition to virtue—this would not prevent the first analogate of such an analogy from being the scientific judgment that man can form, and even better, the human judgment of immediate evidence, which would, in its own turn, be the lowest analogate of this much vaster analogy having the Divine Truth as its pinnacle. Certainly, it is because it is a participation in the Divine Truth that human truth realizes its own, proper concept with more or less perfection. Nonetheless, a pure and perfect type of human truth does exist.

excluded by those who profess them. However, this leads us beyond a direct consideration of judgment so as to turn our attention toward the elements from which judgments themselves are formed, namely, our representations, our concepts.

2. The Various Degrees of Truth Involved in Our "Conceptualizations"

Even though, strictly speaking, concepts are neither true nor false, truth (or the appearance thereof) comes from their combination. In other words, the truth of our judgments depends on the value of their relationship with reality.

Indeed, we can speak of *conceptual truth*, which involves a concept's representation of the intelligible object. So long as this representation is not, of itself, affirmative and cannot be broken down into a subject and a predicate, we cannot yet speak of logical truth but only of this kind of ontological truth of the mind, namely, its fidelity to its nature, with the nature of a concept being to contain its object just as the truth of this object is to be itself. However, clearly, this ontological truth belonging to concepts prepares for the logical truth belonging to judgments. And moreover, more or less implicit judgments are frequently mixed in with this work of "conceptualization" and "definition," which forms the philosopher's own first scientific task.

However, what exactly is meant by the verb "to conceptualize"? "To conceptualize" is to form a concept, to represent and express in a concept what our intellect grasps concerning an object. An outlook concerning the nature of conceptualization, one differing from our own, has been widely disseminated by Bergsonian philosophy. According to the latter, the mind [*esprit*] first grasps its object at a level that is deeper than, and prior to, the distinction between the intellect and the will, doing so by means of a faculty that is completely different from that of conceptualizing and discursive reasoning. This "intuition" of the object, this living experience, is what we would seek to express and formulate in "concepts," in static, solid "images," whose representative value in relation to changing reality is less assured than is their practical value, having only a provisionally-assured correspondence with the living intuition whence they proceed.

We hold, however, that our intellect's first insights are in no way prior to our concepts. The human mind does not think without forming concepts about what it thinks, even in the case of the very first intuitions of being, substance, and of its own existence. A mental fabrication inasmuch as it is a psychological entity, the concept is such—that is, representative of a given thing—only in virtue of a determination impressed upon the mind by the "thing" in question, by the object. The concept is a pure intermediary, "rendering present" the object inasmuch as it is intelligible within the intellect. However, the first concepts, those that are immediate, though not yet reflected upon, being neither elaborated nor compared with each other, are "vague" [*confus*]. Similarly "vague" are the first generalizations by which we seek to group together our experiences and particular notions, which are insufficiently intelligible because they are insufficiently universal.

Comprising in actual fact, at least virtually, a number of interwoven concepts, aiming at many realities without distinguishing them from one another, they lend themselves to judgments that remain equivocal and contain both truth and falsity. The use of vague concepts in our reasoning is extremely dangerous, for we risk passing almost unconsciously from one sense of the term in question to another. "To conceptualize" reality by means of a mental effort of reflection is to obtain a clear, precise, and distinct concept, from a vague one. This is what the ancients referred to as defining. Through this activity, undertaken within the ambit of the mind, we bring to light a notion that is unifying and capable of explaining others.

This is indeed brought about by consulting, in some way, one's own mind concerning what it truly thinks, by interrogating it, by requiring it to, in the words of Socrates, "give birth" to the proper concept of the thing inasmuch as it is distinct from everything else.

There is nothing pejorative involved in this word, "conceptualization," nothing that, of itself, indicates a translation of a superior type of knowledge into an inferior one, nothing that would bring to mind a kind of "degraded," "deficient" representation of a transcendent reality, a representation adapted to our needs and feelings. On the contrary, it involves the perfecting of knowledge as such.

To an extent, it is true to say that there is more in our vague knowledge than in our clear knowledge. At this level of immediacy and non-explanation, concepts and sense experience are mixed together. . . . A kind of more comprehensive view often involves a corresponding, very-strong sentiment, for as St. Thomas saw quite well, although knowledge precedes love, "one can love perfectly that which one knows imperfectly" (*ST* I-II, q. 27, a. 2, ad 2). The feeling of life often intensely accompanies our vague concepts and, along with it, all those connaturalities that give knowledge at least more savor, along with a different kind of evidence. Sedimentation and impoverishment are the price paid for conceptualization, which will need to be pushed to a lofty level of perfection in order for the mind to once again have this feeling of "fullness" in its view of reality, as well as the impression that it has immediate contact with it.

A clear concept is, indeed, always *partial*. It represents this or that aspect of reality, indeed, not always the most essential one. There are generic concepts, and there are others that are specific. Both of these are univocal. Others attain reality only through analogy with another that is more directly graspable, through which we form an analogous concept that is imperfectly abstracted from its inferior analogates. Every *complex* being lends itself to quite diverse representations of itself. This fact becomes striking above all when we are concerned with conceiving of simple but superior realities. Goodness, truth, intelligence, love—all of these are various "views" of the one Divine Reality. *A fortiori* this holds true for concepts wherein supernatural truth is revealed. In a revealed mystery, we forever find ourselves confronted with two "faces" that, at first glance, seem to be opposed, the famous "two ends of the chain," spoken of by Bossuet, two "faces" whose reconciliation is hidden to reason's glance. Quite clearly, the order in which these concepts are present in the human mind, themselves not calling for one another, can vary, thus resulting in different perspectives that nonetheless do not necessarily exclude one another and will both come to be integrated by a perfect theology.[30] Within one and the same domain, there can also be two different analogies that both would have been of use for enabling us to conceive one and the same reality, such as, for example, that of the "Mental Word," and that of "Son" used for enabling us to conceive of the Second Person of the Trinity. However, far from being able to hold that these two analogies are equivalent and interchangeable, they *complement each other* and are mutually illuminative.

Saint Thomas says that the more a being is elevated in the order of intelligence, the less numerous are the ideas that it forms, for such a being has the power to unify its objects of thought or, rather, to perceive their unity. In other words, the more perfect they become, ideas lose their partial character. Intellectual natures that are superior to us see the same things as we do, but they do so in a much vaster ensemble, with *all* their references to the whole

---

[30] A classic example will make our point clear. Faith teaches us of God's absolute unity and, nonetheless, also of the Trinity of Divine Persons. We can first conceive of God's unity and seek to deduce from it the non-impossibility, from a given perspective, of the Trinity of Divine Persons. Or, by contrast, we can first conceive of the Father, the Son, and the Holy Spirit as being God, and look to find in these Three Persons the unity of the Divine Nature. These two conceptualizations of the revealed datum do not allow any aspect of the mystery to be overlooked and are equally legitimate as expressions of faith, though not as a principle of scientific explanation. They will provide the foundations for Trinitarian theologies that have unequal explanatory values and unequal coherence, though the notions and conclusions on either side could possibly not, of themselves—and all the while appearing within a different perspective, expressing an unequal precision—not be opposed to each other, nor mutually exclusive (without, certainly, however, them being able to be true at the same time). The advantage of the coexistence of these two conceptualizations and systematizations is precisely their ability to check each other and mutually enrich each other. Both can be thought by one and the same mind and, ultimately, can be integrated into a single synthesis. The reader will note that, in the chosen example, the difference befalling our conceptualizations has its foundation in the complexity of the revealed datum itself.

in which they are parts.³¹ From one man to the next, we also find such differences in conceptual perfection. We realize that they do not truly bear witness to oppositions and incompatible views, that many non-perfect conceptualizations of a complex reality can exist, and finally that it is often quite difficult to take one judgment formed by one human mind concerning a given problem and then set it in contradictory opposition to a judgment formed by another without needing to find some kind of analogy, properly so called, between their representations.

Up to this point, we have spoken only about one kind of limitation inherent to every form of conceptualization, namely, their *partial character*. However, very often, we will find it necessary to speak of a kind of error, at least one that is virtual and implicit. When I implicitly attribute to the whole of a group of realities, vaguely perceived, a given definition that to my eyes seems to represent their common essence, their deep, essential character [*essence profonde*], while in fact not wholly attaining them, my conceptualization is false and paves the way for an error in judgment.³² However, it does not follow that every concept that is inadequate to the object it claims to define would necessarily be unfit for founding true judgments, nor that two concepts aiming at the same reality, vaguely grasped by two minds, would be contradictorily opposed to each other, as would be the case for two judgments—one *yes*, the other *no*—concerning the same object. If a given conceptualization is imperfect because it has not grasped that which makes up the common essence of a vaguely gathered group of notions or because it has only elaborated a non-essential (though, perhaps, commonly shared) aspect of it, this conceptualization is not, properly speaking, false. It is perhaps applicable to one portion of the notions I wanted to define or perhaps from a given perspective. In judgments that are indeed true, we can make use of imperfect concepts, utilizing all the truth they do contain. This is what explains the

---

31 See *ST* I, q. 55, a. 3:

> Do superior angels understand through more universal species than do inferior ones? Yes. And we can see this to a degree by way of example with something that can be found in us. For there are some who, on account of the weakness of their intellect, can grasp intelligible truth only if it is explained to them part by part in every detail. However, there are others who have stronger intellects and can grasp many things from a few.

32 It is possible that the univocity that Scotus attributes to being is not the same as that which St. Thomas denies of being. However, no more is it the case that Scotus's univocity is St. Thomas's position on analogy. One of their conceptions must have been poorly formulated since, in the presence of the same data concerning unity and diversity vaguely felt and perceived, they arrived at different notions. And consequently, their conception of being also will differ, or Scotus considers it to be univocal whereas St. Thomas holds it to be analogous. The captivating thing to investigate is the precise moment, and on what point, their minds begin to diverge.

possibility of using imperfect philosophical concepts in order to arrive at truths through reasoning that uses such concepts. The use of philosophical concepts in theology provides a particularly illuminative example of this fact. Indeed, there, the philosophical concept is, in truth, only at the service of a truth of faith that desires to be clarified, often coming to rectify "*in actu exercito*" the human concept in question, making use of the truth that it does indeed contain.

Jacques Maritain showed this in detail for the case of St. Augustine, though emphasizing that this theologian's use of imperfect philosophical concepts which, in themselves, were weighed down with errors, presupposed that his faith was illuminated by the gifts of the Holy Spirit.[33] What is so manifestly true for St. Augustine's case can likewise be said in general for the whole of the patristic era of Christian thought, whose specific mission as "builders" and defenders of dogma implied a form of assistance from the Holy Spirit, and their less-scientific methodology likewise implied more intermingling of loving contemplation with rational "*discursus*."[34]

Therefore, our "conceptualizations" involve more or less exactness and success. Nonetheless, let us suppose our mind were to fail in forming for itself a precise and exact concept of what it first thought of in a vague manner. Let us suppose a conceptualization that is actually false, at odds with what I had vaguely in mind. Quite often, in wishing to specify something, I actually deform it. In such a case, it is not necessary that my clearly-defined idea eliminate the vague concept that was prior to it, indeed, presiding over its elaboration.

How often have we come to a halt with a given formulation, a given concept, only then to realize that not only did it fail to account for what it was but even for what we in reality thought. Thus, quite often, we continue thinking something that is vaguely true by means of conceptualizations that are in fact scarcely adequate to reality, thereby, at least when we use them, wielding them in our judgments, discourse, and investigations, quite often implicitly rectifying them, understanding them somewhat differently from

---

[33] See Maritain, *The Degrees of Knowledge*, trans. Gerald Phelan et al. (Notre Dame, IN: University of Notre Dame Press, 2002), ch. 7 (Augustinian Wisdom). To appreciate the degree of truth in Augustinian wisdom, Maritain, in this remarkable chapter, makes allusion above all to this differentiation of "levels" and "dimensions" of knowledge, which we will stress below.

[34] Those who, quite in contrast with our own position, attribute an imperfection of the same sort, perhaps one that is graver, to the Aristotelian concepts used by St. Thomas, should have recourse to the same explanation to justify their correspondence with dogma and even their relative truth. However, these concepts cannot be wholly deprived of some grasp on reality. For example, one cannot say that the notion of substance corresponds only to a *figmentum mentis* without simultaneously professing that the use made of it in theology is wholly devoid of truth.

how we do when we consider them in themselves. This is precisely where we stand in need of Socrates and his method.

Here again, our observation, which could be given infinitely more nuance, holds true quite exactly in the domain of theology. Theology represents an effort of analysis and explanation concerning revealed concepts. This explanation is submitted to the vicissitudes of the rational work undertaken by our mind. However, whatever may be the more or less welcome and successful conceptualizations we manage to form, the revealed concept defined by the Church found at the point of departure of theological thought remains present in our mind. And given that its intelligible content infinitely surpasses the more-precise conceptualizations we could form concerning it, and likewise, given that the light proper to it is the light of faith, an infused light that absolutely transcends the rational light of reason, a light that is the proximate principle of infused contemplation, therefore the psychological phenomenon we noted earlier is observed again, more easily: a poor conceptualization ultimately leading to false judgments, without however destroying the truth that I perceive in a vague, obscure state, through the concepts of faith. A theology that is false in many of its conclusions and outlooks can very well coexist with a faith that is objectively identical to that which presides over an entirely true theology.[35] This brings us back to what we said above concerning the very imperfect consistency habitually befalling the human mind.

Up to this point, we have held that these differences in conceptualizations concerning the same object are formed at the same level of intelligibility. Thus, we can just as well obtain complementary representations of reality or ones that are more or less clear and complete. However, our abstractive way of knowing gives rise to even more profound differentiations within it. The conceptualization formed from one and the same immediate datum can, in fact, exist at multiple levels of abstraction. One and the same objective reality can give way to multiple orders of representations, to multiple systems of conceptualization, to multiple sciences or types of knowing. The physicist who considers being inasmuch as it is realized or realizable in the sensible universe looks upon the universe under a different light than does the pure mathematician who considers it inasmuch as it is submitted merely to the laws of number and quantity, likewise looking at the universe under a different light than does the metaphysician who considers being—even while indeed observing it in the world of that which is sensible—precisely by focusing on that aspect of this reality that transcends matter, quantity, [and so forth]. . . .

---

35 Another example: it is difficult to completely adhere to the Cajetanian conception of personality and not simultaneously perceive that Scotus's conception of it renders a true Hypostatic Union unthinkable. However, at the same time, we can readily admit that both a Scotist mind and a Cajetanian mind both share the same vague insight (which both of them seek to analyze) concerning what Christ's personal unity is.

The danger of error here is to fail to heed the conceptual registers involved, reducing everything to one's most familiar system of conceptualization. In order to speak about realities that reveal themselves only to metaphysical understanding, a physicist will be tempted to retain his experimental language. The metaphysician will be exposed to the risk of reducing everything to concepts that are far too general, thus presenting inadequate responses to questions posed by the mind on a lower level of abstraction. Therefore, a given proposition will be "true" *if* one reads it as being found at a given "register," within a given conceptual "lexicon." According to the sense and, so to speak, the degree of the word "being," two propositions, two apparently divergent world systems, will be equally true, though on different levels of knowledge. The very scope of the word "reality" will not be the same in a science that seeks out the law of observable facts and in that which seeks out the very essence, the "quiddity" of things. We already encounter this difference within one and the same order of abstraction. Between experimental or "empiriological" physics and ontological physics, the qualitative difference in knowledge is clear enough for certain minds to experience the tendency to reduce the latter to metaphysics, reserving the term "physics" for the former. To these two different types of knowing, there correspond, for one and the same object, systems of conceptualization that are not contradictory, though they are fundamentally different: the same words thus encompass quite different notions thatcan give way to definitions and propositions that are disparate and seemingly mutually exclusive. However diverse they may be, these notions nonetheless play analogous roles. The "quiddity" spoken of by the philosopher will be replaced by the physicist with "the possibility of observation," and "conditionality" will be substituted for "causality," properly so called. To reduce observed, measured phenomena, whose laws and conditioning one seeks after, to a philosophical concept of *cause* will seem to be an absolutely non-existent pseudo-response. The "conceptualization" of a problem that seems to be the same, [for example] that of the "intimate constitution" of matter, will be completely different on the empiriological level in contrast to the ontological level of conceptualization. This is because the very idea of "the constitution of matter" is different on these two levels. By contrast, the empiriological physicist is easily subject to the attraction of mathematics—rightly so, given the possibility of translating observable phenomena in terms of quantity. Given that the type of truth he arrives at is mathematical in nature, defined, instead, as a kind of symbolic representation of reality, he will come to form concerning the physical universe propositions that we will need to know how to read in the appropriate register, and in this very register, they remain true.

Let us not insist any further on these matters, though they be of such great importance, matters set forth with great depth and at length by Jacques

Maritain in his *Degrees of Knowledge*. They are of capital importance on the level of the philosophy of nature, and they enable us to perceive the durability not only of medieval metaphysics but also of its natural philosophy, even through the tremendous development of physics on the levels of empiriological and physico-mathematical conceptualization. These same principles help us to perceive, in relation to one and the same revealed datum, the possibility of there being a profound difference in conceptualization when one considers this datum on the level of ontological reflection, in contrast to that of morality or mysticism.[36] St. Thomas does not stand in opposition to St. John of the Cross, or even to St. Augustine, as he does, however, to Duns Scotus.

Moreover, our multiple conceptualizations of reality are reduced to unity. Every time we extrapolate concepts from the level where they are elaborated and understood to a level that is foreign to them, we will ultimately fall into equivocations and errors. And whenever we positively disregard one level of knowledge, we will implicitly fall into error concerning the deep structure and possibilities of the human intellect. In the end, metaphysics (on the merely natural level) and speculative theology (on the level of knowledge of the revealed datum) have the power of reflecting on all the modes and degrees of knowledge, as well as that of constituting a synthesis of the whole of our various forms of knowledge.

3. Conceptualization and Formulation

Still, something is lacking in what we have thus far said concerning the various elements involved in the relativity of human truth. We have not addressed the question of language. And nonetheless, there is no more important equivocation to be dispelled than that involved with the words "expression" and "philosophical language," which are not always clearly identified as referring either to concepts or to words. It is all too clear that great difficulty is involved in trying to separate a concept from the word that serves it both in the mind as well as in its external transmission. However, if a given reality surpasses the concept formed concerning it, the latter is at least a natural representation of it, whereas the word is never anything other than a conventional sign of the concept. A word is truthful only to the extent that it adequately expresses the idea it intends to express. However, the fixity of its signifying value comes from its usage, being wholly assured only in practice thanks to its perpetual contact with concrete things and acts. As soon as one looks to elevate words to the level of signifying general ideas, a kind of fluctuation in their signifying value, along with a kind of arbitrariness in the use

---

[36] Here too, in the *Degrees of Knowledge*, in relation to St. Augustine and St. John of the Cross, Maritain has provided principles for solving this issue, and what he says there deserves wider recognition.

made of them, remain possible. However, what are we to say when it comes to naming philosophical concepts, which have been slowly formed over time, through great difficulty and at the cost of reflections seeking to probe their depths? What are we to say about the person who looks to designate to someone else something that is perhaps being conceived of clearly for the first time ever right here and now? Quite obviously there is something *relative* involved in the value of philosophical vocabulary. We must forever strive to reach the idea behind the words we use. A given vocabulary does not impose itself with the necessity of absolute truth. However revelatory we may find the analysis of words expressing, in a given language, some notion arising from spontaneous philosophical knowledge, it can only serve as a point of departure for the explanation of a concept. But, while the meaning of words does depend in some way on what the philosopher wishes to make them say, we must also conversely note that the philosopher's own thought will inevitably experience the reverberations of the words at his disposal at his particular time and place. It is difficult to use words that are characteristic of a given philosophy so as to express thereby concepts that are different from those usually evoked by such words. However, far be it from us to assert that human thought would be *essentially* dependent upon a language that is essentially variable from one century to the next, as Fr. Le Blond seems to state: "Our thought is expressed by composing and dividing the schemata imposed by various languages, schemata which do not remain wholly external to thought itself."[37] Much to the contrary, thought attains reality only to the degree that it knows that language must serve only as an instrument. The powerlessness of words is its great obstacle, something the historian ceaselessly detects, though the philosopher himself strives to eliminate it.[38] The more one has a sense for the

---

[37] Le Blond, "L'analogie de la verité," 134.

[38] The great obstacle the "word" poses to the idea is its power to substitute itself for the latter. Who will say how often words and images substitute themselves for concepts in imperfect thought? This is why one can very well make coexist within one's own mind vague truths and immediate intuitions alongside conceptions which claim to deny them, though one does not truly "think" them because they are not thinkable. However, sadly, it is quite frequently the case that one does not truly "think"!

This substitution of words for concepts can, moreover, quite well take place where the latter would be full of reality. One thus comes to reason over mental signs, drained of their content. Abstraction is all too often mistaken for being this kind of algebra, this decoupling from reality. In such a case, there is indeed abstraction, though not from the sensible and the particular but, rather, from reality. In this way, one can end up with materially true propositions but not with the *savor of the truth*, which we receive from contact with reality. Thus, is it surprising that minds accustomed to only maneuvering about in words would lose this "sense of truth," which would save them from so many mistakes, misunderstandings, and ignorance of reality in domains that are new for them, as well as so many arbitrary limitations on their own terrain?

natural relativity of language, the more one considers that, in order to attain the perfection of thought toward which the human mind should strive, there necessarily should be established a system of signification that is absolutely objective and fixed, and that we should establish a kind of conventional fixing of language. . . . At least, this is what the Church does for her dogmas and what a scientific theology would itself tend to realize.

Indeed, what immense advantage is drawn from having the conventions of language clearly specified so that we might come to understand each other! The words drawn from a common language are thus endowed with an exactly-determined sense; they can evoke the same concept in all minds. The pitfall is that one can come to play around with them too much, reasoning [merely] concerning these words, dispensing oneself from [actually] thinking and taking up anew the vital work of conceptualization and *personally* grasping reality. If to philosophize is to enter into personal and direct contact with the profound truths that are the foundations of life, great danger is involved in not fashioning a language for oneself. However, to have to express what oneself has seen, doing so in an objectively fixed language whose signifying value is given in advance—what a lofty demand! What a victory over rough approximation! However, [by the very fact of such linguistic expression] philosophy has lost something from its objectivity, its universalism, and its claim to be definitive and in touch with the atemporal. It tends to become the expression of a personal manner—indeed, one wishing to retain this stamp of one's personality—of seeing eternal realities.

The problem of verbal expression is much broader than that of vocabulary. As soon as a thought wishes to express itself, it immediately obeys certain laws of expression. It constructs itself in a given order, that which is more favorable for expression "*ad extra*" and for communication to others. The "order of teaching," the process of placing something into verbal form, and the interconnection of ideas are all constraints that require thought to specify itself but communicate to it a kind of rigidity that does not come from its own proper laws. Here, variations of order, of methods of expositions, and of style will all intervene. One and the same thought can be exposited in very different ways, which cannot fail to reverberate on its own internal order. Differences in formulation can affect conceptualization itself. Here, we could study the variety found in literary genres and styles. However, it seems quite clear that rather profound differences in the form given to thought will not change its intelligible content except, inevitably, in its nuances, and that one can rewrite, for example, St. Thomas in a less didactic and less neat and trim [*découpée*] form, giving his thought a more modern style, without, for all this, changing his concepts.

4. Conceptualization and Systematization

Everything we just said concerning the truth of judgments and concepts becomes more complicated if we come to speak of an organized body of ideas, judgments, and reasoning, of the rational construction that one calls a "system." Here, we are not contrasting "system" with "science." We understand the word in a generic sense that embraces every kind of mental arrangement of thoughts connected to one another, dependent above all upon certain fundamental concepts. Moreover, we have not been able to speak about conceptualization without already glimpsing the interior constructions of these mental arrangements, which can go so far as to desire to reproduce the whole of reality in the human mind in a human manner. However, the truth of a system of science or wisdom obviously cannot be gauged as simply as that of a concept or judgment. In order for a rational construction to be assured of the truth of a great number of the propositions it contains, it suffices that it have sufficient strength for supporting itself in a mind and in a school. Obviously—and this is a basic fact—this truth will need to be appreciated in function of the system's own proper light. The concepts involved in it can be understood in their true sense only if they are considered from within that system. Each philosophical system has its own fabricated language or, at least, one that is modeled on its own concepts, often influenced by the latter even where it serves to express common ideas. Clearly, the statements of each such system concerning the same problems are not purely and simply to be set in opposition to each other but, rather, are to be critiqued and reduced to their true meaning. And yet, the point of departure for various systems is, of course, different. Even when there is only a difference *in via inventionis*, it is rare that this difference not reverberate over the overall arrangement.

However, if the author of a system places at the foundation of his edifice something that in reality represents only some secondary aspect [of reality], he deceives himself in so doing. Nonetheless, many truths remain open to him and some, *per accidens*, will appear to him, as it were, with greater radiance. Methods can also differ and, with them, the way one conceives of the nature of the human mind, science, and wisdom. Even if these conceptions happen to be false (and given their complex nature, if we consider all the details of their content, not everything in them will be false), this does not make everything that appears under their sway invalid. If I deny, for example, the value of the intellect and consequently come to rely above all on an instinct of heart, I will nonetheless—indeed quite often, *in actu exercito*—use my mind as though it does indeed reach reality and will discover no small number of utterly correct things. If I limit human thought to empirically observable objects, my worldview will be false through what it denies, but I will thereby enable myself to greatly perfect my powers of observation.

Let differences in illumination—that is, differences in formal objects—come to be added to these manifold causes of differentiation, and we will find ourselves faced with "positions" before reality whose principal error would be to mutually exclude each other, including the denial of truths that are poorly understood because they are viewed under an unfamiliar intellectual light. A so-called "scientific" outlook (in the modern sense of the word "science") concerning the world is often simply a worldview lacking in philosophical illumination, where the only portion of error that is discernable comes from what is rejected. To put it another way: truth is found in all the great systems. We apologize for making such a banal point, even though it is not nothing to have understood what makes this state of affairs possible. However, this being said, we must come to speak formally not of truths contained in a system but, rather, of *the truth of systems as such*, of the adequation of this mental construction—this "unified" construction, with its unique character and distinction from every other such construction—in relation to the reality that it claims to render intelligible. In this very precise sense, a system will be true if its fundamental principles are true, if they are truly first principles, if the conceptualization implied in these principles is perfect, clear, and formal, that is, going to the very essence of things, and finally, if its method is good, corresponding to the true nature of the mind and its undertakings. We must add that, in order to remain completely true, a system must remain "open," ready to receive all reality, ever-prepared to critique itself and reconstruct itself. A system always has the tendency to lay claim to the totality that is, in fact, its essential aim. It is not in error because it does not embrace *the whole*; rather, error lies in judging that "the whole" is there, that the whole of reality has been captured. The mind forever has the tendency to deny whatever does not find a place in the closed synthesis it has fashioned for itself. Every human mind that remains enclosed within what it has conceived—*a fortiori* within what it has learned—by that very fact distorts the truth it possesses. In its own self-estimation, a system must forever remain aware of that portion of reality that it has not yet assimilated, a portion that could become a principle and ferment in its own turn. This is why the truest [system] must guard against the danger that threatens it precisely because it is a system: to judge everything that is proposed to it in terms of how it corresponds with the overall system rather than through their own proper principles and doubtlessly before long to no longer have a spirit of research but, rather, to be concerned only with presenting an exposition of already-acquired truths. Supposing that this method preserves one from a number of errors, in place of reality, it risks presenting to the mind the system itself as an object, along with this system's coherence. By no longer being aware of any other problems than those that gave birth to this particular system, one risks, through a kind of immobility, relying precisely on what is contingent and accidental in it, its historical conditioning, focusing on what conditioned its historical genesis. It is not a paradox to say that the "truth" and "life" of a system as such must proceed together. However, having thus defined the truth conditions for a system as such, it is obvious that in the face of one and the same object and on one and the same level of knowledge, only one true system is possible, and it is in search of it that the human mind labors through its multiple attempts at synthesis, which time devours only because they have not yet attained their goal, though, all the while leading toward it, indeed, often by error's own path. The word "system" is no longer suitable for describing this ideal mental construction, which would be the true system, the objective possibility of which suffices for justifying all forms of dissatisfactions and investigations. This completely generic word, which above all expresses the internal coherence of a mental whole, equally applies to the true, the hypothetical, and the false. A system deserving of this name is an attempt at science. If it claims it is true and affirms itself as thus, it at the same time declares that it is a "scientific" expression of reality.

As we have seen, there is no reason why the same could not be true for theology and metaphysics. The disproportion between the human mind and its object in theology creates an infinite distance between this object and the representation that it can form of it for itself, thereby making appeal to a supra-conceptual form of knowledge purely and directly through faith. However, this would justify a multitude of theologies only if the human mind were not specifically one or if the divine truths had not been revealed in human concepts.

However, the human mind is so made that the essential itself is partial. No system fashioned by its work can fail to be, in fact, free from error and lacunae. Nor can any system concretely existing in the mind of a man fail to bear his own individual stamp and to lose, in him, the pure nature of perfect science. Although all truths could find a place in the true system, it is often necessary that certain ones appear in the light of other conceptualizations and other methods. This is why, next to Science—indeed as long as it does not come to reach its ultimate state of achievement—there must also forever be systems that force it to perpetually verify, revise, and supplement itself.

5. Mentalities

Moreover, within one and the same science there remain, in addition to the various possible mental outlooks spoken of above, the infinite variations arising from individual mental differences. One mind can completely recopy another mind only if it is itself in touch with reality. Now, one man will never, in fact, embrace all the aspects of reality in their own proper order, without making any personal choice, without any order of preference, without any reverberation of that which, in him, individuates his intellect. The problems he raises for himself, the interest he takes in them, the various kinds of background knowledge that serve as a point of departure, the various influences he has experienced—all of this determines the orientation of his intellect, which can attempt to overcome this order of factors (which, in themselves, are contingent) only after having submitted himself to them. "*Omnis cognitio humana a sensu*." Man reaches eternal essences only by means of realities that pass away and change, by way of mental activity that is deeply involved in the passage of time. Everything that comes from the individual in human thought is only an accidental covering. However, it is essential to this thought that it have this covering and that it see it develop. This is what we must look into more closely by studying, though in a rather summary fashion, what we can call the "mentality" of a thinker.

Indeed, our reflection here would be all too incomplete if, while being concerned with situating the different concepts from which our judgments are formed into the context of great systems of ideas wherein they find their meaning, we did not place these systems themselves into this even-broader—though vaguer and more indefinable as well—context: a "*mentality*." The mentality of a thinker, insofar as it is distinct from his system of thought, involves everything he has in his mind in a non-scientific state, constituting a kind of atmosphere and, at the same time, something presupposed for his intellectual effort. It includes judgments that have not been critiqued, ones that are not scientific or even might be erroneous, general assessments and value judgments, an overall outlook concerning the meaning of life, an *attitude* regarding God and the world, along with one's spirituality. Every new metaphysics comes to birth within a mentality that it sometimes helps to transform by developing itself, though slowly.

And, moreover, many of the ideas one might try to use—though with what difficulty!—to formulate a mentality are themselves accepted ready-made and are introduced uncritically (because they are admitted by all) into a system that otherwise diligently strives to render account of its principles. A "mentality" will not, in fact, ever be entirely defined by a group of ideas but, rather, by ways of feeling, evaluating, seeing, and *imagining* the world, all of which are determined by mores, examples, institutions, and perhaps, the debris left behind by ideological systems that, despite having collapsed, nonetheless reigned for many years.

In order to understand what we mean here by the term "mentality," we must keep in mind what we said concerning the relations between the individual and his race, social category, and general milieu. We forever come back to this condition befalling man, *individuated* through his connection to his embodied nature and thereby *multiplied and begotten*, aspiring to the fullness of his nature through union with his fellow men, the foundation of the family and life in society. The human mind never thinks *alone*. In his intellectual life, he is *dependent*. He is not alone, standing before the object. There are already biases that determine him, which he suffers from or has inherited, and we cannot even always say whether they belong to the order of truth or that of falsity.

However just and true an idea may be, however coherent and substantially adequate to reality a system may be, it is impossible that references to the "mentality" in which it is thought would not come to be added to the pure conceptual datum, marking it with a kind of relativity.

A "mentality" varies even though many of its conceptions remain valid. It is impossible that each thinker and each era would not have a unique mentality, even though the properly scientific attitude of mind seeks to free itself from it, at least by being aware of it. However, if this "mentality," precisely as something transitory, were to affect the essence and "specific nature" of scientific thought, the latter, not having attained the eternal and the necessary, would not be true. A true thought is only accidentally affected by this relativity and by these relations to one's mental context. In it, what is unchanging can be separated from what is variable in the same way that one can, through one's mind, separate what is essential and necessary from something's individuating notes.

In any case, when a mind whose "mentality" differs from that of a thinker from an earlier era thinks the *same* system, when it has the *same* ideas, it must strip them of these references. Otherwise, if it does not know how to do so, relying on this surface-covering, which nonetheless is accidental, it renders itself incapable even of grasping the objective reality that past thinkers grasped and *a fortiori* of adhering to it.

6. Truth and History

Here, we see the role of history, namely, to aid us in distinguishing what is variable and relative from what is essential and permanent, perhaps preserving us from succumbing to the influences of our own era. Far be it from us to disregard the necessity of history for investigation into the truth. Nonetheless, let us here also avoid a strange confusion that so often is allowed to stand when one speaks about the relations between truth and history. Some say: we must make the elements of "history" and "time" enter into conception of human truth. What this meant for Hegel is well known: truth is in the making, as is reality itself, which is the Idea. However, for us, only one meaning is acceptable concerning this affair. There is a history of human thought, a history of truth such as man has seen it. However, there also is a self-identical, atemporal truth, which is the specifying object of human wisdom. Truth, such as a given thinker has seen it, even were this St. Augustine or St. Thomas, depends on history, on time, on everything that conditions his acts of thought, and on its own proper limits. However, the ultimate object of our wisdom is not the Augustinianism of St. Augustine, nor the Thomism of St. Thomas, nor the mind of any thinker whatsoever. It is the truth itself. This is what my own mind must think, aided by those who have contemplated it before it has, though avoiding their errors, surpassing their limits, and striving to see for oneself what they themselves saw.

Can anything more be granted to the element of "time"? Can we think that the duration of humanity, no more than that of the individual, is not only a succession of instants but, rather, a begetting of instants by one another? "Time" would thus have an "orientation." The human species—certainly not in a continuous manner, not without eclipses, backsliding, impasses, and fruitless attempts—would undergo a process of *development*. On account of its incarnation in individual and manifold matter, the human mind would thus progressively reach its maturation and its state of adaptation to its object, its aptitude to see the truth. Man would rise upward toward more spirit, toward more truth, all according to a kind of law, according to a dialectic, and knowledge of this dialectic would be of use in having a better understanding of the thought of this or that moment of this evolution. However, because its nature would not change (nor, consequently, its manner of knowing reality and of adjusting itself to it), this would not mean that there would be a kind of analogy among the successive worldviews that humanity would form. There would only be a progressive elimination of errors, the development of principles, and the acquisition of new, perhaps essential, truths that might be lacking in the very foundations of the edifice. However, we use the conditional mood because facts do not seem to vindicate this way of interpreting the history of the human mind [*esprit*],[39] and no *a priori* could force us to hold that what is *new* would [necessarily] have more truth value. It is already much to say that the novelty of discovery gives thought a greater feeling of life.

In any case, why not see that certain eras are privileged, that certain men are predestined to see realized in themselves the "decisive moments" of human evolution? Others, to the degree that they contribute something new, are only men of their era. The great transcend their era and discover that which is necessary and eternal. They are the true masters. And once the essential is attained, in whatsoever domain, the eternal is also, by that very fact, attained.

---

39 It would perhaps be more exact to say, with Émile Bréhier (*La Philosophie et son passé*) that through so many immense changes, the fundamental attitudes of the human mind remain constant and few in number.

IV.—ST. THOMAS AND THE UNICITY OF THEOLOGY
[LA THÉOLOGIE UNIQUE]

As should be clear, we are in agreement with Fr. Le Blond, as with everyone, no doubt, in admitting that truth can be found in systems of thought and language that are quite different from each other and that, in fact, elements of "relativity" and "variables" are involved in the concrete reality of all human thought. However, in no way can we explain this by claiming that our various representations of reality are necessarily analogical in character. First of all, we find these elements of variability once again in domains where our representations are univocal. Likewise, even where reality infinitely exceeds the proper object of the human intellect [*esprit*], the unity of the latter reduces to unity the kind of analogy by which it knows the Infinite. Where our concepts differ not only through their references to an obsolete system of thought (i.e., one that is recognized as being false, in which case we have a mentality that has been surpassed), but moreover through their essential content itself, we no longer say that it is the same truth, even when the same words are retained. We do not think that many systems whose metaphysical foundations contradict each other can equal each other as expressions of reality. We think the task of the human mind [*esprit*] is to tend toward the unification of knowledge. The effort expended in forming a general synthesis of every form of knowledge, forming a complete and unique worldview founded on faith, does not involve some kind of rationalist tendency but, rather, is an affirmation of the unity of the human mind set before the truth, even the Divine Truth, as well as of the objective value of its grasp upon reality, a grasp that, however partial it may be, nonetheless remains an aspiration toward *wisdom*.

Will we now say that this one [*unique*] theology exists and that our only role is to understand St. Thomas and to repeat what he has said? If this were the case, we indeed could not be pardoned for not dedicating our strength to an exegesis of his thought, armed with all the resources of history. Now, however crucial this work might seem to us, a labor providing enough work to consume teams—how greatly desired they are!—of specialists, we believe it is also necessary to continue to contemplate reality in his footsteps. St. Thomas obviously has neither said everything nor seen everything. He has not delved down into, nor applied, each of his principles [in full]. He integrated into his synthesis false historical and scientific positions that strongly influenced a number of his philosophical conceptions. He held in his own mind many views common in his own era, views that he did not critique, though they did not depend on his own metaphysical outlook. He paid little attention to values that now seem to us to be issues of the first rank of importance. He was not aware of a great number of things that would have inspired great metaphysical insights and admirable theological explanations. He had a determinate end, that of a professor, which slightly inflects even a scholar's own goals. His language is indeed admirable, given how he says exactly what he means, though this language can indeed be significantly enriched. And then there is his spiritual temperament, one that is marvelously conducive for the work of a scholar, though it was that of his own, personal holiness. Finally, if a mortal could be permitted to live for centuries in the full strength of his maturity, accompanied with the full, lively, and innovative curiosity of youth, it is clear that he would not have ceased to progress, to draw to himself for his own self-growth everything that other minds would have felt and discovered concerning the truth. However, St. Thomas is only one man: some years of thought after twelve centuries of Christianity and how many centuries of civilization? Nonetheless, better than anyone before him, he understood the essential truths, those that are first and most fundamental, and he knew how to build everything upon them, fashioning a synthesis that is all the more open to every truth precisely inasmuch as it is more dependent upon a metaphysics, that is, upon the principles of all things. Something very new and very crucial in Christianity began with him. In him and through him, Christian thought succeeded in arriving at a synthesis with the philosophy issuing from mere reason, such as it appeared in Aristotle. How could those who do not believe in the truth of this philosophy, those who do not believe that up to then theology lacked its perfect rational instrument, attach to St. Thomas the importance that we attach to him? We feel how difficult it is for modern thought to affirm that this philosophy is true and, consequently, capable of progressing, extending itself, and assimilating into itself everything that is true, while nonetheless remaining what it is, all on account of the permanence of the principles that define it. If it is true, how many things are false! Yes, even theses that are permitted and taught in the Church. However, the Church only enforces an opinion concerning that which is *de fide* or very immediately connected to faith. Thank goodness! For if this were not the case, who would be orthodox? "Justice and truth are two points that are so subtle that our instruments are too blunt for us to be able to touch them with accuracy. If they reach it, they conceal its very point and press in every direction, more upon falsity than upon truth."[40]

Were we today, in relation to a philosophy that is essentially opposed to the Aristotelianism used by St. Thomas, to strive to do what St. Thomas did in his own day in response to Aristotle's philosophy, we would have but one option: to ultimately repudiate [*nier*] St. Thomas. It is here that we see the equivocation committed by those who speak of imitating St. Thomas by baptizing Hegel or Bergson, Kierkegaard or Marx. For St. Thomas did not intend to provide Christianity with an expression that is provisionally valid for a

---

40 See Pascal, *Pensées* (Brunschvicg, no. 82).

given time when Aristotle was thought to be true. Rather, he intended to provide an objectively rational and ever-true expression of a dogmatic whole, proposed to man's essentially immutable intellect.[41]

In what way is this position *anti-historical*? Are there not decisive moments in the history of the mind, or are things that are accomplished in time always and necessarily perishable? Are there not discoveries on which everything in human history depends? Are they not prepared for by an often-lengthy evolution that suddenly, in a single stroke, gives birth to a new and more perfect form? To go deeper still, did not the Church stand in need of a theology, so that she could safeguard her faith and enable it to bear its rightful fruit? And consequently, was it not necessary that she discover her own philosophy? Thus, we should not be astonished that the Holy Spirit would have guided the development of Christian thought up to a point where the faith of the Fathers would encounter a permanently-true philosophy. For that matter, why name this or that Father, as well as St. Thomas and Aristotle? These are men who, in fact, discovered or decisively expressed this or that truth, placing their stamp upon it. But who thinks of the inventor of the plow? Nonetheless, the plow exists and has become a perfected machine whose principles have not changed. Certain ideas and methods are inventions that are more precious than the plow or any other tool. And I know quite well that Aristotle and the whole of Greek thought itself seem to represent a rather partial view of the human mind concerning things when we think of the world of Hindu thought or even, having become so different from them, that of modern thought. Nonetheless, it is not for nothing that the Divine Truth was revealed and first taught in Hebrew and Greek concepts. Without a doubt, they were adapted to this task and prepared for by the Word who illuminates every man coming into this world. And without a doubt, they were, above all, flexed and rectified, thereby being given more truth, by this Divine

---

41 In his already-cited article in *Nouvelle revue théologique*, Fr. Daniélou once again distinguishes Christian thought and its essential requirements from the various philosophies in which it can be incarnated. To think, as we do, that only one philosophy is true does not prevent us in any way from admitting as well that Christianity contains in itself imperious philosophical requirements that risk bursting the very frameworks of all purely rational systems. These requirements, such as Fr. Daniélou describes them, certainly burst open historical Aristotelianism in those of its elements that were fixed and ultimately closed off to further development; however, just as well, the genius of St. Thomas was to fully and explicitly grant this, without, however, losing the benefit of the positive truths of Greek wisdom. It is true that his God is at once totally independent and—by the same token, accessible to the creature without possible confusion with it—that his entire worldview was penetrated by his awareness of the directionality and meaning of history [*le sens de l'événement et de l'évolution vers un but*], and that he provides a central place for the human person in a universe which we today know to be disproportionate. This is why, in St. Thomas, we speak of an encounter between Christian philosophy and that of Aristotle.

Truth that had to be expressed in them. Plato and Aristotle are our masters, but how transformed are they by the Faith that found in them the concepts needed for its own human expression!

Therefore, in what way would this position be *insufficiently Catholic*? We have said clearly enough that systems that have some error at their foundations, some primordial lacuna, or some confusion between what is secondary and what is essential still can contain many truths. How much more is this true, *a fortiori*, for Christian systems? How much more is this true, *a fortiori*, again, for the thought of the Fathers? Their philosophy and methodology was, perhaps, uncertain, but in them lived the [T]radition, whose first inspiration came from Scripture, which the Holy Spirit illuminated. The fact that the introduction of their great doctrinal themes sometimes seems to break various Thomist frameworks merely proves the fact that we often must deepen the Thomist position in order to integrate them, and we must not confuse either what St. Thomas explicitly thought with what he suggests nor the limitations that his individuality necessarily brings to the fecundity of his thought with the limitations inscribed within the internal possibilities and essence of this thought.

Moreover, quite often, on many points, Fr. Le Blond is right in what he says, and we have taken care to analyze the reasons for this. The oppositions are more so verbal than real, not because the concepts would be equivalent or analogous to each other but because the same idea is hidden under different words, if one knows how to listen to them in the overall light of the system [in which they are expressed]. It is all too obvious that the human mind, despite itself, placed before eternal problems, spontaneously forms concepts that begin to differ from one system to another only after a great deal of explication has been undertaken or by the relations that one makes them sustain with the whole, often at the expense of one's first intuition. It is not always impossible to translate one philosophy into the language of another philosophy, though it is much better to so translate it into the common language of culture than to borrow the technical terms of an essentially contrary philosophy. In any case, we must translate into our own philosophical language many values and realities that have been perceived by thinkers from outside of our own tradition. It is not at all paradoxical to say that the result of this "transposition" may well be more fruitful between systems that are entirely foreign to one another when those systems are not born from a mutual opposition concerning some common datum.

Nonetheless, for the reasons we spelled out above, to purely and simply abandon scholastic language, and even its most essential method of exposition, would involve the loss of one of Christian philosophy's greatest strengths. It merely should be enriched, indeed constantly, by everything that has become common and classic in modern philosophy, which contains many things that are susceptible to finding a fixed sense within the overall Thomist synthesis, expanded as is necessary.

This position commits neither the error of *rationalism* nor that of excessive intellectualism. By setting before the Christian thinker the goal of working on the construction of a philosophy and a single [*unique*] Catholic theology that will never be fully achieved (yet nonetheless has already been given a solid foundation by St. Thomas), we by the same stroke profess the scientific character of theology. However, having said this, scientific theology is not the only form of theology. It is the most perfect kind in the order of pure knowledge. However, it is not the only means of knowledge offered to the Christian soul, and pure knowledge is not the whole of man. A savoring knowledge of the revealed text under the action of the gifts of the Holy Spirit represents a more direct form of contact with God, a more direct form of nourishment for faith. This is even more true for the mystical contemplation of God present in the soul. We also think that "the Word of God in His unique and definitive fullness is the Word made flesh," but to reach and embrace Him as such no longer lies within the ambit of scientific theology. It lies beyond it. Moreover, charity is beyond all knowledge, not only for charity's moral value but also for the union with God it brings about. God forbid that the Church would only contain theologians or that any of us would limit ourselves to being theologians! Conceptual theology can also be less scientific, making itself apologetic in character, "kerygmatic," adapting itself to the needs, possibilities, and (to the degree this is possible within the bounds of truth) to the ways of thinking of those who are to be saved and nourished on the bread of truth. The same is true on the purely rational level. Objective, realistic philosophy, with its scientific structure, does not suppress (and, indeed, much to the contrary, it in a certain manner frees) a philosophy that is more engaged in life and experience, the witness of metaphysical experiences, the analyses that guard against stripping their object of its existence and of everything this existence brings with it, quivering, personal, and impossible to universalize. There is no great metaphysics that is not, in fact, born of and sustained by some spiritual experience. It is good that certain minds [*esprits*] refuse, for their own count, to become detached from it. Poets are necessary as well, in order to recover, through their own unique means, a truth which is not only a truth. Let the wise take heed: "*Noli impedire musicam*." But all of these forms of life must not aim to replace a metaphysics and theology whose rejection would imply, in relation to intelligence and being, a position that is scarcely compatible with the possibility of fixed and permanent dogmas.

Finally, in what way would our position be *anti-missionary*? Certainly, "incarnating" Christian thought in cultures that are entirely different from Latin culture involves great difficulties. However, a great problem is already involved in freeing these cultures from what in them is opposed to Christianity. Even then, even under the pure dominion of faith, reason that has been shaped by Hindu thought would doubtlessly be ill-adapted, in its current state, to assimilate scholastic theology. Doubtlessly, it would think out its new faith in its own manner, and, surely, it would introduce fundamental Christian philosophical conceptions into mental structures that are uniquely its own, into a vocabulary charged with references to a mentality that is quite different from our own. But we must think that not everything would be true, nor complete, nor precise in this theology (even though nothing would prevent faith in the dogmas) until the day when, by dint of its own progress and perhaps of coming into confrontation with Latin theology, and by dint of the latter being obliged to deepen itself and perhaps refashion itself on certain points, indeed, to enrich itself upon everything found in this new contribution, this theology would itself reach a more perfect age, the scientific age.

What every Catholic must believe concerning the permanence and unity of dogmatic formulas through various cultures we likewise affirm by way of necessary consequence in relation to theological science, though recognizing an important difference, namely, that the latter is still unachieved and is not necessary for salvation. Allow us here to cite what we said in our study on the missionary apostolate:

> The fact that the absolute truth of the faith could be expressed in the concepts of substance and person shows that these concepts, in the sense they are understood by the Church's own definition, are certainly true for every man and can be assimilated by every culture. However, if the Church came, to take root, for example, in India and wished (and could) express her faith in concepts familiar to Hindus, this is because these concepts would be true and able to be assimilated in their own turn with more or less effort by Latin thought. Moreover, western philosophy was much more profoundly transformed by Christian faith than the latter was conditioned by western philosophy. And the Christian faith would likewise profoundly transform eastern philosophy. *It would be a factor of unity for the human mind* [*esprit*], which, left to its own devices, does not find in the unity of its own structure sufficient power for dominating the countless elements in which human intelligence, in fact, must exercise its power (nor sufficient power for thus arriving at the fullness of human truth to which it aspires).[42]

Finally, will we need to say that *by being so enlarged our position would cease to be Thomist*? It suffices to recall these fundamental concepts that we

---

42 Michel Labourdette, "Théologie de l'apostolat missionnaire," *Revue Thomiste* 46 (1946): 582–83. [Tr. note: The last parenthesis was added by Fr. Labourdette in this particular article.]

said are essential and permanent in order for us to realize that Thomist thought, however enriched it may be by all of these foreign contributions or by new observations and reflections, will always refashion itself organically on the basis of these fundamental concepts, retaining (within a mental context that is perhaps significantly revised) that which gives Thomist thought its characteristic place among the philosophies and theologies that have been known throughout history: the realism of knowledge, its conception of science, the structure of being, the notions of object and nature, the doctrine of act and potency, that of causality, its anthropology, the relations between knowledge and love, in a word, everything that provides the foundation for a logic, metaphysics, [philosophical] psychology, morality, and finally, the principles and methods that enable it to make use of all this in theology. Moreover, this is why the best introduction to theological science consists in the direct, literal, and profound study of the very work of St. Thomas, in which these principles are implemented in plain sight, principles that remain such a leaven for him who knows how to penetrate into their depths. There we have the full meaning of the place assigned to him by the Church. He is the Master of theological science.

V. CONCLUSION

The pretension to unity and universality implied in the scientific form of St. Thomas's theology is, moreover, a need the mind feels by its very nature.

An attitude of extreme tolerance and theological liberalism can only be provisional. Already, one sees an otherwise-positive ambition dawning. Indeed, already, more or less consciously, one wishes to replace St. Thomas with something else, with another worldview inspired by modern science, by the sentiments of contemporary men, another philosophy and consequently another theology. Why not do for the philosophy of evolution what St. Thomas did for the philosophy of being: why not rethink Christianity in light of this new science, one which believes it contains an entire wisdom? Some still think, certainly, that, thanks to the supple use of analogy, this renewed view of Christianity will ultimately agree with Catholic tradition and even with St. Thomas. Perhaps they expect no more permanence from this "new contemporary expression" of Christianity than from that which St. Thomas championed. Above all, they dream of "drawing" to Christianity those who, in fact, imbued as they are with a positive [sic] and evolutionist mentality, are more comfortable with this sort of conceptualization, so that the Kingdom of God may not be more closed off to them than to a Middle Ages that was suffused with the dangerous Aristotle. However, there are some who have another ambition! They think humanity has finally discovered "science" and that after twenty centuries, Christianity has reached the moment of evolution and culture that will enable it to realize its full agreement with reason. A great enthusiasm courses through these spirits. They feel they are in continuity with many Christian themes that were underexploited in a world of thought that was too marked by the belief that all things are fixed. They truly believe that they finally have discovered the truth. Although they believe it is impossible for us to integrate the results of science and history into St. Thomas's metaphysics and, consequently, into what specifically belongs to his theology, they nonetheless hold in common with him whom they abandon the fact that they are looking to formulate a complete worldview through the union of their faith and reason, as well as the fact that they believe it will be definitive, at least in its essential structure. They should also hold in common with him the fact that they seek after the scientific state of soul, as independent as possible from everything that subjectivity and particularity bring quivering to thought. How can we fail to see that Thomism finds itself at a critical moment—and along with it, all the traditional theological schools, for none of them would survive its ruin unscathed, existing thereafter only in the form of scattered themes taken up and transformed into brand new intellectual constructions? Is it a gangue to be broken up so that Christian Dogma may be thereby freely extracted therefrom? Or, by contrast, does it remain its most perfect and perfectible scientific elaboration? In any case, if it could only survive as an "analogical" relic, then, in keeping with its most essential contention, it would be most appropriate for it to step aside and allow itself to be replaced.

7

Closing Remarks Concerning Our Position

Michel-Marie Labourdette, OP

B y this point, all of our readers are aware of the controversy occasioned by our critical review, "La théologie et ses sources." Each of our subscribers has in hand the small volume in which we wished to gather together the documents involved in this debate. They likewise are doubtlessly aware of the letters that were exchanged between Msgr. Bruno de Solages and Fr. Marie-Joseph Nicolas concerning this matter and published in *Bulletin de Littérature ecclésiastique* under the title "Autour d'une controverse." Regarding this exchange of opinions, which was not taken into account by our *Dialogue théologique*, I will here only say that I would like to thank Msgr. de Solages for having at least having bothered to cite me at length and moreover would like to thank Fr. Nicolas for understanding me so well and for providing such a good defense on my behalf.

Today, apart from any discussion, I would only like to take advantage of remarks that have been made to me and complaints that I have provoked. In so doing, I merely intend to draw into fuller light certain principles that enter into the theological positions taken by the editorial staff of the *Revue thomiste*. I have intentionally used the expression, "*theological* positions" (aware, moreover, of everything they philosophically imply), for I would need to speak in a rather different manner were I to take up a strictly philosophical perspective here. In my opinion, at least, it is important to speak about these two kinds of consideration separately.

1. AUTHORITY IN THEOLOGY

Among all of our sciences, theology has a unique characteristic, namely, the fact that *authority* plays a leading role in it. Essentially ordered to the development of the intelligibility of revealed truths, bringing it to the most perfect state that is accessible to us here-below, theological research absolutely presupposes faith in the theologian. Moreover, in its objective determination, this faith constitutes a rule, a received teaching, which our mind does not control but, instead, accepts. This teaching is something more than a kind of deposit for theology. It calls for something more than obedience from it. It offers a Truth, a spiritual nourishment, an object of contemplation and of life. Nonetheless, it is something proposed by a Transcendent Intelligence concerning a reality that would, of itself, remain beyond our grasp, a reality we come into contact with only through faith. This is not the place to explain how, according to what the Catholic Church teaches, this implies a living and permanent magisterium that is supernaturally assisted and protected against error. However, this means that it falls to this magisterium, and to it alone, to determine authoritatively what is to be believed and to rule out what is incompatible with the true faith.

Theology will need to be particularly attentive to these determinations by the magisterium. This does not mean that its task would consist in recording them. Yes, it must do this, but such a task represents only the first step of theology's task. Through all that it does, theology is essentially an effort to *understand*. To understand what? Not only, on the level of factual history, the reasons for this or that intervention by the Church, its various contextual details, circumstances that are of so great assistance in perceiving its true meaning and scope. Nor does it strive solely to understand, on the level of the history of doctrines, the coherence of this new determination with this or that other one that preceded it and with the whole of the revealed deposit in its various states of authentic proposition. Rather, with all of this being done (and even before this is fully complete), theology applies itself, in the end, to the task of understanding more fully, through analogy and within the mystery, the divine reality itself, which is illuminated for our faith by these objective teachings—the divine reality that we learn about through them, the divine reality in which we will find our beatitude in a knowledge that is filled with joy.

For this effort undertaken in search of theological understanding, every dogmatic clarification (here, understood in a broad sense, meaning every authentic determination made by the magisterium) constitutes a *principle* in the service of scientific knowledge. In a certain line of scholastic [*scolaire*] tradition, one that in fact is quite modern, some have held that "arguments from authority" are the typical kind of argument used in theology, that which characterizes it as a science. By following this line of thought, theological certitude seemed only to belong to that which *is imposed* upon all. By contrast, that which has no other "authority" than *reasoning* is said to remain in the domain of what remains *free*, the opinable, that which belongs to "systems of thought."

The truth of the matter is much more nuanced. If we consider theology throughout all of its scientific efforts, we will see the domain properly belonging to authority is that of theology's *principles*. And certainly, authority can intervene regarding conclusions that have been long contested. The precise effect of such an intervention is to elevate the affirmation in question to the order of those principles that are involved in theological considerations. Of course, this truth, whose certitude henceforth comes to be connected to faith (or to one of the forms of assent that can be required of us by the ecclesiastical magisterium,[1] forms of assent that are more or less certain and more or less reformable depending on the character of its intervention), will not, for all that, be removed from the theologian's consideration. There remains the task of scrutinizing it, the task of developing its own, proper intelligibility, both in itself and within the overall whole of the theological synthesis. Here, we have the effort of speculative theology, which is not a mere affair of opinions but, rather, something that aims at constituting a true science. On this level of speculative theology, authority is not what directly determines the certitude of an assertion. Rather, this certitude is determined by the evidence offered by theological reasoning, by the rigor of the analysis sustaining it. On this level, each person will remain "free" in metaphysics to doubt, in the same sense that one is "free" to be in doubt concerning the transcendental character of the good or concerning the privative character of evil—or, to use the bluntest sort of example, one is "free" here in the same sense that one is "free" in arithmetic to deny that two plus two equals four. In other words, here, one is free from every form of constraint that falls short of evidence.

Thus, when the words "free" and "doubtful" are used in relation to theological assertions, these terms can have two, quite different senses. On the one hand, the terms mean that, because of the lack of a categorical pronouncement by the Magisterium concerning a given matter, one can opine on one side of an issue or on the other without thereby running afoul of the magisterium's measures and without falling into disobedience, thus coming to say that everything that is not determined by authority remains doubtful and contestable. On the other hand, these words simply mean that an assertion has not attained, from the perspective of theological reasoning, a state of evidence sufficing to exclude doubt in the mind that perceives it. (In other words, they mean that one has not provided a decisive proof for the truth of this assertion.) To offer an example, we hold that the theological teaching concerning the instrumental physical causality of Christ's Humanity and of the Sacraments is something perfectly free from the perspective of divine or ecclesiastical authority. However, we do not in the least hold that it is doubtful from the perspective of intellectual evidence. Likewise, we are no more scandalized to see it disputed than we are to see the real distinction between essence and existence in creatures placed in doubt. What is decisive is evidence, the quality of the arguments offered for this position.

---

1 To this are related various "authorities," which have highly nuanced and differentiated weights: that of the Fathers or of certain Fathers, that of the Doctors or of a given Doctor (e.g., that of St. Thomas), etc. . . . In these inferior degrees, an alleged authority always demands respect but forever remains disputable and can obviously be abandoned without fault or error.

Nonetheless, a difference remains between the domain of philosophy and that of theology. In the former, the contested teaching rests only on rational forms of evidence, not only in itself but also in its principles. No authority guarantees the latter. By contrast, revealed assertions are the tools of the trade in theology. The theologian's living intelligence is indeed what analyzes them. It is what manifests their profound implications and consequences. The light that directs it is intellectual (this is the source of theology's particular weakness), though it is drawn into the illumination of a loftier light, which is essentially that of a [supernatural kind of] *faith*. Here, authority remains present alongside faith. However, it is not in virtue of such authority that we adhere to the theological inferences we draw. Nonetheless, our adherence is indeed brought about by coming back into contact with this authority and by analyzing the principles that draw their certitude from it.

Thus, we can see how delicate the work becomes in theological reflection. Reasoning that is undertaken in positive theology will seek (roughly speaking) to determine the authority of a given assertion and to weigh out its scope, as well as the degree to which it is imposed as something necessary. Reasoning that is undertaken in speculative theology will strive to penetrate the depths of its intelligibility, to identify its implications, and to integrate it into a vaster synthesis. In both cases, the theologian *reasons*, and in both cases, he can be mistaken. All too frequently, an author affirms that an assertion is *de fide* when, strictly speaking, it is not. Sometimes it happens, I believe, that an author denies an assertion is *de fide* or proximate to faith when it in fact is. One might think the former defect is more frequent among theologians than is the latter, but nonetheless, the latter exists as well. Standing alongside those who maximize, are there not those who minimize? In a work of speculative theology, it will likewise happen that an author exaggerates the evidence at hand while wishing to manifest the connection that he perceives to exist between a revealed assertion and another assertion that seems to him to be implied by the first. To present his inference as being rigorous and necessary is to affirm, by the same token, that one will not be able to deny its conclusion without, at the same time, denying its principle. And this will be the first objection of the author to anyone who contests his conclusion.

Grave equivocations will be able to follow from this. On the one hand, someone who holds that his reasoning has an authoritative value when it, in fact, does not, will wish to give his conclusion a certitude that is *de fide* or, at least, a certitude that is in some way official, meaning that no "freedom" remains for contesting it. On the other hand, another person, upon hearing it said that his objection places a *de fide* principle in peril because it denies a necessary conclusion, will believe that he is being accused of heterodoxy, being held in suspicion concerning the integrity of his faith, accused of disobedience to the magisterium, which defines the deposit of faith by transmitting it. . . .

To my eyes, this equivocation unquestionably poisons the atmosphere of too many discussions, which could have remained serene and could have led to useful developments. If in any part of my critical review, "La théologie et ses sources"—which I wrongly assumed would be read in the context of what I said in my preceding article, "La Théologie intelligence de la foi," where I thought I had been clear enough concerning the same matter that I am here today explaining at greater length—I seemed to fall into the first kind of defect mentioned above, I here apologize for doing so. Never did I intend to say that any of the authors I critiqued have knowingly departed from orthodoxy, refusing to subscribe to any of its objective determinations. And I ask that my assertions, even those expressed in vigorous language, be understood in this sense. In a theological discussion, I absolutely never wish to contest or suspect the faith of an author whom I critique. For me, what is forever in question is his *reasoning*, his rational analyses. In particular, I did not (and do not) in any way question the *freedom* of various theological schools and various systems.[2] Everyone is *free* to propose his ideas for as long as he believes they are compatible with the Church's teaching and the certitudes presupposed thereby. But, conversely, everyone else is *free* to say to him—on

---

[2] The Church undeniably leaves various theological Schools to retain their *freedom*. However, this means that she does not intend to take a position concerning [their] rationally elaborated constructions, so long as they do not place the faith in danger. This is neither her role nor her mission. This does not in any way imply that all "systems" are equal or that, within a domain into which authority refuses to enter, theological reasoning would not play a decisive role. There is (and can be) only one theological science. According to us, the multiplicity of Christian "theologies" does not come from the impossibility of making one of them prevail [over the others] (not by authority but by theological reasoning). It does not come from some superior reason holding that the human mind could express for itself divine things only by diversifying itself into mutually-irreducible constructions, wherein we would see a testimony to the transcendence of these realities, an effect of the necessary evolution of the mind, or the exigency befalling our various mental structures. Rather, this multiplication arises from our weakness, from the groping character of our research, and from the partial character of our intuitions. The efforts expended in theological science do not aim to multiply them in order to be adapted to new cultures or to different mentalities but, rather, to absorb them, little by little, by elevating itself to a greater level of universality. Even assuming that this ideal terminus could ever be attained (and, it in fact never will be), even then, theological science would in no way claim to be equal to its object and even less to exhaust it. It would remain infinitely deficient in relation to it, being only the analogical, very inferior, and distant human expression of it.—But, in order to justify the equal value of various systematizations, or at least the legitimacy of substituting one for another, let one not argue, as Msgr. de Solages does in defending Fr. Bouillard, on the basis of this [so-called] *analogical* character of our knowledge concerning divine things. Theology does not "work" directly on the divine reality, which we could validly express in successively renewed analogies. It works directly on *revealed notions* which must remain *eodem sensu eademque sententia*, and its task absolutely does not involve replacing them with *other* notions, even were they declared to be equivalent.

the same level and with arguments of the same order—that *in his opinion*, this seeming compatibility is illusory and that a true opposition to his claim can be demonstrated on certain points. I wholly agree that one has every right to proclaim that an assertion is not *de fide* and has no other value than the arguments that support it, but I ask that one have no less a right to say, if one so thinks, that an assertion is connected to faith and cannot be denied without compromising it. Both affirmations belong to the domain properly falling to theological research. A certain kind of demand, asking for a one-sided freedom, itself involves an intolerance that is no less great than that which is contested.

2. RECOURSE TO THE MAGISTERIUM

Authority in theology does not reside only in texts. It is represented by a living magisterium whose essential role on this point is to conserve the revealed deposit, to declare it, define it, clarify it, and also to preserve it from errors that, without being directly related to it, nonetheless compromise it. It falls to this magisterium to watch over the integrity of the faith, and nobody outside of it is authorized to appropriate this office for himself.

We all agree in emphasizing the respect and submission with which the interventions of the doctrinal magisterium must be received. Even if they remain encapsulated [*enveloppées*], more indicative than decisive, they trace out a way forward or at least can prohibit a path that was heading toward error, and no theologian will fail to be grateful for this. However, one does not fail to have either this respect or this submission if one undertakes the effort of trying to *understand* it exactly. This is the very role that properly belongs to theological reasoning. A warning does not intend, by itself, to break up the élan of a given investigation. A condemnation does not necessarily discredit an author, for in the end, the only person who can be sure of never being wrong is the person who says nothing. A doctrinal clarification is not an absolute assertion, requiring theology to be reconstructed anew and in full. Obviously, vehement discussions have led the Roman authorities to make pronouncements concerning secondary points, while many more important truths of faith, truths that are much more central, have not been the object of any extraordinary, official interventions, or at least of very few such interventions, precisely because they are held peacefully [by all]. Nothing would be more misleading than to measure the importance of a truth of faith (or one connected to faith) by merely referring to the number of allusions that are made to it in collections like those of Denzinger or Cavallera. Nothing would be more injurious to our theological thought than to restrict ourselves to commenting on these interventions. For example, it is incontestable that following the immense benefit drawn from the official determinations expressed by the Council of Trent, Post-Tridentine theology too often restricted its concerns, becoming far too specialized in controversy. It is doubtlessly inevitable that this would be true for every era, with its specific riches coming to exist alongside its limitations and consequently, for many minds, its discontents. Therefore, it will always know this ferment of unrest, which will lead it to place many commonly-admitted assertions into question. The Church will nourish in her womb authentic Christians for whom that which has been acquired is not sufficiently satisfying, Christians who seem dedicated to adventure, to the great adventures of the mind [*esprit*]. They seem rebellious and insubordinate; they can be—though not painlessly, nor without bumps along the road—the principle of fruitful renewals.

But all of this still imperiously calls for *freedom of discussion and freedom to criticize*. Forging ahead is not the customary activity of any sort of magisterium—this is not its role. It is not its custom to decide questions before they have been posed and debated. True, the theologian does indeed feel the temptation to immediately appeal to it because his argumentation inevitably leads him, in his principles, to find his support thereupon. However, this does not go without its own dangers. Besides the fact that the attitude of the person who yields to this temptation is, deep down, much less respectful of authority than is the attitude of the theologian who refuses to mix authority in with his own quarrels, this temptation also risks significantly hindering free scientific investigation, to which nothing is more opposed than is an atmosphere of denunciation.

In my opinion, His Holiness Pius XII formulated the golden rule for these matters when he wrote in his Encyclical *Divino afflante Spiritu*:

> Let all the other sons of the Church bear in mind that the efforts of these resolute laborers in the vineyard of the Lord should be judged not only with equity and justice, but also with the greatest charity; all moreover should abhor that intemperate zeal which imagines that whatever is new should for that very reason be opposed or suspected.[3]

I personally knew and venerate Fr. [Marie-Joseph] Lagrange all too well, and all too well could I appreciate the quality of his love for the Church and his admirable submission, not only of heart but also of mind, to the Petrine magisterium, but I also knew all too well, from his own mouth, the atmosphere of suspicion in which his scientific work had to be built up, for me not to be able to feel much closer to those who seek than to those who condemn without any mandate to do so, closer to those who work than to those who denounce.

---

3 [Tr. note: Pius XII, *Divino afflante Spiritu*, no. 47, https://www.vatican.va/content/pius-xii/en/encyclicals/documents/hf_p-xii_enc_30091943_divino-afflante-spiritu.html (accessed August 20, 2022).]

We all submit to the successor of Peter and to the Catholic hierarchy in a complete, filial manner. We are all ready to hear his voice. However, it does not fall to any of us to judge in his place whether it is fitting for him to intervene, even less to suggest to him the direction his intervention should take. However, it is precisely for this reason that we believe free discussion is useful and truly profitable, indeed all the more profitable because it will be loyal and open. It should not be difficult to agree concerning a certain number of elementary rules that make up, so to speak, the "morality" of these discussions.

1° Each person should strive *only to depend on his own arguments*, accepting the possibility of being wrong and, consequently, of being convinced that he is wrong, without seeking, through personal attacks, to disqualify his interlocutor, to cast suspicion onto him, or *a fortiori* to have recourse to indiscriminate denunciations.

2° Each person should know how to take responsibility for what he says or proposes. Msgr. de Solages writes, "When it comes to an accusation, *everything that is anonymous is in bad faith*."[4] I would gladly extend this formula by removing its first part and would ask that it should be clearly understood that we dispense with all clandestine literature widespread among the general public and that we agree to stop its diffusion before it creates, especially in young minds, in relation to the Roman Magisterium, a mentality of suspicion that resembles all too closely that which another clandestinity, one that was all too justified in that case, developed not long ago in our midst in relation to the occupier whose authority, founded as it was upon violence, had no legitimacy.[5]

3° Respect for persons should be safeguarded in the theological discussion, as well as an absolute bias to judge that they are acting in good faith, and that everything should be done to remain on the level of ideas.

Here again, if my critical study failed to observe any of these rules, I apologize for this fact. I reaffirm the proposal I already made (Labourdette, "Theology and Its Sources," p. 138n6 above) to each of the persons whom I critiqued, inviting him to explain himself in our review, even concerning what I believed could be criticized in his thought. I am not one of those people who

---

[4] "Pour l'honneur de la Théologie," extract from *Bulletin de littérature ecclésiastique* (April–June 1947): 8. Since Msgr. de Solages calls upon St. Thomas not only for an example of his methodology but also for his explicit counsels, he will allow me to add to the texts that he gathered together this complaint wherein St. Thomas energetically protested against the clandestine propagation of doctrines outside the ordinary parameters of debate: "If anyone wishes to contradict what I say here, let him not do so by prattling on about it with boys but, rather, let him write and propose his writings in public so that the learned may be able to judge what is true and, by the authority of the Truth, confute what is false" (*Contra pestiferam doctrinam...*, in fine[; *Contra retrahentes*, in fine]).

[5] Granted, this circulation cannot be originally imputable to the actual author of these writings, but when it reaches a certain scale of diffusion, he should indeed be anxious to stop it or to make the necessary adjustments.

believe, on principle, that discussions are useless; they are useful, on the condition that one knows how to stick to the object at hand, without turning such discussions aside to discuss their author, and that one considers such matters in a positive light.—As regards the precise meaning of my critical review, I have already said enough about it and therefore need not return to it once more;[6] I only repeat that the purpose of this review, itself limited in its diffusion and reaching only quite specialized circles,[7] was not to discredit any of those whom I critiqued, men for whom I simultaneously expressed my unfeigned esteem. I only wished to show the tendency underlying the ideas placed in circulation in various writings—then all the sudden united in a single bundle by Fr. Daniélou in a resounding article—hoping thereby to indicate how their convergence leads to certain weaknesses in theological thought and a kind of disdain for the intellectual weapons prepared by St. Thomas.

3. FUNDAMENTALISM [*INTÉGRISME*] AND MODERNISM

Why not say it? Here in France, we still bear the painful weight of the Modernist crisis and the terrible passions it aroused, along with its various social and political repercussions.

Consequently, the word "modernism," in its strict sense, designates at once a doctrine and a method of religious thought, both of which have been solemnly condemned by the Church. The texts exist, indisputably standing in support of this claim. And I do not presume to suspect, *a priori*, that any contemporary Catholic theologians either do not accept this condemnation or knowingly take up this or that error drawn from among those that fall under it.—The term "modernist" also has a broader sense, one that it is undoubtedly dangerous to use without further explanation, and for this reason, I have forbidden myself to make use of it. In this latter sense, the word designates much more so a kind of attitude of mind, a mentality, than a specific method or doctrine. Without a doubt, this term is completely pejorative in the Church and remains an insult. However, it would not, precisely by itself, constitute an accusation of heresy or of a clear case of heterodoxy.

---

[6] See our *Dialogue théologique*.—I myself did not reread without some sadness my own "Réplique" to the anonymous "Réponse" in *Recherches de Sciences Religieuses*. Today, I would prefer to have avoided following my opponents onto the level of polemics and to have held back from personal remarks, which I readily agree do not aid in making progress in debates.

[7] That is, the readers of the *Revue thomiste* (who, allow me to state the truth of the matter, do not quite yet reach the diffusion of being the "general public") and approximately thirty theologians and friends who received my offprint; even the latter doubtlessly would have read the same text in the *Revue*.

The historical sense of the word "fundamentalism" [*intégrisme*] is less precise. Above all, it designates a kind of attitude of mind, a manner of intellectually approaching things (with all that this includes in the way of moral and affective attitudes). Even more quickly than is the case for modernism, whose precise errors are defined, we find that fundamentalism is even more so a kind of general tendency. How can it be described without needing to cite any particular example in a particular author? At bottom, it includes, not perhaps in a formalized way but, rather, in one's attitude, the rejection of that which is *new*, an *a priori* distrust for what places matters into question and for what arouses problems. It implies, more obviously, the desire not to set aside certain formulas or certain frameworks, because one fears that which is not yet proven, or because a secret tendency to a kind of intellectual imperialism drives one to place in the forefront of one's concerns the requirement that there be an external form of discipline, which itself does not go without the risk of some type of conformism. The fundamentalist attitude bespeaks a lack of confidence in the truth and an inexplicable inability to see the world with youthful eyes, with a fundamental assurance that neither the Church nor the truth have such need for our precautions and our prudence, not to mention our deceits.

So-understood, we consider fundamentalism to be a sickness of thought as well as a grave error. I deliberately speak here of "thought" in its personal exercise and not of the mind, because it doubtlessly arises much more from a thinker's moral and affective attitudes than from intellectual defects. The denunciation of it would fall to a well-formulated *ethics of thought*, which must manifest its harmfulness. Though less striking or less immediately obvious, it is no less harmful than is the "modernist" attitude.

* * * * *

In this *Revue*, we are firmly committed to the doctrine, principles, and methods of St. Thomas Aquinas. This is not so that we might thereby cling to a grand past. Nor do we wish to confuse security with truth. And we do not hold this position as a matter of discipline and obedience. Rather, we do so because we believe that St. Thomas's doctrine is true and that it alone can illuminate and guide the renewals needed today without, however, risking the danger of falling into error.

We are well aware that new problems arise, and we feel their weight, along with the anxiety they arouse. We know that if certain minds are easily satisfied with the most classical of solutions, others by contrast—and this is doubtlessly to their honor—are profoundly concerned with the distance that they perceive to exist between many of these solutions and what is expected by scientists, historians, and philosophers trained in the most modern of disciplines. We believe that theology's contemporary task is rendered particularly delicate and arduous by the fact that the great classics of speculative theology and, in the first place, St. Thomas, belong to a different age of culture than our own, as well as by the fact that they are separated from us, in the domain of thought, by the great scientific upheavals of modern times. When we claim, not precisely their authority but, rather, their permanent value, we surely do not believe that the best kind of work would consist in repeating them. No more do we believe that it will suffice to dress them up, somehow or other, in modern vesture. However, we think that one must have a sufficiently lively—and, consequently, sufficiently complete (for this teaching is an *organic* whole)—possession of their essential principles and teaching. We see no other way to avoid losing some aspect of the permanent acquisition they have bequeathed us nor, likewise, today faced with difficulties that they themselves did not know, to benefit from the full luminosity that they were able to transmit to us because of what they themselves received from a continuous tradition engaged in a common labor, in addition to their own rare genius. This inheritance is not only sacred. It is living—quite so—awaiting our efforts, to be sure, but giving these very efforts a point of departure and irreplaceable instruments.

No, we do not believe that theology has completed its task. It will not do so prior to the Last Day. And this is so not only because its "earthly" state is a state of imperfection but, moreover, because human development itself cannot cease to call the mind [*esprit*] toward new aspects of revealed truth, which will forever outstrip our most perfect syntheses.

I believe that the history of thought contains necessary revolutions. However, they do not call for a complete overturning that would reach, in equal fashion, all the various levels of knowledge, thus meaning that everything must be taken up afresh and anew. Rather, the necessity of such revolutions plays out in virtue of great discoveries or, even more, in virtue of great intuitions that have been rendered possible by a given degree of cultural development along with the unique concurrence of circumstances. Modern thought does not require us to bring mere additions to St. Thomas's thought. None of us would agree to endorse so childish an assertion. For example, we believe that the philosophy of Hegel—I take this example precisely on account of his exceptional grandeur as well as his exceptional powers of illusion—presented thought with testimony to a sweeping intuition, even though it was categorized in fundamentally erroneous schemata. I admit that we must say—though, a great number of nuances should be added hereto—that we owe to him the *prise de conscience* of historical movement as an internal dimension of the world, a *prise de conscience* of unique profundity, which speaks to its very novelty. However, I believe that St. Thomas's philosophy alone enables us to grasp the true meaning of this historical dimension of the world. This will not be brought about by abandoning a certain number of Thomist "theses" in order to substitute for them a certain number of

Hegelian doctrines. Indeed, what sort of intellectual monstrosity would that produce? Even less will this be brought about by purely and simply abandoning Thomism in order to adopt the central principles of Hegel. I believe that pure Hegelianism constitutes an absolutely asphyxiating world for Christian faith and a fatal mirage for reason. Moreover, such a choice would involve the loss of the benefits that we draw from values that are loftier still, ones permanently witnessed to by Thomism and finding no place in Hegelianism. The rapprochement we are speaking of here will only be brought about through an effort that is, in truth, more demanding, more difficult, and likewise *of greater duration*. (Time itself is necessary for thought to be able to *mature*. The admirers of Hegel should not be the last people to understand this point, something we have been taught by St. Thomas.) Well aware of the different levels of philosophic and scientific consideration, such an effort will tend to grasp, with the very principles of St. Thomas, an aspect of reality that, historically speaking, became manifest only by following other principles and in accord with other categories. This effort will be neither a form of overly-eager harmonization nor of eclecticism but, rather, an integration that presupposes a vigilant *critique* and constructive effort, and it is unjust to ask Thomism to bring it about more quickly than is actually possible, I mean, in virtue of an effort requiring much collaboration and a *lengthy period of maturation*. Hasty adaptations are disastrous.

I personally believe that St. Thomas's "worldview" and that of the medieval theologians is distant from the worldview imposed upon us by perspectives that are much more profound than the mere framework of a physics that today is obsolete. It is not sufficient merely to abandon this physics. Between them and us—and I in no way claim that I here provide a complete enumeration!—there have been immense discoveries: the discovery of the full dimensions of the earth, with its diversity of cultures and environments; the discovery of this earth's true place in the universe, the representation of which henceforth lacks a common measure with the medieval theologians' own framework for the world's situation in the universe; the discovery of certain stages of human evolution, as well as the recognition of the *temporal* dimension within humanity itself, within ideas and systems themselves; the discovery of certain unconscious depths in man; the discovery of prehistory and a kind of rhythm in the course of history. There have been prodigious perspectival changes in philosophical thought, gradually reconnecting to the same eternal problems, ultimately those that are metaphysical in nature, though by completely different paths. (Whether or not these paths are valid is a completely different question, though they nonetheless remain profoundly instructive.)

What is needed is certainly not the mutilation of St. Thomas's thought, nor even a kind of refashioning thereof. Rather, our concern is to grasp each of his principles in its purity and on its true level, by seeking to distinguish from its true and permanent requirements that which, in its formulation, was adapted to a representation of the world that we no longer can hold in light of the development of our physical and historical sciences. However, this work must be undertaken with infinite seriousness, with neither fevered excitement nor casualness, with respect for the truth, which forbids us to give into intoxication with destruction or with toppling things over for fear of overlooking an acquired truth that has received too little attention. Here, as I already said elsewhere,[8] what we want is a *critical spirit*, persuaded that neither the Church nor Thomism have anything to fear from its effects— though a critical spirit that is not one-way, one that does not take up as it sole mission the overthrowing of the idols of the past but, rather, knows how to avoid the no-less-deceptive (and, for our contemporaries, more seductive) wonders offered by the idols of contemporary relevance. However, even more than the critical spirit, what Christian thought needs today is an immense constructive effort undertaken in order to integrate so many new data into its essential perspectives without losing anything. And we are convinced that no more solid a foundation, nor any better instrument, can be found for this constructive effort than St. Thomas's philosophy.

We know quite well that "this is a hard saying," and that it asks of the modern mind an effort that cannot be undertaken without renouncing inveterate habits and illusions. The philosophy we propose—one that is called "scholastic," taking on the name of its most cruel trial, as Jacques Maritain once remarked—appears to our contemporaries as being something too off-putting to be able to ask them, without thereby requiring the harsh paths of asceticism, to look at things from its perspective and appreciate the depths of its vitality, which we feel is forever-young, like an ever-fresh spring. The historian cannot fail to be amazed when he considers Leo XIII's extraordinary act, at the end of the 19th century, calling Christian thought back to scholasticism. We simply believe that he was right in doing so. By that, we do not in any way intend to claim for our own various remarks the authority of his decision. We do not proclaim any anathema against anyone. It is not by means of recommendations, however august they might be, that we claim to assure and defend St. Thomas's doctrine. It will be fully assured and defended only when it comes to show that *it can accomplish this task by itself.*

* * * * *

If my critical review seemed to some eyes to be something more than a warning call or a taking of positions, being, rather, a rallying cry for a group that would like to be a "party," whether fundamentalist or otherwise, I assure them that they are mistaken. I would not do injury to our regular collaborators

---

8 See Labourdette, "Theology and Its Sources," p. 157 above.

by making them believe that we had them in mind for such a task. For my own part, I believe there could not fail to be some sort of deception or, in any case, incalculable damage, involved in the idea that fidelity to the profound meaning of St. Thomas's thought would come to be crystalized in a group that, no matter how small it might be, would, in the end, be a party or a sect. We have no form of sympathy for this kind of gathering. This is not how we conceive of his School, where love for the truth is the only law guiding the forms of mutual strengthening afforded by such a gathering. We did not wish to trigger off any kind of fratricidal war within French Christian thought, and we do not accept the formation of any "common front." We merely wished to express our sentiment in utter simplicity and frankness, and we will continue to do so on our own proper level [as theologians], persuaded that much more light can be drawn from confrontations and from serene and objective discussions than from artificial unanimity. Moreover, by no means do I believe that those same people who were alarmed by my remarks have any other sentiment than my own concerning this matter. On the contrary, I believe that I have translated rather-common sentiments and remain persuaded that much more unites us than what separates us.

Saint-Maximin, Easter 1947

8

Discussion Surrounding Our 'Dialogue Théologique'

Michel-Marie Labourdette, OP, and Marie-Joseph Nicolas, OP

The most interesting reactions that have been directly aroused by our *Dialogue Théologique* are not coming from within scholastic circles but, rather, from philosophers outside of that outlook and even from Protestant theologians. Pierre Chazel in *Réforme*,[1] Brice Parain in *Le Cheval de Troie*,[2] Emmanuel Mounier in *Esprit*,[3] and Henri Germond in *Revue de Théologie et de Philosophie*[4] all dedicate noteworthy pages to considerations concerning it. Although, to their eyes, our position seems as hard and difficult as it appears to be deserving of respect, we are grateful to them above all for having shed greater light on the reality of the problem, the extent of the debate, and, in their own words, its fascinating relevance:

> Theologians pose the daunting problem anew: how should one speak to the world? When speaking to men who are sensitive to existentialist anxiety or who are accustomed to cast their thought into Marxist dialectic, can one retain a language that remains imprisoned within Aristotelian categories? . . . This fascinating Theological Dialogue . . . sets in contrast not two doctrines as much as it does two temperaments or mindsets, and I will even say two tactics. On the one side, there are those who refuse to accommodate to the world, whatever the cost; on the other, we have strategists on the move, those who, in order to defend what is essential in the Catholic positions, are desirous to maintain their freedom of movement and to engage the enemy on his own terrain.[5]

[1] Pierre Chazel, "Le Thomisme est-il menacé?," *Réforme* (Sept. 6, 1947): 2.

[2] Brice Parain, "Dialogue théologique," *Le Cheval de Troie* (Aug.-Sept. 1947): 329–39.

[3] Emmanuel Mounier, "Aux avant-postes de la pensée chrétienne," *Esprit* (Sept. 1947): 436–44.

[4] Henri Germond, "Dialogue théologique," *Revue de Théologie et de Philosophie* (Jul.-Sept. 1947): 128–33.

[5] Chazel, "Le Thomisme est-il menacé?," 2.

Such is, from the Protestant perspective, Pierre Chazel's estimation concerning this affair. The very title of his article shows the light in which he considers the discussion: "Is Thomism under threat?" His response is very affirmative. For his own part, Mounier concludes his supple and penetrating exposition by expressing the desire that "these debates might move beyond retrospective squabbles and polemics within scholasticism. They participate in the vast effort to simultaneously retrieve a faith that has been lost and a reason that has been dethroned, to retrieve a wisdom wherein intense life does not obfuscate the lights of the mind."[6] While reflecting upon this *Dialogue*, he has recognized "the debate of the nominalists and the realists, along with all the intermediary schools, in the era of great theological discussions," though "renewed by the newfound historical sense that has developed since the time of the 19th century. It expresses the permanent and irreducible tension between Christianity's transcendence and its immanence."[7] For his part, Brice Parain, like the others avoiding the factual question (what exactly does each side say and think?), himself considers "the question that constitutes the foundation of the debate, namely, how can the idea of a timeless truth be maintained within our own mode of human reasoning, which is forever and necessarily temporal. One will here recognize the old metaphysical problem of the finite and the infinite."[8]—"The choice to be made here is one of exceptional gravity.... Today, Christianity finds itself at such a critical moment in its battle against human passions and everything that they invent in order to dominate creation without actually being able to do so that if it does not succeed in providing its truth with communicative power equal to the violence which combats it, Christianity will face very difficult days."[9] Brice Parain's sense for the gravity of what is at stake encourages him to hope for the possibility of a synthesis or, at least, of equilibrium between the two tendencies, which in opposing each other have no choice but to be mutually restrained by each other. As Emmanuel Mounier says, the parties have no "interest in mutually pushing the argument [*se rejeter*] to the point that each party falls into the asymptotic heresy toward which, as is quite clear, each side would lead if pushed to absurdity: on the one hand, a kind of eternalism and of metaphysical quietism, faced, on the other, with a nominalism that would destroy all of faith's continuity and rationality."[10] Here again, our reviewer has understood perfectly that the heresy that is denounced in this kind of debate is a kind of asymptotic heresy, one that is not explicitly willed and, indeed,

---

[6] Mounier, "Aux avant-postes," 444.
[7] Mounier, "Aux avant-postes," 444.
[8] Parain, "Dialogue théologique," 335.
[9] Parain, "Dialogue théologique," 339.
[10] Mounier, "Aux avant-postes," 444.

to the contrary is repudiated, while, nonetheless, each side claims, rightly or wrongly, that, in spite of itself, the opposed tendency provides the foundation for such a heresy. Moreover, we are grateful that Mounier did not succumb to the convenient solution of calling these asymptotic heresies modernism and fundamentalism [*intégrisme*] but indeed even expressly distinguished and treated one after the other in an article dedicated to the "outposts of Christian thought," our own debate "concerning the place of history and the relations of eternity with history," and the debate opened by *Esprit* concerning "The Christian World and the Modern World," which was endorsed [*sanctionné*] by Cardinal Suhard's Lenten Pastoral Letter concerning the "Development or Decline of the Church," wherein modernism and fundamentalism [*intégrisme*] are both denounced.

Here, we believe it is fitting to clarify certain points so as to provide a response to what is awaited from us, not to clarify a controversy that has come and gone but, instead, to specify certain things regarding our own true position in the face of the problem so defined. Brice Parain, kindly taking up one of our own expressions, entreats us not *to leave unquenched the thirst* "of lay philosophers who are not theologians but who are interested, indeed passionately, in the fate of the Catholic Church."[11] For now, let us content ourselves with taking advantage of this request in order to refine our thought.

I. *RÉFORM*

We are asked: "When speaking to men who are sensitive to existentialist anxiety or who are accustomed to cast their thought into Marxist dialectic, can one retain a language that remains imprisoned within Aristotelian categories?"

We must be understood aright. When it is a question of "speaking to men," of bringing the "word of God" to them, this pertains to something different from pure *science*. How can we speak to a man if not by making use of concepts and words with which they are familiar, at least to the degree that such words lend themselves to communication? At this moment, what counts is to bring him whatever portion of the truth he can receive and to save him. Certainly, this presupposes that he abandon those explicit errors that prevent true faith from gaining access to him. However, this does not require him to push onward to the point of becoming a Thomist! The essential and vital witness does not need to be concerned with any truths other than those necessary for salvation, and the number of such truths varies depending on the receptive capacity of those who are being addressed. Theology is not the science or art of "speaking to the world," above all to the world in its present character, to this or that man, or even to this or that class of men. However,

---

[11] Parain, "Dialogue théologique," 330.

this wholly-apostolic science of speaking to the world presupposes theology, which it must know in-depth, knowing even what it contains that is independent of this or that immediate apologetic necessity, in order to be able to adapt it and cast it into categories that lend themselves to such a task only partially and not in a fully adequate or "formal" manner. The term *kerygmatic* has rightly been proposed as a name for this kind of theology, which is wholly ordered to preaching and to the salvation of souls. It presupposes scientific theology. What I cannot do is construct a scientific theology by casting it into the terms of Marxist or existentialist dialectic. . . .

This observation is quite necessary in order to understand a sentence we wrote, which *Réforme* cites as bearing witness to a courageous non-conformism: "Thomist metaphysics cannot be true without being convinced at the same time that there is a foundational evil underlying modern thought, which, however much it may be assimilable on a number of points, is nonetheless fundamentally opposed to it." We certainly do not repudiate this observation. This would represent a quite superficial understanding of the essential characteristics of modern thought and Thomist thought, not acknowledging the profound conflict that sets them in opposition to each other. To say that Thomism is fundamentally true—yes, however painful this might be for those who feel themselves to be naturally occupied with all the tendencies of modernity and would not like to live the life of the mind in separation from the modern world [*ne pas vivre à part la vie de l'esprit*]—is likewise to say that, at its heart, modern thought is affected by a foundational evil, a fundamental error. The choice is necessary, and one must not think, all too readily, that it is really just a question of different forms of the same truth. Nonetheless, we are not here speaking about what is essential to Thomism; and it is not difficult to recognize its insufficiencies when it comes to the perspectives opened up by historical awareness, the falsity of the scientific data that underlie a number of its insights, and its silence concerning problems that are vital for us and were not of interest for it. For us, Thomism goes beyond the explicit and conscious thought that St. Thomas himself had: in addition to being a set of fundamental truths, it is a way of thinking. St. Thomas is its master *par excellence*. This is quite certain. But he is only its master, that is, according to his own teaching, him who *shows* the truth, which is forever vaster than what he himself has seen concerning it, he who teaches us how to find it. Conversely, modern thought seems to us to be brimming with riches. And the drama of Christian thought today is that so many truths have developed outside of its own bounds, on the foundation (and sometimes under the sway) of denials that are unacceptable for it. Therefore, our position does not represent a complete and overarching rejection. It too is "catholic." It too represents a claim to be able to gather together all the various parts of the Truth, though without hiding the intention of transforming and drawing [them] to itself, without hesitating to recognize the differences involved in each of these matters.

Finally, how could we fail to be sensitive to such a sympathetic understanding of our "rejection," so expressed by a Protestant brother who, through his own understanding in this matter, makes us in turn enter more fully into the state of the soul belonging to the Reformation? However, we find ourselves immediately faced with the statement of the great scandal that we are for them: "What these champions defend is St. Thomas's *Summa*, not the Gospel. When they proclaim, 'Their conviction that the abandonment of the main positions of Thomist metaphysics would gradually lead to ruination for the faith,' we are indeed forced to denounce, as a form of scandal, this confusion between, on the one hand, faith, the work of God, the Gospel, and the Word of God, and on the other, a Christian philosophy that is never anything more than one man's own, wondrous construction."[12]

We are not the ones who commit this confusion. Faith is a purely supernatural light, the work of the Holy Spirit, absolutely transcendent to all the reasoning that can accompany it. Nonetheless, there are natural conditions for faith, without which it would be utterly miraculous. One cannot believe with just any indiscriminate philosophy whatsoever in one's mind. Or, if some people can do so, human minds in general cannot, and certainly metaphysical errors rub off on the purity of faith. This is why the Church defends not only faith but also the "*praeambula fidei*," even to the point of proclaiming that the latter are, in fact, confirmed and annexed by the former. We believe that if Thomism were to be considered obsolete, these "*praeambula fidei*" would be endangered. And we think this because we believe it is purely and simply the true expression of metaphysics in its eternal character. However, of course, we do not think, by contrast, that any rational dialectic suffices for giving birth to faith, for the latter remains absolutely beyond the measure of such reasoning. "Faith does not depend upon any dogmatic [theology]," nor upon any philosophy or apologetics. And, moreover, we are convinced that if the Holy Spirit were to allow Thomism to fall into a state of decline, He would remain powerful enough to maintain faith pure and stable within His Church, with defective rational instruments. Therefore, our fidelity to St. Thomas is not a "futile show of strength" or a "heroism without a cause," for his theology is not "one man's wondrous construction" but, instead, is the presentation, in human concepts, of the truth that is founded on God. Quite simply, it is a question of fidelity to what we believe is the truth. Every truth, even natural truth, deserves fidelity, for the whole fits together, and one cannot knowingly deny what reason shows us without thereby running the risk of jeopardizing that very thing which surpasses it and is revealed to us by faith.

---

12 Pierre Chazel, "Le Thomisme est-il menacé?," *Réforme* (Sept. 6, 1947): 2.

However, we do indeed feel that here the possibility of an "imperious synthesis," wherein every truth, both natural and supernatural, would find its place is a properly "catholic" pretention, one austerely repudiated by a Protestant theology. We will return to this point in the final portion of our remarks below.

II. *LE CHEVAL DE TROIE*

Brice Paraine seems to wholly agree with Fr. Bouillard and his famous sentence, "A theology that would not be contemporary would be a false theology." Going further still, he thinks that, through a kind of contradiction, we ourselves approve of it when we write, "Moreover, we know quite well that our most useful work will be to prove the possibility of movement by walking and to resolve the questions that every contemporary Christian thinker asks himself with anguish, doing so with the assistance of St. Thomas's thought."[13] This sentence, writes our gracious [*bienveillant*] reviewer, "is incompatible with the idea of an atemporal truth grasped once and for all in defined concepts. By striving to prove movement by walking, Fr. M.-J. Nicolas does nothing other than promise to give us a contemporary expression of the truths he has discovered within Thomism."

To this, we must first respond that it is not only a question of expressing the same things differently but, more so, on a number of points, we intend to think and say wholly new things, which these past things bear within themselves or at least remain ready to welcome. Provided that the great, foundational metaphysical truths be safeguarded, as well as the very conception of theological science, Thomism forever reconstructs itself from within, from that which provides it with its most specific character, for its essence will be safeguarded and, along with it, the great, characteristic theses that necessarily proceed from it. However, in particular, we must respond to Brice Parain that the "contemporary expression" of the truth must not be confused with its "contemporary conceptualization." To say that, "the entire ensemble of absolute affirmations is distinct from the notions and systems of notions in which these affirmations are incarnated," is not the same thing as saying: "Each era must formulate in its own terms its conception of the Christian truth in conformity with its own experience."[14] In the first formula, Parain summarizes Fr. Bouillard's thought;[15] the second formula is that of Parain himself, who orients the debate from the perspective of formulation and language, going so far as to say that the Thomists, "postulating the transcendence and

---

[13] Marie-Joseph Nicolas, "Theological Progress and Fidelity to St. Thomas," p. 192 above.
[14] Parain, "Dialogue théologique," 336.
[15] Parain, "Dialogue théologique," 336.

permanence of the truth, inasmuch as its truth, behind the various *formulations* that men give for it,"[16] practice a kind of asceticism by choosing "a system of particularly coherent formulations," sticking to it out of distrust for "those aspects of human language that ever remain equivocal," without too much support upon what language supplies in the way of clarity, by placing, on the contrary, their ultimate trust in that which is beyond language, in "the silence that forever envelops coherent systems, and that is always all the denser and closer, by consequence, to what the truth is, in proportion to the tyranny exercised by a system."[17] Parain's thought seems penetrating and very original to our eyes. We must reflect on this interpretation of the "fixism of theological formulation," considering it as being the result of a kind of asceticism, the asceticism of "the gift of a word," rich with a thousand variations, as it were, a kind of hieratic quality that is more befitting to the mystery that one is concerned with expressing. However, one must not forget, when speaking of Thomism, that "speech" [*parole*] is not confused with the "thought" that the former expresses. A concept is something different from a word [*mot*]. It is even something different from a pictorial image [*l'image-tableau*] of a more or less similar external reality. It is the intelligible reality itself in the mind. Weighty arguments can be made in defense of the claim that even St. Thomas's very language should be preserved. However, when we speak of the permanent value of his concepts, we are considering a rather different matter. Ah! We know what intimate and vital bonds join the concept to the word. That is the place where we can speak of an incarnation, rather than when it is a question of the union of the truth to a concept. But also, it is not easy to translate one and the same concept from a philosophical language into a language that is not philosophical, appealing more to imagination and experience, a language that would have the movement, style, and rhythm to which our thought, accustomed to other disciplines, would be habituated. What should we say concerning the case of translating this concept into the language of another philosophy, in other words, looking to find anew, in a completely different system—indeed one that is even completely opposed to the first in its principles—certain concepts, designated by other words, which aim at the same intelligible reality without always adequately covering it? If every translation is difficult, given that a word drawn from one language never has exactly the same meaning as a word drawn from another language, what shall we say about this kind of translation? Nonetheless, it is necessary. It is not concerned with making the truth contemporary [*d'actualiser la vérité*] but, rather, with rendering it *comprehensible* to particular minds *today*.

---

[16] It should be understood that we are taking the liberty to emphasize, in the texts we cite, the sentences or expressions which would like to highlight.

[17] Parain, "Dialogue théologique," 338–39.

But, moreover, let this effort not prevent the theologian from safeguarding its formal expression, its proper and adequate expression, which alone will be its scientific expression and, if I can so speak, the starting point for all translations. . . .[18]

III. *ESPRIT*

The preceding reflections are of use for responding to this warning expressed by Emmanuel Mounier: "Confusing permanence [*pérennité*] with timelessness [*l'intemporalité*], one arbitrarily presupposes that the problem of expression and communication has been resolved, whereas a truth like Christian truth, which is affirmed as being eternal throughout [various] languages, mentalities, and generations, poses this problem with the greatest possible acuity. One accepts the risk of fixing in *formulas of a school that are bound to a given time and place* that which precisely is above time and place. One risks *eternalizing the provisional by refusing to make the eternal contemporary* [*d'actualiser l'éternel*]."[19]

Formulas are bound to time and place, quite clearly, as well as to the concepts that seek to be expressed in them and to inform the verbal matter offered to them. However, these concepts are bound to time and place only in what is *subjective* in them: at a given moment and in a given place, a given man conceived a given thing in a given manner, something that is always explained by a great number of causes external to the very object that he has conceived, a state of affairs that, perhaps, remains undetected for millennia. However, this object itself, this intelligible reality impressed within me, living spiritually in me when I conceive it, is wholly independent of time and place. Nonetheless, we must add that the fact of being conceived in a given, determinate mind [*esprit*]—thereby being introduced into an entire system of partly inexact ideas, ones that are forever partial—will color this intelligible reality with that which the mental whole adds to the simple element. All of a man's conceptions are affected by the worldview into which they are introduced, by what we could call the thinker's "mentality." Indeed, here we see one factor involved in the variation befalling human conceptions, a factor that is related neither to the pure and simple *formulation* of the concept (although the latter will retrain traces from it), nor to the intrinsic content of the concept (although the latter can be obscured and distorted by it), but rather to its integration into a given system of thoughts and sentiments, filled with obsolete and incomplete elements.

---

[18] We explain ourselves more fully on all these points in the article which can be read in this same [volume in English], "The Analogy of Truth and the Unity of Theological Science."

[19] Mounier, "Aux avant-postes," 440.

In fact, Mounier himself understood this difference between "formulation" and "conceptualization" quite well, as can be seen in his excellent summary of the debate: "Differences arise precisely when it is a question of delimiting the frontiers of history and the immutable in the expression of eternal truth. For Thomist thought ... the historical aspect [*indice*] only affects *given secondary regions of the formulation and does not enter, as a component, into the very act* by which the truth is communicated."[20] We would say *the secondary regions of the formulation and the reverberations of the "mindset"* upon the concept; and in place of "the *very act,*" we would say: in the intelligible reality that is *conceptually grasped* through an act of the mind that is historically conditioned.

"By contrast, the other, opposed theologians tend to think that the *systems of notions and of representations through which we grasp eternal affirmations are necessarily bound to circumstances of time and place*, so that through the ages, one and the same immutable truth is expressed through systems of notions which each time translate elementary affirmations, each doing so in its own way, each time in different ways, without ever exhausting those affirmations."[21]

Here we can see the debate placed at its true depth: a modern installment of the conflict between realism and nominalism, with the intermediary schools it generates. But, what does this excellent reviewer think? Here too, he sees quite well, without fear of exacerbating the scope of such a discussion, that the problem arising in relation to the permanence of theology likewise arises in identical fashion for the permanence of dogma. He thus pushes back, as all Catholic theologians obviously do, against the "asymptotic heresy" to which excessive historicism would lead:

> Must one, for all that, hold that every dogmatic formula and every conceptual definition is a mere sign placed upon an unknowable reality, a symbol that defies all illuminating content? The modernist critique tended toward this kind of nominalism, which overturns the entire continuity of the faith. Today, we have a more complex sense of the life of the intellect.[22]

What is this sense?

Therefore, the *formula*, which in itself is valid, *dies* if one does not incessantly seek, *under its structure*, to retrieve the *living movement of thought and faith which deposited it*, [and] on the basis of it, *the con-*

---

[20] Mounier, "Aux avant-postes," 443–44.
[21] Mounier, "Aux avant-postes," 444.
[22] Mounier, "Aux avant-postes," 440–41.

tinuous revelation which *historical and religious experience* gives concerning it, and behind it, *the inexhaustible expressive power* which its *transcendent source* provides for it.[23]

In this antinomy between structure and movement, we can recognize Bergsonian currents, at least in its language. For us, the movement of thought and faith that is the *vital* and subjective intellectual *act* in which the concept is *born* is less important than the *immutable content of this concept*. That said, there can be no doubt that the formula itself dies if one does not make the concept expressed in the formula—indeed, itself the creative source of the formula itself—*live anew* in oneself. The "continuous revelation" in question can be nothing other than our ever-more-actual-and-perfect understanding that the mind draws from the content of the concepts "deposited" in fixed formulas. Precisely because we are here concerned above all with revealed truth, the "transcendent source" of concepts and of their formulation can be nothing other than the Divine Spirit who has spoken within them. Indeed, the First Truth to whom we adhere through faith surely infinitely overflows the concepts that express Him, concepts that can have only a finite—and therefore *infinitely deficient*—grasp upon their object. However, this "infinite expressive power," which cannot be exhausted in the concepts that issue from it, *is no longer exerted*, since God no longer reveals and was only able to reveal through a grace-given, transcendent act, which was by no means homogeneous with the life of our mind. The truth is not expressed in concepts that differ from those in which it was first revealed. They are the basis for whatever reflection might follow thereafter. They are what must be understood and developed. And they set the limits within which the human mind must resign itself to remain.

Perhaps we have distorted Mounier's thought through our commentary. However, our purpose was, rather, to make clear in what precise sense we could subscribe to his words and, consequently, in what sense, perhaps, his thought would differ from ours concerning these matters. In any case, he must be thanked for having expressed with greater understanding how the very foundation of the entire debate concerning the relations between truth and time necessarily involves philosophical positions concerning the nature of conceptual knowledge and of language.

IV. *REVUE DE THÉOLOGIE ET DE PHILOSOPHIE*

We must admit that, for Protestant theologians, the interest in our *Dialogue théologique* is found in the fact that it provides, in full breadth, a "lively image of the oppositions that mark out Catholic thought."[24]

---

[23] Mounier, "Aux avant-postes," 441.
[24] Germond, "Dialogue théologique," 128.

> We can see that, whatever the chosen party, at the very heart of Catholic thought, at the basis of everything that provides it with its apparent solidity, minds [*esprits*] are divided. These divergences can be maintained behind the scenes, but they nonetheless are essential. The façade of the house remains, although its foundations are less secure.[25]

It is true that, in order to appear with such determinate opposition, our respective positions have been pushed to their limits by our reviewer, though this means they have been pushed precisely to that which [we] intended to avoid: on the one hand, disregard for every element of subjectivity and relativity in the constructions wrought by human thought; on the other hand, disregard for the objective and universal value of finite formulas concerning the Infinite Truth. By pushing matters to these extremes, he finds it possible to feel that the Protestants are much closer to the Jesuits, apart from, however, what difficulties could be brought to the purity of their own properly religious witness by intending an even greater conformity with the modern world. However,

> they find it difficult to understand how it is that with such conceptions, the Jesuit Fathers do not press on further and do not bring their criticism to bear upon the absolute value of dogmatic formulas, upon the infallibility of the magisterium which proclaims them, and upon the irrevocable condemnation of every heresy.[26]

What one finds difficult to understand is often what ultimately conceals the solution to problems at hand. What prevents every Catholic theologian from pushing further onward in regard to dogmatic formulas is the fact that whatever he happens to think concerning the relative nature of theological systems, he will forever seek to nuance his position so that he can avoid the implications that others strive to make manifest to him, while he wholly and completely rejects them. When one Catholic theologian attacks another, he shows him—yes, through analysis of the concepts involved—the consequences that faith pushes back against, making clear to his interlocutor how far he must push onward. However, he immediately receives a reply. And if there were some immediate evidence in such implications, if it became psychologically impossible to maintain in his mind, alongside divergent theological conclusions, the very principles of faith understood "*in eodem sensu*," if there were a danger that one would imperceptibly pass from the former to the denial or corruption of the latter, this is when the magisterium would come to intervene, something that it takes care to avoid doing unnecessarily,

---

25 Germond, "Dialogue théologique," 128.
26 Germond, "Dialogue théologique," 132–33.

holding that freedom is one of the necessary conditions for the vitality of the intellect's own work exerted in reflecting upon the object of faith.

One must not, for all this, minimize the importance of certain debates, where the very essential character of Christianity can quite well be put into question.

However, two Catholic positions will forever be prevented from being purely and simply opposed to each other, precisely because of their primordial adherence to the truths that are defined by the Church, an adherence that is not only one of good will but, also, an adherence of the intellect, no more entailing the identity of theological constructions than does the common character of the first intuitions of the mind (or even of certain fundamental truths) entail that various philosophies would need to be identical with each other.

For fear of endlessly repeating ourselves, let us merely note that different positions can be complementary while not being opposed to each other or even that verbal oppositions are often more pronounced than are those on the level of ideas. If one does not sufficiently consider the weight of this distinction between dogma and theology (a distinction commonly held by Catholic theologians), it is understandable that the very idea of a Theological Dialogue at the heart of the same Faith could reveal to Protestant eyes a sign of splintering within the unity of Catholicism, whereas much to the contrary, it manifests just how this unity is placed above every form of contestation for each of us, as soon as matters turn to the truth defined by the Church as being revealed by God, no longer remaining merely something that our reason happens to elaborate concerning this truth.

Saint-Maximin, Nov. 25, 1947

Part 2

The Roman Response: Garrigou-Lagrange on Truth and Dogma

9

Theology and the Life of Faith
Réginald Garrigou-Lagrange, OP

By "the life of faith," we here mean the vitality of Christian faith, whether in the Church in different ages or in each believer considered in his or her intimate relations with God.

It could seem unnecessary to treat of the importance of theology for the life of faith understood in this way, for in principle, it is quite clear that—above all for a priest—the positive and speculative study of Christian dogmas is sovereignly useful to the interior life and to the apostolate. Christian faith is indispensable for salvation, and theology (or, the science of faith) is of great use in becoming well aware of the interrelations existing among the various truths of faith in the *doctrinal body* that is *Christian doctrine* or the teaching of the Savior and of the Apostles.[1] This is so obvious that it is almost tautologous to state the fact.

THE PROBLEM, SUCH AS IT IS POSED TODAY

However, it in fact does happen that one loses sight of this truth and, consequently, of the difficulties that are encountered in the study of theology. Sometimes, these difficulties render this work quite arduous and can fatigue certain minds who are content with a more superficial knowledge of things. From the perspective of positive studies, theology is the patient study of Scriptural texts, the documents of tradition, of various interpretations that have been proposed concerning them, and of errors old and new. From the speculative perspective, it is the thorough study of the notions without which revealed truths would remain unknowable: analogical notions concerning the various divine perfections (Wisdom, Goodness, Mercy, Justice, Providence, Predestination, etc.); the notions of *nature* and *person* in the treatises

---

[1] In its decree *Lamentabili* (Denzinger, no. 3059), the Holy Office condemned this fifty-ninth proposition of the modernists: "Christ did not teach a determined body of doctrine applicable to all times and all men but, rather, inaugurated a religious movement adapted or to be adapted to different times and places." Also, see the proposition that follows.

[Tr. note: The sixtieth condemned proposition reads: "Christian doctrine was originally Judaic. Through successive evolutions it became first Pauline, then Joannine, finally Hellenic and universal."]

on the Trinity and the Incarnation; the notions of *substance* and *accident* in that on the Eucharist; the notions of *freedom, merit, grace, sin, eternal punishment, beatitude*, etc. Some might think that the abstract considerations needed for thoroughly studying these notions are quite distant from our habitual preoccupations. The interior life, we are told, is simpler, above all in its superior parts, and it does not seem necessary that it should get tangled up with the metaphysical study of all these problems. Great saints, like the sublime beggar Benedict-Joseph Labre, lived profoundly upon the Eucharist without ever having read a treatise on the sacraments.

It suffices, some say, that we adhere to the fixity of faith and, for action, to the directions of ecclesiastical authority. As regards *theological opinions—whose ensemble*, they think, *constitutes theology!*—they are merely disputed questions to be investigated by the dedicated teams of laborers belonging to various religious orders. These groups and their doctrines all hold an equally probable certitude, allowing the mind complete freedom in choosing among them and even the possibility of choosing none of them. The vital questions would lie elsewhere.

Some believe that nothing of great importance is involved for the Catholic when it comes to the question of choosing between the *definition of truth* to which St. Thomas always returns (conformity of the intellect with reality) and the definition of truth proposed some years ago by Maurice Blondel when he wrote, "In place of the abstract and chimerical *adaequatio rei et intellectus* [the adequation of the thing, or reality, and the intellect] there is substituted . . . *adaequatio realis mentis et vitae* [the real adequation of the mind and life]."[2]

As the life in question here is human life, which is subject to change, it was then asked how, from this perspective, one can avoid falling under the condemned modernist proposition: *"Truth is no more immutable than man himself, since it evolved with him, in him, and through him."*[3]

Since 1906, Blondel has moved closer to traditional metaphysics. We know that he has formally condemned the manifestly inadmissible excesses that can be found in the posthumous articles of Fr. Laberthonnière.[4] Equally,

---

[2] Maurice Blondel, "Le point de depart de la recherche philosophique," *Annales de philosophie chretienne* 152 (1906): 235.

[3] Pius X, *Lamentabili*, no. 59 (Denzinger, no. 3459).

[4] In his posthumously published articles, one reads in Lucien Laberthonnière, "La société spirituelle," *Archivio di filosofia* 3, no. 3 (July-September 1933): 11: "Without a doubt, St. Thomas kept the letter of Christianity. . .but, by his doctrine, by his fundamental conceptions, by all the orientation of his thought, he is totally and radically outside of Christianity." Also, Laberthonnière, "Dieu d'Aristote, Dieu de l'école, Dieu des chrétiens," *Archivio di filosofia* 3, no. 2 (April-June 1933): 14: "The God (whom he describes for us) is a *being of pride, nothing but pride*" (who has created all things for Himself).

he even retracted the final chapter of *L'Action*, which was most vigorously contested.⁵

However, in his latest work, *La pensée*, we still can find propositions that, understood according to the obvious sense of their terms, seem quite removed from traditional doctrine. In Blondel's thought, which here is preoccupied, on the one hand, with taking into account certain results from the critique of the physical and natural sciences and, on the other, with speaking in opposition to the rationalism of this or that contemporary philosophy, these propositions do not have, we believe, the scope that they appear to have at first sight. Nevertheless, they do not seem to maintain sufficiently enough the *stability* and *ontological value* of the notions necessary for the first principles of reason (including among them that of causality), nor that of those notions needed for the formulas of faith.⁶

Fr. Laberthonnière forgot what is said in Prov 16:4: "The Lord hath made all things for himself," and he has not understood that if God ceased willing everything for the sake of the Sovereign Good, which is Himself, and for the sake of the manifestation of His goodness, God would be, as it were, guilty of mortal sin, a most extremely absurd claim.

5 Blondel said in *L'Action*, pp. 437ff: "*Knowledge, which, before one's option* [or, act of choice], *was simply subjective*, propulsive, becomes, afterwards, privative [sic] *and constitutive of being*" (depending on whether the free choice is morally bad or good). See *L'Action*, 426ff, 439, 463.

6 One reads in *La pensée*, vol. 1, p. 130: "*The objects to which thought is taken and given find their common denominator, their specific stability*, their logical utilization, ONLY BY THE ARTIFICE OF LANGUAGE. . . . We substantize the things that we know not to be substances." If this proposition, thus formulated, is true, how is one to maintain *the stability and real value of the notions of* nature, substance, and person, necessary for *the statement of the dogmas of faith*? [Tr. note: Fr. Garrigou-Lagrange does not cite the edition, but it appears to match the pagination of Maurice Blondel, *La pensée*, vol. 1 (Paris: Presses Universitaires de France, 1934).]

Blondel also says: "*The notion of an object* and the use that is ordinarily made of it is one of these divisions, one of these *illegitimate 'overestimations'* [*majorations*] that we do not cease to denounce as being *the chronic deception* and *ruinous improbity* from which many a philosophy is dying today" (*La pensée*, vol. 1, 131). If one takes this proposition in its obvious sense, how can one determine *the proper object* of our intellect and affirm with the Church (cf. [First] Vatican Council, *Dei filius*, ch. 4 [Denzinger no. 3015]) that the supernatural mysteries of faith certainly *exceed* this [formal] object, which is naturally knowable for us?

Again, we read on the next page: "There are, *not in an absolute fashion* (this would be an illusion), but in a relative fashion, *distinctly subsistent realities* . . . 'substantial forms' that, *without being stably achieved and independent*, nevertheless have . . . a value that is, at one and the same time, objective and subjective" (*La pensée*, vol. 1, 132). Also, see *La pensée*, vol. 1, 136–37 and vol. 2, 30, 57, 74, 196, and 302.

How then is the *nature* of the human soul really and essentially distinct from grace *that is not owed to it*? How is the latter certainly above the exigencies of our nature, contrary to what Baius said?

When Blondel speaks of the dependence of *certitude* upon a *free option* [or, free choice], we greatly desire to see him maintain the profound distinction formulated by St. Thomas[7] concerning the influence of the will upon the intellect, depending on whether or not there is *necessitating evidence* for the object known. In the first case, the influence of the will leads the intellect (*quoad exercitium* [with regard to its exercise]) to *consider* this truth attentively, in a manner that is sustained long enough, likewise *considering everything that should be considered* without neglecting anything. Here, there certainly is room for moral rectitude and intellectual probity. We likewise concede that even when there is necessitating evidence, the influence of the will can *confirm* our intellectual certitude because day-by-day we live ever more in accord with the truth we have already acknowledged. From this perspective, a great difference separates the notion that one can form for oneself, for example, concerning humility after having read an excellent study on this subject from that much more profound notion of humility that a saint has of it at the end of his life. Something similar occurs with regard to the proofs for God's existence.

All this is incontestable and should be clearly distinguished from the influence of the will on the intellect *quoad specificationem* [with regard to specification] *when necessitating evidence* from the object *does not exist*, as holds in the case of faith in the revealed mysteries. Many passages in Blondel related to the free option and to certitude would be admissible if he noted this distinction that is common in St. Thomas and his disciples. By means of it, the role of the will in these very different forms of certitude is easily explained, as are the certitude of science and the certitude of faith or belief.[8] It also sheds light on the character of the kinds of certitude proper

---

We read later in *La pensée*, vol. 1, p. 179: "*Far from deducing the affirmation of the living God from a prior assertion of abstract principles*, these intellectual premises proceed in a more profound sense from the realistic conception of a divine subsistence."

Is this to say that we have a firm certitude of the real and universal value of the principle of causality, necessary for the *a posteriori* proofs of God's existence only *after we believe in God*, which seems indeed to presuppose itself a *free choice*, as Blondel affirms in his book *L'Action* (pp. 437ff, 439, 426ff, and 463), and as voluntarist philosophy of action would require? It is this free choice we see reappearing in the belief of which he speaks in this new work, *La pensée*, vol. 1, pp. 390ff and vol. 2, 65, 67, 81, 90, and 96: "*In our fashion of knowing and affirming*, there is always for the assertion and effective consent *a portion of belief* inherent to vital and intellectual certitudes all together. Not that there would be a hazard [*aléa*] for those who can see and will; but, in the most perspicuous intellect, it is necessary that to the evidence of logical reasons there be joined *the decision* that renders truth the primacy and totality that is owed to it."

7 *ST* I-II, q. 17, a. 6.

8 See *ST* II-II, q. 2, a. 1; q. 4, a. 8.

to prudence,[9] hope,[10] and to the gift of wisdom. In these latter, the role of the will is manifestly much greater than in the certitude born of necessitating evidence.

In order to remain faithful to traditional metaphysics, we absolutely must maintain that, *prior to any free option*, the human intellect can be certain of the truth of the principles of contradiction and of causality, understanding these principles in their *realist* sense.

For the nominalists and consistent [*conséquents*] idealists, the principle of contradiction is only a conditional proposition: *If something is, something is* (*si aliquid est, aliquid est*). However, according to them, perhaps nothing is. Perhaps our idea of being does not have a real value. Perhaps all things become, and perhaps becoming itself is self-explanatory, *ratio sui*. Perhaps God is nothing more than creative evolution.

For the realist, the ontological formulation of the principle of contradiction is categorical: "It is absolutely impossible that, at one and the same time, a thing be and not be." For the realist, a square circle is not only subjectively *inconceivable*. It is *really impossible, unrealizable* outside the mind, whatever Descartes may say about the matter. Similarly, for realism, the denial of the principle of causality leads to absurdity. To claim that *that which begins* (i.e., *the contingent*) is *uncaused* is not only an *unintelligible claim* but, moreover, is absurd and *really impossible* outside the mind. Does Blondel firmly admit, prior to every free option, the certitude of the real value of these principles and that of the principle of finality (every agent acts for an end)? In certain passages, he seems to admit that these certitudes are necessary; however, in others, he attenuates his affirmation and makes it seem like it has some sort of relativity.

Likewise, does he acknowledge, prior to every free option, certitude concerning the *personal existence of the thinking subject* and the truth that *he cannot have the experience of it* without *the existence of the experienced reality*, no sensation of resistance (distinct from hallucination) without something that resists? "Touch and see, for a spirit does not have flesh and bones" (Lk 24:39).[11]

All these primordial questions are manifestly of a great importance for every man who seeks the truth. They are certainly no less important for the intellectual formation of priests according to the mind of the Church.[12]

---

9 See *ST* I-II, q. 57, a. 5, ad 3 (on prudential certitude, *per conformitatem ad appetitum rectum, through conformity to right appetite*, even in the case of invincible ignorance or error).

10 See *ST* II-II q. 18, a. 4.

11 See *ST* III, q. 55, a. 6; q. 57, a. 6, ad 3; *ST* I, q. 51, a. 2.

12 Canon [1917 code] 1366, §2: "Professors shall treat studies in rational theology and philosophy and the instruction of students in these disciplines *according to the system, teaching, and principles of the Angelic Doctor and hold to them religiously.*" Taken from *The 1917 Pio-Benedictine Code of Canon Law*, ed. and trans. Edward N. Peters (San Francisco, CA: Ignatius Press, 2001), can. 1366, §2 (p. 460).

What then must we think about the relationship existing between the speculative and thorough study of theology and the life of faith as well as the interior life itself? In the Church, it has always been taught that the interior life owes much to theology and that the study of this science is, in turn, greatly fertilized by a profound interior life. Here, we find mutual relations whose elementary truths should be recalled, truths which turn out to be very profound when one indeed chooses to penetrate them and make them the rule of one's life with greater intensity each day.

THEOLOGY PRESERVES THE INTERIOR LIFE FROM GRAVE DEVIATIONS

First of all, the study of theology helps the spiritual life avoid two grave, truly ruinous defects: *subjectivism* and *particularism*.

Those who approach God in prayer by allowing themselves to be led too much by the inclination of their own individual nature, temperament, imagination, sensibility, or character often fall into sentimentalist subjectivism.

In our own days, Henri Bergson holds that the mystics are above all dominated by an emotion to which they deliver themselves, one they then express in religious ideas or conceptions, like that of the divine mercy toward us or that of the need to offer reparation to divine justice. However, [according to him] we can make pronunciations concerning *the truth* of these religious conceptions only from the empirical and practical perspective, doing so by the welcome effect they produce, above all if this effect is durable and has an echo in us. Therefore, one could ask oneself whether these conceptions only contain a beautiful dream arising from one's religious sentiment, a consoling reverie, though without its object exceeding the limits of probable opinion, all the while becoming increasingly plausible by the increasing number of welcome results that depend on these conceptions.

It will be responded: However, to be assured of being in the truth, the fixity of faith suffices without needing recourse to theology.

Still, in order to retain the fixity of faith, one must accept the traditional definition of *truth* and not only the pragmatist definition thereof. Otherwise, dogmas would become mere preceptive norms: comport yourself in relation to Jesus Christ *as though* He were God, though without affirming that He really *is* God; comport yourself in relation to the Resurrection as though it really had taken place; comport yourself in relation to the Eucharist as though there really were a transubstantiation and real presence.

Moreover, to preserve oneself from subjectivism in the interior life, to truly live the great mysteries of faith, is it superfluous to meditate seriously on what the masters of theology have written concerning them? Likewise, is it superfluous to know the nature of the spiritual organism of sanctifying grace, the infused virtues and the gifts, the various forms of actual grace, and the signs of a divine inspiration along with its counterfeits?

Have not the great mystics been ever more attentive to the task of placing *truth* in their life so that they might live upon nothing other than the truth?[13]

Of particular note, we have the case of St. Teresa of Ávila, who spoke of the esteem that she had for theology and for learned men:

> In difficult matters, even if I believe I understand what I am saying and am speaking the truth, I use this phrase, "I think," because if I am mistaken, I am very ready to give credence to those who have great learning.[14] For even if they have not themselves experienced these things, men of great learning have a certain instinct to prompt them. As God uses them to give light to His Church, He reveals to them anything that is true so that it shall be accepted; and if they do not squander their talents but are true servants of God, they will never be surprised at His greatness, for they know quite well that He is capable of working more and still more. In any case, where matters are in question for which there is no explanation, there must be others about which they can read, and they can deduce from their reading that it is possible for these first-named to have happened. Of this I have the fullest experience; and I have also experience of timid, half-learned men whose shortcomings have cost me very dear.[15]

* * * * *

Beyond individual subjectivism, theology also preserves the interior life from particularism, which arises from the excessive influence of our environment or from that of the ideas in vogue in our era, ideas that will be outdated in thirty years' time. One can note these deviations in the ages of quietism, Americanism, and modernism. In these deviations, we have passing enthusiasms that last little longer then a fire fed upon straw, and if they are not remedied, they are followed by discouragement.

By preserving our interior life from these deviations, the attentive study of theology gives it a precious *objectivity*, a sane realism, and also, above every narrow, particular, and passing view, *universality*, which is the mark of the great classics of spirituality, whose writings are of value for all places and times. In a way, like something conceived above the flow of time in its continual onward course, these works do not age but, instead, retain a superior relevance.

---

13 On this point, see the beautiful study by Fr. Thomas Deman, "La théologie dans la vie de sainte Catherine de Sienne," *Vie spirituelle*, Vol. 42, Suppl. (1935): [1]–[24].

14 [Tr. note: Fr. Garrigou-Lagrange has in French *les grand théologiens*.]

15 Teresa of Ávila, *Interior Castle*, trans. E. Allison Peers (New York: Doubleday: 1961), 100–101 (fifth mansion, ch. 1). Likewise, see the eighth chapter of the sixth mansion.

THEOLOGY CONTRIBUTES TO PROVIDING THE INTERIOR LIFE WITH THE PROFOUND SENSE OF THE TRUTHS OF FAITH

The study of the great masters of theology not only preserves our interior life from the deviations of which we have spoken. It moreover helps it to know *the mind of the Church* [*le sens de l'Eglise*], which is the same *semper et ubique*. Little by little, it shows us the *profundity of the most elementary truths* of Christianity. It even habituates us to seeing that the elementary truths of Christian doctrine are the loftiest, most profound, and most vital truths we may ever know, provided that they are penetrated well, meditated upon at length, and lived upon. Thus, they ultimately become the *object of contemplation*. Such is the case for the first line of the Catechism: "Why were you created and put into the world? To know God, to love Him, to serve Him, and by these means to obtain eternal life," or, again, this expression of St. John: "God so loved the world that He gave His only Son" (Jn 3:16).

The [First] Vatican Council admirably expresses the importance of theology for the Christian life when it says:

> Nevertheless, if reason illumined by faith inquires in an earnest, pious, and sober manner, it attains by God's grace a certain understanding of the mysteries, which is most fruitful, both from the analogy with the objects of its natural knowledge and from the connection of these mysteries with one another and with man's ultimate end. But it never becomes capable of understanding them in the way it does truths that constitute its proper object.[16]

Theology enables us to arrive at a certain, very fruitful understanding of the revealed mysteries. And this is even its most precious fruit. This is why, in St. Thomas, the first questions of the great dogmatic treatises on the Trinity, the Redemptive Incarnation, the Sacraments in general, and the Eucharist, all first contain *conceptual analysis of these revealed truths* before he is concerned with deducing from them *other truths* of less importance, truths that are theological conclusions, properly so-called, the fruit of objectively *illative* reasoning. All these first questions of the great treatises usually contain only *explicative* reasoning, which explain or deepen the subject and the predicate of the revealed truth, concerning the great mystery in question. In this way, as a result of these explications, the *consubstantiality of the Word* is not, as is sometimes said, a theological conclusion deduced from a revealed truth, but instead, is *the revealed truth* in its exact and profound sense: "*And the Word* (consubstantial to the Father) *was made flesh* (namely, man)." It is the

---

16 [First] Vatican Council, *Dei filius*, ch. 4. Denzinger, no. 3016.

revealed mystery itself in the light of this other expression from the Prologue of St. John: "And the Word was God." The consubstantiality of the Word [to the Father] is incomparably superior to theological conclusions.

Even were theology not to deduce *any* theological conclusions, properly so called, but were only to explain, through a profound metaphysical analysis,[17] the subject and predicate *of revealed truths*, and even were it only to show *their subordination* in order to make us be better aware of the depth, riches, and elevation of the very teaching of the Savior, even in such a case, it would have considerable importance. And this is how theology prepares for the elaboration of increasingly explicit dogmatic formulations of one and the same dogma, that is, of one and the same assertion or revealed truth, before it is a question of deducing from it *other truths* through *objectively illative* reasoning.[18] This deepening of the meaning of a fundamental truth sometimes takes centuries, as with the deepening of this expression: "And the Word was made flesh."

It is utterly evident that theology has contributed much to the elaboration of increasingly explicit formulations of one and the same dogma, an explication often rendered necessary for eliminating heresies.

St. Thomas, who in his Commentary on the *Posterior Analytics* of Aristotle (bk. 2, lect. 3–17) studied so profoundly how one undertakes the *venatio*, the search, for the *real* and distinct *definition* by setting out from the *nominal definition* that expresses the vague concept of the thing to be defined, was certainly not unaware of this *development [progrès] of dogmas*. The most important work of philosophy and theology is found in this methodical passage from the *vague concept* of common sense to the *distinct concept*. The latter is not *deduced* from the preceding like a conclusion. Rather, one and the same concept is given increasing precision through the *division* of the

---

17 [Tr. note: By which he merely means an analysis searching for the most essential definition (or at least what is closest thereto *quoad nos*) of a given reality.]

18 We use the expression "O*bjectively illative* reasoning" for that form of reasoning which leads *to another [objectively new]* truth. For example, from the Divine Intelligence, we can deduce the Divine Freedom through this major premise: every intelligent being is free. By contrast, reasoning is only *explicative* (or at most *subjectively illative*) when it establishes the *equivalence* of two propositions in stating the *same truth*. For example, there is the *equivalence* of these two propositions: "You are Peter and upon this rock I will build my Church; and the gates of hell will not prevail over it" = "The successor of Peter, when he speaks *ex cathedra* to the universal Church, in a matter of faith and morals, cannot be deceived."

See, at the end of this article, an *appendix* concerning the question of knowing whether theological conclusions obtained by *objectively illative* reasoning with the aid of a *natural premise* (even when the latter is the major, that is to say the more universal premise) can be *defined* as *a dogma of faith* to be acknowledged under pain of heresy properly so-called (and not only of error).

genus (or of the most general notion[19]) and through the inductive *comparison of the thing to be defined* with what more or less resembles it. In this way, philosophy comes to obtain precise definitions of substance, man, the soul, the intellect, the will, the different acquired virtues, etc.

In theology, the same kind of conceptual analysis has contributed greatly to the *precision of notions* that are indispensable for *dogmatic formulations*: the notions of created being and uncreated being, those of unity, truth, and (ontological and moral) goodness; the notions of analogy relative to God, of the Divine Wisdom, the Divine Will, love, providence, and predestination; for the understanding of revealed truths concerning the Trinity, the notions of nature, person, and relation; the notions of grace (habitual and actual, efficacious or sufficient); the notions of free will,[20] merit, sin, infused virtue, faith, hope, charity, and justification; the notions of sacrament,[21] character, sacramental grace, transubstantiation, and contrition; the notions of beatitude and punishment, purgatory and hell, etc.

Even before taking up the task of deducing theological conclusions (that is, the task of arriving at new truths distinct from *revealed truths*) an immense labor must be undertaken in the *conceptual analysis* of these revealed truths so as to pass from the *vague notion* (expressed by the current nominal definition or by the terms of Scripture and of Tradition) to *the same distinct and precise notion* in view of eliminating heresy, which deforms revelation itself.

To arrive at this penetration, it is not useless to have studied many times the Treatises on God and on the Incarnation in the work of a master like St. Thomas.

Even those who teach them come to have a command of the subject only after many years; then, little by little, they grasp the profound sense of the principles, as well as their elevation and radiance. Thus, one arrives

---

19 [Tr. note: That is, in the case of analogical notions.]

20 The passage from the nominal definition to the real definition is sometimes quite lengthy. Thus, Thomists and Molinists still do not agree concerning the real (exact or distinct) definition of free will inasmuch as it adds a precision to the nominal definition. Nevertheless, it is a question of the *same concept*, which is at first vague and then is distinct.

21 For *defined doctrine concerning the sacraments*, dogmatic progress is considerable, for the revealed truths relative to the sacraments had been revealed less in an abstract manner than in a *concrete and practical* manner, by the very administration of the sacraments. And thus what is necessary for a sacrament, like baptism, can be considered either from the perspective of being a *sign* (sensible thing and words), or from the perspective of the *subject* who receives it, or from the perspective of the *effects* produced, or from the perspective of the ordinary or exceptional *minister*. Thus, one and the same thing practiced in Church, in accord with the will of Christ, since her beginnings, can be expressed in *multiple propositions* in order to eliminate this or that heresy. And these propositions are not theological conclusions; they are the abstract expression of the concretely *revealed truth*.

at the "fruitful understanding of the mysteries" spoken of by the [First] Vatican Council.

Theology aids in deepening faith so that we may live by it, and below the level of faith, it is gradually constituted as an explanatory *science* of the revealed truths and as a deduction of certain theological conclusions that are nearly universally admitted, with that which contradicts them often having been condemned not as "heresies" but as "errors."

Indeed, it is of great importance not to confuse *theological science* with *theological opinions*. Classics like Bossuet draw from this science with open hands, generally setting aside consideration of the particular opinions of theologians. They are not unaware of these various opinions. However, what they seek in faith and in the science of faith is that which rises above such opinions.

To realize the importance of *the acquisition of theological science*, let us suppose for a moment that St. Thomas's *Summa theologiae* had not yet been written and that the only treatises on God, the Incarnation, grace, and faith that we had were the questions of the Master of the *Sentences*. How much more difficult would we find it to render account of the *mutual relationships that exist among revealed truths* in the body of Christian doctrine, and how much more impoverished would we be for forming a sound judgment concerning dangerous doctrinal novelties, which are sometimes born of a very slight error in a first principle: "*Parvus error in principio magnus est in fine.*" If one distorts in an almost imperceptible manner certain Thomist principles in the question of predestination and reprobation, one can fall into Calvinism (for example, if one does not distinguish clearly enough the divine permission, which precedes sin, and the subtraction of divine grace, which follows at the same instant).

It is of great importance that we know the value of commonly received *theological science*. By having misunderstood it, the nominalists of the fourteenth and fifteenth century fell into grave errors that paved the way for the errors of Luther, who was formed by them. Thus, they conceived of sanctifying grace as being a *quality belonging to the natural order*, which would nevertheless give a moral right to eternal life as a result of a divine institution, like a bank note, which gives us the right to receive a hundred dollars [*francs*], even though it all the while remains nothing more than a piece of paper. Luther came to say that grace and justification are only an *extrinsic denomination* by the imputation of the merits of the Savior unto us.

Finally, as Fr. Gardeil has noted,[22] among the various *theological systems*, we must carefully heed the importance of universal syntheses that set as their

---

[22] Ambroise Gardeil, *Le donné révélé et la théologie* (Paris: Librarie Victor Lecoffre, J. Gabalda et cie., 1910), 252–85.

[Tr. note: Fr. Garrigou-Lagrange lists only the title and pp. 252–85. It appears that he means the third chapter of the second part as cited here, pp. 252–84.]

master idea the very idea of God, the Author of nature and of grace (or, of salvation) and not some particular idea, which is obviously subordinate to the preceding (for example, the idea of man's free will). A given system thus dominated by a particular idea cannot be a universal synthesis, which must be dominated by the idea of God, the proper object of theology.

In its superior simplicity, faith is like an absolutely simple circle. The teachings of the greatest theologians, seeking to explain the dogmas of faith, are like a polygon inscribed within this circle, seeking to elaborate its content and riches. The nominalists draw their polygon in their own particular manner; it is quite different from what had been sketched by St. Augustine and drawn out by St. Thomas.

All this shows what the life of faith receives and can receive from the study of theology when the latter is indeed undertaken with intelligence, penetration, and docility to the great doctors whom the Church proposes to us as Masters.

* * * * *

THE INFLUENCE OF THE INTERIOR LIFE ON THEOLOGY

But if the interior life receives much from the study of theology, it can, in its own turn, greatly perfect such study as well. This fact is not noted frequently enough. Nevertheless, the great doctors of the Church have often mentioned this fact, indeed, in a much truer manner than the current partisans of the philosophy of action.

Too often, the study of theology remains lifeless, either in its positive part or in its abstract and speculative part. It does not truly make felt the superior inspiration existing in it, the breath of the theological virtues and of the gifts of the Holy Spirit, the gifts of understanding and wisdom. Thus, we do not sufficiently find in it this *sapida scientia* spoken of by St. Thomas in the first question of the *Summa theologiae*.

Like a child who studies the piano and cannot yet fathom what gives the works of the masters their value, one comes to a halt too readily at the *formulas* of faith without seeking to pass through them to the Divine Reality they signify, in order to thereby penetrate and taste the revealed mysteries. Here we should recall that saints like St. Francis of Assisi, St. Catherine of Siena, St. Benedict-Joseph Labre, and so many others, who never undertook the conceptual analysis of the dogmas of the Redemptive Incarnation and of the Eucharist and who never studied the theological conclusions that one deduces from them, all profoundly lived upon these mysteries precisely by passing through the formula so as to press onward to the Divine and Living Reality that they signify.

And without calling to mind these great saints who received special graces of contemplation, how many simple but profound Christian souls live upon these mysteries more, perhaps, than many theologians! With a sound and saintly realism, they enter into these heights of God because they are humble, having pure hearts and lively faith, both of which inspire all their conduct from morning to night. As St. Thomas says: "The act of the believer does not find its ultimate terminus in *the statement* but, rather, *in reality*, in the revealed mystery itself."[23]

Now, if this is true of these souls, for how much greater a reason should it be true of a priest who has truly understood the grandeur of his vocation, he who should celebrate the Holy Sacrifice with an ever-livelier faith each day, a purer and stronger love of God, and each day make a communion substantially more fervent than the day before, given that we must not only preserve the charity that is in us but indeed must make it grow, thus disposing ourselves (so long as we do not fall into some form of negligence) to receive our Lord the next day with a fervor of will that is not only equal to the previous day's but, rather, one that is greater still.[24]

When the interior life of a priest thus grows every day, it greatly vivifies his study of theology. These two forms of his activity have the most welcome influence upon one another: *Causae ad invicem sunt causae, in diverso genere* [Causes are mutually causes for each other, though in different genera of causality].

THE FRUITS OF THIS MUTUAL INFLUENCE

When a priest has a great and solid piety, if he also applies himself to study, theology becomes ever-livelier for him. Like the pianist coming to master the necessary techniques of piano playing and to understand the works of the masters, one here comes to perceive the harmonies at play in the works of someone like St. Augustine or St. Thomas.

Then, after *descending* from faith to theology to know its details in its various treatises, the theologian will experience the need to *ascend from theology to faith*, to ascend to the divine source of this science. He resembles a man who would have passed his childhood upon a mountain, like Monte Cassino, then descending into the valley to traverse it in all directions. This man would feel the need to return to the mountain so as to embrace the entire

---

23 *ST* II-II, q. 1, a. 2, ad 2.

24 In his Commentary on Hebrews 10:25, St. Thomas wrote: "The more a natural motion approaches its terminus, the *more is it inclined thereunto*. The contrary is the case for violent motion (e.g., of a stone thrown upward and ascending upward). Now, grace inclines in the manner of nature. Therefore (as the natural motion of the stone falling is ever faster), *the more those who are in grace approach the end, the more they ought to grow [in grace]*." The more they approach God, the more they are attracted by Him, and more rapidly do they press onward toward Him, as we see in the final years of the lives of the saints.

valley in a single glance. The theologian likewise needs to embrace his science in a single glance by finding it virtually contained in the *Credo* or at the end of the Mass in the Prologue of St. John's Gospel.

When the priestly soul has become, as it must, a soul of prayer, the interior life then emphasizes what is most vital and most fertile in dogmatic and moral theology. The gifts of understanding and wisdom render infused faith penetrating and enable it to savor the truths that it knows. . . . And let us remember, infused faith is the root of theology.

One thus discovers increasingly captivating *chiaroscuros* in the doctrines of Christianity, *chiaroscuros* that are the object of the infused contemplation of the saints and of truly interior souls.

Little by little, all the great questions on grace are summarized in the following two principles. On the one hand, "*God never commands the impossible, but in commanding, He admonishes us to do what we can and to ask* [for the grace] *to do what we cannot*," as St. Augustine says[25] and as is cited by the Council of Trent against the Protestants.[26] On the other hand, against the Pelagians and Semi-Pelagians [there are those words of Scripture], "For who sees anything different in you? What have you that you did not receive?" (1 Cor 4:7, RSV); or, according of the terms used by St. Thomas: "Given that the uncreated love of God is the cause of all that is good, nothing would be *better* than something else if it were not more loved by God."[27]

Just as each of these two principles is clear and certain when considered in isolation, so too is their intimate reconciliation obscure on account of the superior obscurity that comes from too-great a light for our weak eyes. To see this intimate reconciliation, we would need to see how infinite justice, infinite mercy, and sovereign freedom are reconciled in the Deity (or, the intimate life of God).

Let us take another example. With the progress of the interior life, one sees more and more fully the loftiness of the treatise on the Redemptive Incarnation and the motive of the Incarnation of the Son of God, "*qui propter nos homines et propter nostrum salutem descendit de caelis et homo factus est* [who for us men and for our salvation descended from heaven and was made man]."

Similarly, again, under the influence of the life of prayer, one gradually discovers what life is hidden in the Eucharist, and, in a domain elevated above all the theories on the sacrifice of the Mass, the sense and scope of these words of the Council of Trent becomes increasingly clear: "For the victim is one and the same: THE SAME NOW OFFERS Himself through the ministry of priests who then offered Himself on the Cross; only the manner of

---

[25] See Augustine, *De natura et gratia*, ch. 43, no. 50.
[26] See Council of Trent, *Decree on Justification*, ch. 11 (Denzinger, no. 1536).
[27] See *ST* I, q. 20, aa. 3 and 4.

the offering is different."²⁸ With ever greater clarity, the Savior appears as the *Principal Priest* "always living to intercede for us" (Heb 7:25), and His interior oblation, ever current, not renewed, but continued and measured, like His beatific vision, by participated eternity, appears as being the soul of the sacrifice of the Mass and of all the Masses that do not cease to be celebrated on the earth's surface.

Thus, little by little, one discovers, in Scripture and the Councils, the most precious stones of the doctrinal edifice. Likewise, in the *Summa theologiae*, one comes to have increasing discernment concerning the *summa capita*, the greatest articles, which are like the most elevated and most characteristic peaks in a lengthy mountain range.

If one truly applies oneself to the study of theology in a spirit of faith and prayer, it becomes living, and then are these words of St. Thomas realized: "Doctrine and preaching (of the divine word) ought to be derived from the fullness of contemplation,"²⁹ as we see, following upon Pentecost, in the preaching of the Apostles.

* * * * *

Understood in this manner, theology is of a great importance in preparing oneself for the ministry of souls. It *profoundly forms the mind* to judge in accord with the Gospel and to exhort souls to true Christian perfection. It shows all the elevation of the ultimate precept: "Love your God with all your heart." It makes one see that this precept does not have limits and that all Christians *must tend* to the perfection of charity,³⁰ each according to his condition, one in marriage, another in the religious state, another in the priestly life.

Now, we cannot arrive at the full perfection of the Christian life if we do not profoundly live the mysteries of the Redemptive Incarnation and of the Eucharist, if we do not penetrate and taste them by a living faith, illuminated by the gifts of understanding and of wisdom. In a subordinate but truly useful way, the study of theology contributes to this, provided that it is inspired not by natural curiosity but by the love of God and desire for the salvation of souls.

In this way, we have an ever-more powerful verification for the beautiful words from the [First] Vatican Council's constitution *Dei filius* cited at the beginning of this article, words which are, at once, a definition and an encomium for theology:

---

28 Council of Trent, sess. 22, Doctrine and Canons on the Sacrifice of the Mass (Denzinger, no. 1743).

29 *ST* II-II, q. 188, a. 6.

30 See *ST* II-II, q. 184, a. 3.

Nevertheless, if *reason illumined by faith* inquires in an earnest, pious, and sober manner, it attains by God's grace *a certain understanding of the mysteries, which is most fruitful*, both from the analogy with the objects of its natural knowledge and from the connection of these mysteries with one another and with man's ultimate end.[31]

The study of theology, which sometimes is difficult and arduous, is thus truly fruitful. It disposes, in a certain way, the faithful and generous priestly soul to receive the light of life, the grace of contemplation and of union, which is, as St. Thomas says, "a kind of beginning of eternal life."[32]

NOTE

With regard to the *definability of theological conclusions*, in the body of this chapter, we distinguished *objectively illative* reasoning, which leads to ANOTHER TRUTH [from that which is expressed in such reasoning's premises], from *explicative* reasoning, namely, that which is, at most, *subjectively illative*, which establishes the equivalence of two propositions that state, the one vaguely, the other distinctly, THE SAME TRUTH (for example, the infallibility of Peter and of his successors).

This leads to the following question: can theological conclusions obtained by *objectively illative* reasoning using a *natural premise* (even when the latter is the major, i.e., the more universal premise) be defined as *a dogma of faith* that one must admit not only under pain of error but, indeed, under that of heresy properly so-called? For example, supposing that the Divine Freedom were not formally revealed, even in a vague manner, could it be defined as a dogma? It would be the conclusion of a process of reasoning whose natural major would be: "Every intelligent being is free." Following with the minor premise, "Now, it is revealed that God is an intelligent being," we would then conclude, "Therefore, God is free, and this is virtually revealed."

We do not think that a theological conclusion, properly so called, as deduced from that which is revealed by means of *objectively illative* reasoning could be defined under pain of heresy, properly so called, as being a dogma of the faith (although the contradictory proposition could be infallibly condemned as erroneous). This is so because—and the great commentators on St. Thomas generally admit the point—it is not *simpliciter* a *revealed* truth but, instead, is a *truth deduced from a revealed proposition* using a natural premise (which even here is the major premise and not the minor).

---

31 [First] Vatican Council, *Dei filius*, ch. 4 (Denzinger, no. 3016).
32 *ST* I-II, q. 69, a. 2; II-II, q. 24, a. 3, ad 2; *De veritate*, q. 14, a. 2.

Even if this conclusion states a judgment concerning God, no matter how rigorous it may be, it cannot be defined as a dogma (unless it is contained elsewhere in some place within the deposit of revelation).

To defend the idea that such statements could be defined, Fr. Marín-Sola said in 1924 in his *Homogenous Evolution of Catholic Dogma*[33]: The truth deduced states a judgment *concerning one and the same Divine Reality*. For example, if one deduced the *Divine Freedom* (presupposing that it not be formally and vaguely revealed) from the *Divine Intelligence*, what is known is one and the same Divine Reality.

It is easy to respond to this. The deduced truth states a judgment concerning the same Divine Reality, *ut res est, concedo; ut obiectum est, nego* [as He is a reality *as such*, I concede the point; as He is an object of knowledge, I deny it], according to the classic distinction explained well by Cajetan in his Commentary on *ST* I, q. 1, a. 3, no. 5.

One and the same Divine Reality is an *object* of many specifically distinct *habitus*: the light of glory, faith, theology, and metaphysics. For all the more reason, *one and the same Divine Reality* corresponds to *many truths*. Some of these truths are *revealed*, while others are *deduced* from the preceding. (*Verum est formaliter in mente, ut conformitas iudicii cum re.* [Truth is formally in the mind, as the conformity of its judgment with reality.]) And for a human intellect, inasmuch as it does not see God, there are *many truths* relative *to one and the same Divine Reality*. Only God forms one, single truth concerning Himself.

Still, one adds: "Two propositions concerning the same subject and *really identical predicates* have a *really identical meaning*." For example: the soul is spiritual, and the soul is immortal. Or again: God is intelligent, and God is free, for there is not a real distinction between the divine attributes.[34]

This would mean that, precisely because they are not *really distinct*, the *divine attributes* have THE SAME MEANING, OR, IN OTHER WORDS, ARE SYNONYMS. Now, this is a nominalist thesis that was refuted by St. Thomas in *ST* I, q. 13, a. 4. It would follow, as the nominalists say, that one could say, "God punishes through mercy and pardons through justice." One would thus arrive at agnosticism.

It sometimes happens, as in the present case, that while believing oneself to combat the nominalist position, and by insisting on the divine reality in which the divine attributes are identified, one ends up in this form of nominalism, holding that *all the divine names are synonyms*, being only verbally distinct. From this perspective, divine justice and mercy would be no more distinct than *Tullius* and *Cicero*, and just as everywhere that the term *Tullius* is written, one could just as well write *Cicero*, so too everywhere that the term *justice* is written, one could

---

[33] Francisco Marín-Sola, *L'évolution homogène du dogme catholique* (Fribourg: Imprimerie et librairie de l'Oeuvre de Saint-Paul, 1924), vol. 2, 332ff.

[34] This is what Fr. Marín-Sola says in *Evolution homogène*, vol. 2, p. 333.

just as well write *mercy*. In-depth investigation into these question of speculative theology is manifestly of great importance concerning all these problems.

However, it is further insisted[35]: In order for an assertion to be defined as a dogma, it suffices that it be revealed *actu implicite*. Now, each divine attribute is contained *actu implicite* in the divine nature conceived as Subsistent Being, as well as in each of the other attributes. Therefore [every divine attribute is revealed and thus can be defined as a dogma.]

In accord with what we have said, we must respond by making a distinction in the claim that in order for an assertion to be defined as a dogma, it suffices that it be revealed *actu implicite*. *I concede* that this is true, on the condition that the truth in question is *the same truth* as the one which is revealed. However, *I deny* that this holds if it is a *new truth that has been deduced*.[36] Now, *I deny* that each divine attribute is contained *actu implicite* in the divine nature and in every other attribute, as *the same truth*. However, *I concede* that they are there as *another, deduced truth*.

Indeed, I concede that a given divine attribute is contained in the divine nature *actu implicite* by reason of the divine reality *ut res est*. However, I make a sub-distinction regarding the claim that there would be *the same truth* as an object of knowledge [*ratione obiecti*]. I concede the point for the case of the divine intellect and that of the intellects of the blessed. However, I deny that it would be the same truth for our intellect [in our current wayfaring state].[37]

Otherwise, all the divine names would be synonyms, and we would need to say: The two statements, "God is just," and "God is merciful," both state the same truth. They state *two truths concerning the same divine reality*.[38] Indeed, truth is formally in the mind. It is the conformity of its judgment with reality. Now, we are here not concerned with the divine mind, nor that of the blessed, but rather with our intellect, in relation to which one speaks of *revealed truths* and *other truths deduced* from the preceding. This is contrary to theologism, which would give, in a way that is similar to philosophism, too much importance to an acquired science;[39] however, this shows, along with the superiority of infused faith, the immense value of *revealed truth*.

---

35 Marín-Sola, *Evolution homogène*, 342ff.

36 Fr. Marín-Sola himself recognizes this in *Evolution homogène*, 333.

37 [Tr. note: Although I have kept some of the scholastic form above, including *nego* and *concedo*, this text required translation, for Fr. Garrigou-Lagrange slipped into Latin after the beginning of the first French sentence.]

38 When one says, "In God, justice is mercy," it is true as a *material*, not a *formal*, attribution or predication.

39 Between infused faith and acquired theology, there is a homogeneity that is not specific but quasi-generic; these are two *habitus* that are specifically distinct by their double formal object (*quod* and *quo*). However, the *theological habitus* has its root in infused faith, even though it is itself acquired, "*acquiritur studio humano*."

10

Where is the New Theology Headed?

Réginald Garrigou-Lagrange, OP

In[1] a recent book, *Conversion et grâce chez S. Thomas d'Aquin*,[2] Father Henri Bouillard writes, "When the mind evolves, an unchanging truth can only maintain itself by virtue of a simultaneous and correlative evolution of all notions, each proportionate to the others. *A theology that would not be contemporary would be a false theology.*"[3]

Moreover, in the pages preceding and following [the above quotation], the author demonstrates that the theology of St. Thomas, in several of its most important sections, is not contemporary. For example, St. Thomas conceived sanctifying grace as a *form* (a radical principle of supernatural operations, which have the infused virtues and the seven gifts as their accompanying principles). "The notions employed by St. Thomas are nothing more than Aristotelian notions applied to theology."[4]

What follows? "By renouncing the Aristotelian system of physics, modern thought abandoned the notions, the schemata, and the dialectical oppositions which only made sense as functions of that system."[5] Thus, modern thought abandoned the notion *of form*.

How then can the reader evade the conclusion, namely, that since it is no longer "contemporary," the theology of St. Thomas is a false theology?

But then, how is it that the Popes so often instructed us to follow the teaching of St. Thomas? Why does the Church say in her Code of Canon Law, Can. 1366, §2, "Professors shall treat studies in rational theology and

---

[1] [Tr. note (Minerd-Kirwan): In general, much of this translation retains the form in which it was found in the *Josephinum* edition cited in the introduction to our volume. However, on occasion, we have made small alterations to it for the sake of consistence with the whole of our volume or in order to correct minor translational issues.]

[2] Henri Bouillard, *Conversion et grâce chez S. Thomas d'Aquin* (Paris: Aubier, 1944), 219.

[3] Emphasis added by Fr. Garrigou-Lagrange.

[4] Bouillard, *Conversion*, 213ff.

[5] Bouillard, *Conversion*, 224.

philosophy and the instruction of students in these disciplines according to the system, teaching, and principles of the Angelic Doctor and hold to them religiously"?[6]

Moreover, how can "*an unchanging truth*" maintain itself if the two notions that are united by the verb *to be* are *essentially variable or changeable*?

An unchangeable relationship can only be conceived of as such if there is something unchangeable in the two terms it unites. Otherwise, for all intents and purposes, it's like saying that an iron clamp could still the waves of the sea.

Of course, the two notions that are united in an unchangeable affirmation are sometimes at first confused and then later distinguished one from the other, such as the notions of nature, person, substance, accident, transubstantiation, the Real Presence, sin, original sin, grace, etc. But if these are not fundamentally unchangeable, how then will the affirmation that unites them by the verb "to be" be unchangeable? How can one hold that the Real Presence of the substance of the Body of Christ in the Eucharist requires transubstantiation if the notions are fundamentally variable? How can one assert that original sin occurred in us through a willed fault of the first man, if the notion of original sin is essentially unstable? How can one hold that the particular judgment after death is eternally irrevocable, if these notions are said to change? Finally, how can one maintain that all of these propositions are invariably *true* if the notion of truth itself must change, and if one must substitute for the traditional definition of truth (the conformity of judgment to extra-mental reality and to its immutable laws) what has been proposed in recent years by the philosophy of action: the conformity of judgment to the exigencies of action or to human life, which is always evolving?

1. DO THE DOGMATIC FORMULAE THEMSELVES RETAIN THEIR IMMUTABILITY?

Father Henri Bouillard responds: "The affirmation which is expressed in them remains."[7] But he adds:

> Perhaps one might wonder if we could even assert that *the notions implied* in conciliar definitions are also contingent? Would this not compromise the irreformable character of these definitions? The Council of Trent (sess. 6, ch. 7, can. 10), for example, in its teaching on justification, employs the notion *of formal cause*. By so doing, did

---

[6] Taken from *The 1917 Pio-Benedictine Code of Canon Law*, ed. and trans. Edward N. Peters (San Francisco, CA: Ignatius Press, 2001), can. 1366, §2 (p. 460).

[7] Bouillard, *Conversion*, 221.

it not enshrine this term and confer a definitive character upon the notion of grace as a form? *Not at all.* It was certainly not the intention of the Council to canonize an Aristotelian notion, nor even a theological notion conceived under the influence of Aristotle. It simply wished to affirm, against the Protestants, that justification is an interior renewal.... To this end, it used some common notion in the theology of its era. *However, other notions can be substituted for these, without modifying the meaning of its teaching.*[8]

Undoubtedly, the Council did not canonize the Aristotelian notion of form with all of its relations to other notions used in the Aristotelian system. But it approved it as a *stable human notion,* in the sense that we speak of everything that formally constitutes a thing (in this case, justification).[9] In this sense, it speaks of sanctifying grace as distinct from actual grace by saying that it is an infused supernatural gift that inheres in the soul and by which man is formally justified.[10] If the Councils define faith, hope, and charity as permanently infused virtues, their radical principle (habitual or sanctifying grace) must also be a permanently infused gift and, from that, distinct from actual grace or a transitory divine motion.

But how can one maintain *the sense* of this teaching of the Council of Trent, namely, that "sanctifying grace is the formal cause of justification," if "*one substitutes another notion for that of formal cause*"?—I did not say, "if one substitutes an equivalent word," but as Father Bouillard says, "if one substitutes another notion."

If it is another notion, then it is no longer that *of formal cause:* then it is also no longer *true* to say with the Council: "Sanctifying grace is the formal cause of justification." It is necessary to be content to say that grace was understood at the time of the Council of Trent as the formal cause of justification, but today it is necessary to define it *differently;* this *passé* definition is no longer "contemporary" and thus is *no longer true,* since a doctrine that is no longer contemporary, as was said, is a false doctrine.[11]

---

8 Bouillard, *Conversion,* 221. [Emphasis is Fr. Garrigou-Lagrange's.]

9 I have explained this more fully in *Thomistic Common Sense: The Philosophy of Being and the Development of Doctrine,* trans. Matthew K. Minerd (Steubenville, OH: Emmaus Academic, 2021), 275–300.

10 See Council of Trent, *Decree on Justification,* ch. 7, Denzinger, nos. 1528–1529 [old no. 799]; Canons on Justification, can. 11, Denzinger, no. 1561 [old no. 821].

11 Further it is defined that the infused virtues (above all the theological virtues), which derive from habitual grace, are *qualities, permanent principles* of supernatural and meritorious operations; it is thus necessary that habitual or sanctifying grace (by which we are in a *state* of grace), from which these virtues proceed as from their source, be itself a *permanently infused quality* and not a motion like actual grace. Well, it was long before St. Thomas that faith, hope and charity were conceived as *infused virtues.* What could be

One will answer: for the notion of formal cause, one can substitute *another equivalent notion*. But this plays too fast and loose with terms (by insisting first on *another* and then on an *equivalent*), especially inasmuch as it is not verbal equivalence but, rather, *another notion*. What then becomes of even *the notion* of *truth*?[12]

Thus, the very serious question continues to resurface: does the conciliar proposition hold as *true* through conformity with being outside the mind and with its immutable laws or, rather, through conformity with the exigencies of human life, which are forever changing?

We can see the danger of the new definition of truth, no longer the *adaequatio rei et intellectus* (adequation of intellect and reality) but *conformitas mentis et vitae* (the agreement of mind and life). When Maurice Blondel in 1906 proposed this substitution, he did not foresee all of the consequences for the faith. He himself would be perhaps terrified or at least very troubled.[13] Which "life" is meant in this definition of: *"agreement of mind and life"*? It means human life. And so then, how can one avoid the Modernist proposi-

---

clearer? Why waste time under the pretext of advancing these questions and of putting into doubt the most certain and fundamental truths? To do so is an indication of the intellectual disarray of our times.

12 Blondel wrote in "Le point de depart de la recherché philosophique," *Les Annales de Philosophie chrétienne* 152 (June 15, 1906), 235: "By rights, in place of the abstract and chimerical 'Adaequatio speculativa rei et intellectus,' we must *substitute* methodical research, the *adaequatio realis mentis et vitae.*" It is not without great responsibility that one calls "chimerical" the traditional definition of the truth accepted for centuries in the Church, and that one speaks of *substituting* another one for it in all domains, including that of theological faith.

Have the most recent works of Blondel corrected this deviation? We are unable to ascertain that. He also says in *L'Etre et les êtres* (Paris: Felix Alcan, 1935), 415: "No intellectual evidence, *not even that of principles that are absolute of themselves*, having an ontological value, imposes itself upon us with a constraining form of certainty." In order to admit the ontological value of these principles, one must exercise *a free option*, and because of this choice, their ontological value is thus only probable. But it is necessary to admit them according to the demands of action *secundum conformitatem mentis et vitae*. It cannot be otherwise if one substitutes the *philosophy of action* for the *philosophy of being* or ontology. Thus truth is defined not as a function of being, but of action. Everything has changed. An error regarding the first notion of truth gives rise to an error regarding all the rest. See also in Blondel, *La Pensée* (Paris: Presses Universitaires de France, 1934 and 1935), vol. 1, 39, 130–36, 347, 355; and vol. 2, 65ff, 90, 96–196.

13 Another theologian, whom we shall cite further on, invites us to say that at the time of the Council of Trent *transubstantiation* was conceived as the changing, the conversion of the substance of the bread into that of the Body of Christ, but that today it has come to be thought of as *transubstantiation, without this changing of substance*, meaning that the substance of the bread, which remains, becomes the efficacious sign of the Body of Christ. And this pretends to conserve *the Council's meaning*!

tion: "Truth is no more immutable than man himself, since it evolved with him, in him, and through him."[14] We can understand why Pius X said of the Modernists, "They pervert the eternal concept of truth."[15]

It is very dangerous to say: "The notions change while the affirmation remains." If even the notion of truth is changing, then the affirmations do not remain true in the same way nor according to the same meaning. Therefore, *what the Counsels meant is* no longer maintained, as one would have wished.

Unfortunately, the new definition of truth has spread among those who forget what Pius X had said: "We admonish professors to bear well in mind that they cannot set aside St. Thomas *especially in metaphysical questions,* without grave disadvantage. 'A small error in principle,' we may thus use the very words of Aquinas himself, 'is a great error in conclusion.'"[16]

A fortiori is this true if one ignores all metaphysics, all ontology, and tends to substitute for the philosophy of being, that of phenomenalism [*du phénomenon*], or of becoming, or of action.

Moreover, is this not the new definition of truth that is found in the new definition of theology: "*Theology is no more than a spirituality or religious experience that has found its intellectual expression.*" And so follow assertions such as: "If theology can help us to understand spirituality, spirituality in turn will, in most cases, burst open our theological frameworks, and we shall be obliged to formulate different types of theology. . . . For to each great spirituality has corresponded a great theology." Does this mean that two theologies can be true, even if their main theses are contradictory and opposite? The answer will be "no" if one keeps to the traditional definition of truth. The answer will be "yes" if one adopts the new definition of truth, conceived not in relation to being and its immutable laws but relative to different religious experiences. This idea brings us remarkably close to Modernism.

We should recall that on December 1, 1924, the Holy Office condemned 12 propositions taken from the philosophy of action, among which was number 5, on the new definition of truth:

> Truth is not found in any particular act of the intellect wherein which there would be had conformity with the object, as the Scholastics have said, but rather truth is always in a state of becoming, and consists in a progressive adequation of the understanding with life,

---

14 Holy Office, *Lamentabili*, no. 58 (Denzinger, no. 3458 [old no. 2058]).

15 Pius X, *Pascendi dominici gregis*, no. 13 (Denzinger, old no. 2080)

16 [Tr. note: this last text refers to Aquinas's reference to Aristotle, which is found both in the opening line of the prologue to Aquinas's *De ente et essentia*, and in the *Summa contra gentiles*, bk. 2, ch. 2.]

namely, a certain perpetual process by which the intellect strives to develop and explain that which experience presents or action requires. However, it is a law that in all progression there is at no time anything which is determined or fixed.

The last of these condemned propositions is: "Even after having grasped matters of faith, man must not take up his rest regarding religious dogmas, adhering to them in a fixed and immobile manner.—Rather, he must forever remain anxious to progress onward to some further truth, namely, by developing a new meaning for what he believes, nay, also by correcting it."[17]

Many who did not heed these warnings have today reverted to these errors.

But then how can it be held that sanctifying grace is *essentially supernatural, gratuitous,* and not at all owed to human nature nor to angelic nature?

This question is clear for St. Thomas who, by the light of Revelation, clearly articulated this principle: faculties, *"habitus,"* and their acts are specified by their formal object; yet, the formal object of the human intellect, and even that of angelic intellects, is immensely inferior to the proper object of the divine intellect: the Godhead or the intimate life of God.[18] But if one puts aside all metaphysics and is satisfied with historical study and psychological introspection, then the text of St. Thomas becomes unintelligible.[19] From this point of view, what can be kept from the traditional doctrine regarding *the distinction,* not contingent but necessary, between *the order of grace* and *that of nature?*

On this subject, in the midst of remarks concerning the probable impeccability of the angels in the natural order, Fr. Henri de Lubac states,

---

17 These condemned propositions are found in *Monitore ecclesiastico* (1925), 194; in *Documentation catholique* (1925), vol. 1. 771ff., and in Fr. Pedro Descoqs, *Praelectiones Theologiae naturalis* (Paris: Beauchesne, 1932), vol. 1, 150; vol. 2, 287ff.

18 See *ST* I, q. 12, a. 4.

19 In Bouillard, *Conversion,* 169ff, arriving at the heart of the matter considered in his volume says, for example, that, regarding the immediate disposition to justification, St. Thomas (in *ST* I-II, q. 113, a. 8, ad 1) *"no longer makes appeal to reciprocal causality,"* as he does in his previous works. To the contrary, it is clear for every Thomist that he does speak of it and that it is what illuminates the whole matter. Moreover (and the point is elementary to recall), reciprocal causality is *always* found where the four causes are involved, that is to say: in all cases of becoming. Here it is said: "On the part of God justifying, by an order of nature, the *infusion of grace is prior to the remission of sins.* However, if we consider matters from the perspective of the man who is justified, *the liberation from sin is prior to the obtaining of justifying grace."* Every theological student who heard an article-by-article explanation of St. Thomas's treatise on grace will agree that this is a truth that cannot be ignored.

in his recent book, *Surnaturel (Études historiques)*:[20] "Nothing is said by St. Thomas regarding the distinction that would be forged later by a number of Thomistic theologians between 'God, Author of the natural order' and 'God, Author of the supernatural order'. . . as if the natural beatitude . . . in the case of the angels would have had to result from an infallible activity, incapable of sin."[21]

On the contrary, St. Thomas often distinguishes the ultimate supernatural end from the ultimate natural end,[22] and as far as what concerns the devil, he says,[23] "The sin of the devil was not in anything that pertains to the natural order but according to something supernatural."[24]

It is by this path that one would become completely disinterested in the *pronuntiata maiora,* or major pronouncements, of the philosophical doctrine of St. Thomas, that is to say, in the 24 Thomistic theses approved in 1916 by the Sacred Congregation of Studies.

Even more, Fr. Gaston Fessard, S.J., in the November 1945 issue of *Études,* speaks of the "blessed drowsiness that protects this canonized (but

---

20 Henri de Lubac, *Surnaturel* (Paris: Aubier, 1946), 254.

21 de Lubac, *Surnaturel,* 275.

22 See *ST* I, q. 23, a. 1:

> *The end to which God has ordered created things is twofold. One exceeds the proportion of human created nature and its powers,* and this end is eternal life, which consists in the vision of God [*divina visione*]. As we said earlier (in *ST* I, q. 12, a. 4), this is above any possible nature whatsoever. *However, the other end is proportioned to created nature*; that is, it can be attained by a created thing in accord with the power of its nature.

Likewise, in *ST* I-II, q. 62, a. 1: "However, as we said earlier (in *ST* I-II, q. 3, a. 2, ad 4; q. 5, a. 5), there is a *twofold beatitude,* or felicity, for man. One is proportioned to human nature, that is, as an end to which man can arrive through his nature's own principles. The other, however, is a beatitude which exceeds man's nature."

Likewise, in *De veritate,* q. 14, a. 2: "*However, man has a twofold ultimate good.* One of them is proportioned to nature . . . and this is the felicity spoken of by the philosophers. . . . The other the is a good which exceeds what is proportioned to human nature." If one no longer accepts the classical distinction between the order of nature and that of grace, one will say that grace is the normal and obligatory achievement of nature, and the granting of such a favor nonetheless would remain, one says, free, like creation and all that follows it, because creation was not at all necessary. To which Fr. Descoqs, S.J., in his little book, *Autour de la crise du Transformisme,* 2nd ed. (Paris: Beauchesne, 1944), 84, very rightly responds: "This explanation seems to us in distinct opposition to the most explicit Catholic teachings. It also contains an evidently erroneous conception of grace. Creation is never a grace in the theological sense of the word, grace only being able to be found in relation to nature. In such a perspective, *the supernatural order disappears.*"

23 *De malo,* q.16, a.3.

24 "*Peccatum diaboli non fuit in aliquo quod pertinet ad ordinem naturalem, sed secundum aliquid supernaturale.*" *ST* I, q. 63, a.1, ad 3.

also, in Péguy's words, 'interred') Thomism, while thought dedicated to its contradiction is full of life."[25]

In the same review in April 1946, it was said that neo-Thomism and the decisions of the Biblical Commission are "a guardrail but not an answer." Yes, what is proposed to replace Thomism, as if Leo XIII in the Encyclical *Aeterni Patris had been wrong* and as if Pius X, in renewing this same recommendation, had gone down the wrong path? And where is this new theology headed, with the new teachers it has inspired? Where but onto the road of skepticism, fantasy and heresy? His Holiness, Pius XII, recently said in a published Discourse in *L'Osservatore Romano,* Dec. 19, 1946:

> There is a good deal of talk (but without a sufficient testing of its character), about a "new theology" which is in constant transformation, following the example of all other things in the world, which are in a constant state of flux and movement, without ever reaching their term. If we were to accept such an opinion, *what would become of the unchangeable dogmas of the Catholic Faith; and what would become of the unity and stability of that Faith?*

2. APPLICATION OF NEW PRINCIPLES TO THE DOCTRINES OF ORIGINAL SIN AND THE EUCHARIST

Some will no doubt say that we exaggerate, but even a small error regarding first notions and first principles has incalculable consequences which are not foreseen by those who are thus mistaken. Therefore, the consequences of the new views, some of which we have already reviewed, must go well beyond what the authors we have cited foresaw. For example, it is difficult not to see these consequences in certain typewritten papers, which have been sent (some even since 1934) to clergy, seminarians, and Catholic intellectuals; one finds in them the most singular assertions and denials concerning original sin and the Real Presence.

At times, in these same circulated papers, before such novelties are proposed, the reader is forestalled by being told: this will appear crazy at first, however, if you look at it closely, it is not without probability and is accepted by many. Those with superficial intelligence are taken in, and the dictum, "*A doctrine that is not contemporary is no longer true*" forges ahead. Some are tempted to conclude: "It seems that the doctrine of the eternal pains of hell is no longer of contemporary relevance, and for that reason it is no longer true." Yet, it is said in the Gospel that one day the love of many persons will grow cold and that they will be seduced by error.

---

[25] Gaston Fessard, [Review of Joseph de Tonquédec, *Un philosophie existentielle. L'Existence d'après Jaspers,*"] *Études* 247 (Nov. 1945): 269–70.

It is a strict obligation of conscience for traditional theologians to respond. Otherwise, they gravely neglect their duty, and they will be made to account for this before God.

In the documents mimeographed and distributed in France in recent years (at least since 1934, according to those which this writer possesses), the most fanciful and false doctrines regarding original sin are being taught.

* * * * *

In these same documents, the act of *Christian faith* is not defined as a supernatural and infallible adherence to revealed truths on account of the authority of God Who reveals them (*propter auctoritatem Dei revelantis*) but as an adherence of the soul to a general perspective of the universe. This general perspective entails a perception of what is possible and *most probable* but not demonstrable. The Faith becomes an ensemble of probable opinions. From this point of view, Adam no longer appears as an individual man from whom the human species is descended but rather as a group of men.

Thus, from that point of view, one can no longer see how it would be possible to hold to the revealed doctrine of original sin as explicated by St. Paul in Romans 5:18: "Therefore as *through the offense of one,* all men are given unto condemnation; so also *through the justice of one,* all men are given unto the justification of life. Just as through the disobedience of one, the many are made sinners, so also through the obedience of one, many are made just." All of the Fathers of the Church, who are the authorized interpreters of Scripture, in their constant sacred teaching, whether ordinary or solemn, have always understood that Adam was an individual man as Christ was after him and not a group of men.[26] But what is now proposed to us is a probability with a meaning opposed to that of the teaching of the Councils of Orange and Trent.[27]

---

26 See Marie-Joseph Lagrange, *L'Épitre aux Romains*, 3rd ed. (Paris: J. Gabalda, 1931), commentary on chapter 5.

27 See 2nd Council of Orange, can. 2 (Denzinger no. 372 [old no. 175]); Council of Trent, *Decree on Original Sin*, can. 2 and 4 (Denzinger, nos. 1512 and 1514 [old nos. 789 and 791]); *Decree on Justification*, ch. 1 (Denzinger, no. 1521 [old no. 793]).

The difficulties for the positive sciences and for prehistory were set forth in the article "Polygenism" in *Dictionnaire de theologie catholique* (Paris: Letouzey et Ané, 1935): cols. 2520–36. The authors of this article, Amédée and Jean Bouyssonie, clearly distinguished, in col. 2536, the purview of philosophy as being "Where the naturalist, as such, is incompetent." It would have been well if, in that same article, the question had been treated from three points of view: the positive sciences, philosophy, and theology, particularly in relation to the dogma of original sin.

Furthermore, following this new point of view, the Incarnation of the Word would be merely a moment of universal evolution.

The hypothesis of the material evolution of the world is now extended into the spiritual order. The supernatural world is in evolution toward the full coming of Christ.

Sin, in so far as it affects the soul, is something spiritual and therefore timeless. Consequently, they say, it is of little importance for God whether it took place at the beginning of the history of humanity or during the course of the ages.

Therefore, original sin in us is no longer a sin that depends on the willful misconduct of the first man, but it comes from the mistakes of men who have influenced humanity.

Following this line of reasoning, one desires in this way to change not only the manner of explaining theology *but even the very nature of theology* and, even more, that of dogma. Dogma itself is no longer considered from the viewpoint of the faith given by divine Revelation and interpreted by the Church in her Councils. It is no longer even a question of the Councils; here one places himself in the point of view of biology, completed by the most fanciful rantings that recall those of Hegelian evolutionism and which retain nothing of Christian dogmas but the name.

In all of this, we but follow the way of the rationalists, and in so doing we do what the enemies of the faith want most: we reduce the faith to ever-changing opinions so that there is no value retained in them. What remains of the word of God given to the world for the salvation of souls?

In these pages, bearing the title, "How I believe," we read (cf. p. 15):

> If we wish, we Christians, to conserve for Christ the qualities that are the basis of His power and our adoration, we can do nothing better or even nothing more than to accept completely the most modern notions of evolution. Under the combined pressure of science and philosophy, the World stands out more and more to our experience and our thought

---

According to several theologians, the hypothesis according to which there were men on earth whose race was extinct before Adam is not contrary to the faith. But according to Scripture, the human race that lives on earth derives from Adam. See Gen 3:5–20; Wis 10:1; Rom 5:12, 18, 19; Acts 17:26.

Moreover, regarding the philosophical point of view, a free intervention of God in creating the human soul was necessary, and even for preparing the body to receive it. The begetting of an inferior nature cannot, however, produce this superior state of his species; more would come out of less, contrary to the principle of causality.

Finally, as is said in aforementioned article (col. 2535): "According to the mutationists (*mutationistes*) of today, a unique seed gave rise to the new species. *The species was begun by an exceptional individual.*"

as an intertwined system of activities gradually lifting itself toward freewill and consciousness. The only satisfying interpretation of this process is that of regarding it as irreversible and convergent. Thus, this convergence has been defined, even before us [Christians], as a *cosmic Universal Center*, where all leads, where all is felt, where everything is ordered. And so, it is in this physical pole of the universal evolution where it is necessary, in my opinion, to locate and recognize *the plenitude of Christ*. . . . Evolution, in discovering the apex of the world, renders Christ possible, just as Christ, in giving meaning to the world, makes evolution possible.

I am perfectly aware of the staggering proportions of this notion, . . . but by imagining a parallel wonder, I do nothing else but transcribe, in terms of physical reality, the juridical expressions in which the Church deposits her Faith. . . . I have unhesitatingly come to the realization that I can only go in that direction that seems possible to me for making progress and, consequently, for saving my faith.

At first blush, Catholicism had disappointed me with its narrow definitions of the World and by its failure to understand the role of Matter. Now, I recognize that by means of the Incarnation of God, which Catholicism reveals to me, that I am only able to be saved by becoming one body with the universe. And, by the same token, these most profound "pantheistic" hopes of mine are fulfilled, reassured and directed. *The World* around me, *becomes divine*.

A general convergence of religions toward a universal-Christ, which, fundamentally, fulfills all of them: this appears to me to be the only conversion possible for the World and the only form imaginable for the Religion of the future.[28]

---

[28] Emphasis added [by Fr. Garrigou-Lagrange]. Ideas that are nearly as fanciful are found in an article by Fr. Teilhard de Chardin, "Vie et planètes: Que se passe-t-il en ce moment sur la terre," *Études* 249 (May 1946): 145–69, especially 158–60 and 168. See also, by the same author, "Un grand Evènement qui se dessine: le Planetisation humaine," in *Cahiers du Monde nouveau* 2 (August 1946): 1–13.

One has recently quoted a text by the same author, ["Comment se pose aujourd'hui la question du transformisme"] in *Études* (1921), 543, where he spoke of "The impossibility of determining *an absolute beginning* of our spirit in the order of phenomena." To this, Georges Salet and Louis Lafont rightly responded in *L'Évolution regressive* (Paris: Éditions Franciscaines, 1943), 47: "Isn't creation an absolute beginning?" Well, faith tells us that God daily creates the souls of babies and that in the beginning He created the spiritual soul of the first man. Moreover, miracles also are absolute beginnings, something that is not at all incompatible with reason. On this point, see Descoqs, *Autour de la crise du transformisme*, 85.

Finally, as Father Descoqs remarked, in *Autour de la crise*, 2 and 7, theologians should not be speaking so much about evolutionism and transformism anymore, since the best minds, such as Lemoine, Professor at the Museum, write: "Evolution is a kind of dogma

Thus, the material world might have evolved toward spirit, and the world of the spirit would evolve naturally, so to say, toward the supernatural order and toward the fullness of Christ. In this way, the Incarnation of the Word, the mystical body, the universal Christ would be moments in the process of Evolution, and based on this view of a constant progress from the beginning, it would seem that there was not a fall at the beginning of the history of humanity but a constant progress of good, which triumphs over evil according to the same laws of evolution. Original sin in us would be merely the sequela of the faults of human beings, which have exercised a deadly influence on all humanity thereafter.

See now what remains of the Christian dogmas in this theory, which distances itself from our "*Credo*" in proportion to its approach to Hegelian evolutionism.

In the above-cited work, the writer said: "I have taken the only road that seems possible to me *for making* progress and *consequently, for saving my Faith.*" This therefore means that the Faith itself is only conserved *if it progresses*, and it changes so much so that one can no longer recognize in it the Faith of the Apostles, of the Fathers, and of the Councils. It is but one way of applying the principle of the new theology: "A doctrine that is no longer contemporary is no longer true," and for some, it suffices that it is no longer contemporary only *in certain quarters*. From this principle, it emerges that the truth is always *in fieri* [in process], never immutable. The Faith is the conformity of judgment, not with being and its necessary laws, but with life, which is constantly and forever evolving. We now see exactly how far the aforementioned propositions condemned by the Holy Office, December 1, 1924 lead: "No abstract proposition can have in itself immutable truth."—"Even after having grasped matters of faith, man must not take up his rest regarding religious dogmas, adhering to them in a fixed and immobile manner. Rather, he must forever remain anxious to *progress* onward to some further truth, namely, *by developing a new meaning for what he believes, nay, also by correcting it.*"[29]

---

which its priests do not believe, but that they hold for their people. It is necessary to have the courage to say so, so that the men of the next generation will conduct their research by other methods" (see Conclusion of vol. 5 of *L'Encyclopédie française* [Paris: Société de gestion de l'Encydopédie Française, 1937]). Dr. Henri Rouvière, professor in the School of Medicine of Paris, member of the Academy of Medicine, also writes in *Anatomie philosophique, La finalité dans l'Évolution* (Paris: Masson, 1941), 37: "The doctrine of transformism has suffered a veritable collapse.... The majority of biologists have distanced themselves from it because the defenders of transformism have never produced the least proof to support their theory and everything known about evolution contradicts their contentions."

29 See *Monitore ecclesiastico* (1925), 194.

* * * * *

We have another example of a similar deviation in the typewritten papers on the Real Presence, which have been circulating for some months among the clergy. These say that, up to now, the true problem with the Real Presence was not well posed: "The response to all of the difficulties that were posed was: Christ is *present after the manner of a substance*. . . . This explanation only side-stepped the real problem. Let us add, moreover, that in its deceptive clarity, it actually suppressed the religious mystery. Strictly speaking, there is no longer a mystery there; there is nothing more than a marvel."

Thus, it is St. Thomas who did not know how to pose the problem of the Real Presence and his solution, that the presence of the Body of Christ *by mode of substance*, would be illusory; its clarity is a *deceptive clarity*. We are warned that the new explication being proposed "evidently implies that we substitute the Cartesian and Spinozan method of reflection for the Scholastic method."

A bit further on, concerning *transubstantiation*, one reads: "This word is not without drawbacks, like that of original sin. It corresponds to the way the Scholastics conceived of and defined this transformation, and *their definition is inadmissible*."

Yet, here the writer distances himself not only from St. Thomas, but also from the Council of Trent,[30] for the latter defined transubstantiation as a truth of faith, and even said: "a change which the Catholic Church most fittingly calls transubstantiation." Today these new theologians say: "Not only is this word unsuitable, . . . it corresponds to an inadmissible understanding and definition."

> In the Scholastic perspective, in which the reality of the thing is 'the substance,' the thing may only really change if the substance changes . . . by transubstantiation. According to the current view, where, by virtue of the offering made according to a rite determined by Christ, *the bread and the wine became the efficacious symbol of the sacrifice of* Christ and consequently of His *spiritual presence, because their religious being was changed,* but not their substance.[31]

---

30 Council of Trent, *Decree on the Most Holy Eucharist*, ch. 4 and can. 2 (Denzinger, nos. 1642 and 1652 [old nos. 877 and 884]).

31 In the same place, we are told: "In the scholastics' perspective, the notion of *thing-sign* was lost. In an Augustinian universe, where a material thing is not only itself, but rather a sign of spiritual realities, one can conceive that a thing, being through the will of God the sign of another thing than what it was by nature, might become *something else* without changing its appearance."

From the scholastic perspective, the notion of thing-sign was not at all lost. Saint Thomas says, *ST* I, q. 1, a.10: "The Author of Sacred Scripture is God, in whose power it lies not

And also: "This is what we can designate by transubstantiation."

But it is clear that this is no longer the transubstantiation defined by the Council of Trent, "that wonderful and unique change of the whole substance of the bread into his body and of the whole substance of the wine into his blood while only the appearance [*species*] of bread and wine remain."[32] It is evident that the meaning of the Council is not maintained by the introduction of these new notions. The bread and the wine have become only "the efficacious symbol of the spiritual presence of Christ."

This brings us singularly close to the Modernist position, which does not affirm the Real Presence of the Body of Christ in the Eucharist, but which only says, from a religious and practical point of view: behave toward the Eucharist the same way you behave with regard to the humanity of Christ.

In these same circulated papers, quite the same is done to the mystery of the Incarnation: "Although Christ is truly God, one cannot say that because of Him, God was present in the land of Judea. . . . God was no more present in Palestine than anywhere else. The *efficacious* sign of this divine presence was manifested in Palestine in the first century of our era, and this is all that one can say."[33]

Finally, the same writer adds: "The problem of the causality of the sacraments is a false problem, born of a false method for posing the question."

* * * * *

---

only to give words their meanings (something that man also can do) but even to do so for things themselves." Thus, Isaac who is prepared to be sacrificed is the figure of Christ, and the manna is a figure of the Eucharist. St. Thomas notes this when speaking of this sacrament. But by the Eucharistic consecration the bread does not only become the sign of the Body of Christ and the wine the sign of His Blood, as the sacramentaries of the Protestants thought. See L. Christiani, "Sacramentaire (controverse)," *Dictionnaire de Théologie Catholique*, ed. Alfred Vacant et al., vol. 14.1 (Paris: Letouze et Ané, 1939), 441–65. However, as was formally defined at the Council of Trent, the substance of bread is *converted* into that of the Body of Christ, which becomes present *per modum substantiae* under the species of bread. And this is not only germane to the theologians of the era of the Council regarding the consecration. It is the immutable truth defined by the Church.

[32] Council of Trent, *Decree on the Most Holy Eucharist*, can. 2 (Denzinger, no. 1652 [old no. 884]).

[33] St. Thomas clearly distinguished the three presences of God: first, the general presence of God in all the creatures that He keeps in existence (*ST* I, q.8, a.1); second, the special presence of God in the just by grace. He is in them as in a temple, as a quasi-experientially recognized object (*ST* I, q. 43, a. 3); third, the presence of the Word in the humanity of Jesus through the hypostatic union. Thus, it is certain that after the Incarnation, God was more present in the land of Judea than elsewhere. But when one thinks that St. Thomas did not even know how to pose these problems, then one goes off into all types of flights of fancy and returns to Modernism with the off-handedness that can be found on every one of these pages.

We do not think that the writers whom we have discussed abandoned the doctrine of St. Thomas. Rather, they never adhered to it, because they never understood it very well. This is saddening and disquieting.

Wouldn't it be that only skeptics can be formed through this type of teaching, since nothing solid is proposed in place of St. Thomas? Moreover, they pretend to submit to the directions of the Church, but what is the substance of this submission?

A professor of theology wrote to me:

> In effect, the very notion of the truth has been put into debate, and without fully realizing it, we return toward modernism in thought as in action. The writings that you have spoken to me about are much read in France. It is true that they exercise a huge influence on the average type of soul. However, they have little effect on serious people. Therefore, it is necessary to write for those who have the sincere desire to be enlightened.

According to some, the Church has only recognized the authority of St. Thomas in the domain of theology but not directly in philosophy. Contrary to their assertions, the Encyclical of Leo XIII, *Aeterni Patris,* speaks above all of the philosophy of St. Thomas. Likewise, the twenty-four Thomistic theses proposed in 1916 by the Sacred Congregation of Studies are of the philosophical order, and if these *pronunciata maiora* of St. Thomas do not have certitude, then how can his theology have value, since they are constantly reiterated in philosophy? Finally, we have already cited Pius X, who wrote in his Encyclical *Pascendi*: "We admonish professors to bear well in mind that they cannot set aside St. Thomas, *especially in metaphysical questions,* without grave disadvantage. *A small error in principle,* says Aquinas, *is a great error in conclusion.*"

What is the source of these trends? A good analyst wrote to me:

> We are harvesting the fruits of the unguarded attendance of university courses. Those who have attempted to attend the classes of the masters of Modernist thought in order to convert them have allowed themselves to be converted by them. Little by little, they come to accept their notions, their methods, their disdain of Scholasticism, their historicism, their idealism and all of their errors. If this is the result for those already formed, it is surely perilous for the others.

CONCLUSION

Where is the New Theology headed? It returns to Modernism because it accepted the proposition that was intrinsic to modernism: that of replacing, as if it were chimerical, the traditional definition of truth, *adaequatio rei et intellectus* [the adequation of intellect and reality], with the subjective definition, *adaequatio realis mentis et vitae* [the adequation of intellect and life]. That was more explicitly stated in the already cited proposition, which emerged from the philosophy of action, and was condemned by the Holy Office, December 1, 1924:

> Truth is not found in any particular act of the intellect wherein which conformity with the object would be had, as the Scholastics have said, but rather truth is always in a state of becoming and consists in a progressive adequation of understanding with life, namely, a certain perpetual process by which the intellect strives to develop and explain that which experience presents or action requires. However, it is a law that in all progression there is at no time anything which is determined or fixed.[34]

The truth is no longer the conformity of judgment to extra-mental reality and its immutable laws but the conformity of judgment to the exigencies of action and to human life, which is always evolving. The philosophy of being, or ontology, is substituted by the philosophy of action, which defines truth as no longer a function of being but of action.

One thus returns to the Modernist position: "Truth is no more immutable than man himself, since it evolved with him, in him, and through him."[35] As Pius X said rightly of the Modernists, "they pervert the eternal concept of truth."

This is what our master, Fr. Marie-Benoît Schwalm, in his articles in *Revue thomiste* (1896 through 1898) foresaw concerning the philosophy of action, the moral dogmatism of Fr. Laberthonnière, the crisis of contemporary apologetics, the illusions of idealism, and the dangers that all of these posed to the Faith.[36]

But while many thought that Fr. Schwalm had exaggerated, little by little they conceded the right of full citizenship to the new definition of truth, and they more or less ceased defending the traditional definition of truth: the conformity of judgment to extra-mental reality and to its immutable laws of non-contradiction, of causality, etc. For them, the truth is no longer *that which is* but *that which is becoming*, and it is constantly and always changing.

---

34 See *Monitore ecclesiastico* (1925), vol. 1, 194.

35 Decree of the Holy Office, *Lamentabili*, no. 58 (Denzinger, no. 3458 [old no. 2058]).

36 Marie-Benoît Schwalm, "L'acte de foi, est-il raisonnable?" *Revue thomiste* 1 (old series) (1896): 36–63; "Les illusions de l'idéalisme et leurs dangers pour la foi," *Revue thomiste* 1 (1896): 413–41; "L'apologétique contemporaine," *Revue thomiste* 2 (1897): 62–92; "La crise et l'apologétique," *Revue thomiste* 2 (1897): 239–71; "La croyance naturelle et la science," *Revue thomiste* 2 (1897): 627–45; "Le dogmatisme du coeur et celui de l'esprit," *Revue thomiste* 3 (1898): 578–619.

And yet to cease to defend the traditional definition of truth, allowing it to be said that it is merely *chimerical* and that one must substitute for it a vitalist and evolutionary definition, leads to complete relativism, and that is a very serious error.

Moreover, although we do not always reflect on it, this leads to saying what the enemies of the Church wish to hear us say. When one reads their recent works, one sees that they are completely content and that they themselves propose interpretations of our dogmas, whether it be regarding original sin, *cosmic evil*, the Incarnation, Redemption, the Eucharist, the final universal restoration, *the cosmic Christ*, or the convergence of all religions toward a universal cosmic center.[37]

One understands, therefore, why the Holy Father in his recent speech published in the September 19, 1946, issue of *L'Osservatore Romano*, said, when speaking of the "new theology": "If we were to accept such an opinion, *what would become of the unchangeable dogmas of the Catholic Faith; and what would become of the unity and stability of that Faith?*"

Moreover, since Providence only permits evil for a greater good, and since we see all about us an excellent reaction against the errors we have emphasized herein, we can hope that these deviations shall be the occasion of a true doctrinal renewal, achieved through a more profound study of the works of St. Thomas, whose value is more and more apparent when compared to today's intellectual disarray.[38]

---

[37] Authors such as Téder [i.e., Charles Détré] and Papus [i.e., Gérard Encausse] in their explanation of the *Martinist doctrine* [*Rituel de l'ordre martiniste* (Paris: Dorbon-Aîné, 1913)], teach a mystical pantheism and a neo-gnosticism by which all beings come from God by emanation (thus, there is a fall, a *cosmic evil*, a *sui generic* original sin), and all aspire *to be reintegrated* into the divinity, and *all* shall arrive there. This is in many recent occultists' works on the *modern Christ* and his *fullness in terms of astral light*, ideas not at all those of the Church and which are blasphemous inversions, because they are always the pantheistic negation of the true supernatural and often even the negation of the distinction of moral good and of moral evil in order to allow only that which is a useful or desired good and of cosmic or physical evil, which *with the reintegration of all, without exception*, will disappear.

[38] Certainly, we admit that *true mystical experience*, which proceeds in the just from the gifts of the Holy Spirit, particularly the gift of wisdom, *confirms the faith*, because it shows us that the revealed mysteries correspond to our highest aspirations and arouse even higher ones. We recognize that there is a truth of life, a conformity of the spirit, with the life of the man of good will, and a peace which is a sign of truth. But this mystical experience *presupposes* infused faith, and the act of faith itself presupposes the evident credibility of the revealed mysteries.

Likewise, as the [First] Vatican Council expresses it, we are able to have, by the natural light of reason, *the certainty that God exists as the author of nature*. Solely because of that, it is necessary that *the principles* of these proofs, in particular that of causality, be *true* per *conformitatem ad ens extramentale*, and that they are demonstrable through *objectively sufficient certainty* (prior a *priori* to the free choice [*option*] of men of good will), and not only through a *subjectively sufficient certainty*, like that of the Kantian proof of the existence of God.

Finally, *the practical truth* of prudence (*per conformitatem ad intentionem rectam*) supposes that our intention is truly rectified in relation to the ultimate end of man and the judgment of the end of men must be true *secundum mentis conformitatem ad realitatem extramentalem*. See *ST* I-II, q. 19, a. 3, ad 2.

11

Truth and the Immutability of Dogma

Réginald Garrigou-Lagrange, OP

In the April–June 1947 issue of the *Bulletin de littérature ecclésiastique*, published by the Catholic Institute of Toulouse, Msgr. Bruno Solages examined the article we recently published in *Angelicum*.[1] In this article, we would like to briefly respond, in an objective manner, to the objections that have been registered against us.[2]

* * * * *

Above all, we critiqued the new definition of truth proposed by Maurice Blondel when he wrote in the *Annales de philosophie chrétienne* in 1906: "By

---

[1] See Reginald Garrigou-Lagrange, "La nouvelle théologie, où va-t-elle?," *Angelicum* 23 (1946): 126–45.

[2] As in our first article, our sole perspective remains on the level of ideas, attempting to speak about persons as little as possible. Such was the method used by St. Thomas, who generally did not name the theologians of his era whose opinions he could not accept. He was content with saying, "*Quidam dicunt*...."

We regret the fact that we must once again cite Maurice Blondel, with whom we have had friendly relations in private letters. However, we feel compelled to do so, for a number of people build upon his most ruinous theses and upon a dangerous use of vocabulary, which lends itself to equivocation. What forces us to cite him is the obvious influence his philosophy of action is having, above all in apologetics, upon the thought of a number of contemporary theologians. Nonetheless, the reader should understand well that we are solely concerned with the objective meaning and logical implications of Blondel's assertions, without in any way attributing to him the way they are applied in domains that are no longer his own. Thus, *a fortiori*, we do not question his personal faith nor even the good that has been brought about by his philosophy for certain minds [*esprits*]. We recognize that his last works indicate a manifest intention to remedy issues that existed in his earlier writings and that they express thoughts having an undeniable loftiness.

In order to understand what will follow in our discussions here, it is necessary to see clearly, against nominalism, the measureless distance separating *the intellectual idea of intelligible being* from a sensible image accompanied by a common name, as well as that separating judgments, whose soul is the verb *to be*, from empirical associations of two images, and finally, the measureless distance separating reasoning, which manifests a *raison d'être*, from empirical sequences of facts [*consécutions*], which do not render *intelligible* the empirical conclusions to which they lead.

rights, in place of the abstract and *chimerical 'Adaequatio speculativa rei et intellectus,'* we must *substitute* methodical research, the *adaequatio realis mentis et vitae*."³

When we referred to this text in the past, we forgot to include the word "speculativa." However, this does not change its meaning in any way, for it is clear that this traditional definition is concerned with speculative truth. Our criticism thus stands as before. Can we call this traditional definition "chimerical," and must we "substitute" another definition for it, namely: the conformity of the mind with the requirements of life and action? Does not this new definition of truth slide toward pragmatism, as Émile Boutroux noted in his criticisms of the philosophy of action in 1908?⁴

Thus, a number of questions arise for both the metaphysician and for the theologian.⁵

The traditional definition of truth, holding that it is *conformity to reality and its immutable laws*, is commonly admitted for the truth of first principles,⁶ the conclusions of the proofs of God's existence,⁷ the affirmation of the fact of revelation along with the probative force of miracles,⁸ and the truth of all revealed dogmas.⁹ If this traditional definition of truth is proclaimed to be "chimerical," and if another definition must be "substituted" for it, what will be the value of the Conciliar definitions that presuppose it? For all these truths, must we content ourselves with the *conformity* of the

---

3 Blondel, "Le point de depart de la recherché philosophique,"*Annales de philosophie chrétienne* 152 (June 15, 1906): 235.

4 See Émile Boutroux, *Science et religion dans la philosophie contemporaine* (Paris: Flammarion, 1908), 296.

5 No doubt, we do not know *everything* that exists in reality, even in infinitely small affairs [*dans les infiniments petits*], a fact that marks out the great difference separating our knowledge and that had by the angels and, above all, by God. However, truth formally exists in judgment, and here we are concerned with knowing the nature of the truth belonging to judgments that are universally recognized in the Church as being *true*.

6 Through the *necessitating evidence* of their real value.

7 They do not have a merely *subjectively sufficient* certitude, like Kant's proof of God's existence but, rather, have an *objectively sufficient* certitude based on the very strength of the demonstration in question, *independent of the requirements of action*.

8 The fact of revelation is affirmed by the probative force of the various signs that confirm it and not only because it corresponds to our aspirations, which find a satisfaction in the Christian religion. See [First] Vatican Council, *Dei filius*, ch. 3 (Denzinger, no. 3009 [old no. 1790]) and canon 3.4 (Denzinger, no. 3034 [old no. 3034]); Pius X, *Sacrorum antistitum* / Anti-Modernist Oath (Denzinger, no. 3542 [old no. 2145]).

9 That *Jesus is God* is affirmed on account of God who reveals and not only because we should behave toward Him as though we were faced with God.

mind (or of judgment) with the *requirements of life and of human action, which forever evolves*?[10]

* * * * *

In his last works, did Blondel retract the words "chimerical" and "substitute"? We answered: we cannot hold that he has done so, and we can indeed cite a text from his work *L'Être et les êtres*. Here it is in a more complete form:

> *No intellectual evidence, not even that of principles* that are absolute of themselves, having a necessary ontological value, *imposes itself on us with a spontaneously and infallibly constraining certitude*, any more than does our real idea of the absolute Good act on our will, as though we already had the intuitive vision of perfect goodness, which alone is able to captivate our utterly free love.[11]

Thus, as we said, given that our love for God here-below is *free*, it follows that the option [or, choice,] by which we adhere to the ontological value of the principle of contradiction is likewise *free*, contrary to what is announced by the title of this same page, which speaks of an intellectual option that is "prior to the application of free choice." Moreover, we are told several pages later: "We now see what initial elaboration and what kind of an intellectual *option* are at work in minds depending on whether they allow themselves to be taken in by worldly seductions or, instead, *free themselves by giving preference to* the truth in a wholly-disinterested fashion."[12]

Is not this preference free? The fact that the exercise of such an option is free was affirmed many times by Blondel in his earlier works, as we will point out.[13] Here, in *Être et les êtres*, we find him laudably striving to reconnect with

---

10 This is why 12 propositions extracted from the philosophy of action were condemned by the Holy Office on Dec. 1, 1924 (cf. *Monitore ecclesiastico* (1925), 194ff). As we have shown elsewhere, among them is numbered the new definition of truth, which leads to two modernist propositions. One of them denies the immutability of truth: "Truth is no more immutable than man" (Pius X, *Lamentabili*, no. 58; Denzinger, no. 3458 [old no., 2058]). The other pertains to the nature of dogmas: "The dogmas of the faith are to be held only according to their practical sense; that is to say, as preceptive norms of conduct and not as norms of believing" (Pius X, *Lamentabili*, no. 26; Denzinger, no. 3426 [old no., 2026]).

If the Christian religion were only the most incontestably lofty form of the natural evolution of religious sentiment, its dogmas and precepts could forever evolve in an intrinsic fashion. However, it is incomparably superior to this. It has an essentially supernatural origin, and the doctrine that it teaches is the immutable word of God.

11 See Maurice Blondel, *L'Être et les êtres* (Paris: Felix Alcan, 1935), 415.

12 Blondel, *L'Être et les êtres*, 419.

13 Moreover, what would a non-free option even be? "Option" means choice, and properly speaking, a choice is free. Blondel, pressed by objections coming from theologians, no

traditional realism and to respond to the constant objection registered against him: "However, the first principles have a necessitating evidence."[14] He ends by acknowledging that this is so for those who stand at a superior perspective and "look upon things from on high," namely, for the wise.[15] However, we say that the only way that the wise could arrive at this reflective metaphysical certitude is if every man's natural understanding already spontaneously adheres to this truth: no being can exist [sic] and not exist at the same time.[16] To deny this truth or to place it in doubt is to dash the intellect against rocky shoals, thereby leading to its death.[17]

Thus, in order to sympathetically interpret this chapter from Blondel, we must at least admit that the proposition from page 415 cited above, "*No intellectual evidence ... imposes itself on us. ...*," is not true in itself. Only the following is true: "*Certain* minds are *so poorly disposed* that they seek *to pull back from the natural evidence* of the principle of contradiction as a law of being." Led by their prejudices and their own sophistical dialectic to deny the real value of this principle or to place it in doubt, even Protagoras, Kant, or Hegel themselves admitted that, at one and the same time, Protagoras cannot simultaneously be and not be Protagoras.[18]

---

longer speaks of a free option here. Nonetheless, he forever continues to hold onto the word "option" and, contrary to what would be desired by classical theologians, he does not speak of *a natural and necessary* adherence to the real value of the first principles on account of their necessitating evidence.

14 Blondel, *L'Être et les êtres*, 415–22.

15 Blondel, *L'Être et les êtres*, 418.

16 See *ST* I-II, q. 17, a. 6.

17 We have been accused of wishing to impose Thomism upon all. Here, we are only asking whether one admits the real value of the principle of contradiction. Nothing less could be asked for.

18 Often enough, Blondel confuses, even in his last works, *accidental deformations* with the *nature* of a faculty that is essentially related to its proper object. Thus, he writes in *La Pensée*, vol. 2 (Paris: Felix Alcan, 1934), 431:

> So-called sense intuition is deceptive ... and the so-called intuition of consciousness is deceptive ... if it is subject to subjective illusions. ... *Deceptive as well is the too-clear intuition of mathematical and rational truths* which can mark out the relays of knowledge ... in order to make room for renovations under the double pressure of further experience and of greater plasticity in understanding.

Likewise, in *La Pensée*, vol. 1, 131: "*The notion of an object* and the use that is ordinarily made of it is one of these divisions, one of these *illegitimate* 'overestimations' [*majorations*] which we do not cease to denounce as being *the chronic deception* and *ruinous improbity* from which many a philosophy is dying today."

However, then, how are we to preserve the teaching of the [First] Vatican Council, which says that the order of supernatural knowledge is distinct from that of natural knowledge,

Every so often, Blondel returns again to his first orientation, which was expressed in the 1893 edition of *L'Action*: "The knowledge of being implies the necessity of the option: *being in knowledge is not prior to the freedom of choice but, rather, comes after it.*"[19] There you have it, the *free* option, and even according to the very context of this remark, it is the option which freely prefers God to every created thing, which prefers "the Being who illuminates every reason and before whom every will must make its self-declaration."[20] This assertion constantly returns to his pen in the 1893 edition of *L'Action*.[21] We have cited these texts elsewhere at length in our work *God: His Existence and His Nature*.[22]

---

not only through its principle but also through *its object*, which is inaccessible to the natural knowledge that is had by man and the angels: "The perpetual common belief of the Catholic Church has held and holds also this: there is *a twofold order of knowledge*, distinct not only in its principle but also *in its object*" (*Dei filius*, ch. 4, Denzinger, no. 3015 [old no. 1795]). Also, see *Dei filius*, canon. 4.1 (Denzinger, no. 3041 [old no. 1816]).

In a number of places in the two volumes of *La Pensée* (1934), one can find assertions that are no less deserving of criticism. See vol. 1, 130–36, 170–72, 175, 179, 180, 349, 355; vol. 2, 39, 66, 67, 90, 96, and 196.

In *Pensée*, vol. 2, 66–69, see what is said concerning *free option* and its role in knowledge, even in that of the real value of the first principles.

19 Blondel, *L'Action* (1893), 435.

20 Blondel, *L'Action* (1893), 435.

21 See Blondel, *L'Action* (1893), 297, 341, 350, 426, 435, 437, and 463.

22 See Reginald Garrigou-Lagrange, *Dieu, son existence et sa nature*, 6th ed. (Paris: Beauchesne, 1936), 44–52. [Tr. note: See Reginald Garrigou-Lagrange, *God: His Existence and His Nature, A Thomistic Solution of Certain Agnostic Antinomies*, trans. Bede Rose (St. Louis, MO: B. Herder, 1949), 43–54.]

In the 1893 edition of *L'Action*, one could read, on 297: "*Metaphysics has its substance in the acting will. It only has truth in this experiential and dynamic form.* It is *less a science of what is* than one that brings about being and becoming."

Blondel, *L'Action* (1893), 341: "*A proof which is only a logical argument* forever remains abstract and partial. *It does not lead to being.* It does not necessarily corner thought within real necessity. A proof which stems from the total movement of life, *a proof which is action itself*, will have, on the contrary, 'this constraining force.'"

Blondel, *L'Action* (1893), 350:

> *The notion of a first cause* or of a moral ideal, the idea of a metaphysical perfection or of a pure act, all these conceptions of human reason, which are *empty, false, and idolatrous* if one considers them only as abstract representations, are true, living, and efficacious as soon as they are seen to be in solidarity with one another. Then, they are no longer a kind of mental game but, rather, *a practical certitude*.

In other words, they are true by way of conformity with the requirements of life and action and not through the objective power of the proofs of God's existence. See Blondel, *L'Action* (1893), 437 and 438. We have not seen the author retract these propositions.

Blondel cannot forget what he wrote in his first book: "*Only action* is concerned with *the whole. That is why it alone is the source for the unquestionable presence and constraining proof of Being.* No matter how lengthy and brilliant dialectical subtleties may be, they are nothing more than stones tossed by children at the sun."[23]

Consequently, for someone who has so conceived of the philosophy of action and has had this pattern of thought his whole life long, it is very difficult now to retract what he wrote in 1906 regarding speculative knowledge: "By rights, in place of the abstract and *chimerical 'Adaequatio speculativa rei et intellectus,'* we must *substitute* methodical research, the *adaequatio realis mentis et vitae.*"

This is what separates the philosophy of *action* from the philosophy of *being*. The former, which represents a superior form of pragmatism, defines truth in terms of action, as one would expect, whereas the latter defines it in terms of being. Otherwise, the philosophy of action ceases to be what it is in order to be the same as the philosophy of being.

The latter is characterized by this assertion made by St. Thomas in *De veritate*, q. 1, a. 1, stating something utterly different from all the citations presented above: "*What the intellect first conceives, as it were, as that which is most known and that into which all of our conceptions are resolved, is being.*" What is first known by the intellect is being, as the colored is what is first known by sight and sound by the sense of hearing. This conception of being is immediately followed by two judgments. 1° *Being is contradictorily opposed to non-being*; that which is cannot at the same time be and not be. 2° *Aliquid existit*, something exists: the thinking subject and extra-mental reality, for example, my body, the earth that carries me, or the food on which I nourish myself. These affirmations are prior to every free choice [*option*]. We cannot freely admit or reject them. As soon as we consider them, we necessarily adhere to them.

---

23 Blondel, *l'Action* (1893), 350. He wrote again in the 1893 edition of *L'Action*, 463: "*For science*, what difference can one discover between that which seems to exist forever and that which is? And *how can it distinguish reality itself from an invincible and permanent illusion* or, so to speak, from an eternal appearance? The situation is different *for practice: by acting as though it were so* it alone possesses *what is if it is truly so.*"

Blondel, *L'Action* (1893), 437ff:

> The knowledge that before the option was simply *subjective* and propulsive becomes, *after it*, privative or constitutive of being (depending on whether the option was evil or good). . . . The second of these forms of knowledge, *that which follows on the freely taken determination* . . . instead of placing us in the presence of what is *to be done*, gathers from that which has been done *that which is*. Therefore, it is truly an objective form of knowledge. . . . The will resolves the problem proposed by the understanding.

St. Thomas likewise says in *ST* I, q. 5, a. 2: "*Being first falls into the intellect's conception*. . . . Thus, it is the proper object of the intellect, just as sound is the proper object of hearing. Therefore, according to its formal character [*rationem*], *being* is prior to the *good*."

Now, this fundamental assertion by the philosophy of being, or ontology, is not found in the philosophy of action. The latter represents, as it were, a transformation, not of ontology, but of ethics, which is the philosophy of human action [*agir*]. Now, ethics requires an ontological foundation. Indeed, the notion of the good presupposes those of being and of truth. Otherwise, we can only speak of an apparent good and not of the *true* good in action's own movement, which could perhaps only be a form of sentimentalism and not a true and authentic love.

In order for the will to tend toward the true good and not toward one that is illusory, it must be profoundly *rectified* by the *intellect*, which alone can *know* being, reality, the truth, and also the true good (and not only an apparent one). Only the intellect can *judge* concerning it by means of a *true* judgment, that is, one that is conformed to reality, in accord with the traditional definition of truth.

We would fall into a vicious circle if we here wished to content ourselves with a prudential judgment conformed to a right will (that is, to a good intention [rectified by the virtues]) since here we are quite precisely concerned with explaining *the rectitude of the will* through its tendency to *the true* good.[24]

And therefore, we cannot allow the traditional definition of the truth, "*adaequatio rei et intellectus*," the conformity of the judgment with reality and its immutable laws, a definition presupposed by all the Councils, to be called *chimerical*. Likewise, we cannot admit the claim that we would need to "substitute" for it another definition that slides toward pragmatism, as Boutroux rightly noted with as much clarity as a good number of theologians.

In the very essence of the intellect, there is an immediate relation to *intelligible being*, its object, and not only a relation to that which is *to be done*. Consequently, if we remove from the intellect this immediate relation to being, we mortally wound it in its very nature.

---

24 This is what St. Thomas said in *ST* I-II, q. 19, a. 3, ad 2: "In the means to be chosen, rectitude of reason (here, of prudence) consists in conformity to right intention of the end [*appetitum finis debiti*]. However, this right intention of the end [*appetitus finis debiti*] presupposes right apprehension of the end, which is had through reason." This latter knowledge is *true* through conformity to reality, not to right intention. Émile Boutroux registers a similar objection against the philosophy of action in *Science et religion*, 296. "*But the will requires an end*," indeed, an end that would be judged by the intellect according to its conformity to reality. Otherwise, how could one be sure of avoiding the sentimentalism of false mystics? The Encyclical, *Pascendi* (no. 14; Denzinger, no. 3484 [old no., 2081]), noted this fact: How is one thus to discern true religious experience from false religion?

THE IMMUTABILITY OF DOGMATIC FORMULAS

According to Msgr. Bruno de Solages, when Fr. Bouillard wrote in his *Conversion et grâce chez S. Thomas d'Aquin*, "A theology that would not be contemporary would be a false theology,"[25] he

> in no way affirms the monstrous notion that a theology that would have been true at a given moment becomes objectively false 'when the mind evolves' but, rather, that it will be *subjectively false*, meaning that it would be *interpreted in a false sense* by a mind that, as a result of its own development, would no longer give the same meaning to the various notions used by this theology.[26]

I will respond: if Fr. Bouillard meant only this, then he has expressed himself poorly in a question of great importance, one requiring the greatest attention to the proper use of terms. Moreover, this would come down to this truism: a theology that is no longer contemporary is poorly understood by those who no longer grasp the notions in which it is expressed. In reality, Fr. Bouillard said: "In order for theology to continue to be meaningful to the mind [*esprit*] and to be able to impregnate it and progress with it, it *must* also *abandon* these notions."[27] He means: like how we abandoned the Ptolemaic system of astronomy.[28]

He speaks to us about the relativity of the notion of *formal cause*, which "modern thought abandoned when it renounced Aristotelian physics."[29]

---

[25] Henri Bouillard, *Conversion et grâce chez S. Thomas d'Aquin* (Paris: Aubier, 1944), 219.

[26] Bruno de Solages, "Pour l'honneur de la Théologie. Les contre-sens du R.P. Garrigou-Lagrange," *Bulletin de Littérature Ecclésiastique* 48 (1947): 75.

[27] Bouillard, *Conversion*, 224.

[28] He also says on Bouillard, *Conversion*, 211:

> If authors are aware of the fact that theology did not always exist in its contemporary state, as it is known by theologians today, they at least unconsciously imagine that it was already given as such *in the domain of eternal truths* and that discursive intellection only had to *discover* it and gradually reconstruct it. By contrast, a historical study reveals . . . *the relativity of notions*.

When Leo XIII spoke in his encyclical *Aeterni patris* about the stability of St. Thomas's doctrine, considered in what is primordial and essential in it, he quite surely meant that what the Holy Doctor taught is true in *the domain of eternal truths*. This is not a prejudice that contemporary theologians should abandon. Rather, they should reread this entire encyclical on this subject.

Likewise, His Holiness, Pope Pius XII, in a discourse published by the *L'Osservatore Romano* on 23–24 Sept. 1946, in opposition to certain new opinions, spoke of the immutable principles on which St. Thomas's doctrine rests.

[29] Bouillard, *Conversion*, 224.

Now, *if we would need to abandon* this *notion*, which is found *all throughout* St. Thomas's theology, this theology would be *objectively false*, and indeed not only in many of its important parts but *as a whole*, for according to St. Thomas *no nature* would be conceivable any longer, neither that of sensible beings nor that of angels nor that of God. One could no longer speak about what formally constitutes them, and along with the formal cause, the notion of the other causes would likewise disappear: the material, efficient, and final causes. Behold what a metaphysician sees all at once. Indeed, moreover, we clearly cannot confuse scientific laws (which progressively replace one another) with immutable truths.

In order to avoid relativism, Fr. Bouillard says: "*While notions*, methods, and systems *change with the times, the affirmations* that they contain *remain*, even though they are expressed in different categories."[30]

Finally, in speaking about the Council of Trent, which employed the notion of *formal cause* in its teaching concerning the notion of justification (cf. sess. 6, ch. 7, can. 10), he says: "By so doing, did it not enshrine this term and confer a definitive character upon the notion of grace as a form? *Not at all*.... To this end, it used notions commonly used in the theology of its era. However, *other notions* can be *substituted* for them without modifying the *meaning* of what the Council declared."

With great care, I have read over what comes before this quotation and what follows it, but this context does not render it more acceptable. I repeat the point again: how can we maintain *the meaning* of this Conciliar teaching, "Sanctifying grace is the formal cause of justification," *if we must abandon* the notion of formal causality, substituting *another* notion for it, even one that is analogous to it. (The uncreated gift that is the Holy Spirit is analogous to a created gift. Nonetheless, one cannot say that habitual grace is the uncreated gift of God.)

If *another notion* is substituted for the Council's own notion, what it affirms no longer will have *the same meaning*. We would need to be content with saying: "At the time of the Council of Trent, grace *was conceived of* as being the formal cause of justification, but, today *we must* conceive of it *in a different way*. This *past* conception is no longer contemporary. Therefore, it *is no longer true*, for a doctrine that is no longer contemporary, as has been said, is a false doctrine, 'which is no longer meaningful to the mind,' one that would be able to 'impregnate it and progress with it.' Therefore, it can no longer be admitted, just as an adolescent no longer can wear the clothing of a child, nor can the ancient claims of astronomy be admitted any longer."

Here again, we have not misinterpreted anything.

---

[30] Bouillard, *Conversion*, 220.

Nonetheless, we find ourselves faced with the objection: Fr. Bouillard does not speak of two notions united by the verb *to be*.

I respond that he says, "While *notions*, methodologies, and systems *change* with the passing of time, *the affirmations* that they contain remain,"[31] adding that even the Council's notions can change.

But then, I ask, what is *an affirmation* if not the union of a subject and a predicate by means of the verb *to be*? For example: grace is the formal cause of justification; transubstantiation is required by the real presence. An affirmation presupposes two notions united by the verb *to be*.

Therefore, if notions change and if we must abandon the notion of *formal causality* and *substitute another* for it, even one that is analogous, how can *the meaning* of this affirmation by the Council of Trent remain: "Grace is the formal cause of justification"? *One and the same relationship* cannot remain between two notions if they are essentially unstable and changing. As we said before, one might as well say that an iron clamp can still the waves of the sea. Therefore, we stand by our criticism.[32]

* * * * *

As regards Fr. de Lubac's assertion in *Surnaturel*, "There is nothing in St. Thomas that declares [*annonce*] to me *the distinction* that a certain number of Thomist theologians will come to draw between *God the Author of nature* and *God the Author of the supernatural order*, etc.,"[33] the four texts from St. Thomas that are cited in a note, when read in their obvious and commonly-received meaning, show that St. Thomas not only declared this distinction but also admitted it himself. We have cited many other texts related to this matter in the first volume of our treatise *De revelatione*,[34] and in that text,[35] we examined and refuted the theory of the supernatural proposed in the 18th century by Noris and Berti, to which Fr. de Lubac on the whole returns today.[36]

---

[31] Bouillard, *Conversion*, 220.

[32] The best of contexts does not suffice for saving a proposition if it is false by itself. Indeed, even the gravest errors are often proposed in a context that gives them some appearance of the truth. Thus, we would deceive ourselves if we spoke of them as though they had a true intuition or an animating truth, whereas, in fact, they only have a parcel of the truth in themselves, turned away from its meaning, thus rendering the error more seductive and more dangerous, as happens in the most specious sophisms.

[33] Henri de Lubac, *Surnaturel: Études historiques* (Paris: Aubier, 1946), 254.

[34] See Reginald Garrigou-Lagrange, *On Divine Revelation*, vol. 1, trans. Matthew K. Minerd (Steubenville, OH: Emmaus Academic, 2021), 475–562.

[35] See Garrigou-Lagrange, *On Divine Revelation*, 543–45.

[36] It is asked where St. Thomas spoke about natural beatitude—not in this life, which was spoken of by the greatest pagan philosophers, but rather, after death. He made allusion to it in speaking of the state of the souls of children born without baptism. According to him, they do not have perfect natural beatitude but, rather, a kind of imperfect, natural

* * * * *

Some other remarks.

When, in *Les études*, Fr. Gaston Fessard spoke "of the blessed drowsiness that protects this canonized (but also, in Péguy's words, 'interred') Thomism,"[37] we are told that he was only referring to the Thomism of Fr. Tonquédec and not Thomism itself.

However, Fr. Tonquédec's Thomism has not been canonized by anyone, and Péguy was not speaking of him, at least as far as I can tell.

If we asked, "Can two theologies be true at the same time if they are contradictorily opposed to each other in their capital theses?," we did so because in recent days there has been talk of the simultaneous truth of Thomism, Scotism, and Molinism, as though the truth, in its integral and full form, were a kind of polyhedron. Thus, we recalled that Thomism and Scotism are opposed contradictorily on many of their principal theses, as are Thomism and Molinism as well, given that, for example, one affirms that grace is efficacious by itself, whereas the other denies this assertion. Here again, we have not misinterpreted anything.

Finally, we are told that there is a lack of probity involved in citing mimeographed sheets clandestinely distributed to the clergy since 1934. Nonetheless, this state of affairs is something known by all. Likewise, we are well aware of the harm they cause for those youths who get caught up in all of this. If a lack of probity does exist here, who is guilty of it: the person who denounces a source of scandal or the person who provokes it?[38]

It seems that if we had been alive in the 13th century, we would have called for St. Thomas's condemnation! However, such a claim presupposes that this or that contemporary theologian, whose conclusions we cannot admit, is the St. Thomas of our own era. We will see in a century or two how

---

beatitude. See *De malo*, q. 5, a. 2, and 3. I have explained this in Reginald Garrigou-Lagrange, *Grace*, trans. Dominican Nuns of Corpus Christi Monastery (St. Louis, MO: B. Herder, 1952), 410–12. Like Noris and Berti, Fr. de Lubac does not seem to preserve the *true notion* of *human nature*. It seems he holds that this nature does not have a determinate limit (receiving such determination from our intellect's proper object). Rather, it seems he holds that it is open as a nature in such a way that it is no longer clear where the natural ends and the supernatural begins, where nature ends and where grace begins. This is the source of the criticisms addressed to St. Thomas who himself has a determinate notion of *nature* and of human nature, such that the supernatural truly exceeds nature's powers and demands, in contrast to what Baius said. We have spoken at length about these questions elsewhere. See the text of *On Divine Revelation* cited above.

37 See Gaston Fessard, [Review of Joseph de Tonquédec, *Un philosophie existentielle. L'Existence d'après Jaspers*,"] *Études* 247 (Nov. 1945): 269–70.

38 We have not at all spoken about the unknown person who has taken the responsibility for distributing these texts. However, along with many others, we have been able to observe the effect they have produced (and still produce) in many of those who read them.

history will judge this matter. In any case, these two St. Thomases would hardly agree with one another.

A theologian is not forbidden to say that, to his eyes, a given new position leads to heresy and even that it seems to him to be heretical. He only says this from the perspective of theological science and its deductions, without *authoritatively* speaking like a judge in an ecclesiastical tribunal.[39]

As regards the problem of evolution, it is important to clearly distinguish between the domain of scientific hypotheses proposed for examination (i.e., that of sensible appearances) and the domain of being, which is that of metaphysics, where we must hold that God specially intervened in the production of vegetative life, sense life, and intellectual life and, *a fortiori* in an utterly special way, in order to produce the life of grace in man.

Finally, we absolutely cannot admit that the Incarnation of the Word and the Redemption would be moments in evolution. And if this evolution were explained along the lines of Hegelian metaphysics, which was condemned by the [First] Vatican Council,[40] this would properly speaking be a case of heresy. Indeed, it would be even more than a heresy. It would represent complete apostasy, for Hegel's absolute and pantheistic evolutionism does not allow *any* Christian dogmas to survive. In denying the True God, who is really and essentially distinct from the world, he denies *all* the revealed mysteries and can only preserve their verbal forms.[41]

* * * * *

Therefore, we find ourselves forced to maintain what we have said, in particular, what pertains to the traditional definition of truth as "*adaequatio*

---

39 In what we have written, we have critiqued ideas, leaving persons to the side as much as is possible. This is an entirely different perspective from that which would be taken up by someone writing a plea on behalf of persons.

A number of representatives of the new theology whom we have cited were already pointed out to us by some of their friends, in particular in *Études* (Sept. 1946): 253ff. [sic]

We are quite well aware that in his Constitution, *Sollicita ac provida* (July 9, 1753), Benedict XIV, in fixing the discipline for the prohibition of books, requires one to attentively read a book in its entirety and not judge it by one or two of its propositions taken out of context, for it is possible, he says, that "that which is obscure in one place would be more clearly stated in another," thus giving it an acceptable sense. This is indeed certain. However, without rendering a judgment on an entire book, one can cite one or several propositions that are (or at least seem) manifestly false or dangerous on account of the consequences that can be drawn from them, above all when they are not explained and made acceptable in another place that is clearer and more explicit.

40 See [First] Vatican Council, *Dei filius*, can. 1.4 (Denzinger, no. 3024 [old. no., 1804]). Also, Jean-Michel-Alfred Vacant, *Études sur le Concile du Vatican*, vol. 1 (Paris: Delhomme, 1895), 213, 344, 362: "The pantheistic evolutionism of Hegel."

41 This is what we have shown elsewhere in *On Divine Revelation*, vol. 1, 389–444.

rei et intellectus, the conformity of judgment with reality and its immutable laws." This definition is not chimerical, and it must not be replaced by another definition that slides toward pragmatism. Were it so replaced, the intellect would be mortally wounded, and one would forget that this traditional definition is presupposed by all of the Councils and is required in order for dogmas to be immutable. Therefore, one cannot be too attentive to the words of His Holiness Pope Pius XII in the discourse published by *L'Osservatore Romano* September 19, 1946:

> There is a good deal of talk (but without a sufficient testing of its character), about a "new theology," which is in constant transformation, following the example of all other things in the world, which are in a constant state of flux and movement, without ever reaching their term. If we were to accept such an opinion, *what would become of the unchangeable dogmas of the Catholic Faith; and what would become of the unity and stability of that Faith.*

At the present hour, in the midst of profound disarray of minds [*esprits*], more than ever, we stand in need of a firm, living, penetrating, and radiant faith. It would cease to be living and strong if it lost its firmness, as well as its immutable adherence "*to the words that will not pass away*," which are expressed in human notions that are stable enough to remain immutably true throughout all the ages.

(*) Even in *La philosophie et l'esprit chrétien*, published by Blondel in 1946, we still find, in the midst of beautiful reflections, assertions like the following:

> One realizes all the more that the idea of supporting the *obsequium rationabile fidei* on abstract arguments, on a *fixity of notions*, without a plastic relationship with the normal development of the methods of thought and of mindsets that are ever in movement, risks leading to a static and closed, formalistic conception of things, which was suited to one moment of history, or to *a wholly extrinsic idea of a religion imposed once and for all* by witnesses marked by the time and mental habits of their own eras, making abstraction from problems that are at once permanent and changing, as well as from the vital roots of the truths to be believed and of obligations to be observed, thrust down into the depths of human souls and of the constructive elements of the moral and metaphysical conscience....[42]

> Therefore, nothing is more contrary to the living idea of Christianity than the twofold thesis that certain people have wished to make into a *sine qua non* condition for a fundamentalist [*intégriste*] orthodoxy: *a summary literally fixed* in dependence on a terminology and *a doctrine*

---

[42] But who, therefore, we ask, has made *such an abstraction*? Certainly not traditional theologians.

constructed with notions as its materials, as well as a pure and simple super-imposition of the supernatural order upon a self-sufficient philosophy, enclosed within itself without even a small window opening, if but darkly, toward a loftier clarity and a more abundant life.[43]

Nonetheless, we must acknowledge *the fixity of the notions of revelation, of the supernatural, of faith, of evident credibility, of the divine signs* of revelation, and *of miracles*. Certainly, these notions are at first vague [*confuses*] and then distinct, but nonetheless, they must be *stable* if we are to maintain the irreformable character of the judgments that unite them by means of the verb *to be*. This is required by the very teaching of the Church concerning *the nature* of *revelation and its object*, a teaching that is summed up in these immutable propositions drawn especially from the [First] Vatican Council, which are correctly presented by Denzinger as follows:

— *Revelation* strictly speaking, that is, God's speech to man, is:
- *possible* and useful (3027ff [1807ff])
- supernatural (2778 [1637], 3006 [1787], 3420ff [2020ff]),
- necessary, regarding morally necessary natural religious truths, as well as regarding absolutely supernatural truths (3006 [1786], 3028 [1808]);
- *and it can be made credible through external signs* (2751ff [1622ff], 2757 [1627], 2779 [1638ff], 2813 [1651], 3009 [1790], 3012 [1793], 3033 [1812]);
- it is neither imperfect nor, as such, to be perfected through progress (2778ff [1637ff], 2829 [1656], 2905 [1705], 3020 [1800]),
- nor is it to be changed in any way into some other meaning (3043 [1818]).

— Beyond truths that can be known by reason,
- Christian revelation contains mysteries both *in the broad sense* such as God's eternal decrees (3004 [1785]) and *strictly speaking*, namely, ones that altogether cannot be known by reason alone (2732ff [1616ff], [1642ff], 2828 [1655], 3015 [1795], 3043 [1818]);
- however, they nonetheless do not contradict reason but, rather, exceed it (2854 [1671], 3015 [1795]),
- and they forever remain obscure for as long as we are pilgrims in this life separated from God, for we walk by faith and not by sight (2 Cor. 5:6) (3016 [1796]);

— Moreover, faith requires certain knowledge concerning the fact of revelation (2752 [1623], 3009 [1790], 3033 [1812], [2106]).

All of these propositions are immutably true and can only be so if the notions they unite by means of the verb "to be" are themselves perfectly stable as well.

---

[43] Maurice Blondel, *La philosophie et l'esprit chrétien*, vol. 2 (Paris: Presses Universitaires, 1946), 261.

12

Concerning Notions Consecrated by the Councils
Réginald Garrigou-Lagrange, OP

In an article recently published in *Angelicum*,[1] we said that one cannot hold that *the notions implied in Conciliar definitions* are contingent or unstable (for example, the notion of *formal cause* used by the Council of Trent [sess. 6, ch. 7, can. 10] in teaching that habitual or sanctifying grace is the formal cause of our justification). Were we to hold that this notion is unstable, we would ultimately compromise the unchangeable character of this Conciliar teaching, and as we said in our earlier article, *another* meaning cannot be substituted for it without thereby modifying the meaning of the Council's teaching.

THE GRAVITY OF THE PROBLEM

Now, one could object: the notions that certain people say are contingent in the Conciliar definitions are only *technical notions*, Aristotelian notions closely connected to a system of thought that has been obsolete for some time now.[2]

However, what shall we say concerning the way that we must distinguish between the technical notions used by the Councils and those that are not technical? Must we say that, in order to preserve its immutable value,

---

[1] See Reginald Garrigou-Lagrange, "Verité et immutabilité du dogme," *Angelicum* 24 (1947): 124–39. [Tr. note: See the previous chapter in this volume.]

[2] We have always responded: they can seem *obsolete* to a chemist who judges all things solely "according to sensible appearances; however, they are not so if one judges them from the perspective of *being* and the ontological value of the first notions of being, unity, identity, substance, and that which formally constitutes a given substance (e.g., hydrogen or oxygen), making it to be *one and the same being* with given properties and not others. Substance (and therefore the substantial form) is wholly in the whole and wholly in each part (e.g., of a molecule of water). Similarly, the substance or nature of oxygen is wholly in the whole of an atom of oxygen and wholly in each of its parts, which, however, are mathematically divisible *ad infinitum*. Considered from the perspective, not of chemistry, but of the philosophy of nature, the notion of *formal cause* is *no more obsolete* than are those of matter, end, or efficient cause. Moreover, formal causality is found not only in the order of bodies but also in the spiritual order and that of grace.

the notion of transubstantiation is a common-sense notion and not a technical one?

Furthermore, it will be objected that the various notions to which the different theological schools have had recourse in order to express one and the same truth are *equivalent* notions. It will be said that, despite their diversity, which is only surface-level, they aim at one and the same reality and truth, meaning that they can be *substituted* for one another.

However, how can this reality and immutable truth be *known with certitude* and firmly believed in if it can only be attained through changing notions? In response, we are told that these successive notions are *equivalent* and *analogous*.

Now, these two last words raise a host of difficulties. Indeed, they involve a most serious problem, which we can't just pass over in silence without seeking to resolve it.

We are told:

> *This immutable thing* is expressed *in a different manner*, depending on the system one chooses. This is the law of analogy, which can be ignored by no Thomist. When *one and the same revealed truth* is expressed in different (e.g., Augustinian, Thomist, Suarezian, etc.) systems, the various notions that are used for translating this truth are neither "equivocal" (if they were, one would no longer be speaking about the same thing) nor "univocal" (for otherwise, all systems [of thought] would be identical) but, rather, "*analogous*." In other words, *they express the same reality in different ways.*

To our eyes, this represents an abuse of the notion of analogy. We have written about this topic for many years, and we can say that, according to St. Thomas, truly analogous notions do not aim at the same reality but, rather, at different realities, which are proportionally similar to one another (e.g., God's existence and that of creatures, the existence of created substance and that of accidents). Likewise, St. Thomas cites the different manifestations of man's health through his complexion, pulse, etc.

By contrast, *different notions* of the *same* reality can differ from each other only as a vague [*confus*] notion and a distinct one concerning one and the same thing. In such a case, they are *univocal*. Or, on the other hand, these different notions can be so opposed to each other that one is the negation of the other (e.g., the notion of *conversive* transubstantiation and that of non-conversive, *adductive* transubstantiation). In that case, they are not even analogical, for the second is the negation of the first, whereas the creature's existence is not the negation of the Creator's existence, which the creature itself presupposes.

Hence, the gravity of the problem becomes clearer for us, helping us to see that we cannot just pass it by.

We would like to examine three questions concerning this subject.

1° In the Councils' teachings, are there notions, indeed even technical ones, which would truly be *consecrated* by them?—It does indeed seem that this is so, for example, for the notions of *the Hypostatic Union, transubstantiation*, and *the spiritual soul*, which of itself and essentially is *the form of the body*, as well as for the notion of sanctifying grace, *the formal cause* of justification.

2° Can we, without modifying the *meaning* of the Councils' teaching, *abandon* these technical notions consecrated by them or leave them fall into obsolescence by *substituting* others that are said to be equivalent and analogous?

3° What would be *the real foundation* for the aforementioned analogy existing between the new notions substituted for those that were previously consecrated? Would it not follow that the *meaning* expressed by the Councils would thus become unknowable or, at least, *uncertain* and merely probable, even for the Church herself? Would not *relativism* be unavoidable?

This problem must be considered in itself with the greatest of attention. If we do not consider it today, it will still exist tomorrow, and its gravity is manifestly clear. The words of the [First] Vatican Council concerning this subject bear being reread: "Hence, also, *that meaning of the sacred dogmas is perpetually to be retained* which our Holy Mother Church has once declared, and there must never be deviation from that meaning on the specious ground and title of a more profound understanding."[3]

* * * * *

1° *In the Councils' teachings, there are notions, indeed even technical ones, that are truly consecrated by them.*

It does not seem that there can be any doubt in this matter. For example, we have: the notions of supernatural revelation, mysteries properly so called (i.e., supernatural truth, which is naturally unknowable and indemonstrable, even after revelation has been made), that of dogma, the notion of naturally knowable, supernatural signs of Divine Revelation; above all, there is the notion of miracles, the notions of infused faith, evident credibility, the biblical inspiration of those books having God as their Author, the notion of divine tradition, as well as the condemnation of heterodox notions contrary to all of those we just cited.[4]

---

[3] [First] Vatican Council, *Dei filius*, ch. 4 (Denzinger, no. 3020 [old. no., 1800]). Likewise, see *Dei filius*, can. 4.3 (Denzinger, no. 3043); similarly, Jean-Michel-Alfred Vacant, *Études théologiques sur les constitutions du Concile du Vatican*, vol. 2 (Paris: Delhomme et Briguet, 1895), 281–321.

[4] We have examined at length the meaning and scope of these fundamental notions (in contrast with the heterodox notions opposed to them) in our treatise *On Divine Revelation*, trans. Matthew K. Minerd (Steubenville, OH: Emmaus Academic, 2021), 205–319, 611–49, 733–63 and vol. 2, 3–63 and 143–57.

Similarly, there is the notion of the Church as a society that is supernatural, perfect, independent, and visible (i.e., knowable through her notes). Likewise, there are the notions of [her] unity, holiness, Catholicity, apostolicity, and that of the hierarchy, as well as the notion of salvation and of that which of itself is necessary for salvation. Moreover, there is the notion of infallibility, the power to teach, the power of jurisdiction, and the power of order.

As regards God, there is the notion of the True God, who is really and essentially distinct from the world, the notions of His principal attributes, simplicity, unity, truth, goodness, infinity, immutability, eternity, God's natural and supernatural knowability, the divine life, His omniscient wisdom, the divine will and freedom, uncreated love, justice, mercy, providence, predestination, omnipotence, and infinite beatitude. All these notions are *analogical* but must be taken in *their proper meaning* and not only by way of *metaphor*, for were we to understand them as being mere metaphors, we ultimately would be led to agnosticism.

These various notions, understood according to their proper and not merely metaphorical sense, are already technical in their own manner. Even more so are the following.

As regards the Holy Trinity, there are the fundamental notions of *the divine processions* (the eternal generation of the Word and the spiration which terminates at the Holy Spirit), *the divine relations* (paternity, filiation, etc.), *divine persons*, the notions concerning their equality, as well as what is proper to each. Without a certain degree of technicality in our theological vocabulary, we cannot avoid contradiction in these matters and will not be able to correctly understand how there are *three persons* in God, that is, three intelligent and free subjects, who nonetheless have the same nature, the same essential intelligence, the same freedom, and the same power, thus meaning that they constitute a single principle of activity [*opération*] ad extra.

Again, let us mention the notions of free creation *ex nihilo* and *non ab aeterno*, the notion of creatures (whether bodily, spiritual, or human) that come forth through free production, *ex nihilo, initio temporis*, and not from the substance of God by way of emanation. Likewise, there is the notion of the human soul, which *by itself and essentially* is *the form of the body*, even though it is spiritual and immortal.

Then, there is the notion of the divine government, as well as that of the distinction between good and evil in relation to this government.

Next, we have the notions of the supernatural order in relation to human and angelic natures, as well as the notion of the supernatural ultimate end and that of the beatific vision.

Likewise, there are the notions of original justice, original sin, and its consequences.

For the mystery of the Incarnation, there is the technical notion of *the Hypostatic Union* and its consequences, the notion of the *communication of idioms* and that of Christ's *impeccable freedom*.[5] Likewise, there are the notions of redemption, sacrifice, universal mediation, and those of the infinite value of the Redeemer's merits and satisfaction. For Mary, there is the notion of the divine maternity and its consequences.

For the life of grace in us, there are the notions of justification, sanctification, and our interior renewal through grace. Indeed, it is quite important that we know that this interior renewal is not *formally constituted* by some other interior principle than grace but, rather, is so constituted by habitual grace, which inheres in the soul as a participation in the divine nature and is the seed of eternal life in us.

The Council of Trent (Denzinger, no. 1528ff [old no. 799]) even teaches us what *the various causes of justification* are: its *final cause* (the Glory of God and of Christ, as well as eternal life), its primary *efficient cause* (the Merciful God), its *meritorious cause* (Jesus Christ, who merited justification for us on the wood of the Cross and made satisfaction for us to God the Father), its *instrumental cause* (the sacrament of baptism), its *sole formal cause* (the justice of God, not that by which He Himself is just but, rather, that by which He makes us just [can. 10 and 11], by which ... we are spiritually renewed [*spiritu mentis nostrae*] ... each of us receiving into ourselves His justice according to the measure that *the Holy Spirit* bestows upon each as He wills [1 Cor. 12:11] and according to each person's own disposition and cooperation.)

In this way, we have an explanation for the *exact meaning* of the Council, as we can see in canon 10: "If anyone says that men are justified without the Justice of Christ, by which He gained merit for us, or that they are *formally* just by His justice itself, let him be anathema" (Denzinger, no. 1560 [old no. 820]). Indeed, it is even more explicitly found in canon 11, which speaks of the grace that inheres in us.[6]

The Councils have likewise consecrated the notions of *prevenient actual grace, operative grace, and cooperative grace*, as well as those of *merit de condigno, satisfaction*, and the notions of *the infused virtues*, in particular those concerning the *theological virtues*. Likewise, they have consecrated the notions pertaining to each sacrament: as regards the Eucharist, those of

---

[5] Thus, Christ is a single intelligent and free subject, even though He has two natures, two intellects, and two freedoms. Here again, without a certain degree of technicality in our theological vocabulary, we cannot grasp *the true meaning* of *the dogma* in question and the true meaning of the Councils.

[6] Here, we must repeat that the notion of formal causality is no more obsolete (in philosophy and theology) than are those of matter, end, and efficient cause.

As we have just seen, the Councils even make use of the notions of meritorious causality and instrumental causality.

transubstantiation and of *real presence* (*vere, realiter, substantialiter*: Denzinger, nos. 1636, 1651 and 1652 [old nos. 874, 883, and 884]), and as regards penance, the notions of attrition and contrition. Finally, as regards the last things: the notions of the immutable particular judgment, of supernatural heavenly beatitude, purgatory, eternal damnation, the resurrection of the dead, and the universal judgment.

Each of these notions, thus consecrated by the Councils, themselves imply many others, many of which are far more precise than what can be attained by common sense (i.e., natural reason, in the natural order), as well as Christian sense, in the order of grace. Through the course of the centuries, philosophical and theological reason have contributed to this precision through the slow passage from vague [*confus*] concepts to the distinct ones, which exclude false conceptions. From this perspective, many notions the Councils have consecrated deserve to be called technical, in particular, the notions of the *Hypostatic Union*, *Transubstantiation*, and that of the human soul, which is spiritual and immortal while nonetheless being "by itself and essentially the substantial form of the human body."[7]

And yet, when the Council of Trent taught that sanctifying grace is the *formal cause* of justification (Denzinger, nos. 1528, 1560, and 1561 [old nos., 799, 820, and 821]), it was not content merely to define habitual grace, as distinct from actual grace, *in relation to the soul* in which it inheres as an infused quality, and *in relation to the final end*, that is, to the glory of which it is the seed. Nor did it limit itself to defining it *in itself* as a participation in the divine nature (Denzinger, nos. 1525, 1528, and 1546ff [old nos., 795, 799, 809ff]). In addition to these definitions, it also taught *what it is in relation to justification*, by saying that it is "the formal cause" thereof (Denzinger, nos. 1528 and 1560 [old nos., 799 and 820]).

And therefore, certain notions consecrated by the Councils are *technical*.[8] Nonetheless, when a Council utilizes and *consecrates* them, it does not

---

[7] See Council of Vienne (Denzinger, no. 902 [old no. 481]); see also Lateran V, sess. 8 (Denzinger, no. 1440 [old no. 738]).

[8] On this subject, we must cite an important text drawn from the *reportatio* read by Johann Baptist Franzelin at the [First] Vatican Council concerning the first schema of the Dogmatic Constitution *De fide*. See Giovanni Domenico Mansi et al., *Amplissima collectio conciliorum*, vol. 50, ed. Louis Petit and Jean-Baptiste Martin [Arnhem and Leipzig: Société nouvelle d'édition de la Collection Mansi, 1924], 321. Quite correctly, Franzelin distinguishes, among errors and heresies to be condemned, those that have a technical form and those expressed in contemporary language, saying,

> Of course, we must distinguish in the very manner of exposition and declaration of a doctrine what must be opposed in the errors of a [given theological] school from the other kind of exposition by which heresies are condemned in sectarian creeds, a distinction that should jump to one's eyes if one were to look at the two chapters

canonize all the various relations that they have to the other notions in the philosophical system that contributed to their precision.

For example, in our earlier article, we said, "The Council of Trent did not canonize the Aristotelian notion of form with all its relations to other ideas of the Aristotelian system. But it approved it as a *stable human idea,* in the sense that we speak of everything that formally constitutes a thing (in this case, justification)."[9]

We have explained this matter at greater length in our book, *Le sens commun: la philosophie de l'être et les formules dogmatiques.*[10] There, we said that, on account of their precision, many of these dogmatic formulas surpass the terms of common sense and even that which is accessible to the Christian sense of simple believers who do not have theological training. However, dogmatic formulas expressed in philosophical language remain in continuity with common sense and Christian sense. Through lofty preaching [élévations] on the mysteries, masters like Bossuet can help fully-docile souls come to understand them, indeed, in a way that is very fruitful.

Firmiter and *Damnamus* from the Lateran Council. In the first, against the Albigensian sect, there is quite simply an exposition of the creed expressly concerned with the doctrine of the Trinity; in the latter, where an error that was introduced in the shape and reasons of a school of thought had to be eliminated, the same Trinitarian doctrine is declared, though in a completely different manner and by means of completely different reasons, which quite obviously corresponded to the error itself, in accord with its own particular character. Here, we first have a lengthy exposition of errors to be condemned, bringing to bear the arguments and texts relied on by its author, the Abbot Joachim of Fiore. Then, a declaration of the mystery follows. Even though this latter text is scarcely suitable for instructing the simple faithful, nonetheless it most certainly is completely suited to its own particular goal and is a declaration that for theologians up to our own days has been, is, and *ever will be the foundation for the entire speculative doctrine concerned with the Trinity.*

It is in this chapter of *Damnamus* (Denzinger, nos. 803–5 [old nos. 431–33]) that this point of doctrine is defined:

because each of the Three Persons is that reality, that is, the divine substance, essence, or nature which alone is the beginning of all things, apart from which nothing else can be found. This reality is neither generating nor generated nor proceeding, but it is the Father who generates, the Son who is generated, and the Holy Spirit who proceeds, so that there be distinctions between the Persons but unity in nature (Denzinger, no. 804 [old no. 432]).

The expression here is learned and technical, like the error to be condemned.

9 Garrigou-Lagrange, "La nouvelle théologie où va-t-elle," *Angelicum* 23 (1946): 128. [Tr. note: See "Where is the New Theology Headed?" earlier in this volume.]

10 See Reginald Garrigou-Lagrange, *Thomistic Common Sense: The Philosophy of Being and the Development of Doctrine*, trans. Matthew K. Minerd (Steubenville, OH: Emmaus Academic, 2021), 275–99.

Thus, far from being submitted to a philosophical system, the Church's faith in Divine Revelation, with the Holy Spirit's assistance, *judges from on high the notions* that were brought to their precision through collaboration with a given system like that of Aristotle.[11] A given notion, like that of formal causality is thus *"taken up"* by the supernatural faith of a Council (through its infused faith, illuminated by the Holy Spirit's gifts and special assistance), consequently receiving, in the supernatural light of Divine Revelation and of infused faith illuminated by the Holy Spirit, *a stability that is superior* to what it heretofore had. Thus, in this superior light, such a notion is judged to be suitable for expressing a divine, revealed truth, which shall not pass away.

*****

2° *Without thereby modifying the meaning of the Councils' teaching, can one abandon the technical notions consecrated by them or leave them fall into obsolescence by substituting for them other so-called "equivalent" or "analogous" ones?*

We must respond negatively to this question. First of all, let us say that, faced with a number of conciliar notions (e.g., for sanctifying grace), we obviously can choose the one that is most suited to our current ends. Indeed, as we said above, the Council of Trent conceived of sanctifying grace in different ways, depending on whether it is considered in relation to the just soul in which it inheres as an infused quality, in relation to the glory of which it is the seed, in relation to the divine nature of which it is a participation, or finally, in relation to justification, of which it is the *formal cause*.

All of these conceptions are simultaneously true and immutable. The last one (in relation to justification) cannot be abandoned, nor can it be allowed to fall into obsolescence by substituting another conception for it (one that is said to be equivalent and analogous), akin to how Ptolemy's astronomical hypothesis was abandoned.

Why? Because the technical meaning of this notion, which was consecrated by the Council of Trent, is not a provisional hypothesis like those of ancient astronomy. If we are truly aware of what such a hypothesis of this

---

[11] This is already true of theology, which judges from on high (i.e., from the perspective of wisdom in the supernatural order) a philosophical truth before making use of it to deduce a theological conclusion. See *ST* I, q. 1, a. 6, ad 2: "This science (namely, theology) does not have the task of *proving* the principles of the other sciences but, rather, is only tasked with *judging concerning them*. For whatever we discover in other sciences to be contrary to a truth held in this science is completely condemned as being false." This is even truer still for a Council, which *judges* with the Holy Spirit's special assistance. Moreover, let us note that normally, in the various orders of nature, the *superior order*, according to its own proper laws, "uses" the *inferior one* without, properly speaking, depending on the laws of the latter. Thus, man assimilates foods like bread and wine because *from on high* he finds them to be *suited* to this assimilation, without being forced to undertake a chemical analysis of these foods, which he has always used.

kind is, we know that it is not proposed as something *true* through a conformity to extra-mental reality and to its immutable laws but, rather, is true inasmuch as it is a *useful means* for provisionally representing and classifying phenomena. Regarding these hypotheses, St. Thomas said in *ST* I, q. 32, a. 1, ad 2: "They do not sufficiently prove what they propose, for perhaps the sensible appearances could likewise be explained by a different hypothesis."

This is not how the Council of Trent affirmed that "*sanctifying grace is the formal cause of justification.*" It affirmed this *proposition* as being true through conformity to extra-mental reality and its immutable laws. This proposition *remains true today* and will remain true forever.

The notion of formal causality cannot be abandoned while still preserving "the meaning of this Conciliar proposition," for the meaning of this *Conciliar affirmation* is inseparable from the notion of formal cause, which is the *predicate* of the aforementioned proposition. If this notion is unstable, the Conciliar affirmation is unstable as well, for it is nothing other than the union of this notion with the subject in question, brought about through the verb *to be*. Therefore, one cannot here say, with Henri Bouillard: "The notions change, while the affirmations remain." In these Conciliar affirmations, the verb *to be* cannot *immutably* unite an essentially *unstable* notion to the subject [in question], just as an iron clamp cannot still the waves of the sea.

Moreover, we must note that one cannot retain the Council's *meaning* by replacing the notion of formal causality with *some other* notion that is said to be equivalent or *analogous*. This would already involve *a different meaning*, for the predicate of the Conciliar proposition would no longer be the same. We would only be able to claim that, at the time of the Council of Trent, it was true to say, "grace is the formal cause of justification," but today, we would need to *abandon* this notion and conceive of it in a different manner.

However, one may object: we must conceive of it in an analogous and equivalent manner, according to the law of analogy.

At the beginning of this article, we already noted that this represents an abuse of the notion of analogy. Two analogous notions do not express the same reality in different ways but, rather, express different realities that have a *proportional* similarity (e.g., the being of God and that of creatures, the being of created substance and that of accidents, or again, complexion as a sign of health and heart rate as such a sign).

By contrast, when two theological notions express one and the same reality in a different manner, they can be *univocal* if they are different only inasmuch as one is vague [*confus*] and the other distinct. Thus, St. Augustine said that the body of Christ is in the Eucharist not as a body in a place but, rather, *spiritually*, whereas St. Thomas later on said much more distinctly that it is there *per modum substantiae*, for he noted that substance, even bodily substance, is wholly in the whole and wholly in each of its parts. Where St.

Augustine only had a vague concept, St. Thomas had a distinct one. Likewise, St. Augustine conceived of habitual grace from the psychological and moral perspective, whereas St. Thomas moreover conceived of it from the metaphysical perspective, that is, the perspective of being, as an accident, an infused quality inhering in the soul. However, this metaphysical concept was already vaguely present in St. Augustine. Here, there is only a passage from the vague to the distinct for one and the same notion. Rather than here having two different, analogous notions, we have one and the same notion becoming more explicit and distinct.

This is not the case for the different conceptions of transubstantiation we find in modern theologians. The Thomists note that in her Councils, the Church first spoke of *the conversion* of the substance of bread into that of the body of Christ and later on more precisely spoke of *transubstantiation*. Thus, they conclude: hence, transubstantiation is *conversive*. By contrast, other theologians speak of a *non-conversive, adductive* transubstantiation, which would be the adduction of the body of Christ in the Eucharist, after the annihilation of the substance of the bread. This would not be the conversion of one substance into another but, rather, the *substitution* of the second for the first. In this case, the new notion of adductive transubstantiation is not equivalent and analogous to that of conversive transubstantiation but, rather, is the negation of it, not preserving the obvious meaning of the Councils, which first spoke of conversion and then, more precisely, of transubstantiation.

In order to preserve the meaning of a Conciliar proposition that brings together two notions through the use of the verb *to be*, these two notions must be maintained. If one of them is replaced by another, even if it is analogous, we no longer have the same judgment, and therefore, the "meaning" of the Council does not remain.

* * * * *

3° *What would be the real foundation for the aforementioned analogy of the new notions substituted for those that were previously consecrated? Would not the meaning of the Conciliar propositions become unknowable or uncertain even for the Church? Would not relativism be unavoidable?*

First of all, one and the same reality, like that of transubstantiation, cannot provide a foundation for two notions that are *contradictorily* opposed to one another, like that of *conversive* transubstantiation and that of *non-conversive* transubstantiation. One of these two notions is certainly false. We do not here have two analogous and equivalent notions, for the second is the negation of the first. By contrast, the existence of the creature that is analogous to that of the Creator is not the negation of the latter but, rather, presupposes it, just as an accident's existence presupposes that of substance. One must not alter the doctrine of analogy, for then confusion would thus be introduced into the very domain one wishes to clarify.

Moreover, would not the *meaning* of the Conciliar propositions become unknowable, or at least uncertain, even for the Church, if one were to say, "*One and the same affirmation* can subsist *through notions that evolve*. Or to put another way, a foundational element, *the essential element, remains through the course of surface-level changes*. In other words, the reality that we aim at forever remains the same."

We respond: however, this essential element remains unknown and even unknowable or at least uncertain, indeed, for the Church herself, for how are we to *distinguish* it from the aforementioned "surface-level changes"? We can only know revealed truth through notions united in a judgment, and if these notions are ever-changing (at least in certain cases), then the truth remains uncertain.

If we take this teaching and proposition from the Council of Trent, "Sanctifying grace is the formal cause of justification," and substitute for the notion of formal causality some *other notion* (even one that is said to be analogous and equivalent), who will ever be able to say *what is the absolute truth* that the Council wished to express?

We are told in response: "Two notions can be *different* inasmuch as they are connected to different systems and *identical* inasmuch as they both aim at the same reality and express an absolute truth."

However, if this absolute and immutable truth can only be expressed by different and successive notions, it remains unknowable and uncertain for the teaching Church herself. Thus, one abandons *traditional realism* in order to fall into *nominalism* and *relativism*.[12] And by abandoning traditional realism, one abandons, whether or not one wishes to do so, the traditional definition of truth, "*adaequatio rei et intellectus*," the conformity of judgment with extra-mental reality and its immutable laws, contenting oneself with the new definition, which slides toward pragmatism: *conformitas mentis et vitae*, the conformity of the judgment with the requirements of life and human action, which forever evolves.

Thus, absolute truth would become unknowable. In order to reach it, we will no longer have anything but provisional and successive technical notions, which are *neither true nor false* but, rather, only *useful* [*commode*] for representing to ourselves, in view of our own activity, a reality that will forever evade our attempts to grasp it, a reality that will never be able to be expressed in a certain and immutable manner.

---

12 And thus, historical works undertaken in this spirit do not in the least help one *understand* St. Thomas's doctrine. What can be their value for Thomists who have passed their life explaining the *Summa theologiae* article by article? They have no desire to dispute the value of the conclusions expressed in these works. This would give way to endless discussions, for it would be undertaken *outside of the light of principles*.

When one reads many contemporary works, one has, as it were, an intuition that this represents their fundamental deviation. Their authors at least implicitly accept some alternative for the very definition of truth. The latter is no longer conceived of as it is by the Church, namely, as the conformity of our judgment with extra-mental reality and its immutable laws but, rather, is thought to be the conformity of our judgment with the requirements of life and action, which forever evolves.

This is what we said in our earlier articles in *Angelicum*,[13] and we find ourselves compelled to maintain what we have stated.

Doubtlessly, in these difficult problems, the authors whom we critique could well have used this or that unfortunate formula, which does not properly translate their thought. However, as these formulas become more widespread, it is important that they be corrected, for otherwise, inexactness in language can lead to a true and very serious error.

From this perspective, we hope that this controversy will not have been useless. It will serve to help us to grasp all the better the Church's teaching concerning the truth and immutability of dogmatic formulas.[14]

---

[13] See Garrigou-Lagrange, "La nouvelle théologie," 126–45; "Verité et immutabilité," 124–39. [Tr. note: See the previous two chapters in this volume.]

[14] In a recent article, obviously written in response to what we recently said on this subject, its author seeks to show that "the absolute character of our truths come to them not so much from the representations to which they are applied as from the affirmation itself," and the author adds, "Through the application of the verb *to be*, whether it is 'copulative' or 'existential,' every judgment implies a positing of the absolute, of unlimited act." In support of this, the author cites *ST* I, q. 2, a. 1, ad 1, where St. Thomas states, "To know *that God exists* is naturally found in us in a kind of general and vague way, namely, inasmuch as God is man's beatitude.... However, this is not the same thing as knowing without qualification *that God exists*."

Doubtlessly, to know and desire beatitude in general is to know God vaguely, for such beatitude can only be found in God. However, this does not mean that "*every judgment* implies a positing of the absolute." For example, the judgment, "this stone or this house exists outside of my mind," does not imply the positing of the absolute, except in the sense that this stone can be of use for me in proving God's existence. See *ST* I, q. 16, a. 6.

Moreover, we have in no way misunderstood the analogous character of the notion of being nor the essential supernaturality of infused faith. For many years we have ceaselessly insisted on these two fundamental points.

[Tr. note: Fr. Garrigou-Lagrange is here citing Jean Marie Le Blond, "L'Analogie de la vérité: Réflexion d'un philosophe sur une controverse théologique," *Recherches de science religieuse* 34 (1947): 129–41 (here, p. 131).]

13

On the Need to Return to the Traditional Conception of Truth

Réginald Garrigou-Lagrange, OP

Today we find ourselves faced with ongoing discussions concerning the point of departure to be taken in philosophical research, the ontological value of the first rational principles, their necessitating evidence as laws of being, the value of the traditional proofs for God's existence, the foundation of moral obligation, the immutability of the notions consecrated by the Councils, the immutable truth of dogmatic definitions, the notion of the supernatural, the notion of original sin, the topic of monogenism vs. polygenism, and the very nature of theology as a science. A fundamental problem of great importance underlies all of these various discussions, a problem that perennially calls for reflection and cannot be set aside or overlooked. It lies at the very foundation of recent discussions that took place at Gallarate from the 16th to the 18th of September, 1947, concerning the point of departure for philosophical research as well as the philosophical thought of Maurice Blondel.[1]

The problem we are speaking of is that of the value of the traditional definition of truth. According to this definition, "*Adaequatio rei et intellectus*," truth is *the conformity of our judgment* not with the subjective laws of our mind but, rather, *with extra-mental reality and its immutable laws* of non-contradiction or identity (what is, is; what is not, is not), of efficient causality (nothing happens without a cause), and of finality (every agent acts for an end, whether or not it knows it).

Such is the fundamental thesis of traditional realism, which holds that our intellect can, by its own natural powers, arrive at metaphysical certitude concerning extra-mental being and even concerning the existence of God, the Sovereignly Perfect Being.

This doctrine was rejected by Kant, who denied that we could have speculative knowledge of the absolute. According to him, we scientifically know

---

[1] *Attualità filosofiche, Aloisianum, Gallarate, Atti del III Convegno di stuid filosofici cristiani tra professori universitarì* (Padova: Editoria Livinia, 1948).

only phenomena, without however knowing anything about *things in themselves, noumena*. For example, the principle of causality has its meaning and scope only in the world of phenomena or of experience (every phenomenon requires an antecedent phenomenon), and it does not enable us to elevate ourselves to certain knowledge of the First Cause.

The positivists go even further down this path, and the pantheistic idealism that came after Kant concluded: given that we cannot affirm with sufficient objective certitude the existence of a first transcendent cause, we must be content with affirming a first immanent cause, which we can call *God who becomes* or who fashions Himself in humanity through its evolution. Thus, *truth* no longer is the conformity of our judgment with extra-mental reality and its supposedly immutable laws, which we in fact cannot know. Instead, *truth is the conformity of our judgment with human life, which forever evolves,* or with the requirements of human action, which manifest themselves through the course of time. In place of the relative and provisional truth of one thesis, the provisional truth of an antithesis will follow, then a superior synthesis, and so on. No longer is there any immutable and absolute truth but, instead, all that remains is a relative and ever-changing truth. (This is what was said in the first proposition of the *Syllabus of Errors*,[2] and it was also said by the modernists.[3])

The point of departure for this outlook can be found above all in Kant. According to him, if truth consists in the agreement of our knowledge with the extra-mental object, my knowledge can only be regarded as being true on the condition that it is in agreement with the latter. Now, given that *I cannot know the extra-mental object except through knowledge*, the act of comparing knowledge with the extra-mental object is itself an act of comparing knowledge with knowledge. Since the object is outside of me and knowledge within me, I am forever limited to rendering one kind of judgment, namely, one stating whether my knowledge of the object agrees with my knowledge of the object. Therefore, man is *enclosed within himself and cannot escape therefrom*. The Greek skeptics already had noted this *vicious circle*, and Sextus Empiricus summarized their arguments, which went back to Protagoras and the other sophists.

* * * * *

Aristotle himself already responded to the sophists, saying that precisely through knowledge the knower becomes, in some manner, *something other* than itself, *quodammodo fit aliud a se*, thanks to the representation, which is *essentially relative* to the object represented, all of this taking place without

---

2 See Pius IX, *Syllabus of Errors*, no. 1 (Denzinger, no. 2901 [old no. 1701]).

3 See Sacred Office under Pius X, *Lamentabili*, no. 58 (Denzinger, no. 3458 [old no., 2058]).

involving any vicious circle. Indeed, the very property of a knower is the fact that it can, in this way, become something other than itself, *aliud a se*. Indeed, this already can be found in the case of animals: whereas the plant *remains enclosed within itself*, through knowledge, the animal is *open* to the external world. When the sun rises, the animal is not only illuminated and heated, as is the plant. Beyond this, *it sees the sun*: *quodammodo fit aliud a se; anima quodammodo fit omnia*.[4]

Moreover, against Protagoras and the other sophists, in *Metaphysics* 4 (III), chs. 3–5, Aristotle wrote his defense of the real value of the principle of contradiction (or, non-contradiction), founded on our very first intellectual knowledge, that of intelligible being in opposition to non-being: "*That which is, is; that which is not, is not.*" Protagoras cannot, at one and the same time, both be and not be himself.

In the same place, Aristotle examines all of the objections raised by the sophists against the real value of the principle of contradiction. He responds to them "*redarguitive*" by showing that these objections do not hold, for they err against the laws of reasoning and are unable to destroy the first natural evidence [of the principle of contradiction]. He adds that were we to doubt the real value of the principle of contradiction, we would be led to suppress all language, every essence (or substance), and indeed, every distinction between things (between a wall, a man, and a trireme). We would likewise be led to suppress movement, for its two *termini* would no longer be opposed to each other. We would arrive at our destination before ever setting forth toward it. Likewise, such a denial would lead us to destroy every form of truth, indeed even every form of opinion, all the degrees of probability, and all of those of error. No longer would there be any difference between a great error and small one. Consequently, we would also in this way be led to suppress every form of desire and action. Thus, we would not only be faced with the death of the intellect but, moreover, with the death of action in all of its domains.

Thus, the fact remains that truth is not only the conformity of our judgment with the logical laws of our mind but, rather, is the conformity of our judgment with extra-mental being and this immutable law of reality: that which is, is; that which is not, is not; being is not non-being.

Moreover, we must acknowledge *the primacy of being over becoming*, for there is *more* in *that which is* than in *that which becomes* and does not yet exist, more in the [fully] begotten adult, than in the embryo still in the midst of its development.

This is why *becoming* is not self-explanatory and, therefore, requires not only *a subject* which passes from potency to act (like the seed which develops) but also an *efficient cause* which actualizes it (begetting it), as well as *an end*,

---

4 See *De Anima* bk. 3, ch. 8; bk. 2, ch 12; St. Thomas Aquinas, *ST* I, q. 14, a. 1.

without which it would not have one given direction for its activity rather than another. Consequently, all bodily and spiritual movements require a Supreme Mover who is ever in act and an Ultimate end for the Universe, He who is Pure Act and the Sovereign Good.

St. Thomas deepened this doctrine. He similarly says in *De veritate*, q. 1, a. 1, "Being is what the intellect first conceives of, as it were, as that which is most known, into which it resolves all of its conceptions," and in *SCG* bk. 2, ch. 83, §32: "Just as sight naturally knows color and hearing sound, so too the intellect naturally knows *being* and those things that *per se* belong to being as such, and our knowledge *of the first principles* is founded on this knowledge." Then, in *De veritate*, q. 1, a. 9, St. Thomas adds

> The intellect *reflects back* upon its own act, not only inasmuch as it knows its own act but also inasmuch as it *knows its proportion to reality* [*rem*], and it indeed could not know this *unless it knew the nature of its act*, which it cannot know *unless the nature of its active principle were known*, namely, the intellect, WHOSE NATURE IS THAT IT BE CONFORMED TO REALITY [*rebus*]. Thus, in this way, the intellect, which reflects upon itself, knows truth.[5]

Our intellect KNOWS ITS OWN NATURE, which is to be ESSENTIALLY RELATIVE TO INTELLIGIBLE BEING, as sight is to color. In this way, the intellect *is not enclosed* within itself but, rather, is opened to the entire domain of intelligible reality. This involves no vicious circle but, on the contrary, is an affirmation which we must hold onto like something more precious than the apple of our eyes, and when this is not maintained, the intellect suffers and dies, as we see in positivism and Kantianism.

* * * * *

This fundamental problem was posed anew to philosophers and theologians when, in his "Le Point de depart de la recherche philosophique," Maurice Blondel wrote: "By rights, in place of the abstract and chimerical '*Adaequatio speculativa rei et intellectus*,' we must substitute methodical research, the *adaequatio realis mentis et vitae*."[6]

---

5 [Tr. note: We have chosen to render "res" as "reality" because this definition of truth applies not merely to purely speculative truth concerning "things" but also to speculatively-practical knowledge of moral truths. Admittedly, Fr. Garrigou-Lagrange most often understands this classical scholastic language of "res" in the sense of "thing" / "things." However, what he says about our knowledge of moral truths indicates something in the direction of this broader translation, which to our eyes is also more correct, theoretically speaking. In any case, let the reader bear in mind the slight interpretive choice that we have thus made, aware of its implications (and its relationship to certain remarks made by Blondel in the letter included in this volume).]

6 Maurice Blondel, "Le Point de depart de la recherche philosophique," *Annales de Philosophie chrétienne* 152 (June 15, 1906), 235. Blondel had already said such in his article,

Theologians, above all Thomists, do not fail to say: *prudence's practical truth* doubtlessly exists *through conformity to right intention, to right appetite,* as Aristotle says (see *EN* 6.2) and as St. Thomas teaches (see *ST* I-II, q. 57, a. 5, ad 3). No doubt, this prudential truth remains true even in the face of speculative error or absolutely involuntary or invincible ignorance, as when we are deceived without being able to discover the deception in question. Undoubtedly, there also is a practical truth of like kind in *mystical experience,* in which we find a conformity of the mind to the life of the man of good will[7] and a *peace* that is a sign of the truth. However, this mystical experience *presupposes* infused faith, and the act of faith itself presupposes the evident credibility of the revealed mysteries, attained through the examination of the signs of Revelation.

Moreover, as the [First] Vatican Council said, through the natural light of reason, we can have *certitude concerning the existence of God,* the Author of nature. However, in order for this to be so, *the principles* of the proofs for God's existence—in particular, the principle of causality—must be true *through conformity to extra-mental being,* with an *objectively sufficient certitude* (prior to the free choice [*option*] exercised by man in his willing [*de l'homme de homme volonté*]) and not only with *a subjectively sufficient certitude,* like that of the Kantian proof for God's existence.[8]

"L'Illusion idéaliste," *Revue de métaphysique et de morale* (Nov. 1898), 12, 17–18 (offprint): "In place of the question of *the agreement of thought with reality*, we must substitute the problem . . . of *the immanent adequation of ourselves with ourselves.*"

The declaration made in 1906 only confirmed what he said at great length in the 1893 edition of *L'Action*, above all in its last chapter, which is quite distant from traditional metaphysics and its proofs for God's existence.

Looking upon this work, many theologians saw (and we still see) thoughts that are much closer to Kant than to traditional metaphysics. However, they acknowledged that the work contained good *ad hominem* arguments addressed to rationalists holding the doctrine of immanence and not wishing to depart from it. Blondel's argument against such rationalists stated that according to the subjective requirements of action, one must freely choose either for or against God, and such a choice will either lead to progress and fecundity in our action or, instead, to its impairment and sterility. As regards this free option, he said, "It will depend on whether God does or does not really exist *for us*—that which alone is absolutely important." See the 1893 edition of *L'Action*, p. 426, as well as 347.

However, Kant could say the same thing to those who would refuse to accept his moral proof for God's existence. And through such an assertion, we will not find ourselves returning to the traditional definition of truth, for in making such claims, one is content with solely affirming that which is conformed to the subjective requirements of action.

7 [Tr. note: In line with what is found near the end of "Where is the New Theology Headed," we are reading "vie de l'homme de homme volonté" as "vie de l'homme de bonne volonté."]

8 According to Kant, we scientifically know only phenomena and do not know things in themselves, *noumena.* The world of noumena is unknown to us. Nonetheless, it is open

Finally, the practical truth of prudence, *through conformity to right intention*, presupposes that our intention is *truly right* in relation to man's ultimate end, and the judgment concerning man's end must be true *according to the conformity of the mind to extra-mental reality* (cf. *ST* I-II, q. 19, a. 3, ad 2).

The best theologians have added: if the traditional definition of speculative truth as "*adaequatio rei et intellectus*" is *chimerical*, and if we must *substitute* another one for it (and not merely complete it through the experience of the Christian life), WHAT IS THE VALUE OF DOGMATIC DEFINITIONS, *which presuppose it?* For all these dogmatic truths, must we content ourselves with the conformity of the mind (or our judgment) with the *requirements of life and human action* which forever evolves? What will thus become of the immutability of dogma?

Hence, we can understand why on December 1, 1924 the Holy Office condemned 12 propositions drawn from the philosophy of action, including (no. 5), the new definition of truth:

> Truth is not found in any particular act of the intellect wherein there would be had *conformity with the object*, as the Scholastics said, but rather truth is always in a state of becoming, and consists in *a progressive adequation of understanding with life*, namely, a certain perpetual process by which the intellect strives to develop and explain that which experience presents or action requires. However, it is a law that in all progression there is at no time anything which is determined or fixed.[9]

* * * * *

This gravely important question constantly comes up in one form or another in a number of contemporary debates.

We find it at the foundation of two problems examined in the recent gatherings in Gallarate.

---

to hypotheses of faith, which themselves are not arbitrary but, rather, are connected to *subjective necessities*. Practical reason posits, *a priori*, the law of duty according to the requirements of moral action, and this law implies postulates of its own: man's freedom, the immortality of the soul, and the existence of God. These postulates are unverifiable in the present world, but they must be admitted, for one does not have the right to renounce one's duty. Thus, according to Kant, *the certitude* of God's existence is *subjectively sufficient*, though *objectively insufficient*. Such certitude does not reach the *noumena*, in particular, concerning the existence of God, except *according to the requirements of moral action*, and not through a metaphysical demonstration. God's existence is true according to the conformity of the judgment, "God exists," with the requirements of action.

9 *Monitore ecclesiastico* (1925), 194; *Documentation catholique* (1925), I, 771ff.—Moreover, as we have noted elsewhere, Émile Boutroux, in his own criticisms of the philosophy of action, likewise noted how it slides toward pragmatism. See Émile Boutroux, *Science et religion dans la philosophie contemporaine* (Paris: Ernest Flammarion, 1908), 296.

Concerning the first of these two problems, "The point of departure for philosophical research," we read the papers offered by professors U. Padovani, F. Sciacca, and C. Mazzantini with particular interest.

The first (pp. 72–76) recalls for us, in an original way, the guiding principle and development of Aristotelian metaphysics perfected by St. Thomas, a metaphysics founded on the intellectual apprehension of intelligible being (of sensible things) in opposition to non-being and, hence, on the principle of non-contradiction, conceived of as the law of being and not only of the mind. This metaphysics is developed through the doctrine of act and potency, which renders becoming intelligible in function of being, leading to Pure Act in virtue of the principles of non-contradiction (or, identity), causality, and finality. According to this paper, as for St. Thomas, the first object known by our intellect is the intelligible being of sensible things, on the basis of which philosophical research ultimately elevates itself to God, with a certitude that preserves the traditional definition of truth.

For Professor Sciacca, who is inspired by St. Augustine (pp. 89ff), the point of departure for philosophical research is our awareness of our individual, existing being, known as an activity and interior dynamism, tending not toward dissolution but, rather, toward self-development, which stretches out, from its very beginnings of activity, toward the Transcendent Being, confusedly known and present, its principle and its end.

In these pages, we can feel the influence of Rosmini's philosophy as well as his own particular conception of being, a conception that is well known by theologians and which is notably different from that of St. Thomas, for according to Rosmini, the idea of being does not arise from abstraction but, rather, represents something of the divine.[10]

In his own unique way, professor Mazzantini (pp. 127–42) defends the Thomist doctrine concerning the point of departure of philosophical research: transcendental being, which emerges from sense experience under the influence of the agent intellect. He defends the objectivity of this doctrine by showing that the objections that have been raised against it remain worthless, and he holds that the first spiritual act necessarily is *to think*, an act prior to our exercise of free choice [*option*], indeed, an act whose value opens up the horizon for willing itself. Before every free choice [*option*], there are evident necessities, above all that of the principle of non-contradiction as a law of extra-mental being.

All of this seems absolutely certain to us: that which is absurd (e.g., a square-circle or an uncaused-contingent) is not only *unimaginable*, nor only *inconceivable*, but indeed evidently *unrealizable*. Here we have a form of

---

10 See Albert Michel, "Rosmini-Serbati, Antonio" in *Dictionnaire de théologie catholique*, vol. 13, pt. 2, ed. Émile Amann (Paris: Letouzey et Ané, 1937), cols. 2917–52.

necessitating evidence, and were we to deny it, we would be faced with the death of the intellect, which would thus be deprived of its own proper object: intelligible being in opposition to non-being. Without this first, certain principle, the intellect no longer has an incentive for passing from what is known to what is unknown and even cannot know anything certain, not even the "*cogito ergo sum*," for if the principle of non-contradiction is not absolutely certain as a law of thought and of being, my thought could at once be mine and not mine. Perhaps, we would need to be content with saying impersonally, "There is thought," just as one says, "It is raining." And still, this would not be certain, for is this impersonal thought really distinct from the subconscious and from the unconscious? Thus, how could we conclude with certitude, *ergo sum*?

Perhaps *I do not exist*. Rather, perhaps *I become*, and perhaps contradictories are identified in a *flow of becoming that has no efficient cause and no true and superior finality*, as is said by contemporary atheistic existentialists.

* * * * *

On the second subject, "The philosophical thought of Maurice Blondel," Professor Sciacca (pp. 255ff and 337ff), a Rosminian by tendency (and thereby a realist), strives to show that Maurice Blondel's philosophy, as found in his last works, attains, with certitude, extra-mental being and the Sovereignly Perfect Being, despite the place that Blondel gives to free choice [*option*], even in our knowledge of the ontological value of the first principles. This would no longer be a philosophy of action, like what we find in Blondel's work in 1893, but rather, a philosophy of mind, thought, action, and being, for the mind is, thinks, and acts.

Nonetheless, we remain faced with the question of knowing whether, according to Blondel's final works, *our certitude* concerning God's existence (which ever seems to be dependent upon our free option) is *objectively sufficient* (like the proofs founded on a necessitating principles) or only *subjectively sufficient*, like the Kantian proof for God's existence.

Fr. Giacon also strives (p. 323) to provide a sensible interpretation of Maurice Blondel's assertions, as though the philosophy of action ultimately rejoins the philosophy of being and as though Blondel no longer defined the truth merely in function of human action but, rather, in function of extramental being. However, would not Blondelism thereby be unfaithful to its first guiding impulse? Or, if it still preserves this impulse, does this not represent a kind of Thomist recasting, which rectifies all of its positions?

Professor Mazzantini (pp. 328ff) maintains, on the contrary, that Blondel's philosophy, which remains a philosophy of action, cannot arrive at metaphysical certitude concerning extra-mental being and its immutable laws, because this philosophy holds that our objective representations are always provisional, likewise holding that there are no necessitating forms of evidence.

Professor Padovani (pp. 328 and 343) also registers a number of objections along these same lines. He asks how Blondel demonstrates the existence of God and how he resolves the problems concerning the relationship between the soul and the body, the value of sense knowledge, and the foundation of morality. Fr. Deza (p. 334) says that if one abandons the path followed by St. Thomas, one no longer will be able to demonstrate the existence of God. Professor Bontandini (p. 346) asks whether Blondel's last books remain faithful to his early thought; if they do, he does not truly prove the existence of God.

Fr. Augustin Valensin notes that one cannot respond to the objections raised except by referring *to the whole* of Blondel's thought, for Blondel never wished to be a scholastic, nor to distinguish problems along the same lines as does classical metaphysics.

Nonetheless, it remains the case that Blondel's thought is a human form of thought that proceeds from the known to the unknown and involves principles, along with the consequences drawn therefrom. Now, the objections raised against his thought are concerned with the *certitude* of his principles. Is this certitude *objectively sufficient* or only *subjectively so*? In the latter case, one would not end up with a true proof for God's existence. Likewise, the traditional definition of truth would not be preserved. Instead, all that would remain is a definition holding that truth is the conformity of our judgment with the requirements of action, as we find in the Kantian proof for God's existence.

* * * * *

In order to respond to the objections raised against Blondelism, Professor Sciacca (pp. 337–51) notes, himself being inspired by Rosmini, that the traditional positions Blondel intends to go beyond are not *false* in his opinion but, rather, are only *incomplete*, taking on their full value only in the superior synthesis presented by him.

We do not see how this can be harmonized with texts in Blondel's work *La pensée*, which we will need to recall below, for example, this one: "It is *deceptive* to speak of an overly clear intuition of mathematical and rational truths."[11]

In order to explain this to us, we are told that every limited truth is only one aspect of the complete truth to which we aspire and that the latter is not merely abstract but, rather, is concrete and living. Certainly, this sort of claim is not new. It is admitted by all philosophers worthy of the name, as well as all theologians, above all if one is thinking of the immediate vision of the Divine Essence, which is promised to us at the end of our spiritual and supernatural ascent.

---

11 Maurice Blondel, *La pensée* (1934), vol. 2, 431.

However, in the discussion at hand, we are situated within the order of philosophical knowledge, not in the order of the supernatural knowledge had through infused faith, which becomes living, penetrating, and, as it were, tasted in authentic mystical experience under the influence of the gifts of the Holy Spirit.

Thus, in the order of philosophical knowledge, if one comes to tell us that the proofs for God's existence given by St. Thomas *do not establish their conclusion* if we also lack the Rosminian primitive intuition or the living and concrete thought of God who is vaguely known and present to us, spoken of by Blondel, we cannot admit such a claim, and the entire problem is raised anew.

As all theologians know, Rosmini's position runs into grave difficulties. To recognize this fact, one merely needs to carefully read the first 17 of the 40 condemned Rosminian propositions. But that is another matter, lying outside of our present concerns.

However, we still must ask whether for Maurice Blondel the *ontological and transcendent value of the principles* of the traditional proofs for God's existence has *a necessitating evidential character*. If it does, why would he still say today, as in his first books, that *an option* must be exercised so that one may admit this evidence, an option properly so called, a free choice.[12] Thus, is *the affirmation* of the real value of these principles *true* according to its conformity with extra-mental being, *independent of the requirements of moral action*, or instead, only *according to the requirements* that are responded to by such an option? In other words, do we here have an *objectively sufficient* certitude or only one that is *subjectively sufficient*, like that found in the Kantian proof for God's existence?

In the 1893 edition of his text *L'Action*, Maurice Blondel said, "*Knowledge of being implies the necessity of the option: being does not exist in knowledge before the freedom of choice but, rather, is there only after it.*"[13] The context even makes it clear that he is speaking of the option that freely prefers God over everything created. This assertion constantly comes up in the 1893 edition of *L'Action*,[14] above all in its final chapter.

However, even in his last works, Blondel remains faithful to his earliest thought. Instead of saying, like traditional philosophers, "*Certain minds are so badly disposed* that they seek to pull back from the natural evidence of the principle of contradiction as a law of being," he writes in *L'Être et les êtres*: "*No intellectual evidence, not even that of principles* that are absolute of themselves, having a necessary ontological value, *imposes itself upon us with a*

---

12 [Tr. note: Reading "ou un choix libre" for "ou un choix est libre."]

13 See Blondel, *L'Action*, 435.

14 See Blondel, *L'Action*, 297, 341, 350, 426, 435, 437, and 463.

spontaneously and infallibly constraining form of certainty."[15]—According to traditional realism, Protagoras himself sees that he cannot at one and the same time be and not be Protagoras. Here, we have a form of necessitating evidence that is not the object of a choice [*option*], as is the case for a proposition that is only probable.

Therefore, Blondel remains quite distant from traditional metaphysics, in particular when he writes in *La pensée*: "It is deceptive to speak of an alleged sensible intuition.... Deceptive too to speak of the so-called intuition of consciousness ... if it is subject to subjective illusions.... *It is deceptive to speak of an overly clear intuition of mathematical and rational truths.*"[16]

One would think that this quote was drawn from Sextus Empiricus's *Adversus mathematicos*.

Likewise, Blondel still writes in the first volume of *La pensée*: "*The notion of an object* and the use that is ordinarily made of it is one of these divisions, one of these *illegitimate* 'overestimations' [*majorations*], which we do not cease to denounce as being *the chronic deception* and *ruinous improbity* from which many a philosophy is dying today."[17] Thus, what could be the value of the assertion made by the [First] Vatican Council concerning the distinction of our supernatural knowledge from our natural knowledge, *on account of their objects*: "The perpetual common belief of the Catholic Church has held and holds also this: there is *a twofold order of knowledge*, distinct not only in its principle but *also in its object"*?[18]

In the 1934 work *La Pensée*, we can find many other assertions that are no less deserving of criticism.[19]

For all these reasons, we think Blondelism is still quite distant from St. Thomas's teaching. However, this does not prevent us from recognizing that it contains very gripping *ad hominem*[20] arguments against the rationalist partisans of the doctrine of immanence, in particular the argument set forth in the 1893 edition of *L'Action* as follows: "It has been claimed that the very notion of revelation does not allow for rational discussion, yet one does not allow this negative conclusion to be debated: *on the pretext of*

---

15 Maurice Blondel, *L'Être et les êtres* (1935), 415.

16 Blondel, *La pensée* (1934), vol. 2, 431.

17 Blondel, *La pensée*, vol. 1, 131.

18 [First] Vatican Council, *Dei filius*, ch. 4 (Denzinger, no. 3015 [old no. 1795]). Also, see *Dei filius*, can. 4.1 (Denzinger, no. 3041 [old no. 1816]).

19 See Blondel, *La pensée*, vol. 1, 130–36, 170–72, 175, 179, 180, 349, and 355; vol. 2, 39, 66–69, 90, 96, and 196.

20 [Tr. note: That is, an argument that concedes the premises of one's interlocutor, for the sake of arguing with that particular person. See Tommaso Zigliara. *Summa philosophica in usum scholarum*, 12th ed., vol. 1 (Paris: Briguet, 1900), 157.]

respect, free examination refuses to be examined."[21] Thus, one finds oneself to be voluntarily enclosed "within a *biased philosophy hostile* to the very notion of revelation and to the possibility and usefulness of every kind of defined dogma."[22]

From this perspective, Blondelism has freed certain minds from their rationalistic prejudices, and we think that Blondel's last works draw close to traditional realism. However, we do not believe that he has been unfaithful to his earliest thought, which is solidly anchored in him, thus keeping him still quite distant from the realism of St. Augustine and that of St. Thomas.

What is certain is the fact that we must absolutely return to the traditional definition of [speculative] truth: *adaequatio rei et intellectus*, the conformity of judgment with extra-mental being and its immutable laws. Dogmas presuppose this definition. It absolutely cannot be called "chimerical," nor can one *substitute* for it a form of truth which would only belong to the practical order.

In other words, we must admit that the real value of the first principles has a *necessitating* evidence, independent of every *free choice* [option]. This is what St. Thomas says in *ST* I-II, q. 17, a. 6: "If there are such things, which the intellect grasps and *naturally* assents to, such as the first principles, then such an assent or dissent *does not lie in our power* but, rather, in the order of nature." It is not through a free option but, rather, through its very nature that our intellect adheres to the ontological value and absolute necessity of the first principles as laws of reality. Only in this way can we maintain the traditional definition of truth which the Church's dogmas themselves presuppose.

---

[21] Blondel, *L'Action*, 392ff.
[22] Blondel, *L'Action*, 393.

14

On the Immutability of Defined Truths, With Remarks on the Notion of the Supernatural

Réginald Garrigou-Lagrange, OP

In the April–May 1948 issue of *Recherches de science religieuse*, Fr. Henri Bouillard looks to explain the correct way that a number of assertions in his book *Conversion et grâce chez S. Thomas d'Aquin* should be understood in relation to the notions used by the Councils. In particular he is concerned with explaining this assertion: "While *notions*, methodologies, and systems *change* with the passing of time, *the affirmations* they contain *remain*, even though they come to be expressed in different categories."[1]

One page later, he adds, in relation to the Council of Trent's teaching that sanctifying grace is the *formal cause* of justification (Sess. 6, ch. 7, can. 10): "In so doing, did it consecrate this use and thus bestow a definitive character upon the notion of grace, considered as a form? *By no means*. . . . To this end, it employed notions that were commonly in use in the theology of that era. However, *others can be substituted* for them without modifying *the meaning of the Council's teaching*."[2]

Likewise, on p. 224: "In abandoning Aristotelian physics, modern thought abandoned the notions, schemas, and dialectical oppositions which were meaningful only in relation to that outlook. In order for theology to continue to furnish the mind with something meaningful, to be able to fertilize it, and progress with it, *it must abandon* these notions."[3] Similarly: "A theology that would not be contemporary would be a false theology."[4]

---

[1] See Henri Bouillard, *Conversion et grâce chez S. Thomas d'Aquin* (Paris: Aubier, 1941), 220.

[2] Bouillard, *Conversion*, 221.

[3] Bouillard, *Conversion*, 224. I [i.e., Fr. Garrigou-Lagrange] have added the emphases.

[4] Bouillard, *Conversion*, 229. Also see what is said (Ibid., 211) about the "relativity of notions" in theology.

To these claims, we responded: If we must "abandon" the notion of formal cause, which is found all throughout St. Thomas's theology, what will remain of this theology?

Of all the aforementioned propositions, one in particular drew our attention, namely: "While *the notions change, the affirmations remain.*" If we must "abandon" *the notion* of formal cause, how can we maintain *the meaning* of the Council of Trent's *affirmation*, "sanctifying grace is the formal cause of justification"?

We apologize for insisting once more on this point, but the importance of this doctrinal problem, one that touches so closely upon the immutability of Christian faith, prevails over every other consideration. This is what was on our mind when we wrote our earlier article, along with the citations it contained. Indeed, this question must not be considered solely from the philologist's perspective and that of the historian but also must be considered from the perspective of the metaphysician and the theologian, and if need be, we will be able to elaborate on the matter [*s'il est necessaire, nous pourrons la développer*].

In order to see things clearly in the problem facing us, we must recall what an *affirmation* is. It is a judgment that, by means of the verb *to be* (the root of all other verbs), attributes a predicate to a subject.[5] Moreover, an affirmation is *true* if it is conformed to reality, and it is *immediately* true if a real, immutable identity exists underneath the logical diversity of its subject and predicate.[6]

Hence, we asked: how can an immutable truth like, "Sanctifying grace is the formal cause of justification," *remain standing* if the notion of formal cause *changes* and must have another notion substituted for it (even if such a notion would be analogous)? We must note that the Council of Trent did not limit itself to the use of terms contained in Scripture but, instead, *specified* that *the formal cause* of justification is not only the imputation of Christ's merits or God's favor, nor is it an interior renewal that would be brought about solely through infused faith or infused hope, which can still exist when one is in the state of mortal sin, but rather, is an interior renewal brought about through sanctifying grace and charity. How can the meaning of this *affirmation* made by the Council be maintained if we must "abandon" the notion of formal cause and *substitute* another, analogous one for it?

---

5 As Aristotle says, *Socrates acts* means *Socrates is acting*.

6 See *ST* I, q. 13, a. 12: "In any given true affirmative proposition, the predicate and the subject must signify something that is, in some way, the same in reality and diverse notionally in reason [*diversum secundum rationem*]."—For example, Peter is the same subject who *is* a man, who *is* large, who *is* learned, who *is* acting, who *is* sick, who *is* the father of three children, etc.—Human nature *is* the principle of given properties and of given specific activities.

Thus, as we said, we would end up having *a different affirmation*. The Council's affirmation would not be maintained, for the immutable truth of a judgment necessarily depends on the immutable value of the notions, which it unites by means of the verb *to be*.

The immutability of the union of two terms presupposes the immutability of these very terms. Two terms that change like waves on the sea cannot be immutably united, and in order for their union to not be immutable, all that is needed is for one of its two terms to change.

(The waves of the sea are only an example for sensibly verifying the principle invoked, one that is self-evident to the intellect.)

Fr. Bouillard seeks to resolve the problem by saying:

> When one and the same revealed truth is expressed in different (e.g., Augustinian, Thomist, Suarezian, etc.) systems, the various notions used for translating this truth are neither "equivocal" (if they were, one would no longer be speaking about the same thing) nor "univocal" (for otherwise, all systems [of thought] would be identical) but, rather, "*analogous*." In other words, *they express the same reality in different ways.*[7]

However, as we already noted [in our earlier article], this does not represent the true notion of analogy. Rather, in place of it, we here have substituted a pseudo-Thomist analogism, which represents an abuse of the notion of analogy, just as philosophism represents an abuse of philosophy.

By proceeding along these lines, one forgets that *notions that are truly analogous* do not aim at the same reality but, instead, *at different realities* that are similar according to a proportion (e.g., the being [*être*] of God and that of creatures, or again, the being [*être*] of substance and that of accidents, or again, pulse and complexion as signs of health).

In the solution that has been proposed to us, the author speaks of "analogous notions expressing *the same reality in different ways*." As we said [in our earlier article], according to this account, the notion of *conversive* transubstantiation could be affirmed as being analogous to that of *adductive, nonconversive* transubstantiation.

Now, this is false, for given that the second of these notions represents the negation (or contradiction) of the first, the notions are not analogous. By contrast, the being [*être*] of [finite] beings does not represent the negation of God's being but, rather, presupposes it.[8]

---

7 Bouillard, "Notions conciliaires et analogie de la vérité," *Recherches de science religieuse* 35 (1948): 254. (Emphasis is Fr. Garrigou's.)

8 Merely because the spiritualist and materialist conceptions of man express the same reality in different ways, it does not follow that they would be analogous. One is the negation of the other.

Moreover, even if this new manner of conceiving of analogy were acceptable, the *meaning* of this Conciliar *affirmation*, "sanctifying grace is the formal cause of justification," *would not remain the same* if one were to "abandon" the notion of formal cause.

If *the notion* of formal cause is obsolete, *the affirmation* founded on this notion is obsolete as well. And if we must "abandon" this notion, we will likewise need to abandon this affirmation, whether or not we wish to do so, just as the Ptolemaic astronomical hypothesis was abandoned as a hypothetical conceptualization that was not true through conformity to reality but, rather, was so only as an *expedient* representation enabling a *provisional* classification of the phenomena observed up to that point of time.—However pure the intentions of the author whom we have critiqued might be, they do not eliminate the consequences of the position he has advanced.[9]

We firmly hold that the notion of formal cause is no more obsolete in philosophy and theology than are those of matter, end, and efficient cause.[10] One

---

Merely because the divine justice and the divine mercy express the same, sovereignly simple divine reality in different manners, they are not analogous to each other. Rather, the divine justice is analogous to human justice and the divine mercy to human mercy. In contrast to what nominalists claim, one clearly cannot write "the divine mercy" in those places where it is necessary to speak of justice, for were one to do that, one would say that God punishes through His mercy.

Let us not forget the definition of univocal, analogous, and equivocal [things]:

"UNIVOCAL [things] are *those whose term [nomen] is held in common*, while the *formal notion [ratio]* signified by the term is *simpliciter* the same. Thus, men univocally are one in species. EQUIVOCAL [things] are those whose term is held in common, while the *formal notion [ratio]* signified through the term is *totally different*, like the dog, which is a domestic animal and the constellation *canis major*."

"ANALOGOUS [things] are those whose *term is held in common*, while the *formal notion [ratio]* signified by that term is *simpliciter diverse* in them, though remaining *proportionally the same*, as being is said of God and of creatures."

9 Moreover, the notions of the four causes are correlative. A mutual relationship exists between the agent and the end, as well as between matter and form, between that which is determinable and the determination given and received for an end.

10 To abandon the notion of formal cause (or, the notion of *the formal constitutive*) would be to abandon the notion of *essence*, as well as the *first principles* that presuppose this notion. It would be to fall into relativism, and the *Ecclesia docens* herself would fall into such relativism if she wished to follow down this path, which her discernment prevents her from taking.

By a necessity at once logical and metaphysical, whether or not one wishes, one erroneous denial would entail many others. We could consider several extreme cases. In Spinoza's *Ethics*, the first error (the assertion that only one substance can exist) entails all the others. This is what makes this book into an extremely tightly-woven web of errors, and once the first error is conceded, one is lost or becomes increasingly entangled. The

will forever speak of the formal constitutive of a given substance, be it bodily or spiritual, as well as that of our faculties, our virtues, and of justification.

Here, we must note that we can consider the notion of formal cause in all its relations with the subsequent or subordinate notions in the Aristotelian system, and from this perspective it has not been consecrated by the Council.

However, we can also consider it *in itself, along with its roots* in the very first, absolutely immutable notions and principles of natural reason (that is, common sense), which were made manifest by Aristotle, notions that are more or less profoundly known by metaphysicians according to how well they penetrate such matters.[11] Understood thus, this notion, along with its roots, is taken up for loftier consideration by theology under the twofold light of revelation and faith accompanied by the [Spirit's] gifts of understanding and wisdom. Theology thus *approves* this notion negatively as not being opposed to any revealed truths and then positively approves it as being *suitable for expressing a number of them in a true manner* (see *ST* I, q. 1, a. 6, ad 2 and 3). From this perspective, a Council can approve such a notion with the *assistance of the Holy Spirit* and can *approve it forever*.

In this sense, as we said, the Council of Trent consecrated this notion by saying that the formal cause of justification is sanctifying grace.

Does or does not Fr. Bouillard believe that the "notion" of *formal cause* "remains" after the downfall of what was obsolete in the Aristotelian cosmology? In other words, according to him, is this notion, along with its roots, a *stable philosophical notion* indicating what we all mean when we speak of the formal constitutive of a given thing—in the case at hand, that of justification?

---

same is true regarding the Hegelian system, which seems to be inspired by an evil genius that was all the more insightful for having formulated the ultimate, necessary consequences of a false principle. Thus, we have these renowned chains of errors which to the eyes of God and of angelic intellects must be absolutely outrageous and ridiculous, indeed, truly insane. Many historians of philosophy mix together great philosophers with great sophists, even though on other occasions they present the generative principle of the greatest truths alongside [*et*] that of the greatest errors. The latter are really contradictions, which are covered over by specious argumentation, like a hidden underwater mine.

11 We have explained this at greater length in our book, *Thomistic Common Sense: The Philosophy of Being and the Development of Doctrine*, trans. Matthew K. Minerd (Steubenville, OH: Emmaus Academic, 2021), 291–394: "How dogmatic formulas are given precision in philosophical terms" (pp. 229–44); "Do dogmatic formulas, thus given precision, remain accessible to common sense?" (pp. 245–74); "Even thus given precision, they do not make dogma subservient to any system" (pp. 275–99). Nonetheless, in a sense, the Church does have a philosophy, which is related to the primitive creed in the same way that "the natural metaphysics of the intellect" is related to common sense (pp. 297–99). Concerning the intellect's first glance over intelligible being, the good, and the supernatural, how this first glance comes to be obscured, and how we are to retrieve it, see pp. 301–19.

Moreover, is this a stable philosophical notion *approved as such forever in a superior light by the Council*? Or, rather, is it only a *hypothesis*, like those formed in the positive sciences, *provisionally accepted* by the Council for as long as this happens to be accepted by philosophy and theology, an acceptance that will no longer hold when this hypothesis is judged to be obsolete and therefore no longer accepted by philosophers and theologians? In the second case, the Church will need to then provisionally accept *another* so-called analogical *notion*. Thus, the meaning of the Council that accepted the first notion will no longer be maintained, since the Church will no longer accept it. However, she will express *a different judgment* in order to accept another, equally provisional truth. In this way, one and the same *Ecclesia docens* will never know what the exact role of sanctifying grace in justification is. On this explanation, the role played by sanctifying grace *will not vary* in itself; however, its knowable meaning would indeed *vary*.[12] In one era, it will be said to play the role of being the "formal cause," and in another, it will be designated by "another notion" (and not only by other, equivalent words).

Indeed, we must carefully distinguish, on the one hand, *the changing of notions*[13] from, on the other, recourse made to different, equivalent words in order to express *the same notion*.

In order to explain, even today, what is meant by the term "form," it suffices to say, as is generally done in the best standard or philosophical dictionaries, that this word has a number of meanings. In its common use, it first of all designates *the various determinations of a body's extension*: a conical form, a spherical form. Then, philosophically, it means *what determines matter in such a way as to constitute a bodily being of this or that species*—for example, an inorganic element (gold, silver), a plant (an oak), an animal (a lion, a bird, etc.). Thus, an animal's sensitive soul is called its substantial form, the principle of its specific activities. St. Thomas often says: "The form in bodily beings determines the matter in this or that species and is the principle of its activity." *In purely spiritual beings*, like the angels, "The form is the very nature of the thing" (cf. *ST* III, q. 13, a. 1).—The dictionary compiled by Littré, speaking first primarily of bodies, says for the word form (lat. *forma*): "That which determines the matter to be such or such a thing." It is less exact when it says before this, "The ensemble of a being's qualities." It would be better to say: in each being, the form is the principle of its specific properties and activities.

---

12 Fr. Bouillard wrote in p. 220 of his book [*Conversion*]: "A new concept is introduced, one that will command the organization of a new system. Never is the divine truth accessible beyond [*en deçà de*] every kind of contingent truth. Such is the law of the Incarnation." This entire page must be read carefully. We respond: an immutable, true affirmation presupposes the immutability of the notions it unites together.

13 [Tr. note: In the original French, "notions" has an opening quotation mark without a closing one.]

Consequently, we say that the rational soul is the form of the human body, the root principle of man's properties and his specific activities.[14] We likewise speak about that which formally constitutes a given virtue (e.g., justice) and, in a superior order, about *that which formally constitutes justification* or *that by which the just man is first and foremost truly just in the eyes of God*. There, we see the verbal equivalences that enable us to understand the meaning of the term "formal cause." However, *this notion is maintained*; it is not replaced by *another*.[15] All of this is intellectually accessible by all in every era.

It is understandable that, sometimes, apologists who are above all preoccupied with the *communication* of Christian and Catholic doctrine to our contemporaries would be particularly attentive to the *adaptation of concepts* to the cultivated men of our era. They sometimes feel a kind of discomfort before a number of concepts used by classical theology, such as transubstantiation and the hypostatic union. Nonetheless, this difficulty is not completely insurmountable if, in the study of traditional philosophy and theology, one strives to *pass methodically from the vague concept known by common sense* and expressed by its nominal definition *to the distinct concept*, which is given greater specification with the progress of philosophy or that of sacred science. On the other hand, one must not forget that, beyond any given apologetic preoccupation, theology's first mission *is to determine and preserve the exact meaning of the truths revealed by God*. To this end, it must make use of *truly universal concepts that are always and everywhere valid*, like those necessary for understanding the first principles. Therefore, it must take care never to slide down the slopes of nominalism toward relativism, even unconscious relativism. One merely needs to recall the excesses that took place because of such nominalism during the 14th century.

This nominalistic outlook came to argue that truths exceeding experience, such as the existence of God, are indemonstrable, that we cannot know, even imperfectly, *the nature of things*, and that the concept of man does not signify *human nature* but, rather, only *individual men*. According to such nominalism, there is no immutable idea of human nature, even in God. Indeed, even for Him, all that remained was knowledge of all individual things. Consequently, even after revelation, one could no longer define the supernatural as, "That which exceeds nature," for *nature* itself would remain unknowable on such nominalistic foundations. In all domains, the only thing

---

[14] In order to affirm the substantial unity of human nature, the Council of Vienne defined that the rational soul is "Of itself and essentially the form of the human body" (Denzinger, no. 902), but it did not define that it is the *sole* substantial form of the human body, as St. Thomas teaches.

[15] In a recent article, Jacques Maritain showed how one can explain this notion of form to contemporary scientists and philosophers. See Jacques Maritain, "Coopération philosophique et justice intellectuelle," *Revue thomiste* 46 (1946): 439ff [434–56].

remaining would be *unstable notions fixed by words and ever-provisional schemata*.[16] This represented nothing other than relativism, which has become even more pronounced with the advent of positivism and evolutionism.—Many of the tendencies of contemporary philosophy could lead us back to it, and certain looseness in language arising from these tendencies could further aggravate them. [17]

In the same book, Fr. Bouillard, speaking of the authors of theological manuals and of more erudite works as well, writes:

> If these authors know that theology has not existed in its contemporary state, as it is found in the theologian's knowledge today, they at least unconsciously imagine that *it was already given as such in the domain of eternal truths*[18] and that discursive intelligence only had to discover it and gradually reconstruct it. By contrast, a historical study reveals the degree to which theology is bound to time, to the becoming of the human mind.[19]

However, traditional theologians are not deceived in thinking that perfect theological science exists *in the domain of eternal truths* in the divine intellect, in the domain of the theologians who have arrived at the beatific vision, and that this theological science existed in an imperfect state (while, nonetheless, already being *immutable* on a good number of points) in the intellect of someone like St. Thomas Aquinas and that of many other theologians while still here-below.

Thus, we can understand why the Holy Father said in a discourse published by the *L'Osservatore Romano* on Sept. 19, 1946:

---

[16] Many speak in a similar manner today.

[17] There are many other points in Fr. Bouillard's text that call for response from us, but we do not have the time to do so. Let us only say that in *ST* I-II, q. 113, a. 8, ad 2, St. Thomas, as ever, makes recourse to the reciprocal causality of the disposition and the form and then writes: "The disposition of the subject precedes the reception of the form in the order of nature; however, it follows the action of the agent through which even the subject itself is disposed. And therefore, *the movement of free choice precedes, in the order of nature, the reception [consecutionem] of grace, although it follows the infusion [infusionem] of grace*." *Consecutio* is said on the side of the subject (namely man), and *infusio* on that of God who infuses.

For merit of eternal life, I meant that what is taught by the Councils is what the theologians call "*de condigno*" and not only a merit of suitability "*de congruo*."

Finally, although I said, "I have no desire to dispute the value of certain historical works," I added, "This would give way to endless discussions, for it would be undertaken outside the light of principles." Hence, I still can judge these works in light of the principles which they neglect.—All the same, I have the pleasure of seeing that the recollection of these principles is not without some effect.

[18] I have added the emphases.

[19] Bouillard, *Conversion*, 213.

Much has been said, though not with careful enough consideration, about the "new theology," which, since it rolls along with all things themselves rolling along in continuous motion, itself will forever be in motion and never will arrive at some destination. If it seemed that such an opinion should be embraced, what would become of Catholic dogmas which must never change, and what would become of the unity and stability of the faith.

THE NOTION OF THE SUPERNATURAL

In the same issue of *Recherches de science religieuse*,[20] Fr. Henri de Lubac wishes to prove that *the natural beatitude* spoken of by St. Thomas is only the imperfect beatitude that falls to the present life, in contrast to the *supernatural beatitude* (or perfect beatitude) experienced in the next life. In support of this claim, he cites a number of texts from St. Thomas that, in fact, make use of examples of natural beatitude precisely in the sense spoken of by Aristotle in relation to the present life.

However, St. Thomas also spoke about the natural beatitude of the angels in their own state as wayfarers [in their first instant of existence, prior to their first free choice],[21] and of a kind of natural beatitude had by children who die without baptism.[22]

Moreover, if the perfect beatitude had in the next life (which is nothing other than the immediate vision of the divine essence, along with the love of God that flows from this) is TRULY SUPERNATURAL, as St. Thomas shows (in *ST* I, q. 12, a. 1 and 4; q. 60, a. 5, ad 4 and 5, etc.), then it is *absolutely grace-given, exceeding the exigencies of every created and creatable intellectual nature*. Consequently, it is *in no way owed* to our nature, as the Church herself said in condemning Baius. Otherwise, the very notion of the supernatural is what would find itself being overthrown.

And thus, in creating man, God *did not owe him* the means needed for leading him to his supernatural beatitude. Therefore, we must conclude that man could have been created in a purely natural state, without sanctifying grace, the seed of eternal life.[23] This means that if man had observed

---

20 See Henri de Lubac, "Duplex Hominis Beatitudo (Saint Thomas, Iª 2ᵃᵉ, q. 62, a. 1)," *Recherches de science religieuse* (April-June 1948): 290–300.

21 See *ST* I, q. 60, a. 5; q. 62, a. 1; q. 63, a. 3.

22 See *De malo*, q. 5, a. 2 and 3.

23 St. Thomas says in *In II Sent.* d. 31, q. 1, a. 2, ad 3:

> God had been able, at the beginning, when He created man, even *to form from the mud of the earth another man whom He would have left in the condition of his nature*, namely so that he would be mortal and passible, likewise experiencing concupiscence's struggle against reason [*ad rationem*]. Were this the case, nothing

the natural law in the present life, God would have owed it to Himself to give man, in the next life, *natural beatitude,* in other words, a beatitude proportionate to our nature, one that is greatly inferior to the immediate vision of the divine essence. It would have consisted in a natural knowledge of God through the reflection of the divine perfections in the created world. Such knowledge would have been certain and unmixed with errors, being likewise accompanied by rational love for God, the author of nature, preferred to all things.

This distinction of the two orders of nature and grace quite certainly is not something foreign to St. Thomas's thought, and it was not "forged by a certain number of Thomist theologians," as Fr. de Lubac claims.[24] Nor is it true to say that I supposedly have reproduced an error committed by Fr. Cathrein. For fifty years, I have studied this problem, and the conception I present is nothing other than what I have found in St. Thomas himself, reading him article by article in light of his own principles and not in light of some preconceived idea. And this is also what I have found said on these matters by all the great Thomists,[25] something likewise laid forth so well by the [First] Vatican Council:

> The *perpetual common belief of the Catholic Church* has held and holds also this: *there is a twofold order of knowledge,* distinct not only in its principle but also in its object; in its *principle,* because in the one we know by natural reason, in the other by divine faith; in its *object,* because apart from what natural reason can attain, there are proposed to our belief *mysteries that are hidden in God that can never be known unless they are revealed by God.*[26]

It is clear that the proper object of the divine intellect, *essentia Dei immediate et clare visa sicuti est,* immensely exceeds the natural powers and *exigencies*

---

would have been detracted from human nature because this would follow from the principles of [his] nature. However, this defect would not have the character of being a form of fault and blame for him because this defect would not have been caused through the [sinful exercise of his] will.

Likewise, see *De malo,* q. 4, a. 1, ad 14.

And again, see *ST* III, q. 1, a. 3, ad 2: "Also, for the perfection of the universe it suffices that the creature be ordered *in a natural manner* to God as to an end." Similarly, see *ST* I, q. 23, a. 1; I-II, q. 5, a. 5; *De veritate,* q. 14, a. 2.

24 See Henri de Lubac, *Surnaturel* (Paris: Aubier, 1946), 254.

25 I set this forth at length in the work *On Divine Revelation,* trans. Matthew K. Minerd (Steubenville, OH: Emmaus Academic, 2021), vol. 1, 475–562, there citing a great number of texts from St. Thomas.

26 [First] Vatican Council, *Dei filius,* ch. 4 (Denzinger, no. 3015).

of every created and creatable intellect. Otherwise, the created intellect in its very nature would be *specified* by the same formal object as is the divine intellect. This would represent the pantheistic confusion of these two natures. Moreover, if the definition of sanctifying grace could thus already hold true for the nature of the created intellect, the latter could not be elevated to a superior order of knowledge.[27]

Thus, we fully accept what Fr. Charles Boyer, S.J., wrote recently concerning the new notion of the supernatural proposed by Fr. de Lubac:

> However, it is now time to examine the internal coherence of this new system. Whatever divergences of opinion might exist among theologians, the supernatural must at least retain the character indicated by its name and attributed to it by the documents of the Church, namely, that of being a reality above our nature: *perfectionem quae naturalem superet* ([First] Vatican Council, *Dei filius*, can. 2.3, *de Revelatione*, Denzinger, no. 3028). Now, an end without which a nature is not conceivable cannot be called an end that is above this nature. Such an end is natural to that nature. It is the end that is owed to it and that God owes to Himself to give to it. It is a properly demanded end, whereas we must all hold that in relation to it, human nature cannot have any demand, properly speaking. Deprived of the means of tending to this single end, nature would exist in a violent, abnormal, and disordered state. All of its movement would be lacking in measure [*déréglé*]. In particular, we can see what would follow for a state of fallen nature.
>
> We are not here concerned with some point of Aristotelianism. Rather, we are concerned with something that reason finds to be necessary: a nature, and above all grace, cannot be ordered to a unique end, without this end entering into its own notion. A nature is an essence, which rests on the good that is proportioned to it or which pursues this very good. It would be contradictory to posit it without placing within its reach the sole good for which it is made. And there is no demand more acute, either for a created nature or for its infinitely wise Creator, than

---

[27] Regarding the text of *ST* I-II, q. 62, a. 1, "However, *there is a twofold human beatitude. . . . One that is proportioned to human nature . . .* whereas the other is a beatitude exceeding man's nature," Fr. de Lubac says on page 291 of his recent article ["Duplex Hominis Beatitudo"]: "This text is suitable for expressing the doctrine of two 'orders,' in the sense that it is spoken of today, only if one already presupposes this distinction."

There are many other, similar texts in St. Thomas (*ST* I, q. 23, a. 1; q. 12, a. 4; I-II, q. 3, a. 4; q. 5, a. 5; *De veritate*, q. 14, a. 2). Moreover, the holy Doctor presupposes what the [First] Vatican Council will come to express later on: "*The perpetual common belief of the Catholic Church has held and holds also this: there is a twofold order of knowledge*, distinct not only in its principle but also in its object, etc." And St. Thomas has shown that the object of the beatific vision immensely exceeds all the powers and exigencies of every created and creatable intellect. See *ST* I, q. 12, a. 4; I-II, q. 5, a. 5.

that of avoiding contradiction, above all when such contradiction would need to be found at the heart of a rational being.[28]

Thus, the matter is clear, and what is said here quite obviously represents an expression of the traditional teaching concerning these topics. Thus, in the same article, Fr. Boyer can conclude:

> The intentions and attestations of an author cannot change anything: as soon as one assigns to a given nature only one possible end, not only is this end natural, but moreover, it is owed to it. It is no longer a grace if it is on equal terms with creation and the other natural gifts. The supernatural has not been exalted; it has been suppressed.[29]

Fr. de Lubac will perhaps respond that, according to him, human nature, or that of the angels, does not involve anything complete and closed up within itself, that it is not an essence that is indeed defined, with necessary properties and a proportionate end. In that case, there no longer is a nature, properly speaking, nor consequently, something supernatural, for the latter can be defined only in relation to nature, which it exceeds. One would thus set out upon the paths of nominalism, and what it led to in the 14th century is known well-enough.[30] It came to doubt the demonstrative value of the classical proofs of God's existence and that of the immutability of the first precepts of the natural law.[31]

* * * * *

[28] Charles Boyer, "Nature pure et surnaturel dans le 'Surnaturel' du P. de Lubac," *Gregorianum* 28 (1947): 379–95, here 390ff.

[29] Boyer, "Nature pure et surnaturel," 392.

[30] Such is the conclusion that we have defended at length elsewhere in *On Divine Revelation*, vol. 1, chs. 11 and 12. In the same place, we set forth what the majority of Thomists hold concerning the character of *our natural desire to see God*: a conditional and inefficacious desire, like that by which the farmer desires rain. This desire certainly does not *prove* that the essentially supernatural vision of God is owed to us, nor even that it is possible; however, it does furnish on behalf of this possibility an argument from befittingness which can forever be deepened, one that the angels know much more profoundly than we do, though it nonetheless remains non-apodictic, for we cannot *naturally demonstrate* even the possibility of an *essentially supernatural* mystery—and the mystery of eternal life is of the same *essentially supernatural* order as those of the Holy Trinity and the Incarnation. Nonetheless, the probability of this argument forever grows as one deepens it. It is like a polygon inscribed within the circumference of a circle. As its sides are multiplied, it forever draws closer to that circumference without, however, ever reaching it.

[31] There is much that could be said concerning this today. We will return to the point only if the necessities of the controversy demand it.

We have not here undertaken a detailed and complete examination of St. Thomas's texts concerning *the twofold beatitude* [of men and angels]. It will be taken up elsewhere by a Thomist theologian who has profoundly studied the matter.[32]

It will be easy to show that St. Thomas fully admits that both we and the angels can have *deliberated-love of God* proceeding from our natural knowledge of Him and from our will, *outside of every aid coming from grace.*

It is false to say that St. Thomas holds that the natural love of God is always reduced to an instinctive, non-free natural movement and that every love of God arising from deliberation must be supernatural and grace-given. St. Thomas always distinguishes two loves, one proceeding from natural knowledge and the will, and the other proceeding from supernatural knowledge and infused charity.[33]

This new examination of the question concerning the supernatural confirms for us, with increasing strength, the traditional positions of the Thomist school, positions which are perfectly conformed to those of St. Thomas.

---

[32] [Tr. note: This is likely referring to the work of his student Marie-Rosaire Gagnebet, "L'amour naturel de Dieu chez saint Thomas et ses contemporains," *Revue thomiste* 48 (1948): 394–446; *Revue thomiste* 49 (1949): 31–102. Also, after this, see Marie-Rosaire Gagnebet, "L'enseignement du magistère et le problème du surnaturel," *Revue thomiste* 53 (1953): 5–27.]

[33] Moreover (and this point has already been noted), by denying man's *natural* last end, *one suppresses* the very principle of *natural ethics*, "*Finis enim est prior in intentione.*" One thus arrives at a very grave error, and it is not clear what means are at hand for avoiding it.—Finally, if, as is claimed, St. Thomas had admitted this position, his doctrine would lead to this error committed by Baius: "*The distinction of a twofold love of God*, namely, a *natural* love whose object is God as the author of nature and a *gratuitous* love whose object is God as beatifying, is meaningless and imaginary; it has been devised as a mockery of the Sacred Scriptures and of the numerous testimonies of ancient authors" (Denzinger, no. 1934 [old no. 1034]).

15
Relativism and the Immutability of Dogma According to the [First] Vatican Council
Réginald Garrigou-Lagrange, OP

In these days of ubiquitous relativism, it is of great importance that we recall what the [First] Vatican Council defined in opposition to Anton Günter's relativism, which the Council believed to contain the gravest of errors. Indeed, this kind of error is graver than any given particular heresy, for such relativism is not concerned with one or several dogmas but, rather, extends to all of them, in the end leading to rationalism itself, indeed, in one of its most inconsistent forms.

The Guntherian Theory: Dogmas are infallibly true, though their truth is only relative to the state of science and philosophy at the time of their definition.[1]

Günther's theory differed from that held by pure rationalists, because he admitted the divine origin of Christianity, as well as a kind of infallibility in the Church's teaching. However, he understood this infallibility in such a way that his conception of dogmatic development barely differed from that held by rationalists properly so called. In the end, his doctrine represents a form of semi-rationalism, and its generative principle is the claim that reason, through its own proper principles, can demonstrate all the truths that God has revealed.[2] In order to justify this new way of looking at things, he had to

---

[1] See Jean-Michel-Alfred Vacant, *Études théologiques sur les constitutions du Concile du Vatican*, vol. 2 (Paris: Delhomme et Briguet, 1895), 282.

[2] Anton Günter was born in Bohemia in 1783. At a rather young age, he sought to build on the writings of Kant, Fichte, and Schelling. This undertaking shook his faith. However, under the influence of Blessed [now, St.] [Clemens Maria] Hoffbauer, he studied Sacred Scripture and theology. His faith was completely placed back on steady footing, and he was ordained to the priesthood in 1820. However, he then gradually came to be persuaded that the philosophical doctrine of the Fathers and of the Doctors of the Middle

interpret dogmas in a new manner, one that was opposed to the statements of the Apostles and to the Church's definitions.

Obviously, weighty objections were raised against this claim, but he believed that he could resolve them by having recourse to the following principle: reason can demonstrate revealed dogmas only after expending extensive efforts in assimilating them. The Apostles and the first Councils understood these revealed data very imperfectly, and their infallibility only had served to enable them to make the best possible choice among the interpretations prevailing in their own particular era. The interpretations the Church has infallibly proposed have always been those that are best in harmony with the scientific, philosophic, and theological culture of the age in which those interpretations were offered. *All these conciliar interpretations were the best ones available at the very time when they came to be defined*; however, with the progress of the sciences, philosophy, and critical theology, *they have come to be replaced by others*, which would, hence, draw closer to truth in its absolute form and would have greater conformity with reason's own natural lights. Thus, reason would gradually come to demonstrate every revealed truth and connect them to the order of philosophical truths.

Thus, according to Günther, the Council of Ephesus, in accord with the psychology of its era, had defined that there is only one person in Jesus Christ. [For Günther,] this statement would have contained a portion of the truth, for Christ's humanity, from the first moment of its existence, was united to the Word of God. However, now that we must (according to Günther) follow the insights of modern philosophy, which makes personality consist in self-consciousness, we must hold that there are two persons in Jesus Christ, one human and the other divine, for there are two consciousnesses in Him. Thus, Christ's holy soul was united to the Word only through knowledge and love, as is the case for the saints, though He would be so united to a loftier degree and with a much more intimate subordination. From this same perspective, Günther called the Council of Trent a kind of *interim* between the ancient

---

Ages no longer sufficed for the needs of our days and believed that he was called to establish a new philosophy, which would provide a correct interpretation for the dogmas of Christianity. His book, *An Introduction to the Speculative Theology of Positive Christianity* was published in 1828 and republished in 1846–48.

Günther's greatest adversary was Fr. Josef Kleutgen, S.J., who from 1852 onward mightily contributed to the restoration of traditional philosophy through his two works *Philosophie der Vorzeit* and *Théologie der Vorzeit*.

Gunther's works were placed on the Index in 1857, and he died in submission to the Church in 1863. Pius IX condemned semi-rationalism in 1857 and 1862. See Pius IX, *Eximiam tuam* to the Archbishop of Cologne, June 15, 1857 (Denzinger, no. 2828 [old no. 1655]) and *Gravissimas inter* to the Archbishop of Munich-Freising, Dec. 11, 1862 (Denzinger, old nos. 1666–76).

Councils and modern times, adding that we could not know whether, in the end, it would be replaced.

As Alfred Vacant observed regarding this matter, "Within Christian revelation itself, he distinguished, on the one hand, *the historical elements* that we must believe on account of God's authority (even when we do not understand *how* they are so) from, on the other hand, *our understanding of these elements*, which he held would consist in knowing the reason *why* they are so."[3] As Vacant likewise notes: "*Thus, he saw in revelation nothing but a kind of outer bark formed out of historical elements*."[4] Hence, the primary object of Divine Revelation would no longer be God Himself, His infinite perfections, and His intimate life, as well as its relations with us in view of eternal life. The revelation given in the Old and New Testaments would only be concerned with *historical facts*, and human reason would seek out the explanation for why they are what they are. Thus, Vacant rightly concludes: "*By this very fact, Christian doctrine ceased to be fundamentally divine and supernatural. The only thing left for the divine and supernatural order was the channel of sacred history, the teachings of the Apostles, and ecclesiastical definitions . . .* which provided him with a *relative and transitory truth* and perfection, *not with a [lasting] truth* and an *absolute perfection*."[5] Thus, we here find ourselves faced with a form of relativism.

As Cardinal Franzelin noted,[6] *this theory replaced the authority of the Councils with the activity of those who cultivate sciences belonging to the natural order*. The progress (or supposed progress) of philosophy became the principal cause of dogmatic declarations, with the Holy Spirit intervening only to give this explanation a *transitory form of infallibility* in accord with the current state of the sciences. Moreover, Günther was thus led to hold that tradition grows *objectively* speaking. Dogma would no longer be intrinsically immutable but, rather, *would undergo intrinsic development, as does philosophy*. By contrast, the Church has always said that dogma is intrinsically immutable and that the only kind of progress involved in dogmatic development is *quoad nos*, through the increasingly-explicit knowledge that we have of dogmas. However, the latter is not perfected in itself, like a human science that undergoes intrinsic development.

---

3 Vacant, *Études théologiques*, 284.

4 Vacant, *Études théologiques*, 284.

5 Vacant, *Études théologiques*, 284.

6 See Johannes Baptist Franzelin, *De traditione*, 2nd ed. [Rome: Sacra Congregatio de Propaganda Fide, 1875], 309.

The definitions of the [First] Vatican Council concerning the absolute and immutable truth of dogmas.

The [First] Vatican Council condemned the two principal errors of Günther when it defined 1° that revealed doctrine is not a philosophical theory to be perfected and 2° that the meaning of the Church's teachings cannot change. Here, we must recall several elementary points that are somewhat forgotten in our own days.

According to the Council, *what is a dogma?* The Council defines what it is by saying: "*All those things are to be believed with divine and Catholic faith that are contained in the word of God, written or handed down, and which by the Church*, either in solemn judgment or through her ordinary and universal teaching office, *are proposed for belief as having been divinely revealed.*"[7]

Moreover, the Council defined the immutability of dogmas as follows:

> For the doctrine of faith that God has revealed has not been proposed like a philosophical system to be perfected by human ingenuity; rather, it has been committed to the spouse of Christ *as a divine trust to be faithfully kept and infallibly declared. Hence, also, that meaning of the sacred dogmas is perpetually to be retained which our Holy Mother Church has once declared, and there must never be a deviation from that meaning* on the specious ground and title of a more profound understanding. "Therefore, let there be growth and abundant progress *in understanding, knowledge, and wisdom, in each and all*, in individuals and in the whole Church, at all times and in the progress of ages, *but only within the proper limits* [sed in suo dumtaxat genere], i.e., *within the same dogma, the same meaning, the same judgment*" (Vincent of Lérins, *Commonitorium primum*, 23, no. 3, PL 50 668A).[8]

Canon 4.3, which corresponds to this declaration, states: "If anyone says that, as science progresses, at times a *sense* is to be given to dogmas proposed by the Church *different* from the one that the Church has understood and understands, let him be anathema."[9]

*****

As Vacant says in the aforementioned work, "In order to fall under the Council's anathema and be guilty of heresy, it suffices that one claim that, on account of the progress of science, there is sometimes room to attribute *another*

---

[7] [First] Vatican Council, *Dei filius*, ch. 3 (Denzinger, no. 3011 [old no., 1792]). Also, see Vacant, *Études théologiques*, 82ff.

[8] [First] Vatican Council, *Dei filius*, ch. 4 (*De fide et ratione*, in fine) (Denzinger, no. 3020 [old. no., 1800]).

[9] [First] Vatican Council, *Dei filius*, can. 4.3 (Denzinger, no. 3043 [old no. 1818]).

meaning to the dogmas proposed by the Church, one differing from the meaning that she once gave for them and, indeed, continues to give for them."[10]

Moreover, as the same theologian notes, this conciliar teaching is *"the consequence of the nature of truth and of infallibility."*

Indeed, *the truth of an affirmation* does not consist in its conformity with the human knowledge attained in each era. Rather, *it consists in its conformity with the reality of things*. If what we affirm *is* [what we affirm it is], our affirmation is true and will forever remain so. Even if this affirmation is concerned with a contingent fact that has already taken place, like, "The Messiah was born in Bethlehem," it will forever remain true that this fact has taken place and that the Messiah was born in Bethlehem.[11] It will remain forever true that He died on the Cross for our salvation. And in the case of truths that dominate time and space, abstracting from the *hic et nunc*, like, "sanctifying grace is the formal cause of justification, that which makes us just in the eyes of God, whether we be speaking of a baptized child or an adult," such a truth will remain forever and immutably true.

Moreover, God's *infallibility*, and that which He communicated to the Apostles and to the Church, consists *in not being able to fall into error*. Therefore, the definitions that are infallibly proposed by the Church cannot be erroneous and never can become such, since the truth is intrinsically immutable. The Savior's words hold true for them as well, "Heaven and earth will pass away, but my words will not pass away" (Mt 24:35, RSV). For example, the Council of Ephesus's definition regarding the unity of personhood in Christ is no less true today (and, indeed, forever) than it was when it was first pronounced. The doctrine of the Hypostatic Union cannot change. It could be proposed in a more explicit manner in response to new errors, but it will not change. What the Church has infallibly affirmed cannot change in meaning.[12]

* * * * *

As Vacant notes, we must add that, "The expressions used by the Council established that *the Church never removes anything from Christian doctrine, nor does she add any element to it.*"[13] Indeed, according to the Council, this doctrine is a divine deposit entrusted to the Church so that she may faithfully

---

[10] Vacant, *Études théologiques*, 286.

[11] A truth is relative to time only when this relativity is mentioned in its statement. For example: "The Messiah will be born in the future in Bethlehem," or even, "The Messiah is being born at this very moment in Bethlehem." However, following this, it will forever remain true that He was born in Bethlehem.

[12] It will forever remain true that in Jesus Christ there is *only one person* ontologically speaking, even though He has two consciousnesses of the same self and two freedoms, one of which is perfectly subordinated to the other.

[13] Vacant, *Études théologiques*, 288.

guard it, leaving it neither fall into ruin nor be forgotten, and so that she may infallibly expound it: *doctrina tanquam divinum depositum Christi Sponsae tradita, fideliter custodienda et infallibiliter declaranda.* This truth's guardian is not *the private reason* of Christian philosophers, however penetrating they may be. Rather, it is *the Holy Church*, established by God and His Christ, *with the special assistance promised to Peter, his successors, and the bishops submitted to him* (Mt 16:8 and 28:19–20). Therefore, the Church cannot leave anything in the divine deposit fall into ruin, for she must faithfully guard it.

No more can she add any foreign doctrine to this divine deposit. Indeed, such new elements could only come from new revelations (which are not part of this divine deposit) or from the human mind's own, ever-fallible discoveries.

This point of doctrine was confirmed by the condemnation of the following modernist propositions in the Holy Office's decree *Lamentabili*:

> (21) Revelation, constituting the object of the Catholic faith, was not *completed* with the Apostles.
>
> (54) Dogmas, sacraments, and hierarchy, both their notion and reality, are only *interpretations* and evolutions of the Christian intelligence that have increased and perfected by an external series of additions the little germ latent in the Gospel.
>
> (58) *Truth is no more immutable than man himself, since it evolved with him, in him, and through him.*[14]

In contrast to these condemned propositions, the Church holds that Revelation, which constitutes the object of Catholic faith, came to a *close* with the death of the last of the Apostles. According to her, dogmas are not mere *interpretations* offered by Christian intelligence but, rather, are immutable truths.

The approval that the Church sometimes accords to certain private revelations, like those related to the worship [*culte*] owed to the Sacred Heart, only provides a guarantee that these revelations do not contain anything that would be contrary to Christian doctrine and that they can be believed without jeopardizing the rules of prudence and piety. However, this approval does not make these private revelations enter into the Church's doctrine.

For all the more reason, the Church holds that Christian doctrine is not proposed to men so that it may receive *perfections* from them, as though it were something akin to *a philosophical theory*. Men would alter the nature of the divine deposit if they strove to bring it to completion. "This is why," as Vacant says, "this deposit was entrusted to the Church and not to philosophers and learned men.... The assistance that God gives her is a sure pledge ... that *she will never present us with a human doctrine as though it were the*

---

[14] Denzinger, nos. 3421, 3454, and 3458 [old nos., 2021, 2054, and 2058].

divine doctrine of Christ."[15] This would be contrary to the *unity of faith*, which unites the faithful of all times and places. In order to have this unity of faith proclaimed by St. Paul (Eph 4:4–6), it suffices that the principal revealed truths be explicitly believed, whereas the others can be implicitly believed.

Progress in knowledge of dogmas.

Revealed doctrine has an inexhaustible fecundity, and it remains forever living. We can forever deepen our understanding of it and discover in it aspects that we have heretofore only implicitly known. Thus, our *knowledge of dogmas progresses, even though those dogmas remain intrinsically immutable*, and this knowledge has indeed progressed *in extent [étendue], clarity, and certitude*—for example, through the infallible proclamation of the dogmas of the Immaculate Conception and that of the Pope's infallibility when he speaks "*ex cathedra*."

This progress in our knowledge of dogmas comes about in particular in the midst of the Church's struggles against errors and heresies, which God permits in order for the truth to be set forth in greater light, just as He permits evil for the sake of a greater good. Preparation for this progress is brought about through private studies undertaken by theologians responding to the needs of souls throughout the ages.

Quite correctly, Vacant notes[16] that this forward march may be slowed down or accelerated by events, but it is never reversed. In it, we see Providence leading the Church onward, and we can distinguish three successive phases within this forward march by distinguishing each of their particular concerns: the positive theology of the Fathers, the speculative theology of the Doctors of the Middle Ages, and the critical theology of modern theologians. The new methodologies are grafted onto the older ones. However, they must not make them disappear, for this would compromise this progress's unity, which in the words of Vincent of Lérins, is comparable to that of a growing human body. The teachings and methodologies of each era correspond to its needs, to the need to combat this or that sort of error.

Thus, the knowledge of dogma progresses for each believer who wishes to be instructed, to pray, and to place his faith into practice, as it also progresses for the Church herself.

St. Vincent of Lerins, who was cited by the Council, said that this represents progress "*in understanding, knowledge, and wisdom*," in opposition to those who every day seek out ever-new novelties, one after another, forever claiming to alter our religion by way of addition, alteration, or removal.[17]

---

15 Vacant, *Études théologiques*, 292.
16 See Vacant, *Études théologiques*, 310ff.
17 See Vincent de Lérins, *Commonitorium*, no. 21.

In this progress, even for the Church herself, the first thing to be done is to *understand* that there is a point of doctrine to be examined (e.g., on account of a deviation that seems to be flaring up in certain places). Then, the question is debated in order to prepare her solution and bring it to full maturation, through [theological] *science*, considering this particular point and looking into what is in conformity with the documents and spirit of orthodox tradition, as was done for the question concerning the privilege of the Immaculate Conception. Finally, the point thus examined at length will be solemnly defined by an act, which will make it a dogma of Catholic faith. In this slow progress by the Church in coming to a definitive declaration concerning controversial questions, we see *her wisdom*, which measures out and weighs all of her judgments so as to assure their harmony. This is indeed what St. Vincent of Lérins said about such progress: progress "in understanding, knowledge, and wisdom . . . within the same dogma, *in eodem dogmate*, the same meaning, *in eodem sensu*, and the same judgment, *in eadem sententia*." This progress will be a passage from what is implicit to what is explicit, as we see in the works that prepared for the definition of the Immaculate Conception and that of the Pope's infallibility.[18]

Theological science can continue to progress in clarity after the definition of a dogma by examining ever more deeply its relations with other truths of faith and with the certitudes of reason. Here again, we will have growth in our understanding of each dogma, knowledge [*science*] of its relations with others, and then wisdom, that is, the superior synthesis connecting all dogmas to God *sub ratione Deitatis*, to His intimate life.

* * * * *

Likewise, in the same work, Vacant rightly states:

> The centuries when *wisdom* will develop will be those of lofty speculation and great faith, such as the 13th century. . . . Theologians even point out that no truth belongs to faith and theology except inasmuch as it is connected to God *sub ratione Deitatis*. Therefore, the wondrous synthesis of Christian doctrine, the *Summa theologiae* of St. Thomas Aquinas, is arranged into three parts, wherein all the dogmas of faith are connected to God who is considered as the principle, to God considered as the end, and to God who became incarnate in order to open to us the supernatural path leading to possession of this same God.[19]

---

18 We must note that the *implicit faith* (or, vague [*confuse*] faith) had by *past saints* was *livelier* (and thus, more profound, despite its still-vague form of expression) than the explicit faith of the theologians of later eras when these theologians do not have as elevated a degree of charity, faith, the other infused virtues, and the seven gifts of the Holy Spirit.

19 Vacant, *Études théologiques*, 319.

The Spirit's gifts of understanding, knowledge, and wisdom contributed to this great synthesis, which quite clearly proceeds from the contemplation of divine things.

Consequences of the Council's Doctrine

When theologians come to devote their labor above all to historical-critical studies, they give the greatest attention to the rules of historical methodology, and they indeed should. Nonetheless, the theologian must take heed that he not become *a mere historian*, as though he no longer needed a philosophical mindset and as though the *habitus* of theological science were no longer necessary for him. This path would gradually lead him to a position similar to that of Günther who, as we have seen, no longer saw in revelation anything but a kind of outer bark of philosophical truths, *a bark formed from the historical elements of the Old and New Testaments,* with human reason, psychology, and philosophical analyses seeking out *explanations* for these elements. Hence, *the primary* object of Divine Revelation would no longer be *God Himself, His infinite perfections, His intimate life*, and its relations with us with regard to eternal life. The Revelation of the Old and New Testaments would no longer be concerned with anything other than *historical facts*, the history of Abraham, Isaac, Jacob, Moses, and the prophets, as well as the history of Jesus Christ and the apostles. And to know the *explanation* for these facts, *theology* properly so called would no longer be necessary. It would suffice to have, along with historical methodology, that of *religious psychology* and *philosophical investigations*, which no longer have the ambition of discovering *the absolute and immutable truth* but, rather, only a *truth that is relative* to the current state of science and, therefore, a truth that is forever *provisional*, perhaps drawing closer to the absolute truth, though without ever attaining it. From this perspective, *theology properly so called* would be suppressed and reduced to philosophy and the history of religions.[20] *The supernatural mysteries* themselves would be *reduced to the order of philosophical mysteries*, as Günther said. And thus, we would find ourselves back at that form of semi-rationalism that denies the very order of essentially supernatural truths and of supernatural life properly so called. The words of Revelation would only have a *phenomenal value* for arousing our *religious experience*, as the modernists said. *It would no longer have an ontological and transcendent value.* Dogmas would only have a practical value. They would tell us to behave toward Jesus as though we were faced with a divine person.[21] *Religious experi-*

---

[20] Instead of making use of history, *positive theology* would, rather, be reduced to *history*, and *speculative theology* would be reduced to *philosophy* (or, rather, to philosophical investigations that no longer hope to arrive at absolute truth).

[21] See *Lamentabili*, no. 26 (Denzinger, no. 3426 [old no. 2026]).

ence, which is found in various degrees in all religions, would be substituted for *infused faith*, which enables us to infallibly and supernaturally adhere *propter auctoritatem Dei revelantis*, on account of the authority of God who reveals, to the *absolute truth* of what He has revealed to us.

This supposed progress in knowledge of dogmas would, in fact, represent a form of utter regression as well as the path leading directly to pure rationalism.

The life of the Infallible Church marches in the opposite direction. As was defined by the [First] Vatican Council, she faithfully guards and infallibly declares the sacred deposit of Divine Revelation concerning the mysteries of God's intimate life, those concerning the Incarnation, the Redemption, and eternal life. And if she progresses in her knowledge concerning dogmas, she does so forever in the same direction and sense. Thus, *the absolute truth of God's word* is preserved in accord with these words spoken by our Savior: "Heaven and earth will pass away, but my words will not pass away" (Mt 24:35, RSV).

However, we must understand aright the profound meaning of this assertion by our Savior. It goes much further and far higher, and in order for it to soar upward, it must have an unshakeable foundation.

In order for Christ's words to not pass away, the notions and judgments they express must have more than a *phenomenal* value (i.e., one limited to the order of external and internal, transitory, *sensible phenomena*). They must have *an ontological and transcendent value* in *the order of being* and *its immutable laws*. Likewise, these notions must be able to express God's intimate life with an absolute truth, despite the imperfections befalling analogical knowledge.

This is what we have shown at great length elsewhere, in the first volume of our *De revelatione*, in the chapters where we critique agnosticism by defending the *ontological value* of the first notions and principles of reason,[22] as well as in in our defense of *the transcendent and analogical value* of the same notions and principles.[23] We have studied this question over the course of many years and are ready to defend what we have said about it.

This twofold ontological and transcendent value of the first notions does not cease to be certain merely because some people who have never studied these problems deeply enough do not understand it and thus are led to a wholly superficial and false notion of analogy. We will return to it [*sic*]. There is no small danger involved in setting aside the task of deeply studying St. Thomas's thought, opting instead to read modern philosophers who, like Henri Bergson and many others, are much closer to *nominalism* than to *traditional realism*.

---

[22] See Reginald Garrigou-Lagrange, *On Divine Revelation*, vol. 1, trans. Matthew Minerd (Steubenville, OH: Emmaus Academic, 2021), 411–23.

[23] Garrigou-Lagrange, *On Divine Revelation*, 423–48.

This would lead one to say that in the era of Modernism, grave problems were posed that the modernists themselves did not know how to rightly resolve, though *the resolution to those problems still awaits discovery*. Indeed, one would thus even be led to place in doubt the demonstrative value of the traditional proofs of God's existence and to say that while human reason *can arrive at* this demonstration (as the [First] Vatican Council stated and as is made clear in the Anti-Modernist Oath), it has, in fact, *never yet arrived at such demonstrative knowledge*.

The preceding pages are only a commentary on these words spoken by our Savior: "Heaven and earth will pass away, but my words will not pass away." This divine affirmation, superior to every denial and existing in a light that immeasurably exceeds that of natural reason, acknowledges that the *notions* needed for the expression of Christian revelation have *an absolutely immutable real value*. Not only does it recognize this fact, but it also confirms it in the loftiest manner, which will be exceeded only by that which will come to us from the immediate vision of the divine essence. No believer places this in doubt.[24]

24 Concerning the first notions and first principles, we are surprised to read the following lines regarding Christian Wolff in the recent text by Étienne Gilson, *L'Être et l'essence* (Paris: Vrin, 1948), 176:
> Wolff's influence over modern scholasticism sometimes goes much further, and we can see it acting even on the philosophical exegesis of Thomism itself. See, for example, Reginald Garrigou-Lagrange, *Dieu, son existence et sa nature*, 3rd ed. (Paris: Beauchesne, 1920), 170–79, where the "principle of *raison d'être*," according to which "every being has a sufficient reason," is there connected to the principle of identity through a *reductio ad absurdum* and, in this sense, made analytic. In this text (p. 175), we are assured that those who hold a different position on these matters in some other way separate themselves "from traditional philosophy." Yes, from what it has become from the time of Leibnitz and Wolff, though it represents the very negation of that of St. Thomas Aquinas.

I have never read the works of Wolff, but I am well-enough aware of the use he made of the principle of sufficient reason, particularly in relation to both divine and human freedom, to be able to say that a great distance separates my thought from his concerning this matter, as can be seen by reading the same book, *Dieu*, 590–672. [Reginald Garrigou-Lagrange, *God: His Existence and His Nature, A Thomistic Solution of Certain Agnostic Antinomies*, vol. 2, trans. Bede Rose (St. Louis, MO: Herder, 1949), 269–354.] What I have called *the principle of raison d'être* is formulated: "*Every being must have its raison d'être either in itself*, if it exists through itself, *or in another*, if it does not exist through itself." This *raison d'être* must be understood analogically in various senses: 1° of the formal cause, in relation to the properties that derive from it, 2° of the efficient cause in relation to what it produces, and 3° of the final cause in relation to the means for which it is the *raison d'être*, as well as to everything that is ordered to it.

Conceived in this way, the principle of *raison d'être* is a general principle commonly received in traditional philosophy. *The principles of efficient causality* and that of *finality* are derived from it, for the efficient cause and the final cause are the extrinsic *raisons d'être* of every contingent being and of its acts. For its own part, the formal cause of a being is the reason for its properties, and matter is the reason for the corruptibility of bodily beings. In this sense, as St. Thomas says, following Aristotle, the four causes each correspond to a question *propter quid*. See St. Thomas, *In* II *Phys.*, lect. 10. Also see Garrigou-Lagrange, *Reality: A Synthesis of Thomistic Thought*, trans. Patrick Cummins (St. Louis, MO: B. Herder, 1950), 31–36.

As regards the subordination of these principles to the principle of identity or of contradiction ("that which is is; that which is not, is not"), I did not find it in Wolff but for years have read it in St. Thomas's Commentaries on Aristotle and in the *Summa theologiae*, which I even cited at considerable length in the pages cited by Gilson.

Indeed, we read in *In* VI *Meta.*, ch. 4, lect 6, that the three conditions for every first principle of reason belong to the principle of contradiction and that the other principles are subordinate to it. The same assertion is made frequently in St. Thomas's writings. For example, see *ST* I-II, q. 94, a. 2:

> *That which first falls into [our intellect's] apprehension is being*, the understanding of which is included in everything that someone grasps. And *therefore, the first indemonstrable principle is* that *we cannot simultaneously affirm and deny* [the same thing of the same subject in the same respect], which is founded on the notion of being and non-being, *and all the other principles are founded on this principle*, as the Philosopher says in *Metaphysics* 4.4.

Likewise, in *ST* II-II, q. 1, a. 7:

> The articles of faith are related to the doctrine of faith as *first self-evident principles* are related to the doctrine that can be had through natural reason. A kind of *order* can be found in these principles, so that certain ones are implicitly [lit. *simpliciter*; Leonine: *implicite*] contained in the others. Thus, *all the principles are reduced to one principle as to the first principle: It is impossible to simultaneously affirm and deny* [the same thing of the same subject in the same respect], as is clear from what the Philosopher says in *Metaphysics* 4.4.

John of St. Thomas, who wrote before Wolff, said in his *Cursus philosophicus, Logica*, q. 25, a. 2:

> It is not contradictory to say that self-evident propositions could be proven through an extrinsic middle term, or *a deduction ad impossibile*, for this is not opposed to there being an immediate and intrinsic connection of subject and predicate. For this reason, *Metaphysics explains and defends all the other principles, indeed not doing so ostensively* (through a demonstrative middle term) *but, rather, by deducing ad impossibile*, indeed, to that supreme principle: "Everything either is or is not."

The Thomist Antoine Goudin speaks in the same manner in his *Philosophia juxta inconcussa tutissimaque D. Thomae dogmata*, vol. 4, pt. 4, disp. 1, q. 1, a. 1 (*On the principles of knowledge* [lit. *cognitianis*; in Goudin: *cognitionis*]): "The first complex principle of knowledge [i.e., in the second operation of the intellect] is this: 'It is impossible that the same thing simultaneously be and not be.' We see this stated by Aristotle in *Metaphysics* 4.4 and by St. Thomas in *ST* I-II, q. 94, a. 2." The first edition of this work by Goudin was published in 1671 in Lyon. Suárez also taught this doctrine in *Disputationes metaphysicae*, disp. 3, sect. 3, no. 9.

Therefore, in the form that we propose it, this principle is something quite earlier than Leibniz and Wolff and certainly does not represent the negation of St. Thomas's doctrine.

Matters would be completely different if we spoke of a principle of sufficient reason, taken in a univocal manner and leading to the psychological determinism of moral necessity, as much for the divine freedom as for human freedom, an outlook that we have forever combatted.

Finally, we can be quite certain that St. Thomas held that it would be *absurd* to claim that *a contingent being* can *exist without an efficient cause* and without an uncaused efficient cause. If this is placed in doubt, the proofs for God's existence *per viam causalitatis efficientis* would no longer be *apodictic*.

Moreover, with St. Thomas and Cajetan, against the line of philosophers who admit the ontological argument, we have always distinguished between *existentia signata*, conceived after the manner of a quiddity (*quid sit existentia*) and *existentia exercita* or *de facto* existence. On this, see *God: His Existence and His Nature, A Thomistic Solution of Certain Agnostic Antinomies*, vol. 1, trans. Bede Rose (St. Louis, MO: Herder, 1949), 68–69. This classic distinction is known by all. It also follows from what we have said that God's rights over human societies are *immutable*, exactly the same today as they were in the past [*sic*].

16

Correspondence
Maurice Blondel and Réginald Garrigou-Lagrange, OP

We received the following letter from Maurice Blondel, along with his request that we publish it. Following it, the reader will find the counter-observations that our colleague feels are necessary.

Out of respect for the truth, I feel duty-bound to respond to the formulas that were critiqued in *Angelicum* 23, no. 3–4, pp. 129–30, and request that the editors of this periodical insert my note for the sake of rectifying this matter.

First of all, my text has been cited in a mutilated fashion. Moreover, the citations thereof overlook the full context of my complete position in these matters, failing to study the various aspects of my outlook, which must be considered as a whole in its unity if it is to be understood aright.

In no domain have I ever placed the immutable character of the truth in doubt or even in danger, above all in matters concerning our essential destiny.

Moreover, I never have substituted a philosophy of action for the philosophy of thought and of being. However, having dedicated two volumes to Thought and intending to deal with the study of beings in relation to Being, I could not fail to be aware of the inviolable role that is played by action, whether faithful or rebellious. Therefore, I felt it necessary to indicate how and why human choice [*option*], in the reality of that very rebellion, can contradict the value of the first principles without ever suppressing this value. Here too, it is not the case that I overthrow either the definition of the truth or its requirements.

Throughout all my works, I have safeguarded the indelible office [*function*] of the truth and have maintained the conciliar propositions in the face of the avenging responsibilities of a false or culpable choice [*option*]. Did not Christ say: "Ego sum via, veritas et via?" Now, does this not show us that mere speculative truth does not suffice and that we must set ourselves in motion, illuminated by this lamp for our feet, *lucerna pedibus*, spoken of in Ps. 118—a forward march and a light that must lead us not only to knowledge but also to eternal life and divine adoption? There is nothing more immutable than this truth, which ultimately leads us to God, and the condemned proposition (Denzinger, no. 3458 [2058]) represents the utter antithesis of the entire effort I have undertaken throughout my philosophical work. Gratuitous consequences are attributed to me, even though they are utterly opposed to my most formally held conclusions.

When the reproach is registered against me, claiming that I overlook the absolute sufficiency of the definition of truth, "*Adaequatio rei et intellectus*," I should be the one to protest against this reduction to the words *res et intellectus*, which do not suffice to exhaust everything involved in these matters: indeed, *res* does not suffice for designating the loftiest realities, and the intellect does not exhaust the science of things and of beings, nor the reality of the intimate activities [*opérations*] of our conscience or our duties, nor the profound truth of our supernatural destiny. Therefore, if there is a deficiency, it is to be found in the doctrine to which one would like to reduce my own position. And even so, does not a Thomist adage itself declare, "*Differentiae rerum sunt innumerae et innominatae*[; the differences of things are numberless and unnamed]"? Indeed, is not this something that we must necessarily admit, lest the secret life of the soul be underestimated, along with the merit of being docile to the divine influence so as to faithfully fulfill our supernatural vocation? Therefore, neither novelty nor fantasy is involved in the idea of broadening out philosophical research so that it may include the study of action, so that we might thereby provide a full account of the truth of the mysterious salvation to which we have been called, at the price of our docile contribution to this appeal, concerning which St. Thomas tells us that the entire movement of nature conspires to multiply the elect, so much so that one of his briefest and most profound formulas is that *omnia intendunt assimilari Deo*; all things strive to be assimilated unto God.

And, without ever having wished to take advantage of the lofty approbations that I have received from Leo XIII to His Holiness Pius XII, allow me to cite here the witness received by the Archbishop Bonnefoy of Aix, who, during his *ad limina* visit in 1912, obtained the following words from the Sovereign Pontiff, Pius X: "I am certain of the orthodoxy of M. Blondel. I instruct you to tell him this." I possess this statement, signed by my Archbishop, recounting at length his discussion with the Pope concerning the encyclical *Pascendi*, and from that time, Archbishop Bonnefoy strongly urged me to make it known.

Maurice Blondel
Aix-en-Provence, Mar. 12, 1947

* * * * *

We will respond to Maurice Blondel as follows.

As we said in an article found in this same issue, we in no way question Monsieur Blondel's personal faith, nor the lofty elevation of his thought, which we have always recognized. Nonetheless, we have examined what can be deduced from certain assertions that he has made, along with what has, in fact, been deduced from them on a number of occasions.

1° Our critique is concerned above all with two words in the proposition that he wrote in 1906: "By rights, in place of the abstract and chimerical '*Adaequatio speculativa rei et intellectus*,' we must *substitute* methodical research, the *adaequatio realis mentis et vitae*."

In order to bring an end to these discussions, which now span over forty years, we kindly asked him to retract the word "chimerical" and to replace the words "must substitute" with "should be supplemented by." Why? Because affective knowledge through connaturality or sympathy does indeed supplement notional truth. Nonetheless, *it presupposes the value of the latter*, through conformity to reality, and does not serve as a substitute for it, at least if one wishes to avoid the pragmatism toward which the philosophy of action tends to slide.

We recognize that this twofold rectification is difficult for Monsieur Blondel, for the aforementioned proposition represents, as it were, a summary of his entire book *L'Action* (1893), where similar formulas can be found repeatedly, indeed, including ones that are even more deserving of critique (see pp. 297, 341, 350, 426, 435, 437, and 463). We pointed out these passages earlier in our own article. Most especially in these formulas, we can see everything that separates the philosophy of action (which defines truth in function of action) from the philosophy of being (which defines truth in function of being). The ultimate outcome of such a position is an ethics (i.e., the philosophy of human action) that lacks sufficient ontological foundation. Now, the good presupposes being and truth [*le vrai*]; otherwise, we cannot be certain whether a given good would be a true good.

2° Moreover, we critiqued a similar proposition found in the more recent work, *L'Être et les êtres* (1935), p. 415: "No intellectual evidence, even that of principles... imposes itself upon us with a spontaneously and infallibly constraining certitude." Above, in our article, we presented this text in full, with its complete context, and we maintain that this proposition, so formulated, cannot be admitted.

Moreover, we recognize easily enough that when, from the perspective of the philosophy of action, one affirms the existence of God *according to the exigencies of action*, this affirmation is *conformed to the divine reality*, though the certitude of this conformity is not *objectively sufficient* (that is, through the demonstrative force of the proofs for God's existence), but, instead, is only *subjectively sufficient*, "according to the exigencies of action," like the Kantian proof for God's existence.

As we have said, this does not suffice. Following this path, one ends up not being able to prove *the fact of Revelation* through the probative force of miracles. Instead, all that will be had is a *subjectively* sufficient certitude concerning this fact of Revelation, thus indeed having at hand a notion of *religious experience*, though one that is not distinguished clearly enough from that had in some form of false religion, wherein sentimentalism and self-reflective concerns [*recherche de soi*] take precedence over true faith and true love of God. The Encyclical *Pascendi* noted this in speaking about that form of religious experience which is not sufficiently founded on the truth, due to what it lacks in regard to the evident credibility concerning the truths of faith (Denzinger, no. 3484 [2081]).

Likewise, it is of utter importance that we maintain *the immutability of the notions* that enter into Conciliar definitions. Now, Blondel writes in *La Pensée* (1934), vol. 2, p. 431, "*It is deceptive to speak of an overly clear intuition of mathematical and rational truths. . . ,*" and in vol. 2, p. 496, "Everywhere that there is a real distinction between essence and existence—in other words, everywhere outside of the divine mystery—*every kind of natural intuition is impossible, as is every kind of direct and exact grasping of reality* [*toute capitation directe et exacte*]." He reduces our concepts to "ever-provisional schemata," drawing their stability from "linguistic artifices" (*La Pensée*, vol. 1, p. 130).

He notes quite surely that even according to St. Thomas, "*Differentiae essentiales rerum sunt saepe innominatae,* the essential differences of things are often unnamed." Yes, but then, not knowing them explicitly and distinctly, *we do not affirm them,* and truth is formally found *only in judgment.*—Are judgments that are universally recognized as being true themselves *true* through conformity to reality? And in the case of first principles, is their *evidence necessitating,* by itself and on account of the very nature of our intellect? Is it evident to every man that he cannot, at one and the same time, exist and not exist?

* * * * *

3° Finally, we examined a number of recent deviations concerning the nature of theology, grace, original sin, and transubstantiation and the real presence. We noted that these deviations come from neglect of—or the more-or-less pronounced abandonment of—*the traditional definition of truth* (the conformity of judgment with reality and its immutable laws), along with the *acceptance of the definition of truth proposed by the philosophy of action* (the conformity of judgment with human life, in accord with the exigencies of action), a definition that, as we have said, slides toward pragmatism.

This is, moreover, what motivated the Holy Office's Dec. 1, 1924 condemnation of 12 propositions drawn from the philosophy of action. [In our article,] we set forth the principal condemned propositions.

In order to explain these various points, we wrote, in this same issue, our article concerning truth and the immutability of dogma.

Fr. Réginald Garrigou-Lagrange, OP

Bibliography

The 1917 Pio-Benedictine Code of Canon Law. Edited and translated by Edward N. Peters. San Francisco, CA: Ignatius Press, 2001.

Antoninus de Carlensis. *Four Questions on the Subalternation of the Sciences.* Translated and edited by Steven J. Livesey. Philadelphia: American Philosophical Society, 1994.

Aristotle. *Posterior Analytics.* In *The Complete Works of Aristotle*, vol. 1. Edited by Jonathan Barnes, translated by Jonathan Barnes, 114–66. Princeton, NJ: Princeton University Press, 1995.

———. *On the Soul.* In *The Complete Works of Aristotle*, vol. 2. Edited by Jonathan Barnes, translated by J. A. Smith, 641–93. Princeton, NJ: Princeton University Press, 1995.

———. *Nicomachean Ethics.* In *The Complete Works of Aristotle*, vol. 2. Edited by Jonathan Barnes, translated by W. D. Ross and J. O. Urmson, 1729–1867. Princeton, NJ: Princeton University Press, 1995.

Aubert, Roger. *Le Problème de l'acte de foi: Données traditionnelles et résultats des controversies récentes.* 3rd ed. Louvain: Universitas Catholica Lovaniensis, 1958.

Augustine of Hippo. *Confessions.* Translated by Vernon J. Bourke. Washington, DC: The Catholic University of America Press, 2008.

———. *On Nature and Grace* in *Four Anti-Pelagian Writings.* Translated by John A. Mourant and William J. Collinge. The Fathers of the Church 86. Washington, DC: The Catholic University of America Press, 2010.

Attualità filosofiche, Aloisianum, Gallarate, Atti del III Convegno di stuid filosofici cristiani tra professori universitarì. Padova: Editoria Livinia, 1948.

Balthasar, Hans Urs von. *Presence et Pensée: Essai sur la philosophie religieuse de Grégoire de Nysse.* Beauchesne: Paris, 1942

———. *Presence and Thought: Essay on the Religious Philosophy of Gregory of Nyssa.* Translated by Mark Sebanc. San Francisco: Ignatius Press, 1995.

———. "Communio—A Program." *Communio* (English edition) 33 (Spring 2006): 153–69.

Benda, Julien. "De la mobilité de la pensée selon une philosophie contemporaine." *Revue de Métaphysique et de Morale* (Juillet 1945): 161–202.

Benedict XIV. *Sollicita ac provida.* Apostolic Constitution. July 9, 1753.

Bergson, Henri. *An Introduction to Metaphysics.* Translated by T. E. Hulme. Indianapolis: Bobbs-Merrill Educational Publishing, 1980.

Bernardi, Peter J. "Maurice Blondel: Precursor of the Second Vatican Council." *Josephinum Journal of Theology* 22, nos. 1–2 (2015): 59–77.

Berthier, Joachim Joseph. *Tractatus de Locis Theologicis.* Turin: Marietti / New York: Benzinger, 1888.

Blondel, Maurice. *L'action: essai d'une critique de la vie et d'une science de la pratique.* Paris: Alcan, 1893.

———. "Le point de depart de la recherche philosophique." *Annales de philosophie chretienne* 152 (1906): 225–49.

———. *L'Être et les êtres.* Paris: Alcan, 1935.

———. *Le pensée.* Paris: Preses Universitaires de France, 1934 and 1935.

———. *La philosophie et l'esprit chrétien.* 2 vols. Paris: Presses Universitaires, 1946.

Boersma, Hans. *Nouvelle Théologie and Sacramental Ontology: Return to Mystery.* Oxford: Oxford University Press, 2009.

———. "Analogy of Truth: The Sacramental Epistemology of *Nouvelle Théologie.*" In *Ressourcement: A Movement for Renewal in Twentieth-Century Catholic Theology,* edited by Gabriel Flynn and Paul Murray, 157–71. Oxford: Oxford University Press, 2012.

Bonino, Serge-Thomas. "Antropologia della tradizione, Prospettive di metodo." In *Persona humana, Imago Dei et Christi in historia, Atti del Congresso Internazionale, Roma 6-8 settembre 2000,* vol. I, *Sentieri, Studi* 1999–2000, edited by Margherita Mari Rossi and Teodora Rossi, 99–109. Rome: Angelicum, 2002.

Bonnefoy, Jean-François, "La théologie comme science et l'explication de la foi selon saint Thomas d'Aquin," *Ephemerides theologicae Lovanienses* 14 (1937): 421–46, 600–31.

———. *La Nature de la théologie selon saint Thomas d'Aquin.* Paris: Vrin, 1939.

Bosschaert, Dries. "A Great Deal of Controversy? A Case Study of Dondeyne, Grégoire, and Moeller Integrating Phenomenology and Existentialism in Louvain Neo-Thomism." In *So What's New About Scholasticism? How Neo-Thomism Helped Shape the Twentieth Century,* edited by Rajesh Heynickx and Stéphane Symons, 131–58. Berlin / Boston: Walter de Guyter, 2018.

Bouillard, Henri. *Conversion et grâce chez S. Thomas d'Aquin.* Paris: Aubier / Éditions Montaigne, 1941.

———. "Notions conciliaires et analogie de la vérité." *Recherches de science religieuse* 35 (1948): 251–71.

Boutroux, Émile. *Science et religion dans la philosophie contemporaine.* Paris: Flammarion, 1908.

Boyssonie, Amédée and Jean. "Polygenism." In *Dictionnaire de theologie catholique,* vol.12, pt. 2, edited by Émile Amann, cols. 2520–36. Paris: Letouzey et Ané, 1935.

Boyer, Charles. "Qu'est-ce que la théologie? Réflexions sur une controverse." *Gregorianum* 21 (1940): 255–66.

———. "Nature pure et surnaturel dans le 'Surnaturel' du P. de Lubac." *Gregorianum* 28 (1947): 379–95.

Bréhier, Emile. *La philosophie et son passé.* Paris: Alcan, 1940.

Brotherton, Joshua. "Development(s) in the Theology of Revelation: From Francisco Marín-Sola to Joseph Ratzinger." *New Blackfriars* 97, no. 1072 (2016): 661–76.

Bruckberger, Raymond-Léopold. *Toute l'église en clameurs.* Paris: Flammarion, 1977.

———. *Tu finira sur l'échafaud: mémoires.* Paris: Flammarion, 1978.

———. *À l'heure où les ombres s'allongent.* Paris: Albin Michel, 1989.

Cahalan, John C. "The Problem of Thing and Object in Maritain," *The Thomist* 59, no. 1 (1995): 21–46.

Cavallera, Ferdinand. "La théologie positive." *Bulletin de litterature ecclesiastique.* (Jan. 1925): 20–42.

———. "À propos de la vie du Dogme." *Bulletin de Littérature Ecclésiastique* 43 (April-June, 1942): 69–79.

Cessario, Romanus. *Christian Faith and the Theological Life.* Washington, DC: The Catholic University of America Press, 1996.

Charlier, Louis. *Essai sur le problème théologique.* Thuillies: Ramgal, 1938.

Chenu, Marie-Dominique. "Position de la théologie," *Revue des sciences philosophiques et théologiques* 24 (1935): 232–57; reprinted as "La foi dans l'intelligence" in Chenu's *La parole de Dieu,* vol. 1, 115–38. Paris: Éditions du Cerf, 1964.

———. *Une école de théolgoie: Le Saulchoir.* Kain: Le Saulchoir, 1937; republished by Éditions du Cerf in 1985.

———. "L'Unité de la foi: Réalimse et formalisme." *La Vie spirituelle* (July–August 1937): 1–8.

———. *Is Theology a Science?* Translated by Adrian Howell North Green-Armytage. New York: Hawthorn Books, 1959.

———. *Faith and Theology.* Translated by Denis Hickey. New York: Macmillan, 1968.

———. *La Théologie comme science au XIIIe siècle,* 3rd ed. Paris: Vrin, 1969.

———. "Vérité évangélique et métaphysique wolfienne à Vatican II." *Revue des Sciences Philosophiques et Théologiques* 57 (1973): 637–38.

Chazel, Pierre. "Le Thomisme est-il menacé?" *Réforme* (Sept. 6, 1947): 2.

Chovelon, Bernadette and Bernard. *Bruckberger, l'enfant terrible.* Paris: Éditions du Cerf, 2011.

Conley, Kieran. *A Theology of Wisdom: A Study of St. Thomas.* Dubuque, IA: Priory, 1963.

Conticulo, Carmelo Giuseppe. "*De Contemplatione* (Angelicum, 1920). La Thèse inédite de doctorat du M.-D. Chenu." *Revue de sciences philosophiques et théologiques* 75 (1991): 362–422.

Conway, Michael A. "Maurice Blondel and Ressourcement." In *Ressourcement: A Movement for Renewal in Twentieth-Century Catholic Theology,* edited by Gabriel Flynn and Paul D. Murray, 65–82. Oxford: Oxford University Press, 2011.

Council of Trent. *Decree on Original Sin; Decree on Justification.* January, 1547.

Council of Vienne. *Fidei Catholicae.* May 6, 1312.

Dalbiez, Roland. *Méthode psychoanalytique et la doctrine freudiene*, vol. 1. Paris: Desclée de Brouwer, 1936.

Daley, Brian. "The Nouvelle Théologie and the Patristic Revival: Sources, Symbols and the Science of Theology." *International Journal of Systematic Theology* 7, no. 4: 362–82.

Daniélou, Jean. Introduction to Gregory of Nyssa, *Contemplation sur la vie de Moïse: ou, Traité de la perfection en matière de vertu.* Paris: Éditions du Cerf, 1941.

———. Introduction to Gregory of Nyssa, *La création de l'homme.* Paris: Éditions du Cerf, 1944.

———. *Platonisme et Théologique Mystique.* Paris: Aubier / Éditions Montaigne, 1944.

———. "La Vie intellectuelle en France: Communisme, Existentialisme, Christianisme." *Études* (September 1945): 241–54.

———. "Les orientations présentes de la pensée religieuse." *Études* 249 (April 1946): 5–21.

———. "Christianisme et histoire." *Études* 254 (1947): 166–84.

———. "La pensee chrétienne." *Nouvelle revue théologique* 69 (Nov. 1947): 930–40.

———. *Dialogues: avec les marxistes, les existentialistes, les protestants, les juifs, l'hindouisme.* Paris: Le Portulan, 1948

———. "Existentialism and the Theology of History." *The Month* 1 (1949): 66–70.

———. "Existentialisme et Théologie de l'Histoire." *Dieu Vivant* 15 (1950): 131–35.

———. "Present Orientations of Religious Thought," *Josephinum Journal of Theology* 18, no. 1 (2011): 51–62.

De Blic, Jacques. "Quelque vieux textes sur la notion de l'ordre surnaturel." *Mélanges de science religieuse* (1946): 359–62.

Deely, John N. "The Immateriality of the Intentional as Such," *The New Scholasticism* 42 (1968): 293–306.

———. "The Absence of Analogy." *The Review of Metaphysics* 55, no. 3 (Mar. 2002): 521–50.

———. *Intentionality and Semiotics: A Story of Mutual Fecundation.* Scranton and London: University of Scranton Press, 2007.

de Lubac, Henri. *Corpus mysticum: l'eucharistie et l'église au Moyen âge (étude historique).* Paris: Aubier / Éditions Montaigne, 1944.

———. *Surnaturel.* Paris: Aubier, 1946.

———. "Duplex Hominis Beatitudo (Saint Thomas, I^a 2^{ae}, q. 62, a. 1)." *Recherches de science religieuse* (April-June, 1948): 290–300.

———. *Corpus Mysticum: The Church and the Eucharist in Middle Ages.* Translated by Gemma Simmons. South Bend: University of Notre Dame Press, 2007.

de Lubac, Henri and Étienne Gilson. *Letters of Etienne Gilson to Henri De Lubac.* Translated by Mary Emily Hamilton. San Francisco: Ignatius Press, 1988.

de Lubac, Henri et al. (anonymously written). "Response to 'The Sources of Theology'[*sic*]." In Patricia Kelly, *Ressourcement Theology: A Sourcebook*, 73–82. London: Bloomsbury T&T Clark, 2020.

de Lubac, Henri et al. (anonymously written), "Théologie et ses sources: Réponse." *Recherches de science religieuse* 33 (1946): 385–401.

Deman, Thomas "La théologie dans la vie de sainte Catherine de Sienne." *Vie spirituelle* 42, Suppl. (1935): [1]–[24].

Denzinger, Heinrich. *Enchiridion Symbolorum: A Compendium of Creeds, Definitions and Declarations of the Catholic Faith.* Edited by Peter Hünermann, Robert Fastiggi, et al. San Francisco: Ignatius Press, 2021.

Descoqs, Pedro. *Praelectiones Theologiae naturalis.* Paris: Beauchesne, 1932.

———. *Autour de la crise du Transformisme.* 2nd ed. Paris: Beauchesne, 1944.

Détré, Charles (pseudonymously as Téder) and Gérard Encausse (pseudonymously as Papus). *Rituel de l'ordre martiniste.* Paris: Dorbon-Aîné, 1913.

D'Ettore, Dominic. *Analogy after Aquinas: Logical Problems, Thomistic Answers.* Washington, DC: The Catholic University of America Press, 2019.

Donneaud, Henri. "La constitution dialectique de la théologie et de son histoire selon M.-D. Chenu." *Revue thomiste* 96, no. 1 (1996): 41–66.

———. "Un retour aux sources cache sous son contraire: Rosaire Gagnebet contre Louis Charlier sur la nature de la théologie spéculative." *Revue thomiste* 119 (2019): 577–612.

Donnelly, Philip J. "Current Theology: Theological Opinion on the Development of Dogma." *Theological Studies* 8, no. 1 (1947): 668–99.

Doronzo, Emmanuel. *Theologia Dogmatica.* Vol. 1. Washington, DC: The Catholic University of America Press, 1966.

———. *Tratatus dogmaticus de sacramentis in genere.* Milwaukee: Bruce, 1946.

Fenton, Joseph Clifford. *The Concept of Sacred Theology.* Edited by Cajetan Cuddy. Providence, RI: Cluny Media, 2018.

Fessard, Gaston. Review of Joseph de Tonquédec, *Un philosophie existentielle. L'Existence d'après Jaspers.*" *Études* 247 (Nov. 1945): 269–70.

———. *Autorité et bien commun.* Paris: Aubier / Éditions Montaigne, 1946.

Fifth Lateran Council. *Apostolici regiminis.* December 19, 1513.

Flynn, Gabriel. "Introduction: The Twentieth-Century Renaissance in Catholic Theology" *Ressourcement: A Movement for Renewal in Twentieth-Century Catholic Theology*, edited by Gabriel Flynn and Paul Murray, 1–22. Oxford: Oxford University Press, 2012.

Fouilloux, Étienne. "Le Saulchoir en procès (1937–1942)." In Marie-Dominique Chenu, *Une école de théologie: Le Saulchoir*, 37–60. Paris: Éditions du Cerf, 1985.

———. "Dialogue theologique? (1946–1948)." In *Saint Thomas au XXᵉ siecle: Actes du colloque Centenaire de la Revue Thomiste; Toulouse, 25-28 mars 1993*, edited by Serge-Thomas Bonino, 153–95. Paris: Éditions Saint-Paul, 1994.

———. "L'affaire Chenu 1937–1943." *Revue des sciences philosophiques et théologiques* 98, no. 2 (April-June 2014): 261–352.

Franzelin, Johannes Baptist. *De traditione*. 2nd ed. Rome: Sacra Congregatio de Propaganda Fide, 1875.

Gagnebet, Marie-Rosaire. "La nature de la théologie spéculative," *Revue thomiste* 44 (1938) 1–39, 213–255, 645–74.

———. "Un essai sur le problème théologique." *Revue thomiste* 45 (1939): 108–45.

———. "Le problème actuel de la théologie et la science aristotélicienne d'après un ouvrage récent." *Divus thomas* 46 (1943): 237–70.

———. "L'amour naturel de Dieu chez saint Thomas et ses contemporains." *Revue thomiste* 48 (1948): 394–446; 49 (1949): 31–102.

———. "L'enseignement du magistère et le problème du surnaturel." *Revue thomiste* 53 (1953): 5–27.

———. "L'oeuvre du P. Garrigou-Lagrange: itineraire intellectuel et spirituel vers Dieu," *Angelicum* 42 (1965): 7–31.

de Gandiallac, Maurice. "À propos de Grégoire de Nysse." *Dieu Vivant* 3 (1945): 123–34.

Gardeil, Ambroise. "La Reforme de la théologie catholique: idée d'une méthode regressive." *Revue thomiste* 11 (1903): 5–19.

———. *La notion du lieu théologique*. Paris: Lecoffre, 1908.

———. *Le donné révélé et la théologie*. Juvisy: Cerf, 1909 / Paris: Librarie Victor Lecoffre, J. Gabalda et cie., 1910; 2nd ed. 1932.

———. "La topicité." Revue des Sciences philosophiques et théologiques 5 (1911): 750–57.

———. "La certitude probable." *Revue des Sciences philosophiques et théologiques* 5 (1911): 237–66, 441–85.

———. *La crédibilité et l'apologétique*. 2nd ed. Paris: Lecoffre, 1912.

———. "Lieux Théologiques." In *Dictionnaire de théologie Catholique*, vol. 9, pt. 2, edited by Alfred Vacant et al., cols. 712–47. Paris: Letouzey, 1926.

———. *La structure de l'âme et l'expérience mystique*. 2 vols. Paris: Lecoffre, 1927.

———. *The True Christian Life: Thomistic Reflections on Divinization, Prudence, Religion, and Prayer*. Translated by Matthew K. Minerd. Washington, DC: The Catholic University of America Press, 2021.

Garrigou-Lagrange, Réginald. *De revelatione per ecclesiam Catholicam proposita*. 2nd edition. Rome: Ferrari, 1921.

———. "La théologie et la vie de foi." *Revue thomiste* 40, NS 18 (1935): 492–514.

———. *Le sens commun: La philosophie de l'être et les formules dogmatiques.* 4th ed. Paris: Desclée de Brouwer, 1936.

———. "Vérité et option libre selon M. Blondel." *Acta Pont. Acad. Rom. S. Thom.* (1936): 46–69.

———. "La notion pragmatiste de la vérité et ses consequences en théologie." *Acta Pont. Acad. Rom. S. Thom.* (1943): 153–78.

———. *De revelatione per ecclesiam Catholicam proposita.* 4th edition. Turin: Marietti, 1945.

———. "La nouvelle théologie: où va-t-elle?" *Angelicum* 23 (1946): 126–47.

———. "Notions consacrées par la Concile," *Angelicum* 24 (1947): 217–31.

———. "Verité et immutabilité du dogme." *Angelicum* 24 (1947): 124–39.

———. *De eucharistia: accedunt de paenitentia quaestiones dogmaticae commentarius in summam theologicam S. Thomae.* Turin: Berruti, 1948.

———. "Immutabilité des vérités définies et la surnaturel." *Angelicum* 25 (1948): 285–98.

———. "Nécessité de revenir à la conception traditionnelle de la vérité." *Angelicum* 25 (1948): 185–98.

———. "Notions conciliaires et analogie de la vérité" *RSR* 3 (1948): 251–71.

———. *The Three Ages of the Interior Life: Prelude of Eternal Life.* Volume 2. Translated by Sister M. Timothea Doyle. St. Louis, MO: B. Herder, 1948.

———. *God: His Existence and His Nature, A Thomistic Solution of Certain Agnostic Antinomies.* 2 vols. Translated by Bede Rose. St. Louis, MO: Herder, 1949.

———. "L'immutabilité du dogme selon le Concile du Vatican, et le relativisme." *Angelicum* 26 (1949): 309–22.

———. *Reality: A Synthesis of Thomistic Thought.* Translated by Patrick Cummins. St. Louis, MO: B. Herder, 1950.

———. "Le relativisme et l'immutabilité du dogme," *Angelicum* 27, no. 3 (Sept. 1950): 219–46.

———. *De revelatione per ecclesiam Catholicam proposita.* 5th edition. Rome: Desclée et Socii, 1950.

———. *Grace.* Translated by the Dominican Nuns of Corpus Christi Monastery. St. Louis, MO: B. Herder, 1952.

———. *The Sense of Mystery.* Translated by Matthew K. Minerd. Steubenville, OH: Emmaus Academic, 2017.

———. "*Cognoscens quodammodo fit vel est aliud a se* (On the Nature of Knowledge as Union with the Other as Other)." In *Philosophizing in Faith: Essays on the Beginning and End of Wisdom*, edited and translated by Matthew K. Minerd, 63–78. Providence, RI: Cluny Media, 2019.

———. "On the Search for Definitions According to Aristotle and St. Thomas." In *Philosophizing in Faith: Essays on the Beginning and End of Wisdom*, edited and translated by Matthew K. Minerd, 21–34. Providence, RI: Cluny Media, 2019.

———. "Theology and the Life of Faith," *Philosophizing in Faith: Essays on the Beginning and End of Wisdom*, edited and translated by Matthew K. Minerd, 421–43. Providence, RI: Cluny Media, 2019.

———. *The Order of Things: The Realism of the Principle of Finality*. Translated by Matthew K. Minerd. Steubenville, OH: Emmaus Academic, 2020.

———. *On Divine Revelation*. Translated by Matthew K. Minerd. Steubenville, OH: Emmaus Academic, 2021.

———. *Thomistic Common Sense: The Philosophy of Being and the Development of Doctrine*. Translated by Matthew K. Minerd. Steubenville, OH: Emmaus Academic, 2021.

Garrigou-Lagrange, Reginald and Maurice Blondel. "Corresondance." *Angelicum* 24 (1947): 210–14.

———. *U potrazi za istinom: korespondencija Blondel - Garrigou-Lagrange*. Edited by Hrvoje Lasic. Zagreb: Demetra, 2016.

Germond, Henri. "Dialogue théologique." *Revue de Théologie et de Philosophie* (Jul.-Sept., 1947): 128–33.

Gilson, Étienne. *Théologie et Histoire de la Spiritualité*. Paris: Vrin, 1943.

———. *L'Être et l'essence*. Paris: Vrin, 1948.

Goudin, Antoine. *Philosophia iuxta inconcussa tutissimaque Divi Thomae Dogmata*. Vol. 4 (*Ethica et Metaphysica*). Urbeveteri: Prelis Speraindeo Pompei, 1860.

Gray, Janette. "Marie-Dominique Chenu and Le Saulchoir: A Stream of Catholic Renewal." In *Ressourcement: A Movement for Renewal in Twentieth-Century Catholic Theology*, edited by Gabriel Flynn and Paul Murray, 204–18. Oxford: Oxford University Press, 2012.

Greenstock, David. "Thomism and the New Theology." *The Thomist* 13 (1950): 567–96.

Grummet, David. "Nouvelle Théologie." In *Cambridge Dictionary of Christian Theology*, edited by Ian McFarland, David Fergusson, Karen Kilby, and Iain Torrance, 348–49. Cambridge: Cambridge University Press, 2014.

Günther, Anton. *Vorschule zur speculativen Theologie d. positiven Christenthums*. Wien: J.B. Wallishausser, 1828.

Haskell, Thomas. "Objectivity is Not Neutrality: Rhetoric vs. Practice in Peter Novick's *That Noble Dream*." *History and Theory* 29, no. 2 (May 1990): 129–57.

John of St. Thomas. *Cursus Theologici*. Vol. 1. Paris: Society of St. John the Evangelist / Desclée et Socii, 1931.

———. *The Material Logic of John of St. Thomas: Basic Treatises*. Translated by Yves R. Simon, John J. Glanville, G. Donald Hollenhorst. Chicago: The University of Chicago Press, 1965.

———. *On Sacred Science: A Translation of Cursus theologicus I, Question 1, Disputation 2*. Translated by John P. Doyle. Edited by Victor M. Salas. South Bend, IN: St. Augustine's Press, 2021.

Johnson, Mark P. "The Sapiential Character of *Sacra Doctrina* in the Thought of St. Thomas Aquinas," Ph.D. Diss. University of Toronto, 1990.

———. "God's Knowledge in Our Frail Mind: The Thomistic Model of Theology." *Angelicum* 76, no. 1 (1999): 25–45.

Journet, Charles. *The Wisdom of Faith: An Introduction to Theology*. Translated by R. F. Smith. Westminster, MD: The Newman Press, 1952.

———. *The Mass: The Presence of the Sacrifice of the Cross*. Translated by Victor Szczurek. South Bend, IN: St. Augustine's Press, 2008.

Kelly, Patricia. *Ressourcement Theology: A Source Book*. London: T&T Clark, 2020.

Kerlin, Michael. "Reginald Garrigou-Lagrange: Defending the Faith from *Pascendi dominici gregis* to *Humani Generis*." *U.S. Catholic Historian* 25, no. 1 (Winter 2007): 97–113.

Kirwan, Jon. *An Avant-garde Theological Generation*. Oxford: Oxford University Press, 2018.

Kleutgen, Joseph. *Die Theologie der Vorzeit*. 5 vols. Münster: Theissing: 1867–1874.

———. *Die Philosophie der Vorzeit*. 2 vols. Innsbruck: Rauch, 1878.

Labourdette, Marie-Michel. "La foi théologale et la connaissance mystique d'après saint Jean de la Croix." *Revue thomiste* 41 (1936): 593–629; 42 (1937): 16–57 and 191–229.

———. "Le développement vital de la foi théologale." *Revue thomiste* 43 (1937): 101–15.

———. "La Théologie et ses sources," *Revue thomiste* 11 (1946): 353–71.

———. "La théologie, intelligence de la foi." *Revue thomiste* 46 (1946): 5–44.

———. "Théologie de l'apostolat missionnaire." *Revue thomiste* 46 (1946): 575–602.

———. "Ferme propos." *Revue thomiste* 47 (1947): 5–19.

———. "Foi et crédibilité (chronique)." *Revue thomiste* 52 (1952): 215–25.

———. "La vie théologale selon saint Thomas, L'objet de la foi." *Revue thomiste* 58 (1958): 597–622.

———. "La vie théologale selon Thomas d'Aquin, L'affection dans la foi." *Revue thomiste* 60 (1960): 364–80.

———. *La foi*. "Grand cours" de théologie morale, vol. 8. Paris: Parole et Silence, 2015.

Labourdette, Michel and Étienne Gilson. "Correspondance Étienne Gilson—Michel Labourdette." Edited by Henry Donneaud. *Revue thomiste* 94 (1994): 479–529.

Labourdette, Marie-Michel and Marie-Joseph Nicolas. "L'analogie de la vérité et l'unité de la science théologique." *Revue thomiste* 47 (1947): 411–66.

———. "Autour du 'Dialogue théologique.'" *Revue thomiste* 47 (1947): 577–85.

Labourdette, Marie-Michel, Marie-Joseph Nicolas, Raymond-Léopold Bruckberger. *Dialogue théologique: Pièces du débat entre "La Revue thomiste" d'une part et les R.R. P.P. de Lubac, Daniélou, Bouillard, Fessard, von Balthasar, S.J., d'autre part.* Saint-Maximin: Les Arcades, 1947.

Lagrange, Marie-Joseph. *L'Épitre aux Romains.* 3rd ed. Paris: J. Gabalda, 1931.

Lang, Albert. *Die Loci Theologici des Melchior Cano und die Methode des dogmatischen Beweises.* München: Verlag J. Kösel und F. Pustet, 1925.

Le Blond, Jean-Marie. "L'analogie de la vérité. Réflexions d'un philosophe sur une controverse théologique." *Recherches de Science Religieuse* 34, no. 2 (1947): 129–41.

Leeming, Bernard. *Principles of Sacramental Theology.* London: Longmans, 1963.

Leo XIII. *Aeterni Patris.* August 4, 1879.

Loughlin, Gerard. "Nouvelle Théologie: A Return to Modernism?" In *Ressourcement: A Movement for Renewal in Twentieth-Century Catholic Theology*, edited by Gabriel Flynn and Paul Murray, 36–50. Oxford: Oxford University Press, 2012.

Magrini, Egidio (Aegidius). *Ioannis Duns Scoti doctrina de scientifica theologiae natura.* Rome: Antonianum, 1952.

Mansi, Giovanni Domenico et al. *Amplissima collection conciliorum.* Vol. 50. Edited by Louis Petit and Jean-Baptiste Martin. Arnhem and Leipzig: Société nouvelle d'édition de la Collection Mansi, 1924.

Mansini, Guy. *What is Dogma? The Meaning and Truth of Dogma in Édouard Le Roy and his Opponents.* Rome: Editrice Pontificia Università Gregoriana, 1985.

———. "The Development of the Development of Doctrine in the Twentieth Century." *Angelicum* 93, no. 4 (2016): 785–822.

———. "The Historicity of Dogma and Common Sense: Ambroise Gardeil, Reginald Garrigou-Lagrange, Yves Congar, and the Modern Magisterium." *Nova et Vetera* (English edition) 18, no. 1 (2020): 111–38.

Maquart, François-Xavier. *Elementa Philosophiae.* Vol. 3 (*Critica*) Paris: André Blot, 1938.

Marín-Sola, Francisco. *L'évolution homogène du dogme catholique.* Fribourg: Imprimerie et librairie de l'Oeuvre de Saint-Paul, 1924.

———. *La evolución homogénea del dogma católico.* Edited by Emilio Sauras. Madrid: Biblioteca de Autores Cristianos, 1963.

———. *The Homogeneous Evolution of Catholic Dogma.* Translated by Antonio T. Piñon. Manila: Santo Tomas University Press, 1988.

Maritain, Jacques. *Le Docteur angélique.* Paris: Desclée de Brouwer, 1920.

———. *Réflexions sur l'intelligence.* 3rd ed. Paris: Desclée de Brouwer, 1930.

———. *De Bergson à Thomas d'Aquin.* New York: Éditions de la Maison française, 1944.

———. "La personne et le bien commun." *Revue thomiste* 46 (1946): 237–78.

———. "Coopération philosophique et justice intellectuelle." *Revue thomiste* 46 (1946): 434–56.

———. *The Degrees of Knowledge*. Translated by Gerald Phelan et al. Notre Dame, IN: University of Notre Dame Press, 1999.

———. *Bergsonian Philosophy and Thomism*. Edited by Ralph McInerny. Translated by Mabelle L. Andison and J. Gordon Andison. Notre Dame, IN: University of Notre Dame Press, 2007.

McCool, Gerald A. *Nineteenth Century Scholasticism: The Search for a Unitary Method*. New York: Fordham University Press, 1989.

McDermott, John M. "De Lubac and Rousselot." *Gregorianum* 78, no. 4 (1997): 735–59.

McInerny, Ralph. *Preambula Fidei: Thomism and the God of the Philosophers*. Washington, DC: The Catholic University of America Press, 2006.

Mettepenningen, Jürgen. "Truth as Issue in a Second Modernist Crisis?" In *Theology and the Quest for Truth*, edited by Mathijs Lamberigts, et al., 149–82. Leuven: Peeters, 2006.

———. "L'Essai de Louis Charlier (1938): Une contribution à la Nouvelle Théologie." *Revue théologique de Louvain* 32 (2008): 211–38.

———. *Nouvelle Théologie, New Theology: Inheritor of Modernism, Precursor of Vatican II*. London: T & T Clark, 2010.

Michel, Albert. "Rosmini-Serbati, Antonio." In *Dictionnaire de théologie catholique*, vol. 13, pt. 2, edited by Émile Amann, cols. 2917–52. Paris: Letouzey et Ané, 1937.

Minerd, Matthew K. "Thomism and the Formal Object of Logic." *American Catholic Philosophical Quarterly* 93, no. 3 (2019): 411–44.

———. "Translator's Appendix 1: Concerning the Formal Object of Acquired Theology." In Reginald Garrigou-Lagrange, "Remarks Concerning the Metaphysical Character of St. Thomas's Moral Theology, in Particular as It Is Related to Prudence and Conscience," 261–66. *Nova et Vetera* 17, no. 1 (2019): 245–70.

———. "A Note on *Synderesis*, Moral Science, and Knowledge of the Natural Law." *Lex Naturalis* 5 (2020): 43–55.

———. "Wisdom be Attentive: The Noetic Structure of Sapiential Knoweldge." *Nova et Vetera* (English ed.) 18, no. 4 (2020): 1103–46.

———. "*Humani Generis* and the Nature of Theology: A Stereoscopic View from Rome and Toulouse." *Saint Anselm Journal* 16, no. 2 (2021): 1–35.

Mounier, Emmanuel. "Aux avant-postes de la pensée chrétienne," *Esprit* (Sept. 1947): 436–44.

Mouroux, Jean. *Sens chrétien de l'homme*. Paris: Aubier / Éditions Montaigne, 1945.

Muñiz, Francisco P. *The Work of Theology*. Translated by John P. Reid. Washington, DC: Thomist Press, 1958.

Murray, Charles. *Human Diversity: The Biology of Gender, Race, and Class*. New York: Twelve / Hachette, 2020.

Nichols, Aidan. "Thomism and the Nouvelle Théologie." *The Thomist* 64 (2000): 1–19.

———. "Garrigou-Lagrange and de Lubac on Divine Revelation." *Josephinum Journal of Theology* 18, no. 1 (2011): 101–11.

Nicolas, Jean-Hervé. "In Memoriam: Le Père Garrigou-Lagrange." *Freiburger Zeitschrift für Philosophie und Theologie* 11 (1964): 390–95.

———. *Dieu connu comme inconnu: Essai d'une critique de la connaisance théologique*. Paris: Desclée de Brouwer, 1966.

———. *Catholic Dogmatic Theology: A Synthesis*, vol. 1 *On the Trinitarian Mystery of God*. Washington, DC: The Catholic University of America Press, 2021.

Nicolas, Marie-Joseph. (*Chronique* / Review concerning *Corpus Mysticum* by Henri De Lubac.) *Revue thomiste* 46 (1946): 383–88.

Ott, Ludwig. *Fundamentals of Catholic Dogma*. 2nd ed. Translated by Patrick Lynch. Edited by James Canon Bastible. Rockford, IL: TAN, 1974.

Parain, Brice. "Dialogue théologique." *Le Cheval de Troie* (Aug.-Sept. 1947): 329–39.

Parente, Pietro. "New Tendencies in Theology." In Patricia Kelly, *Ressourcement Theology: A Sourcebook*, 85–89. London: T & T Clark, 2020.

———. "Nouve tendenze teologiche." *L'Osservatore Romano*. (Feb. 9–10, 1942): 1.

Pascal, Blaise. *Opuscules et Pensées*. Edited by Léon Brunschvicg. Paris: Hachette, 1897.

Peddicord, Richard. *The Sacred Monster of Thomism An Introduction to the Life and Legacy of Reginald Garrigou-Lagrange*. South Bend, IN: St. Augustine's Press, 2005.

Pius IX. *Eximiam tuam*. Apostolic Letter to the Archbishop of Cologne. June 15, 1857.

———. *Gravissimas inter*. Apostolic Letter to the Archbishop of Munich-Freising. December 11, 1862.

———. *Syllabus Errorum*. December 8, 1864.

Pius X (Roman Inquisition). *Lamentabili sane exitu*. Decree of the Holy Office. July 3, 1907.

———. *Pascendi dominici gregis*. Encyclical. September 8, 1907.

Pius XII. *Divino afflante Spiritu*. Encyclical. September 30, 1943.

———. "Il venerato Discorso del Sommo Pontifice alla XXIX Congregazione Generale della Compagnia di Gesù." *L'Osservatore Romano* (Sept. 19, 1946): 1 (AAS 38 [1946]: 381–85).

———. "Fervido Discorso del Sommo Pontifice ai Capitolari dell'Ordine dei Frati Predicatori." *L'Osservatore Romano* (Sept. 23–24, 1946): 1 (AAS 38 [1946]: 385–89).

Portier, William L. "Twentieth-Century Catholic Theology and the Triumph of Maurice Blondel." *Communio* (English edition) 38 (Spring 2011): 103–37.

Régis, Louis-Marie. *L'Opinion selon Aristote*. Paris: Vrin, 1935.

Rouvière, Henri. *Anatomie philosophique, La finalité dans l'Évolution*. Paris: Masson, 1941.

Ruddy, Christopher. "Ressourcement and the Enduring Legacy of Post-Tridentine Theology." In *Ressourcement: A Movement for Renewal in Twentieth-Century Catholic Theology*, edited by Gabriel Flynn and Paul Murray, 185–201. Oxford: Oxford University Press, 2012.

Russo, Antonio. *Henri de Lubac*. Turnhout: Brepols, 1998.

Sadler, Gregory. *Reason Fulfilled by Revelation: The 1930s Christian Philosophy Debate in France*. Washington, DC: The Catholic University of America Press, 2011.

Salet, Georges and Louis Lafont. *L'Évolution regressive*. Paris: Éditions Franciscaines, 1943.

Salm, Celestine Luke. "The Problem of Positive Theology." S.T.D. Dissertation, The Catholic University of America, 1955.

San Severino, Gaetano. *Philosophiae Christianae cum antiqua et nova comparatae*. Vol. 1. Naples: Apud Officinam Bibliothecae Catholicae Scriptorum, 1873.

Schultes, Reginald-Marie. *Introductio in Historiam Dogmatum*. Paris: Lethielleux, 1922.

Schwalm, Marie-Benoît. "L'acte de foi, est-il raisonnable?" *Revue thomiste* 1 (old series) (1896): 36–63.

———. "L'apologétique contemporaine." *Revue thomiste* 2 (1897): 62–92.

———. "La crise et l'apologétique." *Revue thomiste* 2 (1897): 239–71.

———. "La croyance naturelle et la science." *Revue thomiste* 2 (1897): 627–45.

———. "Les illusions de l'idéalisme et leurs dangers pour la foi." *Revue thomiste* 3 (1898): 413–41.

———. "Le dogmatisme du coeur et celui de l'esprit." *Revue thomiste* 3 (1898): 578–619.

Second Synod of Orange. *Canons*. July 3, 529.

Simon, Yves R. "La science modern de la nature et la philosophie." *Revue Néo-scolastique de philosophie* 49 (Feb. 1936): 64–77.

———. "Philosophers and Facts." In *The Great Dialogue of Nature and Space*, edited by Gerard J. Delacourt, 139–62. New York: Magi Books, 1970.

———. *Introduction to Metaphysics of Knowledge*. Translated by Vukan Kuic and Richard J. Thompson. New York: Fordham University Press, 1990.

———. "On Order in Analogical Sets." In *Philosopher at Work*, edited by Anthony O. Simon, 135–71. Lanham: Rowman & Littlefield, 1999.

Solages, Bruno de. "Autour d'une controverse." *Bulletin de littérature ecclésiastique* 48 (1947): 3–17.

———. "Pour l'honneur de la Théologie. Les contre-sens du R.P. Garrigou-Lagrange." *Bulletin de Littérature Ecclésiastique* 48 (1947): 65–84.

Sokolowski, Robert. *The Formation of Husserl's Concept of Constitution*. The Hague: Martinus Nijhoff, 1964.

———. *Husserlian Meditations*. Evanston, IL: Northwestern University Press, 1974.

———. *Moral Action: A Phenomenological Study*. Bloomington, IN: Indiana University Press, 1985.

———. *Introduction to Phenomenology*. Cambridge, UK: Cambridge University Press, 2000.

Sources Chrétiennes (Series). Vols. 1–10. Paris: Éditions du Cerf, 1941–1947.

Sullivan, John. "Forty Years under the Cosh: Blondel and Garrigou-Lagrange." *New Blackfriars* 93 (2012): 58–70.

Teilhard de Chardin, Pierre. "Comment se pose aujourd'hui la question du transformisme." *Études* 167 (1921): 524–44.

———. "Vie et planètes: Que se passe-t-il en ce moment sur la terre." *Études* 249 (May 1946): 145–69.

Théologie (Series). Vols. 1–10. Paris: Aubier / Éditions Montaigne, 1941–1946.

Teresa of Ávila. *Interior Castle*. Translated by E. Allison Peers. New York: Doubleday: 1961.

Thomas Aquinas. *Expositio et Lectura super Epistolas Pauli Apostoli*. 2 vols. 8th edition. Edited by R. Cai. Turin: Marietti, 1953.

———. *In duodecim libros Metaphysicorum Aristotelis expositio*. Edited by M.-R. Cathala and R. M. Spiazzi. Turin-Rome, 1950.

———. *Sancti Thomae de Aquino opera omnia*, Leonine edition. Rome, 1882–. Vols. 4–12, *Summa theologiae*. Vol. 22, *Quaestiones disputatae de veritate*. Vol. 23, *Quaestiones disputate de malo*.

———. *Scriptum super libros sententiarum magistri Petri Lombardi episcopi Parisiensis*. Vol., 1–3. Edited by Pierre Mandonnet. Paris: Lethielleux: 1929–1933.

de Tonquédec, Joseph. *Immanence: Essai critique sur la doctrine de M. Maurice Blondel*. Paris: Beauchesne 1913.

———. *Deux études sur "la Pensé" de M. M. Blondel*. Paris: Beauchesne, 1936.

———. *Les maladies nerveuses ou mentales et les manifestations diaboliques*. Paris: Beauchesne, 1938.

Torre, Michael D. "Yves R. Simon, Disciple of Maritain: The Idea of Fact and the Difference Between Science and Philosophy." In *Facts are Stubborn Things: Thomistic Perspectives in the Philosophies of Nature and Science*, edited by Matthew K. Minerd, 19–39. Washington, DC: American Maritain Association / The Catholic University of America Press, 2020.

Vacant, Jean-Michel-Alfred. *Études théologiques sur les constitutions du Concile du Vatican*. 2 vols. Paris: Delhomme et Briguet, 1895.

Vatican Council I. *Dei Filius*. Dogmatic Constitution. April 24, 1870.

Vatican Council II. *Lumen Gentium*. Dogmatic Constitution. November 21, 1964.

Vollert, Cyril. "Doctrinal Development: A Basic Theory." *Proceedings of the Catholic Theological Society of America* (1957): 45–74.

White, Thomas Joseph. "The Precarity of Wisdom: Modern Dominican Theology, Perspectivalism, and the Tasks of Reconstruction." In *Ressourcement Thomism: Sacred Doctrine, the Sacraments, and the Moral Life: Essays in Honor of Romanus Cessario*, edited by Reinhard Hütter and Matthew Levering, 92–123. Washington, DC: The Catholic University of America Press, 2011.

Zigliara, Tommaso. *Summa philosophica in usum scholarum*. 12th ed. Vol. 1. Paris: Briguet, 1900.

Zorcolo, Benedetto. "Bibliografia del P. Garrigou-Lagrange." *Angelicum* 42 (1965): 200–72.

Index

analogy of truth. *See* truth

Aquinas: and the Church Fathers, 7, 44, 150, 159, 174–75, 235; *De veritate*, 284, 293, 310, 334, 352–53; as example to imitate without mere repetition, 6, 28, 38, 52, 141–42, 182, 232–33, 248, 250–51; enduring value of his thought and metaphysics, 16–17, 23, 128–29, 137, 141, 170, 189–92, 238, 250, 303; and the Eucharist, 38, 270, 288, 299–300, 323, 328; fidelity to, 9, 23–24, 130, 187–92, 259; *intellectus* in, 65–67, 70–72, 201, 292, 310–11; the mind/spirit/wisdom of Thomas, 27, 29, 34, 231; and modernity, 23–24; opposed to nominalism and univocity of being, 20, 29, 198, 200, 203, 210, 219, 277–80, 285, 320, 349; place in history of theology, 31, 44, 131, 159, 197, 230; and proofs for the existence of God, 202, 331, 339–40, 369; "a small error in principle," 279, 291, 294, 301; *Summa contra gentiles*, 291; *Summa theologiae (ST)* I, 75, 200, 219, 273, 280, 282, 285, 292–93, 299–300, 311, 326–27, 330, 333, 344, 347, 351–53; I-II, 66, 125, 217, 272–73, 284, 292–93, 304, 308, 311, 335, 336, 342, 350, 353, 368; II-II, 55, 64, 99, 101, 103, 105, 272–73, 281, 283, 368; III, 184, 348, 352; theology of faith, 64, 101, 103, 289; traditional Thomism as in perfect conformity to Thomas, 314, 352, 355; use of Aristotle, 7, 31, 60, 117, 119, 150, 233–34, 277, 287, 337. *See also* theology; truth

Aristotle, 7, 95; on the intellect, 13, 31, 65, 332–34, 337–38, 343–46. *See also* Aquinas

Aubert, Roger, 11, 375

Augustine, 10, 44–45, 56, 58, 103, 152, 155, 157, 220, 223, 230–31, 280–82, 327, 328, 337, 342, 375, 383, 386

Augustinianism, 40, 42, 220, 231, 299, 320, 345

Benda, Julien, 158, 375

Bergson, Henri, 26, 28, 30–31, 233, 274, 366, 375, 384

Bernardi, Peter, 26, 375

Blondel, Maurice, vii, 26, 28, 33–40, 52–54, 57–59, 84, 170, 290, 317, 318, 331, 334, 335, 371–77, 381, 382, 387, 388; infidelity in later books to his original thought, 339–42; implication for doctrine on the Eucharist, 299–301; theory of truth, implication for original sin, 294–98; on truth, 270–73, 288–94, 305–11, 334–36, 338–42

Boersma, Hans, 22, 25–26, 47, 376

Bonino, Serge-Thomas, 1, 82, 376, 380

Bonnefoy, Jean-François, 11, 81, 372, 376

Bonventure of Bagnoregio, 40, 60, 155, 189

Bosschaert, Dries, 61, 376

Bouillard, Henri, 5–9, 16, 19, 25–26, 33–47, 53, 54, 58–61, 84, 135, 143, 146, 149–53, 161, 168, 169, 173, 176, 179–80, 182, 193, 195–96, 245, 260, 287–89, 292, 312–14, 327, 343, 345, 347, 348, 350, 376, 384; on analogy, 40–42; on dogma, 8, 149–52, 169, 260–62, 262–64, 312–14, 343–51; on judgment, 7–9, 19

Boutroux, Émile, 54, 306, 311, 336, 376
Boyer, Charles, 7, 33, 77, 353, 354, 376
Bruckberger, Raymond-Léopold, iii, v, vii, 5, 15–17, 24, 75, 78, 84, 127, 131, 377, 384

Cajetan, Thomas de Vio, 10, 64, 66, 72, 83, 95, 105, 165, 184, 285, 369, 379
Cavallera, Ferdinand, 103, 120, 246, 377
Cessario, Romanus, 48, 377, 389
Charlier, Louis, 10, 36, 61–62, 77, 81, 377, 379, 385
Chazel, Pierre, 255, 256, 259, 377
Chenu, Marie-Dominique, 10, 11, 25–28, 36, 39, 40, 47, 48, 49, 50, 55, 66, 76, 80–82, 195, 377, 379, 380, 382
common sense, 13, 43, 64, 67, 72–73, 325–27
Congar, Yves, 4, 14, 62, 66, 81, 384
contemporary thought, critique of, 143–52
Conway, Michael A., 26, 377
Council of Trent: *Decree on Justification*, 8–9, 59–60, 323–25; on the Eucharist, 299–300; on formal causality, 37, 43

Daley, Brian, 22, 378
Daniélou, Jean, 5–7, 15–21, 24, 39, 83, 84, 133–38, 141, 142, 144, 145, 153–57, 161, 164, 167, 169, 172, 173, 175, 177, 178–82, 206, 234, 249, 378, 384
de Blic, Jacques, 170, 378
de Carlensis, Antoninus, 55, 375
Deely, John, 64, 69, 378
de Lubac, Henri, 10, 15–23, 25, 28, 33–34, 37–39, 46, 47, 48, 49, 83, 84, 133–38, 147–48, 157, 161, 164, 169, 170, 172, 174, 176, 177, 180–85, 292, 293, 314, 315, 351, 352–54, 376, 378–79, 384–87; on *Corpus Mysticum*, 183–85; response to Dominicans, 20–22; on *Surnaturel*, 314, 351–54
de Tonquédec, Joseph, 112, 294, 315, 379, 388

D'Ettore, Dominic, 65, 379
Descoqs, Pedro, 292, 293, 297, 379
development of doctrine, 63–69, 72–73
dialogue, limits of, 78–79, 127–32
dogma, debate between Garrigou-Lagrange and Bouillard, 33–46
Donneaud, Henri, 28, 48, 56, 57, 81, 83, 379, 383
Donnelly, Philip J., 2, 379
Doronzo, Emmanuel, 56, 62, 379
Duns Scotus, 195, 219, 221, 223

existentialism, 6, 9, 18, 19, 23, 61, 130, 141–42, 156, 157, 177, 181, 191, 255, 257–58, 338, 376–78

faith, 96–104; Church's mediation of, 99–104. *See also* theology
Fenton, Joseph Clifford, 83, 379
Fessard, Gaston, 16, 25, 38, 135, 152, 153, 161, 164, 168–69, 180, 182, 293, 294, 315, 379, 384
First Vatican Council, 57, 63, 89, 90, 97, 178, 335, 360–61
Flynn, Gabriel, 22, 376–77, 379, 382, 384, 387
Fouilloux, Étienne, 1, 9, 10, 15, 19, 20–22, 24, 25, 34, 47, 56, 379
fundamentalism (*intégrisme*), 21, 164, 249, 250, 253, 257

Gagnebet, Marie-Rosaire, 11, 36, 51, 55, 62, 70, 75, 81–82, 116, 118, 355, 379, 380

INDEX

Gardeil, Ambrose, 12–14, 40, 50, 62, 65, 66, 76, 80, 108, 279, 380, 384

Garrigou-Lagrange, Réginald, iii, iv, vii, 5, 8–14, 20, 21, 26, 30, 33–40, 42–77, 80–85, 108, 184, 195, 267, 269, 271, 275, 279, 286–87, 289, 297, 305, 309, 314, 319, 325, 330–31, 334, 343, 357, 366–68, 371, 374, 380, 382–89; on the development of doctrine, 363–65; history of the debate with Bouillard, 33–46

Germond, Henri, 255, 264–65, 382

Gilson, Étienne, 28, 51, 56, 57, 153–55, 175, 367, 368, 379, 382, 383

Grummet, David, 22, 382

Günther, Anton, 34, 57, 357–60, 365, 382

Haskell, Thomas, 3, 382

Hegel, 6, 31, 34, 230, 233, 251–52, 308, 316

historical method, limits of, 74, 143–52

historicism, 18–19, 53, 263, 301

intellectus fidei, 52, 82, 104, 106, 109–10

irrational philosophy, 157–60

John of St. Thomas, 54–56, 62, 69, 77, 95, 368, 382

Johnson, Mark P., 55, 383

Journet, Charles, 9, 21–24, 34, 58, 65, 71, 82, 383

judgment and affirmation, response to Le Blond, 195–96

Kant, Immanuel, 34, 304, 306, 308, 331, 332, 334–40, 357, 373

Kelly, Patricia, 4, 5, 15, 19, 25, 161, 379, 383, 386

Kerlin, Michael, 34, 383

Kirwan, Jon, iii, 1, 4, 6, 22, 26, 28, 34, 37, 48, 50, 80, 82, 287, 383

Laberthonnière, Lucien, 81, 270, 271, 302

Labourdette, Michel, iii, vii, 1, 5, 10–32, 36, 40, 42, 46, 51, 52, 54–62, 66, 70, 73–80, 82–84, 89, 133, 134, 137, 141–42, 144, 150, 152, 153, 161, 187, 193, 194, 210, 237, 241, 248, 253, 255, 383, 384

Le Blond, Jean Marie, 25–29, 330

Leo XIII, 113, 141, 253, 294, 301, 312, 372, 384

Le Roy, Édouard, 13, 36, 384

Mansini, Guy, 13, 14, 62, 64, 66, 72, 76, 384

Maréchal, Joseph, 26, 48

Marín-Sola, Francisco, 59, 62, 63, 80, 285, 286, 377, 384

Maritain, Jacques, 9, 11, 12, 21–26, 30, 34, 51, 52, 65, 69, 71, 75, 94, 96, 115, 131, 168, 182, 210, 220, 223, 253, 349, 377, 384, 388

Marxism, 9, 18, 19, 130, 131, 141, 142, 156, 157, 177; Marxist, 6, 156, 255, 257, 258, 378

McCool, Gerald, 1, 26, 385

McInerny, Ralph, 11, 26, 385

metaphysics. *See* Aquinas

Mettepenningen, Jürgen, 3, 10, 22, 47, 62, 80, 81, 385

Minerd, Matthew, iii, 1, 11, 12, 13, 30, 52–55, 64–68, 72, 75, 76, 78, 85, 108, 287, 289, 314, 321, 325, 347, 352, 366, 380, 381, 382, 385, 388

Mondésert, Claude, 136, 145

Mounier, Emmanuel, 198, 255–57, 262–64, 385

Mouroux, Jean, 135, 138–40, 385
Muñiz, Francisco P., 55, 385

Nichols, Aidan, 2, 19, 21, 34, 49, 386
Nicolas, Jean-Hervé, 64, 69, 70, 75, 386
Nicolas, Marie-Joseph, iii, vii, 1, 5, 15–16, 21, 23–24, 29, 30, 31–32, 42, 56, 57, 75, 79, 82, 84, 133, 147, 180
nouvelle théologie, 4, 16, 23, 25, 26, 28, 38, 39, 47, 153, 179, 305, 325, 330, 376, 378, 381, 382, 384, 385, 386; and the Church Fathers, 18, 79, 82, 111, 132–36, 141, 172, 174, 181, 183, 188, 234–35, 243; implying a denigration of scholasticism as such, 141, 174, 183, 301; praised in its positive aims, 133–143; risks implied modernist epistemology (in particular, in the theory of dogmatic development proposed by Bouillard), 58–59

Parain, Brice, 255–57, 260, 261, 386
Parente, Pietro, 22, 33, 386
Peddicord, Richard, 10, 80, 386
Pius X, 37, 58, 71, 148, 270, 291, 294, 301, 302, 306, 307, 332, 372, 386; on Modernism, 37, 58, 102
Pius XII, 183, 247, 294, 312, 317, 372, 386

Régis, Louis-Marie, 65, 387
relativism: vii, 8, 19–21, 23, 34, 45, 54, 57, 59, 60, 61, 146, 149, 153, 169, 175, 303, 313, 321, 328, 329, 346, 349, 350, 357, 359
ressourcement, 2, 4, 5, 6, 9, 10, 13, 15, 18, 19, 22, 25, 26, 34, 47, 48, 72, 81, 82, 161, 376, 377, 379, 382, 383, 384, 386, 387, 389

revelation, 11, 188–89; closed and unchanging, 63, 206, 318, 367; heresy against, 278; as object of faith, 96–97, 99–102, 119, 204, 264; primarily concerned with God, not facts of history, 359, 365; as source of theology, 75–76, 89–91, 107–8, 110–12, 115, 117, 207; theories of de Lubac and Garrigou-Lagrange compared, 49
Rosmini, Antonio, 34, 337–40
Rousselot, Pierre, 11, 25, 26, 28, 48, 385
Ruddy, Christopher, 82, 387
Russo, Antonio, 19, 37, 387

Sadler, Gregory, 11, 387
Salm, Celestine Luke, 13, 55, 387
Schultes, Reginald, 62, 67, 387
Schwalm, Marie-Benoît, 53, 66, 302, 387
Simon, Yves, 52, 54, 64, 69, 75, 94, 382, 387, 388
Sokolowski, Robert, 69, 388
Sources Chrétiennes, series, 133–38, 164, 167, 172, 180–81
Suarezianism, 42, 60, 79, 195, 320, 345, 368
systems, and conceptualization, 226–28
systems, philosophical, 30–32

Teilhard de Chardin, Pierre, 38, 142, 156, 297, 388
Teresa de Ávila, 275, 388
Théologie series, 135–36, 173–74, 180–81
theology: the act of faith, 105–9; authority in, 241–46; critique of aspects of *ressourcement* attitude, 133–43; as experience, 114–15; and historical method in, 18, 72–74, 141, 144–45, 170; and the interior life,

274–81; mystical, 90–91; positive, 110–12, 244; problem posed by modernity, 269–74; as science, 10, 68–71, 79, 127–28, 206–7; as "speaking to the world," 257–60; structure of, 104–9; systems, 120–22, 188–92

truth: adequation theory (*adaequatio rei et intellectus*), 37, 52–53, 270, 290, 311, 329, 331–32, 336, 342; analogy of, 25–29, 194–98, 203 (in Le Blond); degrees in conceptualization, 216–23; degrees in judgment, 214–16; and history and culture, 208–13, 230–31; logical, 199–203; revealed, 204–6; and the unity of the mind, 203–4

Vacant, Jean-Michel-Alfred, 53, 57, 62, 300, 316, 321, 357, 359, 360, 361, 362, 363, 364, 380, 389

Vincent of Lérins, 61, 63, 360, 363, 364

Vollert, Cyril, 62, 389

von Balthasar, Hans Urs, 16, 83, 137, 145, 159, 161, 164, 169, 173, 179, 180, 182, 384

Wolff, Christian, 367–68

compliance